VALUE AND CONTEXT

Alan Thomas presents an original study of the status of value and its relation to the contexts in which evaluative claims are justified. He articulates and defends the view that human beings do possess moral and political knowledge, but that it is historically and culturally contextual knowledge in ways that, say, mathematical or chemical knowledge is not. His exposition of a 'cognitivist contextualism' in ethics and politics builds upon contemporary work in epistemology, moral philosophy, and political theory to fashion an argument that is relevant to current debates about culture, modernity, and relativism.

Alan Thomas is Professor of Ethics at Tilburg University.

Value and Context

The Nature of Moral and Political Knowledge

ALAN THOMAS

CLARENDON PRESS · OXFORD

OXFORD
UNIVERSITY PRESS

Great Clarendon Street, Oxford OX2 6DP

Oxford University Press is a department of the University of Oxford.
It furthers the University's objective of excellence in research, scholarship,
and education by publishing worldwide in

Oxford New York

Auckland Cape Town Dar es Salaam Hong Kong Karachi
Kuala Lumpur Madrid Melbourne Mexico City Nairobi
New Delhi Shanghai Taipei Toronto

With offices in

Argentina Austria Brazil Chile Czech Republic France Greece
Guatemala Hungary Italy Japan Poland Portugal Singapore
South Korea Switzerland Thailand Turkey Ukraine Vietnam

Oxford is a registered trade mark of Oxford University Press
in the UK and in certain other countries

Published in the United States
by Oxford University Press Inc., New York

First published 2006
First published in paperback 2010

British Library Cataloguing in Publication Data
Data available

Library of Congress Cataloging in Publication Data
Thomas, Alan, Dr.
Value and context : the nature of moral and political knowledge / Alan Thomas.
p. cm.
Includes bibliographical references and index.
ISBN-13: 978–0–19–958727–8 (alk. paper)
ISBN-10: 978–0–19–825017–3 (alk. paper)
1. Ethics. 2. Political science—Philosophy. I. Title.
BJ1012.T53 2006
170′.42—dc22 2006017202

Typeset by Laserwords Private Limited, Chennai, India
Printed in Great Britain
on acid-free paper by the
MPG Books Group, Bodmin and King's Lynn

ISBN 978–0–19–825017–3 (hbk); 978–0–19–958727–8 (pbk)

1 3 5 7 9 10 8 6 4 2

For Kathryn

Acknowledgements

This book originated in a doctoral thesis submitted to the University of Oxford in 1995. It has had a very lengthy period of gestation, for various reasons, and little of the original text of the thesis survives in the present manuscript. I have incurred substantial debts to others over the course of writing the thesis and this book. The late Bernard Williams supervised the thesis on which this book is based and it will be clear from this work how much he shaped my entire conception of philosophy. I take issue with many of his claims about moral knowledge in the course of this book but my indebtedness to him will be equally evident throughout. He was the ideal supervisor of my thesis and became a supportive and wise mentor at the outset of my career. His passing greatly saddened me.

I was very fortunate that my doctoral thesis was examined by Charles Taylor and Roger Crisp. Both of them gave me a great deal of valuable feedback that I have incorporated into the revisions of my thesis to make it more appropriate for publication as a book. I am very grateful to them both. For helpful feedback either on the papers that have been incorporated into this book or on the book itself I am also very grateful to Edward Harcourt, Brad Hooker, Simon Kirchin, Richard Norman, Tom Pink, Martin Stone, and Philip Stratton-Lake.

For financial support during the writing of my thesis I am grateful to Ian Honeyman, the former bursar of St Hugh's College, Oxford; St Hugh's itself for the award of a Senior Jubilee Scholarship; the late Jack Campbell-Lamerton, formerly bursar of Balliol College; and Balliol College itself. Without the support of Ian Honeyman and Jack Campbell-Lamerton I would have been reluctantly forced, on financial grounds, to abandon my doctoral studies many years ago. More recently the Arts and Humanities Research Council supported work on this book and I am grateful to the Board for this support.

I owe a particular debt of gratitude to Peter Momtchiloff at Oxford University Press who has shown a great deal of faith in this project over many years. He was prepared to wait until I was completely happy with the final product. His only comment during this time was that ethics was an area of philosophy in which people took time to get things right!

I am also indebted to Peter for his expert choice of the anonymous readers of the manuscript of this book. The manuscript was reviewed twice, several years apart, by two readers in each instance but with one person performing this task on two separate occasions. While I am grateful to all three readers I do have to single out for particular thanks the individual, whomsoever he or she is, who twice read successive versions of the manuscript. Each time he or she engaged with the arguments in considerable detail, suggesting many improvements and often raising deep issues about contextualism that forced me to rethink my own views. Hopefully one day that person will identify him- or herself so that I can thank them in person. Several footnotes identify particular places where I have responded to his or her suggestions in depth; in those footnotes I refer to him or her (for want of a better phrase) as the 'first anonymous reader'. I would also like to thank Jenni Craig, production editor, and Rowena Anketell, copy editor, for their expert work in the final production stages of this book.

I will conclude with my thanks to three others. Adrian Moore was one of my undergraduate tutors, briefly my thesis supervisor and later a colleague at St Hugh's. His friendship for twenty years has meant a great deal to me and I have learnt more about philosophy from him than from anyone else, including Bernard. Those who know his work will see its pervasive influence throughout this book. My mother, Eira Thomas, was a constant source of moral support throughout my doctoral research; she was delighted when this book was accepted for publication. I very much regret that she did not live to see it published. Finally, the reader has reason to be very grateful to my partner, Kathryn Brown, who has read innumerable drafts of this book over many years and has immeasurably improved it both substantively and stylistically. My personal debt to her goes beyond anything that I can put into words, but I dedicate this book to her. This book would not have existed without her love, support, and practical advice at every stage of its composition.

PERMISSIONS

I am grateful to the editors of the following journals, or collections of papers, for giving me permission to reprint material from previously published papers. I am grateful to Ward E. Jones, editor, for permission to reprint sections from 'Minimalism and Quasi-Realism', *Philosophical Papers* (Nov. 1997), 233–9 which are incorporated into Chapter 5 and to the editors and Edinburgh University Press for permission to reprint substantial parts of 'Consequentialism and the Subversion of Pluralism', in Brad Hooker, Elinor Mason, and Dale Miller (eds.), *Morality, Rules and Consequences* (Edinburgh University Press, 2000), 179–202 which forms the basis of Chapter 8. I am grateful to Roger Crisp and to Edinburgh University Press for permission to reprint material from 'Internal Reasons and Contractualist Impartiality', *Utilitas*, 14/2 (July 2002), 135–54 which forms the basis of Chapter 4. I am grateful to Bob Brecher and Kluwer publishers for permission to incorporate some sentences from 'Nagel's Paradox of Equality and Partiality', published in *Res Publica*, 9/3 (2003), 257–284 into Chapter 11. Finally, I am grateful to Peter Burnell and Peter Calvert, the editors, and to Frank Cass Publishers for the reprinting of passages from 'Liberal Republicanism and the Role of Civil Society', *Democratisation* (Aug. 1997), 26–44 which are incorporated into Chapter 12.

Prefatory Note to the Paperback edition

I have resisted the temptation to make any significant revisions to this paperback edition of what is already quite a long book. I would simply like to direct the reader to three supplementary papers that take forward some of the issues dealt with here. The idea of a so-called "thick" ethical concept plays an important part in the argument of this book particularly in chapter five. It has been the subject of much recent attention by meta-ethicists. My more fully worked out views on this issue are contained in a paper co-authored with my friend and former colleague Edward Harcourt: 'Thick Concepts, Analysis and Reductionism' was presented to a conference at the University of Kent in 2009. (It is forthcoming in a volume to be edited by the conference organizer, Simon Kirchin, provisionally entitled *Thick Concepts*.)

I would also like to direct the reader to a further paper solely authored by Edward: he does an excellent job of characterizing the differences between the versions of minimalism about truth adopted by Crispin Wright and Simon Blackburn in his paper 'Quasi Realism and Ethical Appearances', *Mind*, vol. 114 no. 454 (2005), pp. 249–75. More importantly, Edward shows very clearly the price that Blackburn must pay for adopting his version of minimalism in a way that supplements my argument in this book at pp. 119–20.

Finally, in the course of my liberal-republican interpretation of Rawls I noted the need to respond to G. A. Cohen's well-known critique of Rawlsian special incentives at p. 297, fn. 7 of this work. I now argue that, in fact, the best way to interpret Cohen's views is that the *only* way in which one can secure the content of Rawls's egalitarianism is by adopting the kind of republican emphasis on effective political agency that forms part of the interpretation of Rawls defended here. I defend this interpretation of both Rawls and Cohen in 'Liberalism, Republicanism and the Idea of an Egalitarian Ethos' in Martin O'Neill and Thad Williamson (eds.) *Rawls and Property Owning Democracy*, forthcoming from Blackwell-Wiley. I hope to develop this argument in greater detail in future work.

Alan Thomas
Tilburg University

Contents

A Note to the Reader

Part I of this book sets out the basic assumptions of a cognitivist view of ethics that treats moral properties as anthropocentric but real properties. It explains why there is a problem of moral knowledge and related issues about moral motivation, such as the distinction between internalism and externalism about motivation. Those who are expert in the field and very familiar with these meta-ethical views and the debates that they have stimulated may choose to omit the first three chapters and pick up the argument at Chapter 4.

If it is said that Reason itself, rather than any particular statement of its content, must remain as the final arbiter, then we must wonder what precisely that is. If not as particular content, then the only sense in which reason must endure is as an evolving chain of descent. Reason will endure as whatever evolves or grows out of the current content of reason by a process of piecemeal change that is justified at each moment by principles which are accepted at that moment (although not necessarily later on), provided that each evolving stage seems close enough to the one immediately preceding it to warrant the continued use of the label 'reason' then. (The new stage may not seem very similar, however, to an earlier, step-wise stage.) That degree of continuity hardly seems to mark something which is a fixed and eternal intellectual point.

Robert Nozick, Invariances

Introduction

The aim of this book is to further an ongoing debate between 'cognitivists' and 'non-cognitivists' about the possibility and the nature of moral knowledge. The former assert, and the latter deny, that some of the moral claims we make should be interpreted as claims that are often known to be true. I think this debate is deadlocked. It can only be resolved by re-examining the assumptions underlying our current options. This book develops a contextualist approach to epistemology that I think offers the best way forward for cognitivism. Contextualist models of knowledge have recently received more philosophical attention, even in ethics. However, they have not, so far, explicitly been placed at the service of the defence of moral cognitivism.

The starting point of my work is the innovative form of cognitivism that David Wiggins and John McDowell developed in the nineteen eighties: a view that has been described as 'the most important contemporary challenge to the terms of the standard, and perhaps stalemated, dialectic between noncognitivism and naturalistic cognitivism'.[1] They suggested that we should see moral values as attuned to our particular sensibilities, but none the less as part of our moral experience and as indispensable to our best moral explanations.[2] I sympathize a great deal with the criticisms that they developed of standard non-cognitivist accounts of morality, particularly those varieties of projectivism which see our moral judgements as the projection of values onto an evaluatively neutral reality. The origin of such views is Nietzsche's *The Joyful Science*, although within the analytical tradition this view is particularly associated with the work of Simon Blackburn and Allan Gibbard.[3] Wiggins and McDowell suggested that the attractions of such views are illusory when we focus our attention on so-called 'thick' ethical concepts, such as **courage** or **brutality**.[4] When we examine our use of such concepts from within our ongoing moral practices, we can come to see that there is no possibility of dissociating their descriptive and their normative elements. This seemed to them further to imply that there was no feasible project of separating out our evaluative 'projections' from the non-evaluative reality onto which these judgements were projected.

---

[1] Stephen Darwall, Allan Gibbard, and Peter Railton, 'Toward *Fin de Siècle* Ethics: Some Trends', *Philosophical Review*, 101/1 (1992), 115–189 at 164.

[2] I will refer primarily to the papers collected in David Wiggins, *Needs, Values, Truth*, 3rd edn. (Oxford: Blackwells, 2000) and to the papers collected in John McDowell, *Mind, Value and Reality* (Cambridge, Mass.: Harvard University Press, 2001).

[3] Friedrich Nietzsche, *The Gay Science*, ed. Bernard Williams, trans. Josefine Nauckhoff and Adrian Del Caro (Cambridge: Cambridge University Press, 2002); Allan Gibbard, *Wise Choices, Apt Feelings* (Oxford: Oxford University Press, 1990); Simon Blackburn, *Ruling Passions* (Oxford: Oxford University Press, 1999).

[4] I will adopt the convention of referring to concepts, as opposed to the linguistic terms that express them, in bold typeface.

I have always sympathized both with Wiggins's and McDowell's overall project and with the two analogies they used to illuminate their alternative view: between values and secondary properties, and between moral reasons and mathematical reasons. Their project was to give an account of moral properties in which such properties are construed as anthropocentric, but also as real. They are real in so far as they are indispensable to the explanations we offer of moral phenomena, but not real in the sense that they are grounded in the universe 'as it is in itself' without relation to the interests and concerns of human beings. To explain this unique kind of metaphysical status for moral values, they used analogies between the ontological status of values and that of secondary qualities, such as colours, and between the 'logical space' of moral reasons and the 'logical space' of constructivist mathematics.[5] One of the aims of this latter analogy was to capture the authority of moral reasons; the way in which there appears to be a necessary connection between moral knowledge and the will in an appropriately motivated agent.

However, my sympathy with this theory in its original form only goes so far. My first, less radical, objection, is that the explanation given of the connection between moral knowledge and the will stands in need of revision. I have my own story to tell about how moral reasons motivate an appropriately motivated agent, which I will present in Part II of this book.[6] More radically, however, it seems to me that the account offered of moral knowledge, as it stands, suffers from a major defect, highlighted in the powerful criticism offered by Bernard Williams in his insightful discussion of the view and its limitations in *Ethics and the Limits of Philosophy*.[7] I interpret Williams's criticism as follows: the proposed form of cognitivism can give an excellent account of particular forms of ethical reasoning and judgement as they arise within a given historical community with its culturally specific concepts, practices, and forms of reasoning. However, in its original form, the theory fails to allow for the possibility of a certain kind of radical, distinctively modern, form of reflection in which we

---

[5] The term of art of 'the logical space of reasons' is prominent in John McDowell, *Mind and World* (Cambridge, Mass.: Harvard University Press, 2001). Its contemporary use originated with Wilfrid Sellars, *Empiricism and the Philosophy of Mind* (Cambridge, Mass.: Harvard University Press, 1997), §36. Sellars in turn drew on the discussion of 'logical space' in Ludwig Wittgenstein, *Tractatus Logico-Philosophicus*, trans. David Pears and Brian McGuiness (London: Routledge and Kegan Paul, 1961), 3.42 ff.

[6] Specifically I discuss this point in Ch. 4, below. Another philosopher who shares my view that cognitivism must be revised so as to accept the internal reasons constraint is Adrian Moore in his recent work *Noble in Reason, Infinite in Faculty* (London: Routledge, 2003). See e.g. sect. 3 of the 'Introduction', sect. 5 and 6 of the 'First Set of Variations', and sect. 9 of the 'Second Set of Variations'. However, the main difference between the argument of this book and Moore's is that Moore is more concerned to vindicate a broadly Kantian picture of practical reasons. Such an approach places cognitivism within the wider framework of constructivism about ethical judgements. For a constructivist it is only within a perspective of engagement with the world that is broadly practical (or in Moore's terms 'sense making') that issues about the truth of particular claims arise. I discuss Moore's views in 'Maxims and Thick Concepts: Reply to Moore', presented to the Central Division of the American Philosophical Association, 2005 and available for download at <http://www.logical-operator.com/ReplytoMoore.pdf>

[7] Bernard Williams, *Ethics and the Limits of Philosophy* (London: Fontana, 1985).

take a critical stance towards the practices of our own historical community, or are challenged by the practices and ideals of other communities.

The danger is that we will not be able to face up to such challenges rationally. If our only purchase on moral properties is from within our ongoing form of life, how can we respond if it seems that there is more than one such form of life, each offering access to its own range of moral properties? This is the problem posed to cognitivism by a certain *kind* of ethical pluralism. This is the kind of pluralism that goes beyond the pluralism born of reasonable disagreement that one could expect to find within morality as it has developed within any cultural setting.[8] It is the radical pluralism that seems inherent to any account of morality in a distinctively modern society.

We are, collectively, in the grip of a high degree of 'epochal self-consciousness', to use Bernard Yack's helpful phrase.[9] We think of ourselves as modern in a way that invites scepticism, but in a way that seems, similarly, irresistible. Even if, at the end of the day, we are not convinced by the claim that the ethical is faced with unprecedented challenges in a modern world, the claim is certainly recognisable. It is the claim, or threat, of a kind of radical pluralism that goes beyond a reasonable pluralism within morality, where that latter idea can be seen as a reassuring complement to our ideal of autonomy. The radical pluralism that is, by contrast, a threat, overwhelms us with options that are in some way incomparable, incompatible, and an avenue not to freedom but nihilism. Our modern aspiration to radical freedom has, on this view, spun out of control.[10] If there is anything to this line of concern, and it seems to me foolhardy to deny it, then I believe that addressing it allows one to isolate and to criticize one of the key assumptions driving Williams's critique of the cognitivist position. Anyone sympathetic to cognitivism *ought* to address it. The project of this book is to take Wiggins's and McDowell's original proposals, apparently completely derailed by Williams's critique, and put them back on track by arguing that they can be developed to meet this challenge. However, the way in which cognitivism needs to be developed has to be handled carefully.

---

[8] Reflection on the existence of this kind of objective value pluralism is associated particularly with the work of Isaiah Berlin and Stuart Hampshire. Berlin, *Four Essays on Liberty* (Oxford: Oxford University Press, 1969); Hampshire, 'Morality and Conflict', in *Morality and Conflict* (Cambridge, Mass.: Harvard University Press, 1983), 140–70; 'Morality and Convention', in Amartya Sen and Bernard Williams (eds.), *Utilitarianism and Beyond* (Cambridge: Cambridge University Press, 1982), 145–57.

[9] Bernard Yack, *The Fetishism of Modernities: Epochal Self-Consciousness in Contemporary Social and Political Thought* (Notre Dame, Ind.: University of Notre Dame Press, 1997), 'Introduction', 1–16.

[10] This critique of the modern notion of freedom has generated a substantial literature, of which the best is still Iris Murdoch, *The Sovereignty of Good* (London: Routledge and Kegan Paul, 1970). For a more general context and a more optimistic analysis there is Robert B. Pippin, *Modernism as a Philosophical Problem*, 2nd edn. (Oxford: Blackwell Publishers, 1999). I have also benefited from the contrasting assessments of Hegel's views on modernity in Michael Allen Gillespie, *Hegel, Heidegger and the Ground of History* (Chicago: University of Chicago Press, 1984) and David Kolb, *The Critique of Pure Modernity: Hegel, Heidegger and After* (Chicago: University of Chicago Press, 1986).

I will dissent from one well-established strategy. One way of defusing this worry about the corrosive effects of modern radical pluralism is to argue that all our modes of reasoning and judgement face this problem. The problem comes with the terrain, as it were, and given that ethical reasoning and thought is no worse off than any other area of our knowledge, one can afford a relaxed attitude to the problem. Our aspiration to objectivity is limited, urges the interlocutor, and since it is limited everywhere, it is possible to reimmerse oneself in ethical thought and life with good faith. This move is generally developed from within the perspective towards the realism debate developed by internal realism, associated particularly in the context of ethics with Hilary Putnam and Sabina Lovibond. I explain in Chapter 6 why I do not find this position satisfactory.[11] I agree with Bernard Williams and with others who have further developed and refined his position, such as Adrian Moore, that while our knowledge is indeed conditioned by our perspective on the world, absolute or non-perspectival knowledge is possible in the way that the internal realist denies, in spite of the ubiquity of such human, all too human, conditions on our knowledge.[12] Both our scientific practice and, indeed, our ordinary concept of knowledge implicitly allow that while our ordinary grasp of the world is ineluctably conditioned by our perspective, certain aspirations to knowledge contain the idea that we can detach from any such local perspective. This detachment allows us to form a more inclusive perspective that we hope will be maximally independent of our peculiarities as knowers.

The implication of this view is that physics, for example, can transcend our historical point of view in a way that seems wholly inappropriate for moral reasoning, which seems more tied to a local perspective and its peculiarities. One response to this position is to argue that it once again invites a relaxed diagnosis, perhaps a form of sophisticated relativism. Our local view, conditioned by its peculiarities, is ours, whereas other societies and historical periods have their own particular view. Given that each view is, as it were, hermetically sealed from the others and, further, given that we have abandoned the aspiration for a more than local perspective on ethical practices, the resulting position may be practically uncomfortable, but it poses no difficulties at the level of theory. Such is the position of the postmodern ironists, such as Richard Rorty and Jean-François Lyotard.[13]

---

[11] A position set out in the following works: Hilary Putnam, *Realism with a Human Face* (Cambridge, Mass.: Harvard University Press, 1992); *The Many Faces of Realism* (La Salle, Ill.: Open Court Publishing, 1987); *Renewing Philosophy* (Cambridge, Mass.: Harvard University Press, 1995); *The Collapse of the Fact/Value Dichotomy and Other Essays* (Cambridge, Mass.: Harvard University Press, 2002); *Ethics Without Ontology* (Cambridge, Mass.: Harvard University Press, 2004); Sabina Lovibond, *Realism and Imagination in Ethics* (Oxford: Basil Blackwell, 1983). John McDowell also seemed initially drawn to this line of response to Williams's arguments: see esp. 'Review of *Ethics and the Limits of Philosophy*', *Mind*, 95/379 (1986), 377–88.

[12] Bernard Williams, *Descartes* (London: Penguin Books, 1978); Adrian Moore, *Points of View* (Oxford: Oxford University Press, 1997).

[13] Richard Rorty, *Philosophy and the Mirror of Nature* (Oxford: Basil Blackwell, 1979); Jean-François Lyotard, *The Postmodern Condition: A Report on Knowledge*, trans. Brian Massumi (Manchester: Manchester University Press, 1984).

I am not happy with this view, not because I regard it as shockingly amoral, but rather because I believe a more attractive alternative is available. There is one central claim of Rorty's and Lyotard's with which I agree: namely, that we can no longer overcome this particular intellectual predicament, which has a long history, by appeal to a 'grand historical narrative' of a Hegelian kind. In this book I aim to give this claim a precise sense. I interpret it as the view that while we can form a conception of what it would be for one framework of ethical judgement to be superior to another, we cannot iterate this conception to yield the idea of that framework that cannot be surpassed by any other. This would be an instance of the chain fallacy of arguing from 'all chains have an end' to 'there is an end to all chains'.[14] Expressed in this limited way, the denial that we possess a grand narrative of the legitimation of ethical beliefs steers clear of an obvious pitfall: self-refutation through paradox. From the standpoint of which historical interpretation, the sceptic asks, does one announce the end of all historical narratives, if not from that of the very kind of narrative whose existence is being denied?[15]

This paradox is a variation of a paradox that may be felt to be problematic for Rorty's and Lyotard's deflationary project in its original version: it certainly looks as if the unavailability of a standpoint outside our various language games, the 'God's eye point of view' of a 'final interpretation' is being asserted from somewhere, and a somewhere remarkably similar to the traditional standpoint outside our various language games.[16] This book tries to avoid this paradox, too, by arguing that our conception of objectivity and our conception of what, in a particular case, constitutes an appropriately objective set of standards governing a given subject matter evolve reciprocally.[17] I will discuss this issue throughout the book.

The challenge I have set myself, then, is to find a way of defending the rationality of moral reasoning across entire frameworks of moral belief, across cultures and historical periods, while allowing for the kind of critical insight into moral practices that Williams urged was lacking in the original version of moral cognitivism. Yet this positive account, while acknowledging the historical contextualization of moral knowledge, must also dispense with the Hegelian resources of a grand historical narrative. It is a difficult challenge, but I hope that the contextualist argument that I offer can meet it.

Contextualism is best introduced as a genuine alternative to both foundationalist and coherence theories of knowledge.[18] Both of these alternative approaches to knowledge make the error of imagining that we can treat the system of knowledge as a

[14] Elizabeth Anscombe identified an instance of the chain fallacy (controversially) in the opening chapter of Aristotle's *Nichomachean Ethics*, trans. J. A. K. Thompson (London: Penguin Classics, 2004): Anscombe, *Intention* (Ithaca, NY: Cornell University Press, 1957), 34; Anscombe, *An Introduction to Wittgenstein's Tractatus* (London: Hutchinson, 1967), 15–16.

[15] The idea that the very idea of postmodernism is insuperably beset by paradox is discussed by Yack, *Fetishism of Modernities*, ch. 1.

[16] Bernard Wiliams, 'Auto da Fé', in Alan Malachowski (ed.), *Reading Rorty* (Oxford: Basil Blackwell, 1990), 26–37.

[17] This preserves one (pretty minimal) sense to the philosophical term of art, 'dialectic'.

[18] For a general perspective on the epistemology of contextualism there is an excellent survey in David B. Annis, 'A Contextualist Theory of Epistemic Justification', *American Philosophical Quarterly*, 15 (July 1978), 213–19.

whole. Both view justification as a matter of bringing the entire system of knowledge to bear on particular knowledge claims within it. The standard metaphors used to explain the structure of knowledge are the coherentist sphere and the foundationalist pyramid. In contrast to these metaphors I suggest the contextualist image of knowledge as a 'crazy' or a 'patchwork' quilt. From a contextualist perspective, the system of knowledge is made up of loosely related contexts. Within each one, some beliefs are taken for granted, and provide a fixed framework for the evaluation of other beliefs. However, these framework beliefs are not unchallengeable, as such, because they may be the objects of enquiry in a different context. Indeed, we can be motivated to move to a further context by problems generated within the original context.

I view the ethical understanding of a given society as forming such a loose collection of contexts. From within any particular context we cannot intelligibly ask whether our whole outlook should be scrapped and completely replaced. However, we are in a position to entertain specific challenges either from within our culture or from outside it. In the latter case I argue that we can draw a further distinction, deploying for this purpose Williams's account of the relativism of distance.[19] Williams argued that relativistic confrontations take two forms. In the first a person or group faces a choice between two systems of belief that are genuine alternatives for them. In the second a person or group faces a choice between two systems of belief that they could not mutually inhabit without radical self-deception. Williams calls the former 'real' and the latter 'notional' confrontations. I use this distinction to argue that not every challenge to our ethical understanding originating from beyond itself poses the same kind of challenge to the outlook that we currently endorse. When we observe different ways in which other people have felt, thought, and acted differently not every such case is a challenge to us. Some of them are too far, metaphorically speaking, to be real options for us, alternatives in practice to what we already do. However, when such alternatives are close enough, we have the resources of reason, sympathy, and imagination to assess the alternatives in the light of our own best practices.

The account of moral reasoning I offer has elements in common with theses developed by Alasdair MacIntyre and Charles Taylor.[20] They have both been drawn to a form of historicism as an account of practical and moral reasoning. They each have a very similar picture of such reasoning to mine: it is argument pitched at the level of historically conditioned frameworks of belief. However, alongside this convergence between their position and my own I identify several points of disagreement which I would trace to the residual influence of a form of Hegelian grand historical narrative on their work.[21] This is precisely the kind of narrative that I agree with Rorty and Lyotard we do not possess. Specifically, I will argue that it is too optimistic to view our evolving moral understanding as increasingly comprehensive,

[19] Bernard Williams, 'The Truth in Relativism', in *Moral Luck* (Cambridge: Cambridge University Press, 1981), 132–43.

[20] Alasdair MacIntyre, *After Virtue* (London: Duckworth 1981); *Whose Justice? Which Rationality?* (London: Duckworth, 1988); *Three Rival Versions of Moral Enquiry: Encyclopaedia, Genealogy and Tradition* (London: Duckworth, 1990); Charles Taylor, *Sources of the Self* (Cambridge: Cambridge University Press, 1989).

[21] I will argue for this claim, particularly with regard to Taylor, in Ch. 9, Sect. three.

at the service of an ever-deepening insight, or as capable of overcoming all the conflicting commitments of a modern ethical outlook.[22]

The view I defend may, unfairly, be accused of the besetting vices of any 'internalist' view of ethical reasoning: such views are accused of being inherently relativist and inherently conservative. Both criticisms depend on the belief that the contextualist cannot accommodate the correct form of social criticism: one with sufficient detachment from ideological beliefs to be able to identify and explain them, but without such detachment that it marks a lapse back into a foundationalist perspective. I devote Chapter 10 to explaining why I believe that the contextualist is particularly well placed to explain the nature of social criticism.

I conclude my main argument with a coda that examines the consequences of my view of moral knowledge for social and political philosophy. Contextualism has not been as neglected an option in political philosophy as it has been in moral philosophy, although I believe the argument that I have developed casts further light on the issues involved. I argue that there is a close connection between the model of knowledge that I have defended and Rawls's political liberalism.[23] Rawls's late views seem to me to be a thorough statement of the consequences of adopting contextualism in political philosophy. For his own purposes, Rawls does not quite see things this way, so I explain in Chapter 11 why I think this apparent disagreement emerges. I then explain how Rawls's explicit adoption of contextualism allows one to defend the 'politicization of justice' in his later work from both internal and external criticism. I go on, in the final chapter, to explain how this form of political liberalism can accommodate key emphases taken to be the exclusive preserve of the communitarian, centrally the concepts of citizenship and of civil society. The result is a view that I call liberal republicanism, a form of liberalism that seems to me correctly to exemplify our best, that is, most contextually justified, political theory.

---

[22] Taylor's *Sources of the Self* ostensibly goes no further than a phenomenology of contemporary pluralism, but there is, I will argue, enough evidence to suggest that Taylor envisions a final reconciliation of this kind, at least when we have closely examined which of our contemporary outlooks lack the kind of justification that Taylor demands of them.

[23] John Rawls, *Political Liberalism* (New York: Columbia University Press, 1993).

PART I

MORAL KNOWLEDGE AND MORAL REASONS

1

The Problem of Moral Knowledge

§1: The non-cognitivist positions of Mackie and Harman are interpreted and criticized. Five issues concerning moral knowledge are highlighted as of future importance to the argument. §2: Minimalism about truth is adopted as a framework for discussions of objectivity, which is conceived of more broadly than the issues of either realism or cognitivism.

The aim of this book is to argue that we possess substantial amounts of moral and political knowledge. A necessary preliminary is to bring out some of the peculiarities of the problem of knowledge in these two cases. I will, at this point, focus on the idea of moral knowledge. Bernard Williams, whose views will be acting as a foil to my own throughout this book, pointed out that philosophical discussions of knowledge usually treat the problem in an 'all or nothing' manner.[1] To take one well-worn example, you either know that there is a red tomato in front of you, or it is a visual delusion and you do not. The way in which our knowledge of the external world stands or falls with such mundane examples has attracted some of the most interesting philosophy about the problem of exactly what scepticism amounts to in this case. However, the case of moral and political knowledge is *not* like this.[2] Williams pointed out that moral knowledge raises special problems independent of problems about knowledge per se, not least that its existence or otherwise is properly to be viewed as a matter of degree. This is a consequence, as I will argue in Chapter 6, of his view that social conditions may be

---

[1] Williams, *Ethics and the Limits of Philosophy*, 24–5. Williams contrasted his treatment of this point, in the special case of ethics, with that offered by Renford Bambrough in *Moral Scepticism and Moral Knowledge* (London: Routledge, 1979). Bambrough attempted a Moorean refutation of ethical scepticism that pointed to the existence of a single moral fact whose certainty was greater than that of the sceptic's reasoning to his or her sceptical claim that there were no moral facts. Williams pointed out that there *are* intelligible alternatives to an ethical life whereas it is not clear that scepticism about the external world offers an intelligible alternative to our ordinary conception of an objective world not of our own making. More generally, Williams argued that Bambrough does not establish what makes his representative example truly representative.

[2] This problem of representativeness in samples arises similarly for a view indebted more to Wittgenstein's work than to Moore's, namely, that of J. L. Austin and Stanley Cavell. This argument is well represented by the latter's treatment of scepticism in *The Claim of Reason: Wittgenstein, Scepticism, Morality and Tragedy* (Oxford: Oxford University Press, 1999). This view, too, focuses on the peculiar examples used to sustain what Cavell calls 'the sceptical recital'. Cavell's ingenious attempt to undercut the sceptic will be discussed critically in Ch. 7, Sect. 1 and more positively in Ch. 10, Sect. 4. At this point I note Barry Stroud's observation that this approach to scepticism, too, founders on the failure to specify what counts as representativeness in epistemological examples. Stroud argues for this conclusion in 'Reasonable Claims: Cavell and the Tradition', in *Understanding Human Knowledge* (Oxford: Oxford University Press, 2000), 51–70.

more, or less, hospitable to the existence of such knowledge. (Williams believed that the kind of modern society that we live in is distinctively *inhospitable* to such knowledge.)

In this opening chapter I will consider the views of two philosophers who argue that the existence of moral knowledge is of direct ethical relevance; all the more unfortunate, then, that no such knowledge exists. These are the positions of the non-cognitivist and of the error theorist. In this chapter and the next I will set out the challenges posed by non-cognitivism and error theory to those, such as myself, who want to defend the existence of moral knowledge and will begin to suggest criteria that any satisfactory account of moral knowledge must meet. However, this question—that of the existence of moral knowledge—must first be detached from two others with which it is often confused. These two cross-cutting issues are those of authority and of freedom. I believe that many people who are resistant to the idea that we possess moral knowledge are often motivated by other moral commitments. Those commitments seem to them, paradoxically, to demand the *moral* rejection of the idea that we have moral knowledge (although, unsurprisingly, that tends not to be the way that these objectors would phrase their objection).

The first question concerns the role of authority within moral thinking. One line of resistance to the idea of moral knowledge claims that the existence of such knowledge would place some people in a position of authority over those epistemically less well placed than themselves. Indeed, the non-existence of moral experts has been used as an argument against the existence of moral knowledge.[3] My response to these arguments is to argue that these issues are quite separate from the issues of the existence and extent of moral knowledge. The problems surrounding the epistemic authority of morality can arise only when the case for and against moral knowledge has been separately decided.

Whether or not there is moral knowledge does not make people authoritarian or tolerant. There are plenty of instances of intolerant moral non-cognitivists and equally of tolerant cognitivists. Suppose, for example, that you believe that there is moral knowledge, but that it is an integral part of the good life that people should realize this knowledge in their own lives in their own way. You might, plausibly, believe this on the grounds that you believe an ethical ideal of autonomy is very important. A view of this kind makes it obvious that it is at least possible to be a cognitivist, but to believe that it is very misguided to force moral truth upon other people (if such an idea even makes sense).

My response to the related 'no moral experts' argument is, once again, to separate it out for further consideration. One might, for example, meet it by arguing that if there is moral knowledge, it is not very difficult to obtain and does not require a major cognitive feat on the part of the mature moral agent. Perhaps it simply involves what Kant called 'mother wit'. I am not sure that there is very much one can say about the qualifications for being a moral agent that is both general and informative: people seem to draw on a range of cognitive capacities in moral judgement. A provisional list would include sympathy, appropriate emotional response, careful and conscientious

[3] See e.g. Bernard Williams, 'Who Needs Ethical Knowledge?', in *Making Sense of Humanity* (Cambridge: Cambridge University Press, 1995), 203–12.

judgement and a capacity for reflection, and an appropriate degree of involvement or detachment. But while it seems obviously true that people possess these qualities to various degrees, it seems equally true that most people seem capable of possessing them to at least *some* degree. Moral capacity does not, contingently, seem to be a very demanding psychological accomplishment. (The exercise of this capacity well or badly is, of course, a different matter.)

Relatedly, many people are resistant to the idea of moral knowledge because of their commitment to one of our most deeply held modern moral ideals, radical freedom.[4] If there were moral knowledge, would that not violate such a notion of freedom? Indeed it would, but my response is that it is the conception of freedom that is at fault. On the radical conception being proposed it seems that even theoretical truths violate my freedom: the presence of the cat on the mat impugns my radical freedom to believe it is on the sofa. It seems to me implausible that my freedom can be violated by theoretical truths and if this is so, the moral will may be constrained by moral knowledge in the same way. One could then argue that knowledge of the truth is compatible with freedom in a more defensible sense of the term.[5]

With these two misplaced objections set aside, I will now describe the positions taken by those who have most plausibly argued that there is no moral knowledge. The idea that there is a distinction to be drawn between 'matters of fact' and 'values' has come to permeate common sense. As Hilary Putnam once pointed out, people will continue to think in these terms no matter how hard philosophers try to dislodge these ways of thinking and speaking.[6] But do they have any underlying philosophical rationale? I am not convinced that in the last thirty years anyone has done a better job of articulating error theoretic and sceptical accounts of ethical objectivity than John Mackie and Gilbert Harman, whose arguments complement each other in interesting ways.[7] So I will begin with these classic discussions of the ways in which ordinary moral claims lack objectivity.

---

[4] For insightful observations on how this modern notion of radical freedom emerged from Kant's views without the supporting evaluative framework that would make sense of it see Charles Taylor, 'Kant's Theory of Freedom', in *Philosophical Papers*, ii. *Philosophy and the Human Sciences* (Cambridge: Cambridge University Press, 1985), 318–37. A similar line of argument is presented in Murdoch, *The Sovereignty of Good*.

[5] For a developed presentation of this argument concerning the proper relation of freedom and values see Susan Wolf, *Freedom Within Reason* (Oxford: Oxford University Press, 1990). This account of positive liberty was also defended in more explicitly Kantian terms by Paul Grice in ch. 2 of *The Conception of Value* (Oxford: Oxford University Press, 1991) and by Adrian Moore in the 'Second Set of Variations', in *Noble in Reason, Infinite in Faculty*.

[6] Hilary Putnam once wrote that, 'If the question of fact and value is a forced choice question for reflective people [. . .] one particular answer to that question [. . .] that the dichotomy "statement of fact or value judgement" is an absolute one, has assumed the status of a cultural institution [. . .] it is an unfortunate fact that the received answer will go on being the received answer for quite some time regardless of what philosophers may say about it, and regardless of whether or not the received answer is right.' Putnam, *Reason, Truth and History* (Cambridge: Cambridge University Press 1981), ch. 6, 'Fact and Value', p. 127.

[7] Mackie's error theoretic diagnosis of the claim to objectivity in common sense morality was presented in ch. 1 of John Mackie, *Ethics: Inventing Right and Wrong* (London: Harmondsworth, 1977). Harman's parallel argument was presented in Gilbert Harman, *The Nature of Morality* (Oxford: Oxford University Press, 1977), chs. 1–2, pp. 3–23.

1. MACKIE'S AND HARMAN'S REJECTION OF MORAL KNOWLEDGE

My aim, at this early stage of the argument, is not to prove that there is moral knowledge. I simply want to cast doubt on those arguments which seem to make the idea obviously indefensible while flagging up issues of later concern. Common sense *seems* to draw a distinction between 'the facts of the case' and 'value judgements'. Certainly a dichotomy of this general kind has received many different types of philosophical articulation that draw many different (and non-equivalent) contrasts. I will focus on the work of Mackie and Harman, since between them they offer a case against moral knowledge that is both philosophically highly sophisticated and that succeeds in capturing many of the intuitions that motivate the scepticism of people both within and outside academic philosophy. Mackie's influential *Ethics: Inventing Right and Wrong* set out its agenda in its title. It ultimately defended a social contract view of ethics, which constitutes an attenuated form of moral objectivity. (Mackie did, after all, believe that people have good reasons for acting morally from a standpoint in practical reason.[8]) However, the most influential part of the book has been Mackie's seemingly compelling demonstration of the indefensibility of the idea of moral knowledge from his own robustly empiricist standpoint. From that standpoint, he articulated an 'error theory' of those of our moral claims that purport to be claims to knowledge.

Mackie first classified the entire domain of moral discourse, and then presented three arguments why it could not redeem the credentials that it claimed for itself. Mackie's error theory was striking: he believed both that moral thinking took itself to be robustly objective, indeed 'factual', and that all its central claims are false. This view differs from more orthodox forms of non-cognitivism in its account of the point or purpose of ethical discourse. Mackie takes the putative purpose of ordinary moral thinking at face value—it is trying to state the facts. Error theory also differs from standard non-cognitivism in its acceptance (which follows from its account of the point of ethical thought and language) that the sentences that aim at factual objectivity are apt to be true, even when it turns out that they are all false. This acknowledgement of truth-aptness has further implications for how one treats the syntax of this part of language.

Setting aside for the moment the oddity of Mackie's diagnosis of the claim to objectivity inherent in morality, his actual arguments that there is no moral knowledge were threefold. First, he argued from the existence of pervasive disagreement within and across societies to a lack of factuality in morality's claims. Secondly, he assumed that there was a necessary connection between accepting a moral claim and being moved to act on it, the claim of the *motivational internalist*. He further assumed a basically Humean division of the mind into active and passive faculties. Beliefs being

---

[8] This is another sense in which it would be misleading to classify Mackie as an orthodox sceptic about moral claims. He is not sceptical about such claims if they are understood as grounded in a form of contractarian social contract theory that, in Mackie's view, sufficed to give them rational justification. See *Ethics: Inventing Right and Wrong*, 107–24.

inert, Mackie implied that the motivational force of morality would have to derive from its describing facts that were both in the world, robustly independent of us in the way that primary qualities are, and yet intrinsically motivational. Finding this combination of motivational internalism and primary quality realism implausible, Mackie declared that moral properties would have to be 'queer' entities, whose intrinsic implausibility should dissuade one from postulating their existence. Thirdly, Mackie implied that a subjective basis for morality offered a better explanation of both the actual cognitive status of morality and the factual status it misleadingly claimed for itself.

Before proceeding, let me briefly clarify some of these terms. Motivational internalism and the 'Humean' theory of motivation will be explicitly discussed in the next chapter and in Chapter 4, so at this stage let me offer a brief characterization of these positions.[9] The internalist believes that if a rational agent believes that he or she has a reason to perform action ø, then he or she is thereby motivated to do ø. There is some form of necessity in the link between reasons and agency, and differing forms of internalism differ in the kind of necessity they ascribe to this connection. The opponent of this claim, the externalist, takes there to be no necessary connection between reasons and agency. A related view is that of the Humean in the theory of motivation, who takes all intentional actions to be motivated by a belief and a desire, where the desire is not itself motivated by the belief. All of these positions will be examined in more detail in Part II of this book.

The first point to be made about Mackie's overall case against moral knowledge is that while, on first examination, it seems to represent a sensible empiricist outlook, it is in various ways itself very queer in the sense that it is very counter-intuitive. The first oddity is the tension between the two claims that one ought to classify moral discourse as factual, and that actually all its apparently factual claims are false. Surely the latter point pressurizes the original diagnosis? There is clearly a very fine line between classifying a discourse as factual and entirely false, and deciding that one has misclassified it as aspiring to factuality in the first place.[10]

The second oddity is the queerness of 'queerness'. Mackie's rejection of the idea of moral properties on the basis of their queerness is very misleading. A natural reaction to Mackie's argument is that people have divergent intuitions about what counts as odd, or intuitively queer, and many contemporary scientific postulates such as quarks,

[9] The scare quotes are necessary because there is considerable controversy over Hume's actual views and the phrase 'the Humean theory of motivation' is now often used to describe a set of views that are not Hume's own. See Elijah Milgram, 'Was Hume a Humean?', *Hume Studies*, 21/1 (Apr. 1995), 75–93.

[10] To put the issue in terms that will be used later, there is a tension between two sets of findings: one set relating to *truth-aptness*; the other relating to *truth among the truth-apt*. The first issue is deciding whether an area of thought and language is so structured that we should take its sentences to be apt for being judged true or false. The second issue is deciding what is involved in then attributing the value, true, to truth-apt sentences. It is, at the very least, odd that Mackie should judge all sentences used for making moral assertions to be assertions apt for truth and for them all to be false. This problem becomes even more acute on the conception of truth that I will adopt in the course of this chapter. For extended development of this point see Crispin Wright, 'Truth in Ethics', *Ratio*, 8/3 (Dec. 1995), 209–26, esp. the discussion at 210.

leptons, or the Higgs boson count as queer.[11] This is a fair point, but Mackie simply expressed himself a little clumsily; he in fact gives a precise sense to the term as he uses it and is not at the mercy of people's divergent intuitions as to whether a moral value would be more queer than a superstring. Driving his argument is the combination he presupposes of a conception of a property quite independent of us, in the way primary qualities are, with the internalist's a priori and necessary link between belief and motivation. However, if Mackie's position is understood in this way, it seems to me to run into serious difficulties. First, the position that results from combining primary quality realism and internalism is not 'queer' in the sense of odd or implausible. It is completely unintelligible, given Mackie's implicit commitment to Humeanism in the philosophy of mind. I will explain this in more detail.

If one assumes a Humean view of motivation, it is clear that there may be cases in which beliefs can, as it were, motivationally leave one cold. On this view, beliefs are passive representations of the world and there is no connection between such representations and feelings or motivations that belong to a contrasting active, volitional part of the mind. To borrow a Jonathan Dancy joke, beliefs are, on the Humean view, intrinsically inert whereas desires are intrinsically 'ert'.[12] Beliefs can only motivate in conjunction with desires, whereas desires can motivate alone (in virtue of their 'ert-ness') and there is no necessary connection in the Humean account between the beliefs one holds and the desires that motivate one's actions. So a belief can, motivationally, leave you cold in the sense that it can impact on you with no consequences for how you are motivated. The way the Humean model of the mind is set up explicitly allows for such a possibility.

Now add to this picture Mackie's conception of moral properties as akin to primary qualities, as real in the sense that they are robustly independent of our minds. The beliefs we form about the presence of such properties could, obviously, on occasion leave us cold. But Mackie's commitment to internalism is a commitment to the view that moral requirements, whatever they turn out to be, must be necessarily motivational. So the conjunction of Humeanism, primary quality realism, and internalism is flatly inconsistent in the following way: if moral requirements are construed as beliefs, it demands of them both that they be contingently motivating (to preserve the truth of Humeanism) and necessarily motivating (to preserve the truth of

---

[11] There is another component of Mackie's argument that I will not pursue in detail at this point although some of the relevant issues are broached in Part III, below. This component is well captured by Mackie's remark that 'If there were objective values [properties, facts], then they would be entities or qualities or relations of a very strange sort . . . Correspondingly, if we were aware of them, it would have to be by some special faculty of moral perception or intuition, *utterly different from our ordinary ways of knowing everything else*' [emphasis added]. Mackie, *Ethics*, 38. This is, on the face of it, not a very convincing argument. Superstrings are, by anyone's standards, very strange objects. But they are not known 'correspondingly' using a special faculty of knowledge. We use our general capacity for formulating scientific theories to know about superstrings: this is a case of usual capacities, unusual objects. Furthermore, if one were forced by the very existence of moral knowledge to postulate a *sui generis* mode of knowing such truths, it is hard to see why this faculty would be such as *only* to give knowledge of moral truths. I do not believe that we are, in fact, forced into the drastic step of postulating such a special and dedicated faculty as the arguments of Part III will indicate. See esp. Ch. 8, Sect. 3.

[12] Jonathan Dancy, *Moral Reasons* (Oxford: Blackwell Publishers 1993), chs. 1 and 2.

internalism). Mackie, quite reasonably given his assumptions, has to negate one of his premisses to avoid an inconsistent conclusion, so he rejects the premiss that moral requirements are beliefs.

Little wonder, then, that the only candidate Mackie suggests for a view which meets the constraints he has outlined is strict and literal Platonism, which postulates an independent moral order in the world completely independent of us, yet such that to know its structure is to be motivated in accordance with it (to know the good is to love the good). It is hard to believe that this is the only form cognitivism could take. That this is the only form of cognitivism that Mackie takes seriously should lead one to be cautious in endorsing his assumptions. It is hard to believe that Plato is the only cognitivist in the history of moral philosophy worth taking seriously on the grounds that he is the only moral realist who has fully understood what such a position would have to *be*.[13]

This leads directly to my second criticism, which is that one has the option of contraposing Mackie's claims. His line of reasoning can be used to *introduce* a conception of a property that meets the requirement of an internal link between belief and motivation, and is therefore *not* robustly independent of us in the way that primary qualities are. Secondary properties, which Mackie treats as subjective projections, may prove to be a useful analogy for a property that is anthropocentric and thus 'subjective', and yet also really part of our experience of the objective world. Other cognitivists have contraposed Mackie's reasoning in precisely this way. Paul Grice's comments on Mackie's use of the concept of **queerness** is in my view very helpful:

What strikes me as queer is that the queernesses referred to by Mackie are not darkly concealed skeletons in objectivist closets which are cunningly dragged to light by him; they are, rather, conditions proclaimed by objectivists as ones which must be accommodated if we are to have a satisfactory theoretical account of conduct [. . .] while these queernesses can be used to specify tasks which an objectivist could be called upon [. . .] to perform [. . .] they cannot be used as bricks to bombard an objectivist with even before he has started to fulfil those tasks.[14]

Thirdly, Mackie's account of the internalism requirement is itself idiosyncratic and a very strong interpretation of what internalism requires. Proper consideration of the issue must await a full exposition of the varieties of internalism later in this book. At this point I will cite Grice once more on the subject of how rational agents may be 'bound' by their good practical reasons:

It is perhaps as if someone were to say, [. . .] 'I don't see how there can be such a thing as matrimony; if there were, people would have to be bound to one another in marriage, and everything we see in real life and on the cinema-screen goes to suggest that the only way people can be bound to one another is *with ropes*'.[15]

[13] But for agreement with Mackie see Christine Korsgaard, *The Sources of Normativity* (Cambridge: Cambridge University Press, 1996), 37. I will discuss Korsgaard's views in Chs. 3 and 4, below.
[14] Grice, *The Conception of Value*, 45.
[15] Ibid. Grice's argument in this chapter is directed against both Mackie's and Foot's interpretations of the 'binding force' of morality, and Grice's own Kantian conclusion harmonizes with the defence of internalism in Christine Korsgaard, 'Skepticism about Practical Reason', *Journal of*

The other element of Mackie's argument that seems problematic to anyone sympathetic to cognitivism is the role played in his argument by the idea of disagreement. Mackie's conception of the link between objectivity and disagreement again seems tendentious. In response to Mackie, I would argue that there is no direct link between lack of agreement and lack of objectivity, as any familiar account of the extent of disagreement within perfectly objective disciplines will attest.[16] Mackie himself acknowledged that some extra consideration is required to make moral disagreement peculiarly problematic, but in his account it is unclear what this extra element is supposed to be. One of the innovative proposals that has emerged from the reconception of objectivity in philosophy after Wittgenstein and Davidson is that there is, in fact, an indirect link between core agreements in the meanings of terms, and the truth of certain canonical judgements made using those terms. The presupposition of widespread and interminable disagreement would threaten not just factuality, but the intelligibility of the practices in which the truth claims were embedded. This is a point that I will return to at several junctures in my argument below, so I will not develop it further here. While Mackie's attack on the idea of moral knowledge is superficially compelling, it is, on further reflection, problematic.

Similar considerations apply to the other well-known criticism of the idea of moral knowledge in the work of Gilbert Harman. However, certain aspects of his approach make him a more difficult target than Mackie for the defender of moral cognitivism. For Harman does not hold an error theory, and indeed on one interpretation his argument does not deny that people hold moral beliefs. In Harman's argument, the difference between the kind of objectivity enjoyed by a mature physical science and the status of ethics emerges at a 'meta'-level. The question is not whether or not makers of judgements hold moral, mathematical, or physical beliefs, but what best explains the event of him or her forming that belief. It is at that level, Harman believes, that a suspicion that ethics does not match up to the cognitive status of, say, physics, will emerge as confirmed. He does not deny that in many different cases, observers form beliefs on the basis of their observations, backed up by background theory. There is nothing in this that is, as yet, prejudicial to the moral. Indeed, it offers support to those who wish to explain moral knowledge as a form of observational knowledge by pointing out that observation is informed by background theory. However, it is when we reflect on this process of belief formation and take this process itself as our explanandum that a key difference emerges. The difference is this: in some cases we need to cite the observed fact in both the explanation of the formation of the original belief, and also cite the same fact once again when we give our meta-level explanation of the processes of belief formation. In other cases, Harman contends, the observed fact is only needed for the explanation of the formation of the original belief. It drops

Philosophy, 83/1 (Jan. 1986), 5–25. The conclusion of both discussions is that practical reason motivates the rational agent *in so far as that agent is fully rational*. I will discuss this understanding of internalism and its requirements in Chs. 3 and 4, below.

16 See esp., the Davidsonian argument offered by Susan Hurley, 'Objectivity and Disagreement', in Ted Honderich, (ed.), *Morality and Objectivity* (London: Routledge, 1985), 54–97 and more generally in *Natural Reasons: Personality and Polity* (Oxford: Oxford University Press, 1992).

out of the explanation, given at a reflective meta-level, of the type of belief formation instantiated by the original example. It drops out because it can be successfully reduced.

Harman's actual example is of the contrast between an observer seeing a group of hooligans setting fire to a cat, and a scientist seeing a trace in a cloud chamber that is canonical evidence for the presence of a proton. In both cases, an observer can form a belief informed to a greater or lesser extent by background theory. In the case of the hooligans, Harman argues, the best explanation of the forming of the belief that their action is cruel will rely only on the observer's psychology, plus empirical facts about the circumstances. By contrast, the best explanation of the forming of the belief by the scientist must, indispensably, mention the presence of the proton in both the aetiology and the justification of the belief. The moral property figures only once in the explanation of the original moral belief, whereas the physical property figures twice, in both the explanation of the original belief and in our reflective understanding of how the formation of that belief is best explained.

I think it is helpful to view Harman's argument here in the light of some of his wider commitments, for example, to the idea of naturalized epistemology.[17] This is the view that epistemology can be nothing other than the scientific study of knowledge acquisition processes: a self-vindicating account, in scientific terms, of how the scientific world view is acquired and justified. It is natural, for reasons that Richard Boyd has explained, to cash out these ideas in terms of a causal theory of evidence, and putting Harman's argument in the context of such a theory casts much light, I believe, on how his argument proceeds.[18] Causally, the physicist's belief is justified and explained by the presence of the proton; we need make no such assumption to explain, or explain away, the moral belief that the hooligans were cruel when they burnt the cat. There is no need to cite a property that causes that belief; we have enough when we cite a psychological propensity and facts in the world that are not distinctively moral.

This is a subtle argument, but once again I believe it is possible for the defender of moral knowledge to deflect Harman's argument. The crux of the dispute will not be discussed until Chapter 6, but at this stage I would like to disentangle the various different elements of Harman's position to show once again that they are either question begging, or that their force is debatable. The cognitivist will begin by acknowledging Harman's concession that there can be moral beliefs, so that moral agents at least are in states that are apt to be proper objects of knowledge. Equally useful to the cognitivist is Harman's admission that observation is theory laden: that one can 'see' cruelty is neither more nor less surprising than the fact that an appropriately trained observer can 'see' protons. In both cases, background theory makes available to perception a link between concept, judgement, and canonical evidence. One of the puzzles that

[17] W. V. O. Quine, 'Epistemology Naturalised', in *Ontological Relativity and Other Essays* (New York: Columbia University Press, 1969), 69–90; Gilbert Harman, *Change in View*, (Cambridge, Mass.: MIT Press, 1988).

[18] Richard Boyd, 'Realism, Underdetermination, and a Causal Theory of Evidence', *Noûs*, 7 (Mar. 1973), 1–12.

motivates scepticism about moral knowledge is which cognitive faculty is involved in acquiring such knowledge; the straightforward answer is 'theory laden observation'.[19] (I will discuss this issue further in Chapter 8, Section 3.)

The cognitivist can then point out how many different issues are put together in Harman's objectivity test. On my analysis, there are at least six. First, the claim that the objectivity of an area of thought or language is an issue properly to be raised at a meta-level. Secondly, the claim that our conception of objectivity ought to be 'boot-strapping': in this case, exemplified by the claim that physical science can now vindicate the status of its own claims to knowledge using only concepts vindicated by physical science. (This is a claim central to the project of 'naturalized epistemology'.) Thirdly, the claim that there are no irreducible moral explanations. Fourthly, the claim that moral explanations are never the best explanations of belief. Fifthly, the deployment in Harman's argument of a causal theory of knowledge. Sixth, the suggestion that the concepts deployed in morality are in some sense perspectival, or relative to a distinctively human point of view. All of these different criteria of objectivity are run together in Harman's original argument and in the debate his argument has provoked. Once separated out, they may be rebutted separately. On some points the cognitivist ought to agree, subject to some provisos; other points can be resisted. But the complete package, I will be arguing, adds up to a vindication of a form of qualified cognitivism, not its total rejection.

Amongst the six claims on the list, let me indicate which I think are genuine challenges for moral cognitivism and which I think are not. First and most importantly, I think that Harman has located the issue in exactly the right place. Agents have moral beliefs and any argument critical of the objectivity of those beliefs will be pitched at the meta-level of the best explanation of the holding of them. The second requirement, that our conception of objectivity be, in a sense, 'self-vindicating', does raise a genuine issue, but in a misleading form. I will discuss the point at length in Chapter 6, where I will deny that a conception of objective content requires a similarly objective epistemology and will argue that while objectivity needs a reflective explanation, it does not need a reflexive one.[20]

However, whereas there is a genuine issue here, I do not think battle ought to be joined on the third point, namely, whether there are any irreducibly moral explanations. I share the suspicion voiced by Crispin Wright that what is actually going on in the debate on this point between Harman and his critics is best classified under headings number four and six on the list: whether moral explanations, unreduced, are ever the best explanations we have, and whether it matters that in some way the concepts

[19] This answer is also given by Richard Boyd, 'How to Be a Moral Realist', in Geoffrey Sayre-McCord (ed.), *Essays On Moral Realism* (Ithaca, NY: Cornell University Press, 1988), 131–98, an excellent paper to which I am much indebted.

[20] The point is that naturalized epistemology *can* be used to express an ideal of justification in which the best explanation of how we acquire a justified belief is no less objective or non-perspectival (maximally independent of our perspective on the world and its peculiarities) than the belief itself. This ideal is controversial and Chapter 6 will argue that it is unrealizable in this form. But it seems to me an optional part of the project of naturalized epistemology more generally understood.

and categories we deploy are culturally local.[21] These will prove to be decisive issues in the ensuing discussion, particularly in Chapters 6 and 7 when I discuss Bernard Williams's non-objectivist challenge to moral knowledge.

The aim of this preliminary discussion has not been to defend the claim that there is moral knowledge, rather to defend its possibility. There are four points that I would note as being of crucial interest in the following arguments of this book. The first is methodological and stems from my account of the defects of Mackie's way of approaching the question of moral objectivity. It seems that Mackie's wider empiricist outlook justified several of the presuppositions he brought to his discussion of the cognitive credentials of ethics, in a question begging way. His conception of what it was for a quality to be primary, for example, seems clearly established by a commitment to a prior paradigm of objectivity. This paradigm seems fixed by his understanding of the kind of objectivity exemplified by a mature physical science. I will argue that it is more fruitful to attempt to elicit a range of criteria of objectivity from an appropriate range of disciplines. It is not that we discount the objectivity of science; it is, rather, that mature physical science is one among a range of paradigms, including knowledge in the social sciences, history, and the formal sciences of syntax and mathematics, which may be equally useful in unpacking the cluster concept of **objectivity**. I will offer a further defence of this methodology, drawn from the theory of truth, in the next section.

The next three issues are substantive. First, any defence of moral knowledge must accept the challenge of finding some moral beliefs, unreduced, acting as the best explanations in a domain of moral phenomena. Secondly, this claim must be reconcilable with the admission of a degree of localness or perspectivalness in the concepts deployed in morality. Thirdly, the question of *how much* moral knowledge there is must be addressed. All three points are crucial to the case for cognitivism. In the next section I will set out what I take to be both the best way of approaching the issues of objectivity and realism, via the theory of truth. The minimalist approach to truth that I favour has the advantage that it can act as a methodological guide for the remainder of the argument. It suggests the proper way of formulating questions about the objectivity of areas of thought and language.

2. MINIMALISM, REALISM, AND OBJECTIVITY

In this section I would like further to justify my approach to the issue of objectivity: while the subject of this book is moral and political knowledge, any philosophical account of knowledge quickly becomes involved in questions concerning truth

---

[21] Crispin Wright, *Truth and Objectivity* (Cambridge Mass.: Harvard University Press, 1992), 193–4. For the Harman/Sturgeon dispute see Nicholas Sturgeon, 'Moral Explanations', in David Copp and Dean Zimmerman (eds.), *Morality, Reason and Truth*, (Totowa, NJ: Rowman and Littlefield, 1985), 49–78 and 'Harman on Moral Explanations of Natural Facts', in Norman Gillespie (ed.), *Moral Realism: Proceedings of the 1985 Spindel Conference, Southern Journal of Philosophy*, suppl. 24 (1986), 69–78.

and objectivity more generally. Questions about objectivity seem to me to be properly a matter of degree, involving the placing of different areas of thought and language along a range of degrees of objectivity. 'Objective' and 'subjective' can be fixed by some clear paradigms, but I believe that they are properly to be viewed as subcontraries and not as contradictories.[22] Mature physical science may well represent a paradigm of objectivity and a preference for different flavours of ice-cream a paradigm of subjectivity, but where other discourses are to be placed relative to such paradigms is yet to be determined. Whether this is the most fruitful way to conceive of this issue is a matter only to be determined when my argument is at an end.

Thus, the line of argument I will follow in this book will take as its starting point immanent reflection on the nature of the claim to objectivity internal to ethical thought and language. The force of the Kantian term 'immanent' is that the investigation into the category of objectivity begins from within our ongoing practices and does not require a standpoint external to them, or a predetermined criterion for objective judgement.[23] The contrast intended by Kant was with 'transcendent' forms of enquiry which do attempt to take up such an external perspective (only, in Kant's opinion, to result in paradoxical conclusions that show the whole idea of such a perspective to be an illusion). Pursuing the enquiry in this kind of way compares and contrasts the forms of objectivity exhibited by the ethical with those available in other areas of thought and language.

Traditionally, the issue of objectivity has been approached by examining a series of analogies and disanalogies between ethical discourse, and other discourses such as mature physical theory, aesthetic language, or mathematical discourse. However, the concerns of this strategy are often sceptical, and Mackie and Harman's aim was to motivate what I will call an 'asymmetry thesis' between ethical discourse and their preferred paradigm of objectivity. A discourse is taken as the best case of objectivity and ethical discourse is then downgraded as merely subjective in comparison. However, I am going to pursue an alternative, non-sceptical strategy of placing discourses whose objective status is controversial relative to some better understood paradigms.[24] This task proceeds via immanent reflection on the grammatical features of the discourses concerned. The project is embedded, of course, within the wider issue of realism, and faces the problem that this is a matter of considerable controversy

---

[22] That is, they cannot both be false, though they could both be true. So, for a given subject matter it is either subjective or objective but one might argue that for a controversial case, given the vagueness of the terms, it could be both objective and subjective relative to alternative sets of criteria, each of which might be a reasonable set.

[23] On my understanding of these terms (which is Kant's official deployment of them although this does not stop him mixing them up on occasion) while the immanent is opposed to the transcendent it is compatible with transcendental knowledge. The latter elucidates the necessary conditions of the intelligible experience from which philosophical reflection begins. The 'transcendent' is that which transcends objectifiable experience. The 'transcendental' refers to those a priori conditions which make objectification possible. Immanent metaphysics, which remains within the bounds of objectifiable experience, uses the method of transcendental argument to gain insight into such conditions and to elucidate them.

[24] For this idea of 'placing', see Simon Blackburn, 'Options for the World', unpublished MS, and the parallel comments of Stephen Darwall, Allan Gibbard and Peter Railton, 'Toward *Fin de Siècle* Ethics: Some Trends', 126–7.

and involves essentially contested concepts, centrally that of **realism** itself.[25] Since the wider issue is not my primary focus, I will just set out my approach to the issues of realism and truth in so far as they justify the methodology to which I am committed. Some terminological points must be clarified before I proceed.

I will opt to use the term 'objectivity' instead of 'realism' because there are objective forms of knowledge that we do not want to treat realistically, such as mathematics. I shall restrict the term 'realism', to representation in the limited sense of the causal transmission of information via a representational device, an idea which is problematic in both the ethical and the mathematical case.[26] (However, I accept that a more common usage of the terms takes the terms 'realism' and 'objectivity' to be interchangeable.) The justification for my preferred terminology will emerge as the discussion proceeds; it keeps questions open that need to be kept open. I assume that we can have knowledge in the case of an objective discourse, rather than simply in the case of realistic discourse. This already distances me from Harman's implicit adoption of a causal theory of knowledge. Thus, the separate issue of cognitivism concerns whether or not the mental state expressed by a knowledge claim about an objective area of thought or language is, in its primary dimension of assessment, a belief state, which is apt to be either true or false. When such states are states of knowledge they are, furthermore, true and appropriately justified.

This involves three separate points. First, that the discourse in which the subject makes assertions must involve truth-aptness. Secondly, there is the question of what makes for the truth of truth-apt contents. This leads directly to the third requirement. This is the requirement that what makes truth-apt sentences true should do so in virtue of its being that which makes such contents true. The point of this complication is Dummett's observation that we want to avoid difficulties in the case of successful reduction. If a discourse is successfully reduced to another, are its sentences, couched in the canonical vocabulary of the reduced discipline, still true or false?[27] They are true, but not true in virtue of that in which they were judged apt to be true. The term 'cognition', as the root of the term 'cognitivism', introduces the psychological subject who makes assertions and expresses belief states that embed the relevant contents. This does raise some further difficulties, but to appreciate them it is necessary to set up the framework for my discussion: minimalism about both the truth-apt, and about truth. The remainder of this section will set out my reason for approaching the problems of objectivity within this framework.

Two intuitions about objectivity shape my approach. The first is that I have considerable sympathy with a view of the realism debate, once expressed by Simon

[25] The terminology of essential contestedness was introduced by W. B. Gallie, 'Essentially Contested Concepts', *Proceedings of the Aristotelian Society*, 56, (1955/6), 167–98, repr. in Max Black (ed.), *The Importance of Language* (Englewood Cliffs, NJ: Prentice-Hall, 1960), 121–46.

[26] This leads to one of the key differences between my position and that of Crispin Wright. Bernard Williams pointed out to me Wright's mistaken alignment of the idea of convergence with the idea of a properly functioning representational device. I would agree that convergence is a mark of objectivity more generally, not of representational discourses more narrowly conceived. See *Truth and Objectivity*, 91–4, 169–70.

[27] Michael Dummett, 'Realism', in *Truth and Other Enigmas* (Cambridge, Mass.: Harvard University Press, 1978), 145–65.

Blackburn, to the effect that 'loss of a global issue is not a global loss of issues'.[28] I think Blackburn was quite correct about this, and that the thought that there is little mileage in approaching the issue of realism globally should not lead by default to a quietist position where there is nothing to be said about the different forms of objectivity. There remains the positive task of placing discourses in relation to each other in a manner that goes beyond simply asserting the internal integrity and proper order of each identifiable language game or discourse.

My second intuition is that this first project must be compatible with respecting the univocality of truth. A strategy must be employed which combines 'topic sensitive' analyses of the various marks of objectivity without compromising the unity of the notion of truth. One strategy deployed to this end is the use of the redundancy theory of truth to shift the emphasis from truth to the nature of assertion. It is frequently claimed that Wittgenstein's later work follows this kind of approach. I believe the later Wittgenstein does offer the way forward here, but not via the redundancy theory of truth.[29] (Such a misunderstanding is connected to accusing Wittgenstein of philosophical quietism.)[30] My alternative reading of how Wittgenstein reshaped the debate over the nature of objectivity should, I believe, emerge from the course of my whole argument. At this point I would note that his remarks apparently about the redundancy theory are best interpreted as the view that the platitudes expressed by the redundancy view capture all that can be said in general about the concept of truth, independently, one could say, of how it is used and that Wittgenstein is better viewed as a minimalist about truth.[31]

Blackburn has usefully clarified the issues here by separating out three claims about the truth predicate: that it is 'transparent', that it is 'redundant', and that is it 'minimal'.[32] The transparency claim is that any assertion that a proposition is true can be replaced by an assertion of the same proposition. This is a claim quite distinct from the other two, since it occurs at a given semantic level, within a given language, and is for example, quite compatible with an interpretation of propositions as Fregean Thoughts. It is simply a syntactic remark at a given linguistic level with no semantic bite; all the semantic issues could be presupposed. It is thus easily confused with a different position, which explains that the truth predicate is a syntactic device as opposed

---

[28] Simon Blackburn, 'Options for the World', unpublished MS.

[29] A point made by Peter Winch in 'Im Anfang war die Tat', in I. Block (ed.), *Perspectives on the Philosophy of Wittgenstein* (Oxford: Blackwell, 1981), 159–78. Winch argues that the correct interpretation of Wittgenstein's apparent commitment to a redundancy theory is that truth is not understood antecedently to practices of warranted assertion, nor as being reducible to such practices. They are, rather, constitutively interdependent.

[30] See e.g. the work of Jane Heal, *Fact and Meaning* (Oxford: Blackwell, 1989) and McDowell, *Mind and World*. I will discuss this work critically in Ch. 6. For a response to which I am very sympathetic see the discussion of 'Wittgensteinian quietism', in Wright, *Truth and Objectivity*, ch. 6.

[31] I do not intend the concept of use here to be explanatory. It certainly does not, for example, suggest a speech act construal of the point of truth attributions. I believe that Heal is correct about this point: see *Fact and Meaning*, sec. 8.1 for a convincing criticism of attributing a generalized speech act approach to the later Wittgenstein.

[32] Blackburn, 'Options for the World', 11–13.

to a semantic one with the overall aim of deflating the truth predicate. The transparency thesis is of no assistance to those motivated to deflate or play down the importance of the truth predicate.

The redundancy claim is quite different. It presupposes a hierarchy of languages and meta-languages, and claims that the only function of the truth predicate is to function as a device of both disquotation and semantic ascent. I do not regard this as Wittgenstein's view since he did not believe a hierarchy of languages is possible, but I will not pursue this exegetical issue here.[33] I merely want to distinguish this claim from a third which I do accept, which is that truth is minimal. The two intuitions about realism and truth I want to capture can be reconciled if one assumes minimalism about truth, and such a view provides a framework for my discussion.

Minimalism about truth is the view that an examination of the surface syntax and the internal norms of a discourse will suffice to reveal whether that discourse sustains a truth predicate.[34] However, this point is compatible with attributions of the truth predicate being supported by a range of different considerations relevant to their objectivity.[35] Thus, to take Crispin Wright's example, even if a discourse shows all the internal discipline and syntactic marks of truth-bearing discourse, there remain further issues as to whether the discourse is representational, whether the properties it cites have a 'wide cosmological role', and whether those properties can be characterized independently of human responses.[36] Wright looks to Wittgenstein's *Tractatus* as a paradigm of minimalism, and expresses his form of minimalism in a paragraph worth quoting in full:

> A proposal is being made in a spirit close to what I take to be that of Wittgenstein's insistence in the *Tractatus* that object and proposition are formal concepts. The proposal is simply that any predicate that exhibits certain very general features qualifies, just on that account, as a truth predicate. This is quite consistent with acknowledging that there may, perhaps must be more to say about the content of any predicate that does have these features. But it is also consistent with acknowledging that there is a prospect of pluralism—that the more there is to say may well vary from discourse to discourse—and that whatever may remain to be said, it will not concern any essential features of truth.[37]

I would amend some elements of Wright's proposal: if the aim is to give a nominalist interpretation of Wittgenstein's later conception of logical form, it is important that the proper form of the contrast is between the 'very general' and the particular

---

[33] The point is that the *Tractatus* does not have a meta-language as it has exhausted all the available linguistic resources. Anything that such a meta-language would express is expressed by the symbolism of the Tractarian language via what it shows, rather than what is said. See the insightful discussion of this point by Adrian Moore, 'On Saying and Showing', *Philosophy*, 62 (Oct. 1987), 473–97 and in Wright, *Truth and Objectivity*, 37–8.

[34] Wright, *Truth and Objectivity*, 33–7.

[35] Wright's clearest discussion of how he envisages this proceeding in a particular case is not in fact in *Truth and Objectivity*, but in a paper that applies that framework to the question of realism about the mental: 'Can there be a Rationally Compelling Argument for Anti-Realism about Ordinary ("Folk") Psychology?', in Enrique Villanueva (ed.), *Philosophical Issues*, 6 (Atascadero, Calif.: Ridgeview, 1995), 197–221.

[36] Wright, *Truth and Objectivity*, ch. 5, sect. V.

[37] Ibid., pp. 37–8.

properties of truth, rather than the essential and the accidental, as the closing sentence of this quotation misleadingly suggests.[38] But the quotation from Wright does express succinctly the core of minimalism about truth.

In addition to being a minimalist about truth, Wright is a minimalist about the class of truth-apt sentences. He states that the classification of sentences as assertoric is 'immediately settled just by the reflection that these sentences satisfy certain surface constraints of syntax and discipline'.[39] These surface constraints are further explained (earlier in Wright's text) as satisfying the 'overt syntactic trappings of assertoric content, resources for—apparent—conditionalisation, negation, embedding within propositional attitudes, and so on'.[40] They are also further characterized as exemplifying 'firmly acknowledged standards of proper and improper use of its ingredient sentences'.[41]

I should note immediately that this central point of agreement with Wright is accompanied by a great deal of disagreement. I agree with him about minimalism about truth and about a corollary governing the nature of assertion, on which more below, but we do not agree about much else.[42] I would argue that this is because Wright surrounds his core commitment to truth minimalism with a number of optional alternative assumptions. I further take it that the fact that I can retain minimalism while not sharing these assumptions shows how it is possible to break apart the separable parts of Wright's overall programme. I will note these differences as the argument proceeds.

The most important difference between us is that I am less clear than Wright what the adoption of minimalism rules *out*. He places his minimalism at the service of a broadly Wittgensteinian rejection of a combination of a correspondence theory of truth with 'mirroring realism' and the adoption of a form of internal realism.[43] I reject this general framework for the realism debate in Chapter 6, so I cannot agree with the

---

[38] This is one of the main contentions of Winch, 'Im Anfang'. There may not be any point of dispute between Wright and myself on this point. Wright here speaks of 'very general' features of the predicate and may, by his closing remark, be referring solely to a nominal essence. It depends on how one interprets the use of 'formal concept' in the *Tractatus* at 4.126.

[39] Wright, *Truth and Objectivity*, 35.

[40] Ibid. 29. Wright's views were helpfully clarified by his exchange with Frank Jackson: see Jackson, 'Realism, Truth and Truth Aptness', *Philosophical Books*, 35 (1994), 162–9 and Wright, 'Response to Jackson', *Philosophical Books*, 35 (1994), 169–75.

[41] Wright, *Truth and Objectivity*, 29.

[42] My view is that it is an a priori platitude governing the truth predicate that to assert is to assert as true, where assertion is the expression of a belief. For this reason I am not only *not* an anti-realist, I do not accept that minimalism allows one to be an assertoric non-descriptivist as has recently been argued by Mark Timmons. (David Copp holds a similar view, but on different grounds.) They both want to sever the link between assertion and 'description' so that their non-descriptive views (which are different) can both claim that moral sentences make assertions. In my view it is an a priori truth that to assert is to express a belief and that a belief is a relation between a person and a sentence in the indicative mood. I see no reason at all for denying that such a sentence is 'descriptive'. But I will discuss this issue further in more detail in Ch. 5, below. Timmons's views are in *Morality Without Foundations* (Oxford: Oxford University Press, 1999) esp. ch. 4. David Copp's views are expressed in *Morality, Normativity and Society* (Oxford: Oxford University Press, 1995), ch. 2.

[43] This is clearest in Wright's contribution to Brad Hooker (ed.), *Truth in Ethics* (Oxford: Blackwell Publishers, 1996), 1–18. There are two other assumptions that Wright works with which I will disagree with in the course of my argument: first, that minimalism is of assistance in delivering us from an externally realist package of truth as correspondence, and secondly an

conclusions that Wright draws from his adoption of minimalism. I can see that if you are a minimalist about truth, you are not a correspondence theorist; it is the corollaries of rejecting correspondence theories of truth that are unclear to me. Was the correspondence theory the proprietary possession of the mirroring realist, for example? It will become clear that do not think so, nor that I am either an anti-realist, or a radical revisionary in semantic theory.[44] These auxiliary assumptions do not, in my view, flow from the adoption of minimalism alone.

The striking implication of minimalism for the specific case of truth in ethics is that some debate on the subject seems not entirely to the point. Within minimalism the question of whether or not ethical discourse sustains a truth predicate receives a shallow answer: if the discourse contains norms governing assertions and has the syntactic features of assertoric discourse, then a truth predicate can be defined within that discourse. Now, as I have indicated, these are not trivial requirements: what is needed is the disciplined syntacticism that Wright has described. But debate on the prospects for ethical cognitivism has focused on whether or not ethical discourse sustains regular truth, where truth is given a non-minimalist interpretation. Wiggins's strategy, for example, has been to elucidate the 'marks' of truth, in the Fregean sense of 'marks', and then to establish whether or not ethical truth sustains these marks.[45]

However, this point of disagreement could be lessened if the intuitions motivating Wiggins's approach can be captured within a minimalist framework. The extent to which the residual disagreement between Wiggins and myself about truth affects our different view of the status of ethical discourse as objective also remains to be worked out in the course of this book. However, as I have shown, given the intrinsic plausibility of minimalism, it is more profitable to begin from the assumption that ethical discourse is sufficiently well ordered to allow the definition of a truth predicate over it and then to examine arguments against this assumption.

I view it as a corollary of the minimalist approach that a range of criteria are invoked in classifying an area of discourse as realistic, forming the substance of a truth predicate to be defined purely formally by its governing a priori platitudes.[46] The truth-aptness of a discourse comes cheaply and the substance of the debate concerns whether or not a discourse sustains other intuitions relevant to objectivity. Proceeding in this way substantiates the intuition that we should not expect an exhaustive dichotomy of objective and non-objective areas of discourse, but rather expect differences of degree. Consonant with its Wittgensteinian origins, the upshot

---

associated 'mirroring' realism. I will discuss the first argument in Ch. 2, the second in Ch. 6. On the first point, in particular, see David Wiggins, 'Objective and Subjective in Ethics, with Two Postscripts on Truth', in Hooker (ed.), *Truth in Ethics*, 35–50, esp. at 46.

[44] In Ch. 5 I will point out that minimalism forms part of an attractive package of views that is a strikingly orthodox account of syntax, pragmatics, and a truth conditional semantics. Thus I do not take minimalism to be a route to global anti-realism, nor even to a local and context specific version of anti-realism that applies case by case to particular areas of language.

[45] David Wiggins, 'Truth, and Truth as Predicated of Moral Judgements', in *Needs, Values, Truth*, 139–84 and 'What Would Be a Substantial Theory of Truth?', in Zak van Straaten (ed.), *Philosophical Subjects* (Oxford: Clarendon Press, 1980), 189–221.

[46] For the a priori status of these platitudes see Wright, *Truth and Objectivity*, chs. 1–2.

of this approach is that the practice of immanent philosophical reflection will result in an 'Übersicht' or 'perspicuous surview' of areas of discourse, arranged along a spectrum of degrees of objectivity.[47] Thus, the minimalist approach sits well with the approach to classifying the objectivity of different forms of discourse that I have recommended.

In Wright's developed account, debates over the substance of the truth predicate as opposed to its form, which have a direct bearing on whether one should be realist or anti-realist about a subject area, have two main focal points. They are the issues of cognitive command and width of cosmological role.[48] While I am happy to acknowledge that Wright has focused on the crucial issues, I am not as happy with his actual account of these constraints as applied within the ethical. In particular, his conception of representation as capturing what is intended by reference to convergence among rational enquirers seems simply mistaken. It is, at the very least, question begging in the case of discourses, such as mathematics, where convergence amongst fully rational enquirers following proofs seems central to our conception of mathematics as a rational discipline, but a causal conception of mathematical knowledge remains more controversial as an articulation of that by which the convergence intuition is best explained.

It can reasonably be anticipated that the ethical lacks some of the marks of 'fully realistic' discourse, notably what Wright calls a 'wide cosmological role' for its properties. In Wright's account such width of cosmological role turns on the range of explanatory contexts in which a property is cited without being directly connected to the kind of propositional attitude that takes the property as its object.[49] But reference to a range here highlights, quite correctly, that this width is a matter of degree and seems to me to leave much room for argument over the tie between possessing a wide role and counting as an appropriately objective property. I am happy to accept the view that this way of defending the objectivity of an area of thought or language is dialectical: assumptions about the grammatical features of an area of thought or language and whether this makes it appropriately objective are going to stand or fall together. But I see no reasonable alternative to proceeding in this way.

Wright has, it seems to me, found a way of steering between error theories and projectivist/expressivist theories of ethics. Yet he takes the theory that results to be a form of anti-realism about ethical thinking and as being the shape any future sceptical theory about the ethical ought to take.[50] This point seems worthy of further comment. Why have we been delivered into the hands of anti-realism? First, for the grand strategic reason that this entire approach to truth is motivated by a desire to find a framework to advance anti-realism as a local, as opposed to a global, thesis. In his earlier work, Wright advanced the case for global anti-realism via a global semantic

---

[47] 'Surview' is admittedly an archaism, but it is a better translation of the key Wittgensteinian concept of an 'Übersicht' than the word 'survey'.

[48] Both concepts will be extensively discussed in Ch. 6.

[49] Wright, *Truth and Objectivity*, 196–9.

[50] There is a marked contrast between the later 'Truth in Ethics' and the earlier discussion in ch. 5 of Wright, *Truth and Objectivity*.

programme that foundered on a powerful intuitive realism about truth. Articulable intuitions about truth and its stability vis-à-vis any notion of evidence (powerfully put forward by Strawson) were the central stumbling blocks for this global programme.[51] Wright's response has been to make truth a prize not worth having for either side in the realism/anti-realism dispute. Wright's strategic manoeuvre is to empty the concept of truth of substance, leaving the formal concept defined by its governing a priori platitudes. The argument now shifts to local examinations of the substance of the truth predicate in particular cases and any anti-realism advanced in the particular case will not be rebuttable by 'intuitively realist' intuitions about truth in general.[52]

Because this is Wright's motivation, he sees the framework he is advancing as advantageous to the cause of anti-realism, but it is unclear why we need to accept this gloss on the minimalist strategy. For example, to take a case that I will focus on later, Sabina Lovibond's *Realism and Imagination in Ethics* secures what Lovibond herself takes to be a form of *sui generis* objectivity for the ethical.[53] Yet, by her own admission, Lovibond concedes that, in this case, truth does not outstrip our best assertoric standards. Yet this is, for Wright, precisely the test case for a discourse calling for an 'anti-realist' treatment:

Consider any type of opinion for which we feel we can pretend to no conception of how truth might lie beyond human recognition in principle. Opinion about what is and what isn't funny would seem to provide one example... What seems to make no sense is the idea of a situation being determinate in comic quality, as it were, although human beings are simply not empowered, even in principle, to recognise that quality.[54]

Why should we follow Wright in this gloss on his programme? If, as I have recommended, we shift from talk of realism to talk of objectivity, Wright has essentially afforded a meta-level framework for making such claims as Lovibond's assessable. As Wright concedes, he has not foreclosed the issue of whether what survives in each local area of thought and language is objective or not. It is certainly not always realist, but, as I have noted, Wright tends to place a demanding interpretation on that concept and associates it particularly with the causal transmission of information, a question-begging requirement in this case.

I adopt Wright's framework about truth because it gives us terms of appraisal to work with in specifying objectivist and non-objectivist options in ethics. I do not, however, share other parts of Wright's overall position, mainly concerning what he views as the metaphysical corollaries of his account of truth. However, this claim might be doubted, so I will give it some further consideration. Has it not now all become too easy? Have we not cheaply bought a concept of ethical objectivity so

[51] Sir Peter Strawson, 'Scruton and Wright on Anti-Realism', *Proceedings of the Aristotelian Society*, 77 (1976–7), 15–21.

[52] I take the useful term 'intuitive realist' from the 'Introduction' to Richard Rorty, *The Consequences of Pragmatism* (Brighton: Harvester Press, 1982).

[53] Lovibond, *Realism and Imagination in Ethics*, sects. 12–19.

[54] Wright, 'Truth in Ethics', 217. Lovibond's discussion of this particular point is in sects. 18–19 of *Realism and Imagination in Ethics*.

that with a combination of Wittgensteinian cognitivism and meta-level minimalism, the issue of objectivity has been closed? Certainly, some have argued from these assumptions to the conclusion that the question of ethical objectivity has been definitively settled.[55]

This conclusion is premature. Wright tells us what we need to argue for to secure objectivity in the ethical case:

> Moral truth, for the anti-realist, will be durable justifiability in the light of the standards that discipline ordinary moral thinking. But which standards are those? There is nothing in the proposal to pre-empt all belief in moral progress—belief in the possibility of a gradual refinement of moral thinking and of a gradual convergence in moral points of view, stabilised by the very standards that are the very products of that refinement.[56]

This book attempts precisely this form of defence of ethical objectivity, a task made easier by not sharing exactly the concept of **convergence** Wright uses here (not if he makes his usual connection between convergence, representation, and causation).

That Wright has set up exactly the right framework for the debate without foreclosing on the answer seems to me clear from two facts. The first is that I am going to attempt the defence of a cognitivist view that meets the desiderata he sets out in the passage quoted above. The second is that his work has made possible the expression of a certain kind of historicized scepticism of the kind advanced by Bernard Williams and Jürgen Habermas that is one of my main targets in this book.[57] I discuss their arguments in detail in later chapters, so will not pre-empt that discussion here. The point is that disciplined syntacticism requires core agreements to establish the conditions of sense and that while transcendental conditions may themselves plausibly be taken to be a priori, whether such conditions themselves obtain may be variable according to different historical and social conditions. Thus one question for any defence of ethical cognitivism is whether or not it is hostage to these background social conditions and whether, in particular, there are any aspects of distinctively modern societies that are inhospitable to the existence of such knowledge.

---

[55] e.g. Stephen Everson, 'Aristotle and the Explanation of Evaluation', in Robert Heinamann (ed.), *Aristotle and Moral Realism* (London: University College, London Press, 1995), 173–99; Sergio Tenenbaum, 'Realists Without a Cause: Deflationary Theories of Truth and Ethical Realism', *Canadian Journal of Philosophy*, 26/4 (Dec. 1996), 561–90. (I should note that while Everson seems committed to the view that minimalism is an important complement to moral cognitivism he has some substantive disagreements with Wright's version of miminalism that he also sets out in his paper.)

[56] Wright, 'Truth in Ethics', 219.

[57] Habermas, in particular, has articulated his own sophisticated approach to minimalism and truth in 'A Genealogical Analysis of the Cognitive Content of Morality', *Proceedings of the Aristotelian Society*, 96 (1996), 335–58. Williams showed some sympathy with minimalism in his later works, for example, in 'Truth in Ethics', in Hooker (ed.), *Truth in Ethics*, 19–35; *Der Wert der Warheit* (Vienna: Passagen Verlag, 1998) ch. 1, 'Wahrheit und Wahrhaftigkeit'; *Truth and Truthfulness: An Essay in Genealogy* (Princeton: Princeton University Press 2002).

CONCLUSION

In this chapter I have motivated the central problem with which this book is concerned. I have discussed the positions of Harman and Mackie with a view to highlighting the six claims of central concern, namely (1) whether issues of objectivity should be raised 'reflexively' at the meta-level of enquiry; (2) whether our best account of objectivity will essentially vindicate itself in its own terms; (3) the reducibility of moral properties figuring in moral explanations; (4) whether moral explanations are ever the best explanations of belief; (5) the appropriateness in this context of a causal theory of knowledge; (6) whether the concepts deployed in morality are to a certain extent local or perspectival in the sense of tied in to our particular sensibilities. I will answer all of these questions in the course of this book.

I then explained why I have adopted the framework of minimalism about truth as the best way of prosecuting debates over objectivity. In the next chapter I shall begin to work within the framework I have adopted here. I will assemble the case for cognitivism by examining Wiggins's and McDowell's innovation in the approach to these issues: the view that immanent reflection on the nature of ethical discourse can justify it as appropriately objective via analogies between ethical discourse and secondary property discourse and between moral reasons and mathematical reasons.

2

The Case for Cognitivism

§1: Wiggins's and McDowell's different approaches to objectivity are described. §2: Wittgenstein's account of concept use and the special cases of thick and thin ethical concepts. §3: The virtuous circularity of the tie between property and response. §4: Problems with understanding cognitivism using the idea of response-dependence. §5: Appealing to phenomenology in support of cognitivism. §6: Cognitivist internalism about motivation.

In this chapter I am going to set out the basic motivations for, and contents of, the theory whose critical development provides the starting point of this book. Since the aim of this chapter is mainly to set out ideas, some necessary qualifications are going to be deferred to later chapters. The position which Wiggins and McDowell have developed is one of the most innovative developments in meta-ethics in the last thirty years and it is certainly the option that I have always regarded as the most likely to be finally acceptable, with appropriate revisions. It is a theory that is fatally incomplete, rather than fatally flawed, as I hope that the subsequent discussion will demonstrate. It is also a view of moral truth and enquiry that has been much misunderstood. I hope at the very least to set it out accurately.

There have been several reasons why the position has been misunderstood, not least a failure to appreciate the deep differences between Wiggins and McDowell over the issue of realism. That issue will come into explicit focus in Chapter 6, so I will begin with just enough exposition of the key points to allow the discussion to proceed. I will then set out some important background materials from the work of the later Wittgenstein before explaining the several ways in which cognitivism is grounded in the phenomenology of moral experience and how that phenomenology is best explained.

1. TWO APPROACHES TO OBJECTIVITY

Both Wiggins and McDowell are, most broadly, cognitivists and internalists about moral judgements.[1] As I have noted, the claim of cognitivism goes beyond the mere

---

[1] The works I shall be referring to are primarily the essays collected together in Wiggins, *Needs, Values, Truth*, 3rd edn. I will also refer to David Wiggins, 'Moral Cognitivism, Moral Relativism and Motivating Moral Beliefs', *Proceedings of the Aristotelian Society* (1991), 61–85; 'Cognitivism, Naturalism, and Normativity', in John Haldane and Crispin Wright (eds.), *Reality, Representation and Projection* (Oxford: Oxford University Press, 1993), 301–14; 'A Neglected Position?', in Haldane and Wright (eds.), *Reality, Representation and Projection*, 329–38; 'Categorical

applicability of the truth predicate to moral claims. It extends to the issue of know-ledge and cognition. The question becomes whether the mental state expressed by a moral content is, in its primary dimension of assessment, a belief state. The arguments that Wiggins and McDowell present attempt to secure a *sui generis* form of objectiv-ity for the ethical by eliciting appropriate criteria for ethical objectivity. I aim to show that this approach is commensurate with the approach to the question of objectivity I recommended in Chapter 1 in so far as it involves the placing of discourses around a range of paradigms. But this is where the first and most significant difference between the two versions of the theory emerges.

McDowell, more than Wiggins, is drawn to a quietist position.[2] Quietism denies that there is anything of interest to be said about the relations between the different forms of objectivity exemplified by certain areas of thought and language. It is, as a philosophical position on questions of objectivity, sceptical as to how far our under-standing needs to be reconciled with the demands for explanation. McDowell's quiet-ism is drawn from his interpretation of the later Wittgenstein and is supported by a conception of philosophical methodology as therapeutic and descriptive rather than explanatory. While I will not in this book be engaging directly in exegetical controver-sies over the later Wittgenstein, quietism seems to me independently problematic if it is taken to exclude a proper role for explanatory understanding. Formulating explan-ations is, after all, one of the things that we, in Wittgensteinian terms, 'just do', and do in a way which makes the issue of the relations between different language games unavoidable.

The motivation that McDowell usually gives for quietism is his resistance to reduc-tionism in ethics. Reductionism takes explanation too seriously. Not all explanations are reductive, for example, and none the worse for that; as Bernard Williams pointed out, 'reduces to' is a transitive relation whereas 'explained in terms of' is not. Mis-use of the idea of reduction ties the project of coming up with good explanations to the prospects of a unified sequence of such reductive explanations.[3] However, I am not sure that in the present context such misuse supports quietism in ethics, or else-where. Being committed to explanatory relations of priority and dependence between

---

Requirements: Kant and Hume on the Idea of Duty', *Monist* (1991), 83–106; and 'In a Subjectivist Framework, Categorical Requirements and Real Practical Reasons', in Christoph Fehige and Ulla Wessels (eds.), *Preferences* (Berlin: Walter de Gruyter, 1998), 212–32. In addition, John McDowell's papers are collected primarily in *Mind, Value and Reality*, and *Meaning, Knowledge and Reality* (Cambridge, Mass.: Harvard University Press, 2001). Also directly relevant to this book is McDowell's 'Review of *Ethics and the Limits of Philosophy*', and *Mind and World* (Cambridge, Mass.: Harvard University Press, 1994).

[2] Quietism is an end state of philosophical tranquillity. Common to all the different forms of quietism is the view that philosophy is a descriptive cum phenomenological discipline that should not be concerned with explanation. I shall touch on these issues in subsequent chapters, so will not pursue them here. I have already noted that there is a very insightful discussion in Wright, *Truth and Objectivity*, ch. 6.

[3] There is a passage representative of Williams's views on this issue in *Truth and Truthfulness*, 22–3.

broadly identifiable areas of discourse is simply not the same as being committed to reductionism.

Some of the reasons why McDowell seems to see the issues in these misleading terms will be in closer focus in Chapter 6 when the generic family of internally realist views will be examined: such views structure the debate over objectivity in a very limiting way. My own view is that a form of cognitivism can be developed from the later Wittgenstein which avoids this false dichotomy. But the idea of an approach to ethical objectivity that begins from the later philosophy of Wittgenstein but is neither quietist nor reductionist is already an incomplete description of Wiggins's position. Wiggins's approach to the question of objectivity is, in my view, far more promising. He believes that there is a project of elucidating the marks of truth and central to these marks is the idea of convergence. Exploring these ideas has led Wiggins towards a Peircean conception of objectivity.[4] While I will not pursue this issue fully here, there is a crucial difference in the relations that Wiggins and McDowell postulate between concept possession and interests. Wiggins could broadly be construed as a 'selectional realist'.[5] The selectional realist believes that the world contains a myriad of properties and that which properties are conceptualized by us is relative to our cognitive interests. These interests can, in Wiggins's account, be given a genealogical explanation that offers an intertwined narrative of the co-emergence of interest, concept and associated property.[6] Subjectivity enters into this explanation at the level of presupposed interest: at the level of sense, not of reference. This account takes the relation of concept and interest to be explicably contingent. McDowell, on the other hand, seems drawn to a view in which the relation of concept and interest is a necessary and not contingent one.[7]

This point will come up again in the course of the following discussion when I explain the different things that people can mean by 'thick' ethical concepts. At this

---

[4] Wiggins's explicit discussion of his use of Pierce's conception of objectivity is in sect. 3 of the 'Postscript to Essays I–IX' of *Needs, Values, Truth*. He discusses Peirce's view of truth in 'Reflections on Inquiry and Truth Arising from Peirce's Method for the Fixation of Belief', in Cheryl Misak (ed.), *The Cambridge Companion to Peirce* (Cambridge: Cambridge University Press, 2004), 87–126.

[5] The position, if not under this description, is insightfully discussed in Heal, *Fact and Meaning*, 167–9. She cites as representative of this approach David Wiggins, 'On Singling Out an Object Determinately', in Philip Pettit and John McDowell (eds.), *Subject, Thought and Context* (Oxford: Clarendon Press, 1986), 169–80.

[6] See esp. the discussion in Wiggins, 'A Sensible Subjectivism', in *Needs, Values, Truth*, 185–211, esp. secs. 8 and 9.

[7] McDowell is inclined to treat attempts to disentangle our interests from our concepts as another instance of the scheme/content dichotomy. These attempts are to be rebutted using a combination of Davidson's arguments in 'On the Very Idea of a Conceptual Scheme', in *Inquiries into Truth and Interpretation* (Oxford: Oxford University Press, 1984), 183–98 and Wilfred Sellars's attack on the 'myth of the given' in *Empiricism and the Philosophy of Mind*. The issues here are complex and McDowell's discussion of them insightful, but it is not clear to me that *every* form of immanent reflection on the relation between concepts, groups of concept users, and their interest in having those concepts lapses into the myth of the given or a commitment to a distinction between 'organizing scheme' and 'unorganized content'. I will give some arguments that suggest why this is not so in Ch. 6. For a very helpful discussion of the serious limitations of McDowell's argument strategy see Adrian Moore, *Points of View*, ch. 5, sect. 4.

point I just note that superficially similar approaches to the issue of ethical objectivity are placed in the context of two very different sets of assumptions. I suspect that these differences will ultimately prove to be of more significance than the points of similarity. I shall for the time being present the case for cognitivism in Wiggins's and McDowell's original terms as if it were a composite position, beginning with the background assumptions they draw from the later philosophy of Wittgenstein. Tracing the emergence and development of their views is not an exercise in intellectual history, but a means of bringing out the strengths and weaknesses of the position itself.

2. WITTGENSTEIN, CONCEPTS, AND THICK CONCEPTS

The aim of the cognitivists' strategy is to place the status of ethical discourse among a range of paradigms of objectivity. This argument is developed in the context of a general framework provided by the later philosophy of Wittgenstein. Wittgensteinian assumptions are drawn upon to explain the nature of concept application in general, the application of evaluative concepts in particular, the connection between these issues and realism, and an account of practical necessity.

First, Wittgenstein is drawn upon for a distinctive account of the norms governing concept use.[8] These norms are to be understood as manifested by, but nevertheless authoritative over, communal practice that sustains the use of a concept. A misguided picture leads us to sublime these norms. Harmless Platonic metaphors of the operation of these norms as transcending human subjectivity are misguidedly taken literally: they are taken to be a genuinely explanatory proto-theory of our grasp of conceptual norms.[9] Description of our life with these concepts reveals that our grasp of how to go on in projecting the concept rests on the shared understandings that provide standards of salience, and a sense of what can count as the same case, for a given group of concept users.[10] The general picture of semantic norms is that they are expressed by a form of life, and grounded on agreement in a form of life, although this mutual attunement lies deeper than the type of human agreement found in conventions or contracts.[11] This fundamental agreement in judgements functions as a transcendental ground for, or presupposition of, concept use.

[8] My understanding of the rule following considerations in the later Wittgenstein is indebted to John McDowell's papers, 'Wittgenstein on Following a Rule', 'Meaning and Intentionality in Wittgenstein's Later Philosophy', and 'Intentionality and Interiority in Wittgenstein', all now reprinted in *Mind, Value and Reality* (Cambridge, Mass.: Harvard University Press, 2001) at 221–62, 263–78, and 297–321 respectively.

[9] For this account of the source of philosophical confusions over language I have drawn on the account presented by Warren Goldfarb, 'I Want You to Bring Me a Slab', *Synthese*, 56 (Sept., 1983), 265–82; 'Wittgenstein on Understanding', in Peter French, Theodore Uehling, and Howard Wettstein (eds.), *Midwest Studies in Philosophy*, 17 (1992), 109–22.

[10] For the phrase 'life with concepts' see Cora Diamond's excellent paper 'Losing Your Concepts', *Ethics*, 98/2 (Jan. 1988), 255–77, although the distance Diamond places between her views and McDowell's on p. 206 seems to me highly strained.

[11] For a clarification of the sense of 'agreement' invoked here see the corrective to misreadings of Wittgenstein in the original 1980s rule following debate presented by Stanley Cavell in 'Declining Decline: Wittgenstein as a Philosopher of Culture', ch. 1 of *This New Yet Unapproachable America*,

This general account of concept application leads to the second point, namely, the development of an important argument for sophisticated cognitivism. This is the argument from thick concepts.[12] Bernard Williams introduced the distinction between thick and thin concepts: a judgement involving thick concepts contains more empirical information than a judgement involving thin concepts and thick judgements offer a fusion of empirical content and reason-giving consequences. Thick ethical concepts are concepts such as **brutality** and **cowardice**. Thin concepts, because of their abstractness and generality, give little empirical information about the circumstances in which they are applied and do not, *eo ipso*, provide motivating and defeasible reasons for action. Thus, according to this usage, the concepts **right** and **ought** would be thin, non-world guided concepts.

The argument from thick concepts is restricted to ethical and evaluative concepts. The argument begins with a negative point, resting on the general argument against a Platonic explanation of concept use, but it is important to note that it goes beyond it. The negative point is that the nature of thick concepts forestalls any attempt to give a two-factor analysis of their meaning into a descriptive base with an evaluative 'marker'. Such an analysis would divide the concept into a purely descriptive factor, which is guided by the world, and an evaluative factor.[13] This second, evaluative factor would be construed as a projection or prescription on the part of the concept user. Overall, the point of the proposed two-factor analysis would be to prove that the two elements can be understood independently of each other. The point of the argument from thick concepts is that one cannot grasp the extension of the concept unless one shares the evaluative interests of its users.[14] This crucial argument will be discussed at length in Chapter 6. It will suffice to note at this point that the

(Albuquerque, N. Mex.: Living Batch Press, 1989); 'Scenes of Instruction in Wittgenstein and Kripke', ch. 2 of *Conditions Handsome and Unhandsome* (Chicago: University of Chicago Press, 1990). Cavell's discussions complement McDowell's strictures on descriptions of intentional mental states that go 'below bedrock' in the articles cited in n. 8, above. For a deeper historical diagnosis of such objectified approaches to mind and language see Charles Taylor, 'Language and Human Nature' and 'Theories of Meaning', both in *Philosophical Papers*, i. *Human Agency and Language* (Cambridge: Cambridge University Press 1985) at 215–47 and 248–92 respectively. For Taylor's own view of the rule following debate see 'To Follow a Rule', in *Philosophical Arguments* (Cambridge, Mass.: Harvard University Press, 1995), 165–80.

[12] Williams, *Ethics and the Limits*, ch. 6. The term was also used by Clifford Geertz, but Geertz claims to have taken the term over from Gilbert Ryle who seems a plausible ultimate source. See Clifford Geertz, 'Thick Description: Toward an Interpretative Theory of Culture', repr. in *The Interpretation of Cultures* (New York: Basic Books, 1973), 3–32.

[13] The locus classicus for this argument is McDowell's 'Values and Secondary Qualities', in *Mind, Value and Reality*, 131–50. Bernard Williams dated the emergence of this Wittgensteinian argument to a seminar given by Phillippa Foot and Iris Murdoch in the 1950s. See *Ethics and the Limits of Philosophy*, 217–18 n. 7. The original target of the argument was the prescriptivism of R. M. Hare.

[14] As Roger Crisp has noted the shapelessness charge is a priori: 'The argument against the ethical naturalist is also a priori: given the essentially normative or evaluative character of moral properties, natural analogues (the sheer existence of which any moral theorist will of course permit) must be shapeless', 'Naturalism and Non-Naturalism in Ethics', in Sabina Lovibond and Steven Williams (eds.), *Essays for David Wiggins: Identity, Truth and Value* (Oxford: Blackwells, 1996), 113–29 at 120.

two different understandings of the relation of concept and interest that Wiggins and McDowell disagree over yields at least two forms of the argument from thick concepts, and that Williams may hold a third.

This is the first point at which I think it is helpful to see cognitivism as grounded in phenomenology. For most parties to the current debate accept *that there are concepts of this kind*. For a thick concept *is* a concept such that, when used in whole judgements by the right kind of agent, the judgement as a whole is both responsive to how the world is and gives the agent defeasible reasons for action. Furthermore, thick concepts are concepts whose acceptance and use is holistic, in the putative sense of being embedded in a form of life, a set of ethical practices. I think it is worth registering this point as there are those who have expressed a scepticism as to whether there can be a robust distinction between thick and thin ethical concepts.[15] The point of the argument from thick ethical concepts seems to the sceptically minded merely to repeat, in the ethical case, the very general facts about concept use drawn on in the rule following considerations. But that cannot be correct, otherwise not only would one not be able to distinguish the thick from the thin amongst concepts, one would not be able to distinguish **cruelty** and **oughtness** from the concepts of **hawks** and **handsaws**. Adrian Moore expresses the basic point that a different, and distinctive, point is being made about the use of thick ethical concepts as opposed to concepts in general very clearly:

> Practical reasoning, on this reconstruction, includes a pure element: keeping faith with concepts. Theoretical reasoning also includes keeping faith with concepts. What makes it possible for keeping faith with concepts to have a practical dimension as well as its more familiar theoretical dimension, is, ultimately, the fact that some concepts—thick ethical concepts—equip those who possess them with certain reasons for doing things.[16]

Implicit in this point is the characterization of the concept users and the point that will become crucial, particularly in connection with Bernard Williams's work, is the special demands that the existence of thick ethical concepts place on social explanation. This once again serves to answer the sceptical charge that they do no more than draw on general features of concept use: not all concepts give rise to such special demands.

It is important, then, that the distinction between thick and thin concepts is directly tied in to the demands of social explanation, as will become particularly clear in the discussion of Williams's non-objectivism in Chapter 6 and in subsequent chapters. Thus, the proponents of sophisticated cognitivism are, in Susan Hurley's phrase, 'non-centralists' about ethical concepts: they deny that there is a relation of explanatory priority between very abstract and general ethical concepts such as **good**, and **right**, and very concrete ones such as **brutal, cowardly, ruthless**, such that the former ground or explain the latter.[17] Wittgensteinian cognitivists, such as Hurley

---

[15] See e.g. Simon Kirchin, 'Reasons and Reduction' presented to the conference *The Space of Reasons* (Cape Town, July 2004).

[16] Adrian Moore, 'Maxims and Thick Ethical Concepts', *Proceedings and Addresses of the Central Division of the American Philosophical Association*, 78/4 (Feb. 2005); also forthcoming in *Ratio*.

[17] Hurley, *Natural Reasons*, ch. 2.

herself, argue that there is a two-way explanatory symmetry between the two sorts of concept.

The final aspect of Wittgenstein's thought deployed in the cognitivist theory is the development of an analogy between practical necessity and Wittgenstein's view of mathematical necessity. (Wiggins places more emphasis on this argument than does McDowell.) Wittgenstein's reflections on mathematical necessity suggest that from within the internal understanding of our practices we can discern that necessity arises from our taking certain sentences to be necessary: from the role we assign them in the language game of mathematics. By analogy, the cognitivist account of the necessities of practical reasoning sees such necessities of action as grounded in our practices, as will be further discussed in Section 5 below.

3. THE VIRTUOUS CIRCULARITY BETWEEN PROPERTY AND RESPONSE

With these Wittgensteinian assumptions in place, Wiggins and McDowell develop the cognitivist argument via two analogies.[18] Their hope is that taken together, the analogies forestall the misunderstandings courted by taking either in isolation. Thus excessive concentration on the visual analogies used in connection with the secondary property model has served only to highlight the crucial disanalogy between values and colours, namely that values merit their appropriate response and do not causally evoke them. Concentration on the mathematical analogy dispels that confusion; conversely the mathematical model can encourage the belief that the cognitivist view inevitably involves a global Wittgensteinian quietism or internal realism. The secondary property model is a reminder that the theory need not be taken in that direction. McDowell does take it so, but Wiggins, for the most part, does not.

These two analogies reflect a clear emphasis on the distinction between axiology (the theory of value) and moral deliberation as a dimension of practical reasoning. Both Wiggins and McDowell note that deliberative, normative judgements and evaluative judgements may require different treatment. Secondary qualities reflect the experience of being confronted by value; mathematical reasoning presents the compulsive power of proof, and the hardness of the deliberative 'must', as located within a distinctive space of reasons.

The secondary property analogy brings out a further respect in which the cognitivist appeals to moral phenomenology.[19] The experience of making that which Wiggins

---

[18] The two dimensions of moral thought are described using different metaphors. Wiggins speaks of evaluation as a highlighting of the landscape of choice brought about by the agent, for example, at *Needs, Values, Truth,* 137. McDowell describes the experience of deontic constraints as a matter of other practical reasons 'being silenced', 'Are Moral Requirements Hypothetical Imperatives?', in *Mind, Value and Reality,* 77–94.

[19] These phenomenological arguments for Wittgensteinian cognitivism coverge with those of Maurice Mandelbaum, *The Phenomenology of Moral Experience* (Glencoe, Ill.: The Free Press, 1955). There is one important point of divergence: Mandelbaum's phenomenology covers deontological norms and judgements of virtuousness, but omits experiences of value. Another excellent discussion to which I am indebted is that of William Tolhurst, 'On the Epistemic Value of Moral Experience',

calls 'pure valuations' presents itself to the subject as a case of being constrained by what is true or correct, rather than as a case of deciding or projecting. Cognitivism treats secondary qualities as anthropocentric but perfectly real. They are real in that they pull their weight in explanations of colour experience; they cannot, reflectively, be understood as merely projections. Colour judgements are essentially tied to human sensibility, but colour judgements are cognitive both in the sense that they are apt for the marks of truth and that they involve the exercise of a cognitive capacity.

The plausible intuitions Wiggins and McDowell draw on here are that even though colour discourse is anthropocentric, we can speak of better or worse capacities for making colour judgements. We can give reasons for and argue about such judgements. These distinctions are all embedded in a practice that embodies a distinctive space of reasons. Even though colours do not have a wide cosmological significance, we treat them as fundamental to certain explanations—though not the most fundamental explanations. The projective theorist of secondary qualities takes the lack of wide cosmological role to disqualify the properties as real, but this is a mistake. All that one needs to prove is that there are explanatory spaces that are autonomous of the levels of nature on which they supervene, and which are not rivals of the scientific image of these phenomena, but properly part of the manifest image.[20]

Obvious objections to the analogy with colour experience are that we can easily imagine relativity in such judgements, dependent on variations in physiology, or that there could exist widespread community error in colour judgements. These are obviously unwelcome in the moral case. However, this is a misguided criticism of the cognitivist view, which has the resources to refute it. Ironically, Crispin Wright, no friend of the cognitivist programme, has presented detailed refutations of this set of objections to the proposal.[21] These criticisms pointing to the possibility of relativity or massive error miss the crucial point that what count are the best responses of ideally

Southern Journal of Philosophy, 29, suppl. (1990), 67–87 which I discuss further below in Ch. 8, Sect. 3.

[20] For positions along these lines see John Campbell, 'A Simple View of Colour', in Haldane and Wright (eds.), *Reality, Representation and Projection*, 257–68; Justin Broackes, 'The Autonomy of Colour', in Kathleen Lennon and David Charles (eds.), *Reduction, Explanation and Realism* (Oxford: Oxford University Press, 1992), 421–67. Both of these arguments develop Hilary Putnam's well-known discussion of why a square peg will not go into a round hole. Putnam argues that the correct explanation of this fact is geometric and can only be given at a level of explanation autonomous from that of more fundamental physical theory. See Putnam, 'Philosophy and Our Mental Life', in *Philosophical Papers, ii.: Mind, Language and Reality* (Cambridge: Cambridge University Press, 1979), 272–90.

[21] See Colin McGinn, *The Subjective View* (Oxford: Oxford University Press, 1983). McGinn is concerned with the proper location in our account of the mind of the faculty required to detect such properties. He quite rightly locates the relevant faculty in the understanding rather than sensibility. However, he seems to regard this as a *corrective* to early formulations of Wiggins's and McDowell's cognitivist theory. That seems to me to place too much emphasis on the role of the perceptual analogy in expositing their theories. Crispin Wright's early writings on this problem also looked fruitlessly for a *sui generis* experience of value in the course of effectively dismissing other misunderstandings of Wiggins's and McDowell's arguments. Contrast 'Moral Values, Projection and Secondary Qualities', Inaugural Address to the 1988 Joint Session of the Mind Association and Aristotelian Society, *Proceedings of the Aristotelian Society*, suppl. vol. 62, pp. 1–26 with the treatment of ethical objectivity in *Truth and Objectivity*.

receptive observers and that the content of the concept is indexically tied to such responses using the rigidifying device 'actually'.[22] If the rigidification tactic is then criticized as viciously circular, again this fails to acknowledge the important point that the aim is to be non-reductive about both colour experience and value; the circularity here is the virtuous circularity of a philosophical explication, rather than a reductive definition.[23]

The circularity point is very important. This should become clear as my argument develops, but at this stage I will note that the use of the two analogies is in danger of obscuring the *sui generis* nature of McDowell's and Wiggins's claim. There has been widespread discussion, much of it extremely sophisticated, of the project of formulating provisoed biconditionals to express the nature of response dependent concepts and thereby to clarify the metaphysical status of different areas of discourse. The point that causes the greatest difficulty is the acceptability of circularity in any such account. Boghossian and Velleman, in particular, have challenged any such analysis of colour properties on the grounds that it would leave the nature of the metaphysical interdependence between property and response quite unexplained.[24] A structural relationship is postulated between a sensibility and a property. Without independent characterization different sensibilities cannot be distinguished from each other, and the nature of the relationship is identified attributively rather than referentially. Consider a peg that fits a round hole: it does so in virtue of its particular shape. So does the hole that fits a square peg. 'But what shape in particular do an otherwise unspecified peg and hole have thanks to the fact that they fit each other?'[25]

I do not have to adjudicate this dispute in the case of colour properties; it may not be an unanswerable objection. For example, it may simply require an ascent to a level of abstraction, perhaps the level enjoyed by higher order naturalistic properties. But I think the point of the argument in the present case is to emphasize that the relationship between evaluative property and response Wiggins and McDowell have in mind is an abstract metaphysical interdependence which may well require either a supplementary explanation of how it is known which draws on a general model of knowledge (the approach outlined in this book) or a rationalist conception of the associated faculty (McDowell's preferred approach).[26] The two analogies are heuristic

---

[22] The resources of this device were recognized by Martin Davies and Ian Humberstone, 'Two Concepts of Necessity', *Philosophical Studies*, 38 (July 1980), 1–30.

[23] A point stressed by Wiggins, in *Needs, Values, Truth*, esp. at 142, 188–9.

[24] Paul Boghossian and David Velleman, 'Colour as a Secondary Quality', *Mind*, 98/389 (Jan. 1989), 81–103.

[25] This quotation neatly summarizes the Boghossian/Velleman argument. I take it from Darwall, Gibbard, and Railton, 'Toward *Fin de Siècle* Ethics', 158.

[26] McDowell is certainly explicit about his preference for a rationalist epistemology in his later work. See e.g. *Mind and World*, lecture 4, sect. 7. There is the resulting tension of relating an epistemology for the abstract, modelled on mathematical knowledge, with a phenomenological emphasis on the 'perception' of value. McDowell's emphasis on the phenomenological basis for his views has decreased through time; Wiggins now seems firmly of the opinion that any analogy with secondary qualities has been exegetically unhelpful in that it has simply led to misunderstanding. See Wiggins, 'Moral Cognitivism, Moral Relativism and Motivating Beliefs', 80. For an exposition that firmly downplays the role of any such analogy in Wiggins's version of the theory, see Crisp,

devices, but can obviously mislead if the relationship Wiggins and McDowell want to highlight is unique.

This qualification to the analogies should be borne in mind. Wiggins and McDowell are attempting to give an analogical understanding of a unique relationship, which involves a circularity in its correct philosophical explication that is unavoidable. Sympathetically expositing the colour analogy further, it would be plausible to argue that colour properties are genuinely part of our experience of the external world. We associate a distinctive phenomenology with them, and colour properties pull their weight in explanations of colour experience. This is the requirement imposed by both Wiggins and McDowell for secondary qualities such as colour. McDowell's precise requirement is expressed as follows in a passage worth quoting in full:

A secondary quality is a property the ascription of which to an object is not adequately understood except as true, if it is true, in virtue of the object's disposition to present a certain sort of perceptual appearance: specifically, an appearance characterizable by using a word for the property itself to say how the object perceptually appears.[27]

There are, I would suggest, three different tests for a secondary-like property being genuinely admissible derivable from Wiggins and McDowell's work. First, and strongest, is the test that a property is not comprehensible independently of certain canonical phenomenal experiences, which thereby make the property available to explanations of those same experiences. (This is McDowell's criterion for the case of colour properties.) Secondly, the weaker claim is that a property must feature in a privileged class of explanations which Wiggins calls 'vindicatory explanations'.[28] Thirdly, the weakest claim is that a property should figure indispensably in certain explanatory contexts. It is noteworthy that all three accounts detach the idea of explanation and of a best explanation from a causal theory of knowledge, a crucial point of disagreement with Harman.

It is true that colour properties do not figure in fundamental physical explanations, but this does not seem sufficient reason to adopt a projectivist account of colour properties. The correct explanation of the non-appearance of colour properties in physics is that, because it is fundamental, physical theory is concerned solely with the primary qualities of objects; but omitting an explicit account of secondary qualities is not a

'Naturalism and Non-Naturalism in Ethics', 113–29. McDowell comments further on how limited he takes the use of the analogy to be in Marcus Willaschek (ed.), *John McDowell: Reason and Nature (Lecture and Colloquium in Münster 1999)* (New Brunswick and London: Transaction Publishers, 2000): 'By means of the secondary quality analogy I intended no more than to remove one obstacle to that thesis [that moral judgements can be true] an obstacle that could be formulated by saying truth is objective whereas moral judgements are subjective ... I want to stress that that is all I meant the analogy to show ... The relevant respect of analogy is just the subjectivity of the concepts involved:', 112. I will argue that the cognitivism defended in this book can make a more robust appeal to phenomenology than this in Ch. 8, Sect. 3.

[27] McDowell, 'Values and Secondary Qualities', 111.
[28] Wiggins, *Needs, Values, Truth*, 150–3, 344–6. As I will note below I will not place too much emphasis on this category of explanation in the course of my defence of cognitivism. See Ch. 4 n. 12.

denial of their reality. However, these primary qualities are the physical basis of secondary qualities, which possess an autonomous explanatory basis. In just the same way that different abstract structures in nature can have varying physical realizations, so colour properties can be variably realized. Colour properties are cited in causal explanations of colour experience, but these explanations operate at a level independent of that of fundamental physical theory.[29] As I have indicated I think that this is, indeed, a plausible account of colour properties. However, as I shall show, the problems with applying the account to ethics will arise elsewhere.

In a parallel way to the colour case, Wiggins argues that moral properties pull their weight in moral explanations. In his reply to Harman's argument, which I discussed above, Wiggins argues that if one attempts to supplant moral properties by non-moral properties in such explanations, the point of such explanations is lost.[30] The relevant phenomena are no longer saliently grouped together. In short, moral explanations are relative to our explanatory interests, but none the worse for that since all explanation is, as Putnam puts it, 'interest-relative'.[31] The vocabulary of such explanations is not scientific, but then non-scientific knowledge is not *eo ipso* unscientific. This approach naturally reflects Wiggins's view of the realism issue, as opposed to that of McDowell who is more prepared to argue for a necessary connection between concept and interest.

How are we to make sense of Wiggins's claim that property and response are on his conception 'made for each other'? This seems to be just the way that Boghossian and Velleman argued that colour properties and responses would have to be related. The point is explained in a passage worth quoting in full—a passage which also makes clear that circularity in these kinds of cases is the virtuous circularity of conceptual elucidation rather than the vicious circularity that would arise if Wiggins were proposing a reductive analysis:

Surely it can be true both that we desire x because we think x good [sc. that desiring is made for goodness], and that x is good because x is such that we desire x [sc. that goodness is made for desiring]. It does not count against the point that the explanation of the because is different in each direction. Nor does it count against the particular anti-non-cognitivist position that

[29] See Broackes, 'Autonomy of Colour'. As I noted above, this line of explanation follows a model in the philosophy of mind applied originally to mental properties. For some observations on the disanalogies between mental states and values see the discussion by Paul Snowdon, 'On Formulating Materialism and Dualism', in John Heil (ed.), *Cause, Mind and Reality* (Dordrecht: Kluwer, 1989), 137–58 esp. 139.

[30] Wiggins, 'Truth, Invention and the Meaning of Life', 106. Roger Crisp comments: 'Some Humean mentalists—Humean subjectivists, for example—claim that to say that something has some evaluative feature is to say that it would elicit a certain response under certain conditions. Wiggins's account is richer, in that the properties are to be seen as independent of the responses to them. It is just that understanding the properties requires reference to the responses', 'Naturalism and Non-naturalism in Ethics', 122. For a form of one-way dispositionalism of the kind Crisp mentions here, see Bruce Brower, 'Dispositional Ethical Realism', *Ethics*, 103/2 (Jan. 1993), 221–49; 'Virtue Concepts and Ethical Realism', *Journal of Philosophy*, 85/12 (Dec. 1988), 675–93.

[31] Wiggins, *Needs, Values, Truth*, 157–8; Hilary Putnam, 'Meaning and Knowledge', in *Meaning and the Moral Sciences* (London: Routledge & Kegan Paul, 1978), 9–17.

is now emerging in opposition to non-cognitivism that the second 'because' might have been explained in some such way as this: such desiring by human beings directed in this way is one part of what is required for there to be such a thing as the perspective from which the non-instrumental goodness is there to be perceived.[32]

Putting the case as sympathetically to Wiggins and McDowell as possible, I suggest that the cognitivist position has explained and defended the claim that moral values are subjective, but real. Experiences of value, in both the aesthetic and the moral case, invite a cognitivist, indeed realist, interpretation.[33] Wiggins and McDowell believe that this interpretation is perfectly justifiable. The idea of a subjective, but real, property seems a solecism, but this is not so. The cognitivist view insists on a degree of autonomy to the ethical when it comes to explanation; explanations of what people are doing when they think and act morally are not reducible to explanations drawn from any more objective discipline in enough cases to discredit the initial claim to objectivity.

This explanatory status explains why the primitive idea in an ethical explanation is a pairing of a moral property and a moral response. In a moral explanation essential reference is made both to a subject and to a property to which that subject is attuned; neither can be characterized independently of the other. This does not downgrade the claim to objectivity on the part of the property. We have the same irreducible property/response pairs in the case of moral judgements and in the case of colour judgements. Human sensibility is inevitably involved in fixing the sense of moral language, not its reference.[34]

The underlying metaphysical idea is that certain classes of judgeable contents are only available to judgers of a certain kind.[35] It is crucial to such an account that this kind of deep relativity to our metaphysical point of view does not enter in the very content of the judgements we make, making them explicitly indexical in their very content.[36] The relativity is rather presupposed, so that we can, from a standpoint of engagement with our conceptual scheme, make judgements that are, from our perspective, plainly true. This presuppositional account explains how Wiggins, for example, can see the entire category of value as an anthropocentric category, while not believing that this shows up in the analysis of the nature of ethical judgements as

---

[32] Wiggins, *Needs, Values, Truth*, 106.

[33] I will discuss what is involved in the idea of moral experience in Ch. 8, Sect. 3.

[34] See Wiggins's recapitulation of the argument in the 'Postscript' to *Needs, Values, Truth*, sect. 4.

[35] Where 'available' is not supposed to introduce a relativistic conclusion but to draw attention to the complexities of calling a judgement partly 'subjective', namely, that its constituent concepts may be available only to a class of judgers of a specified kind. That kind is, in turn, determined by the cognitive capacities of the class of judgers concerned.

[36] To borrow a well-worn analogy, one cannot insert into a representation of one's visual field the fact that it is yours. This leads to well-known problems over the expressibility of this kind of perspectivalness in our representations or their constituent concepts. This issue is discussed by Wiggins, 'Truth, Invention and the Meaning of Life', in *Needs, Values, Truth*, 87–137. For a very helpful discussion of different forms of relationality, see Copp, *Morality, Normativity and Society*, 219–20.

a suppressed form of subjectivism. It is not that we are now reflectively aware that in ethics we have truth from a human perspective. It is rather that we are now reflectively aware that in ethics from the human perspective we simply have truth.[37]

Robert Nozick suggests why the word 'response', rather than 'reaction', is appropriate (though his remarks concern a different context):

What is worth exploring is worth responding to. In a response, some action, emotion or judgement is contoured to the valuable panoply that is encountered, taking account of intricate features and fitting them in a nuanced and modulated way. A response differs from a reaction. A reaction focuses upon and takes account of a constricted, standard, and pre-set group of features, and it issues as one of a limited number of pre-set actions . . . . A reaction is a small piece of you reacting to a small piece of the situation by selection from a small and pre-set number of stereotypical actions . . . . In a full response, a large part of you responds to a large part of the situation by selection from a large range of non-stereotyped actions.[38]

Supplementing the secondary property analogy is the analogy between ethical discourse and mathematics. The point of the analogy with mathematics, specifically, mathematics as understood by the later Wittgenstein, is to emphasize how moral reasons operate in a distinctive space of reasons in such a way as to explain how they can be instances of experienced practical necessity. Backing up the surface assertoric form of this area of discourse are appropriate standards of internal discipline governing the assertibility conditions of judgements and mandating certain actions. This form of thinking is, of course, primarily a matter of intellection, not sensing, hence the relevance of the mathematical analogy.[39] Some of the problems with interpreting this analogy and the ways that it deals with the simultaneous contingency and necessity of moral and mathematical practices will come into focus later in my argument in Part II.[40] I think it is safe to say that the analogy with Wittgenstein's philosophy of mathematics is a very general one that needs a great deal of further specification.

4. RESPONSE DEPENDENCE AND 'HARD' VERSUS 'SOFT' FACTS

In the previous section I noted that there has been much discussion in recent philosophy of the idea of response dependence, and an obvious question that arises is the relationship between this type of view and the Wiggins and McDowell proposal for the treatment of moral knowledge. In discussing this relationship I also want to distinguish these two approaches from each other as it seems to me that the aims of the

---

[37] Wiggins, *Needs, Values, Truth*, 107, where Wiggins establishes that 'red is not a relational property'.

[38] Robert Nozick, *The Examined Life* (New York: Simon and Schuster, 1989), 44. (He was, in the original context, discussing yoga.)

[39] It should also be added that Wiggins meant something very specific in his use of the analogy with contructivist mathematics. At one point Wiggins believed that moral reasons exhibited the phenomenon of cognitive underdetermination of the kind defended in *Needs, Values, Truth*, 124–32, but he later changed his mind about that particular point.

[40] In particular when I discuss internalist and externalist accounts of moral motivation in Ch. 4.

substantial literature on response dependence and Wiggins's and McDowell's original proposals have increasingly diverged.

It has seemed to a number of philosophers to be instructive to construe various areas of thought or language as response dependent. One's suspicions should immediately be aroused when this construal is applied to areas of thought and language usually taken to be philosophically problematic, such as causal, modal, and moral facts. We are invited to view these areas as in some way constituted by the response of appropriately specified classes of judgers. Throughout this literature, there is a concern with the direction of dependence between the responses of the specified group of judgers and the class of facts judged that does not figure in McDowell's and Wiggins's argument. McDowell and Wiggins, by way of contrast, ask that one accept an irreducible circularity in their account and the unattainability of a more reductive analysis. They offer no more than a two-way interdependence in the direction of dependence between classes of judger and the relevant range of properties.

Those who see moral facts as reducible to judgements made by a specified class of judgers clearly have deeper ambitions that I am sceptical can be realized without hidden circularity (for example, in the specification of the features of the judgers). There is an unhelpful metaphysical picture in the background that makes it hard to express Wiggins's and McDowell's view without distortion. That is the view that we can usefully separate out domains of fact quite independent of human presupposition and involvement, typically the primary qualities described by fundamental mature physical science, and those domains of fact which are anthropocentrically conditioned: areas of 'soft fact'. (This dichotomy, as we shall see, can even shape the thinking of those who think all facts are 'soft'; some internal realists speak as if they were counterfactual external realists. They deny that any facts are 'hard', but proceed to classify different areas of thought and language as 'more or less soft'. This seems to me to a dubiously coherent strategy.) If one presupposes that Wiggins and McDowell use the secondary property analogy in order to commit themselves to this picture, then they would be far closer to one of the leading positions in the response dependent literature. But this would be a mistake.

The use of an analogy with secondary properties should not be interpreted in the light of a wider commitment to the view that alongside the hard physical facts described by objective science, we have the soft facts corresponding to values, whether moral values or for that matter semantic norms. This view appears to take the evaluative and the normative seriously, by allowing them to be within the domain of the factual, but then qualifies this in such a way as to yield a position that seems ultimately incoherent. My concern has been well expressed by Jane Heal (in the context of a discussion of semantic norms):

there is something extremely strange about assigning a high status ('really true', 'limning the true and ultimate nature of reality' or what not) to some class of utterances, and a different and lower status ('no fact of the matter') to utterances which report . . . the features of the first sort of utterance—their meanings—in virtue of which they were suitable recipients of the honorific seeming label.[41]

---

[41] Heal, *Fact and Meaning*, 115.

It is true that the ethical realist has to adapt this argument. Heal applies it to semantic norms which are more immune to sceptical challenge than moral norms. But it is useful to diagnose the strangeness of the thought Heal has identified by contextualizing it within a wider framework of assumptions. Peter Sullivan has suggested that this thought can be interestingly contextualized in this way.[42] He has a general concern about three aspects of Crispin Wright's approach to objectivity: first, taking truth to be univocal; secondly, of taking the idea of a fact just to fall out from the idea of minimal truth; thirdly, as classifying discourses as more or less subjective according to their orientation around a paradigm of the primary and the secondary. Sullivan points out that an obstacle to any such view is that idealists, such as Kant, can happily accommodate the primary/secondary quality distinction. So how can it capture our intuitive notion of objectivity? Sullivan first describes the line of thought involved in the hope of redeploying the primary/secondary distinction:

This perspective allows us to move beyond the simplistic thought . . . that properties can be divided into two classes, according as there is or is not more to being F than looking F . . . As we think of a colour property, F, it is certain that being F extends beyond being judged to be F in at least two directions, the first allowing for false actual judgements, the second for cases in which no actual judgement is made. However, because of the character of the excess, it seems that it may be encompassed from a subjectivist basis by, first, idealizing the conditions of actual judgement, and second, extrapolating this judged property beyond context of idealised judgement. The equally familiar contrasting thought is, of course, for a primary quality, G, there is yet more to really being G than can be accommodated in this kind of way, the extra deriving from the consequences of supposing something to be G for its involvement and interaction with things other than perceivers of it.[43]

This, then, is the programme. Formulating provisoed biconditionals for judgements that are secondary is a key part of it. That has been the central concern of those inclined to describe ethical discourse as involving response dependence. But Sullivan notes grounds for doubt about the project as a whole:

It is tempting, and no doubt half-right, to speak of a property, G, for which there is more to being G than being (such as to be ideally) taken to be G, as being constituted independently of our best judgements about G-ness. However, if by 'independence' here we were dreamily to imagine some notion of complete independence, then, barring quantifier shifts, that familiar

---

[42] Peter Sullivan, 'Problems for a Construction of Meaning and Intention', *Mind*, 103/410 (Apr. 1994), 147–68. Sullivan detects this strategy in Wright, with some important caveats. See 'ibid.,' esp. 153. How do I escape this charge? Have I not committed myself to minimalism, and to the idea that **objectivity** is a cluster concept picking out different kinds of case? Sullivan explains how to make this position consistent: drop the idea of a single underlying scale of objectivity ranked one-dimensionally. My view is that we can make ordinal, but nothing remotely analogous to cardinal, judgements using the terms 'more objective' and 'less objective'. These are not anchored on a paradigm of the objective identified in terms of primary qualities. Officially, Wright's view does not make this foundational assumption either but those dubious about his constructivism about the intentional point to his commitment to a 'base level' of psychological description that avoids any taint of the secondary. This criticism of Wright was first set out by John McDowell, 'Anti-Realism and the Epistemology of Understanding', in *Meaning, Knowledge and Reality* (Cambridge Mass.: Harvard University Press 2001), 314–43.

[43] Sullivan, 'Problems for a Construction of Meaning and Intention', 152–3.

thought about primary qualities would fall obviously short of establishing the claim. 'Not wholly constituted by X' does not entail 'wholly constituted by things other than non-X'; similarly, that more than X is involved does not deny involvement to X. These points are trivial, but not to be despised for that. They serve as a reminder that gradings of objectivity reached through considerations of this kind are, in comparison with certain other ways of thinking about the mind's relation to reality, a relatively internal matter... This reflection... already gives us reason to doubt whether resources designed to clarify the [primary-secondary] distinction can cut deep enough to assess the objectivity of intentional properties.[44]

I think Sullivan's suspicions, translated into attempts to secure a form of objectivity for moral discourse within Wright's particular framework, are well grounded. At no point in this book will I be putting the secondary quality analogy to work in the way Sullivan criticizes and in the way familiar from the response dependent literature. The form of moral realism I will defend is neither a soft realism, nor an internal realism, nor an external realism; instead it is a realism that acknowledges that the entire category of value presupposes human interests. The short version of this argument is that facts are facts, and there is no philosophically interesting way to qualify the word 'fact'. Whatever the words 'hard' and 'soft' are trying to do in the case of philosophical use of the phrases 'hard facts' and 'soft facts', they cannot succeed. The concept of a fact is as minimal as the concept of truth. I have suggested that when we think about objectivity, we should reciprocally articulate a range of paradigms of objectivity and a range of appropriate criteria for objectivity in any particular case, but I do not take it as a corollary of this project that one is also mapping out different degrees of harder and softer facts.

The position is complicated by the fact that McDowell is independently drawn to a version of internal realism; I would argue that nothing in his view of ethics forces this commitment on him. Certainly, by contrast, Wiggins is an uncompromising realist. The point of the analogy with secondary qualities (which Wiggins is disinclined to use in any case) is to emphasize that the entire category of value is anthropocentric. That is not to say that it is not real, nor that it enjoys some downgraded second-class status amongst the real, nor that the entire category of value is relational. This last point is worth further analysis as it may represent one temptation to combine the view of ethical truth that I will defend here via a distinction between 'hard' and 'soft' facts.

Our relationship to value exhibits several different kinds of relativity.[45] One, obvious case is that evaluative judgements deploy concepts that exhibit perspectivalness. Our peculiarities as a class of judgers enter into the possession conditions for the concepts that are deployed in our evaluative judgements.[46] The metaphysical idea is that certain classes of judgeable contents are only available to judgers of a certain kind. But it is important to realize that in such an account this deep relativity to our point of view does not enter in the very content of the judgements we make, making them

[44] Ibid.

[45] In my view this fact undermines the attempt to define a category of agent-relative values, as any such account seems always to put the relativity in the wrong place. See, for some remarks on this issue, sect. 3 of Alan Thomas, 'Nagel's Paradox of Equality and Partiality', *Res Publica*, 9/3 (2003), 257–84.

[46] Christopher Peacocke, *A Study of Concepts* (Cambridge, Mass.: Bradford Books 1992).

explicitly indexical in their content. The relativity is rather presupposed, so that we can, from a standpoint of engagement with our conceptual scheme, make judgements that are, from our perspective, plainly true.

A useful point of contrast is with the 'intersubjective' view of values recently defended by Christine Korsgaard.[47] Korsgaard's account of the metaphysical status of values is hamstrung by the assumption that we face an exclusive and exhaustive choice in the theory of value between Platonism and intersubjectivism. (Note that, as in Mackie's presentation, the Wiggins and McDowell view does not even make it past the parameters of the debate.) This allows Korsgaard to draw a sharp contrast between an account of value, which places it in no relation to subjective interest, and a constructivist account in which the interests of rational agents enter essentially into the status of values.

This seems to me to ignore precisely Wiggins's aim of explaining the metaphysical status of value as both anthropocentric yet real in the only sense in which anything can be taken to be real: namely, to be cited irreducibly and ineliminably in the best explanations of the formation of moral beliefs. The relation between value and interest here is one of presupposition. There is a sense in which value as a whole stands in a relation to human interest. But this relation does not enter into the analysis of value itself, as Korsgaard insists it does on an intersubjectivist account. This seems to me to place Korsgaard in the unhappy position of insisting that all values are, in a sense, extrinsic.[48] They all derive their value from a process of construction on the part of practically rational agents. Korsgaard has imported this relationality of value into the very nature of values to become a relationality *in* value. Those who view our relation to value as presupposed can avoid this mistake. On Wiggins's and McDowell's view, and on mine, relationality is here figuring in a metaphysical account of what

---

[47] Korsgaard, *The Sources of Normativity*, chs. 1 and 3.

[48] The second anonymous reader for Oxford University Press asked me to defend this claim in the light of Korsgaard's discussion in *The Sources of Normativity*, 109–12. This passage is at the heart of Korsgaard's complex discussion and it properly deserves fuller consideration than I can give it here. However, summarily put my response is as follows. First, I agree entirely with Korsgaard that it is a mistake to identify being explicable with being extrinsic. Both intrinsic and extrinsic values can be explained although, of course, the very fact that they are intrinsic or extrinsic may lead to them being explained differently. (I also agree that it would be a very bad idea to complement that mistake with another, namely, that intrinsic values must be intuitively known 'simples'.) However, these true and important points do not save constructivism from the charge of offering an explanation as to why something is valuable that makes it metaphysically dependent on something outside itself (its source, how it has been constructed) such that the value *itself* depends on an extrinsic relation. An analogy with mathematical truth is no help: we can see clearly in the mathematical case that the relation between being true and being provable could plausibly be understood as constitutive. Independently of metaphysical parsimony for its own sake, the constructivist can simply only assert that this connection between truth and provability (understanding 'provability' here to be equivalent to 'being produced by a process of rational construction'), in the case of truths about ethical value, is a brute fact. However, such a connection is clearly not a brute fact, as the person that Korsgaard calls the 'substantive realist' *can* intelligibly dispute it. (If the world's leading mathematician were to announce, tomorrow, a radically new mathematical truth that she cannot relate by a process of proof to current best theory in mathematics, we may take the view that she has not found any such truth at all. That seems to me clearly disanalogous from our common sense understanding of the ethical.)

makes certain values or disvalues the states they are and in no way suggests that being related to a subject makes these values either relative, extrinsic or instrumental. Pre-supposition, at the level of the whole category of value, does not prevent particular values within that category and their exemplification in particular cases from being intrinsic.[49]

5. PHENOMENOLOGICAL ARGUMENTS FOR COGNITIVISM

The final appeal to phenomenology that I will consider are arguments presented by David Wiggins and Charles Taylor concerning the experience of first personal delib-eration. Phenomenology here is not intended to bear more of a theoretical load than the idea of a description of experience maximally free from prior theoretical presup-positions.[50] Wiggins and Taylor both focus on the experience of deliberation about values and the prospect of reconciling such experience with a projectivist explanation of value.

Wiggins argues that there must be a harmony between one's first personal understanding of moral deliberation and any third personal explanation of that deliberation, such that the latter does not destabilize the former.[51] On that basis he criticizes a wide range of non-cognitivist theories on the grounds that they invite us to combine the realistic intuitions of our first personal perspective on values with a reflective awareness that actually human values are a projection. This, he argues, is schizophrenic. The two thoughts cannot be combined and one cannot take up what is, in effect, an alienating third personal stance towards one's own practical deliberations without abandoning the phenomenology of the experience.[52] Wiggins concludes that projectivists ought to admit that, in fact, the only way in which their view can be made compatible with our first personal experience of value is by abandoning projectivism entirely and becoming error theorists—a conclusion, as Wiggins is well aware, that is not at all welcome to the expressivist/projectivist position that I will discuss in Chapter 5. Taylor has argued for a similar conclusion, with the proviso that he gives the first personal perspective a certain amount of incorrigibility, such that the explanatory costs of reinterpreting this perspective from a non-cognitivist perspective are too high.[53] The general point needs to be handled

[49] For an alternative treatment of the relationship between interest and value that uses the notion of presupposition see my 'Reasonable Partiality and the Agent's Personal Point of View', *Ethical Theory and Moral Practice*, 8/1–2 (Apr. 2005) 25–43.

[50] Maximally free, not completely free; this allows me to give a sense to 'phenomenology' while taking moral knowledge to have implicit theoretical assumptions built in to it. See Ch. 8, Sect. 3, below.

[51] Wiggins, 'Truth, Invention and the Meaning of Life', esp. 98–103.

[52] For a general treatment of the idea that a proper account of self-knowledge must explain both how it can be a non-alienating relation to oneself and yet hold open the possibility of such alienation see Richard Moran's excellent *Authority and Estrangement* (Princeton and Oxford: Princeton University Press, 2001). Moran dicusses, in particular, the relation between false models of self-knowledge and various kinds of ethical evasion in which one fails to take responsibility for identification with oneself.

[53] Charles Taylor, *Sources of the Self* (Cambridge: Cambridge University Press, 1989), ch. 3.

with care; Richard Moran has argued that if self-knowledge is to be seen as a genuine cognitive achievement then both the first and the third personal perspectives have distinctive forms of epistemic warrant but that in both cases each perspective has its insights and its blind spots.[54] However, restricted to beliefs about values, it does seem to me that Wiggins and Taylor are correct to argue that an alternative, projectivist reinterpretation of practical deliberation will be radically destabilizing of our experience of trying to deliberate correctly.[55] I will not go into this class of arguments in any more detail here as they are the explicit focus of my discussion in Chapter 8, section 3.

6. MOTIVATIONAL INTERNALISM AND COGNITIVISM

The final aspect of Wiggins's and McDowell's view that I will set out is their commitment to a cognitivist internalism about motivation. However, that thesis is going to be the focus of detailed examination in the next two chapters of this book, so I will briefly characterize their view in general terms here. A more subtle aspect of ethical phenomenology that the cognitivist position tries to accommodate besides the attraction of axiological value is experience of the deontic modalities, such as moral obligation. McDowell, in particular, has focused on the phenomenology of practical necessity from within the experience of the deliberating agent with the aim of defending a cognitivist internalism.[56]

One of the main reasons for the adoption of non-cognitive explanations of ethical claims is that this seems the best explanation of the tie between such claims and moral motivation. It seems on the face of it to be a necessary truth that if one judges that an act is a case of pointless cruelty, one will be motivated to prevent or impede it or to avoid carrying it out oneself. This was the internalist intuition that Mackie relied on in his argument. (This seems plausible, at least, if one adds the rider 'necessarily motivated insofar as one is fully rational'.[57]) The challenge is to explain how this tie between ethical judgements and the will can be represented by a cognitivist, as opposed to a non-cognitivist, theory.

McDowell's response is that the Humean division of the mind into receptive cognitive faculties and active volitional faculties merely reproduces the two-factor analysis of moral language advanced by non-cognitivism. Both distinctions reflect the same metaphysical picture of morality and agency, and as partners in guilt can offer no support to each other.[58] However, he also has a distinctive positive theory to offer: possession of the sensibility that gives individuals the capacity to discern evaluative properties could necessarily involve possession of the capacities drawn upon in moral motivation.

[54] Moran, *Authority and Estrangement*, pp. xxxiv–xxxv, *passim*.

[55] I discuss a combination of a cognitivist approach to values with models of self-knowledge, inspired by Moran, in 'Reasonable Partiality and the Agent's Personal Point of View'.

[56] McDowell, 'Virtue and Reason' and 'Are Moral Requirements Hypothetical Imperatives?', in *Mind, Value and Reality* at 50–73 and 77–94 respectively.

[57] Korsgaard, 'Skepticism about Practical Reason', 5–25.

[58] This argument is presented most clearly in McDowell, 'Virtue and Reason', sect. 3.

Central to McDowell's theory is his account of the virtuous person: a person for whom moral considerations do not outweigh other considerations, in some common metric of motivational weight, but rather totally silence other practical considerations.[59] This account of a virtuous person preserves the authority of ethical claims in practical deliberation, while there is no claim that these demands arise solely from practical reason. Thus, McDowell claims to have preserved the deep truth in Kant's distinction between hypothetical and categorical imperatives, though in an Aristotelian framework.[60]

This view, it seems to me, cannot be allowed to stand in the terms in which McDowell formulates it, but I will defer these arguments until the next two chapters. At this stage I will merely note the significant differences between McDowell's approach and that of Wiggins. Wiggins is content with the weaker claim that ethical reasons always provide some reason to act, rather than a sufficient and 'silencing' reason.[61] In Wiggins's account the content of moral claims is categorical in that this content makes no reference to a subject's inclinations. I will discuss this view, too, in Chapter 4.

Historically, the upshot of both McDowell's and Wiggins's claims is a position of recognizable ancestry, the existence internalism of the eighteenth-century rational intuitionists Samuel Clarke, John Balguy, and Richard Price. Darwall characterizes such a position as follows:

The other main category of internalisms I call existence internalisms because they are concerned with what must be the case for an ethical or normative proposition to be true or for an ethical or normative fact to exist. On all such views, it is a necessary condition of its being the case that someone should x that that person would, under appropriate conditions, have some motive to x. There is, however, an important distinction between two fundamentally different kinds of existence internalism. According to one sort, although motive is in no way intrinsic to ethical facts themselves, it is a necessary consequence of perceiving or knowing them . . . Motivation is an effect of the knowing encounter with normativity, not part of normativity itself.[62]

The concern expressed in the last sentence of this quotation will be discussed in the next chapter of this book. This is the thought that knowledge of value is not itself inherently normative but that some further impetus to connect knowledge and the practical is required. Both Wiggins and McDowell, by contrast, postulate inherent normativity in the virtuous agent's perception of the appropriate circumstances. This

---

59 Though not necessarily, of course, other moral considerations.

60 McDowell, 'Are Moral Requirements Hypothetical Imperatives?', is intended to reply to some of the arguments of Phillipa Foot, 'Morality as a System of Hypothetical Imperatives', in *Virtues and Vices* (Oxford: Basil Blackwell, 1978), 157–73.

61 See Wiggins, 'Moral Cognitivism, Moral Relativism and Motivating Beliefs', 82–3; 'Categorical Requirements: Kant and Hume on the Idea of Duty', 312.

62 Stephen Darwall, *The British Moralists and the Internal 'Ought', 1640–1740* (Cambridge: Cambridge University Press, 1995), 10. Darwall's assumptions about normativity lead him to focus on the alternative 'constitutive internalism' he finds in Kant and which dominates the historical interpretations of this book. It prioritizes those aspects of the debate that anticipate the emergence of Kantian internalism and existence internalism plays a subsidiary role in Darwall's narrative.

is a central part of both the historical rootedness and radicalism of their view: the idea of a theory of normativity developed independently of the virtuous agent's perception of the circumstances is rendered superfluous.

CONCLUSION

In this chapter I have set out Wiggins's and McDowell's position, treating it, for simplicity's sake, as a composite position. I have emphasized the uniqueness of the relationship that they see between evaluative properties and the response to those properties on the part of the suitably receptive moral judger. That uniqueness is the basis of the non-reductive nature of the elucidations that can be offered of this relationship. This places a considerable degree of distance between the core Wiggins and McDowell proposal and much recent discussion of response dependence and of dispositional theories of value. Similarly, the position I have described here should not be forced into a framework in which it is viewed as positing a *sui generis* domain of soft facts alongside the hard facts postulated as the subvening class of real properties by a physicalist or reductively naturalistic approach to values. I have also tried to bring out the several different ways in which the theory appeals to ethical phenomenology.

But I turn now to criticism, as I must immediately offer a corrective to what I view as a mistaken component of the overall view I have described. My immediate focus is on distinctive features of moral reasons. I have noted that both Wiggins and McDowell are motivational internalists, committed to the existence of inherent normativity. While I agree with them on the latter point, on the former I am inclined to defend a position that departs in significant ways from either of theirs. Ironically, the view I favour has elements that have echoes in both their contrasting positions. Wiggins emphasized two points. First, that we presuppose the category of value. Secondly, that an illuminating analogy for moral reasons might be our understanding of how the necessity of mathematical reasons could be elucidated via the contingent practices in which they are embedded. McDowell emphasizes the importance of the inculcation of values in the context of education within a given social community when he develops his account of the virtuous agent. By combining these elements in a different way I will offer a presuppositional account of the relation between moral knowledge and practical reasons. This first revision of cognitivism is the subject of the remainder of part I of this book.

3

Values, Norms, and the Practical

§1: The idea of inherent normativity. §2: Moral judgements as 'silencing'—importance versus deliberative priority. §3: Wiggins's internalism and the force of good reasons.

In Chapter 2 I introduced Wiggins's and McDowell's cognitivist theory and explained some of the arguments given in its support. I noted that many of those arguments were phenomenological. One aspect of moral phenomenology that Wiggins and McDowell want to capture is the experience of taking practical decisions. This is an experience not of the attractiveness of value, but of the demands of the deontic modalities. These are modalities such as 'oughtness' or 'has to be done-ness'.[1] I have deferred discussion of the nature of practical reasons to this chapter and the next. It raises the wide-ranging and difficult question of what the connection is between the evaluative and the practical, and represents the first major departure from the theory that I have described thus far. My aim is to explore the relationship between the kind of cognitivist theory of moral judgement that I will be defending in this book and our best account of practical reasons. It seems to me that in the light of our best theory of what such reasons are, some amendment is going to be required to Wiggins's and McDowell's theories of moral reasons. (These are, in any case, very different from each other.) But I also want to defend the kind of view I share with them from the objection, found largely in the work of Christine Korsgaard, that any form of moral realism postulates a mysterious form of 'inherent normativity' in moral facts.[2]

Some preliminary clarification of the terminology is appropriate at this point. Any comprehensive, reflective account of moral reasons is going to have to relate three classes of phenomena to each other: the evaluative, the normative, and the practical. The category of the evaluative concerns the attribution to people, actions, and outcomes of evaluative predicates of varying degrees of abstraction ranging from the specific thick conceptualizations that Wiggins and McDowell focus on to thin evaluative concepts such as **good** and **bad**. By contrast, the category of the normative concerns principles whose function is to govern inference: logical relations and the principles underlying practical reasoning. On the view defended in this book, when

---

[1] As Mackie pointed out, moral philosophers seem very concerned to explain the anaemic 'ought', whereas ordinary language has far stronger resources for the expression of moral modality in 'must' and 'has to be done', Mackie, *Ethics*, 64–5.

[2] Korsgaard, *The Sources of Normativity*, 38–42.

the right kind of agent (a virtuous person) makes an evaluative judgement, this directly offers normative governance to the will. This account has been strongly criticized by Kantian theorists, such as Christine Korsgaard, who see such a model as a threat to autonomous will formation. For neo-Kantians, the will must generate normativity from within its own structure, and cannot merely derive its direction from a source outside itself. Korsgaard is, here, objecting to the historically well-developed tradition of existence internalism that Darwall described in the quotation that concluded the previous chapter. Existence internalism seems, to its Kantian critics, to separate knowledge and normativity in an objectionable way. Any view of this general kind seems to imply that knowledge of value is not itself inherently normative, but that some further impetus to connect knowledge and the practical is required. However, I will argue that both Wiggins and McDowell, by contrast, postulate inherent normativity in the virtuous agent's perception of the appropriate circumstances, and I believe that they are correct to do so. A central part of both the historical rootedness and radicalism of their view is the idea that a theory of normativity, over and above the virtuous agent's perception of the circumstances, is superfluous. Being virtuous is a way of knowing certain things in such a way that the virtuous agent's will is already normatively directed.

The kind of normative governance of action offered by an agent's knowledge of value, however, differs between Wiggins's and McDowell's accounts, leading to their differing views of the practical. McDowell seems partly motivated to capture as many neo-Kantian intuitions in his own theory as possible with the overall aim of defending the authority of moral reasons.[3] He stipulates that when an ideally virtuous agent comes to accept an evaluative judgement, this has the effect of 'silencing' all other practical considerations. This, McDowell suggests, captures what people meant by calling moral reasons 'categorical'. They have an unusual and distinctive authority in our practical deliberations. For these reasons, McDowell holds a strong thesis of motivational internalism: for the right kind of agent, the demands of morality are necessarily and overridingly motivating. The necessary connection with practicality is made by noting that while desires sometimes motivate alone, in other cases they are motivated by reasons. McDowell argues that moral motivation falls into this class of motivated desires: such motivation involves desires motivated by reasons, such as the virtuous person's appropriate belief about the morally salient aspects of her circumstances. This is McDowell's adoption of motivated desire theory of a kind first defended by Thomas Nagel in *The Possibility of Altruism*.[4]

Wiggins's views are more modest and so, in my view, more plausible.[5] While he wants to retain an element of internalism in his view, he does not have McDowell's

---

[3] This is clearest in 'Are Moral Requirements Hypothetical Imperatives?', in *Mind, Value and Reality*, 77–94 where, as I have noted, McDowell responds to Foot's externalism.

[4] Nagel, *The Possibility of Altruism*. In spite of many ingenious arguments directed against the motivated desire theory it seems to me to be the most plausible account of moral motivation. It is worth noting that the motivated versus unmotivated desire distinction is *not* the same as the internal/external reasons issue.

[5] Wiggins, 'Categorical Requirements: Kant and Hume on the Idea of Duty', 83–106 and 'In a Subjectivist Framework, Categorical Requirements and Real Practical Reasons', 212–32.

model of the ideally virtuous agent whose moral reasons silence all that agent's other practical reasons. (We shall see below that this is an advantage as McDowell is running together separate ideas that need to be kept apart.) Furthermore, when the agent comes to accept an evaluative judgement, this provides as much normative force as Wiggins thinks is reasonable. It is the force of a good reason. This, as we shall see, is another advantage to his more modest view. But the question of the general relationship between Wiggins's view and the general nature of practical reasons needs further analysis, which I will provide in the course of developing an alternative view of my own.

1. INHERENT NORMATIVITY

Let us assume, for the sake of argument, the existence of an ideally virtuous agent. She has many competing practical concerns: she is late for a meeting with a friend, but she wants to pick up goods from a store on her way to the rendezvous, as they are planning to go to a movie and the local stores will be closed by the time the film is over. Walking down the street, our virtuous agent notices an elderly man ahead of her stop in his tracks, buckle at the knees, and collapse to the ground. She looks around and she is the only person on the deserted street. A question arises: what should she do?[6]

Being ideally virtuous, such an agent has two coordinated features. First of all, she has the conceptual resources and the depth of grasp of those concepts to conceptualize the situation correctly.[7] She forms an evaluative judgement and in the light of that judgement goes to help the person in distress. How did her evaluative judgement engage with her practical reasons? Why, to use McDowell's words, did the ideally virtuous agent see that particular action 'in a favourable light'? On Wiggins's and McDowell's view, the agent was guided by an inherently normative judgement. They diverge in their further accounts of practical reasons, but they agree on this point: the ideally virtuous agent in the example acquires an item of knowledge whose normative governance of the will does not derive from a separable feature of the judgement. This is a recognitional model of the normativity governing practice. Perception of value directly engages with the will.

There is a historically very important position, well represented in contemporary moral philosophy, that is not happy with this claim, namely, Kantianism. Fully engaging with that position would take us far from the main course of my argument, but

---

6 The question is not yet 'what ought she to do', on which see Williams, *Ethics and the Limits of Philosophy*, 19.

7 These two conditions are present to explain away apparent counter-examples of agents with the correct beliefs who fail to be motivated to action. Such agents may be defective in their rationality, either constitutively or in virtue of passing conditions (tiredness, depression, accidie); he or she may not have the appropriate concepts; he or she may have the appropriate concepts but fail to grasp them with a sufficient degree of understanding. For the first condition see, *inter alia*, Korsgaard and Grice as cited in Ch. 1 n. 15, above. The problem of accidie is discussed by Dancy in *Moral Reasons*, 4–6, 45–6. For depth of conceptual grasp see Murdoch's *The Sovereignty of Good*, 28–9 *passim* and its further articulation in Platts, *Ways of Meaning*, 262. See also the highly original discussion of depth of conceptual grasp using the idea of a Platonic scale of forms in Lovibond, *Realism and Imagination*, sect. 8.

it will have to be confronted in a limited way in so far as it suggests that any kind of moral cognitivism is deeply flawed in the account it presupposes of the connections between value, normativity, and the practical. The suggestion that any form of cognitivism is flawed in this way is strongly argued for by Christine Korsgaard. Unfortunately, Korsgaard tends to make her argument easier for herself by only ever attacking moral realism in the form in which Mackie described it, namely as an incoherent combination of primary quality realism and motivational internalism.[8] Korsgaard, like Mackie, takes Platonism as the only viable form of moral realism. She also shares his assumption that the only epistemology available to the realist or cognitivist would be one that postulates a special faculty of moral intuition.[9] However, setting these unfortunate assumptions aside, there are two main lines of argument against moral realism, or, as I would prefer to call it, cognitivism, in Korsgaard's work. (There is a slight terminological complication here, as a Kantian view such as Korsgaard's can also be called 'cognitivist', but I stipulate that I will always use the term unambiguously to refer to 'Wittgensteinian cognitivism'.)[10]

The first of her arguments is that the cognitivist can say nothing in answer to what Korsgaard calls 'the normative question'. According to Korsgaard, all the cognitivist can do is reiterate the values in the situation that bear on the practical decision of the agent. This looks to Korsgaard like stonewalling.[11] She admits that in a case like that of our ideally virtuous agent who stops to help the man who collapses in the street, there is a great deal that the cognitivist can say. The cognitivist will point to the relevant evaluative *features* of the situation that bear on what the agent ought to do: the man is in distress, he may have had a heart attack or a stroke and be in need of urgent attention, there are no other obvious sources of help, and so on. This seems to me to go beyond what Korsgaard calls 'go[-ing] back and review[-ing] the reasons why the action is right'.[12] But for Korsgaard this is not enough. Given her affinities with moral rationalism, Korsgaard is a foundationalist about moral justification and sets a high epistemological standard for ethical demands. Accordingly, what she thinks is required is a reason that will appeal to a person who does not care about morality or its dictates:

If someone finds that the bare fact that something is his duty does not move him to action, and asks what possible motive he has for doing it, it does not help to tell him that the fact that

---

[8] Korsgaard, *The Sources of Normativity*, 37–9; Mackie, *Ethics: Inventing Right and Wrong*, 38–40. In fairness to Korsgaard, she also writes that 'Mackie doesn't really prove that such entities couldn't exist . . . But, he has a point, although I think it is not the point that he meant to make', 38. She then goes on to present her 'stonewalling' argument against realism that I consider below. (Actually, I think that Mackie does demonstrate that moral realism as he conceives of it is not merely false, but incoherent.)

[9] Korsgaard, *The Sources of Normativity*, 38, 112; Mackie, *Ethics: Inventing Right and Wrong*, 38.

[10] Korsgaard's view is cognitivist because, as a constructivist, she takes the object that is constructed as a result of an idealized rational procedure to be a truth evaluable proposition. Therefore, the corresponding mental state on the part of the agent who grasps the proposition is belief (or, on a more ambitious view, the mental state of knowing).

[11] Korsgaard, *The Sources of Normativity*, 30, 38.

[12] Ibid. 38. This point, that the cognitivist can describe in more detail the evaluative factors bearing on decision, has been made very clearly as a response to Korsgaard by Phillip Stratton-Lake in 'Can Hooker's Rule-Consequentialist Principle Justify Ross's Prima Facie Duties?', *Mind*, 106/424 (Oct. 1997), 751–8 esp. at 754–5.

it is his duty just is the motive. That fact isn't motivating him just now and therein lies his problem. In a similar way, if someone falls into doubt about whether obligations really exist, it doesn't help to say 'ah, but indeed they do. They are real things'. Just now he doesn't see it and herein lies his problem... Is it really true that this is what you must do? The realist's answer to this question is simply 'Yes'.[13]

This may look like a demand that is so radical it is hardly surprising that no one can meet it, but Korsgaard demurs. Kant can meet it:

suppose I don't care about being rational? What then?... in Kant's philosophy, this question should be impossible to ask. Rationality, as Kant conceives it, is the human plight that gives rise to the necessity of making free choices—not one of the options that we might choose or reject.[14]

With this radical premiss uncovered, I think the cognitivist can respond that Korsgaard's argument begs too many questions in its own right and rests on too many controversial assumptions. Korsgaard illegitimately places a demand on the acceptance of reasons that no other theory, including her own, can discharge. I will argue in the next chapter that if one is going to use Kant's ideas about moral reasons, even in a revised form, in a theory of moral motivation it is necessary to make a methodological revision to how Kant himself proceeds. The details of this revision will be given there, but I want here to explain the problem Korsgaard faces in employing Kant's argument.

Kant ran two views in tandem: a doctrine and a method. The doctrine, transcendental idealism, finds necessary structures in our experienced world and traces them to the operation of our own subjectivity. The method, transcendental argument, finds necessary conditions for our experience and concludes, on the basis of the necessity of our experience having certain features, that the conditions that ground those features are themselves necessary. Ross Harrison has pointed out that this package can be divided: the method can survive rejection of the doctrine.[15] The method of finding necessary conditions for experience can look simply for conditional necessities, based on contingencies. For example, it is a contingent fact that our world is intelligible to our judgement. One can still seek to establish conditionally necessary claims about what must be the case, if this is to be so. Kant thought he needed to begin with necessary truths about our experience, but he did not. Anyone who wants to retain the method of transcendental argument while rejecting the doctrine of transcendental idealism simply has to observe that a neo-Kantian can begin from contingent truths and establish conditionally necessary constraints applicable to those truths.

In framing her challenge to cognitivism as she has, Korsgaard makes Kant's mistake. Her normative question turns out not simply to be the assumption of motivational internalism, but the more fundamental claim that agents must, necessarily,

[13] Korsgaard, *The Sources of Normativity*, 38.

[14] Korsgaard, 'The Normativity of Instrumental Reason', in Garrett Cullity and Berys Gaut (eds.), *Ethics and Practical Reason* (Oxford: Oxford University Press, 1997), 215–55, quote from 244.

[15] Ross Harrison, 'Transcendental Arguments and Idealism', in G. Vesey (ed.), *Idealisms: Past and Present* (Cambridge: Cambridge University Press, 1982), 211–24.

be subject to rationally necessitating reasons. I very much doubt that Kant can prove this, or that anyone else can. It reflects, as Williams puts it, the desire that rationality itself be some sort of force in the world.[16] Unlike Korsgaard, I do not view it as a defeat for any sensible position that philosophy cannot prove not just that people contingently ought to be necessarily motivated by good reasons, but that they necessarily ought to be necessarily motivated by good reasons. I shall defer a more detailed consideration of this issue until the next chapter.

My second response is that Korsgaard's subsidiary argument makes a tendentious assumption about cognitivism. The cognitivist can do more than state, in response to the normative question, that 'this is your duty'. It is clear that in taking this argument to be an objection to cognitivism, Korsgaard is implicitly attacking a particular type of cognitivism, namely, centralist cognitivism.[17] This is the view that very thin, non-world guided vocabulary is prior to the specific evaluative concepts on which the form of cognitivism which I have defended focuses. It is, indeed, not very helpful to be told if you doubt that a proposed course of action is your duty, that it is your duty because it is right. That does represent the cognitivist as unhelpfully marching on the spot and as not addressing the normative question. But that remark seems otiose because one has implicitly assumed a view in which very thin, general vocabulary is fundamental and prior to thick ethical concepts. Korsgaard never takes seriously the idea that values can be experienced and, as I have noted, seems to assume that a special faculty of intuition is the only available form of cognitivist epistemology. Explaining to someone the 'grounds' of their duty is a trivial matter in Korsgaard's analysis, but that is only because of her prior assumptions.

In the cognitivist position I defend in this book, getting a person to conceptualize their situation in the right way, using the right 'thick' vocabulary, is an important part of practical deliberation. There is clearly a cognitive task in getting people to conceptualize a situation in the correct way, using the appropriate thick ethical concepts, or getting them to articulate (or achieve) an appropriate depth of understanding of the concepts that they have. These are ethical tasks, quite unlike the unhelpful badgering of people to have intuitive insight into the nature of the good and the right when those are insights that they simply do not have. Korsgaard offers the moral cognitivist only the second option as a means of articulating the grounds of moral judgement.

Korsgaard's own view is that the very idea of having a reason involves a reflective agent in the endorsement of his or her mental states. I do not think there is anything in that idea to which a cognitivist need object, provided the thesis is given an undemanding interpretation. Korsgaard, however, gives it a very demanding interpretation. She interprets the reflective structure of consciousness as a reflexive and constant monitoring of one's inner states.[18] Even more implausible claims are made about the basic idea of having a reason: Korsgaard explains the element of

---

[16] Williams, *Ethics and the Limits of Philosophy*, 23.

[17] Notably the only realists that Korsgaard takes seriously are early 20th-cent. intuitionists Prichard and Ross, with a nod to their antecedents in Clarke.

[18] Korsgaard, *The Sources of Normativity*, 91–9. Korsgaard begins, quite correctly, with the Kantian premiss that our human experience is inherently reflective and that this is connected to the normative governance of belief and desire. She then proceeds to make the error of identifying

endorsement involved in this in an unusual way. She considers that to have a reason is to endorse one of your mental states by a self-legislating act of will that is universal in content and coeval with a practical identity to which you commit yourself. This is a general account of normativity that applies equally well to wanting a cold Diet Coke as deciding to sacrifice your life to defend the Alamo. I think this account is very implausible, but I mention it here not to belabour its problems, but to point out that it leaves Korsgaard open to the objection that she criticizes in others the very assumptions that she uses herself. The will is, in her positive account of normativity, functioning as an irreducibly normative entity. The cognitivist was criticized for postulating the existence of such entities. Korsgaard cheerfully admits the parallel:

A good maxim is good in virtue of its intrinsic structure . . . [it] is an intrinsically normative entity. So realism is true after all.[19]

This looks very puzzling, but Korsgaard goes on to explain that her view of intrinsic normativity resists the two objections that may be levelled against 'realist' intrinsic normativity. Korsgaard's first argument may be put as follows: she asserts that her view of 'realist' intrinsic normativity does not make the mistake that if you can explain why something is a value, then it is only an extrinsic value. Neither, she states, does her view make a second, related mistake, which is that intrinsic value, if it must be simple, can only be known intuitively.[20]

Now Korsgaard very insightfully highlights the frequent confusion between the instrumental end/final end distinction (which is about how value is realized in the deliberation of agents) and the intrinsic/extrinsic value distinction (which is about whether something's value is explained by its nature or by something to which it stands in a relation).[21] Realism, she argues, would need in at least some cases a value that was both. Such a value would be both a final end of action and intrinsically valuable, where there is no objection to explaining how that intrinsic value is made up of components (that would not make it extrinsically valuable). An autonomous will is just, in Korsgaard's view, what the realist wants.

In my view this is not a criticism of realism at all. It is a very welcome clarification of that to which a cognitivist is committed. However, he or she will insist that an autonomous will is not the only candidate for an intrinsically valuable final end.

---

the reflective with the reflexive and as taking a reflective consciousness to be a consciousness that scans its own internal states. For an alternative treatment of these themes that takes its origin from Kant but that develops an alternative interpretation of the relation between consciousness and the normative governance of beliefs and desires see my 'Kant, McDowell and the Theory of Consciousness', *European Journal of Philosophy*, 5/3 (Dec. 1997), 283–305; 'An Adverbial Theory of Consciousness', *Phenomenology and the Cognitive Sciences*, 2/3 (2003), 161–85.

[19] Korsgaard, *The Sources of Normativity*, 108.

[20] Korsgaard is assuming something further here, namely, that intrinsic value known by intuition would have to be knowledge of an unanalysable simple. Since the target here seems to be Moore and Moore held the doctrine of organic unities there is some unclarity in how Korsgaard proceeds here that is reflected in *The Sources of Normativity*, 123 n. 23. The issue is explicitly discussed in 'Two Distinctions in Goodness', 192–5.

[21] Korsgaard, 'Two Distinctions in Goodness', in *Creating the Kingdom of Ends* (Cambridge: Cambridge University Press, 1996), 249–74.

I do not think it is incumbent on the realist or cognitivist to deny that a will can, in some etiolated sense, 'make' things valuable *ex nihilo*. However, the better strategy is to say that many other things besides such a will are as Korsgaard describes: intrinsically valuable, final ends, and explicably valuable. In the previous chapter, when I described how the entire category of value presupposed human interest, I argued precisely that the recognition of the explicability of our relation to value did not rule out the existence of intrinsic values. The crucial idea was that such interest is presupposed, so that it does not enter into the content, or any analysis, of values. In her second argument, Korsgaard argues that the realist is committed to an implausible assumption that we possess a special faculty of intuition. I will not be defending cognitivism in this way. For this reason, I shall ignore this argument for the purposes of this book.

Korsgaard remains, therefore, on the receiving end of a *tu quoque* or 'you too' rebuttal. This is an objection that she, too, needs an assumption she criticizes in others. She criticizes realism for postulating inherent normativity when her own position also does so. Just because normativity attaches to the operation of a complex whole, whose parts can be decomposed, this does not avoid a commitment to the inherently normative. The cognitivist will respond that it is the perspective of the virtuous agent that makes values available to judgement, such that this judgement is categorically binding on the agent's will. This too, if you like, can be called a complex whole with describable parts, or 'a reciprocal account of rationality—as some sort of human function or capacity—and of reasons'.[22] Furthermore, it is a view that does not make implausible claims about the very idea of having a reason. This is not the place for a full consideration of Korsgaard's views. It is appropriate, however, to rebut her arguments that moral cognitivism is to be rejected on the grounds that it postulates a form of inherent normativity. As I have pointed out, Korsgaard's view may be criticized on this very ground, as indeed may any view apart from total normative scepticism.

Korsgaard has an important subsidiary line of argument. She argues that the moral cognitivist must be committed to taking reason in action to be primarily an exercise of instrumental reason.[23] I will touch on this argument below, but at this point I want to observe that to the cognitivist this argument is a travesty if applied to the recognitional model of moral motivation as a whole. Values are made available to the moral agent via the perspective of that agent's virtues, but these virtues do not stand to values as a means to an end.[24] Perhaps Korsgaard meant to focus solely on the role of instrumental reasoning in first personal deliberation. However, in Korsgaard's own view the will stands in an instrumental relation to itself. In this way, she, too, is as badly placed as the moral cognitivist; or, to put the point another way, the cognitivist is no worse off than Korsgaard. I conclude that the form of 'existence internalism'

[22] Korsgaard, 'The Normativity of Instrumental Reason', 243.

[23] Korsgaard's excellent paper 'The Normativity of Instrumental Reason', from which I have already quoted, argues that it is incoherent to take the instrumental principle to be the sole principle of practical reason. It is, I think, pretty clear that an internal reasons position is not 'Humean' in *that* very narrow sense and so there is no dispute between the internal reasons theorist and Korsgaard's central thesis in this paper. I will discuss the internal reasons thesis in depth in Ch. 4, below.

[24] I will return to this point, in connection with Bernard Williams's work, in Ch. 6, Sec. 5.

found in Wiggins's and McDowell's account of practical reasons can be defended from the form of neo-Kantian critique developed by Korsgaard.

2. MORAL JUDGEMENTS AS 'SILENCING'

Having explained, and defended, the sense in which both Wiggins and McDowell accept the idea of inherent normativity, it is time to differentiate their positions in a more precise way. I noted above that while McDowell and Wiggins agree about inherent normativity, they disagree over the connections between moral judgement and practicality. This is largely because McDowell has a distinctive and controversial theory of the nature of motivational internalism. Internalism is the thesis that a moral consideration is necessarily connected with the possession of a good reason or a motive: if an agent believes that she has reason to do action A, then she is thereby motivated to do A.

One of the main reasons for the adoption of non-cognitive explanations of ethical claims is that this seems the best explanation of the tie between such claims and moral motivation. It seems on the face of it to be an a priori and necessary truth that if one judges that an act is a case of pointless cruelty, one will be motivated to prevent or impede it or to avoid carrying it out oneself. This was the internalist intuition that Mackie relied on in his argument. This seems plausible, at least, if one adds the rider 'necessarily motivated in so far as one is fully rational'. The challenge is to explain how this tie between ethical judgements and the will can be represented by a cognitivist, as opposed to a non-cognitivist, theory.

McDowell's response to all non-cognitivist arguments of this form (and to Mackie's error theory) is to argue that the question has been begged against a position that is both cognitivist and internalist. The question is whether or not anyone is entitled to assume the truth of the Humean theory of motivation. As I have already stated, the Humean theory states that intentional action is motivated by states of two kinds: a belief state with a direction of fit from the mind to the world and a volitional state with a direction of fit from the world to the mind. These two classes of state are, further, given an asymmetric functional characterization. Desire states are intrinsically motivational in that they can motivate alone (although they may need belief states to give them a 'direction', they are motivationally complete in themselves). Belief states are not intrinsically motivational. If they are to motivate, they must be conjoined with a desire.[25]

This background conception of belief, desire, and motivation is deployed both by the non-cognitivist, who claims that non-cognitivism is better placed to explain the practicality of morality (for the primary content expressed by a moral utterance is, for such a non-cognitivist, an inherently motivational desire state), and, as I described, by the error theorist. Mackie assumed internalism and the Humean theory of motivation and on that basis developed an argument against cognitivism. However, this leaves

---

[25] See the helpful general discussion in Dancy, *Moral Reasons*, chs. 1–3 and in the particular case of McDowell see also R. Jay Wallace, 'Virtue, Reason, and Principle', *Canadian Journal of Philosophy*, 21 (Dec. 1991), 469–95.

open the option of negating one of Mackie's assumptions, which is precisely what McDowell does. McDowell's view retains internalism, adopts cognitivism, and so rejects the Humean theory of motivation, replacing it instead with motivated desire theory. The upshot is his distinctive account of the ideally virtuous agent, a person for whom moral considerations totally silence other practical considerations.

To give an example, reconsider the ideally virtuous agent I described at the beginning of this chapter. At the point of deciding to go and help the man who collapsed in the street, our agent had various practical competing concerns: meeting a friend, going to the store. When her experience makes available to her the relevant moral reason, that the man needs help, does this reason enter into competition with the other practical reasons that our agent had? If so, is the competition decided, for example, by what the agent most wants to do, by the strength of her competing desires? The Humean answers 'yes' to both questions.

McDowell thinks that an account along these lines is mistaken on two counts.[26] First, it suggests that what motivates the agent is not her perception of the facts alone, but the interaction of this perception with a standing disposition to altruistic action. This standing disposition could perhaps be interpreted as a faculty of sympathy that supplies individual desires in any particular case. The perception of the fact alone, being intrinsically motivationally inert, would not suffice to move the agent on this Humean view. Secondly, in McDowell's view, this account suggests that the moral reason enters into a process of balancing with other competing practical reasons. This claim seems to McDowell phenomenologically inaccurate and a threat to the rational authority of morality.

McDowell is certainly drawing on some plausible intuitions, but I am not happy with the way he expresses his objections to the Humean model. McDowell is dissatisfied with the claim that action needs to be motivated by an 'independently intelligible' desire because of his commitment to motivated desire theory.[27] Motivated desire theory assents to the central claim of its apparent rival, the Humean theory of motivation, which asserts that every rational intentional action is motivated by a belief and a desire. But it does so in a particular way, arguing that the Humean theory is correct in the letter, but false in its spirit. It is a truth about explanation, but not about justification. In the case of moral motivation, the belief formed by the suitably cognitively equipped virtuous person, who is rational, in possession of the right set of concepts with an appropriate degree of conceptual grasp, *motivates both the desire and the action*. The perception of the circumstances that the agent would cite as the justification of the action, why she saw helping the man in distress 'in a favourable light', *is the very same proposition* that motivates the desire to help. This contrasts with the case of a basic desire that interacts with a parallel belief to generate action. If I suddenly want a cold drink, and I put money in a vending machine to buy a cold

---

[26] 'Are Moral Reasons Hypothetical Imperatives?', 84 and 90.

[27] The idea of motivated desire theory is, as I have noted, central to the argument of Nagel's *The Possibility of Altruism*. For a general historical perspective on the theory and its ancestry, see Nicholas Dent, *The Moral Psychology of the Virtues* (Cambridge: Cambridge University Press, 1975), ch. 4, 'The Active Powers of Man'.

drink, the belief and the desire are parallel motivations for the action. The desire is not ascribed to me 'consequentially' upon a belief that expresses my perception of the circumstances. This is a view of moral motivation first described by Thomas Nagel that McDowell adapts to his own ends.

While McDowell (and Nagel) have, overall, a plausible case, there are, in my view, two problems with the position that McDowell defends. The first is the peculiarity of the metaphor of silencing. In order to preserve the authority of moral reasons in practical deliberation, McDowell argues that moral reasons silence all other practical considerations when they come into conflict with them on any particular occasion of action. This seems to me an unduly moralistic account of what should be purely an issue in the psychology of motivation. McDowell stipulates an ideal model of a virtuous agent and he can give that agent whatever properties he wants. It is, after all, his stipulation. But one can question the degree of distance this places between McDowell's ideal agent and ordinary agents and the extent to which he has misrepresented ordinary moral reasoning and its different elements. (Some of the problems with the idealizations in McDowell's account will be further discussed in the next chapter.) On the question of silencing Williams pointed out that McDowell seems to have conflated 'importance' with 'deliberative priority'.[28]

As Williams explained these concepts, a consideration can function evidentially in a person's reasoning in a way that makes it clear that such a consideration tends to be very important to that person. Furthermore, the consideration may, in a particular case, receive high deliberative priority. There seems no reason, however, to put these two aspects of a potential moral reason into the composite idea of a silencing reason. They are put together in McDowell's idea of a silencing reason since such a reason is guaranteed always to be important, and always to be given the highest priority in an agent's deliberation. Even if this claim is true, it is a substantive and surprising thesis about the content and role of any particular candidate to be a moral reason, not a thesis that should be stipulated, or derived from the concept of a moral reason. I shall, in any case, be giving reasons in the next chapter why I do not believe that this view is true.

The debate as to whether there can be silencing reasons is the less important of the two issues. All parties can agree that a moral reason could play such a role, but Williams's distinction suggests that this should not be a matter of stipulation. The more serious second concern goes beyond terminology. The idealization built into McDowell's account of moral reasons makes it incompatible with certain general constraints that define the very idea of a practical reason, namely, as Christine Korsgaard puts it: 'to have motives which are caused by the recognition of certain truths which are made relevant to action by one's pre-existing motives'.[29] I will focus on this line of concern in the next chapter. Before doing so, I will explain some of the key differences between McDowell's account and that of Wiggins. This is not merely for completeness, but because Wiggins's view has much less difficulty in accommodating these general constraints on the idea of a practical reason.

---

[28] Williams, *Ethics and the Limits of Philosophy*, 182–3.
[29] Korsgaard, 'The Normativity of Instrumental Reason', 219.

3. WIGGINS'S INTERNALISM: THE FORCE OF GOOD REASONS

Wiggins's account of the psychology of moral motivation is more cautious than that of McDowell's. Perhaps, not coincidentally, it seems to me to have a better chance of being true. Whereas McDowell directly adopts motivated desire theory, Wiggins does so indirectly. Just like McDowell, he develops an account of evaluation and the categorical nature of obligations in parallel, both anchored in the perspective of the virtuous agent. But a community of agents figures more directly in Wiggins's account, as does a basis in the moral sentiments that are genealogically explained as the foundation, but not the content, of a normative perspective from which categorical obligations are generated.

As was discussed in the opening chapters, Wiggins argues that the *sense* of moral language is grasped from the human perspective. These senses are grasped from the perspective of those who also have certain sentiments, grounded in our human nature, that evolve through the pressure of moral learning into the moral sentiments.[30] Just as that grasp of sense makes certain evaluative responses available to the mature moral agent, so the development of this conceptual grasp forces us into the perspective of the social. This perspective is understood as a general point of view for the appraisal of the actions of others.[31] According to Wiggins (influenced by Hume) we come to participate in a common standard for appraising the virtues and vices of others, guided by commonly held sentiments of approbation or disapprobation. The distinctive role of this general perspective and its associated standard is to overcome our limited sympathies. This 'genealogy' elucidates the fact that the common standard has a basis in sentiment, but transcends this basis. For the mature, rational moral agent, the common standard can be the source of categorical requirements that transcend its contingent origins in our moral sentiments:

What the moral standard founded in the affections that is natural and/or promotive of the general interest for human being to feel towards children requires of us as our duty is to give bread, not a stone . . . It does not require that of us hypothetically, or only if we feel affection for children. The requirement is perfectly simple and categorical.[32]

Thus, when the genealogical account is complete, and one has traced the origin of the common human standard which is the source of obligation, we can see that it generates its obligations without presupposing any particular motivation. We have, instead, a general disposition to be guided by the standard. In this way Wiggins updates Hume's standing disposition of sympathy. But as this common standard is *presupposed*, in any particular case we have a judgement that can be both a response to value and a response to a categorical requirement. At this point, the level of particular actions, Wiggins adopts motivated desire theory: when the agent acts on

---

[30] Wiggins, 'A Sensible Subjectivism', in *Needs, Values, Truth*, sects. 8 and 9.

[31] Wiggins, 'Categorical Requirements: Kant and Hume on the Idea of Duty', 83–106 and 'In a Subjectivist Framework, Categorical Requirements and Real Practical Reasons', 212–32.

[32] Wiggins, 'Categorical Requirements: Kant and Hume on the Idea of Duty', 311.

his or her belief, a desire is motivated by its propositional object. But desire comes into the story twice: in the genealogical account of the origin of the moral sentiments and in the motivation of particular actions. It does not intrude where, in Wiggins's view, it should not. Desire does not, for example, occur where the Humean theory of motivation places it. It is not a standing repository of particular motivations for particular actions.

There is much that is very attractive in this account of Wiggins's. Nevertheless, it seems to me that there are problems with the account as it stands. There seems to be some lack of clarity over the role of sentiment in generating categorical obligations. It is clear that Wiggins has avoided the claim that in any particular case of motivated action, a general disposition of sympathy operates to generate a particular desire without which the agent would not act. It is, rather, that the agent has a very general meta-level disposition to be moved to action by considerations of a certain kind. These are considerations guided by the general standard of appraisal adopted through the exercise of the moral sentiments and then transcending them.

My question is how much of the original foundation survives in the general standard, and whether it may not be open to competing explanations? If desire is transcended by the standard, then it no longer distinctively figures in it. My alternative explanation is that what we have in this case is a very general disposition, rooted in our social nature, to justify our actions to others. It is a standard of reasonableness, where that idea is given a social emphasis, as opposed to a standard that is a focus of reasonable convergence, as in Wiggins's proposal. The difference lies between an account that takes the standard to be a focal point of agreement (Wiggins's view) and a version in which the standard is not to be reasonably rejected (my view which I will describe in the next chapter). Borrowing a phrase from Derek Parfit, on this latter interpretation the standard would be an example of a 'complaint model' of standards.[33] It is not positively justified by consensual convergence, but indirectly justified in that no one could bring a reasonable complaint against it. It could not be reasonably rejected. The advantage I would argue for my view is that it copes better with the inherent indeterminacy of the standard: on a complaint model such indeterminacy is more tolerable. We can be more sure that we want to rule out certain forms of conduct than that we want to 'rule them in'.[34] The issue I view as the most interesting, however, is how Wiggins's account integrates with our best account of practical reasons in general. As we shall see, it stands a far better chance of passing this test than McDowell's idealization of the person of sound practical judgement, the Aristotelian *phronimos*.[35]

[33] Derek Parfit originated the phrase 'complaint model' as a general characterization of the contractualist prioritization of individual complaints.

[34] This is one way, and in my view pretty much the only way, in which this contractualist criterion resembles the categorical imperative. The categorical imperative is similarly not a decision procedure but a means of ruling candidates *out* that can hardly, for that reason, avoid further appeal to practical judgement in a full account of verdictive decisions. I discuss this particular point further in 'Nagel's Paradox of Equality and Partiality', 278. For an excellent discussion of the prospects for treating the moral law as criterial, see Philip Stratton-Lake's discussion in *Kant, Duty and Moral Worth* (London: Routledge, 2000), 73–6.

[35] The *phronimos* is Aristotle's person of ideally sound powers of practical reasoning in the *Nicomachean Ethics*.

But it may, in addition, require some modification if it is to meet a general constraint on those reasons that we demarcate as practical. I shall argue for this conclusion in the next chapter.

CONCLUSION

In this chapter I have rejected the view that Wiggins's and McDowell's theories of moral motivation postulate an objectionable form of inherent normativity in a moral agent's recognition of value. Their position is no worse off in this regard than anyone else's (specifically, Korsgaard's). I have described McDowell's position, and the conflation of different considerations in his metaphor of 'silencing' and Wiggins's genealogy of categorical obligations. I turn now to the crucial issue of how both accounts relate to the general issue of the nature of practical reasons. This is with a view to the development of a different approach to moral reasons of my own which also postulates inherent normativity in an agent's perception of the moral circumstances, such that this perception directly governs the will.

4

Internal Reasons and Contractualist Impartiality

§1: Interpreting Practical Reasons as Internal Reasons. §2: Korsgaard's Distinction between Motivational and Content Scepticism. §3: McDowell's Response to the Internal Reasons Argument. §4: Constructing an Alternative and Construing Moral Reasons as Impartially Defensible. §5: Motivation by Structure as the Internalisation of a Relativised A Priori Principle. §5: Classifying the Resulting Theory as Internalist or Externalist.

Chapter 3 set out Wiggins's and McDowell's composite views and their separate commitments to the idea of inherent normativity. I argued that this commitment was entirely defensible. In this chapter I turn to the wider question of assessing their proposals in the light of a conception of practical reasons. Presumably, all sides to the debate over the merits of internalism and externalism about moral reasons agree that whatever our eventual view is, it must harmonize with our best account of practical reasons in general. Now, I concede that there is a complication here: neo-Kantians such as Korsgaard believe that the perspective of moral reasons just *is* the perspective of practical reason in general. But absent this special set of assumptions, any account of moral reasons is presumably going to have to be constrained by our best, general, reflective account of practical reasons. This is so on the understanding that, without Korsgaard's special assumptions, the idea of a practical reason is of wider scope than the idea of a moral reason. They are related as genus to species.

In this chapter I will examine a proposal concerning the nature of practical reasons: that all such reasons are *internal reasons*.[1] It is the first obstacle that was placed in the way of the Wittgensteinian cognitivists' position by Bernard Williams. Part III will examine Williams's scepticism about the claim that we possess moral knowledge and find that claim to be a genuine challenge to cognitivism, but one that can be overcome. In this chapter, however, I am going to be more sympathetic to Williams's arguments. Mainly, this is because I want to present them in a different light from the way in which they are usually understood. Mention of Humeanism in his initial

---

[1] Bernard Williams, 'Internal and External Reasons', in *Moral Luck* (Cambridge: Cambridge University Press, 1981), 101–13; 'Internal Reasons and the Obscurity of Blame', in *Making Sense of Humanity* (Cambridge: Cambridge University Press, 1995), 35–45; 'Postscript: Some Further Notes On Internal and External Reasons' in Elijah Milgram (ed.), *Varieties of Practical Reasoning* (Cambridge, Mass.: MIT Press, 2001), 90–7.

presentation of his ideas led to Williams being viewed as a representative of someone committed to the Humean theory of motivation, or to a Humean view of the self or of the psychological.[2] I do not read Williams this way. I always saw his position as a set of relatively neutral constraints on the very idea of a practical reason. All sides to the debate should be able to accept these constraints in the course of giving our best overall reflective account of moral reasons.

Williams's opponents about the status of moral reasons view them as directly analogous to theoretical reasons in the sense that they are 'there' for an agent, regardless of the prior configuration of an agent's psychology. I will suggest that they are wrong about that claim. However, I will also suggest that one can accept Williams's claim that all practical reasons are internal, and hence that all moral reasons are internal, while also accepting that an important aspect of moral reasons is their impartiality. Impartiality, in my argument, figures as a pragmatic constraint on moral debate. I will then develop a contractualist understanding of impartiality which renders it compatible with the internal reasons argument. In this way a central motivation to viewing moral reasons as external, the desire to provide an objective, critical perspective on an agent's reasons, can be accommodated within an internal reasons position. So, I do not see my view as in any way a threat to the authority of moral reasons in practical deliberation. Those who took themselves to be defending the idea that the moral point of view was an impartial point of view did so on the assumption that this explained the authority of moral reasons. That is (partially) correct, in that being impartial is an aspect of reasons that we value, and an aspect that captures part of what we mean by calling moral reasons 'authoritative'. However, this view should not be supported by the erroneous further assumption that for this view to be true, moral reasons have to be external.

One of McDowell's fundamental motivations was to preserve the authority of moral reasons and I will develop an account that does so as well, but free of any connection to the idea that moral reasons are external. I am not, then, entirely parting company with every part of the cognitivist approach to psychology and motivation that I have described in the previous chapters. The connection that I perceive, between the internal reasons constraint and the defence of a role for impartiality, highlights a connection between my approach and that of Wiggins. He offers a similar 'genealogy' of our moral reasons, as I described in the previous chapter. Our accounts have this in common: they both emphasize the role in reasoning of a presupposed social standard. They both emphasise the development of this standard in the process of moral development and education. They both take this standard to constrain the motivations of agents. The differences, however, are equally important.

I see this presupposed structure as inculcated into individual agents to give their deliberations a certain form. The general disposition I am interested in is that of making one's rational moral actions defensible to others in an impartial way· in a way that they could not reasonably reject. This is different from Wiggins's proposal.

---

[2] I will try in this chapter to detach the internal reasons thesis from the kind of 'Humeanism' defended, for example, by Michael Smith in *The Moral Problem* (Oxford: Basil Blackwell, 1994). See also nn. 18 and 19, below.

Nevertheless, I see the two approaches as interestingly complementary to one another. If the contractualist component of my view rests on an idea of reasonable rejection, I could interpret Wiggins's genealogical account as giving further substance to the relevant idea of reasonableness.

1. PRACTICAL REASONS AS 'INTERNAL'

I will begin by briefly considering Williams's central arguments that spelled out his basic conception of what it is for a reason to be a practical reason. Williams argued that statements about an agent's reasons bear two interpretations, one 'internal' and one 'external'.[3] The 'internal' interpretation operates under a constraint that is not applicable in the 'external' interpretation; in the internal sense, one can assert that 'A has a reason to ø' if the following truth condition obtains:

A can reach the conclusion that he/she should ø (or a conclusion to ø) by a sound deliberative route from, or in virtue of, the motivations that he has in his actual motivational set—that is, the set of his desires, evaluations, attitudes, projects and so on.[4]

Williams believed that this condition is a necessary and sufficient condition for the assertion of 'A has a reason to ø', but argued for the weaker claim that it is a necessary condition. The position of the external reasons theorist is implicitly defined by his or her denial of this constraint: he or she claims that a statement of the form 'A has a reason to ø' can be true in a situation where the internal constraint does not hold. Such statements can be true of A when the constraint is not operative, and therefore the sentence is warrantedly assertible in a situation where A cannot reach the conclusion that he or she should ø by a sound deliberative route from his or her current 'subjective motivational set', which Williams called 'S'. A useful heuristic is to think of the set of motivations that an agent can deliberatively access, via sound practical deliberation, as the indeterminate revised set S*. Williams's argument can then be rephrased as the claim that an agent's practical reasons must either be in S or in S*.[5]

A crucial assumption driving the argument against external reasons is that reasons for an agent, while normative, must be potentially explanatory of action.[6] The external reasons theorist, it seems, violates this constraint. *Ex hypothesi*, a statement

---

[3] Thus, 'internal' and 'external' are not predicates of reasons, per se, but predicates of statements about reasons, and are hence in the formal, not the material, mode. This is a qualification I will ignore in the sequel, speaking for convenience of 'internal reasons' and 'external reasons'.

[4] Williams, 'Internal Reasons and the Obscurity of Blame', 35.

[5] It must be borne in mind that this set can contract as well as expand in the course of revision. For example, by vividly imagining the way you intend to satisfy your desire for an enjoyable evening by going to the theatre, you may lose your desire to go to the theatre. So the revision of S into S* is not necessarily expansion. The indeterminacy of S*, Williams argues, arises from the role in practical deliberation of the imagination.

[6] 'It has been generally recognised that the concept of a reason for action stands at the point of intersection, so as to speak, between the theory of the explanation of action and the theory of the justification of action', Michael Woods, 'Reasons for Action and Desires', *Proceedings of the Aristotelian Society*, suppl. vol. 46 (1972), 189–201, at 189.

that a subject has reason to ø that can be true when the reason is not in the agent's S, nor derivable from that S, cannot be explanatory of that agent's action. However, explained in this way, the argument may seem trivial. In every case where an agent's action is justified by a reason, where that reason is potentially explanatory of the agent's action, external reasons statements will simply collapse into internal reasons statements. However, the point is not trivial, as Williams explained:

it does not follow from this that there is nothing in external reasons statements. What does follow is that their content is not going to be revealed by considering merely the state of one who believes such a statement, nor how that state explains action, for that state is merely the state with regard to which an internal reasons statement could truly be made. Rather, the content ... will have to be revealed by considering *what it is to come to believe* such a statement. [emphasis added][7]

Williams here identifies the crucial issue as how an agent's *acceptance* of a reason is best explained. The external reasons theorist is, Williams argues, committed to the claim that an agent acquires a motivation from coming to accept the external reasons statement, and because this acceptance takes the form of 'seeing matters aright'. This, in turn, establishes an equivalence between the external reasons statement being truly assertible of the agent, and the claim that if he or she rationally deliberated, then whatever motivations they had they would be motivated to ø. The external reasons theorist works from the truth of the external reason, via rational deliberation, to its acceptance and the generation of a motive. In the opposite direction, as it were, Williams works from the initial S, via rational deliberation, to all the true internal reasons statements about the agent. Williams asserts that the external reasons conception is fatally flawed by its violation of the link between normative and explanatory reasons. It is a corollary of Williams's argument that he takes the external reasons theorist's position to be implicitly circular. Every attempt to justify the existence of external reasons as, as it were, the terminus of practical deliberation does so by covertly packing all the necessary assumptions into the idea of an agent's S. The objection to this strategy is that it begs the question by inserting, a priori, whatever is needed in the prior conception of an agent's S to sustain the 'reasons entail counterfactuals' claim.[8]

If this connection between the normative and explanatory senses of reason is so fundamental, how can it be further defended? In my view, it can hardly be defended at all: it is true a priori and self-evident to conceptual reflection.[9] This may explain

[7] Williams, 'Internal and External Reasons', 103.

[8] As John Skorupski points out at pp. 4–5 of 'Internal Reasons and the Scope of Blame', unpublished MS in Alan Thomas (ed.), *Bernard Williams* (Cambridge: Cambridge University Press, forthcoming) the issue is the insertion of such principles into an agent's S. If they are included in the idea of a sound deliberative route by definition, for example if they are either a priori or necessary, then they are going to be reached from anyone's S as they will be part of *any* route from such an S. Williams explicitly argues against this alternative interpretation of the idea of a sound deliberative route in 'Internal Reasons and the Obscurity of Blame', 37.

[9] By contrast, Thomas Scanlon, in his interesting discussion of Williams's argument, takes Williams's thesis to be essentially a substantive normative claim and not an analysis of the idea

why arguments in favour of the principle are so brief, as for example in Allan Gibbard's comments on those who violate the connection:

Some writers speak of 'reasons' in a non-Humean way, and indeed try to ground ethical theory on a non-Humean concept of reasons . . . None of them, so far as I can discover, explains what he is using the term reason to mean.[10]

One way to reject the connection between the normative and the explanatory dimensions of the term 'reason' is to insist that reasons are properly normative and not explanatory. Another way to sever the connection is to treat them as two distinct kinds of reason:

We work with two quite different concepts of reasons for action depending on whether we emphasise the explanatory dimension and downplay the justificatory, or vice versa . . . Let me say a little about the similarities and differences between these *two kinds of reasons*. [emphasis added][11]

I will assume, for the sake of argument of this chapter, that a claim such as this is mistaken (or merely a *façon de parler*).

From exposition, I will now offer some commentary on Williams's argument as it is certainly very compressed and allusive in its original formulations. Consider theoretical reasoning directed towards the acquisition of true belief. A judger comes to accept a belief P, because this is seeing the matter aright, and one way to gloss this remark is that the judger comes to believe P *because* P. A philosophical understanding of this 'because' would take it to be both normative and explanatory: that given the norms of reasoning governing the acquisition of beliefs of this class, and the judger's proper application of these norms, there is nothing else for him or her to think, but P. In addition, from either a meta-level perspective or an explanatory one, an account of the same judger's cognitive economy would see the fact that P as being causally implicated in the aetiology of the judger's belief. In this case we have a compatibility between a justificatory and a causal account and a fully satisfactory philosophical understanding of the 'because'. Not all justifications are of this kind: this is an ideal of a fully self-conscious rational justification.[12] Its key element is a fusion of justification and explanation: the grounds and causal antecedents of a belief fuse to offer a fully satisfactory understanding of the 'because'. This ideal of justification reflects a conception of cognitive autonomy: that the causal antecedents of a belief are within the rational cognitive control of the agent because they are, in addition, its rational

---

of a practical reason. See *What We Owe to Each Other* (Cambridge, Mass.: Belknap Press, 1998), 'Appendix', pp. 363–73, quotation at 365.

[10] Allan Gibbard, *Wise Choices, Apt Feelings* (Oxford: Oxford University Press, 1990), 161 n. 6.

[11] Smith, *The Moral Problem*, 95. (Let me say I am not placing too much emphasis on Smith's choice of words, but it seems to me an interesting choice in this context.)

[12] See e.g. Moore's discussion of this point in *Points of View*, ch. 4. David Wiggins has called ideal justifications of this form 'vindicatory explanations'. They are discussed in *Needs, Values, Truth*, e.g. at 150–3 and in 'Moral Cognitivism, Moral Relativism and Motivating Moral Beliefs', 66–8. I don't focus on this idea at any length in this book, as it seems to me that vindicatory explanations apply to any belief and are part of a constitutive explanation of the nature of a rationally held belief. So they do not, in my view, offer any *extra* argument to the moral cognitivist.

grounds. I have described this account of justification as an ideal. This emphasizes that its unattainability in practice need not impugn its status as a regulative ideal and that it plays a constitutive role in the explanation of the psychologies of rational agents.[13]

The external reasons theorist models his or her account of the agent's acceptance of external reasons on such a model of ideal, autonomous justification, applied to practical reasoning. What, then, of the class of 'basic reasons'? One automatically gets the fusion of cause and justification in the case of beliefs which are epistemologically basic or underived and 'given' in the causal and the epistemic sense. If there is a class of reasons that are basic in the sense that any rational agent must just accept them as input to their belief system on the basis of their self-evident epistemic legitimacy, does this not offer a model for the acceptance of a reason that escapes Williams's criticism? There may be cases where reasons are accepted, but not on the basis of reasoning at all.[14]

This point, however, does seem to rest on a misunderstanding. The acceptance of a basic reason is a simulacrum of the ideal of fully self-conscious rational justification given by the vindicatory schema, as it has the form 'P because P' where 'because' has both normative and explanatory force. But this similarity of form does not prove that the case of basic ethical reasons violates the internal reasons constraint. Williams's argument is that one has to examine the psychological dynamics of an agent's acceptance of a reason. The internal reasons argument applies to this process of acceptance, *whether basic or non-basic reasons are accepted.* Applied to the case of a basic reason, the external reasons account expressed by the 'external reasons claim' implies that however the internal economy of the agent's system of belief is configured, the agent will accept 'P' on the basis of its initial credence. But now how can the agent do this? Only if there is a standing disposition in the agent's S to accept reasons of this kind. This implies that simply in virtue of being a rational agent, an agent has a disposition to acquire true beliefs that are inherently motivating. This simply relocates the very point of controversy.[15]

---

[13] This is famously argued for by Donald Davidson in e.g. 'Actions, Reasons and Causes', in *Essays on Actions and Events* (Oxford: Oxford University Press, 1980), 261–75. McDowell notes these connections in 'Might There Be External Reasons?', in J. E. J. Altham and T. R. Harrison (eds.), *World, Mind and Ethics: Essays on the Ethical Philosophy of Bernard Williams* (Cambridge: Cambridge University Press, 1995), 68–85 at 76 where he expresses the Davidsonian point that the intertwining of the explanatory and the normative in the idea of a reason for action is constitutive.

[14] Elijah Milgram has pressed the second question against the internal reasons position in 'Williams' Argument Against External Reasons', *Noûs*, 30/2 (June 1996), 197–220; John McDowell has pressed the third question in 'Might There Be External Reasons?'. Claims of both these types are made by Milgram and McDowell but it would be a mistake to run together this line of argument with an error in the philosophy of mind which I will discuss below, namely, taking a state that is attributed from an interpretative perspective to be neither phenomenologically accessible nor the bearer of causal properties.

[15] I think this would be the internal reasons theorist's best line of response to the arguments on McDowell's behalf put forward by William J. Fitzpatrick in his interesting paper, 'Reasons, Value, and Particular Agents: Normative Relevance Without Motivational Internalism', *Mind*, 113/450 (Apr. 2004), 285–318 at 309–11. Fitzpatrick there extends Williams's correction for an agent's interest in being well informed to the insertion of knowledge of the relevant good making features of moral actions into everyone's S. I will discuss other aspects of Fitzpatrick's view below.

The point of Williams's 'Humeanism' was that he allowed that one could build into one's model of a sound deliberative route the assumption that all agents have an interest in being factually well informed and in reasoning properly. This much normativity comes for free, as it were, with the idea of a practically rational agent. If, however, there is to be this much latitude allowed in idealizing the contents of agents' subjective motivational sets, why cannot one additionally insert moral or prudential reasons or a standing disposition to accept such reasons, such that they generate motivations?

Williams's reply was that this is perfectly acceptable if one has an argument for such an insertion.[16] I think this is absolutely vital for understanding his position. Take the first claim for the insertion of altruism as a condition of rational agency. There is a long history in moral philosophy of arguing that the very idea of a practically rational agent imports altruistic or prudential motivations as an a priori requirement of practical reason. Williams's contention is that this argument must be proffered and inspected, whereas the 'Humean' claim that a practically rational agent has a standing interest in being fully informed and sound in their practical reasoning is platitudinous. In this matter of the burden of proof, as Williams notes, his 'external reasons' opponents tend to concur with his position. Neo-Kantian theorists offer arguments as to why the very idea of a practically rational agent legitimizes introducing altruistic or prudential motives into every rational agent's S. However, as Williams notes, if this argument for the a priori possibility of pure practical reason is offered and succeeds, his argument simply lapses: altruistic and prudential considerations are guaranteed to be in everyone's S.[17] The more interesting argument for the insertion simply of a standing disposition to accept moral reasons I defer to the next section, as its consideration involves a distinction between different forms of scepticism about practical reasoning.

This issue of a prioricity seems to be overlooked by 'phenomenological' arguments that appeal to the existence of basic reasons and of reasons accepted without reasoning, but even so these arguments should be kept apart from a much more implausible argument in the secondary literature with which they might be confused. McDowell and Milgram emphasize moral phenomenology to press their case, but this must be detached from the further strategy of attributing a Humean conception of the self or the psychological to Williams.[18] Williams does announce that his model is a

---

[16] This issue of the a priori source of moral reasons is ignored by Milgram in 'Williams' Argument Against External Reasons'. Milgram attempts a preliminary dialectical gambit against the internal reasons argument of constructing an analogue of the argument for theoretical reasons, rhetorically allowing him to ask why we should accept an account for practical reasons that fails for theoretical reasons. The answer, presumably, lies in how much we are allowed to assume a priori about practical agents as such. We are allowed to assume, a priori, that a subject has a standing reason to acquire true theoretical beliefs via correct normative deliberation. This requires a further argument for practical reasons.

[17] See Williams, 'Internal Reasons and the Obscurity of Blame', 36–7.

[18] Jonathan Lear, in his otherwise excellent paper 'Moral Objectivity', in S. C. Brown (ed.), *Objectivity and Cultural Divergence* (Cambridge: Cambridge University Press, 1984), 135–70, connects the internal reasons argument to a Humean bundle theory of the self on pp. 139–44, but this seems to me to be a mistake. If there is a conception of a temporally invariant real interest for

'Humean' one, but I do not think that this should be taken to include a commitment to Humean models of the psychological.[19] Ascertaining the contents of one's S is not a matter of inspecting the contents of one's inner mental theatre. Identifying an agent's reasons for action can require all the resources of hermeneutic reconstruction. Williams's 'Humeanism' is compatible, for example, with the agent's reasons being obscure to them at the point of decision. An emphasis on moral decision as a vehicle of self-interpretation and self-discovery is not ruled out in Williams's theory: indeed, he seems explicitly to allow for it.[20]

Williams's approach to the mental is interpretationist and bearing this orientation in mind should prevent the intrusion of irrelevant objections to the argument. The two most important points for rebutting some of the misconceptions people have advanced are that states attributed from an interpretationist perspective can nevertheless be causally efficacious in explaining action and that they can be explanatory without being the bearer of phenomenal properties.[21] 'Phenomenological' refutations of the internal reasons argument cannot proceed via a refutation of a stereotypically Humean conception of psychology as involving immediate self-knowledge of discrete, atomistic mental states which are the bearers of phenomenal properties and are epistemically 'given' without the mediation of interpretation.[22] One the contrary, in

an agent already available, this is no doubt relevant to one's view of an agent's identity (otherwise, whose interest are we assuming this interest to be?). This seems to me, however, to beg the question against the internal reasons view.

[19] Mention of the apocryphal Hume, not the historical Hume, may have led interpreters of Williams astray. This is particularly true of the very broad use that Williams makes of the term 'desire'. That has led to such misdirected criticisms of the internal reasons view as those offered by Derek Parfit in 'Reasons and Motivation', *Aristotelian Society*, Suppl. Vol. 71 (1997), 98–146. Parfit thinks that simply to note that some desires are value dependent poses a problem for the internal reasons thesis: 'We can...have reasons that depend on our desires, since our having some desire may affect what is worth achieving, or preventing', 128. But this seems to me simply to equivocate between a narrow and 'Humean' sense of 'desire' as a discrete occurrent mental state with phenomenal properties, as opposed to a cognitivist treatment of desires as rationalized by their propositional objects. There is no reason to treat Williams's 'formal' use of desire to cover 'desires, evaluations, attitudes, projects and so on' or 'dispositions of evaluation, patterns of emotional reaction, personal loyalties and various projects...embodying commitments of the agent' (Williams, 'Internal and External Reasons', 105), as restricted to a simple Humean view of desires. Parfit's objection trades on a defect in our vague terminology. For an interesting discussion that does not simply assume that the possibility of motivated desire theory *in itself* refutes the internal reasons thesis, see Skorupski, 'Internal Reasons and the Scope of Blame', esp. sect. 2.

[20] There is a very striking passage in Williams's last work, *Truth and Truthfulness*, expressing a scepticism about the transparency of a person's motives to him- or herself in the course of decision, focused on the idea of 'direction of fit': 'To put it more accurately, a content, relating to an outcome or process which is relevant to the deliberation and to the affective state in which the deliberation is conducted, comes before the mind, carrying with it an attitude that is part of the affective state. This does not represent, yet, any commitment of the agent, in the sense that I have used the term: it is not yet either a belief or a desire. *But it may be on the way to becoming either*', 197. See also *Shame and Necessity* (Berkeley and Los Angeles: University of California Press, 1993), 44–6.

[21] These claims are, for example, ably defended by Bill Child in his *Causality, Interpretation and the Mind* (Oxford: Oxford University Press, 1995).

[22] Two papers in the secondary literature seem to offer misguided criticisms of Williams based on their failure to recognize his use of an interpretationist perspective on the mental. The first is Rachel Cohon's 'Are External Reasons Impossible?', *Ethics*, 96/3 (Apr. 1986), 545–56, which turns

the internal reasons argument properly understood, the agent brings to deliberation a subjective motivational set, S, whose contents are as indeterminate as are all such psychological phenomena. Self-knowledge of, for example, intention, may require interpretative reconstruction and probably will require considerable interpretation.

In addition, it should be noted that the internal reasons theorist operates with a flexible, open ended, but none the less normative conception of practical rationality. Pressing the lines of objection I have canvassed to the internal reasons theory need not involve denying this point.[23] Practical reasoning involves, on Williams's view, the exercise of imagination and hence its upshot must inherit the indeterminacy of imagination's operations as a supplement to reasoning.[24] The operation of practical reasoning involves the addition of items to S, and their deletion.

In the interpretation of the internal reasons argument I have offered here, an essential supplement to it is case by case consideration and rebuttal of specific proposals for connecting altruistic motivation or a standing disposition to such motivation with the idea of practical rationality. This is where I turn to applying these considerations about practical reasons in general to the Wittgensteinian cognitivist position developed by Wiggins and McDowell. As a first step, however, I will examine the conflict between the internal reasons requirement and the neo-Kantian position developed by Christine Korsgaard. This discussion will give further insight into the fundamental motivations for the internal reasons position. It will also serve my overall aim of elucidating desiderata for a theory of moral reasons that construes them as internal and yet impartial.

centrally on the point that some of our actions are 'done without reasons'. Cohon cites packing a lunch pack, we might say 'unheedingly' as an example of action done without a reason. The second is Craig D. Taylor's 'Williams on Moral Incapacity', *Philosophy*, 70/272 (Apr. 1995), 273–85, in which Taylor argues that Williams's Humeanism is incompatible with a phenomenologically plausible model of self-knowledge. Taking such cases to be a problem for Williams in my view rests on a misunderstanding. The internal reasons model is not committed to mental states being atomistic, discrete entities phenomenally known, or to any 'inner hydraulics' model of deliberation, or to a higher order perception model of introspection. A similar misunderstanding of the interpretationist perspective seems to lie behind Milgram's complaint that Williams's argument offers an account in which 'being a reason must be made out in terms of giving reasons, that is, in terms of the deliberation and explanation which invokes reasons', 'Williams's Argument Against External Reasons', 199. From an interpretationist perspective this is not an objectionable equation.

23 McDowell is not inclined to do so, praising the flexibility of Williams's account of practical reasoning, whereas Milgram *is* inclined to do so. Williams, in 'Internal and External Reasons', 104 n., cites the influence on his views of the anti-instrumentalist account of practical reasoning presented by Aurel Kolnai, 'Deliberation is of Ends', in *Ethics, Value and Reality* (London and Indianapolis: Athlone Press, 1973), 44–62.

24 Milgram's mischaracterization of Williams's position as solely instrumentalist paves the way for the argument that Williams has an impoverished notion of imagination's role in practical reasoning, correction of which would have revealed the force of Milgram's external reasons alternative. This does not strike me as particularly plausible. Milgram acknowledges the influence on his view of practical reasoning of David Wiggins. Both Wiggins and Williams, in their turn, acknowledge their debt to the work of Kolnai. A central part of this indebtedness is an acknowledgement of the indeterminacy of practical reasoning, because of the role played in it by imagination. So if Milgram thinks Williams is an instrumentalist because of his false view of the role of imagination in practical reasoning, then someone in this historical line of transmitted influence seems to have made an error.

2. KORSGAARD ON TWO KINDS OF PRACTICAL SCEPTICISM

Even the relatively neutral critic is worried that Williams's argument has an air of begging the question. (It will be interesting, in what follows, to identify the number of times the two sides to this debate accuse each other of this informal fallacy.) Brad Hooker has argued as follows: can we not assume that any rational agent will acquire the relevant motive when he or she comes to accept an external reason?[25] After all, the classical natural law formulation is that goodness is the object of rational desire, and can we not presuppose a naturalized version of this formulation which accepts that rational agents have a standing interest in the good, qua rational agents? In this counter-argument, advanced by Hooker, just as rational agents have a standing interest in truth, they have a standing interest in accepting external reasons. Williams's charge against this line of reasoning in defence of external reasons is that it simply deploys a belief whose content is precisely the point of contention. (This charge of question begging proves to be a two-way street.) Williams puts his point in the form of a rhetorical question:

What is it that one comes to believe when he comes to believe that there is a reason for him to ø, if it is not the proposition, or something that entails the proposition, that if he deliberated rationally, he would be motivated to act appropriately?[26]

Hooker objects that this proposed reply is 'question begging' or 'impotent', depending on how one interprets 'deliberated rationally'. If one accepts that the list of possible means of deliberating rationally has already been circumscribed by the resources allowed by Williams's 'Humean' position, then the external reasons theorist can fairly complain that the question has been begged against him or her:

the external theorist is likely to think that (at least some) rational deliberation about reasons for action starts not from the agent's own subjective present motivations, but from some objective ('external') values and requirements, fixed independently of the agent's present motivations.[27]

Hooker offers Williams the alternative route of not begging the question by circumscribing the resources of practical reason, but by taking the resources of practical reason in a neutral way. This allows that the external reasons theorist can add his or her preferred form of rational deliberation to the list of reason's resources. However, if this is permitted, obviously the internal reasons argument just collapses.

This is an interesting response, but I do not believe that the internal reasons argument implodes so quickly. To make some progress here, we need a very insightful distinction that Korsgaard has made between two forms of scepticism about reason in practice.[28] The first is Hegelian scepticism about whether Kantian formalism about

---

[25] Brad Hooker, 'Williams's Argument Against External Reasons', *Analysis*, 47/1 (Jan. 1987), 42–44.

[26] Williams, 'Internal and External Reasons', 109.

[27] Hooker, 'Williams's Argument Against External Reasons', 43.

[28] Korsgaard, 'Skepticism about Practical Reason', 5–25.

practical reasons yields any substantive conclusion: Korsgaard calls this 'content scepticism'. The second is scepticism as to whether a reason grounded on practical reason alone has motivational efficacy, which she calls 'motivational scepticism'. Korsgaard's aim is to argue that any scepticism about the pretensions of practical reasons must be a content based one and that motivational scepticism has no independent force.

Korsgaard begins with some distinctions that are supportive of the internal reasons position. She argues that Hume has two arguments against the authority of reason in practice, a content scepticism and a motive scepticism, and then argues that Williams is updating Hume's motivational scepticism. Second, Korsgaard observes:

Nagel's argument makes from the agent's perspective the same point that Williams makes from the explainer's perspective, namely that unless reasons are motives, they cannot prompt or explain actions . . . Thus, it seems to be a requirement on practical reasons, that they be capable of motivating us . . . Practical reasons claims, if they are really to present us with reasons for action, must be capable of motivating rational persons. I will call this the internalism requirement.[29]

However, this appearance that Korsgaard has borrowed Williams's constraint in formulating her version of internalism is misleading, for Korsgaard regards Williams as the canonical modern motivational sceptic. I think she is mistaken about this and I will explain why.

Korsgaard's central line of argument is that the internalism requirement, as she has outlined it, claims that we can be motivated by reason *in so far as we are rational* as I described in the previous chapter. I would rephrase Korsgaard's point in the following way: there is a difference between the necessitation of a conditional and conditional necessitation. If you are rational, then reason exerts its motivational force of necessity. But you need not be reasonable, any more than the world need be intelligible. This distinction is, in fact, vital for the project of transcendental philosophy as a whole as I described in the previous chapter, although Korsgaard does not make this wider connection.[30] In the present context, the relevance of this observation is that one can no longer argue from failures to act on the basis of pure practical reason to motivational scepticism, although, importantly for my argument, content scepticism still remains open. On this basis, Korsgaard takes herself to have refuted Williams. She argues that he advances a criticism of practical reason based solely on motivational, not content, scepticism. Thus, she writes:

This argument, however, having been cut loose from Hume's very definite ideas about what sort of rational operations and processes exist, has a very unclear bearing on claims about pure practical reason. If one accepts the internalism requirement, it follows that pure practical reason exists if and only if we are capable of being motivated by the . . . conclusions of practical reason as such. Something in us must make us capable of being motivated by them, and this something will be part of the subjective motivational set. Williams seems to think that this is a reason for doubting that pure practical reasons exist, whereas what seems to follow from the internalism requirement is this: if we can be motivated by considerations stemming

---

[29] Ibid. 11.   [30] Harrison, 'Transcendental Arguments and Idealism', 211–24.

form pure practical reason, the capacity belongs to the subjective motivational set of every rational being.[31]

Korsgaard and Williams both agree on internalism and its requirements, but draw very different conclusions from it for the wider issue of internal and external reasons.[32] They are in full accord that the only ground for motivational scepticism is content scepticism; the former is dialectically dependent on the latter. However, Korsgaard has not proved that content scepticism cannot stand alone, as an independent and self-sufficient challenge to the validity of the practical deployment of reason. Her account of motivational scepticism leaves content scepticism untouched as a self-sufficient challenge to practical reasoning. I believe that is why Williams should remain untroubled by Korsgaard's first argument.

In my alternative interpretation, Williams is *primarily* a content sceptic. He does not believe that the S of every rational agent can be argued, a priori, to contain altruistic or prudential reasons *solely* in virtue of the agent's practical rationality, nor that it can be argued, a priori, to contain a standing disposition to accept such reasons. Korsgaard is taking on the burden of justifying these claims and, in my judgement, this burden of proof has not been discharged, though a full assessment of her overall project is beyond the scope of the current book.[33] Hooker's criticism depended on highlighting the impotence of Williams's motivational scepticism when taken alone. Like Korsgaard, he sees the motivational scepticism as either question begging or impotent. But unlike Korsgaard, he does not introduce the dialectical dependency of motivational scepticism on the prior content scepticism, and hence does not consider the force of Williams's critique when the two lines of argument are separated and the content scepticism isolated.

Hooker's argument took the form of a dilemma: either the list of the resources of practical reason is question beggingly circumscribed, or if it is to be open ended, it must take on board the resources of reason required by pure practical reason. But now the proponent of internal reasons can respond that lying behind the argument is the prior content scepticism that says that pure a priori practical reason, being merely formal, can yield no substantive contents for which the motivational issue even arises. Thus, the list of the resources of practical reason, absent a proof from Kantians that one can transcendentally deduce the presence of altruistic or prudential reasons in the contents of everyone's S, or a standing disposition for their acceptance, will only go as far in circumscribing the limits of practical reason as the 'Humean' assumption permits.

---

[31] Korsgaard, 'Skepticism about Practical Reasons', 21.

[32] A cautionary note on the terminology: the issue of internal versus external reasons properly concerns practical reasoning per se, rather than specifically moral reasons. Internalism versus externalism, as discussed in Ch. 1, is a matter specifically of whether the acceptance of moral requirements necessarily generates a motive. The reason there is no equivocation at this stage of the argument is that Korsgaard is working within the tacitly reductive Kantian project of reducing moral to practical reasons.

[33] A project developed in Christine Korsgaard, *The Sources of Normativity*, aspects of which were criticized in Ch. 3.

Korsgaard compares Williams's polemic against Nagel with Hegel's critique of Kant's derivation of substantial principle from a 'formal' moral law. Korsgaard comments as follows:

From considerations concerning the necessity that reasons be internal and capable of motivating us that are almost identical to Williams's, Nagel . . . argues that investigations into practical reason will yield discoveries about our motivational capacities . . . In Nagel's eyes, the internalism requirement leads not to a limitation on practical reason, but to a rather surprising increase in the power of moral philosophy: it can teach us about human motivational capacities, it can teach us psychology.[34]

This is, indeed, a surprising increase in the power of moral philosophy and a very implausible one at that. I will offer a more modest account of the powers of moral psychology below. At this point I draw three conclusions: first, that Korsgaard's refutation of motivational scepticism alone does not suffice to refute Williams's prior content scepticism. Secondly, her analysis has isolated the internal reasons theorist's best response to Hooker and demonstrates that this response does not commit the fallacy of begging the question. Thirdly, given the resilience of Williams's position, any defence of impartial reasons will have to avoid the strictures imposed by his argument, absent a more plausible neo-Kantian proposal for making altruism an a priori condition of rational agency.

This is not, however, the end of my discussion of Korsgaard because in other work she presents another account of Williams, which ends up as much more sympathetic to the internal reasons case. These arguments are presented in 'The Normativity of Instrumental Reason'.[35] On the interpretation of the internal reasons argument that I am developing here, Williams objects primarily to a rationalist conception of an a priori source of practical reasons. I view him as primarily a content sceptic. Constraints are placed on the idea of a practical reason in these ways: an initial statement of an agent's motivational resources; an enumeration of possible extensions of those resources via the instrumental principle; an extension of that principle to 'constitutive reasoning'; and a further account of how an enumeration of the resources of reason is not strictly possible because of a (Kolnai-influenced) view of the indeterminacy of practical reason because of the role played in it by the imagination. But on this view, Williams is, as it were, genuinely open to offers on how the list can be extended, with the sole proviso that any extension not beg the question in a damaging way. The rationalist claim that external reasons simply are part of an agent's motivational set is unacceptable precisely because it cannot be explained in a non-circular way. An agent's capacity to accept any external reason is simply built into the initial starting point of deliberation.

That explains why both Williams's argument and those of his opponents seem circular. (To come down on Williams's side in this argument is to accept that his more minimal conception of a rational agent is the more acceptable starting point.) It is noteworthy that every party to this dispute accuses the others of question begging and

---

[34] Korsgaard, 'Skepticism about Practical Reasons', 23.
[35] Korsgaard, 'The Normativity of Instrumental Reason', 215–55.

this aspect of the debate is worth analysing. I think it is also helpful in understanding the structure of the argument to reflect on Williams's apparently baffling claim that Kant, of all people, represents the 'limiting case' of an internal reasons theorist.[36] This seems very odd: surely Kant, of all people, counts as an archetypal external reasons theorist? But the reason for Williams's classification is now clear: Kant has a reciprocal account of the nature of moral reasons and the nature of moral agents. He acknowledges that his conception of reasons requires reciprocal adjustment in his account of the capacities of practically rational agents. In making this reciprocal adjustment he can be viewed as being guided by the internal reasons constraint in the sense that he tailors his account of moral reasons to his account of rational agency, and vice versa, in a way that reflects his concern for autonomy.[37] With this point made, Kant can, indeed, be a canonical internal reasons theorist in that he is centrally concerned with the autonomy of a practically rational agent and the importance to that agent of acting on reasons that she, qua particular individual, has first personally endorsed.[38]

Whereas Korsgaard was, initially, inclined to challenge the internal reasons argument, in her later paper there is a different approach that offers a more qualified verdict on the internal reasons requirement. Korsgaard is now more critical of what she calls 'dogmatic rationalism' and defends a limited content scepticism in her own right. Korsgaard's later work is implicitly critical of the internal reasons position in so far as such a view takes the instrumental principle to be the sole principle of practical reasoning. However, as we have seen, it is not clear that the internal reasons theorist *is* restricted to seeing reason simply as instrumental and no more.[39] That point aside, Korsgaard now places some distance between her own considered view and pure or 'dogmatic' rationalism:

According to dogmatic rationalism . . . there are facts, which exist independently of the person's mind, about what there is reason to do . . . The difficulty with this account in a way exists right on its surface, for the account invites the question why it is necessary to act in accordance with those reasons, and so seems to leave us in need of a reason to be rational . . . we must still explain why a person finds it necessary to act on those normative facts, or what it is about her that makes them normative for her. We must explain how these reasons get a grip on the agent.[40]

---

[36] Williams, 'Reply', in Altham and Harrison (eds.), *World, Mind and Ethics*, 220 n. 3.

[37] Discussions with Adrian Moore helped me to see the importance of this point, which is central to the argument strategy of his paper, 'Conative Transcendental Arguments and the Question Whether There Can be External Reasons', in Robert Stern (ed.), *Transcendental Arguments: Problems and Prospects* (Oxford: Oxford University Press, 2003), 271–92.

[38] A point made to me separately by two people: the first anonymous reader for Oxford University Press and John Skorupski, 'Internal Reasons and the Scope of Blame', forthcoming in Thomas (ed.), *Bernard Williams*.

[39] Williams does take this to be a paradigm of a principle of practical reason that is, as it were, internal reason preserving. It begins with elements of an agent's S and gives that agent 'new' reasons. But, as I have already noted, Williams extends this paradigm to constitutive reasoning and the question of whether it is the only form of practical reasoning is left as indeterminate, because the role of imagination in practical reasoning makes this conclusion indeterminate. Korsgaard's target is slightly different: as I have noted she thinks it is incoherent to take the instrumental principle to be the *only* principle of practical reasoning.

[40] See 'The Normativity of Instrumental Reason', 215–55, quotation from 240.

Korsgaard traces this defect to dogmatic rationalism's project of deriving reasons for an agent from the reasons of an ideally rational agent. A source in pure practical reason is insufficient because it cannot explain how the reasons statements it generates for an individual agent say something distinctive about that agent. This looks like the adoption of the internal reasons requirement, not its rejection (and, on Williams's interpretation of Kant, it looks like a position that is more authentically Kantian). For this reason also, Korsgaard now no longer views it as acceptable simply to *stipulate* that rational agents are such as to be motivated by principles of reason.[41] This seems to me to be a tactical withdrawal from the argument directed against the internal reasons theory in 'Skepticism about Practical Reason' and, indeed, to constitute a form of content scepticism in its own right.

So, overall, what desiderata for my positive account of impartial reasons that I will be developing later in this chapter can be elicited from both of Korsgaard's discussions, the earlier and the later? From the first argument, the desideratum is that impartial reasons must be compatible with the plausibility of content scepticism. They cannot be derived a priori from a 'pure' conception of practical reason. From the second argument, that any account of practical reasons must explain how they get a grip on the practically rational agent and thus, indirectly, how they could not possibly be explained by dogmatic rationalism. These two arguments seem to converge, significantly, on an overall endorsement of the internal reasons constraint.

I conclude that the internal reasons position has proved to be durable. It has survived Hooker's and Korsgaard's attempted rebuttals, and these critics have contributed to the clarification of the nature of the internal reasons constraint. But I have interpreted Williams as primarily a content sceptic, not a motivational sceptic. Why, then, is there any dispute between the internal reasons claim and McDowell's version of neo-Aristotelianism? Ought they not to agree? As we shall see, consideration of why they do still disagree leads to new issues arising. They lead, in my view helpfully, to new constraints on a finally acceptable theory of moral reasons.

3. MCDOWELL'S RESPONSE: DISCONTINUOUS MOTIVATIONS AND MORAL CONVERSIONS

Given the differences between their approaches described in the previous chapter, there is clearly more disagreement between McDowell and Williams than between Wiggins and Williams on the issue of internal reasons. However, a problem for my reading of Williams as a content sceptic is that if my interpretation of him were correct, then one would predict little disagreement between his position and that of McDowell. For McDowell argues that Kant's insights into the binding nature of moral obligations should be separated from the project of deriving moral reasons from

---

[41] Ibid. 219 n. 11, 'I believe that in "Skepticism about Practical Reason" I may give the impression that I think a stipulation of this kind sufficient to meet the worries of those who complain that moral principles do not meet the internalism requirement. I don't believe that . . . the internalism requirement may be met by such a stipulation, but . . . this does not resolve the real worry'.

the perspective of pure practical reason. If McDowell shares a commitment to content scepticism with Williams, I have to explain why they disagree over the possibility of external reasons. The mere existence of the dispute between them challenges the interpretation of the internal reasons constraint that I have offered.

McDowell has three criticisms of the internal reasons argument. His first argument is that the internal reasons argument is defective because it is *psychologistic*: the list of the resources of practical rationality implies that the idea of a sound deliberative route is implicitly conditioned by the psychological materials from which the agent started. (Far from denying this implication of his account, Williams makes a virtue of it.) McDowell argues that this makes the contents of the admittedly normative conception of practical reasons hostage to its starting point.[42] McDowell dramatizes his point by appealing to cases where a person can be brought to acknowledge the force of moral reasons in a way quite discontinuous from their existing S or its possible expansion, namely, cases such as conversion in which one cannot be brought to see the force of external reasons without a discontinuous break in the resources of practical rationality.

This first issue is the most important for my project of trying to break the deadlock over the internal reasons problem by eliciting relatively neutral constraints on practical reasons from the internal reasons argument. McDowell's general approach to the psychological is to see it as an interpretative construction out of intersubjective norms, located in the realm of Fregean sense.[43] His naturalized Platonism sees us as able to align with this intersubjective structure owing to our 'second nature'; given this picture, it is clear why McDowell feels free to assume that this structure will be defined for us by the motivational and rational structures of the *phronimos* (Aristotle's ideal of the person of sound practical wisdom) and why it will be culturally invariant. It is also the basis of McDowell's rejection of psychologism in the theory of practical reasons, but the acceptability of this argument is less clear.

Williams is happy to plead guilty as charged, as he does not regard psychologism as an appropriate criticism of a theory of practical reasons. I agree with Williams that while the structure of truth-evaluable contents may exist independently of our capacity to grasp that structure, and one can only come to see our interaction with that structure via the realm of sense as the grasp of pre-existing truth, the same constraint does not apply to what one has most reason to do. The internal reasons argument *begins* with the intuition that in the sphere of practice, our engagement with content is shaped by the psychological starting point of practical enquiry. This minimal form of psychologism seems inherent in the very idea of a theory of practical reasons, which does not share the mind-independent structure of constructivist mathematics. The obscurity lies in why McDowell thinks a view of this kind is psychologistic, given his own Davidsonian emphasis on the constitutive connection between norm and explanation implicit in psychological interpretation.[44]

---

[42] McDowell does not make the error of treating Williams as an instrumentalist about practical reasoning. He recognizes that the conception of practical reasoning Williams deploys reflects the influence on both Williams and Wiggins of Aurel Kolnai. See nn. 23 and 24, above.

[43] McDowell, *Mind and World*, lecture 4.

[44] Given McDowell's sympathies both with Williams's Davidsonian approach to the mental and to his normative conception of practical reasoning, this charge would have to rest on the

If the theory that McDowell defends is intended to be 'anti-psychologistic' as McDowell intends that phrase, it will fall foul of the internal reasons constraint in one of two ways. First, it assumes that one can build the idea of moral reasons into an expanded account of a practically rational agent's motivational set by appealing to every agent's real interest in flourishing. Secondly, it further assumes a single unitary space of reasons that applies both to those agents properly aligned with that space and those outside it. Rejecting these assumptions, as the internal reasons theorist does, is only psychologistic in the minimal sense of relating an agent's normative reasons to the potential explanations of his or her actions. In such a guise, this minimally psychologistic constraint seems to me acceptable. It is certainly not psychologistic in the sense that it abandons a normative conception of reasons for a merely explanatory one. I agree that if the internal reasons position incorporated psychologism in this form, it ought to be immediately abandoned, but it clearly does not.

McDowell has a second argument against the internal reasons claim. That argument challenges the equivalence of the external reasons claim and the reasons entail counterfactuals claim: the equivalence between the assertion, by an external reasons theorist, that an external reason is true of (or for) an agent, and the assertion that if the agent rationally deliberated, regardless of the make up of their S, they would be motivated to ø. It does so by arguing that one may be brought to accept a reason regardless of the prior economy of one's S by a non-rational process, whether conversion or being 'properly brought up'. Conversion is not, I think, McDowell's preferred model for moral development. He takes it as a supplement, to accommodate drastic cases, to his more general model of the inculcation of a simultaneous sensitivity to value and the acquisition of the motivational dispositions that treat moral reasons as automatically overriding. McDowell eliminates the need for such dramatic discontinuities in motivational resources by locating agents in a situation where they have been properly educated, in an Aristotelian community of virtue, such that their external reasons—their objective interest in human flourishing—are accessible to everyone's S. But those agents outside the community of virtue may still be viewed in McDowell's theory as having external reasons statements about their real interests being true of them. He is thus committed to the external reasons model. He denies, however, that he has violated Williams's constraints because of his prior rejection of the claim that there is an equivalence between an external reasons statement being truly assertible of the agent, and the claim that if she rationally deliberated, then whatever motivations she had she would be motivated to ø.

The pressing question is why Williams should dissent from any of this. The answer lies, in part, in Williams's insistence that he holds a *relativized* conception of practical reasons. Reasons must, on his view, say something distinctive about the agent they purport to characterise.[45] It is this corollary of the internal reasons claim that

importation into Williams's argument of a stereotypically 'Humean' position which I have argued has little bearing on the internal reasons argument.

[45] Williams, 'Reply', in Altham and Harrison (eds.), *World, Mind and Ethics*, 189–190. This aspect of the debate has recently been analysed in Fitzpatrick's 'Reasons, Value, and Particular

poses problems for McDowell's second argument. Williams suggests that this argument rests on the mistake of believing that the material equivalence between the truth of the external reasons claim and the reasons entail counterfactuals claim is something that could figure *in the first personal deliberations of the agent*. The false interpretation of the internal reasons position is that an agent of whom the external reasons claim can be truly asserted could, through deliberation, come to see the reasons entail counterfactuals claim as true of themselves also. But if that point does rest on an exegetical misunderstanding on McDowell's part, it modulates quickly into McDowell's third argument. That is the argument that the content of an external reasons claim, for an appropriately specified agent, can derive its content from an appeal to the idea of a *phronimos*.

Williams denies that the content of an agent's reasons is to be explained by relating their S to the S of such an ideal Aristotelian agent, the *phronimos*.[46] Williams does not believe that there is just one ideal S, upon which all agents should converge, because he is sceptical as to whether there is a single, determinate form of life available to modern theory of the kind Aristotle was able to draw upon.[47] That general worry about McDowell's 'objectivism' will be discussed in Part III, below. For the present argument what matters is that Williams believes that there is a further, special point about McDowell's neo-Aristotelian position that is separable from the general concern about the kind of objectivity available to neo-Aristotelianism:

[It] raises a problem which is as much ethical as analytical . . . what A has most reason to do in certain circumstances is what the *phronimos* would have reason to do in those circumstances. But in considering what he has reason to do, one thing that A should take into account, if he is

Agents: Normative Relevance Without Motivational Internalism', sects. 6 and 7. He notes that this aspect of Williams's view is crucial to the dispute with McDowell but claims that it can be accommodated from McDowell's value oriented account of practical reason by noting that a person can be just as 'normatively alienated' from the internal reasons that they actually fail to grasp as from external reasons. My response to this suggestion is that given that Williams's conception of reasons is a normative one, clearly it leaves open the fact that people can make mistakes, hence have internal reasons that they fail to grasp. But it seems to me to make a very radical difference to our ordinary practices surrounding blame and responsibility to treat mistakes as normatively alienating in exactly the same way in which Williams argues that external reasons are normatively alienating. I think Fitzpatrick is simply equivocating over two senses of 'could' in his account of those reasons a person does not act upon but could have acted upon had he or she not made a mistake or, from the external reasons perspective, 'seen things aright'. Once again, to make this claim plausible, Fitzpatrick has to assume that there is a sense in which the agent could 'see things aright' in the sense of coming to accept an external reasons statement that, once again, assumes the truth of that which is to be proved. If you assume that the external reasons thesis is correct, then that which Williams calls 'optimistic internal reasons statements' will be assumed to be external reasons. It will seem to you that they stand to a person's actual deliberations, which may or may not extend to such reasons, in a relation analogous to that between a person's actual reasons and the good internal reasons available in their S*. But that analogy, once again, begs the question: from the internal reasons perspective external reasons are *more than* deliberatively *inaccessible* to poorly reasoning agents. They violate the constraints on what it is to be a practical reason and are therefore impossible. Happily, they are redescribable as optimistic internal reasons statements.

[46] Williams, 'Reply', in Altham and Harrison (eds.), *World, Mind and Ethics*, 189–90.

[47] I will discuss this issue later in this book, with particular reference to the debate on this point between Williams and Martha Nussbaum. See Ch. 6 n. 86.

grown up and has some sense, are the ways in which he relevantly fails to be *phronimos*... The homiletic tradition, not only within Christianity, is full of sensible warning about the dangers of moral weightlifting.[48]

The charge, then, is of illegitimate idealization in the theory of practical reasons, an idealization that severs the link between justifying and explanatory reasons.[49] The best reply to Williams's argument is that of Anthony Price, who has argued that the *phronimos* will not advise the morally weak to do what the *phronimos* would do if located in their situation; the *phronimos* will, rather, tailor his or her advice to the feebler moral powers of the advisee.[50] Point taken, but this seems to concede to Williams the relativity of moral reasons, which is simply another way of expressing the internal reasons argument. Moral advice tailored to individual circumstance implies that we cannot read off the reasons for the agent from the reasons of the *phronimos* without relativization. This seems to concede that the agent's reasons are internal in the required sense. What is the *phronimos* doing, when he or she tailors moral advice to the person being advised, if not observing the internal reasons constraint?

An immediate response is to say: doing what any prudent moral adviser does, namely, tailoring the content of one's advice to the circumstances of the person being advised. Any theory of normative explanatory reasons would do as much.[51] However, this does not seem to me to be a decisive consideration. If the moral adviser is tailoring moral advice to its addressee, is this not in the hope that the content of the reason will say something distinctive about the agent to whom it is addressed? Is there any clear sense, now, of the role of the *phronimos* in giving us the *content* of such a reason, construed as the external reasons theorist must construe it?

Nevertheless, this crucial point does seem to me to be the location of the most promising way of breaking out of the impasse between the internal and the external reasons theorist. The question is: how does one take up an objective, critical perspective on an agent's reasons? Williams says, by launching an 'optimistic internal reasons statement' that goes beyond the contents of the agent's existing 'S' (or presumably such advice would be redundant) but remains within his or her expanded 'S*'. We hope that it is a reason they can metaphorically reach by sound practical reasoning. The external reasons theorist says more: the reason is there for him or her, regardless of their starting point, because it was there for them all along. Williams is primarily sceptical about the explanation of this external reasons claim that takes reason itself to be a source of motivations. In addition, he is secondarily critical of the Neo-Aristotelian position that finds this source in an ideal model of the practical reasoner.

[48] Williams, 'Reply', in Altham and Harrison (eds.), *World, Mind and Ethics*, 190.

[49] Fitzpatrick, in 'Reasons, Value and Particular Agents', denies that McDowell's neo-Aristotelian position can be analysed using the model of a *phronimos* as the idea of a normative reason is itself simple and unanalyzable. In this he follows Derek Parfit's argument in 'Reasons and Motivation'. I would simply note that counter-assertion that a concept is unanalyzable is not an argument and that, in any case, it is not clear that Williams *is* offering an analysis in quite the sense these critics intend. This point is very helpfully discussed by Skorupski in 'Internal Reasons and the Scope of Blame', n. 14.

[50] A.W. Price, 'Reasons and Desires', unpublished MS, presented at a University of London seminar on practical reasoning (1995).

[51] A point that I owe to Brad Hooker.

I would respond, however, that we can borrow a pair of distinctions that Kantian theorists make without emulating their claim that pure practical reason is itself a normative source. The first distinction is between taking an objective perspective on reasons as itself a generator of reasons, as opposed to merely a filter on a person's existing motivations. The second (connected) distinction is between the legitimacy of abstraction and of idealization.[52]

For the sake of argument, assume that taking up an objective perspective on an agent's reasons is to take up an impartial perspective on such reasons which nevertheless respects the relativity of reasons to an agent's expanded 'S*'. It does so by ensuring that the impartial perspective is not itself a generator of new motives but a matter of endorsing already accepted motivations, or deleting accepted motivations that fail to withstand reflective scrutiny. Further, add the desideratum that an impartial theory of moral reasons must avoid Williams's critique of neo-Aristotelian theory by neither assuming that we all share the same motivational set/real interests under idealization, nor by idealizing our capacities to be motivated by moral reasons. I suggest that the alternative is to imagine our reasons as constrained by an abstract procedural constraint, applied to our existing normative motivations, the content of the agent's revised S'. The role of imagination in practical reasoning may be expanded to include the application of this procedural constraint.

To avoid making too strong a claim, and thus to invite Williams's reformulated critique, this constraint on our reasons must *not* attempt to capture the normative force of moral reasons via an idealized theory of the practically rational agent. There is an important difference between the legitimate procedure of abstracting and the illegitimate feature of idealizing. Abstraction selects and deletes, but it does not introduce characterizations of the phenomena it models which are, in the actual world, false.[53] McDowell's ideal theory attributed to all agents the fiction that we should all come to converge on the subjective motivational set of the ideal agent, the *phronimos*. This does seem a proper target of Williams's criticisms, but it is unclear that a conception of a constraint on practical reasons that is abstract, rather than ideal, need fall foul of this aspect of Williams's argument.

There is, I suggest, a chain fallacy in McDowell's argument. For any given individual, we need both to obtain some critical purchase on the reasons that agent actually has (McDowell's point) while saying something distinctively about that individual (Williams's point). But the way McDowell has obtained this critical perspective is by postulating that ideal individual who can provide optimal critical grasp on any other, namely, the *phronimos*. This now loses the sense in which critical purchase on the individual says something distinctive about that individual. Price attempts to bridge that connection by tailoring moral advice to the particular agent while arguing that the idea of the *phronimos* remains, as it were, the *source* of our normative purchase on the motivations of individuals.

---

[52] Onora O'Neill, 'Constructivisms in Ethics', in *Constructions of Reason* (Cambridge: Cambridge University Press, 1989), 206–18.

[53] Ibid., esp. 209–10.

But why do we have to take that route? Why do we need to say that the idea of a normative criticism of an agent's actual reasons that offers us a critical distance from that particular individual's motivations takes us all the way to the idea of the *phronimos*? Rather than showing us how to tailor the idea of advice drawn from an ideal to a non-ideal, actual individual, can we not dispense with such an idealization? I would argue that we can. We still have the resources of abstraction. In the course of taking up a critical perspective on his or her own reasons, an agent can be objective about such reasons without *idealization*. We can view our reasons as subject to a form of abstract procedural constraint. How would this view work, and does it take us beyond the content of the optimistic internal reasons statements that are all that Williams permits us?

4. INTERNAL AND IMPARTIAL REASONS

The external reasons theorist operated with a particular model of how to take up an objective perspective on an agent's existing reasons: a perspective modelled on the psychological dynamics of the acceptance of theoretical truths. There is an ultimate critical perspective on the S of any agent, namely those reasons statements that are true of the agent, as it were, 'all along'. But this argument proves too much: it iterates the fact that we want critical leverage on any agent's perspective in order to generate that perspective that will give us a critical perspective on any agent. This fiction is then substantiated either by a source in pure reason, or by the contents of the S of the *phronimos*. There seems room for a conception of the objective criticism of an agent's reasons that offers less, while offering more than the content of an optimistic internal reasons statement.

My positive proposal detaches the idea of an impartial reason from that of an external reason; the historical connection between the two conceptions is contingent and unfortunate. Humeans, too, can talk about impartiality, and contemporary contractualism represents a view of this kind. Contractualism is usually presented as being of Kantian origin. It is a comprehensive, reflective account of moral rightness and wrongness which seems to derive such properties from a construction procedure in an ontologically modest way. This construction procedure can be viewed as a way of cashing out the motivational efficacy of reason and, therefore, as being supportive of a Korsgaardian view of practical reason.[54]

This is not my understanding of contractualism. For the purpose of developing my argument, the limited amount that I want to take from it is that it offers a pragmatic, rather than a semantic, account of impartial reasons. It presupposes that agents with an interest in morality, that is, socialized and moralized agents, possess a certain kind of internalized psychological structure. That structure grounds a fundamental ethical disposition: the disposition to justify one's actions to others on grounds they could

---

[54] For an interpretation of this kind see Samuel Freeman's 'Contractualism, Moral Motivation and Practical Reason', *Journal of Philosophy*, 88/6 (June 1991), 281–303. For a contrary view of contractualism as basically Humean and externalist, see R. Jay Wallace, 'How to Argue about Practical Reason', *Mind*, 99/395 (July 1990), 355–85.

not reasonably reject. However, that is not a functional characterization by which the agent need first personally regulate his or her deliberation. Nor does this constraint impose any distinctive content. Instead, as I will argue, a constraint that functioned in this way would combine the elements of necessity and contingency in the structure of moral reasoning in a promising way.

The general contrast between a 'semantic' and a 'pragmatic' account of a concept lies in whether one looks to intrinsic features of a concept to explain its distinctive features, or to its extrinsic, functional role.[55] The contractualist, promisingly, does not elucidate impartiality by looking to intrinsic features of a certain class of reasons, but rather to the role of a certain kind of pragmatic constraint on the acceptance of reasons. Agents with an interest in morality view it as a constraint on their own reasons that they can be put to reasonable interlocutors without reasonable rejection. The impartial point of view functions here, as Rawls urges in a related context, as a 'device of representation'.[56] It is a heuristic device which invites us to take up a certain perspective towards already existing moral knowledge and moral principles and our consequent motivations.

An important value to those inculcated into morality is avoiding appealing to partial interests in moral debate and argument. Conversational maxims of reasonableness, wholly context dependent and informal, sustain our recognition that one dimension of those moral claims that impinge on the interests of others is impartial defensibility.[57] Recasting this traditionally Kantian ideal of impartiality into a Humean framework involves two major departures from the traditional project of grounding moral reasons. First, it departs from the identification of the moral point of view with the perspective of practical rationality per se. Secondly, it abandons the attempt to ground a norm internal to the practice of moral deliberation on a deeper norm that is external to that practice. Underpinning such attempts is a mistake about the nature of objectification and what is involved in offering an objective grounding for a reason.

Reflection on the way in which our judgements are tied to a point of view suggests that a more objective conception of the world involves 'perspectival ascent'; namely, the forming of a conception that is less dependent on perspectival modes of conceptualization.[58] However, any such ascent should in my view be interpreted as a 'Hegelian' rather than 'Cartesian' model of objectification.[59] The salient difference is between a pattern of objectification which strips appearance away, revealing it to be an illusion, and another form of objectification which embeds an 'appearance' in a wider context.

[55] I take the distinction from Edward Craig, *Knowledge and the State of Nature* (Oxford: Oxford University Press, 1990), 33–4.

[56] Rawls, *Political Liberalism*, 24–8.

[57] Jeremy Waldron invokes the idea of placing appeals before an individual's 'tribunal of reason' in his 'Theoretical Foundations of Liberalism', *Philosophical Quarterly*, 37 (Apr. 1987), 127–50. The phrase 'reasonable rejection' is Scanlon's: the first presentation of this form of contractualism is in 'Utilitarianism or Contractualism', in Sen and Williams, *Utilitarianism and Beyond*, 103–28.

[58] I take the useful phrase 'perspectival ascent' from Mark Sacks, *The World We Found* (La Salle, Ill.: Open Court Publishing, 1989), 95.

[59] There is a particularly helpful discussion of this distinction in Dancy, *Moral Reasons*, 147–53.

The traditional defence of impartial reasons is unhappy with its contingent grounding as a norm internal to moral argument and attempts to ground it on a more objective basis. The standpoint of the practical is tacitly assumed to be a standpoint of engagement, of subjectivity and of appearance, to be defended by taking up a new perspective that is external to practice, disengaged, 'objective', and capable of stripping away false appearance. However, this approach then severs the link between norm and explanation and immediately runs into the internal reasons constraint. If, however, the constraint of impartiality is vindicated not by Cartesian but by Hegelian objectification, the result is quite different. There is no, in principle, difficulty in the objective perspective endorsing already existing motivations. The perspective it offers is an abstract rather than an ideal perspective. This point, in essence, explains my belief that impartial reasons can be internal reasons.[60] If the impartial point of view is understood as a device of representation, a conception of impartial reasons can be developed that harmonizes with the internal reasons constraint. My concluding task is to suggest how the account of impartial reasons I have offered can be related to an independently plausible account of moral psychology.

5. STRUCTURAL MOTIVATION AND THE RELATIVISED A PRIORI

If the previous section described the *possibility* of a form of objectifying theory, which takes the normative goals of the external reasons theorist and attaches them to a certain view of impartial reasons, much remains to be explained. The claim is that normally socialized individuals with an interest in morality are disposed to take up a certain kind of perspective on their reasons. This perspective is an abstract perspective in which the agent filters his or her reasons in the light of his or her standing disposition to justify such reasons to reasonable interlocutors, such as not to anticipate reasonable rejection. What is the status of this disposition? Has it not just been inserted a priori into the S of every practically rational agent? The claim that we are all motivated to be impartial is just as implausible as the claim that we all have a standing disposition to accept external reasons.

The outline I am offering accepts the internal reasons theorist's strictures on the source of practical reasons. No attempt is being made here to ground our ethical reasons on a source in pure practical reason, nor to insert them, a priori, into the S of every practical agent solely in virtue of his or her practical rationality. That would be, as Williams has pointed out, entirely circular. We are dealing with those agents who have an empirical interest in morality and, as McDowell would urge, are 'properly

---

[60] Williams himself seems to have been led to reject an impartialist account of moral reasons because he associated it, quite plausibly, with a Cartesian model of objectification in Nagel, *The Possibility of Altruism*. In that text moral reasons are 'objective', achieved by a process akin to perspectival ascent, and can be interpreted as both 'external' and impartial. Nagel's later work on this issue constitutes a reply in that he no longer conceives of the objective standpoint as capable of generating motivations in its own right. It is merely a heuristic device. This more defensible position is presented in *The View from Nowhere* (Oxford: Oxford University Press, 1986), ch. 9.

brought up'. These fully socialized agents have a standing disposition to justify their acceptance of reasons in the light of an abstract conception of themselves as parties to a certain kind of procedurally specified moral dialogue. *This disposition, however, is not itself best viewed as a motive akin to other motives.*[61] Given its role in the psychological economy of fully socialized agents, the disposition to impartiality is better viewed as a structural constraint. It functions as a principle would function were it an instance of the relativised a priori.[62]

Let me offer an analogy.[63] Kant claimed that geometry was made up of synthetic a priori principles and was Euclidean. It turned out, however, that the physical world was best described by a geometry that was Riemannian. What ought the Kantian to say? Well, one thing that he or she can do is to make a distinction and thereby to introduce the idea of a relativized a priori. In Michael Friedman's words, we can separate out two concepts of the a priori: 'necessary and unrevisable, fixed for all time, on the one hand, "constitutive of the object of [scientific] knowledge", on the other'.[64] Kant's account of geometry should be understood as a priori in the latter sense, but not in the former. This general strategy can, I suggest, be applied to the current problem too. I suggest that our standing disposition to act on reasons that we can put before others without reasonable rejection is an internalization of a relativized a priori principle.[65]

---

[61] Thus I do not want to rehabilitate the unpromising idea of an externalist 'desire to be moral', recently defended by Sigrun Svavarsdottir in 'Moral Cognitivism and Motivation', *Philosophical Review*, 108/9 (Apr. 1999), 161–219. Any such idea is vulnerable to Michael Smith's objection that while we may desire to do the right thing, we don't desire to do so under that description. See *The Moral Problem*, 74–5. Not for the only time in this book I think the idea needed here is one of presupposition at the level of a commitment to a moral life as a whole.

[62] An idea that originates with Hans Reichenbach, *The Theory of Relativity and A Priori Knowledge* (Berkeley and Los Angeles: University of California Press, 1965).

[63] Here is another analogy that I owe to Adrian Moore. What role does the norm of consistency play when you investigate the structure of the physical world? It plays a presupposed role. You do not explicitly adopt a principle of consistency, but if you accepted inconsistent representations of the world, investigating what there is not a project in which you could intelligibly be engaged. I suggest that the disposition to contractualist impartiality functions as presupposed in a similar way.

[64] I cannot enter here into the intriguing recent debate over a prioricity well represented by the essays in Paul Boghossian and Christopher Peacocke (eds.), *New Essays On The A Priori* (Oxford: Oxford University Press, 2000). However, in that anthology Michael Friedman extends his defence of the role of the relativized a priori (indebted to Reichenbach's account) as an account of the a prioricity of mathematics in 'Transcendental Philosophy and A Priori Knowledge: A Neo-Kantian Perspective', 367–83. In the same volume Phillip Kitcher, in 'A Priori Knowledge Revisited', 65–91, accepts that this is a viable notion of the a priori, but makes two further points that seem to me to be true and interesting. First, that this notion cannot do all the work that the tradition demanded of a stronger conception of a prioricity (one that Kitcher favours) and in particular it cannot establish an authoritative, experience independent framework for future enquiry, 75–7. Secondly, Kitcher's further (and related) point is that the assumption doing the work here is of the truth of historicism, 90–1. While I recognize that Kitcher is pointing to controversial features of mathematical knowledge it seems to me that in the case of moral reasons recognition of these two features makes the account more, not less, plausible.

[65] The kind of view suggested here can be applied not to the structure of an individual agent's deliberations and his or her grasp of a principle, but to the objective structure of knowledge itself. Construed in such a way, it can be taken to represent a form of historicized Kantianism that is a close competitor to the kind of contextualist model of knowledge defended in this book. I have in

In the light of this analogy, let me put my claim this way: our practical deliberations are shaped by a certain deliberative structure, which we may third personally characterize as a commitment to the impartiality of our reasons. But this is not to build into every agent's S a motive to impartiality. To explain what I mean by this, let me return to the contrasts between the view I am outlining and the traditional project of grounding moral reasons on pure practical reason. I have accepted the independent plausibility of content scepticism.[66] Content scepticism is directed to two peculiar features of Kant's theory, the purity of practical reason, and its a priori derivation. I have already argued that Korsgaard's reformulation of internalism ought to parallel wider discussions of Kant's theoretical philosophy that attempt to separate the method of transcendental argument from the doctrine of transcendental idealism. On this view, Kant was misguided in believing that he had to begin his transcendental argumentation with necessary truths about experience. Contingencies, combined with conditional necessities, support the method of transcendental argument without requiring the doctrine of transcendental idealism.[67] However, an 'analytical salvage' along these lines would avail us little when it comes to content scepticism: any such project would have departed from the target of Williams's pessimism and Korsgaard's optimism. For there are reasons internal to the Kantian system as to why Kant is driven to an extreme position on the overdetermination of moral action by both empirical causation and pure moral motive.[68]

Nevertheless, while one would openly depart from Kant's extreme view on these matters, one could attempt an ethical equivalent of the analytical salvage with more modest ambitions. Paralleling its theoretical counterpart it would look not for a priori knowledge of necessary truths about human psychology and motivation, but relativized a priori knowledge of truths that are only conditionally necessitated postulates of the theory.[69] Such a theory avoids the excessive anti-psychologism inherent in McDowell's illegitimate idealization of moral psychology. The theory is compatible with the minimal psychologism of the internal reasons argument position that requires no more than a link between the explanatory and justificatory senses of the phrase 'practical reasons for an agent'. It would thus have met the desiderata

mind the application to ethical knowledge of the kind of model of historicized reason developed in Michael Friedman's recent work, notably *The Dynamics of Reason* (Stanford, Calif.: Center for the Study of Language and Information, 2001). I discuss these parallels throughout Part III, below.

[66] Thus, I am not suggesting that the constraint of impartiality determines any specific content for moral reasons. I mean two more precise things by this. I do not believe that moral reasons are essentially public and *hence* altruistic in content—a very obscure connection. Nor do I believe that impartial reasons can be explained as both agent-neutral and universal, as I do not believe that the agent-relative/agent-neutral distinction is a tenable one. I argue for both of these claims in 'The Scope of the Agent-Relative', unpublished MS (2005).

[67] I have already drawn upon the arguments of Ross Harrison's paper, 'Transcendental Arguments and Idealism', 215–18, further discussed below.

[68] Charles Larmore, *Patterns of Moral Complexity* (Cambridge: Cambridge University Press, 1989), 85–90; *The Morals of Modernity* (Cambridge, Cambridge University Press, 1996), 35–40.

[69] This is the neo-Kantian strategy replicated in the case of his theoretical philosophy, for example, by Hans Reichenbach, *The Theory of Relativity and A Priori Knowledge*. The leading contemporary developer of this approach is Michael Friedman, see nn. 64 and 65, above.

established both from Williams's critique of neo-Kantianism and his critique of
neo-Aristotelianism in such a way that it could offer an account of the harmony
between impartial reasons and human motivation that satisfied the internal reasons
constraint.

The version of impartialism I have outlined takes this form: it defends the impartiality of reasons, but does so in a framework that observes the psychologistic constraint, and it needs to be supplemented by a moral psychology which is an instance
of the relativized a priori, not a priori as Korsgaard required. It evades Williams's
critique of neo-Aristotelian theory by not assuming that we all share the same motivational set/real interests under idealization, but it is permitted to view us as capable of
an abstract representation of our reasons and their structure.

A theory which grounds impartial reasons in a realistic psychology builds on the
following points: first, that we should replace the Kantian assumption that our interest in morality is non-empirical with a conception of our moral interests as inescap-
ably empirically conditioned and subject to contingency.[70] Secondly, we should take
from Thomas Nagel not a commitment to a similarly a priori and pure conception of
moral motivation to that of Kant's original theory, as Korsgaard mistakenly does, but
rather a commitment to structural explanations in moral psychology.[71] Moral motivation should postulate within the agent an authoritative structure which embeds non-
desire driven motivation which Scheffler calls authoritative motivation. He turns to
psychoanalysis as an example of a psychological theory that is in broad outline naturalistic, postulates such a structural source of motivation, and captures the twin phenomena of the resonance and the fragility of moral demands in our lives, factors which
in turn reflect the susceptibility of moral motivation to familiar deformations.[72]

This is the precise point at which the contractualist position I have discussed can
draw on the traditional project of grounding external reasons. It does not postulate
that alongside a fully socialized agent's reasons there exists a further first order reason,
the desire impartially to justify one's actions. Furthermore, we do not need to view
this disposition as a higher order desire either, not, that is, in the sense of a 'higher
order' functional state. I do not believe that it is misleading to call this internalized
principle a higher order disposition.[73] However, this is on the understanding that

---

[70] Larmore, *Patterns of Moral Complexity*, 87–9.

[71] I have already noted that Korsgaard, in 'Skepticism about Practical Reason', esp. at 32, takes
the moral of Nagel's *The Possibility of Altruism* to be that moral philosophy can teach us psychology,
which should come as news to psychologists. For the alternative proposal of interpreting Nagel as
having isolated the role of structural motivation in moral psychology see Samuel Scheffler, *Human
Morality* (Oxford: Oxford University Press, 1992) ch. 5. I agree with Scheffler that this is one of
the most promising lines of argument in *The Possibility of Altruism*. The current chapter can be
seen as a development of one of Nagel's lines of thought, taking my lead from Scheffler's insightful
discussion.

[72] Scheffler, *Human Morality*, 86–8.

[73] I refer to a 'higher order disposition' as it is plausible to maintain that particular dispositions
of character, such as virtues, have distinctive patterns of motivation associated with them. The
disposition I am concerned with has a regulative status over such particular motivations. Williams
himself has a similar story to tell about how, given the truth of the internal reasons thesis, blame
actually operates. His account invokes a 'proleptic mechanism' whereby one appeals in moral

such a disposition is part of the cognitive architecture of the agent's practical reasoning.[74]

Compare an analogy that I used earlier: the presupposed role of the norm of consistency when you investigate the structure of the physical world.[75] You do not explicitly adopt such a principle, but if you accepted inconsistent representations of the world, you could not intelligibly be viewed as engaged in the business of representation. Similarly, the fully socialized agent does not have some meta-level desire to have moral reasons that are impartially defensible. But if such a meta-level norm cannot be interpreted as applying to such an agent, then the enterprise of giving moral reasons is not one in which he or she can intelligibly be viewed as engaging. Let me emphasize that I do not view this constraint as itself determining content—that is why I view it as formal—but this does not mean it is vacuous. This is, I think, as much content as remains to the idea of a 'moral point of view'.[76]

A moral psychology of this kind contains principles that are instances of the relativized a priori and thus perfectly matches the desiderata for an acceptable theory that I have developed. Its postulated explanatory structure is only a priori relative to a postulated body of theory. It locates, within this naturalistic perspective, a psychological explanation cum vindication of an impartial constraint on moral reasons. In order for this to be possible, it is important that the theory must *not* attempt to capture the normative force of moral reasons via an idealized theory of the practically rational agent. McDowell's ideal theory attributed to all agents the fiction that we should all come to converge on the subjective motivational set of the ideal agent, the *phronimos*. This does seem a proper target of Williams's criticisms, but it is unclear that

criticism to 'the desire to be respected by people whom, in turn, one respects', 'Internal Reasons and the Obscurity of Blame', 41. This invokes a reason proleptically as it makes it true that a person has a reason motivated indirectly by this desire. The difference between his account and the one I have offered here is that the disposition I cite is more minimal: the motivation to want to be respected by others is a substantial ethical motivation, whereas the desire to advance reasons to others without reasonable rejection goes less deeply into ethical motivations. But merely because my notion is the more minimal, it does not, for that reason, allow one simply to presuppose its universality of scope and in that I agree with Williams. (By way of contrast, Scanlon, in *What We Owe to Each Other*, takes the universality of moral reasons as a premiss from which one can argue *against* the idea that moral reasons are internal.)

[74] Freeman, 'Contractualism, Moral Motivation and Practical Reason', 298–9, makes a similar suggestion concerning the role of the central disposition that contractualism attributes to agents, but he takes his proposal to vindicate the Kantian origins of the theory. This is because it demonstrates that such motivations have a 'formal basis in practical reasoning'. I do not see that the sense of 'formal' Freeman explains has this consequence. I agree, rather, with Scheffler that we are dealing with structures which I explain as instances of the relativized a priori. They are compatible with a broadly naturalistic account of motivation. I leave it open whether this position is better traced back to Hume or to the philosopher that Grice once called 'Kantotle'.

[75] See n. 63, above.

[76] I should add that as I do not regard my view as supplying particular motivations but rather as shaping the architecture of deliberation, it is distinct from neo-Kantian attempts to make impartial reasons a class of reasons with a distinctive 'fail safe' role in moral deliberation. I have in mind here a contrast with Barbara Herman's deservedly influential position in 'On the Value of Acting from the Motive of Duty', in *The Practice of Moral Judgement* (Cambridge, Mass.: Harvard University Press, 1993), 1–22.

a conception of practical reasons that involves abstraction, rather than idealization, need fall foul of this aspect of Williams's argument.

We are, therefore, supplementing Williams's account of the resources of practical reasoning. Such reasoning centrally involves imagination. However, in fully socialized agents with an interest in morality this includes the capacity to view one's reasons as subject to an abstract procedural constraint, a constraint built into the structure of practical deliberation. An agent's existing deliberative standpoint, the content of his or her S, provides the matter of deliberation, but a higher order disposition structures its form. This allows one to explain how one could subject an agent's reasons to an objective constraint, the constraint of impartiality, and thereby have critical leverage on his or her motivations. This constraint does not invoke the fictions of pure practical reason, nor of an ideal reasoner who provides independent critical purchase on any actual reasoner. The form of our criticism is not to argue, to take a Williams example, that a man who is cruel to his wife has an external reason statement for him not to do so to be true of him 'all along'. Our purchase on his motivations is to argue that he himself has reason to accept only those reasons that, were he fully rational, he could put to co-deliberators without the prospect of reasonable rejection. That is to say more than we can only put optimistic internal reasons statements to him.

I have analysed Williams's argument against external reasons and have endorsed both his underlying content scepticism and his relativization of an agent's reasons to his or her expanded set of internal reasons. I have accepted that a theory of such reasons must be minimally psychologistic. However, I have presented an account of impartial reasons, contractualist in inspiration, that can harmonize both with these constraints and with an independently plausible account of moral psychology. The result gives us the resources to take up an objective perspective on an agent's reasons, while dispensing with the fiction of a maximally objective perspective, such that any agent could be criticized on the grounds that he or she is not 'seeing matters aright' and failing to acknowledge an external reason.

6. INTERNALISM, EXTERNALISM, AND 'MORAL LIFE'

What the external reasons theorist seemed to want was an a priori truth about the fundamental role that moral reasons play in deliberation. That truth was secured by placing such reasons, a priori, in every agent's S. I have offered, instead, a relativized a priori truth instantiated in moral psychology of fully socialized agents. For such agents, morality has a psychological authority rooted in the cognitive architecture of their practical deliberation, based on a general psychological disposition to want to hold moral reasons that are impartially defensible. This seems to me to give us all that an exponent of external reasons could want without making implausible claims about how much we can derive from the very idea of a practically rational agent a priori.

What 'force' ought a moral reason to have? The force of a good reason, a force that is not contrary to rational freedom, but expressive of it. Stuart Hampshire attributed the following view to Spinoza:

A man is most free...and also feels himself to be most free, when he cannot help drawing a certain conclusion, and cannot help embarking on a certain course of action in view of the evidently compelling reasons in favour of it...The issue is decided for him when the arguments in support of a theoretical conclusion are conclusive arguments.[77]

I think this is a very plausible and attractive view, one shared in the present context by Wiggins. Nevertheless, views of the kind that I have proposed have been heavily criticized. Scanlon, originator of the contractualist element of my composite theory, cites two grounds for *not* taking contractualism in an externalist direction. He argues that people who lack the disposition in question to view their reasons as impartially defensible suffer from a 'particularly grave moral fault' and any such view involves what Scanlon regards as a discredited Humeanism about desires. On the first point, I would, conditionally, accept it. People who lack the disposition I have described do indeed suffer from a particularly disabling moral fault. However, that does not seem to me to be, directly, any reason to give up the view that I have described. Perhaps Scanlon is suggesting that the intuition that he is appealing to gives us grounds for looking for an alternative view, but I have looked at the alternative views and found reasons to reject them.

On the second point, I have demonstrated that the internal reasons constraint has no essential connection with a Humean theory of the self or a Humean conception of the psychological. I have conceded that the general disposition to hold impartially defensible reasons which shapes the deliberations of mature moral agents would have to be put in a category of mental phenomena whose direction of fit is from world to mind. Hence will be classified in the same category as desires. But this is a defect in our current broad terminology: having the cognitive architecture governing one's deliberation shaped in a particular way really is not like suddenly wanting a peach flavoured ice cream. Nothing in the internal reasons position rests on 'Humeanism' about individual desires.

The account I have presented attempts to bracket the motivational internalists' intuitions about the authority of morality. Once again, it seems to me that the best way to put this is via a claim of *presupposition*. Moral life involves a commitment to treating certain considerations as authoritative, but this general commitment is not a non-cognitive state called upon on particular occasions. It was, perhaps, the misleading suggestions of his terminology that made Rodger Beehler's claim that moral life involved a pre-commitment to 'caring' about morality sound more non-cognitivist than it was; in every other respect his account is close to that which I have defended here.[78]

---

[77] Stuart Hampshire, 'Spinoza on the Idea of Freedom', *Proceedings of the British Academy* (1960), 195–215, quotation from 198.

[78] Rodger Beehler, *Moral Life* (Oxford: Basil Blackwell, 1978) a book which heroically steered a course between Hare's prescriptivism and a Wittgenstein-influenced social practice view of ethics that represented the 'Moralitat'/'Sittlichkeit' antinomy at the time of its composition (for a representative of the latter view see Dewi Phillips and Howard Mounce, *Moral Practices* (London: Routledge, 1970)).

I concede that what makes this account of motivation look closer to the traditional view of the motivational externalist is that our overall picture of morality is going to be, in a sense, disjunctive. There is going to be one account about how moral agents acquire knowledge of value and a separate account about how properly brought up agents are psychologically disposed to attach special authority to such reasons. The neo-Kantian wanted to preserve the autonomy of the will by excluding any such external determination entirely. Wiggins and McDowell preserve the inherent normativity of evaluative judgements, but have a separable account of the nature of the practical. My view has taken this degree of separation one step further with the aim of respecting an intuition that the internal reasons constraint gives us insight into the very nature of practical reasons in general.

CONCLUSION

In this part of this book I have engaged in the first major revision of the cognitivist argument I described in the opening chapters. In my view, it can be made compatible with our best account of what it is for reasons in general to be practical reasons. This is possible, however, only by embedding the motivated desire theory at the heart of the view in a more general, presuppositional story about the general disposition we have to explain our actions to others on acceptable grounds. This paralleled, as I have demonstrated, the presuppositional structure of Wiggins's version of the theory.

With this revision in place, it is time to resume the main line of argument for the proposed cognitivist position as the best account of our knowledge of value. Part II turns to new challenges that the view must face. In my view, the proposed cognitivist theory, in Wiggins's and McDowell's original presentations, convincingly made the case for the *sui generis* objectivity of the ethical. However, I contend that the interesting stage of the argument arises when the cognitivist position is forced to meet the challenge of equally sophisticated non-cognitivists. Both Simon Blackburn and Bernard Williams offer defences of the motivations behind non-cognitivism while attempting to avoid the Wittgensteinian critique. The crucial argument is the argument from thick concepts, since it forms the crux of the cognitivist position while also, Williams alleges, trading on a crucial ambiguity.

The next stage in my account of the cognitivist theory is to highlight the centrality of thick concepts to the argument, brought out by considering the projectivist alternative. For while the case I have expounded so far has considerable *prima facie* plausibility, it remains to be seen whether the case for non-cognitivism could be developed along similar lines, undercutting the cognitivist case. The key argument between the projectivist and the cognitivist concerns our aspiration to a reflective explanation of the ethical. The centrality of this point will emerge at the next stage of the argument. The conflict between Wittgensteinian cognitivism and the general programme of expressivism will advance the argument in two key ways. First, it will emphasize the point that the case for cognitivism rests essentially on moral beliefs being irreducibly the best explanations of some core moral phenomena. Secondly, it will further clarify how far the idea of explanation can be applied to the case of our moral responses and moral knowledge. My discussion of Harman's various objectivity tests emphasized that it is essential for the cognitivist position to prove that moral properties can meet the 'best explanation' requirement and can do so unreduced. Further reflection on the argument from thick concepts will sharpen the point of dispute between the cognitivist position I have described and its more sophisticated non-cognitivist rivals. These are the themes of Part II of this book.

PART II

NORM-EXPRESSIVISM AND NON-OBJECTIVISM

5

A Critique of Expressivism

§1: A default starting point for the discussion is established, namely, the orthodox Fregean treatment of 'action guiding' uses of language as a distinction between the forces of an utterance. §2: Blackburn's projectivism is evaluated in the context of his wider commitment to quasi-realism and the conflict between this theory and cognitivism is assessed. §3: Blackburn's and Timmons's recent "twin track" approach of assertoric non-descriptivism plus an account of the ethical use of language. §4: Gibbard's norm-expressivism assessed and the denial of emotional cognitivism.

In part II I examine the challenge to the revised form of cognitivism that I have developed so far from two sophisticated forms of non-cognitivist strategy. The first, which is the focus of this chapter, I label the expressive/projective strategy. The second, non-objectivism, is the focus of Chapter 6. As will become clear, the expressive/projective strategy covers a family of views with interrelated common themes. I shall primarily focus on the two most highly developed: norm expressivism (defended by Allan Gibbard) and projectivism (defended by Simon Blackburn). They both focus on the crucial issue of how we should understand our desire to explain the ethical within a generally naturalistic framework.

One way in which the theories that I am going to discuss in the chapter differ from historically earlier forms of non-cognitivism is that they are intended to constitute a general theory of normativity, which, while it is supposed to bolster some of the intuitions underlying the prevalent conception of **value**, does not exactly match the extension of that term. To borrow the useful examples of David Copp: the norm of truth telling is not a value, and calling his car 'battered and slow' is an evaluation which is not normative.[1] The non-cognitivists whom I am going to discuss in this chapter operate with a descriptive/normative distinction, not a fact/value distinction.

1. THE DEFAULT FREGEAN STARTING POINT

The starting point of the debate between cognitivism and non-cognitivism is an aspect of our ordinary practice that both sides wish to explain: the linguistic practices that we draw upon when we discuss morality. The cognitivist can claim some marginal advantage here, for the surface structure of our use of language strongly

---

[1] Copp, *Morality, Normativity and Society*, 11, n. 6.

suggests that it is an area of language fit for the making of assertions. This, combined with the a priori platitude connecting assertion and the expression of belief, strongly supports the cognitivist diagnosis of how we think and speak in this area. All parties agree that the surface appearances do indeed support a cognitivist interpretation of how we think and speak about morality.

Non-cognitivists are not impressed and suggest that we simply need to develop an account of why the surface structure of language is misleading in this case. They promise an account of the underlying structure of language that comports better with a non-cognitivist account of ethics. Slightly muddying the waters, some non-cognitivists appeal not only to how we speak in this area but, importantly, how we think, at least in terms of characterizing the mental state primarily expressed by moral judgement. This introduces a tangential connection between non-cognitivism and the position discussed under the heading of 'internalism' in Part I. Happy to seize any dialectical weapon to hand, some non-cognitivists claim that the non-cognitive account of the mental state typically expressed by moral utterances harmonizes better with internalism.[2] He or she argues that given that the mental state concerned is intrinsically motivating, having the direction of fit of an attitude or desire, it is, as it were, of the right general character intrinsically to motivate action.[3] Internalism, in turn, is viewed as the making more precise of the vaguer intuition that moral utterances are 'action guiding'.[4] So while these two issues of moral psychology and the reconstruction of our linguistic practices are, in principle, distinct, they are usually closely tied together in non-cognitivist views. (The cognitivist appeals to his or her own connection between the mental state typically expressed by a moral assertion and the 'surface' linguistic expression of such states, namely, the a priori connection between assertion and belief.)

In this chapter I will be persevering with what I have always taken to be a sound response to this non-cognitivist line of argument: namely, that it unhappily runs together issues in pragmatics (that is, issues about speakers' use of a language) with issues in semantics.[5] Semantic issues concern the contents expressed by utterances when that utterance is evaluated in a certain, limited, way. To adapt slightly an argument of Alasdair MacIntyre's, suppose two Secret Service agents rush into the

---

[2] The general connection here was discussed in Chs. 2 and 3. For example, if the 'Humean' theory of motivation takes the form of arguing that there is a type of mental state whose tokens are intrinsically motivating, then the demand that moral requirements (whatever they are) must necessarily supply an agent with a motive would seem to comport well with Humeanism. Needless to say I am not convinced by arguments of this general form.

[3] See Blackburn, *Spreading the Word*, 188–9, for a particularly clear expression of this argument and some reservations about it, noting that it must be supplemented by an account of 'what it is about an attitude that makes it a moral one'.

[4] This intuition about 'action guidingness' originated with Patrick Nowell-Smith, *Ethics* (Oxford: Blackwell, 1957), 86.

[5] I am indebted to Rawls's discussion in *A Theory of Justice* (Cambridge Mass.: Harvard University Press, 1971), sect. 62: 'A Note on Meaning'. Rawls acknowledges the influence on his presentation of John Searle's discussions of the problem specifically in 'Meaning and Speech Acts', *Philosophical Review*, 71/4 (Oct. 1962), 423–32.

President's bedroom in the White House, both ignorant of each other's action. One is a friend of the President; the other dislikes him intensely. They both utter the true sentence, 'Mr President, your bed is on fire'. On hearing both utterances the President leaps out of bed. In both cases we have a use of language that is 'action guiding'.[6] The utterances caused an action to occur. If the utterances had not been made, the President would not have acted. As uttered by the hostile agent, the utterance had the force of describing; as uttered by the benevolently disposed agent, it had the force of a warning. But in both cases the embedded content of the utterance was a core descriptive component: a sentence in the indicative mood. An orthodox Fregean treatment of this case would take the speech acts of the two agents to be utterances with different forces. The theory of force in general involves the conventional transformation of those embedded sentences that are the invariant transforms across the different cases. It is assumed that speakers of a language grasp the conventional rules that take such core components, embed them in utterances with different forces, and thus allow us to carry out various actions with language, such as describing, recommending, warning, and so forth. This idea of a separable theory of force is an important part of a Fregean theory of meaning.[7]

This diagnosis clearly supports cognitivism as it breaks the connection between the content of the utterance and the speech act in which it is embedded. The connection is broken in this way: action-guiding language (more precisely, speech acts that can be appraised in a particular context as action guiding) do not have to embed a content in any particular grammatical mood or to express a content with any particular psychological content. My purely factual utterance of 'there is a bull behind you' may warn you and guide your action (if we are picnicking in a field) or inform you and not affect your actions at all (if we are buying in the cattle market); but these are aspects of the force of the utterance that are essentially dependent on a speaker's grasp of the conventional forces of utterances in various contexts. So cognitivism, which claims that the embedded content of such speech acts is truth-apt and connected a priori to the expression of belief (when asserted) can accommodate the action guiding character of language perfectly well. No advantage is conceded to the non-cognitivist from the fact that language can be used in an action guiding way. Uses of language may be appraised, on particular occasions, as action guiding, but it would be a confusion to infer from this that we need to postulate a different kind of content at the level of embedded contents.

As Rawls pointed out in his classic, and very perceptive, discussion of this issue, this does not mean that the cognitivist cannot, in principle, accept the claim that moral utterances are *typically* or *primarily* action guiding (although personally I do not see why we should accept this claim and I shall say more about this below).[8] If this claim

---

6 Alasdair MacIntyre, *A Short History of Ethics* (London: Routledge Classic, 2002), 261.

7 Michael Dummett, 'What Is a Theory of Meaning II?', in Gareth Evans and John McDowell (eds.), *Truth and Meaning: Essays in Semantics* (Oxford: Oxford University Press, 1976), 67–137.

8 Rawls, *A Theory of Justice*, 406–7.

is true, then cognitivists can not only explain this claim, they can offer a better explanation of it than non-cognitivists:

> The meaning of 'good' and of related expressions does not change in those statements that are counted as advisory. It is the context that converts what we say into advice even though the sense of the words is the same . . . constant descriptive sense together with the general reasons why persons seek out the views of others explain these characteristic uses of 'good'.[9]

Indeed, the cognitivist is now equipped to prepare a counter-attack. Peter Geach focused on a particular aspect of our ordinary use of language that is especially problematic for the non-cognitivist about ethics: the phenomenon of the combination of sentences to form more complex sentences that contain conditional connectives. Geach begins from the following fundamental claim, the 'Frege point':

> A thought may have just the same content whether you assent to its truth or not; a proposition may occur in discourse now asserted, now unasserted, and yet be recognizably the same proposition.[10]

On the basis of this point, Geach constructed an objection to those analyses of ethical language that understood what appear to be assertions in the indicative mood to be something else, namely, an expression or the taking up of a practical stance:

> In all the kinds of case that I have mentioned, the very same sentence can occur in an 'if' clause; and to such occurrences the anti-descriptive theories will not apply . . . Of course, the anti-descriptive theorist will reply that his theory was not intended to cover such cases—that the same form of words, after all, may have different uses on different occasions. This possibility of varying use, however, cannot be appealed to in cases where an ostensibly assertoric utterance 'p' and 'If p, then q' can be teamed up as premises for a modus ponens. Here, the two occurrences of 'p', by itself and in the 'if' clause, must have the same sense if the modus ponens is not to be vitiated by equivocation.[11]

To use one of Geach's examples, if I say that 'doing a thing is bad' using the sentence in an indicative mood, I can usually have been taken to have asserted the sentence (although, as Geach points out, ordinary language does not have a device for the explicit marking of assertions). However, that very same sentence can occur unasserted, as, for example, when I say that 'If doing a thing is bad, then getting your little brother to do it is bad'. Here, 'doing a thing is bad' occurs as the antecedent of a conditional and in this context it is not asserted. Suppose that we have a sequence of sentences expressing a 'piece of moral reasoning':

If doing a thing is bad, getting your little brother to do it is bad.
Tormenting the cat is bad.
Ergo, getting your little brother to torment the cat is bad.[12]

---

[9] Rawls, *A Theory of Justice*, 406.
[10] Geach, 'Assertion', *Philosophical Review*, 74/4 (1965), 449–65 at 449. See also 'Ascriptivism', *Philosophical Review*, 69/2 (1960), 221–5.
[11] Geach, 'Assertion', 462–3.
[12] Ibid. 463.

Geach points out that for this to be a piece of reasoning that we can follow without its being guilty of the fallacy of equivocation, the occurrence of 'bad' needs to mean the same in all four of its occurrences in this piece of reasoning. But the expressivist or prescriptivist insists that calling something 'bad' is not to describe it, but to carry out the speech act of condemnation. But on that interpretation, this piece of reasoning involves meanings for 'bad' that shift as it occurs in asserted and non-asserted contexts. The whole argument is, by expressivist lights, guilty of a fallacy of equivocation. But it seems intuitively clear that it is not defective in this way.

Geach here represents the Fregean orthodoxy, also defended by Searle and Rawls. I have emphasized these points as I want to defend the cause of such semantic and pragmatic orthodoxy throughout this chapter. I have one very simple argument which I think is decisive: that every attempt to rebut this account of our 'moral use of language' (whatever that use is supposed to be) involves costs far greater than the proposed benefits of the non-cognitivist's 'deep' analysis. In each case, the non-cognitivists's strategy of reinterpreting the surface structure of our use of language incurs theoretical commitments that are unduly burdensome. I do not doubt that it is technically possible to devise a means of representing this area of language along non-cognitivist (expressivist) lines. The question, then, is what reason we would have for adopting such a proposal? It is at this point, I argue, that the expressive/projective strategy fails by its own lights.

2. PROJECTIVISM

I will begin with the proposal most precisely focused on the problem to hand. The crucial emphasis on naturalistic explanation is central to the projectivist view of Simon Blackburn. His projectivist theory of the ethical, combined with a strategy towards realism called 'quasi-realism', tries to accommodate the positive points made by the cognitivist theory while retaining the fundamental motivations of the fact/value dichotomy.[13] I will discuss the dispute between the cognitivist position and Blackburn's projectivism further to focus on what will become the crucial issue for cognitivism: the challenge of how we explain radical ethical pluralism and the implications that such pluralism has for the argument from thick concepts.

Blackburn's overall strategy is important for the details of my subsequent argument. He conjoins a projectivist account of moral discourse with a defence of that position in metaphysics and the philosophy of language pitched at a more reflective level. This second level defence is termed 'quasi-realism' and it is intended to defend

---

[13] Blackburn's earlier position is set out in the following papers: 'Opinions and Chances', 'How to be an Ethical Anti-Realist', and 'Attitudes and Contents', all in *Essays in Quasi-Realism* (Oxford: Oxford University Press, 1993) at 75–93, 166–81, 182–97 respectively; 'Non-Cognitivism and Rule Following', in Holtzmann and Leich (eds.), *Wittgenstein: To Follow a Rule*, 163–87; 'The Land of Lost Content', in Ray Frey and Katherine Morris (eds.), *Value, Welfare and Morality* (Cambridge: Cambridge University Press, 1993), 13–25. The earliest presentation of the theory was *Spreading the Word* (Oxford: Oxford University Press, 1984), ch. 6. There have now been significant changes in his views, expressed by the considerable differences between *Spreading the Word* and his most recent book, *Ruling Passions* (Oxford: Oxford University Press, 1999).

projectivism from the charge that it is a familiar form of scepticism about the discourses which it claims are 'projected'. The quasi-realist argues that reflection on the nature of the commitments of our various discourses reveals a fundamental dichotomy between those that are fully realistic and those that we reflectively understand to be projected. However, the 'real versus projected' dichotomy need not be at the service of scepticism. The projectivist claim is that certain discourses, such as the causal, the modal, and the evaluative, are projections on to reality rather than a fully cognitive response to it. However, the quasi-realist also argues that recognition of the projected nature of these discourses is fully compatible with continued engagement in the practices constitutive of them. This engagement should be supplemented by a demonstration that projected discourses can inherit many of the marks of truth possessed by the fully factual discourses. Diagnosing an area of thought or language as projected clarifies its status, but it need not be taken to undermine it.

Thus, in the case of the ethical, Blackburn's presentation of the projectivist theory is straightforward.[14] When we reflect on our ethical judgements, we come to see them as expressive of two different classes of psychological state, belief states and attitudinal states. The projectivist argues that the *distinctive* and primary element of moral judgement is the expression of a non-intellectual affective state, rather than a grasp of the nature of reality. When one judges ethically, one takes oneself to be recognizing an external state of the world. Reflection reveals that this extra component is a projection of our own minds, and hence what one is actually doing all along is expressing an attitude, not judging facts—at least, not in the distinctively evaluative part of the judgement. The projectivist claim is that evaluative properties are correctly understood as projections of our attitudes, construed as more stable than passing emotions.

I would argue that it is important to be clear about the motivations of the theory for reasons that will become apparent when I present some counter-arguments on behalf of cognitivism. Its primary motivation is ontological economy, part of a wider commitment to naturalistic explanations.[15] Blackburn argues that as in the practice of science, so in philosophy, theory choice is to be guided by a principle of ontological economy. The wider commitment to naturalism comes in not simply to make such a scientific methodology appropriate for philosophical contexts, but also to restrict the kinds of objects and properties that can figure in such explanations.

Blackburn argues that a projectivist account of the ethical is well placed to explain the metaphysical status of value, notably its supervenience upon the non-evaluative, and to explain the plausibility of motivational internalism.[16] Projectivism explains the

---

[14] It has actually evolved through three different versions, as clearly distinguished by Mark van Roojen, 'Expressivism and Irrationality', *Philosophical Review*, 105/3 (July 1996), 311–36, at 314–18. I focus here on the third, most recent and the most sophisticated proposal.

[15] The importance of this point to the projectivist strategy was brought home to me by Jane Heal, 'Ethics and the Absolute Conception', *Philosophy*, 64 (1985), 49–65.

[16] Blackburn also has an argument that the moral realist *cannot* explain the supervenience of the moral on the non-moral, but this argument was, in my view, successfully rebutted by James Klagge in 'An Alleged Difficulty Concerning Moral Properties', *Mind*, 93/371 (July 1984), 370–80. See also Wiggins, 'Moral Cognitivism, Moral Relativism and Motivating Beliefs': 'moral properties do not vary independently of physical properties . . . this is simply an instance of the perfectly general

supervenience of moral properties on natural properties as reflecting constraints on our projections which we impose to make them a reliable practical guide to decision making. This takes the allegedly non-cognitivist intuition that the function of moral language is action guiding, and puts it, in Blackburn's opinion, to fruitful explanatory work.

Motivational internalism is also satisfactorily explained, Blackburn suggests, because the content of a moral judgement is the expression of an attitude, not a cognitive belief. This harmonizes with the standard belief-desire model of the explanation of intentional action, and offers an explanation of a necessary motivational link between moral reasons and action. Blackburn is only a weak internalist, however. He notes that a moral attitude, in the projectivist account, is not directly tied to choice and action. Nevertheless the mediating factors are themselves attitudes, suggesting to him that the account is on the right track. The strategy is that if one makes the content of moral judgements attitudes or sentiments, one can easily connect the two dimensions of moral thought. They are both world-directed and yet connected to motivation.

This is a sophisticated presentation of a basically Humean account, which in itself is a familiar option in meta-ethics. The novel arguments are those that Blackburn deploys to defend the position against equally well-known objections to it. This meta-level defence of projectivism, quasi-realism, is the theoretically innovative centrepiece of Blackburn's project. Some familiar criticisms have been assumed to prove projectivism's inadequacy as an explanation of ethical practice.[17] The moral phenomenology of both our experience of value and our ordinary linguistic practices, seems to place serious obstacles in the path of the non-cognitivist. In particular, the Frege/Geach objection seems to offer two distinct threats: first, any proposed non-cognitivist analysis of the deep structure of our use of moral language would have to be internally very complicated. Alternatively, one would be forced to adopt a sceptical stance towards ordinary moral practice and to offer one's non-cognitivist reconstruction as part of a 'sceptical solution' to the problem of explaining the defective factuality of moral claims. (In a solution of this general kind, one conditionally concedes the strength of the sceptic's case and works out a solution compatible with it.) Both consequences would make it less clear that the projectivist option was tenable.

I have already argued that the surface syntax of moral utterances forces the classification of this area of discourse as assertoric and have described the Frege/Geach argument. Briefly to recapitulate for present purposes: if moral sentences do not have a truth value but instead primarily express an attitude, why do sentences embedding

---

truth that, given a particular object x in a particular context, there will be all sorts of causal and conceptual interdependencies between a property of x in one's range and x's properties in other ranges. If that is the truth in supervenience, let us not deny it! But there is *nothing the least bit special here to moral properties*', 83 [emphasis added].

[17] In addition to the papers by Geach, cited in n. 10, above, see Bernard Williams, 'Imperative Inference' and 'Consistency and Realism', in *Problems of the Self* (Cambridge: Cambridge University Press, 1973) at 152–165 and 187–206 respectively.

them unasserted appear to obey the ordinary rules of classical logic when the sentences are unasserted? A speaker can assent to the conditional sentence, 'If stealing is wrong, then you ought not to steal the money' without attitudinally endorsing the sub-component, 'stealing is wrong', and thereby giving it a truth value. But if it lacks a truth value, how can we assess the cogency of arguments in which the entire conditional may figure as a premiss? Or, to put the point less question beggingly from an expressivist perspective, why do normal patterns of inference seem to be valid, when they involve inference across unasserted contexts embedding sentences primarily expressing non-cognitive contents, if the standard way of explaining such inferences (in terms of propositional truth and validity) is not available to us?

This need not be the claim that projective theories cannot explain unasserted contexts as there is the weakened (but still very damaging claim) that the expressivist can do so only by ad hoc explanations tailored to individual types of context. Blackburn's most developed response is to introduce a revised logic where the idea of a proposition is replaced by the generic notion of a commitment, which covers both beliefs and attitudes, and where the idea of truth is replaced by the notion of acceptance. Thus, in the case of conditionals, one would use them to trace out the relations between beliefs and attitudes as part of our general interest in evaluating and analysing the moral sensibilities of others.[18]

Blackburn's arguments have been subjected to very rigorous scrutiny and the consensus is that in spite of their technical ingenuity, they do not succeed in meeting the Frege/Geach challenge.[19] In addition, Mark van Roojen has argued that it seems possible to draw general morals from their failure.[20] First, that Blackburn's revised notion of consistency seems to smuggle controversial moral assumptions into what are, intuitively, matters of logic. Secondly, there is a lack of fit between the revised notion of 'inconsistency' that Blackburn wants to develop and our intuitive notion of logical inconsistency. Thirdly, there are general difficulties in getting an account of the rational relations between contents (whether truth-evaluable or not) to mirror the normative relations that hold between contents as described by logic.

The irony of the failure of Blackburn's solution to the problem of unasserted contents is that older forms of non-cognitivism faced a structurally parallel problem. The problem of embedded contexts led to Hare's distinction between neustics and phrastics operating over a 'monadic transformational component'.[21] Such a

---

[18] This is the account first sketched in Blackburn, *Spreading the Word*, ch. 6.

[19] Critical work on Blackburn's early work includes papers by G. F. Schueler, 'Modus Ponens and Moral Realism', *Ethics*, 98/3 (Apr. 1988), 492–500; Bob Hale, 'Can there be a Logic of Attitudes?', in John Haldane and Crispin Wright (eds.), *Reality, Representation and Projection* (Oxford: Oxford University Press, 1993), 337–64; Mark van Roojen, 'Expressivism and Irrationality', *Philosophical Review*, 105/3 (July 1996), 322–35; and Nicholas Unwin, 'Quasi-Realism, Negation and the Frege-Geach Problem', *Philosophical Quarterly*, 49/196 (July 1999), 337–52.

[20] Van Roojen, 'Expressivism and Irrationality', 324 ff.

[21] Hare's distinction was first presented in *The Language of Morals* (Oxford: Oxford University Press, 1952). It was the target of Williams and Geach's critical articles: Geach, 'Assertion'; Williams, 'Imperative Inference' and 'Consistency and Realism', in *Problems of the Self* (Cambridge: Cambridge University Press, 1976) at 152–65, 187–206 respectively. The expression 'monadic transformational component' I take from Gordon Baker and Peter Hacker's *Language Sense and*

component forms the common element which is operated on in grammatical mood transformations, and should therefore be the key element which is truth-evaluable when one wants to capture the validity of inferences composed of sentences with different grammatical moods. Hare, too, seems to have been motivated by the belief that it was not enough to make the primary dimension of assessment for moral language the pragmatic values of in/appropriateness or 'felicity conditions'. Intuitively, within the theory of force one is concerned with norms licensing moves in a game that are answerable to such felicity conditions. The penalty for making the wrong move is inappropriateness to context. However, Blackburn is going even further than Hare in removing truth from the core theory of sense, replacing it with commitments that may or may not have a truth condition, and this more radical theoretical strategy seems to me even less attractive than Hare's.

It does not seem to me appropriate to review all the intricacies of the arguments that Schueler, Hale, and van Roojen have levelled against Blackburn's proposed logic of the attitudes, as I want to supplement them by taking a new line against Blackburn. I am prepared to concede that he may in the future find a way to formulate his proposal in such a way that rational relations between attitudes can be used to mirror normative logical relations in such a way that all and only inferences judged in/consistent by our intuitive common sense understanding of logic are judged as in/consistent by Blackburn's generic logic of commitment. Even if he were to succeed (and I doubt that he will) my argument applies at a later stage to provide a new obstacle for his analysis.

For Blackburn's proposal globally to revise logic is, in my view, a surprising strategy for him to adopt. I would argue that the rationale for Blackburn's approach, when fully analysed, leads to the conclusion that the overall quasi-realist project in which projectivism is embedded is misguided. Its essential motivations are better represented in the minimalist framework I introduced in Chapter 1. Both theories can be viewed as research programmes and one response to the task of evaluating their respective merits would be to adopt a wait and see strategy. The extent to which the two theories meet their respective criteria of success will emerge from continuing debate and the evidence is not, as yet, complete. However, the aim of my argument is to suggest that we can decide, now, that minimalism is superior to quasi-realism because the latter theory can now be judged to have failed in its own terms. The emergence of minimalism as a viable theoretical option in its own right has transformed a minor anomaly within the quasi-realist programme into a fatal defect.

Thus, it is important to my argument to establish clearly the rationale for quasi-realism, a rationale which is internal to the theory. As I have noted, the

---

Nonsense (Oxford: Basil Blackwell, 1984), though I do not share their scepticism as to whether such theoretical postulates exist. Hare wanted to discriminate between:

The rug is in the room	The rug is in the room
Everything in the room will be destroyed	Destroy everything in the room!
The rug will be destroyed	The rug will be destroyed

The indicative inference is valid, the 'imperative inference' invalid.

quasi-realist package contains two components: a projectivist analysis of problematic discourses, and a meta-level defence of this projective analysis, quasi-realism. The specific projectivist analyses offered of problematic areas of thought and language are defended by re-earning for these analyses all the marks of fully objective discourse. This latter task is the distinctive aim of quasi-realism. The background motivation for the overall theory is a general commitment to naturalistic explanations and for ontological parsimony. In evaluating theoretical commitments at any level, the balance sheet is to be drawn up in terms of cost and benefit. The benefits of smoothness and economy of theory are to be balanced against costs in terms of ontological commitment.

The central point of dispute between this quasi-realist project and minimalism concerns the availability of the truth predicate. The minimalist thinks that it does not take much to re-earn the truth predicate. It comes so cheaply that this enterprise is trivial. Any discourse with a sufficient degree of internal discipline to sustain a robust syntax for its assertoric sentences sustains minimal truth. Even the problematic discourses of the causal, moral, and modal, the objects of projectivist reinterpretation, sustain a minimal truth predicate. For the minimalist, the matters that concern the projectivist are better addressed as issues concerning the 'matter' of the truth predicate as opposed to its 'form'. Its form is captured entirely by its syntax; if one can give 'syntax' a strong enough reading.[22]

I would argue that very general considerations about the overall strategy of each of the two programmes determine the superiority of minimalism if we take, as a representative test case, the Frege/Geach objection.[23] This objection essentially turns on the fact that the surface syntax of moral utterances forces the classification of this area of discourse as assertoric. Blackburn's response to this challenge is, as I have described, to introduce a revised logic.[24] The standard conception that truth-evaluable propositions, expressed by indicative sentences, are embedded in logical contexts is replaced by the generic notion of a commitment to embedded attitudes/beliefs. This concept covers both beliefs and attitudes and permits the replacement of the theoretical role of truth with a new concept of **acceptance**. Thus, in the case of conditional sentences about moral matters, Blackburn's suggestion is that one would use them to trace out the relations between beliefs and attitudes as part of our general interest in evaluating and analysing the moral sensibilities of others.[25] This avoids Geach's charge of being ad hoc by offering a principled solution to the problem, but the way it does so leads directly to an inconsistency within the quasi-realist project.

My argument for this claim runs as follows: first, projectivism must be a *local* as opposed to a *global* thesis about discourse. It can only be developed as a claim specific to discourses such as the modal, the causal, and the moral. Global formulations of the theory, which Blackburn quite correctly avoids, would leave obscure what element of thought was being projected, and what it was projected 'on to'. Thus, to grasp the

[22] Crispin Wright, 'Reply to Jackson', *Philosophical Books*, 35 (1994), 169–75.
[23] Geach, 'Ascriptivism'; 'Assertion'.
[24] Blackburn, 'Attitudes and Contents', in *Essays on Quasi-Realism*, 182–97.
[25] This is the account first sketched in Blackburn, *Spreading the Word*, 218–20.

fact/projection contrast we need an explanation of what it is for a discourse to be robustly factual. Projectivism is essentially a contrastive and local thesis.

Secondly, how is one to explain the status of non-projected areas of thought or language? The obvious candidate explanation is the claim that they truly represent the facts. However, if this idea of truth to the facts is to contrast with projected discourses, it must go beyond the globally applicable minimal truth predicate, or there is no point to the contrast. This concept of truth must be substantial. With a substantial concept of truth available, more than enough resources are in place to define a classical logic with standard connectives and a standard model theory.

Thirdly, the logical connectives are *univocal*. The surface grammar of language seems to draw no distinction between 'projected' and 'detecting' discourses. This is the intuition driving the Frege/Geach objection. The meanings of ordinary language counterparts of logical connectives seem univocal across, for example, talk of physical facts and causal contexts. The minimalist response to this point is to accept it. If the internal discipline of discourse concerning modal, moral, and causal facts sustains a minimal truth predicate, then so be it. This, in turn, sustains a classical interpretation of logic and hence the univocality of logical connectives across all discourse.

With these assumptions in place, one can address to the projectivist the following *ad hominem* question: why should one adopt a quasi-realist rather than minimalist framework for the overall strategic aim of placing the relatively objective status of discourses given the relative costs and benefits of their respective solutions to the Frege/Geach problem? This is not the claim that projectivism cannot solve that problem. My challenge arises when projectivism has *already* solved the Frege/Geach problem. The point is that it can only do so at too high a cost. The minimalist, by contrast, simply has no problem at all. The point is that given the local nature of his or her subsidiary projectivist account of problematic discourses, the quasi-realist must have available a substantive notion of truth and a classical logic for the other non-problematic discourses. But he or she cannot, perforce, offer such a classical interpretation of modal, moral, or causal discourse. The norm governing assertion in these discourses cannot, by projectivist lights, be truth. The availability of truth has been suspended, until the right to use the predicate is re-earned by detailing the governing norms of the discourse concerned. The unpalatable dilemma facing the quasi-realist is thus either the abandonment of the univocality of logical vocabulary across discourse as a whole, or retaining univocality and offering a global reinterpretation of logic. Classical logic will have to be replaced for all areas of discourse and replaced with a generic logic of commitment of which truth conditional commitment is a species. The *ad hominem* point is that for a view motivated by a naturalistic aspiration to a streamlined explanatory account of thought and language, quasi-realism is driven by its central commitment to a projectivist account of problematic discourses globally to revise logic *in spite of the fact that a robust concept of truth is already available to the overall theory.*

His or her conception of philosophical methodology commits the projectivist to viewing the adoption or rejection of theoretical options as a matter of balancing costs and benefits. We may be driven globally to revise logic for strong theoretical reasons, such as the paradoxes of physical theory. However, this is not a case of this kind. The quasi-realist proposal for global revision is motivated solely by requirements internal to the theory of quasi-realism itself. It seems paradoxical that the grounds for such revision should be a logic that abstains from truth, when the internal structure of quasi-realism commits it to a non-minimal concept of truth. Contrast the happier position of the minimalist, untroubled by the Frege/Geach objection and able to offer an account of the univocality of logical vocabulary via a standard classical interpretation of logic.

This argument should be added to the doubts I have cited about the feasibility of Blackburn's logic of the attitudes.[26] The effect of doing so is to make those doubts look more serious: if the global revision of logic is not well motivated in any case, how much weaker is Blackburn's rationale if we cannot even be guaranteed to succeed in our aim of avoiding the Frege/Geach argument? Blackburn chooses what he considers the lesser of two evils when he formulates a logic that will cover all discourses, including 'projected' discourses. The resultant challenges are how to elucidate acceptance independently of truth and how to reconstruct the idea of deductive validity. It is not mere realist prejudice that leads me to argue that a logic of acceptance, like a logic of provability, must ultimately be explained via truth. The alternative is a return to a psychologistic account of logic, the norms of which arise from psychological transitions we are disposed to make. Not only is this inexplicable as a logic, but it is a curiously unmotivated position to take if a robust concept of truth must be available, as dictated by the strategy of Blackburn's quasi-realism.

However, these points can remain moot. My argument is that even if we concede to the quasi-realist his or her most promising solution to the Frege/Geach problem, he or she is still hoist by his or her own petard. The final irony is that this point emerges when we adopt the quasi-realist's preferred philosophical methodology for the evaluation of philosophical theories. Evaluation of a theory may be contextually sensitive to the plausibility of available competitors. Just as in the case of scientific enquiry, the internal anomalies of a theory can be judged to be fatally disabling only when a competitor theory emerges which beats the predecessor theory on its own terms. In the overall dispute over the superiority of minimalist or quasi-realist accounts of these problematic discourses, I believe it is clear that we can judge, now, that the minimalist has a dialectical advantage.[27]

This seems to me to be a decisive argument. However, it is open to Blackburn to make an internal adjustment to his position. Can he not simply downplay the importance of this argument from ontological economy and his general methodology of assessing the costs and benefits of revisions of logic? It seems to me that he cannot for interesting reasons that I will go into in more detail. But I will first of all comment a little further on the argument I have presented and defend it from possible objections.

---

[26] For a searching discussion, see Hale's 'Can there be a Logic of Attitudes?'. There is a later, updated, critique in Bob Hale, 'Can Arboreal Knotwork Help Blackburn Out of Frege's Abyss?', *Philosophy and Phenomenological Research*, 65/1 (July, 2002), 144–9.

[27] When I first published this argument, in 'Minimalism and Quasi-Realism', *Philosophical Papers*, 26/3 (Nov. 1997), 233–9, it pre-dated *Ruling Passions* and Blackburn's (surprising) adoption of minimalism. Hence, the further arguments of this chapter.

The first objection is that I should admit that minimalism is not clearly superior to projectivism, or expressivism more generally, in its treatment of unassserted contexts. There is a further issue yet to be determined: the nature of the link envisaged between assertion, truth, and belief. Proponents of non-cognitivism have attempted to refute minimalism by arguing that the a priori link between truth and belief integral to the theory cannot be sustained: that the state expressed by a moral content is to be explained in the context of a theory of representation which will assign it the direction of fit characteristic of desire not belief.[28] This would obviously undercut my argument completely. I will not pursue this issue in detail here, but I would argue that this non-cognitivist counter-argument is in my view much weaker than its proponents claim. It seems straightforwardly rebuttable if one argues that an a priori platitude governing a minimal truth predicate connects assertion and *minimal* belief. There seems little reason to concede that a general theory of representation which is fundamentally teleological directly imports 'desires' into all action explanations and thus a fortiori into the explanation of moral contents.[29] Far from being a striking exception to ordinary models of rational action in being uniquely confirmatory of a Humean theory of motivation, moral action seems to offer the strongest case against such theories as I argued in Chapters 3 and 4.

The second objection is that if the general strategy I have adopted in this book is derived from the later Wittgenstein, does not a similarly Wittgensteinian spirit lie behind Blackburn's proposals? For it is consonant with the spirit of the later Wittgenstein to insist that normativity is involved in characterizing any intentional mental state and that the issue of normativity should be detached from the concept of truth. Truth is one dimension of normative assessment of contents, but the theory of representation should not be seen as structured around a single key concept. Stanley Cavell

[28] Michael Smith has pursued a variant of this argument to develop a general case against minimalism about truth in a series of papers. See 'Why Expressivists about Value Should Love Minimalism about Truth', *Analysis*, 54/1 (Jan. 1994), 1–12; 'Minimalism, Truth-Aptitude and Belief', *Analysis*, 54/1 (Jan. 1994), 21–6; Frank Jackson, Graham Oppy, and Michael Smith, 'Minimalism and Truth Aptness', *Mind*, 103/411 (July 1994), 287–302. The central line of attack is that minimalism assumes an a priori platitude which connects sincere assertion and the expression of belief; Smith *et al.* argue that the link is far from platitudinous. For a rejoinder that the appropriate conception of belief assumed by the minimalist framework is itself minimal, capturable by the same strategy of implicit definition via a priori platitudes, see John Divers and Alex Miller, 'Platitudes and Attitudes: A Minimalist Conception of Belief', *Analysis*, 55/1 (Jan. 1995), 37–44. For a slightly different tack from Smith see n. 29, below.

[29] Michael Smith argued in 'The Humean Theory of Motivation', *Mind*, 96/381 (Jan. 1987), 36–61 that the teleological character of action explanation led directly to the truth of the Humean theory of motivation. For an effective reply to Smith, pointing out that one and the same state can have different 'directions of fit' as regards different propositional objects, see Phillip Pettit, 'Humeans, Anti-Humeans, and Motivation', *Mind*, 96/384 (Oct. 1987), 530–3. For a clarification of the 'direction of fit' terminology using the idea of a background controlling intention, see the analysis of I. L. Humberstone, 'Direction of Fit', *Mind*, 101/401 (Jan. 1992), 59–83. Another (to my mind) convincing reply to Smith is Mark van Roojen's 'Humean Motivation and Humean Rationality', *Philosophical Studies*, 79/1 (July 1995), 37–57. The issue of whether action explanations are irreducibly teleological goes beyond the scope of this book, but my inclination is to say that they are not, on the grounds that this leaves nothing one can say about what it is for an agent to *have* a purpose, as opposed to be ascribed a purpose. See Andrew Woodfield, *Teleology* (Cambridge: Cambridge University Press, 1986), ch. 10.

once remarked that Husserl's de-psychologizing of logic was followed by Wittgenstein's de-psychologizing of psychology.[30] Contraposing this remark, it can be argued that Wittgenstein logicized psychology, and the point of, for example, the remarks on rule following is to stress how any intentional state with content can only be identified as such if it stands in normative relations to other states and the world. Hence the idea of a truth-conditional commitment is replaced in Wittgenstein's later thought by the generic idea of a commitment, with truth-conditional commitment as a species of the genus. So Blackburn's account is more faithful to Wittgenstein's intentions than mine and represents a powerful reinterpretation of the idea of objective content.

I believe that structuring the issue this way misplaces Wittgenstein's insight into the de-psychologizing of logic and lapses into a psychologism that he would have rejected. The key point is that the a priori link between truth and assertion is lost. Without truth it is not possible to characterize the norms that govern the relations between contents as norms, rather than as registering psychological dispositions of acceptance with no normative content.[31] Wittgenstein neither rejected truth conditional semantics nor replaced it with pragmatist assertion conditional semantics. While I cannot enter into the exegetical issues here I believe that he was a minimalist about truth and reference in both his early and later thought. This is not to abandon the concept of truth, but to illustrate how it actually functions to regulate discourses. The distinction between truth and idealised rational acceptability is a grammatical distinction that is internal to all our objective practices. Wittgenstein's scattered remarks about truth should be interpreted as a form of minimalism, not as a form of redundancy theory. This interpretation preserves the link between truth and normativity essential to my argument.

With these objections set aside, let me return to the main line of argument and formulate a third objection. Granted that, given Blackburn's commitment to a streamlined, ontologically economical conception of how we should motivate the projectivist/quasi-realist package, the counter-argument I have offered is a pragmatic embarrassment. But that is all it is and Blackburn can respond by downplaying this motivation for his position. Let the technical analysis of the deep structure of unasserted contexts stand on its own and our overall commitments can follow from the success of these analyses. I think that is a promising line of defence, but unfortunately Blackburn, of all people, *cannot* adopt it. I will now explain why.

The suspension of truth in Blackburn's logic of the attitudes leads directly to the central point of conflict between projectivism and Wittgensteinian cognitivism: the argument from thick concepts. McDowell and Wiggins argue that an interpreter of a community's thick concepts will be unable to understand the extension of the concept without sharing the evaluative interest of its users. To the external observer who is not part of the form of life of the group who deploy the concept, the extension of

    [30] Stanley Cavell, 'The Availability of Wittgenstein's Philosophy', in *Must We Mean What We Say?*, updated edn. (Cambridge: Cambridge University Press, 2002), 44–72.
    [31] Compare John McDowell's account of how one introduces the norms governing psychological contents, the norms of the realms of sense, throughout *Mind and World*, but summarized at 179–80. I have discussed McDowell's views, relating them to those of Kant, in 'Kant, McDowell and Consciousness'.

the term seems 'shapeless'. If the reaction that these objects and properties in the world evoke is supposed to be characterizable in the vocabulary of one who does not possess the concept, such a vocabulary is impossible. I would argue that Blackburn's central metaphor of 'projection' becomes inexplicable if such an independent characterization is not possible. If we cannot identify the base onto which the evaluative response is projected why should we accept that a two-factor analysis of such concepts is correct?

Blackburn anticipates this line of attack on projectivism, supplemented by a related consideration:

Projectivism in moral philosophy is open to attack on the grounds that the reaction of the mind that is supposedly projected is itself only identifiable as a reaction to a cognised moral feature of the world. The specific attitudes and emotions . . . can, it is argued, only be understood in terms of the perception of right and wrong, obligations, rights, etc., which therefore cannot be reflections of them.[32]

Thus the projectivist is forced to continue to use the concept which is revealed to be an expression of attitude, rather than offer an independent account of it. This concession seems to me fatal to Blackburn's case. He is, after all, offering an analysis. But he does not believe that this objection is fatal. His response is:

It is unsurprising that our best vocabulary for identifying the reaction should be the familiar one using the predicates we apply to the world we have spread.[33]

Blackburn argues that the unavailability of an independent account of the projected feature of a judgement does not, per se, refute the projectivist picture if one bears in mind the overall strategy of the position. He responds with a restatement of his overall strategic aims: if non-realism about the ethical was to be established by the projectivist explanation alone, Blackburn admits the problem would be serious. However, there are strategic arguments in the background that carry the onus of proof here. His primary argument is the argument from ontological economy. Thus, the non-availability of an independent identification of the attitude expressed does not, in Blackburn's opinion, refute projectivism.

But this takes him from one unpalatable alternative to another that is equally so: his solution to this problem forecloses the suggested manoeuvre for responding to my criticism of his treatment of unasserted contexts. For if Blackburn resists offering a reductive analysis of his analysandum, allowing the same term to figure in the analysans, on the grounds of his master argument from ontological economy, he is committed to a master argument that fatally undermines his treatment of unasserted contexts. There seems no way to square this circle.

Setting aside for a moment the charge that the entire structure of Blackburn's argument is inconsistent, Blackburn's denial that he is obliged to give a reductive analysis of our thick ethical concepts does not, in my view, address the concern that motivates the criticism. An argument from explanatory parsimony will not suffice. Blackburn's Humean naturalism seems simply to have assumed a certain view of what

---

[32] Blackburn, 'Opinions and Chances', 180.   [33] Ibid.

kinds of properties can properly figure in explanations, and to have brought these restrictions to bear in the case of the ethical. This begs the question as to whether the relevant issue is whether a real property is one that pulls its weight in a causal account of the world.[34]

The proponents of a sophisticated cognitivism could simply say that they intend no causal gloss on the idea that moral properties are real. They could dispute the general idea of a causal theory of knowledge (as I would) but even so, it is more question begging to make causal efficacy a criterion for a real property. One can argue this even if one believes, as Wiggins does, that moral properties are causally efficacious (McDowell does not believe that they are under the relevant descriptions that pick out properties and responses as standing in the irreducible relation of *meriting*).[35] Blackburn's analysis of the ethical now seems to be issuing promissory notes on a comprehensive philosophical naturalism. Provisionally, we are left trying to appreciate a projectivist analysis that cannot characterize the projections involved in the ethical independently of the original concept. The circularity involved seems to compromise the claim that projectivism offers an explanation of the ethical. Thus the argument between cognitivism and projectivism is simply a stand-off. I hope I have added a decisive argument to this stand-off: that Blackburn's strategic commitment to an ontologically parsimonious naturalism undermines his treatment of unasserted contexts. His treatment of unasserted contexts, if it weakens his naturalism, undermines his claim that he need not offer an analysis of our thick ethical concepts. So a cognitivism allied to minimalism, in fact, has a decisive edge in this argument.

However, while these arguments seem to me to be decisive, there is a new set of considerations arising from Blackburn's most recent work on ethics, *Ruling Passions*. It has been central to my argument strategy here that Blackburn has to avoid a commitment to minimalism. In this book I have argued that a commitment to minimalism is only a starting point for a defensible cognitivism, but, nevertheless, it does allow one to use the Frege/Geach problem as a weapon against rival expressivist accounts of ethics. I have applied this argument to Blackburn's work, conjoined with the claim that he has to offer a two-factor analysis of ethical judgements. But in his most recent work, Blackburn announces that he is happy to be committed to minimalism. In addition, he has argued that the distinctive part of a naturalistic explanation of ethics is not the development of analyses of ethical judgements, but the provision of synthetic, genealogical explanations focused on functional role. Clearly, I need to explain why I do not think Blackburn can make these moves without incurring costs to his own position that he ought not to accept, or the arguments I have presented so far lapse.

---

[34] I would not want to adopt a position where properties are defined by their causal role—as intrinsic causal powers—as this would certainly beg too many of the relevant questions. However, one of the most famous and influential discussions of properties makes a powerful case for this claim: Sydney Shoemaker, 'Causality and Properties' in the revised and expanded edn. of *Identity, Cause and Mind* (Oxford: Oxford University Press, 2003), 206–33.

[35] Wiggins, 'Strictly speaking, properties themselves can cause nothing. Not even the primary qualities can. In that sense all properties are inert. But in another they are not inert. For properties figure indispensably in many explanations that are causal explanations', *Needs, Values, Truth*, 355.

3. BLACKBURN'S NEW 'TWIN TRACK' STRATEGY

Blackburn's most recent work on ethics pursues that which I will call a 'twin track' strategy. As part of its ambition naturalistically to place ethics (not to offer a reductive account of it), it offers a naturalistic genealogy of the role of ethical claims in people's lives. Such an explanation is a synthetic account of the concept, similar to the synthetic account given of the disposition to impartiality in Chapter 4, above. This macro-level account of ethics as a whole, cast in functional and genealogical terms, is accompanied by a micro-level acceptance of minimalism as the correct account of truth in general and hence of the truth of ethical claims in particular.

I am going to discuss Blackburn's view in tandem with that of Mark Timmons. Timmons acknowledges that his view, which owes a great deal to Hare, is similar to Blackburn's.[36] Timmons's basic idea is that the adoption of minimalism allows one to abandon the idea that assertions must be, in his terms, 'descriptive'. He associates 'description' with a certain account of truth as correspondence, which minimalism shows to be an incorrect account. This then allows Timmons to claim that ethics involves assertions, but assertions construed as part of an 'assertoric non-descriptivism'. That which is distinctive about ethical claims, as in Blackburn's account, is going to come in at the very general level of the pragmatics of language, its 'point and purpose'. He argues that this distinctive point is to be action guiding.[37]

Clearly these two strategies are very similar. At the micro-level, one uses minimalism to detach the practice of assertion from either distinctively expressing belief as opposed to attitude (Blackburn) or from expressing 'descriptions' (Timmons). That takes care of the annoying problem of unasserted contexts. Then, prove the truth of non-cognitivism, but do so at the level of the 'point or purpose' of moral language as a whole, or at the level of a genealogy for the practices that embed this part of thought and language.

I will set out and criticize each view in turn before offering criticisms of this composite position. First, Blackburn's view: the first track of his twin track strategy is to claim that what we need to do to solve the Frege/Geach problem is to look at how ethical sentences function in such contexts. By examining this function, Blackburn hopes to motivate a piggyback strategy where the role that we expect to be filled by beliefs is instead filled by belief/attitude combinations. (Gibbard tries a similar approach, as I shall discuss in the next section.) The background to this strategy is a commitment to functionalism in the philosophy of mind, where states are attributed holistically and in terms of their functional role. These characterizations are made from an interpretative perspective: Blackburn holds the view that the normativity of the mental can be captured fully in functionalist terms. But his main aim is to exploit these holistic and normative relations to argue that the 'propositional structure' that we use to express our commitments mirrors that of a 'functional structure of commitments'.

---

[36] Timmons, *Morality Without Foundations*, 129.
[37] Ibid., ch. 4, *passim*, e.g. at pp. 132, 138.

Blackburn begins his argument by noting that the problem posed by indirect contexts extends even to beliefs, and that the Fregean approach takes for granted a proposition that is the common element in both an asserted and unasserted (indirect) context. But Blackburn's point is that this attribution of a common element can be seen as, in a way, a functional characterization:

In the Fregean story a 'proposition' or 'thought' is simply introduced as the common element between contexts . . . why not say the same about an 'attitude'? . . . Just as we want to know the implications of a proposition or a thought, so we want to know the implications of an attitude.[38]

This idea uses the generic notion of commitment to belief/attitude combinations, and explains logical connectives as expressing constraints on such combinations. It inherits its normativity from the normativity of the enterprise of mental interpretation in which it is embedded. Psychologized logic tracks 'intelligible combinations of commitment'.[39]

This part of Blackburn's view is not new, but what is new is the claim that it leads directly to a commitment to a form of minimalism. The challenge that I have made central to this chapter is that Blackburn must avoid minimalism if projectivism is to remain a contrastive thesis. In Blackburn's view, a view such as mine would take his proposed treatment of ethical claims as not in any way distinctive; it simply invites him to take his minimalist position 'through one more turn'. Blackburn motivates his own approach by comparing his views to those of the later Wittgenstein.

In various areas of thought or language, Wittgenstein suggests that it is a misrepresentation of that area to view it in representational terms. It has, instead, a different function. For example, first person uses of the sentence 'I am in pain' are better viewed as expressive avowals than as descriptions. Challenged by the representationalist, Wittgenstein replies that the idea of truth simply goes with that of a commitment that we are prepared to assert. Blackburn goes on to note that Wittgenstein had the resources to avoid a contrast between language games which 'express' and those which 'represent'. If minimalism is true, then all the trappings of 'fact', 'representation' and 'truth' attach solely to assertion, and Blackburn argues that what Wittgenstein ought to have said is that to assert is to express a commitment.[40]

Of course, once this move is made, all the talk that seemed to mark off the cognitivist project from the quasi-realist/projectivist project comes flooding back in. Blackburn's new position allows him, he claims, to speak of knowledge, truth, reality, and representation. Responding to an objection similar to that which I have developed in this chapter against his earlier position, he says:

Superficially, this might seem like an objection to the investigation, as if the 'quasi-realist' construction has bitten its own tail. It starts from a contrast between expressing belief and expressing an attitude, which it then undermines, by showing how the expression of attitude takes on all the trappings of belief. Since we can handle the ethical proposition exactly like any

[38] Blackburn, *Ruling Passions*, 71.   [39] Ibid. 72.   [40] Ibid. 77–83.

other, it is not mistaken to say that we voice belief in it, when we do . . . But in fact this is no objection, and there is no tail biting . . . Just because of miminalism about truth and representation, there is no objection to tossing them in for free, at the end. But the commitments must first be understood in other terms.[41]

This seems to Blackburn a superior strategy to the cognitivist one, which will, he claims, 'draw a blank'. Needless to say, I am not happy with Blackburn's response to the criticism that his position is self-undermining (or has 'bitten its own tail'?). I think Blackburn's new defence of his position involves an equivocation. There is certainly a spiral of reflection in his new position: we *begin* by understanding quasi-realism as a local and contrastive thesis, involving centrally a contrast between areas of thought and language which represent and those that do not. More sophisticated reflections on the nature of truth move this issue to the philosophy of mind and to two classes of mental state with different directions of fit. But, at that stage, Blackburn introduces his generic logic of commitment. To assert is to hold as true, and that is no more than the expression of a commitment. At this level of reflection the initial contrast between representation and expression falls away.

This is not, as it seems, the complete abandonment of expressivism. The crux of the issue is that Blackburn holds a different version of minimalism from that of Crispin Wright, which I adopted in Chapter 2. In Wright's version of minimalism, if a discourse exhibits disciplined syntacticism then it sustains a truth predicate. If it sustains a truth predicate, then its sentences have truth conditions. Blackburn demurs. His version of 'deflationism' accepts that exhibiting disciplined syntacticism is equivalent to sustaining a truth predicate, but denies that this latter is equivalent to having a truth condition. In Blackburn's deflationism, to assert a commitment as true is to assert it. So the only available contrast is now at the level of mental states. Syntax, the availability of the truth predicate, and indeed truth-aptness are relatively neutral features that do not pick out, contrastively, discourses that represent from those which express. Minimal beliefs and minimal attitudes are to be explained via the generic idea of commitment.

Blackburn thus collapses two steps in his argument and the attractions of the first step seduce one into taking the second. The entire discussion has been moved upwards into an interpretationist approach to the mental, supplemented by the view that a form of functionalism about the mental is true. From within this perspective, Blackburn says a great deal that is congenial to cognitivism. But the cognitivist cannot and must not follow Blackburn in so hollowing out the idea of cognitivism that the distinction between cognitivism and expressivism is eliminated. All the distinctions that one might want to make, in any case, reappear. The proper arena for these discussions in Blackburn's most recent work is the theory of acceptance conditions for mental contents. Under what conditions is one to undertake different classes of commitment?

In pursuing this question, various distinctions emerge. For example, one way of understanding the discussion of the claim that all practical reasons are internal, set out

---

[41] Ibid. 79–80.

in Chapter 4, is that the external reasons theorist sees the acceptance of practical reasons as modelled on the acceptance of theoretical truths whereas the internal reasons theorist does not. In this way, the theory of acceptance conditions for different classes of content will give evidence of distinction between representations and expressions. There is, I would argue, a simple and compelling explanation of such a distinction that uses the minimal concept of truth, *understood in Wright's sense and not Blackburn's*. The systematic pattern of divergence between classes of contents with the direction of fit of beliefs and classes of contents understood as having the direction of fit of desires cannot be explained if assertion is merely the reiteration of a commitment.

The number of issues that will emerge as problems for the logic of commitment will multiply: why is it that in theoretical reasoning, evidence is subsumed under a successful hypothesis, whereas moral evidence not acted upon continues to be a source of regret? To use another concept from Wittgenstein, the idea of a contrast between two classes of mental content will show itself, even if it cannot be said. Whatever one's pre-theoretical views, it does not seem helpful to iron out these distinctions and to see them as a non-contrast between a set of commitments, all of which earn the courtesy title 'representations' and so, for that matter, are equally deserving of the courtesy title 'expressions'.

In conclusion, I would note that throughout the arguments of this section, I have taken at face value Blackburn's claim that it is feasible globally to revise logic as a psychologized generic logic of commitment. But that has been solely for the sake of a clear understanding of Blackburn's argument in his own terms. I have not withdrawn my original charge that our only motivation for adopting this global revision of logic is to escape various problems internal to the quasi-realist/projectivist package. That seems to me to be a weak reason to adopt it. Nor have I withdrawn any of the suspicions that such psychological materials, even viewed 'normatively', are inappropriate contents for a logic. If those concerns are added to the objections that I have raised in this section, I believe we have good reason to take Blackburn's most recent proposals as no more successful against cognitivism than his earlier arguments.

The next twin track strategy that I want to consider is that of Mark Timmons. Timmons argues that a novel option for the non-cognitivist is to sever the connection between assertion and description and so to open up the prospect of assertoric non-descriptivism:

> the presumption about genuine moral assertion combines with the reasons for rejecting descriptivism to suggest a view about moral statements that embraces both non-descriptivism and the contention that moral discourse is fully assertoric—a view claiming that the evaluative meaning of moral sentences subserves genuine assertion, but also claiming that evaluative meaning is not a species of descriptive meaning. Such an approach . . . cries out for articulation and defence.[42]

Timmons argues as follows: there are two kinds of assertion, descriptive and evaluative. The latter play an 'action guiding' as opposed to a descriptive role. Evaluative assertions are truth-apt; their assertion, however, makes 'minimal demands of the

---

[42] Timmons, *Morality Without Foundations*, 129.

world'.[43] In order to see the possibility of this view, one has to highlight and reject the assumption that all assertoric sentences have 'robustly descriptive content'.

I would like to begin my criticism of this proposal by examining the claim that Timmons wants to reject: that assertions have 'robustly descriptive content'. One thing that hamstrings Timmons's entire discussion is that he is tacitly working with a certain framework for the realism debate that will meet with much criticism in Chapter 6. At this point, let me say that it involves the assumption that our only options are internal realism, external realism, and relativism. External realism, which I will discuss below, seems to me to be so implausible a position it is not clear to me anyone has ever held it, but in Timmons's argument it essentially involves commitment to a correspondence theory of truth. Furthermore, he takes this to be *the* central commitment of realism.[44] Timmons, like me, is drawn to minimalism about truth, but he is a lot more certain than I am what this rules *out*. Surprisingly, for Timmons, it seems to rule out realism per se; of course it does, if all and only realists are correspondence theorists. The move to minimalism then debars you from being a realist.

I see no reason to structure the issue in this way and cannot see why you cannot be a non-correspondence realist (as, indeed, I am).[45] This background assumption exerts pressure on the current issue of the feasibility of assertoric non-descriptivism. It loads what Timmons means by 'description', in my view quite unfairly. It is part of cognitivism to claim that assertion is to assert as true; it is no part of cognitivism to make this a commitment to a correspondence theory of truth, and hence external realism and hence a 'robustly descriptive' view of assertion. This is plain wrong, and lines up the cognitivist for an ill-founded refutation. I think this entire approach is in danger of trafficking in the illegitimate currency of 'hard' and 'soft' facts that I criticized in Chapter 2. The cognitivist should not be drawn into this discussion and, properly understood, this discussion is not representative of Wittgenstein's views either.

Timmons sees very clearly that this view is going to need two supplementary assumptions: something like the 'hard fact'/'soft fact' distinction and the psychologizing of semantics.[46] Just as Blackburn made his functionalism in the philosophy of mind prior to semantic issues, so Timmons assigns parallel status to a form of 'psychologistic semantics'. Precisely what this semantics enables one to do is to cash out intuitions about 'hard' and 'soft' facts. This is not the place for a comprehensive assessment of Timmons's 'psychologistic semantics', worked out in collaboration with Terry Horgan, but I would say that minimalism simply hopes to bypass any such question as to whether sentences about symphonies represent softer facts than sentences about quarks.[47]

[43] Ibid. 129 and 133.
[44] Ibid. 116 and 153 ff.
[45] As I discussed in Ch. 1, n. 43, this point has been forcefully made by David Wiggins in the case of Wright's minimalism.
[46] See Timmons, *Morality Without Foundations*, 117–19 for the application of these ideas.
[47] I have already described the critique of any such 'hard fact' versus 'soft fact' distinction in Ch. 2; e.g. in Jane Heal, *Fact and Meaning*, at 115. In Timmons, *Morality Without Foundations*, e.g. at 119–20, his semantic theses are explicitly *contrastive*: referring to superstrings differs from referring

With this false assumption that minimalism is solely a rejection of a correspondence theory of truth removed, Timmons's argument slowly starts to unravel. There is no longer any basis for his claim that assertion should be detached from description, or rather from the idea of 'robustly descriptive content' as the distinctiveness of that latter idea cannot be made out. There is no room for, let alone a plausible rationale for, a special kind of evaluative assertions. That proposal inherits all the problems posed by Rawls for such views that I discussed at the beginning of this chapter. The view proposed is simply not explanatory enough when placed alongside a cognitivist competitor.

I have criticized both Blackburn's and Timmons's versions of the twin track strategy. I now turn to treating Timmons's and Blackburn's case as a composite, criticizing those views that they hold in common. My arguments against this composite view are as follows. First, the project of isolating a distinctively ethical use of language is hopeless. Secondly, if there are ethical uses of language, they are better and more simply explained by cognitivism than non-cognitivism. Cognitivism offers a better explanation because of the pre-emption thesis implicit in non-cognitivism: the view that if a content is expressive, it cannot also express a belief. This preemption thesis fatally disables non-cognitivism's capacity to explain the full range of ethical language. My next objection is that even if the non-cognitivist offers a pragmatic account of the genealogy of ethical concepts, it is a non sequitur to argue that since ethics originates in sentiment, it terminates there. My next objection is to Blackburn's and Timmons's treatment of minimalism. It would, in my view, be seriously implausible if the adoption of minimalism led one to reject the a priori connection between assertion and belief.

First, I will argue for the hopelessness of finding a distinctively ethical use of language. Blackburn argues that it is cognitivism that gets in the way of a truthful account of how we use ethical language:

When we voice our ethics we have distinct conversational dynamics. People are badgered. Reproaches are made and rejected. Prescriptions are issued and enforced. Resentments arise and are soothed. Emotions are tugged. The smooth clothing of statements produced as true or denied as false disguise the living body beneath.[48]

This is, it seems to me, the very opposite of the truth. Here are some ethical uses of language: first, contemplating the wrong you did a friend, who is now dead, by misinterpreting his actions as selfish when in fact he was acting for your own good in a way you could not, at the time, appreciate. There is, now, no way to make amends. Secondly, thinking to yourself about the destruction and loss of something of value. Thirdly, the contemplation, in a disinterested way, of the goodness of a person far from you in either time or space. Perhaps, in each case, we can think of you as having these thoughts in silent soliloquy so that no one else knows that you have them. (Not in any philosophically problematic sense. You would avow them if asked. But,

to symphonies and that is a distinction *within* our reflections on our use of a particular natural language.

[48] Blackburn, *Ruling Passions*, 51.

as it happens, no one does ask.)[49] Are these instances of the ethical use of language? I would say that they were. But whereas every instance on Blackburn's list prejudges the issue, since he only gives examples where a person tries to change another person's attitudes, in none of these cases do you try to change another person's attitudes. Indeed, these cases do not seem to have much to do with action or the practical at all.

Anyone can come up with a list that suits his or her case. But the real issue is that the cognitivist can explain all the examples on Blackburn's list, but he cannot explain the examples put forward by the cognitivist. And the cognitivist's real aim is to cast doubt on the idea of an 'ethical use of language' at all. Blackburn is going to have to cast doubt on whether the list I have suggested is a true account of ethical uses of language, or he is going to have to treat such cases as marginal, or in some strained way connected to practice. (There is a non-strained way in which they might be connected to practice. They might, for example, be connected to ritual. But ritual is not connected to 'the changing of attitudes' that is Blackburn's sense of 'practical'.) The cognitivist, on the contrary, need not deny such 'practical' uses of language as changing someone's attitudes, or giving them advice which motivates them to a different form of action, or other instances of the philosopher's obsessive concern with the 'adviser stance' where someone gets someone else to do something.[50] All that the cognitivist insists upon is that such uses have the simple and compelling explanation offered by the Fregean orthodoxy: that these are different speech acts that embed transformations of indicative sentences which, when asserted, express beliefs. That was Rawls's original point and I see no reason to abandon it.

The problem here is the pre-emption thesis.[51] Throughout, I have emphasized that cognitivism only claims that the content expressed by an asserted moral judgement is a belief in its primary dimension of assessment. It can have a further, secondary dimension of assessment in which the same use of that sentence can be seen as the expression of an attitude or non-cognitive state. But the non-cognitivist cannot accept the converse claim, and that is why it is explanatorily weak compared with cognitivism. Cognitivism can explain all cases equally well; non-cognitivism has to

---

[49] In this sense you have a distinctive kind of first personal warrant for your current thoughts, in the sense described by Charles Siewert, *The Significance of Consciousness* (Princeton: Princeton University Press, 1998), 33.

[50] As Richard Norman has interestingly observed, one of the problems generated by this obsessive focus on the 'adviser stance' is that it ignores how much ethical thinking focuses not on getting a person to do something, but on the prior question of who is to act. (He gives the example of deciding which of us should tell a work colleague that her husband has been injured in a car accident.) See Richard Norman, 'Particularism and Reasons', *Journal of Moral Philosophy* (forthcoming). Bernard Williams also criticized the 'local advisory model of reasons', 'Who Needs Ethical Knowledge?' 208–9.

[51] The idea that classifying an utterance as an expression pre-empts assigning it descriptive content is a thesis that has been both isolated and challenged in a series of interesting papers by Rockney Jakobsen, to which I am indebted: 'Semantic Character and Expressive Content', *Philosophical Papers*, 26/2 (Aug. 1997), 129–46; 'Self-Quotation and Self-Knowledge', *Synthese*, 110/3 (Mar. 1997), 419–45; 'Wittgenstein on Self-Knowledge and Self-Expression', *Philosophical Quarterly*, 46/182 (Jan. 1996), 12–30.

gerrymander the examples to set some aside as not 'really' ethical uses of language as they are not 'really' practical or involved in the changing of attitudes.[52]

The pre-emption thesis underlines the doomed attempt to find not an ethical use of language but a *distinctively* ethical use of language. If ethics is a matter of prescribing to others, then ethics can be *only* a matter of prescribing to others and cannot, for instance, also be a matter of describing. As Bernard Williams pointed out some time ago, in Hare's original version of prescriptivism, the treatment of aesthetic language it implied turned everyone into a collector. You could not, within Hare's prescriptivism, say that a painting is a good painting without an entailed imperative dictating action towards it. (Collect it!)[53] But if there are uses of language in ethics that are disinterested in an analogous way to aesthetic disinterest, then ethical language is no more 'distinctively' prescriptive than descriptive. Cognitivism can accept that it can be both, and have other functions besides, in a way that suggests overlaps and continuities with other uses of language with other kinds of content. For example, our dealings with value need not be exclusively moral, nor exclusively ethical, let alone exclusively involved in its realization or responses to it, such as 'honouring' or 'promoting'.[54] From a cognitivist perspective, the whole idea of an ethical use of language looks hopeless. But that is an advantage to the view, not a drawback. From an explanatory point of view, cognitivism is the ecumenical broad church here, whereas noncognitivism is the schismatic sect!

Cognitivism is the best explanation of all aspects of the ethical, so, for that reason, it is the best explanation of how it functions. It functions as it does partly because it is a matter of acquiring knowledge and moral truths and sees being virtuous as one of the ways in which we come to know things. On that basis, its practical functions have a simple and compelling explanation, whereas the expressivist is hard pressed to come up with explanations of morality's cognitivist features. This asymmetry in the capacity to explain all of the features of ethics is central to the case for cognitivism.

At the level of the top track of the twin track stance, pitched at the level of ethical language as a whole, Blackburn could reply that he is not so much interested in the pragmatics of ethical language as in giving a genealogy of ethical language. This is not only a non-reductive account, it is about the synthesis of a concept, not its analysis. In a genealogical narrative of this kind, ethics has its origins in the moral

---

[52] This does involve a general commitment to a representationalist as opposed to an expressivist conception of language. I am quite happy to go along with such a commitment, given the understanding of expressivism defended by Charles Taylor in 'Theories of Meaning', in *Philosophical Papers, i. Human Agency and Language* (Cambridge: Cambridge University Press, 1985), 248–92. Such a generalized version of expressivism does figure in Taylor's defences of cognitivism and in the work of those that he has influenced such as Sabina Lovibond. See Lovibond, *Realism and Imagination in Ethics*, sects. 7– 10. I critically discussed a variant of such a pragmatic/expressive treatment of language, indebted to Hegel, in my review of Robert Brandom's *Making It Explicit*, *European Journal of Philosophy*, 4/3 (Dec. 1996), 394–6.

[53] Williams, *Ethics and the Limits of Philosophy*, 124.

[54] A point well made by Anthony Quinton, 'The Varieties of Value', in Grethe B. Peterson (ed.), *The Tanner Lectures on Human Values* (Salt Lake City: University of Utah Press, 1988), 185–210 who argues against the focus solely on morally relevant values in philosophical discussions and the consequent constriction of the field of practical philosophy.

sentiments in the way that Mill described. Non-cognitive states play a distinctive role in this genealogy.

Once again, however, the cognitivist can agree. It would be a very odd account of ethics that had nothing to say about guilt and shame, anger and righteous indignation, *ressentiment* and other moral emotions. But once again the question arises as to whether we need generally to introduce the propositional object that rationalizes such non-cognitive states. The question then remains open as to whether these states figure in a genealogy of ethics, only to be transcended by a later stage of its development. Wiggins's genealogy began with desire, but his common standpoint of judgement transcended it and supplied non-desire driven motivation in any particular case.[55] Thus, the appeal to genealogy can be disarmed: there are cognitivist and non-cognitivist genealogies of ethics and the non-cognitivist has conclusively to prove that a non-cognitive state implicated in such a diachronic account does not evolve into a state with a different direction of fit at a later stage of the narrative.[56]

Finally, I will consider Blackburn's and Timmons's commitment to minimalism. The form of minimalism that I have adopted preserves the intuitive, a priori connection between assertion and belief. Blackburn severs this connection by adopting deflationism, not minimalism, and Timmons can only make minimalism supportive of assertoric non-descriptivism by detaching the idea of description from its normal sense and making it the proprietary possession of the correspondence theorist. As regards Blackburn's view, I do not follow him in distinguishing deflationism from minimalism and hold a version of minimalism where the a priori connection between assertion and minimal belief is preserved.

As regards Timmons's view, I would concede that I am less clear than either Blackburn or Timmons about that which the adoption of miminalism rules out: from minimal assumptions non-minimal consequences may flow. But I am happy to agree with Timmons that adopting minimalism rules out a theory of truth as correspondence. What I cannot follow him in is the assumption that all and only correspondence theorists are entitled to the concept of **description**. I believe that a partial motivation for this assumption is a constraining framework for the realism debate which sees our only alternatives as external realism (involving a correspondence theory of truth), internal realism, and possibly relativism, where the first two positions are exclusive and exhaustive of the possible positions one can take. If that is the essential presupposition of Timmons's claim that description only makes sense if truth is correspondence truth, then I will suggest reasons to dispense with that assumption in the next chapter.

I conclude that there is no version of expressivism that has, as yet, posed a serious challenge to the cognitivist view that the indicative use of sentences about ethical or moral issues expresses contents which are, in their primary dimension of assessment, belief states. But there is another, equally sophisticated version of expressivism yet to be considered: norm-expressivism.

---

[55] Wiggins, 'Categorical Requirements: Kant and Hume on the Idea of Duty', 83–106; 'In a Subjectivist Framework, Categorical Requirements and Real Practical Reasons', 212–32.

[56] Which is precisely the point of Wiggins's 'genealogy' of morals.

4. THE NORM-EXPRESSIVIST PARADIGM

The theory presented by Allan Gibbard in *Wise Choices, Apt Feelings* was explicitly developed to avoid some of the shortcomings of Blackburn's projectivism.[57] Whereas Blackburn is inclined to develop projectivism as a local theory of the contested discourses of the moral, the modal, and the causal, Gibbard's much more ambitious programme aims to develop a general theory of the norms of rationality along expressivist lines. It is not my aim here to present a general account of Gibbard's views; rather I want to assess his contribution to the present problem of the possibility of a two-factor analysis of thick ethical concepts and, relatedly, the cognitivists' a priori 'shapelessness' argument.

The first thing to say about Gibbard's work is that its primary focus is not morality. Its primary focus is rationality.[58] That is why, unfortunately, in spite of the exemplary clarity and complexity of the theory Gibbard presents in *Wise Choices, Apt Feelings*, it is difficult to extract from his work a solution to the problem of shapelessness which seems to be the key point of dispute between cognitivists and projectivists. Gibbard has, however, devoted two subsequent papers to the topic of thick concepts so they seem to be the best source to consult for his approach to this problem.[59]

Gibbard seems, on the face of it, happy to accept that there *are* such concepts as thick concepts. However, he also notes that, 'a full characterization of thick concepts might have to be fairly theory laden, and the theories compete'.[60] For this reason, like other theorists, Gibbard approaches the nature of thick concepts from the perspective of his own theory and this is my first concern about Gibbard's approach to the problem of shapelessness. When I introduced the idea of a thick concept, in a usage that was intended to be faithful to the Wittgensteinian cognitivists and to Williams's use of the phrase, I spoke of a concept whose use in a judgement was both world guided and supplied defeasible reasons for action. That usage makes clear that talk of thick concepts should direct us to a certain range of judgements, namely, those that use thick concepts. The giving of defeasible reasons, for example, is clearly a feature of a whole judgement. (Some meta-ethicists have, by contrast, taken to speaking of thick 'features', as though there is some one-to-one correspondence between concepts and features. That seems to me an unhappy usage; it is not Gibbard's.) However, in Gibbard's initial discussion, use of thick concepts is identified as picking out features or properties and as expressive of an *attitude*.[61] That does seem to me to begin to shape

---

[57] Gibbard, *Wise Choices, Apt Feelings*.

[58] For an excellent general discussion of Gibbard's norm-expressivist account of *rationality* see Paul Horwich, 'Gibbard's Theory of Norms', *Philosophy and Public Affairs*, 22/1 (1993), 67–78.

[59] Allan Gibbard, 'Thick Concepts and Warrant for Feelings', *Proceedings of the Aristotelian Society*, suppl. vol. 66 (1992), 267–83 and 'Reasons Thin and Thick: A Possibility Proof', *Journal of Philosophy*, 100/6 (2003), 288–304.

[60] Gibbard, 'Thick Concepts and Warrant for Feelings', 268.

[61] This is the terminology of 'Thick Concepts and Warrant for Feelings'; it has changed by 'Reasons Thick and Thin' but as the latter paper is concerned largely with the exposition of another person's views (Williams's) Gibbard continues simply to assert that the explanation of why people use, or dissent from, certain thick concepts is explained by his or her attitudes.

that which needs to be explained in a way that invites a norm-expressivist analysis. I concede that both Gibbard's papers on thick concepts contain an extended discussion of why any two-factor analysis of a thick concept will not succeed, given a certain understanding of what 'descriptive' and 'evaluative' mean in this context, in such a way as to lend support to the cognitivists' case.[62] However, the centrepiece of Gibbard's presentation is a norm-expressivist analysis of the thick concept **lewd**, whose key elements are as follows:

'Act X is lewd' means this: L-censoriousness towards the agent is warranted, for passing beyond the limits on sexual display such that (i) in general, passing beyond those limits warrants feelings of L-censoriousness toward the person doing so, and (ii) this holds either on no further grounds or on grounds that apply specially to sexual displays as sexual displays.[63]

Where 'L-censoriousness' has already been explained by Gibbard as follows, 'we don't have a special name for the feeling of outraged shock and censure that goes with finding something lewd, but call it L-censoriousness'.[64]

This is not, strictly speaking, an *analysis* but even this reflective account of a thick concept sees it as involving warranted standards for the expression of attitude, plus a classificatory component. The main problem for this account, it seems to me, is explanatory circularity. Gibbard's pattern of analysis for moral terms is that it contains a methodological assumption that seems to place his theory in the same predicament as Blackburn's. That assumption is the denial of emotional cognitivism—Gibbard is perfectly open about this and the potential disagreement between his view and that of the Wittgensteinian cognitivists.[65] The basic idea of Gibbard's theory is that moral judgements concern which moral sentiments are morally justified or warranted: this account then receives the important supplementation of an expressivist theory of rational warrant. To describe a moral sentiment of shame or guilt as warranted is to express one's acceptance of the system of rational norms that permit the feeling. It is crucial to Gibbard's account, if he is to avoid circularity, to be clear about which of its elements require a reductive account and which do not: the moral sentiments themselves, of guilt and impartial anger, cannot be treated cognitively as directed to propositional objects. These distinctively moral feelings must be analysed in a way that does not require a prior understanding of moral judgements.

For this reason it does not seem that his account offers a means of breaking the circle relating descriptive and evaluative components postulated in the cognitivist

[62] Gibbard, 'Thick Concepts and Warrant for Feelings', 274–8 rejects 'conjunctive', 'licensing', and 'presuppositional' accounts of how the descriptive and the evaluative components of thick concepts are related. 'Reasons Thick and Thin' takes issue, as I will in Ch. 6, with some of the ways in which Williams both resists projectivism and yet separates the two dimensions of assessment of thick concepts, namely, their role in truthfully classifying and their role in supplying defeasible reasons. (My reasons for dissenting from this way of setting up the issue differs from those of Gibbard.)

[63] Gibbard, 'Thick Concepts and Warrant for Feelings', 280–1; he returns to this sample analysis in 'Reasons Thin and Thick', 303 and assumes its correctness.

[64] Gibbard, 'Thick Concepts and Warrant for Feelings', 279–80.

[65] Ibid. 272 n. 7.

account of thick concepts. The content of moral judgements, for Gibbard, is that moral feelings are rationally warranted by accepted norms, but the link between the rationality of the feeling and the descriptive content of the judgement cannot be substantiated without circularity under the constraints of Gibbard's naturalistic theory. By contrast, Wiggins and McDowell are precisely concerned to argue that while the user of a judgement deploying a thick concept must take up a pro-attitude to an action or be committed to a certain range of feelings, these items are not 'independently intelligible', let alone explicable. Certainly they would further contend that the warranted emotion must have a cognitivist interpretation, as directed to the same propositional object as the moral judgement, but under a different mode of presentation.

Perhaps a projectivist response to the problem of shapelessness requires further work within the norm-expressivist research project. But certainly my provisional conclusion is that the cognitivist position can deflect both Blackburn's and Gibbard's analyses of moral judgements. In particular their failure to identify the alleged projection constitutively involved in our truth valued judgements deploying thick concepts is fatal to the explanatory ambitions of the projectivist and norm-expressivist account.

My final concern about norm-expressivism is that the argument that I levelled against Blackburn's overall strategy, to the effect that his solution to the Frege/Geach problem contradicted the rationale of his own theory, can be extended to Gibbard's similar attempt to solve the problem of unasserted contexts. In *Wise Choices, Apt Feelings*, Gibbard adapts the standard semantics for the alethic modalities to give a notion of 'factual-normative worlds'. He basically adopts the device of substituting for any normative occurrence of a phrase in a sentence the non-normative sentence that relativizes the occurrence of that phrase to the system of norms that permit it. Thus, normative sentences, sentences in which normative phrases occur, get a non-normative rewrite so that the logic of such discourse can piggyback on standard logic. The problem is that this solution looks ad hoc, compared even to Blackburn's version, and brings unwarranted complexities in its train as David Copp has convincingly argued:

Gibbard's account implies that various sentential contexts are ambiguous, with the semantics depending on whether p is normative. A cognitivist theory could avoid this kind of complexity . . . A variety of complex constructions give rise to problems, since it appears that a non-cognitivist theory must treat them differently, depending on whether an embedded sentence is one that would standardly be used to make a normative claim. At best, then, Gibbard's way of dealing with the Frege point adds an unwanted complexity and disunity to our semantics, our logic, and our psychology of belief, complexity that would not be needed by a cognitivist account of normative claims.[66]

I have developed a similar point in Blackburn's case and it is unclear to me that Gibbard's alternative strategy offers any theoretical advantage. I conclude, then, that the general case against norm-expressivism in both its main varieties succeeds.

[66] Copp, *Morality, Normativity and Society*, 18.

CONCLUSION

So far, so good, then, for the Wittgensteinian cognitivist: the first attempted non-cognitivist refutation has not proved successful. However, there is another line of criticism the cognitivist theory has to meet: the challenge of 'non-objectivism'. The challenge of how one best explains our ethical beliefs is approached in a different way in the powerful and subtle criticism of the cognitivist argument presented by Bernard Williams. It is to Williams's arguments that I now turn.

6

Non-Objectivism and Internal Realism

§1: The non-objectivist strategy is introduced. §2: The internal realist criticism of the aspiration to absoluteness is rejected. §3: The non-objectivist challenge to cognitivism is interpreted. §4: The possibility of an indirect vindication of moral knowledge is assessed. §5: Can objectivity be derived from the perspective of practical reason?

The line of argument so far has demonstrated that the practical, the evaluative, and the descriptive are inextricably intertwined in the use of thick concepts such that ethical judgements using them are capable of truth. They are, therefore, appropriate objects of knowledge. This is so even within the demanding framework set up by the cognitivists themselves that requires more of a judgement for it to be properly called 'cognitive' than I required when I adopted minimalism as the framework for my discussion. With projectivism and norm expressivism successfully rebutted, the cognitivist argument set out in Chapters 1 and 2 seems to have won the day. It seems that moral cognitivism has been vindicated.

However, there are alternative interpretations that can be placed on the conclusions defended up to this point that pose new challenges to cognitivism. Thus far, I do not believe that they have been met. Certainly the literature on these issues shows every sign of having reached an impasse, with no new options having been developed in recent years. Wiggins and McDowell have further developed and reiterated their positions, but have not allayed the concerns of their opponents. The opposition, mainly Crispin Wright, Bernard Williams, and Jürgen Habermas, have sharpened their critiques, making their composite case even more formidable.[1] I will describe the challenge to cognitivism from their 'non-objectivism' before setting out

---

[1] Wright, *Truth and Objectivity*, esp. ch. 5, and 'Truth in Ethics'; Williams, 'Who Needs Ethical Knowledge?', in *Making Sense of Humanity* (Cambridge: Cambridge University Press 1995), and 'Truth in Ethics'. Habermas offers his own critical discussion of cognitivism in *Truth and Justification*, trans. Barbara Fultman (Cambridge, Mass.: MIT Press, 2003). Habermas has in several places also endorsed Williams's scepticism about moral knowledge, although with the strategic aim of strengthening the case for Habermas's discourse ethical alternative based on a dialogical conception of rationality. For representative discussions see 'Remarks on Discourse Ethics' and 'Lawrence Kohlberg and Neo-Aristotelianism', both in *Justification and Application: Remarks on Discourse Ethics*, trans. Ciaran P. Cronin (Cambridge, Mass.: MIT Press, 1993) at 19–111 and 113–32 respectively. While Habermas has not explicitly adopted minimalism, a theoretical statement of his discourse ethical approach adopts Wright's notion of superassertibility as an explication of Habermas's general notion of discursive validity: Jürgen Habermas, 'On the Cognitive Content of Morality', *Proceedings of the Aristotelian Society*, 96 (1996), 335–58.

my own criticisms of Wiggins and McDowell's position. I will then set out, in Part III, the basis for an alternative view that avoids these criticisms. However, there is a subject that must satisfactorily be dealt with before I can proceed to deal with the non-objectivist argument in detail. These opening sections, forming an excursus from the main line of my argument, deal with this subsidiary issue.

This issue concerns the nature of objectivity and returns us to the discussions of Chapter 1, specifically the viability of global internal realism. In order even to frame the non-objectivist criticism of the cognitivist position I have set out, I have to demonstrate that our conception of objectivity is misrepresented by a group of philosophers all of whom defend a version of internal realism, across the board, for all areas of thought and language that meet some minimal requirements for objectivity. From the perspective of these internal realists, I have already done enough to secure the idea of ethical objectivity, and the argument of this book could stop at this stage. I disagree, however, and the aim of this chapter is to explain why. To locate how and where this disagreement arises I will begin by outlining the non-objectivist position.

1. NON-OBJECTIVISM EXPLAINED

The cognitivist argument seems to have demonstrated that specific value judgements can be true or false, that the mental states expressed by moral contents are belief states and thus properly cognitive, and that as a consequence there can be moral knowledge. The remaining challenge comes from those philosophers who argue that while all this is perfectly true, there are, one might say, truths and truths.

Crispin Wright, Bernard Williams, and Jürgen Habermas have all developed criticisms of cognitivism that share this basic strategy. Wright and Williams came to share the minimalist framework for the debate over objectivity I outlined in Chapter 1.[2] Within such a framework whether or not a truth predicate can be defined over a particular discourse ceases to have the importance it seemed to enjoy in previous discussions of the metaphysical issue of realism. Within the general ambit of minimalism, a range of discourses can have a truth predicate defined over them if they enjoy the requisite internal discipline. That internal discipline has to sustain standards of warranted assertibility for indicative sentences and constitute the relevant social practice *as* an assertoric practice. These discourses may be formally similar, but this similarity will be accompanied by substantive differences in the internal discipline of each practice. Thus, the force of minimalism is to place a much weaker emphasis on the Wittgensteinian cognitivists' use of such terms as 'know' and 'true', with the result that the corresponding concepts are, perhaps, hardly worth having.

I have already examined Blackburn's and Timmons's unsuccessful attempts to exploit this minimalist framework on behalf of non-cognitivism by developing their respective versions of assertoric non-descriptivism. Non-objectivists, however, follow a different strategy. Williams and Wright describe differences between areas of thought and language in a perspicuous surview of a range of discourses that uses

---

[2] As their respective papers in *Truth in Ethics* indicated.

Wittgensteinian means to reach an un-Wittgensteinian end.[3] Such a strategy results in a commentary on the relative status of discourses, which proceeds by immanent reflection on their substantive standards of assertoric warrant. Wright and Williams are presenting another way to develop Blackburn's insight that 'loss of a global issue is not a global loss of issues'.[4] In particular they emphasize that truth is no longer the central issue. That concept has lost its metaphysical bite, and thus should not, within a minimalist framework, be the locus of metaphysical disputes.[5]

Bernard Williams's criticism of the cognitivist argument in *Ethics and the Limits of Philosophy* followed precisely this strategy of eliciting criteria that will bring out a difference in the status between 'the scientific' and 'the ethical'. Williams's approach was to show that the cognitivist argument for the existence of moral truth and moral knowledge achieved far too little. Immanent reflection on different areas of discourse brought out the fact that certain distinctions can still be made which express the intuitions underlying the fact/value dichotomy. They do so while avoiding 'the more positivistic formulations that have gone into defining each side of such a distinction'.[6]

These intuitions are not directly concerned with truth, but rather with the nature of representation. They are intuitions about the meta-level distinction between absolute and perspectival representations.[7] 'Absolute' and 'perspectival' should here be understood as predicates of modes of presentation of contents, rather than as predicates of contents themselves. One way to approach the distinction, as it has come to be deployed in recent philosophy, is via a theory of concepts, which will explain how perspective enters into the acquisition and use of concepts.[8]

A theory of what it is to understand a content in thought will give an account of how the content is grasped and will be built up from an account of how its constituent concepts are grasped. The theory of concepts explains how a subject acquires and possesses concepts. For a perspectival concept, such an account will essentially mention an indexed, perspectival, point of view in the possession conditions for concepts of that kind.[9] Some concepts have possession conditions tied to points of view that are peculiarly ours, such as concepts connected to our distinctive sensibilities. Others, however, are available to judgers less peculiarly like us. One of Williams's intuitions is that the concepts of mathematical physics will not have our distinctive peculiarities written into their possession conditions.[10] Such concepts would be graspable from a

---

[3] As I explained in Ch. 1, this archaic word is undergoing a limited revival in English as the correct translation of Wittgenstein's key term 'Übersicht'.

[4] Blackburn, 'Options for the World', 1.

[5] For similar claims to those of Wright and Williams see Richard Rorty, 'Pragmatism, Davidson, Truth', in *Objectivity, Relativism and Truth* (Cambridge: Cambridge University Press, 1991), 126–50, and Michael Williams, 'Do We (Epistemologists) Need a Theory of Truth?', *Philosophical Topics*, 14/1 (Spring 1986), 223–42.

[6] Williams, *Ethics and the Limits of Philosophy*, 134.

[7] Adrian Moore, 'Points of View', *Philosophical Quarterly*, 37/146 (Jan. 1987), 1–20; *Points of View*.

[8] See e.g. Christopher Peacocke, *A Study of Concepts* (Cambridge, Mass.: Bradford Books, 1992) for a theory of concepts and concept possession of this kind.

[9] McDowell's account of secondary qualities, quoted above on p. 41, offers an account of the possession conditions for secondary quality concepts of this kind.

[10] Williams, *Ethics and the Limits of Philosophy*, 152.

wider range of points of view which could take narrower points of view within their scope. So the idea of a point of view in this discussion is tied to the idea that there are different classes of judger, picked out in terms of different repertoires of epistemic capacities.

In my discussion of Gilbert Harman's sceptical argument against the idea of moral objectivity in Chapter 1, I argued that Harman's test for objectivity conflated several different issues. Three in particular were of central importance: whether the best explanations of phenomena ever cite moral properties, unreduced; the local or perspectival character of ethical concepts; finally, the issue of *how much* moral knowledge there is. If the argument of this book thus far has made a prima facie case, using the argument from thick concepts, that there are unreduced best explanations of moral phenomena that cite moral properties, this chapter switches the focus onto the remaining two challenges. But it will prove essential in the course of the discussion clearly to distinguish Harman's argument from those of Williams and Wright. As we shall see, much misguided energy has been expended on attempting to defend cognitivism by attacking Harman's position and that of the non-objectivist (particularly Williams) together. They are in fact very different arguments as this chapter will demonstrate.

I will focus on Williams's argument as the representative form of non-objectivism. The essence of his argument was as follows: if you reflect not on the contents of judgements, but on the meta-level issue of the best explanation of our holdings of those judgements, a distinction emerges which captures an asymmetry between the scientific and the ethical. This immanent reflection classifies discourses as more or less perspectival in how they represent the world. It must be emphasized, again, that this classification concerns the 'how' of representation, not the 'what': 'absolute' and 'perspectival' make no sense as predicated of contents, as opposed to predicates of modes of presentation of contents.[11] Williams did not deny that very perspectival concepts can be used to form judgements which are true, and which can figure in knowledge claims.[12] But, in Williams's argument, cognitivism claimed too much. It claimed much more than the minimal claim that there is perspectival ethical knowledge. For the cognitivists met the tracking condition for theoretical knowledge by assuming that it was anchored, at the reflective level, by considerations that stabilize the practices which deploy the knowledge concerned in *just the same way* that factual truth anchored belief. Williams believed that this claim of strict parity was false.

The title Williams gave to his position was revealing, 'non-objectivism'. His choice was clearly intended to mark out a position between 'subjectivism' and 'objectivism'. As I noted above, Williams did not denigrate ethical objectivity by claiming that it was merely subjective. His scepticism was more indirect. It was, rather, that Williams believed that he could substantiate an ideal of objectivity and then demonstrate that our ethical understanding differs grammatically in certain key respects from that ideal, such that we can declare it to be non-objective, but not necessarily subjective

---

[11] See the extended discussion of this point in Moore, *Points of View*, 42–60.
[12] Williams, *Ethics and the Limits of Philosophy*, 139.

either. 'Objective' and 'subjective' are subcontraries, not contradictories, that is, they can both be true together and can both be false together, when applied to a particular domain. (For example, when applied to a domain that is truly described by 'non-objectivism'.) This point cuts orthogonally across the separate issue of cognitivism versus non-cognitivism, given that Williams allows that we can have knowledge even in highly perspectival discourses. So the basic argument against the Wittgensteinian cognitivism that I have defended is that its attempt to secure moral knowledge was undermined by the strength of the objectivist model of objective ethical practice that it uses to do so. Non-objectivism undermined this model.

I will set out Williams's argument in detail in Section 3 of this chapter, since it requires interpretative work to combine Williams's complex and varied lines of argument and to assess his intriguing suggestion that a kind of ethical objectivity survived a non-objectivist understanding of the ethical. I have sketched his argument in order to motivate an objection of principle to Williams's argument that is both very influential and in my view completely misguided. The issue is properly located within metaphysics. However, given that the cross-purposes and confusion surrounding Williams's argument are a major barrier to further progress on the issue of moral objectivity, I am going to consider these arguments. I shall discuss the internal realist critique of Williams, both for its intrinsic interest, and to identify its relevance for the question of the objectivity, specifically, of morality.

Williams's argument, as I have characterized it, drew on an ideal of objectivity. Several philosophers have taken Williams's stance on objectivity to be typical of a form of dogmatic realism that invites scepticism and makes our ordinary conceptions of objectivity hostage to corrosive sceptical doubt. Their general line of attack is to argue that Williams's ethical views are an updated asymmetry thesis which downgrades moral objectivity by elevating the realistic status of science. Thus, these critics do not consider Williams's views on ethics worth considering on their intrinsic merits. They argue that it is a better strategy to undermine the general account of realism and so indirectly to subvert Williams's account of ethical objectivity.[13] I would not deny that these critics have one sound point here, namely, that Williams's views come as a package. It is not that his realism forces him to be a 'non-objectivist' about ethics. It is, rather, that his realism makes the expression of his non-objectivism in the particular form it takes possible as Adrian Moore has argued.[14] Nevertheless, these criticisms motivated by internal realism seem to me notably

[13] The number of philosophers who have argued in this way is quite large, suggesting widespread misunderstanding of Williams's argument. See Richard Rorty, 'Introduction', in *The Consequences of Pragmatism*; Hilary Putnam, 'Objectivity and the Science/Ethics Distinction', in *Realism With a Human Face*, 163–78, and 'Bernard Williams and the Absolute Conception of the World', in *Renewing Philosophy*, 80–107, McDowell, 'Review of *Ethics and the Limits of Philosophy*'; Warren Quinn, 'Truth and Explanation in Ethics', in *Morality and Action* (Cambridge: Cambridge University Press, 1994), 109–33, and 'Reflection and the Loss of Moral Knowledge', in *Morality and Action*, 134–48; Jane Heal, 'Ethics and the Absolute Conception', *Philosophy*, 64 (1985), 49–65, and *Fact and Meaning*, chs. 2, 7.

[14] On this point see Adrian Moore, 'Realism and the Absolute Conception', unpublished MS, forthcoming in Alan Thomas (ed.), *Bernard Williams*: 'What Williams is presenting us with, it seems to me, is a package of ideas that need to be understood together', 9.

uncharitable in their exegesis of what Williams said and occasionally mistaken in their understanding of the substance of Williams's arguments. These criticisms also seem to me intrinsically implausible whether or not they get Williams right. I have my own substantive disagreements with Williams that will emerge clearly from the subsequent discussion, but accusing him of holding a very implausible position labelled 'external realism' is not one of them.

2. THE 'ABSOLUTE CONCEPTION' VERSUS GLOBAL INTERNAL REALISM

Several philosophers have argued that Williams's criticism of the cognitive claims of ethics can be set aside since he has already begged the relevant questions by making tendentious metaphysical assumptions. These critics include Jane Heal, Warren Quinn, John McDowell, Hilary Putnam, and Richard Rorty. The controversial assumptions allegedly made by Williams concern the very nature of realism and truth. These philosophers usually add that, in this respect, Williams's position is identical to Gilbert Harman's. Both forms of scepticism about moral objectivity can be undermined by a single argument that undercuts Harman's and Williams's allegedly shared commitment to a scientistic external realism.[15]

Williams consistently argued that reflection on the idea of realism committed us to the idea of an absolute conception of the world. This idea is supposedly a gloss on our ordinary intuitions about knowledge of an external world that is there, 'anyway', independent of our practices of enquiry. Williams believed that these intuitions lead directly to an absolute conception of the world, namely, conceiving of the world in a way that is *maximally independent of our perspective and its peculiarities*.[16] Williams's argument began with an account of how judgements are grasped in thought. Reflection on the perspectival character of judgement suggests that a more objective conception of the world involves perspectival ascent: the forming of a conception of the world that is less dependent on perspectival modes of conception.[17] Two points are very important to forestall misunderstanding. First, this ascent should be

---

[15] The connection between Williams's argument and Harman's is most clearly made by Warren Quinn, 'Truth and Explanation in Ethics' and 'Reflection and the Loss of Moral Knowledge'. The connection between Williams's argument and analogous arguments in Nagel and Sellars is made by Richard Rorty, 'Representation, Social Practice and Truth', in *Objectivity, Relativism and Truth* (Cambridge: Cambridge University Press, 1991), 151–61.

[16] The original presentation was in *Descartes* (London: Penguin Books, 1977), chs. 7, 8, and 10. See the further refinement of the idea in *Ethics and the Limits of Philosophy*, 134–40. There is further reflection on the idea and helpful clarification of it in 'Terrestrial Thoughts, Extraterrestrial Science: Review of Hilary Putnam, *Realism with a Human Face*', *London Review of Books* (7 Feb 1991), 12–13 where, in particular, Wiliams wrote 'We can, I suggested, by a reflection within the resources of our human understanding, identify amongst our various descriptions of one and the same world some that, in order to be understood, make more demands on experience that is peculiarly human, and others that make less', 13. It is also briefly discussed in Williams's 'Reply', in Altham and Harrison (eds.), *World, Mind and Ethics*, 208–10 and in 'Philosophy as a Humanistic Discipline', third annual Royal Institute of Philosophy Lecture (2000), repr. in *Philosophy*, 75/294 (Oct. 2000), 477–96 at 481–5.

[17] I take the useful phrase 'perspectival ascent' from Sacks, *The World We Found*, 95.

interpreted as a 'Hegelian' rather than a 'Cartesian' model of objectification, to use once again Jonathan Dancy's terminology and his very useful distinction between these two ways thought may be objectified. (I put this distinction to use in Chapter 4 in the account offered there of impartial reasons.) The salient difference is between a pattern of objectification which strips appearance away, revealing it to be an illusion, and another form of objectification which embeds an appearance in a wider context. Williams, it seems to me, clearly intends the latter view of how one contextualizes the more perspectival in terms of the less perspectival. In forming a less perspectival account of a subject matter previous perspectives are not thereby downgraded as illusory.

The second important caveat is that the perspectival is here explained in terms of the local or the peculiar, in the sense of connected to the particular nature of the knowing subject. It is not merely the idea of the *relational*. Thus, for example, the observer-dependence of physics is not an instance of the metaphysically perspectival, as Putnam mistakenly asserts.[18] Were there intelligent life on Mars, Martian physics would not share our perspective because our imaginary Martians would form a different class of judgers with a distinctive set of epistemic capacities. But their physics would be observer-relative, just like our physics. We do not believe that the observer-relativity of physical theory results from any limitations connected to our peculiar character as knowers. It is a problem, if that is how it is best described, for *any* judgers making physical measurements. Thus, Williams's account of the absolute/perspectival distinction clearly separates the ideas of being relative to our point of view and being constituted by such a point of view.

Williams's controversial suggestion was that the very idea of objective knowledge suggests that this procedure of perspectival ascent should be iterated, to generate the idea of a conception of the world 'to the maximum degree independent of our perspective and its peculiarities'.[19] Transcending a more perspectival view and supplanting it with a less perspectival view is a process that can be repeated. This absolute conception, he argued, was implicit in the ordinary idea of knowledge, and explained why it contained a 'standing invitation to scepticism'.[20] Williams went on to claim that it is possible to present an account of realism that avoids the usual dichotomy presented by proponents of internal realism. Internal realists typically assert that the concept of **the world as it is in itself** is an empty one. They offer the following unappealing dichotomy: either the world as it is in itself is the empty noumenal cause of our experiences, or it can be identified only by reiterating our current best theories of the world and its structure. In neither case, it is argued by internalists, does their opponent, the external realist, offer any insight into the relation between thought and the world. They conclude that whatever is picked out by the phrase 'the world' is

---

[18] Putnam, 'Objectivity and the Science/Ethics Distinction', 170–4, is a representative passage. Williams commented as follows, 'If quantum mechanics presents these features, then it presents them to observers using a similar theory elsewhere in the universe. The "absolute conception" is one that abstracts to the maximum degree from the *peculiarities* of any set of observers', 'Terrestrial Thoughts, Extraterrestrial Science', 13.

[19] Williams, *Ethics and the Limits of Philosophy*, 139.

[20] Williams, *Descartes*, 64.

dispensable in its philosophical role as the noumenal dough structured by our conceptual 'cookie cutter'.[21]

Williams intended the absolute conception to be an alternative to this false dichotomy that nevertheless substantiates our realist intuitions. It does not take our existing best representations at face value, nor does it refer to some noumenal structure which may, for all we know, lie beyond them. As Williams said, there has to be an alternative to either putting all our representations together as our world view or taking them all away leaving no one's world view which are the only two choices offered by internal realism. Immanent reflection on our existing representations classifies them as more or less perspectival in how they represent the world. From *within this perspective*, Williams argued, the intuitions of the realist can be captured by the idea of an absolute conception of the world. This immanent approach rejected the idea of a noumenal structure underlying our representations that is forever beyond our knowledge. However, neither did it retreat to a quietist reiteration of our existing commitments. There is still a positive task of elucidating different degrees of objectivity using a method of immanent reflection.

The nerve of Williams's basic argument was this: reality is unitary, and knowledge, if it is to be such, must be answerable to such a unified and independent reality (save where that which is known is itself a mental item).[22] For this reason, if we have two candidate pieces of knowledge, there must be a conception of the world that 'indicates' what makes each item of knowledge true.[23] This conception can be drawn upon to explain how they are coherent representations of the same reality. But to play this role the conception drawn upon must not, itself, be perspectival in the way that the two items of knowledge are. It must be non-perspectival in the sense of not being from any point of view *in particular*.[24] (This remains compatible with its being perspectival up to a point.) Scientific representations of the world attempt to play this role.

As Adrian Moore points out, there is nothing, so far, in this argument that invokes explanation. Thus far, it is an expression of what Moore calls Williams's 'basic realism'.[25] Williams then added considerations about the explanation of the

---

[21] The image is Putnam's; see *The Many Faces of Realism*, 19, 33, 36.

[22] I have been very much helped in my interpretation of Williams's account of the absolute conception by Adrian Moore. The account I give here of the essence of Williams's realism captures an aspect of the subtle interpretation of Williams's argument given in Moore's *Points of View*, esp. ch. 4, sect. 3. There are, it should be noted, some differences between Moore's version of the argument and Williams's own, but I take myself to be describing the uncontentious core of the argument common to both their versions.

[23] I take the crucial word 'indicates' from Moore; he carefully explains this use of it in 'Realism and the Absolute Conception': 'By "indicates" here, I do not mean "makes reference to"; I mean "expresses". Thus consider someone who knows that gold is a precious metal. In order to indicate the fact that makes this item of knowledge true, the conception must actually incorporate the claim that gold is a precious metal—or else a claim that entails that gold is a precious metal. It cannot just incorporate some claim about the fact that makes this item of knowledge true', 9 n. 37.

[24] This conclusion is ambiguous between 'the conception cannot itself be from any point of view'—see e.g. Moore, 'Realism and the Absolute Conception', 10—and the conception cannot be from any point of view *in particular*. I will explain why I take this distinction to be important below.

[25] Moore, 'Realism and the Absolute Conception', 3.

knowledge that we have, and it is at this point that he added sufficient resources to his account to make the distinctions he wanted to draw between the scientific and the ethical. Williams was not directly concerned to argue that we do not have ethical knowledge. He was perfectly happy with the idea of perspectival knowledge that ineluctably draws on a point of view and ethical knowledge is clearly perspectival in this way. The point is, rather, that at the reflective level the best explanation of putative ethical knowledge does not *directly vindicate* that knowledge. By contrast, in the scientific case, the best explanation at the reflective level of that knowledge does directly vindicate it. I will now explain this distinction between direct and indirect vindication and its significance for Williams's argument about ethical objectivity.

The best case scenario for cognitivism, the claim that we have ethical knowledge, focuses on repertoires of thick concepts drawn upon in the making of moral claims. It is the use of such concepts that makes it most plausible to argue that we have moral knowledge. Williams's fundamental thought about the ethical was that there is a deep-seated plurality of such repertoires, each of which serves to give sense to the idea of an individuable social world. This idea of an individuable social world plays a crucial, destabilizing role in the claim that we have ethical knowledge. For, on Williams's understanding of the idea, different social worlds represented different, incompatible, ways of conceptualizing social reality. As Moore glosses the claim, 'although we need to inhabit some social world, there is no one social world that we need to inhabit'.[26]

So, when we have competing ethical knowledge claims, and ascend to the level of reflection, we need an account of a presupposition of the claims that explains why each is made from an incompatible social world. This explanation is going to draw on the resources of the social sciences and maybe history and psychology too, but it is debarred, by its own explanatory ambitions, from directly reusing the thick ethical concepts in question. It needs sufficient explanatory leverage such that it must be outside the relevant social world. Obviously, direct vindication of the perspectival knowledge, as in the scientific case, is ruled out. Moore puts the argument very succinctly:

A good reflective explanation for someone's having a given item of scientific knowledge can make use of the very concepts exercised in the knowledge, and so can straightforwardly and directly vindicate the knowledge, by revealing that the person has come by the knowledge as a result of being suitably sensitive to how things are. Thus Williams's realism about science, but not about ethics . . . Inhabiting a social world means having a certain point of view. What prevents a good reflective explanation of someone having such knowledge from directly vindicating it is the fact that the explanations must include an account of why they have the relevant point of view (where this does not itself consist in their knowing anything). By contrast, there can be scientific knowledge that is not from any point of view. A good reflective explanation of someone's having such scientific knowledge need not involve the same kind of indirection.[27]

I will examine the argument, as extended to ethics, in more detail in the next section. At this point I will restrict myself to a consideration of Williams's basic realism and

———
[26] Moore, 'Realism and the Absolute Conception', 3.   [27] Ibid.

the strategy of Williams's critics. This strategy has been to reject this approach to realism, and thereby to undercut Willliams's criticism of ethical cognitivism. These critics want to defend a global internal realism and structure the debate in such a way that the only alternatives to this view are Platonism or external realism, brought together by the thought that according to these views the world is, in a sense, 'self-interpreting'. They therefore expend considerable exegetical energy proving that Williams holds such a view, to my mind fruitlessly. The result is a hollow victory for an internally realist form of cognitivism purchased at the cost of misrepresenting the strongest argument against it.

The case against Williams, in particular, has been vitiated by crucial misunderstandings. The first is the assumption that Williams's argument is essentially identical to Harman's, a point to which I will return. The second is the initial divisions that internal realists impose on dialectical space. They take it to be completely occupied by three positions: internal realism, external realism, and relativism, which are mutually exclusive and jointly exhaustive.[28] A connected assumption is that certain models of reason and rational practice are corollaries of models of realism. Thus, it is claimed that external realists are committed to a rationalistic or Platonic view of reason, though this expresses itself in contemporary terms as an algorithmic concept of scientific method.[29]

This assumption motivates the claim that Williams's scientistic model of objectivity must give an equally reductive account of its own epistemology. It is argued that, since Williams introduces the idea of the absolute conception via the idea of explanation at the reflective level, the aspiration to an absolute conception must reflexively apply to itself. This leads to the claim that Williams does not simply want an absolute and austerely physicalist description of the world but that he must add the extra requirement that it offer a similar physicalistic account of its own epistemic legitimacy. This simply runs together claims about the contents of knowledge and claims about their justification. It assumes non-perspectival contents must have non-perspectival component concepts and a non-perspectival epistemology. This is both false and a misguided leap over the use/mention distinction.

Putnam and Quinn criticize Williams in this misguided way.[30] They claim that Williams must be hoping for the completion of Quine's programme of naturalized epistemology as the aim of the absolute conception is to give a non-perspectival account of the holding of its own non-perspectival contents. Williams's opponents conclude that with this metaphysical conception of realism in play it is no wonder that ethics fails to meet this standard of objectivity. Williams's arguments specifically

---

[28] Putnam at least makes this assumption explicit: the entire argument strategy of *Reason, Truth and History* presupposes it. That work operates with an exclusive and exhaustive trichotomy of internal realism, external realism, and 'self-refuting' relativism; see e.g. ch. 3, 'Two Philosophical Perspectives'.

[29] This connection between external realism and Platonic or algorithmic conceptions of the scientific method is explicit in Putnam's *Reason Truth and History*, 188–200; McDowell's 'Review of *Ethics and the Limits of Philosophy*'; and Heal's *Fact and Meaning*, chs. 2, 6, and 9.

[30] Putnam, 'Objectivity and the Science/Ethics Distinction', 174. Quinn, 'Reflection and the Loss of Moral Knowledge', 200.

about ethics can, therefore, safely be ignored. Unfortunately, these assumptions do not stand up to either philosophical or exegetical scrutiny. First, there seems little reason to concede that the only two possible stances on the realism issue are external and internal realism, particularly as those terms are defined in the debate. Secondly, in several texts Williams introduces his views as an explicit alternative to these options. Thirdly, it is a misunderstanding to take Williams either as a reductive physicalist or as reflexively applying the absoluteness constraint to the best explanation of the holding of judgements.

Williams accepted a holistic and normative conception of the intentional, and nowhere did he expect such idioms to be eliminated.[31] There is no suggestion that the holding true of ethical beliefs will be given a reductive explanation. The explanation of why people legitimately hold beliefs will relate the holding of those beliefs to the acknowledgement of the internal standards governing assertoric utterance within that discipline. This will, in turn, involve the platitudes governing the truth predicate. Williams's point was that reflection on these assertoric practices will bring out a disanalogy between the scientific and the ethical. These reflective explanations are not themselves absolute. They will be perspectival narratives about the holdings of all kinds of content—whether perspectival or absolute. Williams could even concede that standards of rational appraisal are socially and historically embedded, requiring strongly perspectival techniques of engaged hermeneutic enquiry to elucidate them. This does not affect his central argument. While the absolute conception is elucidated using the idea of explanation this does not in turn require a reductive account of explanation.[32] The internal realists' non sequitur is to argue that explanations of absolute representations must themselves be absolute in the same way.

Thus, as I argued in Chapter 1, it is crucial to draw a distinction between the way Harman and Williams introduce the connection between objectivity, explanation, and reflection. Harman's test for objectivity does introduce a bootstrapping test, whereby our best theory of objectivity, physical science, offers via naturalized epistemology an account of the conditions of its own acceptance. A physicalistic world view completes itself, via a virtuous circle, by replacing the old discipline of epistemology as first philosophy with a successor discipline, naturalized epistemology.

---

[31] Admittedly, the closing chapter of *Descartes* looks more to Quine than Davidson, but even there eliminativism about the mental is not adopted. Putnam asserts the contrary in 'Objectivity and the Science/Ethics Distinction', 173. Williams in a later work noted that 'I do accept that some formulations of the idea [of the absolute conception] have implied a poorly considered causal theory of knowledge. I believe that the general idea is independent of such a theory.' 'Reply', in Altham and Harrison (eds.), *World, Mind and Ethics*, 209.

[32] Thus the two issues conflated by Quinn and Putnam are the relevance of 'best explanation' tests for ethical objectivity and the quite tangential issue of the perspectival/absolute distinction. Further disentangling of the argument would have to separate out the theory/observation distinction, the science/non-science distinction, and the role played by the causal theory of knowledge. Thus I suspect that Quinn in particular was motivated by the belief that the argument of Gilbert Harman in *The Nature of Morality* was in no essential respects different from that of Williams. In both his critical essays on Williams's account of objectivity Quinn associated Williams's position closely with Harman's. But I have demonstrated that both the structure of Harman's position and his understanding of its component elements are completely different from the arguments of Williams and in my view require quite separate treatment.

In this version of a naturalized epistemology, physicalism gives a physicalistically acceptable account of its own aetiology and justification. Here the aspiration to *reflective* explanation transmutes into a requirement for *reflexive* explanation. What I mean by this is that Putnam and Quinn assume that our most objective view of the world can only explain itself using concepts drawn from our most objective view of the world: the absolute conception is here conflated with an all-embracing physicalism. By contrast, it seems to me that Williams seemed committed only to a reflective explanatory test, not a reflexive one: we want, reflectively, to explain all our knowledge, even our most absolute knowledge, but we can do this without this explanation itself being cast in the most objective terms.

As Moore points out, the most that Putnam and Quinn have proved is that our meta-level representations must be perspectival, not that all our representations must be.[33] *Representations about representations* will deploy all the resources of hermeneutic interpretation and hence will involve perspective, but that would not have troubled Williams.[34] His claim is that some first order representations aspire to the kind of objectivity appropriately called absolute, not that all do so, or that the intentional idioms called upon to elucidate the idea of representation itself do so.

The idea of the absolute conception does not seem a proper target of the criticisms it has received from its Wittgensteinian critics. Moore has recently offered an extended discussion and defence of this conception of objectivity that could hardly be improved upon, taking the discussion to a new level of sophistication, and I will not pursue this issue further here.[35] I would simply note that you do not have to be a Wittgensteinian quietist to hold that one should offer no comment on how representations hook on to the world. Williams's refusal to explain how the absolute conception 'mirrors' reality is surely a surprising omission for an alleged external realist.[36] Williams has no substantive comments to make about how the absolute conception is true, or of how its component representations hook on to the world, unlike Wilfrid Sellars's neo-Tractarian account of 'picturing'.[37] In this, he parallels Davidson, who similarly treats reference below the level of the sentence held true as an auxiliary, instrumental concept in his overall account of language and truth.[38]

---

[33] Adrian Moore, *Points of View* presents the strongest arguments yet developed for the necessity of absolute representations. In the course of his argument he presents penetrating criticisms of the Putnamian line of argument I have examined, notably throughout ch. 5.

[34] Ibid., p. 88.

[35] Ibid., chs. 4 and 5.

[36] Heal has an extensive account of how Williams's absolute conception involves the use of special purified 'super concepts' which reflect nature carved at its joints at a subsentential level in *Fact and Meaning*, ch. 2, 'Varieties of Realism'. I do not believe that this interpretation is adequately supported by the texts cited.

[37] Wilfred Sellars, *Science and Metaphysics: Variations on Kantian Themes* (London: Routledge and Kegan Paul, 1968), ch. 5. That Rorty has run together Sellars's position and Williams's is clear from his paper 'Representation, Social Practice and Truth'.

[38] Davidson, 'Reality Without Reference', which contains the famous passage: '[T]he essential question is whether [reference] is the, or at least one, place where there is direct contact between linguistic theory and events, actions, or objects described in nonlinguistic terms. If we could give the desired analysis or reduction of the concept of reference then all would, I suppose, be clear sailing. Having explained directly the semantic features of proper names and simple predicates, we could go

It seems that all too often Williams's critics knew what he must be saying using the method of guilt by association, the two guilty partners being Sellars and Nagel.[39] Thus, it was claimed that Williams held a neo-Peircean view of knowledge which identifies truth with idealized warranted assertibility; that he was a representational atomist and believed in ideally purified concepts which picture the world as it really is and that his Cartesian conception of objectivity strips the world of perspective by dismissing it as mere appearance. These are all views held at some stage held by Sellars and Nagel, whether globally or about a particular issue, but not held by Williams. Meanwhile, to be on the side of the angels, one must now deny that truth has any theorizable essence at all. Qua minimalist, Williams must surely just have agreed with this claim. Unfortunately, this alleged criticism leaves all the interesting parts of his view unscathed.

If anything, Williams's account stands closer to internal than external realism. This is hardly surprising, though, given the position which internalists foist on their opponents. Their account of external realism with a ready-made world which our representational vocabulary carves at the joints is a caricature of that to which any careful realist is committed.[40] There is, admittedly, an ambiguity in Williams's presentation of his theory. This concerns the idea of the absolute conception being maximally independent of a point of view. This could be interpreted as the requirement that the conception be *totally* independent of a point of view, or that it *is* so dependent, but *minimally* so. As I have indicated above, both exegetical and philosophical reasons lead me to argue for the latter, more internalist reading.[41] Moore's interpretation of Williams's basic argument also seemed to allow that the distinctive kind of role of the idea of the absolute conception in substantiating our belief in a unitary and objective reality could be secured by representations that were,

---

on to explain the reference of complex singular terms and complex predicates, we could characterize satisfaction (as a derivative concept), and finally truth. This picture of how to do semantics is (aside from the details) an old and natural one. It is often called the building-block theory. It has often been tried. And it is hopeless.', 219–20.

[39] Sellars, *Science and Metaphysics*; Thomas Nagel, 'The Limits of Objectivity', in Sterling M. McMurrin (ed.), *The Tanner Lectures on Human Values*, i (Cambridge: Cambridge University Press, 1980), 75–139.

[40] To be fair to Putnam he had a very specific target in mind, David Lewis. Lewis's solution to Putnam's model-theoretic critique of realism, the introduction of elite classes into the Lewisian ontology, did seem to invite the charge of presupposing a 'ready-made world'. See e.g. Lewis, 'Putnam's Paradox', *Australasian Journal of Philosophy*, 62 (Sept. 1984), 221–36, at 228. Lewis credited the general form of this solution to G. H. Merrill, 'The Model-Theoretic Argument Against Realism', *Philosophy of Science*, 47 (Mar. 1980), 69–81. But there are other forms of realism besides Lewisian realism.

[41] In a sense that is the only available reading: Williams commented both that, 'If we use Putnam's contrast, this idea [of an absolute conception] belongs with internal realism' and that, 'In calling the acceptable and banal kind of realism "internal", Putman implies that the vital contrast is between a standpoint inside human experience and one outside it . . . We seem to have a boundary, but no conceivable idea of anything outside it. If we put it like this, however, and insist that the only standpoint is "inside" human experience, we are still, in fact, using the idea of a boundary . . . But as Wittgenstein insisted, there is no such boundary—the very idea of it is unintelligible . . . An *internal* realism must be inside something, but what we have learned is that there is nothing for it to be inside'. 'Terrestrial Thoughts, Extraterrestrial Science', 13.

themselves, perspectival to some degree. I would suggest both that this is Williams's preferred option and that his opponents have over-hastily attributed the former interpretation to his work.[42]

Finally, given Williams's criticisms of a rationalistic conception of rationality in social and political philosophy it seems very implausible to attack him for holding an algorithmic conception of scientific method.[43] I suggest that this implausible interpretation arose because of the prior assumption that the absolute conception must give an absolute account of its own epistemology. This would give grounds for believing that physical science must generate the theory of its own acceptance conditions. This would presumably be a description, in physicalistically acceptable terms, of how theories are generated and accepted. An algorithmic account of scientific method might meet this requirement, but there is no reason to believe Williams was committed to it.

My aim in this section has not been to prove that Williams's view of realism is the final word on that issue, but to prove that his account of ethical objectivity does not suffer from presupposing an implausible account of realism. His arguments cannot be dismissed as quickly as Quinn and Putnam suggest. There remain several substantive points of disagreement between Williams and myself on the general issue of realism. I endorse what I will call the internalist interpretation of an absolute conception, which I take to represent a regulative ideal of a minimally perspectival, but nonetheless perspectival, representation of reality from our point of view.[44] I would endorse many of the claims made by the internalists, although I reject the constraining structure they bring to the realism debate which generates their caricature of external realism. (Indeed, in developing a contextualist model of moral knowledge I will draw a great deal on the pioneering development of such an approach found in Putnam's work.) At this point, my aim has simply been to prove that Williams's account of ethical objectivity represents a real threat to the cognitivist argument I have traced thus far, rather than being made up of a set of obvious mistakes about the nature of objectivity.

Both Wright and Williams are able to resist the pressure towards a quietistic stance towards realism by allowing truth to be a minimal notion, but also allowing grammatical investigation of which of its governing platitudes constitute a particular discourse to do all the work. Conclusions which can only be shown, and cannot be said, are enough for the minimalist. More work will have to be done if the non-objectivist challenge is to be deflected by a revised form of cognitivism. I will now

---

[42] In fairness to Williams's critics I have already in n. 31 above quoted the passage where Williams acknowledges that his early version of the idea of an absolute conception was not originally presented as independent of a causal theory of knowledge, but he did later come to argue that the two ideas were clearly independent. Moore's separation of Williams's basic argument from the idea of explanation (let alone the connection between explanation and a causal theory of evidence or explanation) makes that clear. Moore, 'Realism and the Absolute Conception', 11–12.

[43] Williams, *Ethics and the Limits*, 18, 100–1, 197.

[44] If there is an overtone of idealism to this formulation, but then it is a form of idealism equivalent to empirical realism. See Adrian Moore, 'Transcendental Idealism in Wittgenstein, and Theories of Meaning', *Philosophical Quarterly*, 35/139 (Apr. 1985), 134–55. Moore's *Points of View* is an extended explanation of why this kind of idealism is, in fact, nonsense while also indirectly communicating an ineffable insight.

set out Williams's argument for undermining the full objectivity of the ethical from what I think could fairly be described as his Hegelian starting point.

3. THE NON-OBJECTIVIST CHALLENGE TO COGNITIVISM

In this section I turn to Williams's specific arguments for the prospects for an object-ive understanding of the cognitive claims of ethics as opposed to his wider approach to objectivity more generally. In the remaining sections of this chapter I hope to sub-stantiate my view that non-objectivism poses the deepest challenge to the form of moral cognitivism outlined in Chapters 1 and 2. Providing an adequate response to non-objectivism is one of the central tasks of this book.

Much of the difficulty in interpreting Williams's critique arises because he seemed, as it were, always one step ahead in his argument against cognitivism. I briefly sketched above two lines of argument on Williams's behalf. The first did not mention explanation and proceeded from Williams's basic realism to the claim that scientific claims could be directly vindicated, whereas ethical claims could not. There is a parallel argument couched in terms of explanation (which I will shortly describe). But underlying both arguments is a set of assumptions. This is an account of a distinctively modern society and what it is like to try and lead an ethical life in such a society. It is this vision that clashed head-on with the Wittgensteinian cognitivists' position and that seemed to Williams to show that non-objectivism is a more truthful model of ethical practice than the objectivism that he claimed was implicit in the cognitivists' position.

That which I described as the best case scenario for cognitivism was a case where repertoires of thick concepts are drawn upon in the making of moral claims in such a way as to make knowledge claims about values and to offer defeasible practical reas-ons. This suggested to Williams a model of knowledge that is at home in a certain conception of society, but one fundamentally at odds with his own account of a mod-ern society. His competing view of a modern society assumed that any description of such a society would find a deep-seated plurality of whole schemes of thick ethical concepts. This pluralism helped to substantiate his concept of an individuable social world. Such worlds are different, incompatible ways of conceptualizing social reality, and it is the role of such social worlds in Williams's argument that was responsible for destabilizing the cognitivists' position. But Williams was well aware that, at this point, all we have is a clash of intuitions.

So, to resolve the deadlock in way that he regarded as advantageous to the non-objectivist diagnosis of our ethical life, he brought in some of his prior assumptions about how the cognitivist argument must be understood. It seemed to Williams that the proposed form of cognitivism most closely resembled a form of neo-Hegelianism. He had already assumed that the most plausible form of cognitivism is going to take a transcendental turn and view its proprietary notions of agreement, sense, and necessity as rooted in a form of life in a way developed by Wittgenstein, but with antecedents in Hegel. On that basis Williams made various assumptions not only about the proposed cognitivist argument, but also about how it might be developed in response to his objections.

Williams's critique began from the internal grammar of a discourse, in the Wittgensteinian sense, with the aim of demonstrating that the cognitivist argument for the existence of moral truth and moral knowledge achieved far too little. Issues of truth and knowledge did not, on his view, exhaust the issue of objectivity. Immanent reflection on different areas of discourse brought out the fact that certain distinctions could still be made which expressed the intuitions underlying the fact/value dichotomy.[45] The disanalogy that Williams perceived between the scientific and the ethical was the following:

In a scientific enquiry there should ideally be convergence on an answer where the best explanation of the convergence involves the idea that the answer represents how things are; in the area of the ethical, at least at a high level of generality, there is no such coherent hope.[46]

This was Williams's conclusion, which he reached at the end of a long and complex line of argument. Its starting point was Williams's long-standing suspicion of the ideas drawn from the later Wittgenstein on which Wiggins and McDowell based their arguments.[47] Williams argued that Wittgenstein conflated two ways of taking the term 'we', when he posited a constitutive relation between sense, truth, and 'our' form of life. On the one hand, a use of 'we' can pick out a determinate group in the world, which gives it empirical content at the cost of inviting relativistic interpretations of Wittgenstein's claims about the role agreement plays in grounding truth.[48] Alternatively, the 'we' can be given a transcendental reading that introduces a form of pluralized idealism.[49] This empties the term of empirical content, avoids relativism, but gives the term very wide scope. This reading must take 'we', in Kantian fashion, to apply to all makers of judgements who are potential participants in our form of life. Even if this constitutes an intelligible approach to realism, which I believe, but Williams doubted, the crucial point is whether it was an appropriate model for moral knowledge. Williams's perspectivalism classified ethics as involving both concepts and epistemic norms more local than the categories of the understanding. That was the basis for his view that the model for moral knowledge that Wiggins and McDowell took from Wittgenstein's work was an inappropriate model for the ethical.

---

[45] Williams, *Ethics and the Limits of Philosophy*, 134.

[46] Ibid. 136.

[47] A suspicion first expressed in the arguments of Bernard Williams, 'Wittgenstein and Idealism', in *Moral Luck* (Cambridge: Cambridge University Press, 1981), 144–63.

[48] Canonically expressed by the *Philosophical Investigations* passage, 'If language is to be a means of communication there must be agreement not only in definitions but also (queer as this may sound) in judgements. Strange as it may seem, this requires not only agreement in judgements, but also in opinions. This seems to abolish logic, but does not do so'. Wittgenstein, *Philosophical Investigations* (Oxford: Basil Blackwell, 1958), sect. 242.

[49] Williams was implicitly critical of this development in the later Wittgenstein. However, this line of interpretation has been developed and defended in its own right by Adrian Moore and Jonathan Lear. See Moore, 'Transcendental Idealism in Wittgenstein and Theories of Meaning'; Lear, 'The Disappearing "We"' and 'Transcendental Anthropology', both repr. in *Open Minded: Working Out the Logic of the Soul* (Cambridge, Mass.: Harvard University Press, 1998), at 282–300, 247–81 respectively; 'Leaving the World Alone', *Journal of Philosophy*, 79/7 (July 1982), 382–403; 'On Reflection: The Legacy of Wittgenstein's Later Philosophy', *Ratio*, 2/1 (1989), 19–45.

On the first reading of the term 'we' in the expression 'how we go on' with ethical concepts, it has a narrow and empirical scope. If interpreted as possessing this narrow scope Williams argued that the appropriate Wittgensteinian conclusion should be moral relativism of a strong kind: a relativism transcendentally grounded in a form of life. Williams rejected the second reading of 'we', with wide scope, on the ground that the evident facts of ethical diversity would have to be dismissed. He clearly assumed that the role of transcendental considerations is to guarantee a single necessary structure to thought and that the ethical presents too many intelligible structures for this to be a plausible account of the structure of ethical thought. Williams assumed that the kind of consideration intelligible to all makers of judgements would be the non-perspectival (or maximally non-perspectival) concepts of physical theory. That is clearly an inappropriate basis of comparison for ethical concepts.

I believe that this background assumption shaped much of Williams's argument as presented in a compressed and allusive form in *Ethics and the Limits of Philosophy*. It centrally motivated the dispute with Wiggins and McDowell.[50] The key issue was, predictably, the argument from thick concepts and relating the existence of such concepts (which Williams did not deny) to the demands of explanation. Williams was quite happy to use the argument from thick concepts to refute the projectivist, but he denied that it offered conclusive support to the cognitivist position. As I explained in summary form in my discussion of Gibbard's views in the previous chapter, Williams's argument was that the claim that understanding an evaluative concept involved sharing an evaluative viewpoint with its users is ambiguous. The ambiguity of the word 'share' supports two readings for this claim: a weak one which is true and a far stronger one which is, in Williams's view, false.[51]

On the weak reading, to share an evaluative viewpoint is to be 'sympathetic but not identified'. Williams called such a position the 'ethnographic stance'.[52] To make sense of why a group uses an evaluative concept to structure its experience in a certain way, one must to a certain extent have sympathetic insight into how it goes on with that concept. But this falls short of the stronger reading of the argument, where what was required to share an evaluative viewpoint was total identification with the group of concept users. In the next chapter I will discuss at some length the connection Williams identified here between his criticism of thick concepts and his account of the Wittgensteinian origins of the idea. At this point it is necessary to note that the total identification requirement is easily accommodated within the Wittgensteinian perspective: there is just one point of view, that of all participants in the given form of life. But Williams claims that such a development of the Wittgensteinian position cannot accommodate the ethnographic stance, which involves a relation between languages that cannot be explained within the scope of the Wittgensteinian cognitivists' theory.

---

[50] This also suggests that McDowell and Wiggins may differ in how well placed they are to respond to this argument. As I have already noted, McDowell is much more drawn than Wiggins to a constitutive account of the relation between concept and interest.

[51] Williams, *Ethics and the Limits of Philosophy*, 142–7.

[52] Williams, 'Reply to Blackburn', *Philosophical Books*, 27/4 (Oct. 1986), 203–8.

However, Williams's explicit discussion of the cognitivist theory in *Ethics and the Limits of Philosophy* proceeded far more obliquely. He developed his Hegelian model of objectification via the perplexing fable of the hypertraditional society.[53] The members of this society met the requirements of the cognitivist account of moral knowledge. They conceptualized their moral experience using thick ethical concepts and they made judgements and withdrew them in the light of discussion and criticism. But they did not have a certain kind of thought; they did not, in Williams's model, have the thought that their way of going on was *just* local. This prepared the way for Williams's surprising conclusion: that if the hypertraditionalists reflected on what they did, this would destabilize their practice and they would lose their knowledge. Williams reached the paradoxical conclusion that reflection, far from being the factor that converts opinion to knowledge, can destroy the knowledge that the hypertraditionalists had.

This twist to Williams's account baffled his commentators. It seemed to ignore a central property of the truth predicate; that the property of truth is stable and that, unlike evidence or justification, it cannot be lost.[54] These critics claimed that Williams's conclusion was a *reductio ad absurdum* of his own argument. If the hypertraditionalists lost their knowledge on reflection, surely they never had it in the first place? They had local standards of warranted assertibility which turned out to be unreliable guides to truth. Whatever they had, it certainly was not knowledge.

This is, however, a misunderstanding of Williams's argument. The hypertraditionalists lost not their truths, but their concepts. They were unable to endorse the concepts they originally used without irony. They could not form the perspectival judgements, using perspectival concepts, which articulated the truths that had been available to them. Williams was able to set up the model because of his belief in perspectival knowledge, where the subjective conditions of a judger enter into the possession conditions of the relevant concepts. The case he envisaged is analogous to cases of presuppositional failure, where one hesitates to endorse a sentence because one does not accept a key presupposition of its becoming a candidate for truth or falsity.[55] For example, someone who rejects the concept of **chastity** as a means of conceptualizing sexual behaviour may refuse to judge a sentence deploying the concept as either true or false as a means of registering the rejection of the concept.

McDowell has argued that the model of the hypertraditional society confuses reflection and detachment.[56] That seems to me to be a line of criticism well worth developing, and one which I will develop throughout this book in my development of a contextual model of moral knowledge. However, put forward without qualification, McDowell's objection can seem misleading. Naturally, if the perspectival is identified

---

[53] Williams, *Ethics and the Limits of Philosophy*, 142. I use the term 'Hegelian' as a reminder that the form of objectivity to which perspectival ascent aspires, as discussed in Ch. 4, is Hegelian and not Cartesian. The less perspectival is not relegated to some kind of second class status in the course of perspectival ascent.

[54] Putnam, *Reason, Truth and History*, 55, Wright, *Truth and Objectivity*, 38–9.

[55] This is my interpretation, not Williams's. He has a reason for resisting the analogy, see 'Truth in Ethics', 238.

[56] McDowell, 'Review of *Ethics and the Limits of Philosophy*', 383.

with a 'point of involvement', to use Moore's useful phrase, introducing *detached* reflection would be fatal to the cognitivists' position.[57] As Moore points out, a subclass of perspectival judgements are those made from a standpoint of engagement, often involving expression of one's involvement in that point of view.[58] But this idea of a point of involvement does not exhaust the category of the perspectival by any means. But Williams did not make this identification of the perspectival with the necessarily engaged or involved. He allowed for reflection within the model, but did not allow a particular form of reflection, namely, that this local way of going on is *just one form of life amongst other equally valid possibilities*. Williams presented the same line of criticism against the Wittgensteinian cognitivists that he deployed against the model of objectivity he found in the later Wittgenstein. Williams suggested that what would guarantee ethical knowledge would be a consideration, at the reflective level, that legitimated one form of life from amongst others as uniquely the best life. This is a separate target for Williams's scepticism: the modern world has made us familiar with a pluralism which makes the prospects for such a uniquely privileged form of life seem hopeless.

I think there is an illuminating comparison between Williams's non-objectivist argument and the explicitly Hegelian development of the Wittgensteinian cognit- ivists' position in Sabina Lovibond's *Realism and Imagination in Ethics*. Lovibond explicitly envisages the hypertraditionalists' predicament in the development of her own cognitivist position. Her response is to invite these participants in ethical life to reimmerse themselves in a transcendental parochialism:

[A]n acquiescence in what we might describe as a 'transcendental parochialism': a renunci- ation of the (ascetically motivated) impulse to escape from the conceptual scheme to which, as creatures with a certain kind of body and environment, we are transcendentally related.[59]

I believe that it is helpful to put Williams's critical argument, expressed via the thought experiment of the hypertraditional society, alongside Lovibond's model as it is precisely this reimmersion into our local and particular perspective that the hypertraditionalists cannot achieve, at least if they want to keep thinking of their particular form of ethical life as a way of acquiring objective (that is, non-local) knowledge.

Besides this central line of argument, Williams offered supplementary attacks on the cognitivist position. He pointed out, for example, that the secondary property analogy failed at precisely the point one would predict on the basis of his argument.[60] Reflection on how our senses deliver reliable knowledge of the colours of objects deploys, at the reflective level, explanations as to how our sensory capacities operate. A reflective account of colour perception, even one which gives us the theoretical possibility of observers with very different colour concepts from ours, will not undermine our confidence in our practice of making colour judgements. The

[57] Moore, *Points of View*, 3.
[58] Ibid., ch. 2.
[59] Lovibond, *Realism and Imagination in Ethics*, 210.
[60] Williams, *Ethics and the Limits of Philosophy*, 149–50.

key point is that the explanatory issue will equally answer the issue of epistemic justification. But Williams argued that this is not so for the case of ethical judgements. Nor is it the case, he further argued, for those specific evaluative judgements, involving thick concepts, most favourable to the cognitivist case.

Williams implied that the reliabilist approach to knowledge, which takes the causal explanation of the functioning of our colour perception to support the epistemic legitimacy of knowledge acquired through these mechanisms, has no analogy in the ethical case (I will challenge this claim in Part III, specifically in Chapter 10.) All the work would be done by a reflective ethical justification and, returning to his central line of argument, Williams argued that no such justification was possible. Williams's comments on the mathematical analogy for moral reasons, again, followed his overall strategy.[61] There are, he argued, too many explicable differences in ethical outlook which have no parallel in the mathematical case. There can only be one space of reasons in mathematics, which is not the case for ethics. In the background here is one of Williams's key assumptions, namely the prospects, at the reflective level, of a systematic theory of ethical error parallel to a reflective account of theoretical error. I will discuss this crucial issue below and, once again, return to it in Chapter 10.

4. THE INDIRECT VINDICATION STRATEGY

Intriguingly, in spite of these considerations Williams *did* hold out a prospect for a defence of moral knowledge. His view, after all, drew distinctions not between knowledge and non-knowledge but primarily about how forms of knowledge were best explained.[62] Understood in these terms, resolutely internalist terms, as one might call them, the grammatical placing of discourses would not show that we did not have ethical knowledge. It would, rather, change our conception of what this amounted to, such that Williams's scepticism would be allowed to show, rather than say, that our understanding of our knowledge would be have to be a non-objective understanding.

Passages in *Ethics and the Limits of Philosophy* suggest this interpretation.[63] The conscientious deployment of thick concepts makes judgements available that are properly items of knowledge. But in every such case Williams noted that this knowledge is deployed in the context of *a* social world, not *the* social world, and this places demands on how the relevant practice is to be explained. Williams characterizes repertoires of thick concepts functionally, in terms of finding one's way around a social world. The user of a set of scientific concepts can give a reflective account of that use that redeploys the original concepts: such knowledge can be directly vindicated.

---

[61] Williams' argument on this point converges with the criticisms of the cognitivist position offered in Jonathan Lear's important paper, 'Ethics, Mathematics and Relativism', *Mind*, 83/92 (Jan. 1983), 38–60.

[62] Moore, 'Realism and the Absolute Conception', 12–14.

[63] In my concern primarily to analyse Williams's arguments against moral knowledge, I overlooked this possibility of indirect vindication in the doctoral thesis on which this book is based and I am grateful to Adrian Moore for making me realize that I needed to consider this argument in more detail. See also Moore, 'Williams on Ethics, Knowledge and Reflection', *Philosophy*, 78/305 (July 2003), 337–54.

But the user of ethical concepts cannot do this. Once we have progressed beyond the point of lost hypertraditional innocence, his or her judgements are relative to a presupposed social world. Thus, a person reflecting on such judgements cannot *directly* vindicate them in quite the same way. But that leaves open the prospect of *indirect* vindication. It is entirely compatible with everything Williams says, his entire battery of arguments against cognitivism, that such a form of indirect vindication is possible, as Moore makes clear.[64] Both Moore and Miranda Fricker have attempted to develop a view of this kind from Williams's starting point.

I am sceptical that any argument of this general kind will work, and the key point, from my perspective, is that our hypothetical group of concept users looking for an indirect vindication of their outlook must not find themselves in the disaster scenario of the hypertraditionalists. They cannot come to a realization that their knowledge is from a point of view that delivers them into a cosmic exile from which any return to a point of view, especially their own, would be in bad faith. If this were so, then their realization would permanently estrange them from any set of thick concepts, from any available knowledge. So if we are to go down this route of indirect vindication we have, it seems to me, to find fault with Williams's hypertraditionalist scenario. That is the strategy I follow in this book. But even *if* a group of thick concept users could not avoid this predicament, in Williams's own terms there *might* be an indirect vindication strategy available to them. (This is the possibility that Moore and Fricker explore.) It would work as follows. If we have two items of knowledge, the role of the absolute conception of the world is to be able to indicate that which makes them both true. In the scientific case we can form the idea that such knowledge is from incompatible perspectives, but 'incompatible' here has an undemanding sense. In the scientific case we can always, from one such point of view, indicate (from that perspective) what makes the claim formulated from the other perspective true. That is what it is for the absolute conception to provide us with knowledge from no point of view in particular.

Alternatively, in the case of ethical knowledge, Williams is going to relativize such knowledge to a social world and the incompatibility between such worlds has to be, as Moore points out, of a more radical character:

given two incompatible social worlds, even if (improbably) it is possible to use the thick ethical concepts associated with one to indicate what makes an item of knowledge involving the thick ethical concepts associated with the other true, it is out of the question to use this indication of what makes the second item of knowledge true in giving an account of how the two items of knowledge cohere. To give an account of how the two items of knowledge cohere, and in particular to frame that part of the account that indicates what makes both the items of knowledge true, requires at very least the sort of detachment from either social world that would be needed to indulge in some suitably reflective history, psychology and/or anthropology.[65]

[64] Moore, 'Realism and the Absolute Conception', 10. Moore immediately adds after this quoted passage 'I am not now trying to defend the position, just to clarify it'. Interestingly, the argument Moore reconstructs from Williams's text is different from Williams's own argument in this way: Williams emphasizes the crucial role of explanation in distinguishing different kinds of knowledge whereas Moore's argument does not.

[65] Moore, 'Realism and the Absolute Conception', 12.

Now as Moore points out in his insightful analysis of this argument, the prospect ruled out is *direct* vindication of an item of ethical knowledge.[66] No account pitched at the level of 'no point of view in particular' can exercise *the very same* ethical concepts deployed in the original judgement. But it does not rule out an account, from no point of view, which has as one of its consequences the fact known by the group of ethical judgers. Such an account has to go beyond the austere resources of the absolute conception, not least in its account of how it, itself, is possible. It is going to be a perspectival, interest laden story provided by such hermeneutically committed disciplines as history, sociology, psychology, and epistemology.

There are passages in which it seems that Williams was question beggingly conjoining an account of the unitary structure of the world known by the scientific with a plural, incommensurable approach to our many social worlds. But that is, Moore argues, to get his view precisely back to front. He took his view to be more explanatory than that of the Wittgensteinian cognitivists because their position has to develop into either a single unitary structure for the ethical or a plurality of incommensurable ways of conceptualizing the world ethically. Williams believes that it is his view that preserves the claims of social explanation, whereas if cognitivism takes the transcendental turn then it is debarred from offering any illuminating explanations of ethical practice. The question he posed was: 'how do we explain both the unity of the scientific and the "difference within unity" of the ethical?' Williams believed that we can answer that question only by adopting his approach to the scientific and the ethical, such that we can make room for an illuminating and explanatory ethnographic stance towards diverse ethical practices. Williams's basic aim seemed to be a transcendental deduction of the possibility of a social scientific account of the ethical. The consequences of Williams's position are twofold: one implication is for the social scientific observer and another is for us, in our reflective predicament as people who want to make ethical knowledge claims.

What the social scientist will have is the ability indirectly to indicate what a group of concept users know. He or she cannot directly use their knowledge to make judgements, nor can he or she come up with neutral equivalents for the concepts that the group uses. Williams was quite happy to acknowledge that the prospects for a projectivist two-factor analysis of ethical concepts are very dim. But the use of an appeal to thick concepts to refute projectivism does not mean that cognitivism is true and, importantly, the converse does not hold. As I mentioned in my discussion of Gibbard's account of thick concepts, Williams argued that the possibility of an ethnographic stance does not mean that one could glue on to the correct ethnographic (or, more generally, a social scientific) explanation of a practice that deploys a thick ethical concept a thin, non-world guided ethical principle. Thus, there is no prospect of recovering a projectivist analysis for one very good reason:

Centralism is a doctrine about language and linguistic practice, and there is no reason at all to think that people could substitute for a linguistic practice the term in which that practice was psychologically or sociologically explained.[67]

---

[66] Ibid. 13.
[67] Williams, 'What Does Intuitionism Imply?', in *Making Sense of Humanity*, 187.

This explains something that seems, at first sight, puzzling; namely, that Williams borrowed the argument from thick concepts to refute the projectivist, but then undermined the Wittgensteinian cognitivists' position too even though the latter is based on an argument from thick concepts. Williams's intermediate position was possible because of how he understood thick concepts and their best explanation. Williams's internal realist critics accused him of running together claims about the content of judgements with claims about how they are best explained. As Moore pointed out very clearly, that is a mistake: representations about representations can be perspectival without, as it were, some of the object level representations having to be perspectival too. Extending the point, Williams's treatment of thick concepts envisions the highly perspectival concepts of ethical practice explained by the less perspectival concepts of social science, without the implication that participants in the ethical practice could simply accept the explanatory 'descriptive equivalents' of their original judgements and carry on as before, but using the social scientific explanation supplemented by other, thin, ethical concepts expressed in the form of ethical principles.

Nevertheless, the envisioned social scientist has an understanding of the practice described, but this is neither a direct vindication of the knowledge deployed within it (the scientist is not a member of this social world) nor the provision of 'neutral equivalents' for that which is claimed (that is the truth in the argument from thick concepts). But from the ethnographic stance the observing social scientist can indirectly indicate that which the concept users know (if they do, indeed, know it). Moore explains how:

He may be able to understand enough about the community, about their social world and its history to be able to see how their use of these concepts enables them to live in that world, and he may be able to say ... how their circumstances warrant the exercise of the knowledgeable judgements they make using these concepts ... if he does succeed in doing this, he might still not have carved out the same chunk of logical space as they do in making any of the relevant judgements. But carving out the same chunk of logical space must not be confused with carving out a chunk of the same logical space. He will have done the second of these, which is all that Williams requires. In particular, he will have said enough to entail what they know.[68]

What of us, from our engaged perspective as reflective ethical agents? What remains possible for us, on the indirect vindication story, is the prospect of living in the light of truth, the truth of our situation. Williams's realist framework was particularly suited to giving a particular kind of account of this prospect, which Moore summarizes as follows:

Williams's realism gives us ... a richer understanding ... of the nature of our ethical experience. By enabling us to see that our ethical knowledge is from a point of view that admits of equally legitimate and compatible alternatives, in a way in which our scientific knowledge is not—and by enabling us to see how history, psychology and/or anthropology are needed to explain why we have the ethical point of view we have, where this is not itself a matter of knowing anything.[69]

---

[68] Moore, 'Realism and the Absolute Conception', 17.   [69] Ibid. 21.

That is, as it were, the general truth of our predicament. But more specific truths are possible even if this 'disenchanted' view is correct. Even if it is a sociological matter, and not simply an issue of philosophical analysis, to determine the extent to which a given society relies more heavily on thin, non-world guided concepts, it is true that a modern society such as ours *does* rely more heavily on thin concepts. This stock can be bolstered by the remnants of our cultural supply of thick concepts that have survived the corrosive effects of reflection. We could still know ethical truths, but only if we can draw upon the resources of a phenomenon that is itself social, and that Williams called 'confidence'. From within this account, there is a way forward that Williams offers: the cultivation of confidence. Within a non-objectified ethical life, we could even have knowledge if we could retain confidence in our ethical outlook. How would that be possible? What is confidence? In *Ethics and the Limits of Philosophy* it is characterized as 'basically a social phenomenon' and a normative one.[70] It appears to be form of conviction and Williams later explained his invocation of it as follows:

What is done by confidence? The answer I had in mind was that, granted the nature of modern societies, we would face a good number of ethical tasks with the help of unsupported thin concepts, and, since there was not going to be knowledge in that connection, it would be as well if we had confidence.[71]

Confidence is a social phenomenon in the strong sense that it depends, for its existence, on certain social conditions: we need to live in a certain kind of society. But it does not, itself, play a role in making such a society come into being. Once again, Williams's invocation of the concept rests on a background theory of modernity and of the nature of a modern society. Confidence is a key concept in Williams's attempt to reconcile us to a life, lived in the light of truthfulness, in non-objectified ethical conditions.

Some have tried to take this indirect vindication strategy forward in a positive way. Miranda Fricker has attempted to build on the form of indirect vindication that Williams offers us here and has suggested that the correct development of the argument is to view confidence as an irreducibly social notion.[72] Moore has developed a parallel set of arguments, developing an indirect vindication strategy summarized as follows:

---

70 Williams, *Ethics and the Limits of Philosophy*, 170.
71 Williams, 'Reply', in Altham and Harrison (eds.), *World, Mind and Ethics*, 207.
72 I am not convinced by the arguments given in Miranda Fricker's 'Confidence and Irony', in Edward Harcourt (ed.), *Morality and Ideology* (Oxford: Oxford University Press, 2000), 87–112. The account given of what confidence *is* in this paper is very broad. While it is at one stage presented as an 'adverbial proposal', the activity it seems to qualify is nothing less than tradition-informed rather than tradition-bound critical thinking itself. This seems to me too broad a definition of what it is to have confidence in continued use of a practice involving thick concepts. Fricker suggests that by analogy with linguistic and other forms of division of labour, confidence is an irreducibly social state distributed across social groups as a whole. While I can see that people very often defer to social critics on matters of social criticism, or full mastery of a technical concept, it seems to me that Williams's argument uses a narrower understanding of confidence as a form of solidaristic identification or commitment. I do not see how this can avoid being an irreducibly individualistic notion. If the closest analogy is to trust, I can defer to your knowledge and expertise on many matters but I do not see how you can *trust* for me.

The concept of being intrinsically wrong is not itself a thick ethical concept. Its applicability is not 'world-guided' in the way that, say, the concept of being a racist is. My conviction that racial discrimination is intrinsically wrong is not an item of knowledge. But—and this is the point—it does enable me to know such things as that Wagner was a racist. The clumsy appeal to the fact/value distinction obscures this. Williams' more layered view makes it very clear. It also makes clear what kind of thing I need, or more generally what kind of thing we need, if we are to maintain our point of view and continue to have such knowledge, from that point of view. We need confidence. Not that Williams' realism itself gives us confidence. On the contrary, it contributes significantly to undermining our confidence—not least, by making us aware of our need of it. But that is the predicament that we must learn to face if we are to live in light of the truth, something we have every reason to do.[73]

Moore and Fricker here indicate the upside of Williams's apparently pessimistic narrative. If we can foster confidence in our ethical point of view, then we can retain a commitment to unshakeable convictions, such that racism is wrong, while recognizing that this is not knowledge. But in the light of that conviction we can know particular things. And this entire account places us in the position of living in the light of truth. We can view our relations between reflection and practice as transparent, and the authority of morality and the conviction we attach to it as a matter of, to borrow a Rortyan term, collective solidarity.[74]

However, I am not convinced by this more optimistic strategy of securing indirect vindication. Because, earlier in my narrative, I noted that Williams's own version of the indirect vindication strategy was acceptable *if* we could avoid the disaster scenario of the hypertraditionalists. But I do not see how we can, in Williams's own terms. (This entire essay is predicated on an avoidance of those terms, but that is a different matter.) Williams's understanding of non-objectivism, it seems to me, leads inevitably to the conclusion that what is lost is lost and cannot be recovered by cultivating the social phenomenon of confidence. The crucial point is that Williams envisages the survival, at the reflective level, of *some* ethical knowledge. We have less ethical knowledge than we took ourselves to have, but we retain some, and these resources are bolstered by the invocation of confidence. As Bernard Yack has pointed out, a characteristic of recent philosophical discussions of modernity is that modernity is treated as a total concept, contrasted monolithically with pre-modern understandings of what it is to be modern.[75] But, on a more historically and sociologically nuanced view, modern practices and ideologies exist alongside pre-modern equivalents. Williams's global account of a modern society as reliant on thin concepts plus redemptive confidence is challenged by his own more nuanced acknowledgement that we still possess considerable amounts of ethical knowledge that relies on thick concepts.

Confidence is, then, essentially a supplementary device to these resources of ethical knowledge, knowledge that still puts thick concepts to use. But, as Jeremy Altham has pointed out, it is precisely this scenario that makes the invocation of confidence

---

[73] Adrian Moore, 'Maxims and Thick Ethical Concepts', forthcoming in *Ratio*. Quotation from the version presented to the Central Division of the American Philosophical Association (Mar. 2005), 22.

[74] Rorty, *Contingency, Irony and Solidarity*, ch. 9.

[75] Yack, *The Fetishism of Modernities*, 4–8, 40 ff.

so puzzling.[76] If we have some knowledge, made possible using thick ethical concepts, how can we also have other ethical commitments sustained not by knowledge but by confidence? The combination looks very unstable. Williams's response is to press confidence into two roles, not one: to supplement thin, non-world guided commitments in their application and also, when we have thick concepts, to give us confidence in continuing to be committed to them when we know that others have incompatible sets. But Altham's argument, which I think is a very good one, is that if we have knowledge, we have no need to bolster it with confidence. If we do not have knowledge, we do need confidence. But the situation we cannot be in is that of having some knowledge and bolstering it with confidence while at the same time replacing our lost knowledge *with* confidence. Confidence is being called upon to play two very different roles that seem clearly incompatible. They can both be called 'knowing how to go on' with our concepts, but this is envisaged in two contrasting and ultimately incompatible ways.

Consider once again the best case scenario where we accept the existence of principles 'that are not items of knowledge, but allow one to know particular things', as Moore put it. We are clearly in the situation of 'shaken realists'.[77] But where, I would ask, in *this* indirect vindication model for ethical judgements are thick ethical concepts? Moore, in particular, hopes to secure a form of practical objectivity for the ethical, in spite of the failure of pure reason to be practical, by the existence of judgements using concepts of this kind.[78] This practical objectivity is secured by seeing how, as Moore puts it, our concepts can withstand, on occasions of their use in judgements, rational challenges.[79] These challenges lead to internal development that keeps faith with the fact that these are the concepts we live by. But it seems to me that if we do retain them after such rational scrutiny, how we may go on with their development is at least as dependent on their world guidedness as on their practicality. Furthermore, if we lose them, we cannot retain the inherent practicality of such judgements without those very conceptualizations that made 'world guidedness' and 'action guidingness' available within one and the same judgement. In summary, my concern is that if the strategy of indirect vindication rests on an appeal to confidence, it is going to fail. And if it fails, we cannot see ourselves as being in a situation where we have principles, which are not knowledge, in the light of which we know particular things, without invoking those thick conceptualizations that secure moral cognitivism alongside the practicality of judgement. If those thick conceptualizations are simply not available, both Moore and the cognitivist are in serious trouble.[80]

Moore, in particular, agrees with my conclusion in Chapter 4 that all practical reasons are internal and the corollary that pure practical reason offers no independent

[76] J. E. J. Altham, 'Reflection and Confidence', in Altham and Harrison (eds.), *World, Mind and Ethics*, 156–69.

[77] I take the quote from Williams's epigraph to *Ethics and the Limits of Philosophy*, taken from Wallace Stevens's *Aesthetique du Mal*, 'How cold the vacancy | When the phantoms are gone and the shaken realist | First sees reality', p. x.

[78] This argument is presented in detail in Moore, 'Maxims and Thick Ethical Concepts'.

[79] Ibid. 8–9.

[80] I here summarize some of the argument of my 'Maxims and Thick Ethical Concepts: Reply to Moore'.

source of justification for thin ethical principles.[81] But it seems integral to the indirect vindication strategy that it is principles of that kind, combined with confidence, that sustain particular claims to knowledge such as 'Wagner was a racist'. The availability of the indirect vindication strategy is itself hostage to the availability of thick concepts and so it is an unreliable means of recovering such concepts once they have already been lost. This argument will only work if we can, as this book argues, undermine Williams's model of a hypertraditional society. We cannot accept it and work with what remains available in a non-objectified understanding of the ethical.

My view is that the indirect vindication strategy cannot succeed and in suggesting a strategy of this kind Williams simply highlighted where the overall structure of his argument began to break down. A contrast that has been in the offing throughout the argument so far needs to be made explicit. It is a contrast that will be central to the arguments of Chapter 7, namely, the local/global distinction. Is it really the case that for those thick concepts which have survived reflection, our attachment to them is simply that we continue to find a use for them and that we are always reflectively aware of alternative conceptualizations? Or is it simply more likely that Williams's account applies locally, to some concepts but not to all? This issue, which I think is the crucial one here (together with, I admit, the prospects for a theory of error) will come into explicit focus in the next chapter and in other chapters in this book, notably Chapter 10.

In response to Altham's argument, Williams's response was to change the role that confidence plays.[82] However, the change was so striking as to be a change of subject: confidence was not a substitute for knowledge, but confidence in a practice that sustains knowledge. Williams seems in later work to have envisaged confidence as operating presuppositionally. But now the genuine concern, which I will discuss further

---

[81] Moore's subtle strategy is to combine Williams's argument for internal reasons with Williams's concession that there are thick concepts, so as to emphasize that while pure practical reason supplies no motivations in its own right, our use of judgements involving thick concepts involves defeasible practical reasons. That is simply what *it is* for there to be concepts of that kind. Moore believes that the resulting position can be developed in such a way as to converge with aspects of Kant's views and its underlying model of objectivity can follow the pattern of Williams's indirect vindication for the ethical.

[82] In his response to Altham, Williams made more precise the role that he intended the invocation of 'confidence' to play. Williams, 'Reply', in Altham and Harrison (eds.), *World, Mind and Ethics*, 207–10. Even when pockets of ethical knowledge survive reflection, as Williams agrees that they do, they are not buttressed by a further item of knowledge at the meta-ethical level, for example, that this is a uniquely best way of structuring the social world. What confidence does in this revised account is act as a counterbalance to the reflective awareness of radical plurality and the relativism of distance that Williams thinks is characteristic of authentic reflection in the conditions of a modern society. These reflections make us aware of a condition on our knowledge—that does not enter into its content—namely that it is from our social point of view. But this need not destabilize the knowledge and we express our continuing commitment to that knowledge that is ours by having confidence in it. Qua contextualist, I agree entirely with this rejection of the sceptical trope that reflective awareness that we hold one view amongst others is not, per se, to abandon our view. But I would argue that is because, in this case, we have knowledge and once again confidence is idling. However, if we lose our knowledge, an appeal to confidence is not going to recover it. This repeats Altham's objection to the original idea at the meta-level of reflective awareness of which thick concepts we remain committed to and which we have abandoned.

in the next chapter, is that confidence is relegated to a marginal role and is applicable only to marginal cases. Where we find a group of thick concepts that has *survived* reflection, in Williams's minimal sense of their still being in business, and yet we view those concepts as ethically optional, we can describe our commitment to them as 'confidence'. Survival here is a pretty low level achievement. It is not some vindicatory stability under reflection, but simply an awareness that a concept meets an ethical purpose even though we are aware that use of that particular concept is optional for us. It seems to me unobjectionable to call this an instance of having confidence in a practice that sustains a concept, but this usage seems to presuppose that those thick concepts that have survived reflection in a modern society lead a marginalized existence at the periphery of our ethical thought. The core of our thinking is better described by the 'shaken realist', who describes it as a combination of thin principles and particular knowledge claims just as the indirect vindication strategy envisages. In this sense, confidence has been relegated to a marginal phenomenon, just as the thick concepts it sustains have become marginal. They are always an optional way of meeting certain ethical demands. Being bolstered by confidence, in this case, falls a long way short of stability under reflection.

I noted earlier the striking parallels between Williams's scepticism and Sabina Lovibond's cognitivism. The predicament of the unhappy consciousness strikes at Lovibond's position, too, in her call for a transcendental parochialism where the estranged community reaffirms its particular and contingent form of life. But in both her case and Williams's it seems to me too late for irony. While irony is a complex phenomenon at its heart lies a degree of unsuspecting confidence on the part of an involved agent. The confidence that Williams calls for cannot be unsuspecting without bad faith and the suspiciousness that his account of reflectiveness engenders is destructive of confidence. If it is not to be a purely non-cognitive stance, we need something for confidence to be confidence *in*. It has to be rationalized by its propositional object, and that object, in this case, can be nothing other than moral knowledge that has survived the process of reflection in the strong sense that it has proved stable under reflection. So this process cannot be correctly modelled by the scenario of the hypertraditionalists because, as I have argued, what they lose in that thought experiment is irrecoverably lost. But nor can it be correctly modelled in the way envisaged by those drawn to an indirect vindication of our ethical outlook.

Is there no way forward? I believe that there is, but unlike Moore and Fricker I don't believe it can lie in the direction that Williams seemed to indicate with his account of indirect vindication. The lacuna in Williams's argument is that his basic realism, allied with claims about explanation, allows him to express with great force a certain model of ethical thought which shows how moral knowledge could not be possible, given those assumptions. The way forward is not to contest the model of basic realism, but to point to the looseness of fit between this model and Williams's picture of the ethical. It allows him to express his assumptions very clearly, but offers no independent support for them.

What I have in mind is this: there is a powerful and persuasive picture expressed by Williams's model of ethical thought with deep roots in the tradition of philosophical reflection on modernity. It stems ultimately from a theory of modernity as a historical phase in which reflection has so corroded traditional forms of life that we moderns are left with a thin, non-world guided ethical vocabulary and pockets of thick ethical vocabulary that form discrete parts of modern social reality, in the latter case driven to the cultural margins of our collective life. Where we have unity and generality in ethics, we do not have knowledge; where we have knowledge, we cannot have unity and generality, so that even that knowledge is ultimately lost to us. This apocalyptic picture of our current ethical life is one made familiar by Alasdair MacIntyre, but Williams's version seems to have dispensed even with MacIntyre's residual optimism.[83] (As I shall describe in Part III, MacIntyre's residual optimism is based on his belief that one of these discrete pockets of moral knowledge, 'Neo-Neo-Thomism', has the resources to restore coherence and rationality to those other views that contain elements of truth. Williams, clearly, does not have an equivalent deus ex machina in his own theory of modernity). What we should not do, I think, is accept this picture of ethical thought in the distinctive conditions of a modern society.

How can this be possible, though? Doesn't Williams's basic realism entail his non-objectivist understanding of the ethical? I said that I was not going to contest Williams's basic model of realism. I am not, because I think it is ambiguous in a way I can explain. It can be given both an internalist and an externalist interpretation. Williams's central idea was that of developing a conception of the world maximally independent of our perspective and its peculiarities. I suggested that the word 'maximally' made this formulation ambiguous. It could either mean: a conception of the world independent of our perspective and its peculiarities to the maximal extent possible in any case (but not totally so); or, a conception of the world totally independent of our perspective and its peculiarities.

The ambiguity is important because of the way in which direct vindication is supposed to succeed in the case of the scientific and to fail in the case of the ethical. Whatever point of view is implicit in two scientific representations, we can find a representation from no point of view that describes that which makes both perspectival representations true. But the ineluctability of the perspective of social worlds prevents this direct vindication in the ethical case. So the role of the non-perspectival representation is, as it were, that of explanatory umpire. It shows how two perspectival representations can be integrated into a unitary overall conception of the world.

Now one kind of representation that is guaranteed always to play this role is a representation that is from no point of view. But I would suggest that another kind of representation that might be capable of playing this role is a representation from no point of view *in particular*. It is possible to adjudicate between two standpoints immanently, without the neutral referee, if a view can both indicate what makes its true sentences true, what made the true sentences of its rival view true, and what made the false sentences of its rival false. Both representations can still be perspectival. They

---

[83] There were after all, in the apocalyptic scenario of *After Virtue*, communities that still lived according to the Aristotelian virtues in pockets of counter-modern forms of life. That is an acknowledgement, at the level of reality, of Yack's theoretical point: modern and pre-modern practices coexist side by side in contemporary life even if they cannot coexist happily at the level of 'theory'. Yack's argument that **modernity** is not a total category is central to *The Fetishism of Modernities*.

could still play this role (they are not guaranteed to do so, as the idea of an absolute representation is) but whether they do so or not is going to depend on the content of specific perspectival candidates. Nothing in Williams's argument rules this out.

Even if direct vindication of ethical knowledge, as Williams understands that process, is ruled out, there are alternative conceptions of how one might adjudicate between representations from different ethical outlooks that differ also, in significant respects, from Williams's envisaged strategy of indirect vindication. When two ethical outlooks come into a real confrontation, a possible interpretation of the situation is that we have two sets of perspectival knowledge claims and that the true view will indirectly vindicate those claims of its competitor that it can indirectly vindicate and abandon those that it cannot. This process will look more plausible if we can represent the transition between ethical outlooks as a narrative progression of incremental gains and losses, where it is not the case that any complete ethical outlook has been totally scrapped (although significant parts of it may have been). From a contextualist perspective, all we need is a chain of rationally overlapping outlooks equipped with the ordinal rankings of 'better than' or 'worse than'. There even remains a role in such a conception for an externalist understanding of the absolute conception. It functions solely as a regulative ideal, which operates as a reminder that reason is context breaking and potentially transcendent of any particular context.[84]

Can our ethical outlook be represented in such a way, purely contingently? Williams can fairly protest that the case needs to be made out that ethical knowledge fits this model rather than his own. In particular, he thinks that the prospects for a substantive and illuminating theory of error, which my view is clearly committed to, are dim indeed. I will have more to say about this below in Part III, especially in Chapter 10.

Let me say immediately that I am not endorsing an argument in the cognitivist literature which makes it an a priori truth that there is a common core of true ethical representations.[85] Nor am I endorsing the argument, adapted from Aristotle, which argues that there will always be, because of the common constraints and circumstances of human life, a core of ethical truth that is invariantly true across all times and places.[86] Both arguments, the one a priori and the other a posteriori, make

---

[84] I will develop this account in Ch. 8.

[85] This argument extends Davidson's reflections in 'On the Very Idea of a Conceptual Scheme' to argue that there are limits to how much inexplicable disagreement between our ethical outlook and the outlook of a rival group that we are interpreting can be tolerated. That argument, it seems to me, trades on a 'local' versus 'global' equivocation: there must be a basis of shared agreements to make sense of disagreement, but the location of this scaffolding is open to question and it begs the question if *ethical* representations are simply assumed to form part of this a priori common core of representations. Perhaps the load is carried by other parts of the structure; I don't see, for example, why the argument in this general form need trouble the expressivist. This Davidsonian argument forms one of the many complex strands of Susan Hurley's *Natural Reasons: Personality and Polity*.

[86] An alternative tack argues that substantive agreement across ethical outlooks is simply empirically very plausible, forming part of a comprehensive naturalism in which very general natural conditions of human life sustain a broad commonality across human needs and interests and hence across ethical outlooks. For a representative discussion between a proponent of this view and Williams see the exchange between Martha Nussbaum and Williams in *Mind, World and Ethics*. Williams is surely correct that a neo-Aristotelian naturalism had better be more sensitive to changes in that which Aristotle conceived of as **nature** to run the argument in quite this form. Martha

the mistake of meeting Williams on his own terms. They attempt to find a core of representations always available to play the role of neutral umpire when two ethical outlooks are in competition. But we must dispense with such a guarantee and make do with what is contingently available in any particular case. This is the central claim of the epistemological contextualist. What we are ultimately going to need in order to resist Williams's arguments is a rejection of the epistemological foundationalism underpinning his account of the hypertraditional society. Developing such an alternative model will be the task of Part III. However, before proceeding, there is yet another line of criticism from Williams that the hard-pressed cognitivist has to try and meet.

5. THE PERSPECTIVE OF PRACTICAL REASON

Before I can begin to set out the elements of a contextualist moral epistemology there are further critical arguments against cognitivism put forward by Williams that I have to consider. That is because Williams had two arguments against the idea of ethical objectivity which he ran in tandem, frequently switching from one to the other. They are both a threat to cognitivism. Paralleling the way he introduced the distinction in *Ethics and the Limits of Philosophy,* one could say that Williams was sceptical both about the idea of reason itself as a source of objective requirements over practice, and about the idea of ethical objectivity where that notion is modelled on the kind of objectivity exemplified by the scientific. The first strand of his scepticism was touched on in Chapter 4, but it arises interestingly in the present context too.

Because Williams *did* offer a further argument as to why there cannot be moral knowledge at the reflective level, which I mention here for its importance for the subsequent development of his position. Williams's criterion for an adequate solution to this problem is that, at the reflective level, there would have to be a piece of knowledge to the effect that just one development of the ethical, one set of thick concepts, and one space of moral reasons, was the best life for people. Williams's best candidate for a piece of knowledge of this kind was an Aristotelian theory that stated that a single kind of life is grounded on a determinate theory of human nature. Williams's comments about this model are all of considerable interest.[87]

The first is that Williams held open the prospect for a kind of ethical objectivity, a kind which is a recurrent feature of the tradition and has been defended recently by Christine Korsgaard. The kind of objectivity on offer involves reflective endorsement and convergence within the domain of practical reasoning. Korsgaard describes the project as follows:

The reflective endorsement method has its natural home in theories that reject realism and ground morality in human nature . . . the question is a practical one and can only be answered in practical terms.[88]

Nussbaum, 'Aristotle on Human Nature and the Foundations of Ethics', in Altham and Harrison (eds.), *Mind, World and Ethics,* 86–131; Williams, 'Reply', ibid. 194–202.

[87] Williams, *Ethics and the Limits of Philosophy,* ch. 3, 'Foundations: Well Being'.
[88] Korsgaard, *The Sources of Normativity,* 50.

In Korsgaard's exposition, such a view will have two components. It naturally begins with an anthropological account of persons, and the role that morality plays in our lives. Critical philosophical reflection on this role, from within our moral experience, sees if morality will stand up to the required test from a standpoint that is itself normative. If morality is vindicated from every such normative standpoint, it will have survived the project of reflective endorsement and a distinctive kind of practical objectivity will emerge. Korsgaard draws attention to Williams's use of the reflective endorsement model. Williams presented an account of how such a model would work, taking the case of Aristotle:

> If he [the agent] is to conduct any reflection in which he stands back from his dispositions, it is important whether there is anything in the view of things he takes from the outside that conflicts with the view of things he takes from the inside. For Aristotle, the virtuous agent would find no such conflict. He could come to understand that the dispositions that gave him his ethical view of the world were a correct or full development of human potentiality . . . when the agent reflects, even from the outside . . . he will find no conflict with his ethical dispositions.[89]

Williams was prepared to pay the view a back-handed compliment: it is a view that could intelligibly have been true. Contingently, however, it is false:

> Here again we meet the many modern doubts that weaken this account. Our present understanding gives us no reason to expect that ethical dispositions can be fully harmonised with other cultural and personal aspirations that have as good a claim to represent human development . . . a potential gap opens between the agent's perspective and the outside view.[90]

This looks like the claim that the two lines of argument Williams has distinguished, a line of argument that draws on a model of theoretical objectivity and a line of argument that draws on a model of practical objectivity, are not in fact distinct. For what would it be for the inside view and the outside view to harmonize if it is not for the virtuous agent to see him- or herself as responding to value in the world? (This is, I suggest, why Korsgaard underestimated Williams as discussed in Chapter 4 when she took him to be a motivational, as opposed to a content, sceptic.)

Williams's next comment suggests that he did indeed take himself to be blocking this route for the cognitivist. He was aware that a cognitivist strategy he has not addressed could begin with the perspective of practical reason, but not end there (I will defend a view of this kind). The perspective of practical reason would be a device the cognitivist would deploy in the context of a transcendental argument of this form: given that our practical engagement with the world gives us objective reasons, what must the world contain to support that fact? The cognitivist answer is that the world must contain value to which we respond and which we do not project. That was, in general terms, the argument strategy shared by the general class of phenomenological arguments for cognitivism in Chapter 2.

Williams anticipated this move: he argued that even if something like a neo-Aristotelian account were true, it may still not be what was required for the cognitivists. He claimed that the result would be an artefact of our practical

---

[89] Williams, *Ethics and the Limits of Philosophy*, 52.   [90] Ibid.

engagement with the world. It would yield not truths, but dispositions to hold certain beliefs as a precondition of practical enquiry. I surmise that Williams's objection to this was that it would involve a form of detachment, or alienation, from one's own epistemic attitudes:

> The excellence or satisfactoriness of a life does not stand to that life as premiss to conclusion. Rather an agent's excellent life is characterised by having those beliefs... Reflection on the excellence of a life does not itself establish the truth of judgements using those concepts or of the agent's other ethical judgements. Instead it shows that there is good reason (granted the commitment to an ethical life) to live a life that involves those concepts and those beliefs.[91]

To make sense of these compressed and allusive remarks it is necessary to reintroduce Williams's version of the distinction between theoretical and practical reasoning discussed in part two. The account he gave of the asymmetry of the scientific and the ethical was reflected in his account of epistemic norms and the nature of reasoning. In a development of his earlier argument against external reasons, *Ethics and the Limits of Philosophy* claimed that practical reasoning is essentially first personal, whereas theoretical reasoning is, if first personal, only contingently so.[92] Williams argued that only a misguided assimilation of the two forms of reasoning would lead one to say that there was a reason available for agents that they could not access via sound practical deliberation from their existing 'S'. However, no such constraint operates in the case of theoretical truth.

But it does seem to me that Williams underestimated the resources available to the cognitivist in this argument. The analogy with transcendental arguments is instructive and I have already touched on how such arguments ought to be understood in Chapters 3 and 4. As Kant deployed this strategy, you begin with necessary truths about experience, and argue that various necessary conditions must hold for this experience to be possible. Two very powerful objections have been levelled against this strategy: first, that assuming necessary truths about experience begs the question by assuming the idealism that Kant sought to prove by this method (an argument particularly associated with Ralph Walker); secondly, that the entire strategy is question begging in that transcendental arguments prove only that one must hold certain beliefs, not that those beliefs are true (an argument associated particularly with Barry Stroud).[93]

Stroud's general point about transcendental arguments seems very similar to Williams's specific objection to what looks like the transcendental argument strategy in ethics.[94] Practical objectivity can only give one a reason to hold certain beliefs, not

---

91 Williams, *Ethics and the Limits of Philosophy*, 154.
92 Ibid. 67–9.
93 The key papers in the literature on transcendental arguments (for my purposes) are by Barry Stroud, Ross Harrison, and Quassim Cassam: Stroud, 'Transcendental Arguments', *Journal of Philosophy*, 65/9 (May 1968), 241–56; Harrison, 'Transcendental Arguments and Idealism'; Cassam, 'Transcendental Arguments, Transcendental Synthesis and Transcendental Idealism', *Philosophical Quarterly*, 37/149 (Oct. 1982), 355–78.
94 In this respect there seems to me to be a clear parallel between Stroud's argument against transcendental arguments and Williams's critique of the idea of a practical vindication of an ethical outlook. For the very idea of offering a transcendental argument in defence not of a cognitive

a reason to take those beliefs to be true. If Stroud's argument can be met, perhaps Williams's can too. Can the moral cognitivist avail him- or herself of a transcendental argument about what objective reasons we must recognize? I believe the answer is yes, but first it is necessary to deal with Walker's objection. I have already described Ross Harrison's argument that while Kant may have developed his arguments as part of a dual strategy of transcendental idealism and transcendental argument (both a doctrine and a method), he did not have to do so.[95] There is nothing in the methodology of transcendental arguments itself that stops such arguments beginning from contingencies (an argument I exploited in Chapter 4). We do not have to begin with necessary truths about our experience: contingent facts will suffice. In the present case, I would put the point this way: reflection is entitled to begin from the fact of a life virtuously lived.

What of Stroud's objection? The answer here is similarly direct: it is Stroud who is begging the question against those who believe that transcendental arguments establish that the subject concerned indeed has knowledge, not simply beliefs.[96] Why is it assumed, without defence, that all a transcendental argument can do is establish that one must hold certain beliefs? The correct reply is to say that such arguments prove that one must hold certain justified true beliefs that constitute knowledge, not just beliefs that fall short of their object in the way that Stroud is clearly envisaging that they will. Stroud asserts that a sceptic will be able to accept the method of transcendental argument as all this will do is prove the necessity of holding non-world involving beliefs. But why should one accept that claim without further argument? I will argue that it is fruitful to try and develop an analogous response to Williams's parallel argument about the use of transcendental arguments in ethics.

His argument had three stages:

> (1) 'The excellence or satisfactoriness of a life does not stand to that life as premiss to conclusion. Rather an agent's excellent life is characterised by having those beliefs'.[97]

The cognitivist can agree with this, but then it is also integral to the strategy of transcendental argument to be immanent and phenomenological and to begin from a virtuous life as it is lived. Kant did have the unfortunate tendency to place artificial

state such as belief but a mental state with the general direction of fit of a desire, commitment, or practical plan see Moore, 'Conative Transcendental Arguments and the Question Whether There Can Be External Reasons'.

[95] I have already drawn upon Ross Harrison's insightful paper 'Transcendental Arguments and Idealism' in Chs. 3 and 4.

[96] As Quassim Cassam remarks about Stroud's original paper, '[It] is simply asserted, without anything in the way of supporting argument, that the sceptic can always "very plausibly" substitute his weaker claim for the stronger one made by the original transcendental argument. Once such a substitution has taken place, there will indeed be a gap to be bridged but the substitution will be resisted by the Kantian. He or she might insist, for example, that it is the *existence* of physical objects and not merely belief in their existence which constitutes a necessary condition of the possibility of experience, and if this is *true*, there will simply be no gap to be bridged, by the verification principle or otherwise.' 'Transcendental Arguments, Transcendental Synthesis and Transcendental Idealism', 356.

[97] Williams, *Ethics and the Limits of Philosophy*, 154.

distance between his ethical view and that of Aristotle by representing him as holding the view that a virtuous life stood to a good life as a means to an end. But he need not be followed in that error and the cognitivist can acknowledge that we begin from a virtuous life lived 'from the inside'. We are not to see a virtuous life as a means to the end of a good life. Living virtuously is not the means to the end of leading a good life; it *is* to lead a good life. Reflection begins from the contingent starting point of a life virtuously lived and asks what makes that possible, without taking as a starting point an agent standing outside his or her life and seeing its excellence as a premiss to which that life is selected as an appropriate conclusion. That whole idea is clearly a non-starter, but the cognitivist is not committed to it.

Williams's second premiss was as follows:

> (2) 'Reflection on the excellence of a life does not itself establish the truth of judgements using those concepts or of the agent's other ethical judgements'.[98]

The question here is, simply, why not? This premiss needs some further unpacking. Perhaps the idea is this: intuitively, one can take up a practical stance independently of truth. Practical stances have the direction of fit of world to mind, not mind to world. They can thus be held independently of whether or not they are true. But the cognitivist will insist that this is beside the point, for as Williams went on to point out, we are talking here about an agent's beliefs. Furthermore, they are beliefs that are rationalized by their propositional object. Each virtue has its characteristic domain, or scope of operation, and one way to pick out the appropriate domain is in terms of the values to which the exercise of the virtue is responsive.

Williams's conclusion was:

> (3) 'Instead it shows that there is good reason (granted the commitment to an ethical life) to live a life that involves those concepts and those beliefs'.[99]

What is the force here of the word 'instead'? If we are talking about ethical beliefs, which are rationalized by their objects, and if there is good reason to lead a life which deploys such beliefs, what would lead Williams to insist on the 'instead'? In the case of Stroud's similar undercutting of transcendental arguments about beliefs in the external world, what moved Stroud was the thought that a sceptic could deploy such an argument within a narrow conception of empirical experience, proving to Stroud's satisfaction that the transcendental argument must fall short of its object. Perhaps Williams is envisaging a parallel undercutting strategy in the ethical case: a person could lead the life of a sound practical reasoner with no answering moral properties in the world, no external view to underpin the perspective of a virtuous life.

This view seems to assume that a virtuous agent could lead his or her life within a non-objectified ethical perspective, but that is assumed rather than proved. The assumption runs through Williams's concluding line of argument. He *did* allow that sound practical deliberation could lead to convergence on a given form of life. We would thus be in a situation analogous to those of people inhabiting a social world which embodied the cognitivists' model for ethical knowledge. The difference would

---

[98] Williams, *Ethics and the Limits of Philosophy*, 154.   [99] Ibid.

be that unlike the hypertraditionalists we would, collectively, know that we were living the best life qua humans, in the uniquely best social world for us. But it would not be knowledge comparable to the scientific case, for the consideration keeping the form of life on track on the reflective level would not be another piece of knowledge, but rather a matter of practical convergence, based on sound practical reasoning. There could be convergence, but it would not, at the reflective level, be world guided.

Hence, we have arrived back at the starting point of Williams's discussion: the asymmetry between the best case scenario for the objectivity of the ethical and of the scientific. He took that point to have been established, even if one is opposed to his pessimism about the availability of the thinner model of practical objectivity. It is, of course, central to this argument that it rests on the Hegelian model of objectification I set out above, not the Cartesian objectification to which Williams's critics object. Note also the proviso 'granted the commitment to an ethical life', a proviso that returns us to the discussions of Chapter 4 where I accepted the necessity of presupposing such a commitment.

I will conclude this exposition of Williams's subtle and intertwined lines of argument with two observations: first, that he assumed that a non-objectified ethical life is a possibility. It was demonstrated when I analysed the indirect vindication strategy that this is too optimistic an assumption. My view, like Altham's, is that if we grant Williams the assumptions that lead to his non-objectified diagnosis of our ethical life, there is no way back. No appeal to confidence will replace what we have lost. Secondly, if such a non-objectified form of ethical life is not possible, Williams was not entitled to assume that the beliefs that are revealed, by reflection, to the virtuous agent seeking an internal understanding of her life are anything other than true. They are items of ethical knowledge. Such an agent would thus not have been shown, 'instead', that there was merely good reason to lead her life *as if* the corresponding beliefs are true.

My analysis of Williams's arguments has identified two ways forward for the cognitivist, which in my view are interestingly complementary. One way forward challenges the model of the hypertraditional society by attacking Williams's model of knowledge. The other way forward attacks the underlying assumptions of Williams's critique of deriving ethical beliefs by bootstrapping arguments based in the perspective of practical reason. My aim is not just to develop both arguments, but to suggest that they can be interestingly interrelated and can be made mutually supportive.

CONCLUSION

Freed from the illusions of external realism, or the belief that the absolute conception provides a reflexive test of objectivity, the non-objectivist argument can be located in the proper place. It emerges from an immanent, transcendental placing of the various ways in which we conceive of different areas of thought or language. Rather than announcing itself as a sceptical conclusion, the sceptical line of reflection that emerges can be allowed, in Tractarian fashion, to show its truth. It is in this way that the non-objectivist critique emerges as the most powerful means of undermining the cognitivist argument traced so far. Underpinned by a worked-out programme in the philosophy of truth, namely minimalism, non-objectivism is also powered by a distinctive vision of a modern society, a point which will emerge more fully in the chapters to come. The suggestion is that the conditions of such societies are hostile to the possibility of moral knowledge. This point is well expressed by Williams's fable of the hypertraditional society and the corrosive effects of reflection. The pressing question is whether the cognitivist argument I have outlined has any answer to this deep and subtle challenge, and that is the subject of my next chapter. It opens Part III of this book, where a model for moral knowledge is developed that both defends the possibility of such knowledge and defends the claim that we possess significant amounts of such knowledge, even in the inhospitable conditions of society characterized by extensive reflectiveness.

PART III

CONTEXTUALIST MORAL JUSTIFICATION

7

Epistemological Contextualism

§1: Contextualism is motivated as our best response to scepticism. §2: Different varieties of contextualism are distinguished. §3: Contextualism is compared to coherence theories and two different versions of justification are discriminated, 'systematic' and 'relational'. §4: A challenge from moral pragmatism is described and rebutted §5: Contextually justified beliefs are distinguished from Kantian synthetic a priori principles.

This part of the book develops proposals for the solution of the problems described in Parts I and II (with the exception of my account of practical reasons, which has already been presented in Chapter 4). In the previous two parts I have set out an account of cognitivism, revised its view of moral motivation, and described what I take to be the strongest challenge to cognitivism, non-objectivism. I suggested that there are two ways forward if one wants to develop a revised and more plausible cognitivist position. The first is to suggest that Williams's commitment to the absolute conception concealed an ambiguity that would allow one to retain his arguments for such a conception while giving that commitment an internalist interpretation. (That internalist interpretation was to aspire to a conception of the world maximally independent of our perspective and its distinctive peculiarities, but not completely so independent.) This interpretation, I have argued, can be extended to ethical representations such that an appropriate degree of objectivity for such representations can be secured. Secondly, and intimately connected to the first proposal, I believe that the model of knowledge underpinning Williams's critical arguments must be challenged and replaced. The predicament of Williams's hypertraditionalists must be avoided, not accepted and then repaired by the invocation of social confidence.

It would be imprudent, however, not to learn from the non-objectivist challenge. Any acceptable account of moral knowledge is going to have to accommodate Williams's requirement that we need an account of moral knowledge that has the critical resources to engage with ideological beliefs. A revised cognitivist theory is going to have to explain how this would be possible within its theory of error. In this part of the book, I am going to argue that a single model of moral knowledge has these advantageous features and should be the preferred model of moral knowledge. First, in this chapter, I will characterize the model as a whole. In the next chapter I will apply it to the special case of ethics, comparing and contrasting it in particular with the methodological proposal known as reflective equilibrium. In Chapter 9 I will address the crucial question of how one defends the idea of rationality across tradition bound contexts of moral belief. I will then conclude this part of the book in Chapter 10 with an account of both how one develops an error theory for moral beliefs and how such a theory might be put to critical use by a social theory. The epistemological model that I am going to present and defend in this part is contextualism.[1] Contextualism is drawn from the pragmatist tradition, but the greatest impetus to contextualism in recent philosophy has come from Wittgenstein's *On Certainty*.[2]

1. CONTEXTUALISM AS OUR BEST RESPONSE TO PHILOSOPHICAL SCEPTICISM

A critic might note that it is all very well to argue that the adoption of contextualism allows one to defend the possibility of moral knowledge. Indeed, adopting contextualism might pave the way for an argument that we possess considerable amounts of such knowledge in spite of the inhospitable conditions for such knowledge prevalent in a modern society. This simply begs the deeper question of why one ought to adopt contextualism as one's best reflective account of knowledge in the first place. If it cannot be motivated as an independently plausible account, my use of contextualism will look opportunistic. There had better be more to be said in favour of contextualism than that it wards off the non-objectivist critique of moral knowledge. There would be a marked lack of perspective in urging that we adopt a model of knowledge as a whole in order to extricate ourselves from a comparatively local difficulty within meta-ethics.

However, this book is not primarily an essay in epistemology. It tries to put an epistemological outlook to work in connecting together problems in different areas of enquiry, namely, morality and politics. The overall aim is to establish contextualism's overall superiority to the foundationalist and coherentist models that represent the orthodoxy in these areas. So, in this part of the book, I shall try to steer an appropriate middle course between sketching in no more motivation for being a contextualist than the argument so far and offering a complete defence of contextualism as an epistemological model. The latter is a more ambitious task that goes beyond the scope of this book. I would note that some distinguished contemporary epistemologists are now defending contextualist theories, and a fuller defence of the view has been offered by others.[3]

---

[1] A concise survey of the leading historical contextualists is provided by Annis, 'A Contextualist Theory of Epistemic Justification'. In ethics the leading contextualists about justification are Larmore, in *Patterns of Moral Complexity* and Timmons, *Morality Without Foundations*. I have learnt a great deal from both of them. In epistemology more generally the greatest impetus to the development of contextualism in recent philosophy has been the pioneering work of Michael Williams, especially in *Unnatural Doubts: Epistemological Realism and the Basis of Scepticism* (Oxford: Blackwell Publishers, 1991), a work to which I am also indebted.

[2] Ludwig Wittgenstein, *On Certainty* (Oxford: Blackwell Publishers, 1975). Of the many critical studies of *On Certainty* by far the best are Marie McGinn's *Sense and Certainty: The Dissolution of Scepticism* (Oxford: Blackwell Publishers, 1989) and Thomas Morawetz, *Wittgenstein and Knowledge: The Importance of On Certainty* (Brighton: Harvester Press, 1980).

[3] Primarily by Michael Williams, but there has also been recent interest in the different version of contextualism defended by David Lewis and Peter Unger. The Lewis/Unger view spans issues in epistemology and the philosophy of language, particularly the nature of semantic competence and analogies between uses of the term 'know' and the use of indexicals. As this chapter develops

With this limited aim in view I will trace the origin of contextualism to Wittgenstein's *On Certainty* and develop it as a distinctive epistemological model while drawing on the important interpretative and critical work of Michael Williams.[4]

The fundamental reason for being a contextualist in epistemology generally is that contextualism offers the only fully satisfactory response to philosophical scepticism. This response is worked out, amongst a great deal of other cross-cutting themes, in Wittgenstein's *On Certainty*. Any interpreter of that difficult work has to admit that it is one of Wittgenstein's most recalcitrant texts. Nevertheless, there is plenty of material to be mined for those who wish to develop a contextualist account of justification in such a way as to offer a satisfactory response to philosophical scepticism. One aspect of *On Certainty* is Wittgenstein's bafflement at the confrontation between philosophical scepticism about the external world and G. E. Moore's attempted refutation of such scepticism. It is one of very few places in Wittgenstein's work where he confronts a philosophical tradition, philosophical scepticism about the external world, that is both highly developed and very sophisticated.

Crispin Wright has commented that realism about external reality combines modesty with presumption.[5] Modestly, we take ourselves to be embedded in a world, not of our making, that transcends both us and our cognitive capacities. This is, as Bernard Williams once put it, the world as it is 'anyway'.[6] Presumptuously, we take ourselves to have a great deal of knowledge of the world, if not personally, then by deference to the collective cultural achievement of organized cognitive enquiry such as the institutions and practices of modern science. Such are the facts of our situation as knowers from our everyday perspective. Philosophical scepticism typically adds to this quotidian perspective a commentary on its deeper underlying features.[7]

it will be clear that I have considerably more sympathy with Michael Williams's dissolution of scepticism than with the Lewis/Unger line of argument that accuses the sceptic of exploiting the context relativity of knowledge claims covertly to shift epistemic standards. For a useful anthology describing the new wave of semantic/epistemic contextualism, see Gerhard Preyer and George Peter (eds.), *Contextualism in Philosophy: Knowledge, Meaning and Truth* (Oxford: Oxford University Press, 2005). Duncan Prichard labels Michael Williams's view, with which I will be primarily concerned, as 'inferential contextualism'; see his 'Wittgenstein's *On Certainty* and Contemporary Anti-Scepticism', in Danièle Moyal-Sharrock and William H. Brenner (eds.), *Readings of Wittgenstein's On Certainty* (London: Macmillan, 2005).

 [4] In addition to *Unnatural Doubts* see Michael Williams, 'Still Unnatural: A Reply to Vogel and Rorty', *Journal of Philosophical Research*, 22 (Apr. 1997), 29–39; for a critical argument that specifically takes Williams as its target see also Stephen Jacobson, 'Contextualism and Global Doubts about the World', *Synthese*, 129/3 (Dec. 2001), 381–404.

 [5] Crispin Wright, 'Introduction', in *Realism, Meaning and Truth* (Oxford: Blackwell, 1986).

 [6] Bernard Williams, *Descartes: The Project of Pure Enquiry* (London: Penguin Books, 1978), 65.

 [7] Setting out the sceptic's position in the way returns us immediately to the discussion of Bernard Williams's work in, Ch. 6, above. Williams seems to take scepticism seriously in precisely this way. He connects the impulse to scepticism with the idea of a reflective, detached examination of our knowledge as a whole in the light of our concept of objectivity. That concept of objectivity is, in turn, expressed by the absolute conception. This at least seems to be true of the treatment of the issue in *Descartes*, ch. 2, 'The Project'. It further suggests why critics of Williams are misguided in arguing that he aspires to an absolutely 'self-transcendent' conception of the world which would involve concepts applied without any underlying interest. The idea is, rather, that concepts are shaped by interests, but interests marked by a certain philosophical ideal of 'purity'. In fact, I

This characterization is congenial to a certain kind of critic of our ordinary knowledge claims, the philosophical sceptic about the external world, at least in his or her modern, post-Cartesian guise. The sceptic begins by noting that ordinary knowledge claims *are* contextualized in these ways: ordinary knowledge claims are relative to a context. The sceptic then adds that it is implicit in such a context that we have a reflective capacity for transcending any such context. This is all to the good, the sceptic continues, as the context of ordinary enquiry is constitutively *impure*. Many of its ordinary features mask its real point. All we have to do in order to come to this realization is engage in philosophical reflection on what we are doing when we claim to know. Such reflection will reveal an underlying purpose to knowledge claims which ordinary epistemological contexts partially conceal (this is an aspect of their impurity). That is why we are honouring our everyday, initial, commitments and respecting an ideal of authenticity when the sceptic coaxes us out of the limitations of our everyday epistemological perspective to a purer one. The exigencies of the ordinary perspective draw us away from a deeper purpose with which we are implicitly identified. That deeper purpose is the disinterested search for truth.[8]

So the sceptic claims that ordinary contexts of enquiry both presuppose, and yet mask, such a pure interest. Yet, once the sceptic has convinced us that this is indeed our implicit commitment when we make knowledge claims, the very same context that seems to bring out the essential nature of knowledge proves to be severely damaging to the knowledge claims we wish, in fact, to make. Without going into the details of familiar sceptical procedures any further, suffice to say that the special context of philosophical reflection that the sceptic urges upon us seems both essential to, and destructive of, our ordinary claims to know. In accepting the sceptic's characterizations of our ordinary epistemic standpoint we fall victim to a gambit. Perhaps it is an instance of that which a chess player would call a 'poisoned pawn' variation, where your opponent 'carelessly' leaves a pawn in a position where it can be taken only for disaster to strike when you do.

The idea that the sceptic is asking us to honour our pre-existing commitments, by placing them in a special context which highlights what is essential about knowledge, suggests why some important lines of response to scepticism seem ultimately unpersuasive.[9] The suggestion that the sceptical project is the imposition of arbitrary or

---

think the absolute conception as a regulative ideal for certain of our representations survives the abandonment of this ideal of purity, but that wider issue goes beyond the scope of this book where I am only concerned with the idea that the absolute conception is part of an asymmetry thesis used to downgrade the status of ethical representations.

[8] Jane Heal, 'The Disinterested Search for Truth', *Proceedings of the Aristotelian Society*, 88 (1987–8), 97–108.

[9] Michael Williams catalogues, and rejects, these standard 'Wittgensteinian' strategies against the sceptic in *Unnatural Doubts* in sect. 1.4. For example, it is urged that the sceptic has changed the meanings of words or our intuitive understanding of the concept of factuality, such that in the course of the sceptical argument the sceptic can no longer mean what he or she says that they mean. Given the way in which the sceptic motivates an unusual context for the assessment of all our knowledge, this line of argument may draw upon a connection between meaning and context, such as the priority of pragmatics to semantics, or the invocation of presupposed implicit standards that the sceptic has arbitrarily violated. But Williams persuasively argues that the views of meaning

unwarranted demands on our ordinary epistemic practices seems to miss the point. If the sceptic is right, these are demands that arise naturally from our epistemic practices. These demands are not an external imposition, or arbitrary. The related idea that the sceptic is changing the meaning of words such as "know" looks similarly misguided. We seem to understand the sceptic only too well: if his or her assertions lacked sense, we would not be as troubled by them as we are. More sophisticated views about meaning which tie the pragmatics of utterance to context do not fare any better if precisely what the sceptic insists upon is that he or she has set up a novel context for our ordinary knowledge claims which highlights the underlying point of their utterance.[10] Utterances may indeed have to be 'felicitous' or 'pointful', prior to being assessed as true or false, but the sceptic can take that point on board. He or she has constructed a context which brings out what he or she takes to be 'the point' and that context *is* our everyday context, but freed from extraneous presuppositions.[11] Similarly ill-fated are verificationist responses to scepticism which seem to tie our concept of objectivity to our epistemic capacities in ways that seem to be an acknowledgement of the truth of scepticism rather than its denial.[12] It is difficult to find a formulation of the verification principle, for example, that is not more implausible than the simple and natural reasoning of the sceptic.

Wittgenstein's work has usually been associated with these different ways of undercutting the sceptical line of argument, ways that seem ultimately untenable. However, there is a distinct line of argument in *On Certainty* that promises to be more successful. It challenges the very idea that we have a context invariant epistemic position from which we can assess our knowledge as a whole. This argument strategy, developed out of Wittgenstein's work by Michael Williams, resists the sceptical line of argument that I have described by attempting nothing less than the dissolution of the traditional object of epistemological enquiry.[13] When the sceptic moves to the

and factuality such a view will draw upon are more implausible than the sceptic's arguments: we seem to understand the sceptic perfectly well. The rejection of the 'change of standards' argument in particular makes Williams different from the kind of contextualist represented by Lewis and Unger, *Unnatural Doubts*, 48–9. In particular, the Lewis/Unger focus on conversational contexts suggests a construal of what counts as a 'regress stopping' belief as a 'perhaps negotiated social matter', as David Henderson puts it in 'Epistemic Competence and Contextualist Epistemology: Why Contextualism is Not Just the Poor Person's Coherentism', *Journal of Philosophy*, 91/12 (Dec. 1994), 627–49 at 634. In the structural or inferential contextualism defended by Williams, Henderson, and in this book it is the functional role of a belief in inferential contexts that fixes the analogues of Wittgenstein's 'hinge propositions'.

[10] This line of argument, associated particularly with Stanley Cavell, is discussed very insightfully by McGinn, *Sense and Certainty*, 93 ff. Given Michael Williams's rebuttal of the view I am not convinced by Duncan Prichard's attempt to marry the two forms of contextualism, inferentialist and semantic, in 'Two Forms of Epistemological Contextualism', *Grazer Philosophische Studien*, 64 (2002), 19–55. Once again the point turns on whether or not Michael Williams permits the sceptic to make a pointful assertion of global sceptical doubt; I read Williams as understanding the sceptic as attempting to do just this, but with the falsity of epistemological realism there is no context available in which these assertions could be made. See nn. 17 and 23, below.

[11] Williams, *Unnatural Doubts*, ch. 4.

[12] Ibid., p. 132.

[13] Ibid., p. 145:, 'In tying scepticism to foundationalism, I will not be tying it so much to a particular theory of knowledge as to the idea that knowledge is the sort of thing that could be an

special context of enquiry that he or she has elaborately constructed there is nothing left to discern from such a standpoint. It is not surprising, then, that from such a standpoint knowledge is impossible.

In that sense, Michael Williams argues, there is no such thing as knowledge. At least, not in the sense that the sceptic must understand knowledge for his or her strategy to make sense.[14] He believes that this is an application of Wittgenstein's meta-philosophical moral that most philosophically interesting terms have only 'family resemblance' intensions. At the reflective level, the sceptic must treat knowledge as a theoretically integrated kind, whereas it is not. I cannot, here, treat of all of Michael Williams's subtle and detailed arguments for his conclusions. However, his overall strategy is to shift the burden of proof such that sceptical doubts no longer appear as 'natural', arising naturally from our human perspective as knowers or demanded by the concept of knowledge itself.[15]

object of knowledge *at all*'. There is a subtle difference here between the arguments Williams derives from *On Certainty* and McGinn's interpretation of that work in *Sense and Certainty*. McGinn's procedure is to undermine a key presupposition of the sceptic's enquiry, namely, that our relation to 'taken for granted' truisms that both structure and give point to our epistemological enquiries is an epistemic relation. McGinn argues that in the relevant sense our relation is not epistemic but *practical*. This interpretation seems to me to give rise to three problems. The first, stressed by Williams, is that on this reading we have only shown that our relation to these framework sentences is not usually epistemic, and we have not prevented the sceptic insisting that we embed them in a special context in which our relation to framework judgements changes to an epistemic one: see *Unnatural Doubts*, 27–30. Second, Williams also points out that claiming that framework judgements are both groundless and yet factual threatens to put us in the unfortunate position of engaging in an unmotivated revision in the idea of factuality: see *Unnatural Doubts*, 28. I would add a third argument, namely, that McGinn's response to the sceptic looks like a second order dogmatism, namely, a dogmatic insistence on the priority of practice over theory. See also *Unnatural Doubts*, 65–6. This line of interpretation of *On Certainty* as involving a 'non-epistemic', practical relation to our world view is continued in Danièle Moyal-Sharrock's *Understanding Wittgenstein's On Certainty* (London: Macmillan, 2004).

14 Thus, as Michael Williams clearly argues, his position sounds remarkably like a conclusion of the 'New Humeans' he opposes: Barry Stroud, Thomas Nagel, and Sir Peter Strawson. There is no such thing as **knowledge** as that concept is ordinarily understood. The central claim of his book is that this conclusion can be defused by being relativized to a context, but in a sense the New Humeans remain conditionally correct in their conclusion. *If* knowledge is understood as the sceptic understands it, or as the traditional philosophical approach to knowledge is forced to represent it, then there is no such thing as knowledge. But one can reject the antecedent by adopting inferential contextualism.

15 One of the most appealing motivations for Williams's project is that it is a response to the 'New Humean' conclusion that philosophical scepticism is the inevitable outcome of certain questions that are natural to us and expressive of our humanity. Further, such scepticism yields results about human knowledge that are both devastating and yet incredible; that the common sense certainties of ordinary life remain unscathed from the quotidian perspective. The result is a position which Williams dubs 'bi-perspectivalism'. It is philosophically threatening in two ways: it both suggests that sceptical doubts arise naturally from our ordinary epistemic perspective and also insinuates that the main lines of philosophical response to scepticism are, by contrast, artificial products of theory. Compared to the minimal assumptions that the sceptic draws upon, the various baroque constructions in the philosophy of mind and language needed to rebut sceptical claims place the anti-sceptic in a difficult dialectical predicament. What remains of great value in the New Humeans' position is, as Williams notes, that it highlights the context sensitivity of sceptical doubt, *Unnatural Doubts*, 10, 35.

In Williams's own terms he offers a 'theoretical', as opposed to a 'therapeutic', diagnosis of the errors of scepticism.[16] This is the contrast between therapeutic-ally dissolving sceptical arguments and tracing their deficiencies to false theoretical assumptions, centrally assumptions about knowledge itself. The aim is to demon-strate that the case for scepticism rests not on innocent platitudes that no one could reject, but on contentious theoretical assumptions in the guise of such platitudes. This theoretical diagnosis begins from Barry Stroud's canonical characterization of the four key elements of the traditional epistemological project as involving the *assessment* of the *totality* of our knowledge of an *objective* world from a *detached* perspective.[17] This project is, Michael Williams argues, deeply connected to a commitment to founda-tionalism such that the project cannot be sustained without it.[18] But the foundation-alism flows not just from a prior commitment to viewing experience of the world as prior to knowledge of it, *but from the totality condition*.[19] This is the idea that we can assess our knowledge of the world taken as a whole. The sceptic's desire for a general account of our knowledge evolves into a demand for the assessment of the totality of our knowledge. A requirement of generality thereby becomes a requirement of total-ity. Obviously, in the light of my developing argument about moral knowledge, this is a crucial assumption about the structure of sceptical arguments that I can exploit for my own ends. Bernard Williams's hypertraditionalists assumed that, at the reflective level, they could survey all possible developments of the ethical and see which of them constituted a form of ethical knowledge for them. The counter-argument is that at that level there *is* no object of epistemological reflection to examine. This is, of course, the local application of a general truth, given that the hypertraditionalists were, after all, just asking a question about moral knowledge, not knowledge as a whole. But if the general idea of taking up such a standpoint is flawed, an analogous problem arises for the issue of surveying moral knowledge as a whole. But I accept that the analogy must be further specified.

To undercut the idea that it is possible to survey knowledge as a whole, a positive model of the structure of knowledge is required which explains why this is impossible. It is that model that helps me to identify the particular error made by the hypertradi-tionalists. Contextualism supplies such a model, and its account of the local character of justification is the basis for taking the general conclusion that knowledge cannot be surveyed and applying it to the particular case of Bernard Williams's hypertradition-alists. The hypertraditionalists are taken, by reflection, from a perspective within their ordinary knowledge acquiring practices. Those practices embody a history of success-ful knowledge acquisition and in that way the standards internal to their tradition are

---

[16] This important distinction is made initially at p. xvii of the 'Preface' of *Unnatural Doubts* and is discussed again at pp. 35–7, *passim*. It is reiterated in Williams, 'Still Unnatural: A Reply to Vogel and Rorty'.

[17] Williams assembles these characterizations of scepticism from Barry Stroud, *The Significance of Philosophical Scepticism* (Oxford: Oxford University Press, 1989), 81–2, 209 at *Unnatural Doubts*, 22.

[18] Williams, *Unnatural Doubts*, 41: 'No matter how natural or intuitive sceptical arguments appear, or can be made to appear, they cannot be divorced from epistemological foundationalism'. See also n. 13, above.

[19] Williams, *Unnatural Doubts*, 89–93.

warranted as reliable. (I will discuss these presuppositions of their practice in the next two chapters.) The hypertraditionalists are, in Williams's extension to the thought experiment, taken to the new perspective of hyperreflection and now those within the hypertraditional society are no longer guaranteed to have knowledge at the reflective level. However, I would argue that this is simply a reflection of the more general truth that knowledge claims are context specific. The conclusion in the moral case reflects more general features about knowledge. The 'loss' of knowledge in this case is traceable to false foundationalist assumptions about knowledge built into the model. In the original argument Bernard Williams set up the question in this way:

The very general kind of judgement that is in question here—a judgement using a very general concept—is essentially a product of reflection. . . . In relation to this society, the question now is: Does the practice of the society, in particular the judgements that members of the society make, imply answers to reflective questions about that practice, questions they have never raised?[20]

Before transferring the onus of proof in answering it to the cognitivist:

There are two different ways in which we can see the activities of the hypertraditional society. They depend on different models of ethical practice. One of them may be called an 'objectivist' model . . . we shall see the members of the society as trying, in their local way, to find the truth about values . . . *We shall then see their judgements as having these general implications.* [emphasis added][21]

That particular knowledge claims have 'general implications' impels the move to the hyperreflective standpoint. But this move is foreshadowed by how Williams described ordinary practice in this case. Williams had a precisely specified model of how knowledge was deployed in a hypertraditional society that contrasted the ordinary perspective of the hypertraditionalists with their hyperreflective perspective. But while this argument favoured the conclusion that we should treat the hypertraditionalists' ethical practices in a non-objectivist way, it should be clear that a contextualist response to this model is that its use in this case is contentious. From the contextualist's perspective it is not clear that at the hyperreflective level there is, any longer, an object of knowledge to be assessed. But the dissolution of the object of epistemological enquiry at the hyperreflective level merely indicates the context sensitivity of knowledge claims. The contextualist charge, then, is that foundationalism appears built into Williams's description of the hypertraditionalists and their relation to their moral knowledge.

In order to forestall the sceptical ascent to a pure context of enquiry, Wittgenstein suggests that we need a more phenomenologically accurate account of how we typically make and defend knowledge claims. This description would allow us to resist the sceptic's seductive account of the implicit commitments of our ordinary epistemic context. In the context of our everyday epistemic enquiries we take the knowledge claims that are to be assessed to be framed by judgements that do not themselves come into question, namely, 'framework judgements':

20 Bernard Williams, *Ethics and the Limits of Philosophy*, 146.   21 Ibid., 147.

I did not get my picture of the world by satisfying myself of its correctness; nor do I have it because I am satisfied of its correctness. No: it is the inherited background against which I distinguish between the true and the false . . . if I were to say 'It is my unshakeable conviction that, etc.', this means that in the present case too that I have not consciously arrived at the conviction by following a particular line of thought, but that it is anchored in all my questions and answers, so anchored that I cannot touch it.[22]

These judgements are at the centre of Wittgenstein's attention in *On Certainty*. They are important to his diagnosis of the confrontation between Moore and the sceptic. It seemed to Wittgenstein that Moore was entering his claims one stage too late in the argument such that Moore's claims sound as absurd as the sceptical doubts they are attempting to deny. Wittgenstein means more than that framework judgements are a presupposed range of judgements, which provide a context for the particular judgements that we are evaluating on any particular occasion. He is going further than suggesting that our judgements are normally assessed in the light of other judgements that 'stand fast'. He is, in other words, going beyond coherentism in order to argue for a controversial thesis about the status of presupposed 'judgements of the frame' or 'hinge propositions'.

Such judgements have the following puzzling features: while they do not, in any given context, normally come up for testing, they are only contingently true. They can themselves, in different contexts, come up for assessment. Yet they seem to be context determining, playing a peculiar functional role. It is perfectly in order for a historian, attempting to assess whether Napoleon died on St Helena from natural causes or from poisoning, to assess a range of relevant hypotheses about the cause of Napoleon's death. But should her enquiries encompass the possibility that the world only came into existence half an hour ago, complete with all the evidence suggestive of what we take to prove its correct age? After all, if that hypothesis were correct, her researches about Napoleon would have to take a very different turn. But we do not think that when the historian announces the results of her research, she is negligent in not discounting this possibility. The best summary of the point Wittgenstein wants to explain is that given by Meredith Williams:

The truth of this methodological proposition (that the Earth has existed long before my birth) is a causal condition for doing history and is logically assumed by historical enquiry. It is not, however, an epistemic condition. In other words, in order to do history and to be justified in one's findings, it is not necessary to establish or determine the truth of that proposition. It simply does not figure in the justification of an historical claim.[23]

So, far from making a coherentist point, Wittgenstein is drawing attention to a class of cases that pose a problem for coherentism. According to the coherentist, such framework judgements are part of our corporate body of beliefs that comes up for testing as a whole, even if only tacitly or indirectly. This seems to miss the puzzling features of framework judgements on which Wittgenstein focused. They

---

[22] Wittgenstein, *On Certainty*, §34.
[23] Meredith Williams, 'Wittgenstein, Kant and the Metaphysics of Experience', *Kant-Studien*, 81/1 (1990), 69–88 at 80–1.

do not function as the coherentist says they should and so coherentism fails to take into account all aspects of their puzzling functional role. (I will say more on how coherentism misrepresents the character of justification below.)

As a phenomenological description of our ordinary epistemic practices Wittgenstein's account seems accurate. But how can this pose a problem for a sceptic who accepts the appearances, but who argues that our ordinary epistemic context implicitly commits us to its own transcendence? Michael Williams suggests that it is, in fact, the sceptic who is embarrassed, when it turns out that he or she levers us out of our ordinary epistemological contexts by adopting false theoretical assumptions, primarily foundationalist assumptions. As Michael Williams puts it, 'The sceptic tries to assess all our knowledge of the world, all at once'; but this presupposes that at that level of generality there is such a phenomenon to assess.[24] Williams urges, instead, irrealism about such an object of general epistemological reflection, suggesting that the sceptic's error is to treat the concept of **knowledge** as a natural kind concept.[25] The sceptic assumes that we are studying, in epistemology, fixed and stratified relations of epistemic priority and dependence that are independent of our explanatory and classificatory interests. Michael Williams calls this the doctrine of 'epistemological realism'.[26] It is the rejection of this doctrine that underlies his insistence that the rejection of foundationalism, and hence of the traditional sceptical project, does not lead one to a form of coherence theory:

The only alternative to epistemological realism, hence to foundationalism, is a contextualist view of justification. This is because contextualism alone takes issue with foundationalism's deepest theoretical commitment, which is to the idea that beliefs possess an intrinsic epistemological status . . . a contextualist epistemology brings with it a partly 'externalist' conception of knowledge . . . [which] is acceptable only in the aftermath of a successful theoretical diagnosis of sceptical problems . . . My contextualist view of knowledge explains the context sensitivity of the sceptic's results and threatens to convict him of a fallacy: confusing the discovery that knowledge is impossible under the conditions of philosophical reflection with the discovery, under the conditions of philosophical reflection, that knowledge is generally impossible.[27]

The aim, then, is to resist the idea that we can examine the totality of our knowledge from a special epistemological standpoint by denying that from that standpoint there is anything to examine. The traditional object of epistemological enquiry has been

---

[24] Williams, *Unnatural Doubts*, p. xx.
[25] Ibid., ch. 3, sect. 3. I think this aspect of Williams's view is overlooked in Duncan Prichard's otherwise helpful discussion in 'Wittgenstein's *On Certainty* and Contemporary Anti-Scepticism', where Prichard focuses on Williams's apparent concession that the sceptic's claims are true and warrantedly assertible in her context. Taking that claim as established, Prichard then argues that what does the work in Williams's view is externalism, but if one can rebut scepticism by being an externalist we don't need the further details of Williams's inferentialist view. I think this overlooks Williams's treatment of the totality condition and his dissolution of the traditional object of sceptical enquiry. At the level of assessing 'all our knowledge of the world, all at once' there is nothing to assess. I think Williams clearly takes the view that his externalism plays a supplementary role in his overall argument against the traditional sceptic.
[26] Williams, *Unnatural Doubts*, ch. 3.
[27] Ibid., p. xx.

dissolved. From the contextualist perspective, there are a variety of appropriate stand-points each shaped by the multiple interests of enquiry and all we can pick out is a multiply realized functional kind—the class of 'taken for granted' statements that are fixed by the direction of the enquiry at hand.

Thus, Williams's contextualism makes two basic claims: first, that Wittgenstein's 'hinge propositions' pick out a functionally defined set of beliefs, in that one and the same belief may function in one context as a hinge proposition that helps to identify the inferential structure of that context while in another context it may itself come up for testing. Secondly, there is no pure context of enquiry underpinning our ordinary practices of enquiry and that in moving from one context to another they are, simply, different contexts that do not conceal an underlying inferential structure. The hinge propositions, combined with substantive truisms that are also taken for granted (but in a different sense), serve to individuate contexts.[28]

While I am not entirely happy with every part of Michael Williams's view, these seem to me to be interesting and important distinctions about knowledge as a whole. I would not, as Williams does, put his main point in terms of the rejection of the idea that **knowledge** is a natural kind concept, which he further identifies with the idea of picking out a referent with a theorizable essence. There are, after all, many theories of phenomena that do not have underlying essences in the sense fixed by Williams's paradigm of a natural kind term, and that paradigm is itself a subject of controversy.[29] It is not clear, for example, how closely the philosophically idealized notion of a natural kind term in recent philosophy of language corresponds to the actual classificatory practices of contemporary science. The main component of the view that I do want to endorse is viewing the objects of epistemic appraisal func-tionally, in terms of their extrinsic, relational properties. If that is what the denial of epistemological realism is primarily directed at then I am happy to deny it. These are certainly very general reasons for adopting contextualism in epistemology. It offers a uniquely satisfying response to the philosophical sceptic. One can also add, however, that contextualism offers the most accurate phenomenological account of our ordin-ary epistemic practice and elucidates several of its key features. In the next section I will further explain why contextualism should be our preferred reflective account of our ordinary practice of entering knowledge claims by supplying some of the addi-tional necessary detail to my account of contextualism.

---

[28] Prichard, in 'Wittgenstein's *On Certainty* and Contemporary Anti-Scepticism', takes which propositions are functioning as hinge propositions in a context to individuate contexts. That seems to me exegetically faithful to Wittgenstein but it seems to me that for a fully convincing account of how one individuates contexts one has to add the role played by the kind of topic-specific truisms central to Richard Miller's account of substantive rationality in *Fact and Method: Explanation, Confirmation and Reality in the Natural and the Social Sciences* (Princeton: Princeton University Press, 1987), 219–22. I will discuss this further element of contextualism below. A similar idea features in Williams's account as 'topical' or 'disciplinary' constraints, see e.g. *Unnatural Doubts*, 117–19, 122–3.

[29] See e.g. the insightful discussion of natural kind terms in John Dupré, *Disorder of Things: Metaphysical Foundations of the Disunity of Science* (Cambridge, Mass.: Harvard University Press, 1993). I take it that it is strategically inadvisable for Michael Williams's argument to be hostage to the correct view of the nature of theoretical kinds.

2. ANALYSING CONTEXTUALISM

There are now several different views in the secondary literature, all of which merit the title 'contextualism'.[30] At the outset, we have to be clear about whether or not we are discussing the epistemology of first personal belief systems, or the system of knowledge, impersonally or collectively considered. This is a particularly important point for the contextualist. An issue that will recur throughout the discussions of this part is whether or not contextualism can be reduced to a set of pragmatic constraints, operative in actual enquiry, that are not reflected at the level of the knowledge system as a whole. It is not surprising, says the critic, that the first personal belief systems of agents appear to be accurately described by contextualism. Agents have limited resources and cannot aspire to a full or complete justification of all their beliefs. They operate with defeasible, taken for granted, principles in order to avoid cognitive overload; this does not mean that such pragmatism is justified. Ordinary agents need to free themselves from ordinary concerns in order to align their beliefs with the structure of genuine knowledge. One way in which one might formulate this contrast is by using the positivist distinction between a 'context of discovery' and a 'context of justification'.[31] Applying this distinction to a person's beliefs, first personally considered, might be one way to formulate this rejoinder that contextualism is, as it were, a shallow view that does not look beyond the pragmatics of belief acquisition to an underlying context of justification that is coherentist in form.

Note the assumptions of this line of argument: that our ordinary knowledge gathering activities involve practical compromise over their essential point and that it is essentially a cost/benefit matter how much care one takes over the ratio of truth to falsity in one's beliefs. These are both assumptions that play directly into the hands of the sceptic in the manner I described above. Nevertheless, this is a plausible rebuttal (or deflation) of contextualism, so I will immediately address it. In my view, contextualism derives a great deal of plausibility from its realistic account of actual first personal belief systems and of first personal justification. But it takes such systems as an accurate reflection of the structure of knowledge claims as a whole even when they are reconstructed in a context of justification that eliminates pragmatic constraints. The way that beliefs are represented and justified in individuals is analogous to the way in which knowledge claims are embedded in impersonal or collective contexts of justification. I will make two assumptions in this book: that contextualism is very plausible as the most realistic account of the psychologies of actual knowers and that contextualists should place little weight on this. The important argument is whether or not this first personal account accurately mirrors an objective account of the structure of the knowledge system.[32]

[30] See Timmons's extremely helpful analysis of the different forms of contextualism in *Morality Without Foundations*, ch. 5.
[31] For a classic formulation of the distinction see Hans Reichenbach, *Experience and Prediction: An Analysis of the Foundations and Structure of Knowledge* (Chicago: Chicago University Press, 1961), sect. 1, 'The Three Tasks of Epistemology'.
[32] This is a clear point of contrast with Timmons. He focuses on the idea of holding an individual epistemically responsible and is very much concerned to ensure that most people's

Putting the point in this way might suggest that I have not absorbed Michael Williams's central point: the rejection of epistemological realism. I seem to be talking about the knowledge system as though it possessed a structure that is independent of the practice of enquiry. To use that unhappy term, I am talking like an 'external realist' about the knowledge system. But it was that kind of talk that Williams wanted therapeutically to dissolve. This concern is misplaced; my view is that it is still useful to talk about the structure of knowledge, but that this is not a commitment to viewing it as a structure independent of enquiry to which such enquiry must conform. That is the realism Williams rejected. More generally, while I concede that contextualism has its origins in the pragmatist tradition, I do not want to associate contextualism too strongly with pragmatism and the pragmatic refutation of scepticism.[33]

There are various reasons why I want to call my view 'contextualism' and to distance it from pragmatism, even when those with very similar positions, such as Putnam and Larmore, call themselves moral pragmatists. Two of the main reasons for my rejection of pragmatism is the belief that there is not much point in discussing the aim of enquiry in general, and that in ethics the very idea of an end of enquiry is particularly problematic as I will argue in Chapter 9. In this particular context, the reason for not calling my view pragmatist is that the pragmatic refutation of scepticism is usually a variant of the change of standards argument. The sceptic is presented as arbitrarily imposing an unduly high set of standards or costs on the ordinary agent, an argument rebutted by an appeal to the different standards implicit in the pragmatics of our ordinary practice. That does not seem to me, as I have said, to be a satisfactory response to the sceptic and in that sense contextualism represents an advance on one standard pragmatic refutation of scepticism. Contextualism understands the sceptic's basic strategy as asking us to respect the underlying commitments of our actual practice. He or she does not arbitrarily demand different standards or costs, other than those that authentically represent our position as people offering, challenging, and assessing knowledge claims. Pragmatism does not understand the sceptical case in this way, so it is unable to rebut it. (None the less, I will return to this issue of the relationship between contextualism and pragmatism in Section 4, below.)

---

epistemic credentials pass the kind of requirements for knowledge that he imposes. He also makes the apparently odd claim that the claims to knowledge of individuals do not have to be derived from their knowledge of a true moral theory. The reason for this seems to be that he takes moral theories to be always generalist, whereas the moral judgements of individuals are particularist, and that in fact people do not reason from moral theories to their particular judgements. My view is that while I owe the reader an account of holding an individual epistemically responsible, that should be a derived requirement from one's account of propositional justification. In Ch. 8 I will also argue that there need be no presupposition of the truth of generalism about moral principles and that we might want to say different things about the general basis for moral verdicts (evidence) and 'all things considered' practical verdicts themselves.

[33] Some of these distinctions between contextualism and moral pragmatism will come into explicit focus in Ch. 9. The most developed application of pragmatist ideas to these issues is in Cheryl Misak, *Truth, Politics, Morality: Pragmatism and Deliberation* (London: Routledge, 2000) a work which, like this one, shows the influence of Wiggins and explicitly applies Peircean ideas to morality and politics.

I want to focus not so much on the belief systems of individuals, as on the structures of enquiry within which individuals work, sometimes as individuals, more usually as members of cooperative teams. I do not doubt that the knowledge of the vast majority of people about moral issues is, in fact, derived from learning and testimony. I am not, in this book, going to focus on the limited cognitive resources of individual thinkers, but on our collective resources of knowledge to which they defer.

Furthermore, a little more needs to be said about dependence on context, namely, the externalist part of contextualism. Contextualism is, as Michael Williams argues, both partially reliabilist and partially externalist.[34] From within an ordinary epistemic context, a responsible knower only has to rule out relevant alternatives to his or her knowledge claim. A view implicit in Wittgenstein, but more fully developed in Austin, according to this argument knowledge involves justification only relative to relevant alternatives. The consideration of such alternatives is grounded on the two principles of 'reasonable sufficiency' and 'definite lack'.[35] This view is externalist in that to know, one has only to know in normal conditions. One does not, in addition, have to know that the presupposed conditions are normal. The framework judgements that are presupposed by the entering of an ordinary claim to knowledge are not epistemologically prior to such knowledge in the sense that they must be known before the knowledge claim can be legitimated. This is precisely what the externalist denies. Similarly, the view is partially reliabilist: in normal circumstances, ruling out relevant alternatives is a reliable way of forming true beliefs.[36]

In the position that I will develop, these aspects of contextualism are clarified by being placed in a particular kind of social context of enquiry. The context is afforded by a tradition of reliable knowledge acquisition. In order to know, one has to be embedded in an epistemic context which involves the following elements: a presupposed set of framework beliefs, a set of disciplinary parameters, and, in the case of ordinary worldly knowledge, one's embodied and embedded engagement with the world. Part of such engagement is those normal conditions that are presupposed by an externalist account of knowledge.

That leads on to the key and definitive thesis of contextualism: following Mark Timmons, I will call this the claim of 'structural contextualism'.[37] It is a position that is a rival to foundationalist and coherentist models of epistemic justification as a thesis about the structure of justification. Justification can legitimately terminate

---

[34] Williams, *Unnatural Doubts*, 294: 'Externalism is not to be equated with pure reliabilism . . . a theory of knowledge is externalist if it allows us knowledge (or justified belief) provided that certain conditions on knowledge are in fact met, rather than known (or justifiably believed) to be met. To count as externalist, a theory need not claim (as do pure reliabilist theories) that all conditions on knowledge or justification are of this character, only that some are'.

[35] The classic paper by J. L. Austin is, 'Other Minds', *Proceedings of the Aristotelian Society*, suppl. 20 (1946), 148–87, repr. in Austin, *Philosophical Papers* (Oxford: Oxford University Press, 1961) and it is frequently cited by those contextualists influenced by Lewis and Unger who want to press the 'change of standards' argument against the sceptic. Let me reiterate that I agree with Michael Williams that that argument, on its own, will not trouble the sceptic without a prior dissolution of epistemological realism.

[36] Williams, *Unnatural Doubts*, 96.

[37] See Timmons, *Morality Without Foundations*, 186–90, 206–12.

on beliefs that are basic relative to a given context of enquiry. This answer to the regress of justification problem is, like coherentism, holistic. But, in a phrase that seems oxymoronic, it is only 'locally holistic'. The kind of holistic relations between beliefs characteristic of coherentism occur in local pockets of beliefs, bounded by framework judgements. Those judgements function 'foundationally', but do not have the intrinsic mark of epistemic merit characteristic of foundationalism and can themselves play a different functional role in a different context. The distinctive contextualist claim is that to understand the functioning of a contextually basic belief we need to understand its role in a larger functioning structure, namely, a context of enquiry.

The best explanation of why contextualism is the neglected option in epistemology is that it has been unable to break the orthodox dichotomy between foundationalist and coherentist models of justification. But in fact, the way contextualism abandons the key assumption that structures both of these theories and the debate between them is one of its most revolutionary features. Contextualism abandons the idea that we can discuss knowledge as a whole, and a conception of the system of knowledge as a unified and integrated system with global and systemic features. Underpinning this, in turn, is the rejection of epistemological realism, in Michael Williams's sense.

At the level of individual beliefs, contextualism claims that a belief is justified if it is legitimated in a context of enquiry via the elimination of competing alternatives. Thus the epistemic status and epistemic role of a belief *varies with context*. Thus beliefs, in contextualism, have no intrinsic epistemic status. Contextualism shares with a coherence theory the assumption that the epistemic legitimacy of a belief is an extrinsic, functional property of that belief rather than an intrinsic property. By contrast, foundationalism must regard a class of beliefs as intrinsically epistemically privileged, to terminate the regress of justification. This assumption of intrinsic merit within foundationalism leads to three unfortunate consequences. The first is that beliefs are assumed to fall into natural epistemic classes; the second is that methodology must conform to an intrinsic order of reasons; the third is that knowledge can be secured only if an intrinsic mark of epistemic merit can be identified in individual beliefs. This third requirement leads naturally to the demand for certainty.[38] The foundationalist view encourages rigid, hierarchical models of epistemic justification. As we have seen, the three requirements, taken together, invite global scepticism, since the attempt to find an appropriately basic class of self-justifying beliefs has been beset by sceptical challenges. This point will be discussed in more detail in the next chapter when I discuss different interpretations, within moral epistemology, of Rawls's method of reflective equilibrium.

Contexts function as the framework of enquiries. They are themselves structured by a given problem solving situation. The advantages of such an account, applied in general epistemology are these: we can explain how the focused point of an enquiry can explain the structure of a context. Within a context, we can explain how some beliefs structure a context while others come up for appraisal. Furthermore, we can

---

[38] This is brought out very clearly in Bernard Williams, *Descartes*, ch. 2.

within a context explain which relevant alternatives a person must exclude in order justifiably to hold his or her beliefs. This local character of contextual justification is an important feature of the view for my purposes as it puts pressure on the idea that in epistemological enquiry we can survey knowledge as a whole. While an important part of the view, it is also controversial and merits further consideration.

3. CONTEXTUALISM, COHERENTISM, AND KNOWLEDGE AS A WHOLE

The key advantage of contextualism is that it rejects Stroud's totality condition. It abandons the idea that we can discuss knowledge as a whole, and the related conception of the system of knowledge as a unified and integrated system with systemic features that transcends the actual practice of enquiry. The traditional alternative to foundationalism, coherence theory, replaces this model with a holistic model of justification. To introduce some of the key elements of contextualism, I will contrast it with a version of coherence theory, the corporatist version developed by Quine. The reason I select Quine's unusual version of coherentism, in spite of its much criticized defects, is that his version focuses attention on a salient point for the purposes of my argument. That is the way in which a coherentist must view the knowledge system holistically and globally even when justification is viewed locally.[39]

The coherentist takes a belief to be justified if it coheres with other beliefs already taken to be justified. Justification cannot proceed unless some beliefs are taken to be legitimate. So the coherentist does *not* regard beliefs as falling into natural epistemic classes, nor does methodology conform to an intrinsic order of reasons. In the coherentist account, beliefs need not possess an intrinsic mark of epistemic status, since they inherit this status from their relations to other legitimate beliefs, or from forming part of a total system that is maximally explanatory. I will return to this important ambiguity below.

Coherentism faces two central objections. The first is that it cannot tell the difference between a legitimate belief system and a coherent fairy story and thus must rely on a pre-established harmony between knowledge and the world left unexplained in the theory.[40] This objection rests on which concept of empirical content the theory deploys. Since that is a matter of considerable controversy I will rest little on this first objection, which seems resistible in one way or another. Nevertheless it seems to raise

---

[39] W. V. O. Quine, 'Two Dogmas of Empiricism', in *From A Logical Point of View*, 2nd edn. (Cambridge, Mass.: Harvard University Press, 1980). I have not taken Quine as representative of coherentism in order to beg any substantive questions against coherentism. I am well aware that Quine's view has been strongly criticized because of its 'narrow' conception of empirical content. I have selected it because ethical coherentism cannot, as I have noted, appeal to a conception of empirical content and Quine's view focuses on the global and holistic model of the knowledge system implicit in all coherentist theories.

[40] For those who view this as a tired response to coherentism there is a powerful version of the objection in Ralph Walker's account of coherence theories of knowledge and of truth in *The Coherence Theory of Truth: Realism, Anti-Realism, Idealism* (London and New York: Routledge, 1989) esp. chs. 9–11.

an issue in the ethical case that has no analogue in the more general epistemological debate.[41]

It seems to me to be very unlikely that those interested in applying a coherence theory to ethical justification can supply any analogue for a representational theory of perceptual content in which we are to see our perceptual input as constituting fragments of an objective, three-dimensional world, as opposed to sensory data.[42] Coherentism seems vulnerable to the coherent fairy story objection only if empirical content is viewed in austerely empiricist terms as not intrinsically intentional or representational. Our task is then the construction of a mosaic in which the pattern (the representation of the objective world) is a matter of our design, rather than the constrained construction of a jigsaw puzzle, as in a more realistic account of empirical content. However, there seems to be no sense in which the ethical coherentist can explain our ethical experience in similar representationalist or intentionalist terms. So while the coherent fairy story objection is not much of a problem for a coherentist about empirical knowledge, I suggest that it is a little more problematic for the coherentist in ethics, who is looking for coherence amongst theoretical beliefs which are, as it were, unsupported in their coherence. So even if one does not set much store by the 'coherent fairy story' objection as a general criticism of coherentism, it has a little more force in the case of coherentist models of ethical knowledge. (This issue will be raised again in the next chapter when I examine interpretations of reflective equilibrium as a coherentist theory.)

The second, more damaging, set of objections, which apply to coherentism generally, is that it makes justification practically impossible and that it misrepresents the practice of justification. These are, for my purposes, the most important objections. Contextualists pick up on the second point to develop their genuine alternative to coherentist models as a whole. To see the necessity for a revision of the coherentist argument, it is necessary to demonstrate a representative failure of a coherence view, such as Quine's corporatist epistemology that emphasizes the holistic nature of justification. Quinean holism extends not only across all the sentences in the corporate body of knowledge, but also to those second order sentences that describe our policies of legitimation. Methodological principles governing belief revision, ranging from tactical ad hoc principles to strategic principles of logic are equally revisable if the resulting system is maximally explanatory. Adopting arguments from Duhem, Quine argued that recalcitrant experiences could lead to the revision of any sentence in the total fabric of beliefs that we hold true, and could lead us to any revision of our methodology. Methodological principles are as likely to be revised as any of our beliefs.

The contextualist objects that this approach makes justification practically impossible. Such a thoroughgoing holism leaves us unable to set up a context of enquiry and hence makes knowledge impossible. For any given enquiry, some beliefs must be assumed to be held fixed in that context otherwise every investigation would

[41] See Michael DePaul's discussion in *Balance and Refinement: Beyond Coherence Methods of Moral Inquiry* (London, Routledge: 1986), ch. 4.
[42] Michael Williams offers a defence of this view of the content of perceptual knowledge in an earlier book, *Groundless Belief* (Oxford: Basil Blackwell, 1977,) e.g. at 101–15.

involve testing the whole of knowledge.[43] I will draw on an argument of Crispin Wright's which proves that such global holism is not just a pragmatic embarrassment, but in truth self-defeating.[44] Wright argues that Quinean 'recalcitrance' in our willingness to surrender central beliefs can mean only that we are spontaneously inclined to accept two observation sentences 'P' and 'not-Q', while also accepting a theory T, the underlying logic of which L incorporates the principle 'if P then Q'. The Quinean now argues that we have a choice in the face of recalcitrant experience: we can revise T, 'P', or 'not-Q'. But Wright responds that Quine should also add the logic, L, as a candidate for revision. If this is so, then we should add the meta-meta-theoretical principle W: 'theory T plus logic L entails that "if P then Q" '. So now everything is revisable: theory T, logic L, observation statements 'P' and 'Q', and meta-meta-principle W. But now the only point to our choice is minimizing future recalcitrance, and Wright points out that now everything is revisable this decision is just relativized to our choices. So far so good for Quine, who would simply argue that minimizing future recalcitrance is indeed our only guide. But Wright presses the argument home: whichever choice we make will involve the acceptance or rejection of the meta-meta-principle W, but the acceptance or rejection of W determines *whether or not P or Q is blamed for recalcitrance*. Once everything is a matter of choice, the sense of a constrained rational policy is lost.[45] In my view this is a decisive argument against Quinean holism, which focuses on a defect in his theory which does not rest on controversial assumptions about empirical content.[46] It is a central defect of coherentism per se, namely, treating the knowledge system as a global and unified system.

Quine might seem to have an answer to this problem since his model of science is covertly hierarchical. Recalcitrance is passed through the web of belief to its core, namely, our most fundamental logical and mathematical beliefs.[47] But here I would argue that one is being misled by the metaphor. Quine can substantiate the centrality or fundamentality of such beliefs only in terms of behavioural reluctance to abandon

[43] This is, of course, a conclusion that Quine accepts.

[44] Crispin Wright, 'Scientific Realism, Observation and the Verification Principle', in Graham MacDonald and Crispin Wright (eds.), *Fact, Science and Morality* (Oxford: Blackwell, 1986), 247–74.

[45] Ibid. This point marks one of the losses Quine incurred in totally dismantling Carnap's approach to analyticity. The arguments of 'Two Dogmas' undermines not simply the analytic/synthetic distinction but also Carnap's internal/external questions distinction that allowed Carnap to justify methodological precepts pragmatically. For suggestions as to how one might defend a metaphysically innocent notion of analyticity which would not fall foul of Quine's strictures, nor support the conception of a priori knowledge that was his ultimate target, see McDowell, *Mind and World*, 156–61 but esp. 157.

[46] Although Quine's 'narrow' conception of empirical content is undoubtedly deficient in that regard also, on which see further McDowell, *Mind and World*, 156–61.

[47] I have presented Quine's theory as a form of coherence theory and I believe Quine himself would view his theory in this light. But on this point—possessing an internally hierarchical structure—the theory is covertly hierarchical in a foundationalist manner. On this point see Diderik Batens, 'Do We Need a Hierarchical Model of Science?', in John Earman (ed.), *Inference, Explanation and Other Frustrations: Essays in the Philosophy of Science* (Berkeley and Los Angeles: University of California Press, 1992), 199–215.

such beliefs. This psychologism cannot represent the normative authority we attribute to the centrality of these beliefs, nor is it an independent explanation for such centrality. The fact that we find it difficult to imagine abandoning them is all that their supposed centrality amounts to, and this is to abandon their normative authority altogether.[48]

The contextualist counter to the considerations Wright adduces is that we should conceive of the practice of enquiry differently. The holistic body of knowledge is devolved into multiple contexts of enquiry where beliefs are held fixed in order to structure a context in which a relevant range of alternatives can be considered. Furthermore, these contexts stand in a horizontal rather than a vertical arrangement: there is no hierarchical relation between the contexts of enquiry. Justification in a context is a matter of eliminating alternatives in a closed, problem oriented environment.[49]

This view shares elements of foundationalism (in a context, certain beliefs are held fixed to frame the enquiry, so they are 'relatively' foundational) with elements of coherentism. However, it is not a matter of pragmatic compromise with a fundamentally coherentist model of justification. Contextualism is a genuinely alternative view. Borrowing a paradoxical formulation from systems theory, the contextualist sees the knowledge system as a whole that is less than the sum of its parts. Coherence theories, because of their implicit commitment to global holism and hierarchical justification, retain a residual desire to legitimate knowledge as a whole. This is a project that is as much a hostage to global scepticism as the foundationalist project that it rejected.

The contextualist claims that justification is essentially local and contextual. The coherentist sees this as the elevation of merely pragmatic constraints on justification into a misguided obstacle for a process that is actually coherentist. Justification may appear to be devolved into a plurality of contexts of justification, but this is a surface appearance, presented by the context of discovery, that is shown to be illusory in the rationally reconstructed context of justification. For a denial of the distinctness of the contextualist option specifically applied to ethics, I can cite the discussion of contextualism by David Brink. Brink dissents on precisely this point, arguing that contextual justification is 'merely local' and must be backed up by a coherence theory. Brink's main premise is that justifying beliefs have themselves to be justified:

The coherentist needs to distinguish between two different kinds of justification: systematic and contextualist. Systematic justification is absolute or complete justification and results from

---

[48] The problem ultimately lies with the naturalization of epistemic norms and the resultant psychologism which Quine accepts, but which I believe we should reject. Naturalized epistemology is a matter of taking the results of one kind of scientific enquiry, psychology, as vindicatory of epistemic status of all scientifically provable results, which constitutes a vicious circle. So Quine's position lapses into psychologism. I accept that this is a question begging response to Quine, for whom all questions of epistemic legitimacy are issues in naturalized epistemology. For a development of this criticism see the excellent discussion of Quine's views in Barry Stroud, *The Significance of Philosophical Scepticism* (Oxford: Oxford University Press, 1989), ch. 6. The vicious circularity of naturalized epistemology's 'justification' of its own practices differs from the 'virtuous spiral' of a contextualist's bootstrapping justifications.

[49] See e.g. Batens's model in 'Do We Need a Hierarchical Model of Science?', esp. sect. 3, 'Contextual Problem Solving'.

consistently applying the epistemological requirement that justifying beliefs be justified. Contextualist justification, by contrast, is partial or incomplete justification and results from refusing to apply the epistemological requirement consistently.[50] [emphasis added]

Brink argues that moral justification must be seen as fully coherentist, yielding a form of naturalized moral realism.[51] I believe that Brink's counter-argument can be resisted, if one is clear about the sense in which contextualist justification is a form of relational justification and if one disambiguates the claim that justifying beliefs must themselves be justified. I will defer the second point until Section 4. On the first point, Michael Williams notes that,

Although officially 'coherence' designates a property of our belief system taken as a whole, it often gets treated as the name of a relation that a candidate belief may or may not bear to some antecedently given system . . . We may call the two versions of coherence 'systematic' and 'relational'.[52]

Relational justification can be accepted by my view, but systematic justification cannot. That is because it is systematic justification that introduces the global holism that characterizes coherentist systems of justification. Contextual justification is not the poor relation of foundationalism or coherentism. In particular, it is not a coherence theory that has been insufficiently developed. When coherentists argue that contextual justification is merely local and must be backed up by the global system, their use of the terms 'local' and 'global' misunderstand the possibilities offered by contextualism.[53]

It is obviously central to the case for contextualism that it should dislodge false models of the system of knowledge. The foundationalist model of knowledge as a pyramid, and the coherentist picture of knowledge as a free floating structure like a raft, require replacement with the contextualist picture of a patchwork or crazy quilt. The knowledge system is a devolved and differentiated structure. The traditional sceptical concern as to whether knowledge as a whole could come apart from the represented world makes no sense in the contextualist account. Knowledge does not possess the unified structure that allows one to ask questions about knowledge as a whole.

There are certainly elements of commonality across both coherentist and contextualist models of justification. Both deny that beliefs have intrinsic epistemic status. Furthermore, both insist, in the ethical case that the justification of ethical beliefs involves our best beliefs, and that there is no requirement that these other beliefs

---

[50] David Brink, *Moral Realism and the Foundations of Ethics* (Cambridge: Cambridge University Press, 1989), 123.

[51] Ibid., 122–5.

[52] Williams, *Unnatural Doubts*, 276. For a canonical statement of a coherentist account of justification for individual beliefs, see Laurence Bonjour, *The Structure of Empirical Knowledge* (Cambridge, Mass.: Harvard University Press, 1985), 92.

[53] A point emphasized by Henderson, in 'Epistemic Competence and Contextualist Epistemology: Why Contextualism is Not Just the Poor Person's Coherentism'. Henderson's contextualism is focused on reconstructing an individual's epistemic competence in the context of a naturalized epistemology. This gives it both a first personal focus and leads to a more purely externalist and reliabilist form of contextualism than Michael Williams's version. However, Henderson's 'in principle' critique of coherentism is insightful and cogent, esp. the discussion at 632–4, 646–9.

should not, themselves, be ethical.[54] However, these similarities are less important than the radical differences, which have to be emphasized as contextualism has for too long been obscured by its closest competitor. I would in fact argue that contextualism should be the theory of knowledge adopted across the board, and there are strong arguments that mature physical theory, our most objective form of discourse, has such an epistemology. However, that issue can be left undecided here, as I need prove my claim only for justification in ethics. Proving the wider claim is not a task that I can undertake in this book. Before beginning my analysis of moral epistemology I want to discuss how contextualism views the structure of enquiry. This is for two reasons. First, there is an important challenge to the status that contextualism attributes to framework beliefs from moral pragmatism. Second, there is an additional concern that the kind of view that I am putting forward represents an unacceptable rehabilitation of the Kantian idea of the synthetic a priori.

4. A CHALLENGE FROM THE MORAL PRAGMATIST

I have given some reasons why I am not inclined to describe my view as a form of moral pragmatism, reasons that I will both expand upon, and add to, later in this book. But, clearly, the kind of view that I am describing here is very close to the views of other philosophers, such as Isaac Levi, Charles Larmore, and Hilary Putnam, who describe themselves as pragmatists in general or moral pragmatists in particular. The concept of pragmatism is clearly a complex cluster concept, and one might weight various elements in the cluster so that the view I describe might reasonably be taken to be a form of pragmatism. However, I have indicated why I want to resist that move. Nevertheless, there is an issue of substance that goes beyond a matter over which reasonable speakers might disagree over a choice of terminology. Contextualism faces a powerful challenge from pragmatism. Addressing that challenge is the subject of this section.[55]

The challenge focuses on the role, within contexualism, of those background beliefs that form the context of enquiry. It takes the form of a dilemma. Are these background beliefs themselves justified? In the quotation from Wittgenstein I cited above, and in the comment on the status of background beliefs I cited from Meredith Williams, it seems that the answer is 'no'. Wittgenstein spoke of 'the inherited background against which I distinguish between the true and the false' that does not itself seem to involve truth and falsity; Meredith Williams described background beliefs as 'causal' not 'epistemic' conditions of enquiry. If one takes that view, however, one does seem open to a powerful objection, namely, the justification *ex nihilo* objection.

Let me be clear that this objection is not levelled at those normal conditions that feature in any externalist theory of knowledge as presuppositions of enquiry; it is an objection levelled at claims that seem, plausibly, themselves to be beliefs. (They are

---

[54] An important point made by Larmore, *Patterns of Moral Complexity*, 29–30.

[55] This pragmatist challenge to contextualism originates from the first of my anonymous referees for Oxford University Press. In formulating my response I am grateful to Edward Harcourt for discussion of some of the issues involved.

plausibly relata of the relation 'x is justified by y', not presuppositions of justification at all.) On the view that I have attributed to Wittgenstein, background framework beliefs supply justification to other beliefs, but are not themselves justified. The *ex nihilo* objection is that this is completely mysterious: a claim that is not justified cannot generate a justification for another claim that it is called upon to support.

The *ex nihilo* objection is one horn of the dilemma. The other horn is that if one denies the principle that background framework beliefs supply justification *ex nihilo*, one is thereby committed to the view that justifying beliefs are themselves justified. But that, the moral pragmatist urges, is precisely what the coherentist believes. If one adopts this view then the contextualist is forced to concede that the distinction between contextualism and coherentism is, as the coherentist always urged, illusory. Certainly the claim that all justifying beliefs are justified was Brink's reason for rejecting contextualism and adopting coherentism, as the passage quoted from Brink above indicated.

The way to avoid contextualism collapsing into coherentism, my pragmatist interlocutor urges, is to take a step taken by Peirce and by contemporary pragmatists such as Isaac Levi and Charles Larmore. That which is justified in enquiry is not a set of beliefs, but a *change* in a set of beliefs. So, in any given context of enquiry, we can evade the coherentist assumption that all justifying beliefs are justified by maintaining that the taken for granted background beliefs are not justified. They are, though, true. Justification cannot attach to them, and it is a category mistake to believe that it can. Justification only attaches to changes in belief and as, in this context, the background beliefs are not candidates to be changed they are not the objects of justification. They are still true and, Levi claims, known certainly to be true:

> To regard some proposition as certainly true and as settled is to rule out its falsity as a serious possibility for the time being . . . As long as the proposition is taken for granted, any [. . .] test presupposes the truth of the proposition
> But from this it does not follow that good reasons will not become available in the future for a change of mind and for calling into question what is currently considered to be true . . . Certainty does not imply incorrigibility.[56]

The neo-Peircean, then, claims that my contextualism cannot answer the *ex nihilo* objection or that it faces a collapse into coherentism when it concedes that justifying beliefs are themselves justified. That latter claim can be avoided, the pragmatist argues, by carefully distinguishing the proper objects of justification: changes in sets of beliefs, not sets of beliefs. To believe is to believe as true, but not, properly speaking, to be justified when it comes to background framework beliefs. Justification comes into play only when doubt arises and a proposed change of belief is considered.

This is, clearly, a powerful objection. My response is to agree that the contextualist, like the pragmatist, focuses on the actual structure of enquiry and also on processes of belief revision. However, I do not want to abandon the claim that those background

---

[56] Isaac Levi, *The Fixation of Belief and Its Undoing: Changing Beliefs through Enquiry* (Cambridge: Cambridge University Press, 1991), 3.

beliefs are themselves justified: the alternative put forward by the pragmatist seems to me to come dangerously close to succumbing to his or her own dilemma. The pragmatist claims that background framework beliefs are true, but not justified, but once doubt is raised they justify transitions from them. That looks to me very like justification *ex nihilo*.

How, then, does my claim that background framework beliefs are themselves justified differ from Brink's coherentist claim that all justifying beliefs are justified? It does so by exploiting an ambiguity in Brink's claim. It is ambiguous between.

(1) For any belief, B, if there is a context C in which that belief is justifying, then there is some context C* in which that belief is justified. [C and C* may, or may not, be identical.]

(2) For any belief B, if there is a context C in which that belief is justified, then it is justified in that very same context C.

Clearly, qua contextualist, I do not assert 2 as my explanation of 'all justifying beliefs are justified'. But then 2 is simply a denial of contextualism: it denies that contexts are a relevant parameter in justification.

But what about proposition 1? The key issue, it seems to me, is that the contextualist believes that there is an irreducible plurality of contexts, such that for many beliefs C and C* are not identical. (I don't think that the contextualist has to assert that there are *no* contexts in which C and C* are identical, as that takes a position on, for example, the possibility of a priori knowledge about which the contextualist does not have to commit him- or herself. A limited agnosticism is more prudent.) But the coherentist *does* commit him- or herself on this point, as the key dispute between the coherentist and the contextualist is not the possibility of context relative justification, but the fact that the coherentist believes that when it comes to justification there is only one, global, context of justification. Hence C and C* in proposition 1 are *guaranteed* to be identical for the coherentist. (Proposition 1 is, therefore, extensionally equivalent to proposition 2.) The coherentist should, in fact, come clean and assert 1*:

(1*) [For any belief B, if there is a context C in which that belief is justifying, then there is some context C* in which that belief is justified] and [C = C* because in the relevant sense of context there is only one, global, context.]

In my view, therefore, the pragmatist's charge that accepting the claim that 'all justifying beliefs are justified' leads to coherentism is not true. It only does so if you add the claim that there is only one global context, which the contextualist does not.

I believe, then, that the pragmatist's objection can be avoided. But the valuable point about how background beliefs come into question can be adopted by contextualism independently of the claim that they are true but not justified. Within a context of enquiry they come into question when they become objects of a specific and focused doubt, as Peirce, Levi, and Larmore claim. Contextualism is happy to adopt that insight from the pragmatist tradition, but I still do not believe that it is helpful to view contextualism as a form of pragmatism.

5. CONTEXTUALISM, ANALYTICITY, AND THE 'SYNTHETIC A PRIORI'

Contextualism shares the pragmatist's focus on processes of belief revision, even if the motivation for doing so is not, as the previous section demonstrated, the same motivation as that of the pragmatist. An examination of the actual process of enquiry shows how enquiry is structured by background framework beliefs. But does not this merely rehabilitate the Kantian idea that we can identify a fixed framework for enquiry in the form of synthetic a priori principles? There is a neo-Kantian interpretation of *On Certainty* that attributes precisely this view to Wittgenstein.[57] Furthermore, Michael Friedman has recently defended a historicized and 'dynamic' form of neo-Kantianism that looks like a very close rival to the kind of contextual view that I have defended.[58] I think it is worth explaining in some detail how the contextualist, like the pragmatist, focuses on those processes by which beliefs acquire warrant, while not adopting the view that we can identify even relativized a priori principles in enquiry, identified in terms of their content.

I believe that the best way to clarify both points is to examine the way in which the distinctive role of contextual judgements emerges from considerations about analyticity. It would go beyond the scope of this book to offer anything other than a brief characterization of the problem of analyticity. But there is an aspect of Putnam's critique of Carnap's account of analyticity that indirectly addresses both issues.[59]

Critiques of analyticity are largely critiques of the attempt to define that notion in the classic presentation of the idea in Carnap.[60] Carnap believed that it was possible, using a precisely defined concept of analyticity, to isolate those parts of a language that constitute its analytical meaning postulates and thus constitute the linguistic framework of that language. This account had consequences, he believed, for the issue of scepticism. If these postulates involve the concepts of, and lay down rules for, a material object language, then it is analytic that there are material things and that there are procedures for verifying this in particular cases. A sceptic who questions this fact is either raising this question internal to this language, in which case he or she is just confused, or we have to understand them as raising this question externally, about which linguistic framework we ought to deploy. Here, Carnap believes, we have to accept a meta-level pragmatism about the adoption of frameworks and assess the sceptic's proposal on such grounds.[61]

[57] Morawetz, *Wittgenstein and Knowledge*.

[58] Friedman, *The Dynamics of Reason*.

[59] Hilary Putnam, 'The Analytic and the Synthetic', in *Mind, Language and Reality* (Cambridge: Cambridge University Press, 1975), 33–69.

[60] Rudolf Carnap, *Meaning and Necessity: A Study in Semantics and Modal Logic*, 2nd edn. (Chicago: University of Chicago Press, 1988).

[61] There is a very clear discussion of this anti-sceptical aspect of Carnap's views in Stroud, *The Significance of Philosophical Scepticism*, ch. 5.

This position appears paradoxical. It postulates a meta-level framework in which these external questions can be debated that is not itself a framework. Carnap hoped to evade this paradox by assuming that this level of enquiry was purely syntactic, but that ambition rapidly faded.[62] However, the real problem is that as a reconstructive model of actual scientific practice, there are important elements of such practices that the model cannot represent.[63]

The problem lies in the account of analyticity. Carnapian analyticity forms part of a project of reconstructing the context of justification atemporally. It is precisely this point that became the focus of Hilary Putnam's well-known critique of Carnapian analyticity in 'The Analytic and the Synthetic'. Putnam deconstructed Carnap's analytic/synthetic distinction from within (unlike the strategy of Quine's parallel critique) and argued that it misrepresented our ordinary practice, which cannot be described if one adopts Carnap's version of the analytic/synthetic distinction. Putnam's invocation of 'our linguistic practices' here is explicitly intended to include processes of enquiry.[64] Putnam began his argument by accepting the idea of a semantic rule in a formal language, but objecting to the corollary that *if a sentence, S, of L, is not true in virtue of L's semantic rules, then it is synthetic.*

Carnap justified this corollary using the following empiricist principle: if it is reasonable to hold a sentence S of language L immune from disconfirmation by all empirical evidence, this is so only if S is true in virtue of the rules for L. Putnam's response to this principle is to give examples of sentences which are not analytic, and which were held to be immune from disconfirmation by all empirical evidence at a certain time. They are therefore not analytic in Carnap's sense, nor are they synthetic. They are not synthetic, because of their peculiar role in enquiry: they are held immune from empirical disconfirmation. Putnam argued that if you ignored this class of sentences, certain kinds of disagreement cannot be described, particularly those that occur in radical scientific changes.[65] He argued that to describe such changes, it is necessary to introduce the class of 'contextually a priori' sentences. This is a class of sentences that are 'necessary relative to a body of knowledge'. None of these sentences is thus necessarily true. If a sentence S is contextually a priori it is reasonable to hold S immune from disconfirmation even if S is not analytic. By taking a synchronic view of enquiry, Carnap is prevented from seeing that we can commit ourselves to the outcome of investigations into the truth of given sentence S even when we do not know precise rules for the discovery of its truth value.

---

[62] The syntactic programme is set out in Rudolf Carnap, *The Logical Syntax of Language*, trans. Ameath Smeaton (London: Routledge, 2000). This aspect of Carnap's views is discussed by Michael Friedman, esp. in 'Carnap's *Aufbau* Reconsidered', *Noûs*, 21 (Dec. 1987), 521–45 and 'Philosophy and the Exact Sciences: Logical Positivism as a Case Study', in Earman (ed.), *Inference, Explanation and Other Frustrations*, 84–98.

[63] I have benefited from the discussion of this aspect of Putnam's critique of Carnap by Gary Ebbs, *Rule-Following and Realism* (Cambridge, Mass.: Harvard University Press 1997), ch. 6.

[64] See, e.g. ibid., sect. 83 for a discussion of this aspect of Putnam's view.

[65] Putnam, 'The Analytic and the Synthetic', 42–54.

Putnam hoped that this distinction allowed for rational discussion across Kuhn style framework changes that are rational and not merely pragmatic, changes in belief, not in the reference of words. We are still able, Putnam argued, to recognize a class of analytically true sentences. Analyticity is possible for 'one criterion' terms in natural language, where we can change a criterion only by changing the meaning. These terms are unlike 'law cluster' terms. Thus, overall, Putnam's account allows us to describe all aspects of the practice of enquiry and preserves our belief that while there are analytical sentences, they are trivialities involving one criterion terms.[66]

From a contextualist perspective, there are two important aspects to Putnam's claims that can be exploited within contextualism. First, in isolating a certain functional category of beliefs in enquiry, Putnam seems to be recognizing the distinctive role of contextualism's framework judgements. Secondly, Putnam's examples involve the historicality of knowledge. It was Carnap's atemporal concept of justification that invited Putnam's critique.[67] Focus on processes of belief revision gave Putnam the kind of examples he needed to argue that Carnap's overall account misrepresented actual practices of enquiry. This justifies the contextualist's (and the pragmatist's) focus on the essentially temporal aspect of actual processes of enquiry.

Putnam's arguments allow one to make headway with the second claim that contextualism rehabilitates the Kantian idea of the synthetic a priori. This line of argument claims that the contextualist's framework principles are a restatement of Kant's synthetic a priori principles in a contemporary guise. I do not think that the contextualist should welcome this characterization of his or her project. One could envisage a similar response to Putnam's arguments. The sentences that Putnam isolates as functionally equivalent to framework judgements are non-analytic and immune to confirmation or disconfirmation. On the grounds of this latter feature, Putnam does not call them 'synthetic'. But those sympathetic to Kant might argue that this is merely a terminological point: these are not sentences where the subject term contains the predicate, so they are synthetic.

Dealing with this objection requires two clarifications which both need careful specification and whose mutual relation also needs to be specified. The first clarification is to point out that while contextualist frameworks of belief function like a set of synthetic a priori principles, they are neither themselves synthetic a priori, nor for that matter picked out substantively at all. Such truths are contingent, not transparent to conceptual reflection, and function like the class of analytic truths while not, in fact, being analytic. Similarity of function masks differences of content. The contextualist picks them out solely in terms of their functional role in justification.

The second important clarification of contextualism required to rebut this objection that it merely rehabilitates the synthetic a priori runs as follows. The Kantian hopes not merely to state that there are synthetic a priori principles, but to list such

[66] Ibid. 65–8.

[67] A point emphasized by Ebbs, *Rule-Following and Realism*, 158–63, esp. his description of Putnam's 'diachronic picture of shared commitments', 162, on the part of enquirers compared to Carnap's 'synchronic view of enquiry', 161.

a set of principles that function to objectify an area of thought or language. But this ties together content and function in precisely the way that contextualism urges we ought not to do. The contextualist does not believe that we can, once and for all, give a substantive, content based list of those principles that function as judgements of a frame. But that is because the role of such judgements is, once again, context specific and functionally specified.

While I think that these two clarifications do help to distinguish contextualism from a neo-Kantian rehabilitation of the synthetic a priori, the relation between them needs to be handled with care. This is because, as will become apparent, what actually makes up a context of enquiry in any particular case may well involve a commitment, on the part of a group of enquirers, to a shared background framework of beliefs. So contexts may be picked out substantively, in terms of what Richard Miller has called a set of 'topic-specific truisms'.[68] But this does not undercut the distinctions that I have introduced as the nature of these topic-specific truisms is, once again, picked out on a case by case basis depending on the particular problem solving context at hand. These topic specific truisms are certainly not synthetic a priori judgements, even though they are both substantive and function in a particular case as if they were the kinds of beliefs traditionally called 'synthetic a priori'.

Putting together the case for the prosecution, the charge would be that the contextualist is going to have to offer a substantive set of criteria for individuating frameworks of enquiry. This conclusion is over-determined: it can be derived both from the reflections on analyticity that I have cited, and from reflection on what it is to substantiate standards of reasonableness. Richard Miller appealed to topic-specific truisms in his account of confirmation in order to correct what he sees as the inadequacy of positivistic accounts of rationality. Rationality, he argues, involves a commitment to these substantive truisms.[69] I would defend contextualism from these problems by arguing that, while it is not a form of pragmatism, it does share with that view an emphasis on actual processes of enquiry. It is the process of enquiry that gives rise to a problem solving context which determines which beliefs, in that context, are *functioning* as framework judgements and which are up for testing. Qua contextualism, the view can accept Miller's claim that substantively rational enquirers believe a set of topic-specific truisms about a particular subject matter while remaining completely agnostic as to what they are in any particular case.

Drawing the various threads of the discussion together, the upshot of these arguments would seem to be this. Viewed diachronically, contexts typically involve framework judgements. Such judgements individuate frameworks on a case by case basis. There is no hard and fast delimitation of these framework beliefs independently of

---

[68] Richard Miller, *Fact and Method: Explanation, Confirmation and Reality in the Natural and the Social Sciences* (Princeton: Princeton University Press, 1987), 219–22.

[69] Ibid. 221: 'In philosophy, it is more common to take general logical principles and general principles of inference as marks of rationality. But, on the face of it, the truistic responses are marks of rationality as well'; 223: 'What is valid a priori is that a reasonable human being with standard experiences is committed to the truisms, in all their vagueness and with all their hedges. Or perhaps one should say "committed to the basic validity of the truisms, as a whole"'.

the point of the enquiry in that particular context. They function as contextually basic beliefs, and without an acknowledgement of their role the rationality of belief revision in such contexts cannot be reconstructed. Such principles mimic the traditional role assigned within Kantian theories to the synthetic a priori, but they are better viewed as contextually basic beliefs playing an unusual, context determining role. They are not, in fact, instances of the synthetic a priori.[70]

If contextualism makes contact with one idea in the literature on justification, it is not the idea of the synthetic a priori, but Kuhn's ambiguous notion of a paradigm. Some recent work has argued that a form of neo-Kantianism, of the kind I have just criticized, makes the best sense of Kuhn's notion of a paradigm, but in fact I think that contextualism can give a better account of that multiply ambiguous idea. A distinctive role that background frameworks to specific contexts of enquiry play is perspicuously to structure the options available for testing. This has emerged from recent discussions as the best interpretation that can be placed on one important sense of a Kuhnian paradigm. John Earman has argued that before applying standard rules for belief revision by conditionalization, scientists may have to revise their background frameworks of belief and by so doing reconceptualize the matrix of possibilities within which they have to decide:

The exploration of the space of possibilities constantly brings into consciousness heretofore unrecognised possibilities. The resulting shifts in our belief functions cannot be described by means of any sort of rule of conditionalization. The most dramatic shifts occur during scientific revolutions when radically new possibilities are introduced, but the same point holds for the less dramatic, workaday cases.[71]

I would argue that contextualism is particularly able to describe these cases, since it takes as central to the process of belief revision the role of such frameworks in 'bounding' epistemic contexts. Moral discourse, I will go on to argue, exhibits the truth of a general contextualist model of discourse applied to a particular case.

CONCLUSION

I have, in this chapter, attempted three tasks. First, I have suggested that contextualism should be adopted as our best epistemological theory on the grounds that it represents our most satisfactory response to philosophical scepticism. Secondly, I have set out distinctive advantages that contextualism has vis-à-vis alternative models of knowledge. Thirdly, I have begun to characterize the key elements in a contextual model of justification. The following chapter narrows the focus from general issues

---

[70] Nor the relativized notion of the a priori defended by Michael Friedman that I used in Ch. 4. Given that the overall position that Friedman develops is very similar to the account of the relativized a priori about moral psychology defended in Ch. 4, must I not then concede that my account of moral knowledge is a historicized form of Kantianism about theoretical knowledge? For the reasons I have given in this section I think the contextualist can resist the claim that his or her claims about moral knowledge are a rehabilitation even of this revised notion of the relativized a priori.

[71] John Earman, in *Bayes or Bust* (Cambridge, Mass.: MIT Press, 1992), 183.

in epistemology to explain which elements play this role in moral justification, and how the advantages of the contextualist approach meet the constraints on any plausible model of moral knowledge. In the next chapter I attempt such a project, while I shall also undertake the task of comparing the model developed here both with regard to important rivals, such as the reflective equilibrium model, and with regard to traditional views with which it might be confused, such as intuitionism.

8

A Contextual Model of Moral Justification

*§1: A contextualist model of moral knowledge is compared to a coherent-
ist interpretation of reflective equilibrium. §2: It is explained how reflective
equilibrium can be given a contextualist interpretation. §3: Support for cognitivism from ethical phenomenology is defended from circularity. §4: It is
argued that a justificatory theory focused on belief can still give an account of
expression and articulation in moral justification. §5. The connection envisaged between contextualism and non-prioritist pluralism is described.*

I have suggested both that the non-objectivist criticism of cognitivism can be deflected and that its central insight can be accommodated if cognitivism is combined with
a contextual model of justification. Having set out the basic elements of a contextual epistemology I shall now develop an application of contextualism in the specific
case of moral knowledge. The overall aim is the final vindication of a contextualist account of moral justification that supports a cognitivist interpretation of morality. In this chapter I will, first, explain how contextualism compares and contrasts
with the dominant coherentist model of moral epistemology in contemporary ethics,
namely, an understanding of Rawlsian reflective equilibrium as a coherence theory
of justification. I will argue that contextualism can, in fact, be seen as arising from
Rawls's methodological assumptions if one retains the assumption that considered
moral judgements retain a direct source of moral justification even when they derive
further warrant from their embedding in a context of justification. The next section
justifies this appeal to direct warrant, based on theory laden moral experience, before
providing a fuller example of how contextualist justification proceeds. Further reasons
are given for seeing contextual justification as primarily directed to beliefs in a way
that explains a derived emphasis on articulation and the expression of a moral point
of view. Finally, the connections are analysed between the contextual model of moral
justification described in this book and the first order view known as non-prioritist
pluralism.

1. METHODOLOGY: FROM REFLECTIVE EQUILIBRIUM
TO CONTEXTUALISM

In Chapter 7 I discussed the contrast between contextualism and coherentism in
general terms. In this chapter the debate between them is focused more precisely on
a single issue. For a contextualist moral epistemology has to displace a very well-
entrenched competitor, namely, Rawls's method of reflective equilibrium, which

is usually assumed strongly to support a coherence model of moral justification. Contextualism has, it seems, got its work cut out even to appear to be a serious competitor to this entrenched view. However, in this section I will argue that the appearances are deceptive and that contextualism can, in fact, flow naturally from Rawls's initial methodological assumptions. Following the lead of DePaul, Ebertz, and others, I will argue that reflective equilibrium does not constitute a coherentist model of moral justification, but is better understood in contextualist terms.[1] Before setting out in detail how I believe a contextualist model of moral justification can meet the desiderata I have established for a satisfactory reflective account of moral knowledge, I would like to focus on the contrast between a contextualist and a coherentist model of justification in ethics.

In order to develop this contrast some important terminological issues have to be clarified before proceeding as some of the terminology in this area is confusing. In particular, I need to explain the distinctions between *epistemological intuitionism, methodological intuitionism,* and *pluralism.* These distinctions, in turn, are underpinned by the corresponding distinctions between an epistemological model, a methodological model, and a normative ethical theory (or, in this last case, any similarly reflective account of ethics that denies that it is appropriate to speak of a 'theory' of ethics as many pluralists do). An epistemological model is an account of how a certain class of knowledge claims is justified. I have put forward contextualism as a model of this kind. It is a reflective account of the nature of knowledge claims in a particular area. A methodological model is something slightly different. It is a proposal about how, before one develops an epistemological model, one ought to set about collecting data that the epistemological model will interpret and justify. Finally, a normative ethical theory is a substantive view as to what constitutes right and wrong. For the purposes of this book, I will also include under this third broad heading views that are, strictly speaking, 'anti-theoretical'. Such views are a reflective account of what constitutes our judgements of right and wrong, even as they deny that this account should take the form of a moral theory as moral philosophers typically use that term.

The first distinction that needs to be made is between two views called 'intuitionism'. Both Rawls and Bernard Williams made it very clear that we need to distinguish *epistemological* intuitionism from *methodological* intuitionism.[2] Epistemological intuitionism is the epistemological thesis that certain moral truths are known

---

[1] Michael DePaul, 'Two Conceptions of Coherence Methods in Ethics', *Mind*, 96/384 (Oct. 1987), 463–81; Roger Ebertz, 'Is Reflective Equilibrium a Coherentist Model?', *Canadian Journal of Philosophy*, 23/2 (June 1993), 193–214.

[2] Rawls, *A Theory of Justice*, 34–40. Rawls argued that 'various other contentions are commonly associated with intuitionism, for example, that the concepts of the right and the good are unanalyzable, that moral principles when suitably formulated express self-evident propositions about legitimate moral claims, and so on ... These characteristic epistemological doctrines are not a necessary part of intuitionism as I understand it', 34–5; see also Bernard Williams, 'What Does Intuitionism Imply?', in *Making Sense of Humanity* (Cambridge University Press, 1995), 182–91, where Williams wrote, 'Intuitionism in ethics is nowadays usually treated as a methodological doctrine ... The use of the term to stand for this kind of view represents a change from the practice of the 1950s and 1960s when it was taken for granted that intuitionism in ethics was an

via a faculty of rational intuition comparable to the faculty of intuition that gives us knowledge of a priori truths in the special sciences. This was a view that, it is usually assumed, was held by Moore, Prichard, and Ross.[3] Methodological intuitionism is the view, held by Urmson and Williams, that the starting point of ethical enquiry should be a phenomenological description of the plural sources available in our ethical experience.[4] Such an unprejudiced phenomenology will, it is argued, reveal a plurality of commitments both at the level of moral knowledge and at the level of principles.[5] Rawls holds a similar view about how a reflective account of moral justification ought to proceed that I will describe in more detail shortly.

It is now possible to introduce the third distinction between a methodological proposal and a normative ethical theory, or those 'anti-theoretical' views that also offer a general and reflective account of morality. Urmson, Williams, and Rawls broadly share a similar view of how, methodologically, we ought to proceed, but differ in the outcome that they predict will result from the application of this method. Urmson and Williams emphasized that not only is the starting point of ethical reflection deeply pluralistic in the range of plural and sometimes conflicting values and principles to which it gives rise. They also suggest that reflection will not take us very far in imposing or discovering any underlying unity to this pluralism. Thus they are, from the perspective of normative theory, non-prioritist *pluralists*.[6] Pluralism is the view that our first order ethical beliefs constitute a plural set of commitments; it is thus one amongst the many different kinds of first order normative theories, such as consequentialism or contractualism. It is, though, a good example of a general, reflective account of morality that is sceptical as to whether it can constitute anything like a theory of morality. This is particularly true of the non-prioritist pluralism developed by Urmson and Williams that denies that we can come up with any kind of ranking of our plural moral commitments, particularly in cases of moral conflict.[7] I will discuss this important point further below.

I think, in fact, that there are a set of natural connections between how we should set about ethical reflection, which epistemological model we should choose, and what the upshot is likely to be in terms of the resulting normative theory—or 'anti-theory'. But while each of these three components is closely connected, they remain distinct.

---

epistemological doctrine . . . It seems to be mainly the influence of Rawls that has brought about this change in the understanding of the term', 182.

[3] Although Urmson makes the point that this classification, with the benefit of Rawls's hindsight into the past, was not the understanding of intuitionism prevalent amongst the intuitionists who taught Urmson, who took Moore to be an arch-enemy because of his consequentialism! See J. O. Urmson, 'A Defence of Intuitionism', *Proceedings of the Aristotelian Society* (1975), 111–19 at 111–2.

[4] Williams, 'What Does Intuitionism Imply?'; Urmson, 'A Defence of Intuitionism'.

[5] Furthermore, a non-prioritist pluralism, a point to which I will return below. This is the main focus of Urmson's discussion in 'A Defence of Intuitionism'; see the 'Summary' at 119.

[6] See ibid. 116–17 for the critique of prioritist pluralism.

[7] This is slightly misleading in that it suggests that the Urmson/Williams view is that there are a plurality of moral principles but no relation of priority between them. It is more accurate to say that there are a variety of inputs into ethical decisions, including more than principles, but no means of determining a priority relation between any of these elements. I will describe a view of this kind in Sect. 5, below.

I concede that I have an ulterior motive in emphasizing this point. I want to detach Rawls's methodological proposal, the method of reflective equilibrium, from the presupposition that it leads us ineluctably to a coherence model of moral justification (which it does not) and to a particular kind of normative ethical theory (the sort of non-prioritist pluralism that Rawls did *not* believe acceptable for the particular and restricted case that he considered, the theory of justice). My own view is that adopting Rawls's methodology does lead us to a non-prioritist pluralism, as I will argue below.

My main focus in this chapter is on how Rawls intended to advance from those descriptive results that captured the pluralist phenomenology of our moral experience by using reflective equilibrium. Rawls's interpretations of the method changed through time, but broadly speaking both Rawls and Norman Daniels (whose formulation of the methodology has become standard) put considerable distance between the method and the *epistemological* intuitionism they attributed to Moore and to Ross.[8] To emphasize how different their proposal was from that of the epistemological intuitionists they emphasized that the initial class of considered moral judgements do not possess even prima facie epistemic privilege.[9] They argued that the status that any class of judgements enjoys cannot be determined until the entire process of moving from narrow to wide reflective equilibrium has been completed. In this way, it seems, any direct support for moral judgements from experience itself is not part of Rawls's and Daniels's view. This rejection of any direct support seems to them important to avoid their view being confused with epistemological intuitionism. I will argue that this motivation was misguided and that taking this route overlooks the possibility of a contextualist interpretation of reflective equilibrium.

Reflective equilibrium is a general reasonable procedure for adjusting moral principles to moral intuitions. As canonically formulated by Daniels, the method of reflective equilibrium begins by isolating a class of considered moral judgements. These judgements are moderately subject to reflection in that they are filtered in the light of presuppositions about the appropriate contexts for reliable belief formation and are thereby shaped by a preliminary and moderately reflective theory of error. (In Rawls's original formulation, these beliefs were picked out by the subject's degree of confidence in them.) The transition to narrow reflective equilibrium begins when these considered moral judgements are related to a set of principles that both justify and give insight into them. These principles are strict and exceptionless, with no *ceteris paribus* clauses in their formulation.[10] This involves a process of mutual

---

[8] The major point of difference between Rawls and Daniels is that while both see the method of reflective equilibrium as a form of coherence theory, in Rawls's eyes this allows one to construct ethical truth, whereas Daniels leaves open the option of combining of a coherentist epistemology with a form of realism in the manner of Boyd and Brink. Daniels's methodological papers now form part I of *Justice and Justification: Reflective Equilibrium in Theory and Practice* (Cambridge: Cambridge University Press, 1996).

[9] This is particularly emphasized by Daniels, 'Wide Reflective Equilibrium and Theory Acceptance in Ethics', in *Justice and Justification*, 21–65.

[10] This point is emphasized in Daniel Bonevac's excellent paper, 'Reflection Without Equilibrium', *Journal of Philosophy*, 101/7 (July 2004), 363–88, to which I am indebted. Bonevac notes that 'I follow R. M. Hare in interpreting Rawls as seeking principles that are strictly universal, without *ceteris paribus* or similar clauses... If we could rest content with... principles... with

adjustment that can involve the revision of either considered moral judgement or of general principles. The conclusion of this process is *narrow* reflective equilibrium. However, this is not the end of the process of justification.

Further reflection draws on background theories in the human sciences relevant to the project at hand. These include theories of social stability drawn from sociology in the case of deliberations over social justice or theories of the person or social and moral psychology in the case of moral deliberation.[11] Rawls and Daniels accept that these background theories need not be value free and may be significantly shaped by prior moral presuppositions. Daniels hopes that it is possible to disjoin those of our considered moral beliefs implicated in these background theories from the majority that are not so implicated. Only then, he believes, can the transition to wide reflective equilibrium uncover the full structure of reflective ethical justification without introducing a damaging circularity into the process.[12]

I will argue in this chapter that the application of this methodological proposal should be detached from the separate claim that it leads to a coherence theory of moral justification. From the earliest critical discussions of the method a succession of critics have argued that this understanding of reflective equilibrium could not be sustained. It has variously been argued that considered moral judgements must possess prima facie epistemic status for the methodology to make sense; that the contrast between narrow and wide reflective equilibrium has been overdrawn by Daniels; that some judgements must function relatively foundationally in the process of establishing reflective equilibrium, thus making the overall theory not a coherence theory at all; finally that there can be no presumption that such a process of reflection could be completed in a finite time at all.[13] I agree with these critics that reflective equilibrium must presuppose some direct justification of ethical beliefs, does not form a coherence theory of justification, and

ceteris paribus or similar clauses . . . there would be no dispute between Rawls and the intuitionist', 365–6. (Bonevac is referring here to the methodological intuitionist.)

[11] Bonevac notes a further constraint on reflective equilibrium when it is applied in the case of Rawls's theory of justice (ibid. 367). The process of adjusting considered moral judgements to principles is also constrained by the formulation of the device of the original position itself. As this constraint is only needed in this special case of Rawls's modelling of justice I will set it aside for the purposes of the generalized use of the reflective equilibrium model as an epistemological model for ethics discussed here.

[12] Daniels, 'Wide Reflective Equilibrium and Theory Acceptance in Ethics'. It will prove important to bear in mind a further complication: that the method of reflective equilibrium is applied to a person's moral experiences at a given time and that expanding experience will lead to the process of revision being repeated. Thus while reflective equilibrium itself tailors considered judgements in the light of exceptionless principles, that entire process is open to adjustment in the light of new, expanded, moral experience. For a discussion of this see Bonevac, 'Reflection Without Equilibrium', 363 n. 2; Geoffrey Sayre-McCord, 'Coherentist Epistemology and Moral Theory', in Walter Sinnot-Armstrong and Mark Timmons (eds.), *Moral Knowledge?: New Readings in Moral Epistemology* (Oxford: Oxford University Press, 1996), 137–89 at 141–2; DePaul, 'Two Conceptions of Coherence Methods in Ethics', 470–2.

[13] Stefan Sencerz, 'Moral Intuitions and Justification in Ethics', *Philosophical Studies*, 50 (July 1986), 77–95; Margaret Holmgren, 'Wide Reflective Equilibrium and Objective Moral Truth', *Metaphilosophy*, 18 (Apr. 1987), 108–24 and 'The Wide and Narrow of Reflective Equilibrium', *Canadian Journal of Philosophy*, 19 (Mar. 1989), 43–60; Bonevac, 'Reflection Without Equilibirum', 369–73, 377–80.

is compatible with a modest foundationalism.[14] Unsurprisingly, this latter idea turns out, in my account, to be better reinterpreted as a form of contextualism. To support this interpretation I will focus on two key points. First, that the method of reflective equilibrium should not be given a rationalist and epistemologically realist interpretation in the senses of those terms I introduced in Chapter 7. Secondly, that considered moral judgements can be of any degree of abstraction. Taken together they form a decisive criticism of the view that the method of reflective equilibrium leads inevitably to a coherence theory of moral knowledge.

On the rationalist conception of how one applies reflective equilibrium to the data supplied by methodological intuitionism that I have in mind the two accounts essentially complement each other. When conjoined this leads to a coherence theory of moral knowledge.[15] Methodological intuitionism lists our plural moral commitments, assigning no rank order of epistemic priority to this list of commitments. Reflective equilibrium is an essential supplement in that it allows one to determine relations of epistemic priority amongst the items of the list and to render the list of commitments a coherent set.

The process is as follows: the concrete and specific materials yielded up by methodological intuitionism are described by a set of abstract principles which takes us as far as narrow reflective equilibrium. We then hope that some of our initial considered judgements can be separated by disjunction from the rest. This is so that they can offer non-circular support to those background theories of the person, of the role of morality in society and in the psychology of the individual that lead to further revisions as we enter into wide reflective equilibrium. The end point of the process is a list of concrete intuitions harmonized, systematized, and rendered coherent by the ideal set of strict and exceptionless abstract principles, in the light of established background theories in the human sciences. The conjunction of methodological intuitionism and reflective equilibrium thus yields a coherence theory of moral knowledge. Methodological intuitionism is here playing the role of a methodological preliminary to the full application of reflective equilibrium. Its plurality of principles and judgements are not violated by any attempt to reduce it to a single principle. This plurality is rather, by application of the reflective equilibrium method, woven into a different kind of unity. This is the unity of a set of judgements standing in relations of mutual coherence, or standing in a certain kind of relation to any proposed addition to the overall set.[16] I regard this view of methodological intuitionism and reflective equilibrium as seriously mistaken.

[14] DePaul, 'Two Conceptions of Coherence Methods in Ethics'; 'Reflective Equilibrium and Foundationalism', *American Philosophical Quarterly*, 23 (Jan. 1986), 59–69; Ebertz, 'Is Reflective Equilibrium a Coherentist Model?'.

[15] A position explicitly defended by Kai Nielsen in 'Reflective Equilibrium and the Transformation of Philosophy', *Metaphilosophy*, 20/3-4 (1989), 235–46, in addition to the construal of reflective equilibrium as leading to a coherence theory of justification combinable with an independently motivated realism cited in n. 8.

[16] A distinction explained by Michael Williams in *Unnatural Doubts*, 'Although officially "coherence" designates a property of our belief system taken as a whole, it often gets treated as the name of a relation that a candidate belief may or may not bear to some antecedently given system . . . We may call the two versions of coherence "systematic" and "relational" ', 276.

My diagnosis of what has gone awry with this line of argument draws on the arguments of the previous chapter. This line of reasoning is both *rationalist* and *epistemologically realist*.[17] It brings to its discussion of moral knowledge the following familiar and contentious assumptions: in every body of knowledge there is an underlying epistemic order of relations of epistemic priority and subordination. The postulation of such an underlying order explains why the subjective order of enquiry should align with this underlying objective order of reasons. In this overall process, degrees of concreteness and abstraction directly co-vary with the classification of phenomena as data and theoretical principle. The concrete is equivalent to the evaluative and the contestable whereas the abstract is equivalent to principles of right and the foci of rational incontestability. These are the traditionally rationalist assumptions that were uncovered in Chapter 7 and if unchallenged they make the misunderstanding of the relations between methodological intuitionism and reflective equilibrium inevitable.

This rationalist picture misconceives the structure of methodological intuitionism in the following way. It takes the list of our commitments to be exhausted by concrete, conflict-ridden intuitions whose disorder conceals an underlying theoretical order or unity awaiting *discovery*. These intuitions are evaluative and thereby essentially contested in the face of the kind of evaluative pluralism familiar in modern societies. Rationality, in the face of conflict, is restored by uncovering the underlying epistemic order of principles structuring the surface diversity of our plural commitments. The formulation of principles, the foci of rational agreement, assists in the practical task of problem solving and the formulation of moral advice.

It is clear from Rawls's own work, restricted to the limited case of justice, that there are important background assumptions about practical rationality and conflict shaping his arguments about the mutual relationships between methodological intuitionism and the choice between prioritist and non-prioritist pluralism.[18] It would be unfair to generalize from his consideration of the limited case of principles of justice, but Rawls clearly believed that it was desirable to find relations of priority within the plurality of strict exceptionless principles that harmonized our considered judgements. This was for two reasons: to eliminate the role of intuition in the balancing of the claims of different principles, that apply in a particular case, and because it is a desideratum that such a conflict is resolved by practical reason when possible. But it is possible to hold a different view on both issues. In an important paper Daniel Bonevac has argued that it is difficult to see how one sets about the processes of revision internal to reflective equilibrium without intuitive judgements about the order in which the process is to proceed. Yet these judgements are themselves shaped by an intuitive grasp of the relative importance of the considerations to be assessed.[19] Furthermore, Bonevac argues that Rawls's view of conflict is also contestable:

---

[17] See Ch. 7, Sect. 1, above.

[18] This is noted by Bonevac, 'Reflection Without Equilibrium', 387–8.

[19] Bonevac notes that 'the decisions that have to be made [during the process of determining equilibrium] are distinctly ethical decisions, requiring intuitive judgement as well as (or as a part of) general considerations of belief revision', ibid. 370.

Rawls looks at conflicts as problems that an adequate theory must solve . . . That violates the intuitionist's sense that we perpetually operate in the face of unresolved conflicts. Solving the priority problem is not an adequacy condition for a conception of justice or ethics. It is an ongoing task that forms one of the chief enterprises of such a conception in practice.[20]

I will return to this point when I discuss non-prioritist pluralism, below. Clearly, the rationalist treats conflict as ideally eliminable: it is a feature of our conflict-ridden intuitions that an appeal to abstract principles will resolve. If such principles conflict, priority relations must be discerned between *them* by appealing to priority relations between them.

I think such a rationalist and epistemologically realist interpretation of the reflective equilibrium method, if generalized, ought to be resisted.[21] This interpretation also overlooks a second point, emphasized by Scanlon, which is that considered judgements are picked out not by their relative concreteness, but *solely* by our degree of initial confidence in them.[22] They can be of any degree of abstractness or concreteness. Further, this initial class of considered moral judgements can be expanded to include judgements as to the relevance of considerations for and against judgements. Both points lead Scanlon to emphasize that the relation between considered judgements and principles is not that of 'extensional fit', and hence that the role of principles in this model is to provide a fuller understanding of our initial reasons for making our considered judgements. Thus, it is a misunderstanding to treat the relation of considered judgement and principle on the model of data and theory in a scientific theory:

Such modification is not a matter of abandoning data points which are too far from the line . . . but rather a matter of coming to believe that we have misunderstood the reasons we had for accepting certain conclusions . . . The revisability of the class of considered judgements thus illustrates the fact that the search for Reflective Equilibrium is essentially a first person enterprise; if the judgements in question were those of other people, treated as a kind of sociological fact, then they would not be susceptible to this particular kind of revision.[23]

The relevance of this point for my purposes is that it brings out the way in which Rawls's method fails to meet a rationalist conception of 'theory'. Reflective equilibrium does not look for underlying structures in a body of neutral data in the way that scientific enquiry seeks underlying explanatory structures. It offers insight into existing commitments from an internal perspective that takes our moral commitments as

---

[20] Ibid. 387. He cites in support of his position the complementary arguments of Isaac Levi, 'Conflict and Social Agency', *Journal of Philosophy*, 79/5 (May, 1982), 231–47.

[21] 'If generalized'—it seems to me very plausible to argue that Rawls succeeded in describing a set of principles in the correct lexical order in the special and restricted case of justice. But a correct model of justice need not be in a form that generalizes to all forms of ethical justification, not even when it is the claims of justice that are being balanced against other claims.

[22] Thomas Scanlon, 'The Aims and Authority of Moral Theory', *Oxford Journal of Legal Studies*, 12/1 (Spring 1992), 1–23. Rawls's earliest presentation of the reflective equilibrium method restricted considered judgements to judgements about particular cases; it was generality that was allowed into the method later. For the earlier version, see 'Outline for a Decision Procedure for Ethics', *Philosophical Review*, 40/2 (Apr. 1951), 177–97.

[23] Scanlon, 'Aims and Authority of Moral Theory', 9–10.

a going concern.[24] I will concede that reflective equilibrium does seek *generality*.[25] However, as Scanlon notes, reflective equilibrium takes within its scope principles of evidential salience as well as principles of judgement. It seems to me plausible to argue that such general principles have a role in moral reasoning that can be acknowledged and described.[26] Full discussion of the issue would take me beyond the confines of this book, but recent, revisionary, readings of W. D. Ross contest the view that he offers a theory in the form of a list of prima facie duties that use a thin, deontic vocabulary.[27] Perhaps, instead, what matters is what Ross calls the 'grounds' of duty. On such grounds of duty Ross can plausibly be represented as an Aristotelian particularist. The general element in ethical deliberation is a list of principles of evidential salience that dictate what tends to count as evidence in broad classes of case. Taken in this way, there is a distinctive role for such principles, and this can be incorporated within the reflective equilibrium method.

This point, that reflective equilibrium seeks generality but not abstraction, can be separated from the claim that reflective equilibrium should be viewed as a coherence theory of moral justification. It should, by my lights, be reinterpreted as offering that which I have called, following Wittgenstein, a perspicuous surview ('Übersicht') of existing commitments rather than a theory of them in the rationalist sense. It is a form of modest foundationalism.[28] This view can, from my perspective, be reinterpreted as exemplifying a contextualist theory of justification, as I will argue in more detail in the next section.

To what extent does the reflective equilibrium methodology lend itself to the contrasting rationalist and epistemologically realist interpretation? Admittedly, proponents of the method have frequently warned against interpreting it as exemplifying what Dworkin called the 'natural model', as in any way akin to the formulation of scientific generalizations or laws from observational evidence.[29] My point, however, is that the rationalist/epistemologically realist understanding of the method can survive

---

[24] Scanlon describes the aim of 'Philosophical Enquiry' into morality as 'explain[-ing] more clearly the kind of reasons those who accept morality have for doing so', ibid. 14.

[25] This leads directly into the contemporary dispute between particularists and generalists about moral judgement. It seems to me that the particularist, with whom I have a great deal of sympathy, can concede that there is obviously a role for general principles of evidential salience. But these principles are precisely that, to use Philippa Foot's distinction: general in their role as determining the relevance of evidence bearing on a moral decision. This is no concession, as particularism is a thesis about that which Foot called verdictive judgements. See Foot, 'Moral Beliefs', in *Virtues and Vices*, 182.

[26] My own views on this issue are (briefly) set out in 'Practical Reasoning and Normative Relevance', *Journal of Moral Philosophy* (forthcoming).

[27] Sir David Ross's work in particular has been defended by Philip Stratton-Lake (interpreted, it has to be said, in a distinctive way) in *Kant, Duty and Moral Worth*. I discussed Stratton-Lake's view, alongside other innovative reinterpretations of Kant's practical philosophy, in 'Kant's Practical Philosophy Reconsidered' presented to a conference of the same title at the University of Kent, 2004.

[28] As argued for in DePaul, 'Two Conceptions of Coherence Methods in Ethics'; Ebertz, 'Is Reflective Equilibrium a Coherentist Model?'. I will discuss their views in more detail below.

[29] Ronald Dworkin, 'The Original Position', in Daniels (ed.), *Reading Rawls*, 16–52. The disanalogy between the adjustment of considered judgement to principle and the adjustment of observational evidence to covering law in a scientific context was stressed by Daniels in sect. 3B of 'Wide Reflective Equilibrium and Theory Acceptance in Ethics'.

even when explicitly distanced from an overly scientistic understanding of the procedure. This mistaken understanding of reflective equilibrium will take the phenomenological data supplied by methodological intuitionism as input and yield a Ross-style
list of discursive abstract principles as output, in the light of some standing background theories in the human sciences.

Again, it would overburden this book to go into too much detail, but some recent
sophisticated views combine this kind of approach with a further derivation of the
discursive principles from a more fundamental or abstract principle akin to the categorical imperative.[30] At this point the rationalist treatment of reflective equilibrium
shows its true colours. Kant claimed that he could derive the moral law from reflections on practical reason or from analysing the common moral consciousness. In these
recent sophisticated proposals reflective equilibrium takes our ordinary moral judgements and then converts them into a list of abstract principles so that they can then
plausibly be derived from a higher order principle of reason.[31] But in my view, we
have reason to resist every part of this proposal. The starting point of this process,
our ordinary moral judgements, is misdescribed. It is then misrepresented by a list
of abstract principles in a 'thin' deontic vocabulary. So the process used to launder
our first order judgements, to prepare them for rationalist derivation from an abstract
principle, is suspect. So is the fundamental motivation: to move away from the evaluative and the specific, which is assumed to be conflict-ridden and of no assistance in
solving practical problems, to the thinner air of abstract principle. But, as Williams
points out:

> [R]eflective criticism should basically go in a direction opposite to that encouraged by crit-
> ical theory. Theory looks characteristically for considerations that are very general and have as
> little distinctive content as possible, because it is trying to systematize and because it wants to
> represent as many reasons as possible as applications of other reasons. But critical reflection
> should seek for as much shared understanding as it can find on any issue, and use any ethical

---

[30] There are three discernible versions of this strategy in contemporary moral epistemology:
those of Brad Hooker, 'Ross-Style Pluralism versus Rule-Consequentialism', *Mind*, 106/420 (Oct.
1996), 531–52; Robert Audi, 'A Kantian Intuitionism', *Mind*, 110/439 (July 2001), 601–35 and
The Good in the Right: A Theory of Intuition and Intrinsic Value; finally, Philip Stratton-Lake in
Kant, Duty and Moral Worth (London: Routledge, 2000), ch. 5. Hooker, Stratton-Lake, and Audi
all take as their starting point Ross's list of prima facie duties. Hooker argues that they can be
systematized and justified by a higher order consequentialist principle. Audi derives them more or
less directly from something akin to the moral law. Stratton-Lake has a particularly subtle view in
which the prima facie duties retain a particular kind of role distinct from that of the moral law
proper, which is he argues a constitutive principle that explains how deontic modality is so much
as possible. I cannot do full justice to these subtle views and all the issues that they raise in this
book. However, I have discussed Hooker's derivation in some detail in 'Consequentialism and the
Subversion of Pluralism', in Brad Hooker, Elinor Mason, and Dale Miller (eds.), *Morality, Rules and
Consequences* (Edinburgh: Edinburgh University Press, 2000), 179–202 and Stratton-Lake's view in
'Kant's Practical Philosophy Reconsidered'. The reasons I give for not viewing the account of moral
knowledge defended in this book as a kind of historicized Kantianism suggest some reasons as to
why I see my view as importantly different from these versions of Kantianism or consequentialism.

[31] That the rationalism underpinning these views misrepresents the most plausible form of
pluralism will be argued in Sect. 5, below; see also 'Consequentialism and the Subversion of
Pluralism', 186–90.

material that, in the context of the reflective discussion, makes some sense and commands some loyalty.[32]

So much for how one should *not* view the relation between methodological intuitionism and reflective equilibrium. How ought one to see them as related? A description of this relation is the task of the next section of this chapter.

2. FROM REFLECTIVE EQUILIBRIUM TO CONTEXTUALISM

It seems to me important to emphasize that the reflective equilibrium method is in fact compatible with a degree of modest foundationalism, a point established by both Michael DePaul and Gary Ebertz.[33] DePaul, like Bonevac, focuses on situations where a person's moral beliefs face expansion in the light of new experience.[34] This kind of case allows DePaul to contrast a 'conservative' and a 'radical' interpretation of reflective equilibrium. On the conservative interpretation, the grounds of a person's judgements may be further understood, but the judgements function themselves relatively foundationally, vis-à-vis the other judgements in the course of synchronic reflection. On the radical interpretation, a person revises his or her judgements not solely on the basis of the need to eliminate internal incoherence in his or her beliefs as a whole. He or she may simply 'change his [or her] mind about a proposition'.[35]

DePaul argues that the radical interpretation is the only sustainable one as it acknowledges the role of new beliefs with direct support from ethical experience, for example, beliefs based on moral conversions. He describes his version of the radical position as follows:

In a truly radical moral conversion changes in belief or degrees of belief are not dictated by some strongly held considered moral judgements or background philosophical belief... The distinctive feature of the radical conception of reflective equilibrium is that a person can just change her mind about something.[36]

Discussing the more general epistemological features of his view, DePaul notes that 'my more radical coherence method may seem to be more a version of foundationalism'.[37] I believe that the contextualist can take this general description and make it more precise: it is a description of a contextual model of moral justification. But to see why, it is helpful to focus on Ebertz's parallel conclusions to those of DePaul. His argument begins with the claim that 'some beliefs must be justified in virtue of some source or sources of direct prima facie justification'.[38] He then offers two arguments against the purely coherentist interpretation of reflective equilibrium which focus on

---

[32] Williams, *Ethics and the Limits of Philosophy*, 116–17.

[33] DePaul, 'Two Conceptions of Coherence Methods in Ethics'; Ebertz, 'Is Reflective Equilibrium a Coherentist Model?'.

[34] Bonevac, 'Reflection Without Equilibrium', 371, 377; DePaul, 'Two Conceptions of Coherence Methods in Ethics', 469–471.

[35] DePaul, 'Two Conceptions of Coherence Methods in Ethics', 463.

[36] Ibid. 469.

[37] Ibid. 472.

[38] Ebertz, 'Is Reflective Equilibrium a Coherentist Model?', 201.

the role of considered moral judgements. First, on a conservative understanding of the process of reflection, 'both considered judgements and common presuppositions *function as* foundational beliefs'.[39] They are based on an individual's moral capacity to make firm judgements, 'to respond evaluatively to situations around them'.[40] They are subjected to reflection, but, crucially, this does not change their role:

> they have a prima facie privileged justificatory status in the structure, a status which is not derived merely from their relationship to other beliefs... they have prima facie direct justification... In the reflective process they may be defeated or thrown out. Nevertheless, if they do survive the process, we have no reason to believe they somehow lose their direct justification.[41]

However, this leaves open the possibility of global replacement of such judgements in the more radical model of reflective equilibrium suggested by DePaul. DePaul himself clearly does not take this line of envisaging the radical extension of a person's considered moral judgements such that the latter are all replaced by directly supported judgements; that would be to abandon the vestigially coherentist aspect of his view and move over fully to a foundationalist view. There is no reason to believe that reflective equilibrium can be given an interpretation that is *that* radical. However, the contextualist can point to an argument put forward by Ebertz: if a sequence of contextually motivated transitions totally replace the considered moral judgements from which enquiry began, that has not eliminated the role of a class of considered moral judgements in the process of enquiry as a whole. Ebertz points out that some set of judgements will *still* play the role of considered moral judgements and he picks out that class functionally:

> the fact that an individual's initial considered moral judgements are all rejected as she seeks reflective equilibrium does not entail *that in the end there are no considered moral judgements in the system*. In fact, it is crucial to Rawls's understanding of reflective equilibrium... that when reflective equilibrium is reached the resulting system of beliefs involves a balanced set of considered moral judgements and other moral and theoretical beliefs.[42] [emphasis added]

So reflective equilibrium seems compatible with a degree of modest foundationalism. I would describe the result differently. It is best interpreted as a form of contextualism. When new, directly supported, moral beliefs are added in the process of reflection some subset of all beliefs are, nevertheless, 'held fast' as considered moral judgements. In my view the real interest of this fact arises when it is combined with a second point: that initial judgements, which become firmly held considered judgements in the course of reflection, can be concrete ethical judgements. They deploy thick concepts and are guided by something akin to theoretically informed observation. That takes us all the way to the kind of contextualism that I want to defend.

---

[39] Ibid. 204. My italics, to emphasize the contextualist reading of this remark, which would highlight how beliefs can function foundationally within a context.

[40] I interpolate the term 'firm' into Ebertz's theory, taken from Audi's 'Intuitionism, Pluralism and the Foundations of Ethics', in Mark Timmons and Walter Sinnott-Armstrong (eds.), *Moral Knowledge?: New Readings in Moral Epistemology* (Oxford: Oxford University Press, 1996), 101–36 at 109–10. For justification for this and further discussion of Audi's paper see Sect. 3, below.

[41] Ebertz, 'Is Reflective Equilibrum a Coherentist Model?', 202.

[42] Ibid. 203.

On this alternative understanding of reflective equilibrium, hypothesized to start from a class of judgements that includes concrete judgements deploying thick concepts, it proceeds as follows. Methodological intuitionism supplies a set of judgements that reflect a true description of our moral experience. A degree of reflection on conditions of error leads us to revise this class into the class of considered moral judgements. These judgements vary from specific judgements, which largely deploy thick concepts, to general judgements more reliant on thin vocabulary. We have to take this initial set of judgements to possess some degree of belief worthiness. It must possess some direct justification. We now seek on the basis of further reflection to determine if any further degree of generality (not abstraction) can be derived from reflection on the class of considered moral judgements. The course of reflection may lead us to dismiss some of this set of considered moral judgements, but it does not follow that those that remain have lost what direct justification they possessed (I take this final and very important point from Ebertz).

Now comes the transition from narrow reflective equilibrium to wide. The first question that arises is what motivates this next stage. Holmgren, in her critique of Daniels, points out that the move to wide reflective equilibrium is justified by Daniels by one central argument: that wide reflective equilibrium is a superior strategy to narrow reflective equilibrium for ensuring that we do not accidentally generalize over our considered moral judgements but are, rather, discerning a theoretically insightful and explanatory structure in our moral beliefs. Holmgren points out that this justification is not wholly convincing.[43]

We need to draw on moral background theories that are independent of the class of considered moral judgements in the sense that Daniels explained. They are independent because they are supported by a disjoined subset of our considered moral judgements, not the set as a whole. So the general principles that narrow reflective equilibrium has drawn up now have two forms of sources of support: their relation to considered moral judgements and their relation to moral background theories. These sources are independent of each other. But even if this proposal is realizable, and I do not personally believe it is (for reasons which I will go into in more detail in Chapter 10), why should this come as a surprise to the more orthodox intuitionist, disinclined to move beyond narrow reflective equilibrium? He or she can point out how much is achieved by reaching narrow reflective equilibrium: considered moral judgements have been screened by a theory of error. They have been reflectively revised in the light of such general principles, hedged with *ceteris paribus* clauses, as are available in a particular case. (This is already to depart from Rawls's ambition to find strict, exceptionless, principles.) Holmgren argues,

> If wide reflective equilibrium differs from narrow reflective equilibrium only in the use of background moral theories, the proponent of wide reflective equilibrium must acknowledge, with the moral intuitionist, both that our considered moral judgements have a prima facie

---

[43] Holmgren argues, in a manner parallel to Ebertz, that, 'In attributing prima facie credibility to our considered moral judgements, we need not claim that any of them are in principle immune to revision. We need only claim that they must be regarded as credible unless we have good reason to revise or discard them', 'The Wide and Narrow of Reflective Equilibrium', 46 n. 8.

credibility and that moral theories derive their credibility from the fact that they systemat-
ize these judgements. In this case wide reflective equilibrium should be regarded simply as a
more sophisticated methodology to be adopted by the intuitionist rather than as a methodology that allows us to bypass moral intuitionism, along with whatever difficulties this position
may entail.[44]

She adds that narrow reflective equilibrium has its own resources for avoiding
accidental generalization over considered moral judgements, namely, seeking as small
a number of judgements that are maximally explanatory. Whether this resource is
preferable to drawing on the background theories cited in wide reflective equilibrium
is, she argues, an open question.[45] A methodological and normative non-prioritist
pluralist, such as myself, agrees that the question is open in principle, but is sceptical
as to the degree of further generality discernible in our considered moral judgements
and is similarly sceptical as to the required independence of background theories in
the human sciences. The reflective equilibrium method is an addition to the armoury
of the moral epistemologist, but its deployment is not guaranteed to take us much
beyond an unsystematic pluralism that offers us deeper insight into our previous
ethical commitments, akin to a Wittgensteinian perspicuous surview of our pre-
existing commitments and our degree of confidence in them.

We have really been returned, I suggest, to Rawls's original, modest, methodological proposal. When we take methodological intuitionism as a starting point and
apply the method of reflective equilibrium to this initial data, the outcome is open.
Either a comprehensive coherence theory, or a contextualist theory, is an attempt at a
reflective explanation and justification of the ethical phenomena. How far each view
can realise its conflicting ideals is to be judged on the merits of particular proposals.
Rawls never denied this, not least for the restricted case that particularly concerned
him, namely the theory of justice. He only rejected non-prioritist pluralism in that
case because he thought he could do better by devising lexically ordered principles for
the particular case of a theory of justice. The key difference between Rawls's interpretation of reflective equilibrium in the particular case of theories of justice and the
contextualist account of reflective equilibrium that I have defended here involves the
extent to which considered moral judgements possess a direct evidential warrant that
they do not lose. Explaining how such direct warrant is possible is the task of the next
section.

[44] Ibid. 57.
[45] On the basis of her interesting argument (ibid. 58–9) that if a single principle in narrow
reflective equilibrium, P, captures a wide range of considered moral judgements which is captured
by a plurality of background theories Q, R, S, T in wide reflective equilibrium, the latter must
be more internally complex because of the independence constraint. So a theory which was based
on P would be preferable to the theory based on Q, R, S, T. Holmgren concludes that 'the
strategy narrow reflective equilibrium embodies for avoiding accidental generalisation is in fact
more basic . . . than the strategy embodied in wide reflective equilibrium. However, [the latter] is
clearly workable . . . it seems appropriate for the sophisticated moral intuitionist to regard these two
strategies as complementary rather than competing techniques', ibid. 59.

3. PHENOMENOLOGY, THEORY, AND THE CHARGE OF CIRCULARITY

I noted in Chapter 2, in my exposition of the original cognitivist theory, that some of the strongest arguments for the theory were phenomenological, that is, based on an appeal to our moral experience. Yet I have also made the following three claims: that cognitivism is not committed, via the secondary quality analogy, to the claim that there is a *sui generis* 'moral experience'. Secondly, that one cannot buttress an account of justification in ethics by appealing to a privileged account of empirical content, as one can combine coherentism with a representationalist account of empirical content in explaining our perceptual knowledge of an objective world. We seem to have in the ethical case pure coherence, standing alone, not tacitly drawing support from a combination of coherence and externalism in the theory of empirical content.[46] Thirdly, moral knowledge is a form of theoretical knowledge and that observation is theory laden, a claim accepted both by a sceptic like Harman and endorsed by the canonical Cornell realist Richard Boyd.[47] I will put that final claim to some positive work in the next section. How can all these claims be combined?

The problem is that any defensible account of phenomenology must take phenomenology to be an appeal to a relatively neutral conception of experience. (To the extent that one inflates claims about the content of moral experience, so one invites rejection of the claim that we have moral experiences in *that* sense.) Yet if experience is theory laden, any deployment of the idea of experience in a justificatory role begs the question against those who deny the view of moral experience to which one is appealing. So an appeal to phenomenology is debarred. The unpalatable choice is to abandon an attractive way of conceiving of our moral knowledge as a form of knowledge with prima facie direct support in experience, plus indirect support from its incorporation into a contextualist model of justification, or, alternatively, to abandon the basis of the theory in moral phenomenology. If I am appealing to experience, I do not need theory; if I am appealing to theory, I do not need experience.

That dichotomy is, fortunately, too simple. I want to argue that there is a clear sense in which experience provides direct support for moral judgements and that such judgements can be further reinforced by theory or disconfirmed by it. But this reflects my view that the case for cognitivism is an overdetermined one. One strategy, to which I am obviously sympathetic, would be to eschew any appeal to phenomenology and to let the theory I have defended stand alone. This strategy would work, first, by pointing to the implicit commitment to cognitivism in the surface syntax of moral discourse as a default setting, an entitlement authorized by the adoption of minimalism. Secondly, one would construct an epistemological theory that vindicated this claim to objectivity while also undermining the assumptions of any sceptical analysis

---

[46] Externalism in this sense has no relation to externalism in the theory of moral motivation and the duplication of terminology is merely unfortunate.

[47] Boyd, 'How to be a Moral Realist'.

of that area of thought and language. The argument of this book works partly in this way, but I do not believe that I have to abandon appeals to phenomenology entirely. It all depends on how one explains the idea of theory dependence. If I can vindicate such an appeal to phenomenology, this book will offer more than the undermining of sceptical arguments against the objectivity of morality (a negative line of argument); it will offer, in addition, positive presumptive grounds for such objectivity grounded in the phenomenology of our moral experience.

The role of the appeal to theory is simply this: that it is no more surprising or philosophically problematic to assume that a person can judge that what the hooligans did to the cat was cruel, on the basis of observation, than that a physicist can judge from the presence of a trace in a cloud chamber that a proton is present. The point is a negative one, namely, that we do not have to appeal to a dedicated special faculty to explain this kind of knowledge. We have only to appeal to the capacities of the appropriately trained judger deploying a general capacity we possess for theory formation and the inculcated and developed capacities of the scientific observer/virtuous agent.

Now the two cases undoubtedly differ. If I were to look through an electron microscope I would not, in the relevant sense, 'see' anything as I have not been trained as a laboratory technician.[48] Observation in scientific contexts may require a highly skilled exercise of one's capacities as a result of lengthy training and development. The demands for making ethical judgements do not seem to require that level of skill and training. Furthermore, ethical judgement draws on a much wider range of general capacities, such as capacities for clear judgement, imagination, sympathy, an appropriate degree of involvement or detachment and for appropriate emotional response. Finally, we have the internalism requirement, at least in so far as it survived the discussions of Chapters 3 and 4 in an attenuated form. This is the requirement that for an appropriately disposed judger who is fully rational, moral knowledge supplies an important, indeed authoritative, disposition that guides which evidential considerations that agent will put to others.[49] But nothing in this suggests the model of a special faculty of moral sense for the acquisition and deployment of moral knowledge, nor should it. It is a non sequitur to argue from the fact that we only have one way of accessing a realm of facts to the conclusion that this requires a dedicated epistemological faculty specifically for that purpose.

What, then, of theory dependence? The problem is one of circularity and this is a charge that contextualism has to confront in two distinct forms. Circularity enters into the relation between theory and evidence and also into the intra-theoretic relationship between beliefs that are vindicated relative to a context and those that are

---

[48] This is taken by some social constructivists to be proof that the scientific world picture is manufactured—look at how that technician is being inculcated into the relevant form of life—whereas it seems to me to prove the very opposite. Observing real things in controlled conditions just is the very difficult exercise of a highly skilled capacity and it is difficult precisely because it is trying to get something objectively right.

[49] This points precisely to one of the differences between dispositions of character that are skills and those that are virtues, namely, the implication of the latter with characteristic patterns of motivation. See Williams, *Ethics and the Limits of Philosophy*, 'One can be a good pianist and have no desire to play, but if one is generous or fair minded, those qualities themselves help to determine, in the right contexts, what one will want to do', 9.

merely presupposed. Rebutting these circularity charges requires the introduction of some internal complexity to the contextualist model that I have defended so far.

The issue of theory dependence is, in my view, resolved in three stages. First, the kind of case for which the problem arises must be isolated; we are dealing with inputs to theory. This is the class of cases that function as basic, relative to a context, in which a judger deploys thick ethical concepts. Second, it must be noted that theory dependence comes in positive and negative forms, as explained by Robert Audi, to whose work I am indebted on this issue. Audi attempts to explain what Ross intended by treating our intuitions on the model of sense perceptions as an analogy for the way in which they provide data for moral generalizations. He first defines a notion somewhat misleadingly (for my purposes, not his) called 'pre-theoreticality':[50]

Not only will an intuition not be an inference from a theory, it will also not be epistemically dependent on a theory even in the general sense that the theory provides one's justificatory ground (even a noninferential ground) for the intuition.[51]

However, Audi goes on to develop the idea further in a way that allows me to steer between the horns of the dilemma confronting my positive argument for phenomenological prima facie support for cognitivism:

This point does not entail that intuition has complete independence of theory: an intuition may be defeated and abandoned in the light of theoretical results incompatible with its truth, especially when these results are supported by other intuitions. This is a kind of negative epistemic dependence of intuition on theory: the justification does not derive from the impossibility of such untoward hypothetical results, but it can be destroyed by them if they occur. Such defeasibility on the part of intuition is not a positive justificatory dependence on any actual theory: it is a negative dependence on—in the sense of a vulnerability to—disconfirmation by theories, whether actual or possible.[52]

This explains the limited sense in which judgements of experience that are basic, relative to a context, in which a judger deploys thick concepts to conceptualize a situation, can act as inputs into theory while being vulnerable to disconfirmation by theories. Theory dependence is only being presupposed in a negative rather than a positive form. Thirdly, as Audi notes, even if no moral perception meets this strong

---

[50] Audi, 'Intuitionism, Pluralism and the Foundations of Ethics', 110–11. Let me explain why I take this account to be misleading from my perspective. Audi is, at this point in his argument, explaining why he takes intuitions to be 'pre-theoretical'. Am I not thereby distorting his account into an account of theoreticality precisely counter to his intentions? No, because he goes on to make the following important qualifications to his account of 'pre-theoreticality': 'The perceptual analogy is also misleading because intuitions need not be about observable: rights are not observable, yet we have intuitions about them. We may see them in the sense of recognising them, as when one sees a right to refuse feeding tubes, but they are not seen visually. *If what is both nonobservable and significantly complex is thereby theoretical, then we certainly have intuitions about theoretical entities*; but such "theoretical" intuitions need not be epistemically dependent on any theory', 111 [emphasis added]. I am using 'theoretical' in the broad sense Audi concedes, whereas he is defining a more restricted concept. I take Audi's 'pre-theoreticality' to mark off a restriction *within* the theoretical as I am using the term 'theoretical'.

[51] Ibid. 110–11.
[52] Ibid.

requirement of only negative dependence, one need not abandon the idea of moral generalizations being supported by perceptions:

If . . . to have concepts sufficient for judging a theory one must be biased by either the theory or another one relevant to judging the theory . . . One would hope that even if every judge has some biases, there are some judges who at least have no biases that vitiate their decisions on cases they must resolve . . . perhaps some [cognitions] may be pre-theoretical [i.e. only negatively dependent on theory] with respect to a moral generalization needing appraisal.[53]

This would constitute my defence of continuing to appeal, from within the contextualism I have developed, to the phenomenological arguments of Chapter 2.[54] However, I note again that strictly speaking I do not need this argument to work in order to defend the overall position I have set out. However, defence in depth is usually a prudent strategy.

To avoid misunderstanding, let me once again explain that I do not mean, by the term 'theory', that which many moral philosophers mean by the term. I do not, in this book, defend a general, constitutive account of the nature of rightness and wrongness using abstract and thin ethical concepts in the way that, for example, contemporary contractualism does. Such a view would welcome Williams's non-objectivism, or Harman's scepticism, as usefully clarifying our ethical position. All that we have, the contractualist argues, are thin ethical concepts. All the better, then, that one can construct a theory out of them. By a 'theory' I refer simply to a reflective account of ethical knowledge that begins with the thick evaluative vocabulary implicit in our ethical experience and seeks that generality which is to hand, just as non-prioritist pluralism suggests. We may gain insight into our existing commitments by finding some degree of generality in our moral principles that are related to our more concrete judgements, but, equally, we may not.

Secondly, I do not believe that the role I have given to moral experience in this account resurrects foundationalism, nor makes ethical justification modestly a priori. Possessing a prima facie direct support from experience only gives an ethical belief

---

[53] Ibid. 111.

[54] Were I to develop the argument further, I would draw on the subtle and interesting paper by Tolhurst, 'On the Epistemic Value of Moral Experience', whose central contention the author summarizes as follows: 'moral experience always involves the experience of fittingness . . . we must distinguish two different ways in which the concept of fittingness figures in the explication of moral experience. First, there is the experience of deontic value: to experience an action as obligatory is to experience it as being required by or fitting the circumstances in which it would be performed . . . In addition to deontic moral experiences, we also have experiences of moral goodness and badness which cannot adequately be analysed in this way . . . To experience something as being good is to experience it as calling for or demanding some sort of positive response from us', 78. Tolhurst attributes this conception to Mandelbaum and Brentano, in addition to McDowell. I would like to note the points of difference between Tolhurst's account and my own: Tolhurst identifies 'moral experience' with concomitant emotion, rather than belief, and seems to assume that the direction of justification in basic cases is from general to particular. On the former point, it seems to me that the only invariant moral experience is precisely the experience of fittingness and that a separate account must be given of emotions such as guilt and shame. On the latter point, I would argue that the basic cases are particular judgements that are the basis of (evidential) general principles. I will discuss this point in detail in the following sections.

a provisional degree of support that can be overturned by its relation to the background context of beliefs. Contextualism is happy with the view that beliefs *appear* to function foundationally, particularly within first personal belief systems. But any such belief is open to revision given the standing of the other beliefs drawn upon in that problem situation, a situation set up when that particular belief comes to be doubted for some specific reason.

Some moral philosophers appeal to theory, others to experience, but it is unusual to do both. So some further clarification of how I intend these two aspects of the view defended here to be integrated (where that is an appropriate goal) seems necessary. Appeal to moral experience here is intended as a pretty minimal notion. Given that many contemporary analytic philosophers have a healthy dose of empiricist scepticism even when they are not card-carrying empiricists, any appeal to ethical experience can seem akin to an appeal to experience of the paranormal. But the idea should be understood in as mundane a way as possible. John McDowell, in his original formulations using visual metaphors, spoke simply of 'seeing situations in a certain light' and of the 'perception of saliences'.[55]

Given that minimal and hopefully unexciting account of moral experience, how can such an appeal to experience be combined with the methodology of reflective equilibrium? Very simply, by heeding the reminder that Rawls's proposal was merely methodological and that it does not, automatically, lead one to a coherence theory of justification. Coherentism ought, in its pure form, to insist that epistemic status is always a relational property of beliefs and thus it ought to find problematic even the idea of a prima facie support for a belief in ethical experience. But I have described an alternative understanding of Rawls's proposal that allows for the idea that the inputs to reflective equilibrium can have direct epistemological support. Having described my account of the prima facie direct justification of ethical judgements using specific thick ethical concepts, I will explore in more detail the phenomenological arguments cited in Chapter 1 as a source of support for cognitivism in the next chapter. A preliminary task is to elucidate the relationship between the view I have defended here and non-prioritist ethical pluralism. That discussion will conclude this chapter.

4. BELIEF, ARTICULATION, AND A CONTEXTUALIST MODEL OF JUSTIFICATION

It may be helpful, at this point, to put some flesh on what may seem to be the bare bones of a rather abstract proposal. How, exactly, does a contextualist about ethical justification see such justification as proceeding? Specifying the process in more detail will also allow me to address an important further issue as to whether or not the process is misrepresented if it is seen as being analogous to the justification of theoretical *belief* at all.

---

[55] For independent, deflationary accounts of that in which moral realism consists see e.g. Stuart Hampshire, *Innocence and Experience* (Cambridge, Mass.: Harvard University Press, 1989), 90; Richard Norman, 'Making Sense of Moral Realism', *Philosophical Investigations*, 20/2 (Apr. 1997), 117–35.

In summary, the moral contextualist views justification as follows: moral justification occurs relative to a context. An agent defending a particular moral judgement can draw either on the intrinsic status of the judgement if it is an experiential judgment or the overdetermined evidential support available from the relation between that judgement and a background framework of beliefs. The verdict of moral experience is positive presumptive: it offers direct support for judgement, but it is negatively dependent on theory because background theory can overturn it. (I explained how this works above.) Contexts are complex functional organizations of beliefs of different degrees of particularity and generality that serve several distinctive functions. They articulate a moral ontology: they offer the concepts to conceptualize the world, including moral ideals and identities, in certain ways salient to ethical judgement. These conceptualizations permit the derivation of a class of relevant reasons bearing on moral judgements. By supplying a basis of topic specific truisms such contexts sustain substantive judgements of reasonableness. For an appropriately receptive judger, they make certain kinds of ethical experience possible. Finally, such contexts exhibit the dependence of moral judgement on established, intra-traditional methods of moral reasoning.

Many of these functions seem to have constructivist overtones. If this is indeed, as in a certain style of Wittgensteinian writing about ethics, a matter of bringing moral agents to the point where they 'see matters aright', ought we not to see this whole issue in more aestheticized terms? The point of this alternative picture is to suggest that the contextualist view I have described is too focused on something akin to theoretical belief. The issue is, rather, articulation and expressive power. The point is, the critic urges, to articulate and express a conception of the world and of our identities within it, rather than offer a theoretical description.

I agree with a great deal of this, except the phrase 'rather than'. There is clearly an important role, within a contextualist model of moral justification, for those very perspectivally local and expressively powerful images of the world that depend on one's capacity to articulate them. But they are still best viewed as sets of beliefs. The line between making and finding in setting out such a view of the world may be unclear, but in my view 'finding' is clearly prior to 'making'. These challenges to a model focused exclusively on beliefs have been raised very acutely by Charles Taylor in *Sources of the Self*. In his account of this first function of a background framework, that of articulating a moral ontology, Taylor emphasizes the connection between such articulation and our powers of expression. Articulation is important to our capacity adequately to describe situations to make them objects of judgement.[56] A range of subject terms and predicates are made available to the judger to conceptualize the range of relevant moral objects of appraisal. For example, if I want to extend your moral sympathies to the lives of animals, I may try and make you see them as sharing a life with you as part of a natural world in which you should live in harmony, not as a set of resources for exploitation.[57] The first task played by a background framework is to articulate an ontology, so that the question arises as to whether such a framework is adequate in its expressive power.

---

[56] Taylor, *Sources of the Self*, ch. 1, pp. 5–8.
[57] J. M. Coetzee, *The Lives of Animals* (Princeton: Princeton University Press, 2001).

Nevertheless, it does seem to me that in this case, as in other areas of Taylor's philosophy (such as his general philosophical anthropology which sees us as 'self-interpreting animals') we make best sense of Taylor's account of interpretation by taking it to be a cognitive process that articulates beliefs: that is why 'articulate' is the correct verb.[58] Articulation unpacks the features of a real object, whose identity is held fixed throughout the process of articulation so we have to view that object and its properties as picked out by beliefs.

As a special case of this ontological articulation, background frameworks of belief can express personal moral identities. For his own Hegelian purposes, Charles Taylor lays great stress on this role of background frameworks in morally orienting the self towards the good and essentially orienting the self towards other people.[59] Such frameworks can articulate the relevant features of our moral identity. However, it seems to me that this is a particular instance of what a background framework of belief can be used to do, as opposed to anything inherent to its structure. One important role that such frameworks can play is to give us beliefs about our own moral identity. I would prefer to classify this as an aspect of articulation of a moral ontology, with the proviso that a limiting case is where the object articulated is one's own identity. (In such cases, Taylor's emphasis on expressive power and the blurred line between finding and making summed up by his central metaphor of articulation is well placed.)

In principle, one can separate this articulation of an ontology from a class of general evidential principles, but in fact the two go hand in hand. In making you see the world as made up of certain morally relevant objects, I make you see a range of concerns as relevant to them. Certain aspects of the world now register as evidentially salient to you. It matters, as a result of our articulation, that this animal is feeling pain in a way it did not do so when that animal was an exploitable resource, or a morally indifferent part of the workings of the natural order. A background framework of moral beliefs thus equips a moral judge to respond to certain features of the world as morally relevant, both at the level of the 'constituency' of morality, the idea that these things morally count, and at the level of that which may be relevantly predicated of these objects so conceived. A relevant range of reasons has been articulated.

There is a further important function provided by such frameworks: they supply a context of substantive topic-specific truisms. Paralleling Miller's account of theoretical reasons, moral reasoning across background frameworks of belief requires the support of substantive topic-specific truisms.[60] The role of such commitments will be further considered when I discuss practical reasoning across frameworks of belief in the next chapter. Examples of such truisms would be that animals can feel pain, but they cannot be held responsible; animals can exhibit intelligent behaviour and

[58] Richard Moran, *Authority and Estrangement* (Princeton and Oxford: Princeton University Press, 2001), ch. 2, contains an extended discussion of Taylor's account of articulation and argues that the best interpretation of that view sees it, as Taylor sometimes seems not to, as committed to an objective and realist conception of the mental. Thus the mental states involved must be cognitive states, if we are to understand what a process of articulation is supposed to be.

[59] Taylor, *Sources of the Self*, sects. 1.4, 1.5, 2.1.
[60] Miller, *Fact and Method*, 219–22.

'higher' animals can exhibit the higher forms of mental distress akin to psychoses (anyone who has seen the disturbed behaviour of some zoo animals would attest to the latter). Nothing yet, of course, adds up to a theory of what Foot would call verdictive judgements. All parties can agree that there is a gap between the conflicting data supplied by the world, even the world of morally salient values, and the final executive decision of the agent. A moderate particularism is, it seems to me, probably the most plausible account of practical verdicts, but cognitivism is a theory about the evidential input to such verdicts.[61]

Three issues immediately seem to arise for the responsible and reflective agent. First, for an appropriately receptive agent, a person with the right sensibility and virtues, a certain range of experiences has become available to the agent, experiences with a direct ethical justification. The cruelty of the treatment of an animal can be 'seen'. Secondly, the experienced world can present (as I have noted) conflicting evaluative aspects. Thirdly, the agent possesses an allegiance to more than one background framework of moral belief. The second and third points introduce moral conflict into the picture.

It is certainly true that when pushed to justify their moral beliefs beyond a certain point, most people respond by citing those beliefs that function 'foundationally' for them in their personal justifications. These are not beliefs about specific cases, but beliefs about the moral constituency and about the relevance of moral considerations. If you cannot see the moral harm of exploiting an animal, if you do not see that consideration as relevant, most agents are inclined to shrug their shoulders and say that they take the relevance of such considerations as a given and they are not unseated in this by the fact that you cannot 'see'. They are not wrong to respond in this way, but it also seems to me that a more complete or full explanation of these responses is possible, where this is not understood in a coherentist way. (This is connected to my view that contextualism is very plausible as an account of first personal justification, but that no fully defensible contextualism can rest on that point alone.)

We are reflectively aware that our ethical outlook is internally complex and reflects a diverse historical deposit from many different traditions of ethical enquiry. This does not, in itself, commit us to some form of the genetic fallacy. (This would be the fallacy of inferring from the contingent origins of our beliefs that they are in some way unjustified.) Our current background frameworks of belief have historical explanations and the question arises in this case of whether those explanations will have a damaging impact on the background frameworks to which we are committed. This is the question, as Bernard Williams put it, of the stability under reflection of the beliefs that make up those frameworks.

Thus, justification in an everyday context, as in the imagined dialogue about the ethical status of animals, naturally leads in the direction of the justification of the relationship between background frameworks themselves. Additional justification is available to those who have direct, phenomenological support for their moral beliefs

---

[61] I have suggested that the evidential/verdictive distinction may be of some assistance in explaining the disagreements between moral particularists and generalists; for a denial that it is any help, see Jonathan Dancy, *Ethics Without Principles* (Oxford: Oxford University Press, 2004), 16 n. 2.

if they can, on reflection, see themselves as located within a tradition of enquiry that makes the source of their beliefs, and their methods of reasoning, reliable.

This broad account suggests two pressing problems for the kind of view that I want to defend. I have appealed to two theses that have not yet received sufficient defence. The first is the claim that the inputs into reflective equilibrium can possess a direct justification in our experience. The second is the claim that they can possess indirect justification from the reflection that they are acquired by deploying reliable, tradition based, methods of knowledge acquisition. A defence of the first claim will constitute the rest of the argument of this chapter. The defence of the second claim, however, will take the next chapter to articulate in full. It is a recurrent focus for scepticism as to whether any view of this kind is ultimately defensible.

5. THE CONNECTION BETWEEN CONTEXTUALISM AND PLURALISM

The discussion of reflective equilibrium has already suggested another connection worthy of exploration, namely, the link between a contextual model of moral justification and the position in first order normative ethics known as non-prioritist ethical pluralism. I suggest that the two positions are naturally complementary and that contextualism provides a vital supplement to the insights afforded by those philosophers who have defended this form of pluralism. In particular, the role of thick ethical concepts in the argument for a *sui generis* account of moral objectivity I have developed, via contextualism, is important in presenting pluralism in its most plausible form. Pluralism is often assumed to take the form of a list of general duties, couched in thin ethical vocabulary. I have argued that this is not the form a pluralist theory need take and, indeed, that the most plausible version of the theory does not take this form.[62]

Non-prioritist moral pluralism is the view that a correct account of the resources of moral thinking will find an irreducible plurality of principles of moral salience and basic ethical considerations.[63] I take basic ethical considerations to be the exemplification of values by situations, persons, and actions. These judgements will typically be conceptualized by drawing on a range of thick ethical concepts. This class of judgements offers the basic class for the justification of other kinds of moral judgement. Thus, I regard thin ethical concepts as ultimately grounded on evaluative judgements

---

[62] In 'Consequentialism and the Subversion of Pluralism'.

[63] If one sets aside the issue of whether or not pluralism describes a plurality of general or abstract principles or more concrete values (or both) then it is a widely held account of first order normative ethics, defended by Ross, Davidson, Nagel, Williams, Berlin, Taylor, and Gaut. Berys Gaut's 'Moral Pluralism', *Philosophical Papers*, 22/1 (Apr. 1993), 17–40, contains further bibliographic references. Another very valuable characterization of pluralism is Christine Swanton's 'The Rationality of Ethical Intuitionism', *Australasian Journal of Philosophy*, 65/2 (June 1987), 172–81. Gaut has an extended defence of pluralism, including the claim that it is a probable upshot of applying the process of reflective equilibrium, in 'Rag Bags, Disputes and Moral Pluralism', *Utilitas*, 11/1 (Mar. 1999), 37–8 and 'Justifying Moral Pluralism', in Philip Stratton-Lake (ed.), *Ethical Intuitionism: Re-Evaluations* (Oxford: Oxford University Press 2002), 137–60.

primarily deploying thick concepts. Principles of moral salience dictate which reasons typically function to ground specific verdicts in particular cases. They are statements of the tendency of reasons to function as evidential considerations across a range of different contexts of judgement. The role of this class of judgements will be discussed further below. The constitutive features of pluralism which make it distinctive vis-à-vis other reflective accounts of morality have been expressed by Rawls:

> [Pluralist] theories, then, have two features: first, they consist of a plurality of first principles which may conflict to give contrary directives in particular types of cases, and second, they include no explicit method, no priority rules, for weighing these principles against one another: we are simply to strike a balance by intuition, by what seems to us most nearly right. Or if there are no priority rules, these are thought to be more or less trivial and of no substantial assistance in reaching a judgement.[64]

As we have seen, Rawls believed that the only means of rebutting moral pluralism, which he took very seriously as a theory of moral judgement, was to construct a set of principles which can do better from the point of view of developing lexically ordered priority rules in the particular case of justice.[65] In Rawls's account, the pluralist, on the contrary, does not believe such a lexical ordering can be discovered (or imposed).[66]

Two of the main advantages of pluralism are its close tie to moral phenomenology and its phenomenological plausibility. These features directly relate pluralism to the more general theory of methodological intuitionism: the view, held by Urmson and Williams, that the starting point of ethical enquiry should be a phenomenological description of the plural sources available in our ethical experience.[67] Such an unprejudiced phenomenology will, they argued, reveal a plurality of commitments both at the level of moral knowledge and at the level of principles. Thus, the evidence of unprejudiced phenomenology, which is the starting point of methodological intuitionism, and the findings of the reflective account of morality, which is represented by pluralism, match precisely.

The claim that methodological intuitionism is phenomenologically plausible may not seem to be much of an advantage for the view on the grounds that since it simply redescribes our existing commitments, the pluralism that it yields does no more than reproduce a pluralism inherent in the original material. If it does try to do more than this, moral pluralism runs into two problems: it confuses explanation with justification and it faces the problem that it may simply be reproducing a parochialism inherent in the original data.[68]

---

[64] Rawls, *A Theory of Justice* (Cambridge, Mass.: Harvard University Press, 1971) 34. Strictly this is a definition of 'non-prioritist pluralism', as Urmson, Swanton, Williams, and Gaut note.

[65] Rawls has in addition a series of 'in principle' arguments against pluralism, well dealt with by Swanton, Gaut, and Bonevac in their respective papers: Swanton, 'The Rationality of Ethical Intuitionism'; Gaut, 'Moral Pluralism'; Bonevac, 'Reflection Without Equilibrium'.

[66] Philip Stratton-Lake has pointed out to me that this Rawlsian critique of pluralism is controversial: the pluralist could, for example, assign lexical priority to perfect over imperfect duties. Furthermore, not every priority claim need be as strong as lexical ordering.

[67] Urmson, 'A Defence of Intuitionism'; Bernard Williams, 'What Does Intuitionism Imply?'.

[68] I take the first line of objection from those critics of Rawlsian reflective equilibrium who objected to what they took to be the lingering intuitionism of Rawls's commitment to starting

However, we are now in a position to refine the sense in which methodological intuitionism is phenomenologically plausible. It is plausible in that it takes up an internal perspective on our existing moral practices. I have argued throughout this book that any acceptable moral view must further undertake to entertain specific, grounded doubts about the deliverances of any moral phenomenology without thereby being open to global doubts about our moral knowledge as a whole.[69] Pluralism must be open to correction from social theory, put to a critical use, whose workings will come into explicit focus in Chapter 10. Its results are thereby normative and do not merely reflect the de facto content of the ethical materials it seeks to describe. It can entertain specific, grounded doubts about the deliverances of any moral phenomenology, without thereby being open to global doubts about our moral knowledge as a whole. As a reflective account of the ethical, pluralism, like any other acceptable account, must be open to correction from social theory put to a critical use.

While Williams and I disagreed over the availability of ethical knowledge, we agreed on the plausibility of non-prioritist pluralism. Williams's form of pluralism was, unsurprisingly, to a significant degree historicized. Its account of moral phenomenology took that phenomenology to reflect the historical development of different sets of ethical ideas which have to various degrees fused or remained incommensurable with each other. Once again Williams argued that the degree to which the social reality described has proceeded along a path of typically modern reflection would determine the extent to which participants in sets of ethical arrangements deployed thick or thin concepts in describing their experience.

Nevertheless, one can expect that the description of this phenomenology will deliver judgements of any degree of abstraction or concreteness, including the concrete deliverances of thick specific evaluations as well as thinner vocabulary, where this thick versus thin distinction is one of degree. I argued above that only a misapplication of the reflective equilibrium model would lead one to overlook this. Williams himself had a tendency to present his hypertraditionalist fable solely in terms of the thick being displaced by the thin. A more realistic thought experiment makes the upshot of reflection far less clear. It seems to me more likely that an

from 'our' considered moral judgements: Richard Hare, 'Rawls's Theory of Justice', in Norman Daniels (ed.), *Reading Rawls* (New York: Basic Books, 1975), 81–107; Peter Singer, 'Sidgwick and Reflective Equilibrium', *Monist*, 58 (July 1974), 490–517. It should be clear from what follows that my sympathies lie with Rawls, not his critics. This line of objection seems to conflate the requirement that we should be able critically to challenge any claim to moral knowledge with the claim that we must be able critically to challenge all such claims. Hooker is not committed in this way to global scepticism about our considered judgements, nor to defending consequentialism in such a form that it would evade such a global form of scepticism. I take the charge that pluralism conflates justification and explanation to be implied by Hooker's remarks on the 'genetic fallacy' on which see Hooker, 'Ross-Style Pluralism', 546–7.

[69] Gaut's 'Moral Pluralism' similarly emphasizes that any defensible pluralism must build into itself safeguards against the distortion of moral thought by power and interests, in the course of rebutting an envisaged objection on behalf of Rawls. Gaut builds into his theory the quasi-contractualist idea of 'generative reflection'. There are similarities between this idea and the constraints I invoke in this book, notably in Ch. 10. I am indebted to Gaut's valuable discussion of the resources available to the pluralist.

unprejudiced pluralism will find a range of concepts demanded by our experience all along the range from the thick to the thin. All of these materials form the starting point for reflection and Williams further argues that the outcome of reflection will be a combination of a non-prioritist pluralism and a particularist account of judgement. The grounds for his particularism is the ubiquity of judgements of importance:

> Judgements of importance are ubiquitous, and are central to practical life and to reflection at a more general level about the considerations that go into practical decision ... It may be obvious that in general one kind of consideration is more important than another ... but it is a matter of judgement whether in one particular set of circumstances that priority is preserved: other factors alter the balance, or it may be a very weak example of the consideration that generally wins. Last, there is no reason to believe that there is one currency in terms of which all relations of comparative importance can be represented ... [For] any such currency ... it will make sense to ask whether, on a given occasion or more generally, it is more important than something else.[70]

I noted, above, Daniel Bonevac's argument that if Rawls's motivation in rejecting non-prioritist pluralism was to avoid appeals to intuition, or such judgements of importance, then his arguments have to be judged a failure as any realistic account of the application of reflective equilibrium is going to have to appeal to judgements of this kind.[71] That criticism seems very plausible; we do seem unable to do without judgements of this kind.

What would be the upshot of applying reflective equilibrium to the phenomenological data that Williams invokes? In my view, the vindication of contextualism: the method is applied to beliefs whose contents are of any degree of concreteness and abstraction and do not automatically form an ascent from the thick to the thin. My argument has been that applying reflective equilibrium in this way will find generality and a degree of system in principles of moral salience. However, as Rawls allows, its application will leave non-prioritist pluralism intact as both the most plausible reflective account of morality and as compatible with particularism as the best account of verdictive ethical judgement. Reflective equilibrium is not particularly at the service of coherentist or abstracting theory, but is better viewed in Wittgensteinian terms as offering insight into the reasons that we already hold.

The ubiquity of importance and the need for judgement figure in the explanation of why the reflective equilibrium method can have no implications for the degree of abstractness/concreteness of the content of the belief. Any plausible phenomenological description of the various evaluative beliefs we would reflectively endorse will find that those beliefs range from a wide variety of judgements deploying thick ethical concepts, which we can confidently take to express moral knowledge, to other

---

[70] Bernard Williams, *Making Sense of Humanity*, 190. Williams elsewhere rejects 'the general additive model of moral considerations or reasons in terms of the resolution of forces: if a type of consideration ... ever in itself exerts an influence, then it always exerts an influence, and the method of agreement and difference can be used to isolate the influence it exerts. I see no necessity to accept this idea; there are surely many examples of non-moral practical reasoning, and also of aesthetic judgement, that tell against it', 'Acts and Omissions, Doing and Not Doing', in *Making Sense of Humanity*, 57.

[71] Bonevac, 'Reflection Without Equilibrium', 370, 386.

evidential or verdictive judgements employing thinner deontic vocabulary. All of this vocabulary can figure in judgements of any degree of abstractness or concreteness.

These beliefs are functioning modestly foundationally, that is, as initial considered judgements possessing a direct justification as exemplifications of moral knowledge. They are further buttressed by reflection that does not overturn the direct justification of the beliefs but deepens their ground or status as 'firm' beliefs for the subject. They may be couched in thick or thin concepts: a belief in an abstract principle of right may yield to a vivid appreciation of a betrayal of a friend. Conversely, an appreciation of suffering caused may have to be outweighed by a commitment of principle, such as the need to avoid negotiation with evildoers in coercive crises, for example. The need for importance and an ineliminable appeal to the practical use of reason reflects the multi-dimensionality of such judgements. This aspect of the view is compatible with Rawls's original proposal solely to measure degrees of belief, but not with taking the wide reflective equilibrium model to have an epistemologically realist structure. Nor is it compatible with taking the upshot of wide reflective equilibrium to be a set of abstract principles, as in Ross's version of pluralism, even allowing for the application of the reflective equilibrium method. In my view pluralism should not be restricted to a thesis that has already taken the phenomenological data and reduced it to a list of abstract discursive principles couched in thin vocabulary.

I conclude that reflective equilibrium, applied to the phenomenological materials to which Williams appeals, applies to beliefs whose contents are of any degree of concreteness and abstraction and do not automatically form an ascent from the thick to the thin. My argument has been that applying reflective equilibrium in this way will find generality and a degree of system in principles of moral salience, but (as Rawls allows) will leave pluralism intact as the most plausible reflective account of morality and compatible with particularism as the best theory of ethical judgement. Reflective equilibrium is not particularly at the service of coherentist or abstracting theory, but is better viewed in Wittgensteinian terms as offering a perspicuous surview of our existing ethical commitments, offering insight into the reasons we already hold. When extended to belief change where we add to the stock of beliefs directly supported evaluative judgements it is best interpreted as a form of contexualism. It is certainly no challenge to contextualism, rather it is an essential complement to it.

I have offered a proposal that captures the essentials of a contextualist model of moral knowledge and have related this model to the supplementary model of reflective equilibrium. The resulting reflective account of morality has been demonstrated to be compatible with pluralism as a theory of moral judgement. In the next stage of my argument I want to deepen the motivation for being a contextualist by addressing the issue of the maintenance of rationality in the face of conflict between traditions of enquiry.

9

Tradition Based Moral Enquiry

§1: The argument thus far leaves open the possibility of ethical knowledge grounded in traditions of enquiry. §2: A model of tradition based moral reasoning is described and contrasted with Putnam's moral pragmatism and Timmons's contextualism. §3: MacIntyre's and Taylor's narratives of moral knowledge in modern conditions are analysed.

The previous chapter set out the basic elements of a contextualist moral epistemology. However, further argument is necessary as I have claimed that there are two distinct sources of support for one's ethical beliefs. First, they have a direct grounding in experience. Secondly, they have indirect support from their role in a background framework of moral beliefs. That framework is itself further embedded, temporally, in a reliable tradition of moral enquiry: a tradition that reliably delivers the moral truth. I gave more details about the first form of support. However, if anything, the second claim is more controversial, because it invites an even more corrosive form of scepticism.

It has become almost a contemporary commonplace in ordinary moral thinking that there is no adjudication between competing traditions of moral thought. (I concede that sometimes this attitude reflects a confused commitment to an ethical practice of universal tolerance, grounded unhappily on a belief that there are no universal values of any kind.) But there are also sophisticated versions of this argument: one of the distinctive claims of non-objectivism was that it, alone, made social scientific explanation of the ethical possible. For that reason, it was an apt vehicle for a certain kind of historicist scepticism that sees modern societies as scenes for a kind of radical pluralism that undermines the claim that we have moral knowledge. In this chapter, I will explain how a contextualist can argue for rationality both within a tradition of moral enquiry and, equally importantly, across such traditions. An essential part of the latter task is reiterating why, in some cases, an apparent challenge to our ethical outlook does not constitute a challenge at all, a part of the overall argument that will come into focus in the next chapter.

1. THE IDEA OF TRADITION BASED MORAL REASONING

Throughout this book I have taken the challenge of non-objectivism to be the strongest challenge that an account of moral knowledge has to meet. However, I have also argued that there were ambiguities in Williams's position that could be exploited in order to deflect the non-objectivist critique of the claim that we possess substantial amounts of moral knowledge. Earlier I tried to deflect his argument concerning practical objectivity and the contrast he saw between such a view and objectivism. In this chapter I return to the proposal to interpret his ideas about absoluteness in such a way that a defence of moral knowledge remains possible. Most moral philosophers drawn to a contextualist view of moral knowledge have been internal realists, sceptical about the aspiration to absoluteness. I have, by contrast, accepted that some of our representations aspire to absoluteness in the way that Williams describes. Perhaps representations in physical science are of this kind. But this aspiration is simply not appropriate to ethical representations. The open question is why this is a defect in representations that can hardly be understood as even trying to represent the world 'from no point of view'.

Williams never denied that such representations could be knowledge. However, I want to bolster that concession by focusing on the point that such representations can, in spite of their perspectivalness, be given an explanation that falls within the general schema that Williams described. They can play one of the roles that absolute representations typically play. I argued that the idea of an absolute representation was ambiguous between two ideas. First, there is the idea of a representation maximally independent of our perspective and our peculiarities in the sense that it is *totally* independent of our perspective. Secondly, there is the idea of a representation that is maximally independent of our perspective *without* being totally independent of our perspective. The latter idea seemed to me much more plausible than the former. I pointed out that in the master argument for the absolute conception that Moore developed out of Williams's work (downplaying, until a later stage in the argument, the role of explanation) the key idea is that of a representation acting as an umpire in the case of apparent conflicts between two other perspectival representations.

That suggests the following loophole to be exploited: that since Williams accepts the existence of perspectival knowledge, some of this knowledge can be viewed as playing this distinctive role when the representations are ethical and hence relatively closely tied to 'our perspective and its peculiarities'. Representations that are 'absolute' in the strong, perspective transcending sense are always available as neutral umpires, but representations that are perspectival in the weaker sense *may* also be available to play this role in a particular case. Absoluteness is introduced, in the argument Moore considers, as playing a certain kind of cognitive role. That is the role of 'context breaker'. As contextualists such as Larmore and Timmons have emphasized, a contextualist epistemology explains how reason can be both immanent in our actual, contextualized practices of enquiry and yet locally transcendent. For any context of enquiry, a fully worked out competitor can lead us to abandon most of the beliefs that form that context by a series of gradual transitions. But it is the chain fallacy once again to argue from that to the conclusion that there is some one context that is guaranteed to lever us out of any other. The contextualist account of objectivity has been well characterized by Robert Nozick:

If it is said that Reason itself, rather than any particular statement of its content, must remain as the final arbiter, then we must wonder what precisely that is. If not as particular content, then the only sense in which reason must endure is as an evolving chain of descent. Reason will endure as whatever evolves or grows out of the current content of reason by a process of piecemeal change that is justified at each moment by principles which are accepted at that moment (although not necessarily later on), provided that each evolving stage seems close enough to the one immediately preceding it to warrant the continued use of the label 'reason' then. (The new stage may not seem very similar, however, to an earlier, step-wise stage.) That degree of continuity hardly seems to mark something which is a fixed and eternal intellectual point.[1]

The process of comparing two perspectival representations of the world and accepting one and rejecting the other, or constructing a third that transcends one or both, is a mark of an objective discipline. But that role in enquiry can be played by representations that are, themselves, still perspectival to a significant degree. The idea is, then, that more inclusive representations can play a role that less inclusive ones cannot. But they can play this role even if they reflect, to a very significant degree, our perspective and its distinctive peculiarities, as ethical representations inevitably must do.

Nozick describes a contextualist view of the evolution of rationality in the context of traditions of enquiry. The contextualist compares representations in the light of a background of taken for granted judgements embedded in such traditions. The context breaking nature of reason may suggest that to resolve a particular problem, significant parts of that background may themselves have to come into question and become the object of enquiry. But the contextualist insists that all we have to work with here are the concepts of **better than** and **worse than**. Outlooks are compared in such terms, and those terms do not support an extrapolation to the idea of an outlook such that no other outlook is better than *it*. We can give substance to the idea of a conception of the world maximally independent of our perspective and its peculiarities in the sense of maximally independent but not totally so. However, on contextualist grounds, the point of this idea is not whether or not it is true (which, on this internal interpretation, it certainly is). The point, rather, is that it functions in enquiry as a cognitive ideal that encapsulates the idea of the context transcendence of reason.

This line of argument looks promising. But the argument from the possibility of absoluteness in representation was not Williams's only argument, and indeed most attention has been focused on the ideas of explanation and convergence that appear to be derived parts of his view. But, even if they are derived from more fundamental considerations about the possibility of perspectivalness, these ideas have some force. Surely they are also very damaging to the idea of ethical objectivity? In fact, I think the opposite: the demand for convergence can be used helpfully to explain the nature of ethical objectivity. Many components of Williams's view can be reinterpreted in a way congenial to the cognitivist and be redeployed in the context of a positive model of the nature of moral knowledge. This is certainly true of the aspiration to convergence.

Convergence was explained via the idea of the functioning of a reliable cognitive mechanism. The crucial question, for Williams, turned out to be not whether ethical convergence occurs. It was, rather, how it best explained when it does occur. Part of Williams's critique was that such knowledge must be justified by its own reflective explanation. This explanation must, in turn, harmonize with an independent account

---

[1] Robert Nozick, *Invariances* (Cambridge, Mass.: Harvard University Press, 2001), 2–3.

of reliably functioning cognitive mechanisms. 'World-guidedness', in its objectivist sense, was the proposed candidate to fit this bill and for Williams it was an unacceptable candidate. But with his foundationalist model of the knowledge system undermined, perhaps a better understanding of how ethical judgements could have this world guided role is once more available within the ambit of contextualism.

A defensible view needs to establish two things: a degree of ethical convergence, plus the explicability of divergent cases in a complementary theory of error. The starting point in explaining how these are possible must be the acceptance of Williams's account of reliable belief formation. These involve the deployment of rational methods that need not be integrated into a causal theory of knowledge. It was Williams who pointed out that in connecting his convergence platitude with the idea of a reliably functioning representational device, Crispin Wright was conflating two ideas: covergence and a causal theory of representation.[2] In an important paper, Nicholas Jardine has argued that there is a core proposal extractable from Williams's argument that is worth preserving as an insight into the nature of objectivity:

It is an important insight that an objective convergence of belief is one that is justified by its explanation . . . the justification required for objectivity is in terms of reliability . . . Is world guidedness the only way in which these stringent demands on a standard of objectivity can be met?[3]

Jardine defends the following proposal as a reply to his rhetorical question:

Let us distinguish two ways in which a belief can be justified or vitiated by appeal to considerations of reliability. In a causal justification the methods or techniques which have engendered and sustained the belief are spelled out in causal terms in such a way as to demonstrate their reliability; conversely, in a causal vitiation the causal account of the relevant methods or techniques is such as to demonstrate their unreliability. In a justification by precedent the reliability of the methods and techniques that have engendered or sustained a belief is demonstrated by testing against independently warranted precedents and standards; conversely in a vitiation by precedent the unreliability of the relevant methods and techniques is demonstrated by testing against precedents and standards.[4]

In other words, it is possible to retain the connection between objectivity and convergence and between convergence and the reliable functioning of a cognitive mechanism. However, while the latter idea *could* be explained causally it need not be so. It can also, legitimately, *be explained in terms of independently warranted rational standards*. Such standards are tested against precedents and standards internal to a tradition of enquiry. The invocation of precedent suggests a legalistic model for moral objectivity and although Jardine does not mention this example, there is a long established tradition which emphasizes this form of 'internal' objectivity, namely

---

[2] As I have already noted, one can infer from Williams's critical comments on Wright that Williams did not intend to go on to explain reliably functioning cognitive mechanisms exclusively in causal terms.

[3] Nicholas Jardine, 'Science, Ethics and Objectivity', in Altham and Harrison (eds.), *World, Mind and Ethics*, 32–45 at 38.

[4] Ibid. 38.

the casuistical tradition.[5] Rationally warranted standards may be a reliable source of knowledge without such reliability being explained causally via a precedent based defence of (at least) ethical objectivity.[6]

This proposal, it seems to me, dovetails happily with the idea that justification is contextual. Its ultimate tenability rests on the construction of narrative accounts of ethical reasoning in which reasoning can be seen in a precedent guided, intra-traditional way. The equally important issue, however, is vitiation by precedent and the possibility of a theory of error. It would be imprudent not to acknowledge that this remains an important disanalogy between ethical and other forms of objectivity. Precedent should not only function as a model for convergence on ethical truth but also be used to vitiate divergent beliefs as substantially in error. To what extent is it possible to explain away conflicting beliefs as 'products of unreliable methods and procedures'? Williams raised two basic problems for any such theory: the problem that for those ethical options which are not real options for us appraisal is not relevant and that ethical reflection 'cannot generate an adequate theory of error and account generally for the tendency for people to have what, according to its principles, are wrong beliefs'.[7] I will be discussing both the relativism of distance and the possibility of ethical error in the next chapter. At this point I would like to examine the claims of two other philosophers who understand the challenge to cognitivism here very much as I do.

2. A MODEL OF TRADITION BASED MORAL REASONING

I will begin my account of tradition based moral reasoning by focusing on Putnam's model of moral knowledge and some criticisms of that view levelled by Mark Timmons. They are two of the philosophers whose views are closest to my own: Putnam is a realist, albeit an internal realist, but is not inclined to describe his epistemological views as contextualist (he prefers the term 'pragmatist'). Timmons is avowedly a contextualist, but as I have described he is an 'assertoric non-descriptivist' about moral assertions. This section will allow me to clarify where I think they both go astray, and how a revision in some of their assumptions leads to a view which I believe is more acceptable: unsurprisingly, a combination of a cognitivist account of moral assertions with a contextualist moral epistemology.

Putnam's views about moral knowledge have, it seems to me, unfortunately been overshadowed by the way in which he has attempted to prove that the non-objectivist critique is motivated by a form of external realism. But there is a great deal of interest and value in Putnam's positive account of moral knowledge detachable from this mistaken strategy, which was criticized in Chapter 6, above. It is, furthermore, detachable from his own commitment to 'internal' or 'pragmatic' realism. Since I failed to

---

[5] Such casuistic or 'neo-specifist' models of practical reasoning have been defended by Henry Richardson and Susan Hurley. See Richardson, *Practical Reasoning about Final Ends* (Cambridge: Cambridge University Press, 1997); Hurley, *Natural Reasons: Personality and Polity*.

[6] Again, I have not in this book pressed the case for extending this model further in order to develop an account of scientific objectivity.

[7] Williams, *Ethics and the Limits*, 151.

identify any view as clearly classifiable as external realism, I have comparable difficulty understanding what internal realism is supposed to be. In addition, I have throughout suggested that contextualism ought to be detached from its origins in the pragmatist tradition, whereas Putnam is inclined to stress the similarity between his view and pragmatism. These differences notwithstanding, there is a great deal in Putnam's account of moral knowledge with which I agree.

His account is non-reductive about key critical notions, such as rationality and truth. They are to be elucidated in terms of how they are *used*.[8] With the increasingly Wittgensteinian turn of Putnam's later work, such concepts are to be elucidated by examining their use in specific contexts of enquiry. These contexts set the relevant standards of epistemic appraisal for moral claims, which, post-*Reason, Truth and History*, are now construed as 'sufficiently good' relative to context as opposed to 'ideal' standards.[9] As Putnam now puts it, 'there are better and worse epistemic situations with respect to particular statements'.[10] Epistemic appraisal is context sensitive, as are the epistemic norms underpinning such appraisals. This seems to me to integrate straightforwardly into the kind of Austinian account of personal justification, in terms of the context sensitive norms of 'reasonable sufficiency' and 'definite lack' described in Chapter 8. Timmons extracts an underlying model from Putnam's discussion to which I am very sympathetic:

Norms involved in our conception of ideal warrant . . . are, in a dual sense, 'open-ended'. First, viewed synchronically, they represent a battery of ceteris paribus norms for which it is not possible to specify, in terms of an algorithm, all of those conditions under which ceteris is paribus. Second, viewed diachronically, the current set of ceteris paribus norms are liable to change; current norms may be rejected . . . others may be added. In short, our conception of ideal warrant with regard to empirical sentences may be rather loose and fluid—not something for which we have necessary and sufficient conditions—but nevertheless serviceable.[11]

The evolution of Putnam's views and Timmons's articulation of his underlying commitments are of the greatest value to the project I am pursuing in this book.[12] I have, throughout, sought to distance contextualism from pragmatism and some of these key issues allow contextualism to put clear blue water between itself and pragmatism

---

[8] For a representative set of passages describing Putnam's later views on epistemic justification and warrant see Putnam, *Representation and Reality*, 115; *Realism with a Human Face*, pp. viii, 42.

[9] Putnam, *Representation and Reality*, 115.

[10] Putnam, *Realism with a Human Face*, p. viii.

[11] Timmons, *Morality Without Foundations*, 98–9.

[12] Timmons's sympathetic treatment of Putnam's work may seem curious, given that Timmons is an irrealist (for my own purposes, I prefer the term a 'non-cognitivist'). Timmons's view (with which I entirely agree) that there is no reductive treatment available of critical concepts like truth and rationality (the view he shares with Putnam) is combined, in Timmons's work, with a belief that Putnam, too, is an irrealist. The first thing to be said about this is that Putnam is going to be far from happy with this description. His internal realism, described in Ch. 6, is supposed to deliver a global verdict that all realist discourse receives the same internalist treatment (a point that Timmons acknowledges). Timmons's revisionary treatment of Putnam's views rests, once again, on Timmons's restrictive view that there is a single essential feature marking out realism, namely, a correspondence theory of truth. Anyone who denies that truth is correspondence is thereby an irrealist by Timmons's lights. That does not seem to me a helpful way of dividing up the available positions, as I argued in Ch. 6.

as I argued in Chapter 8, above. Both contextualism and pragmatism insist that we have to begin from a realistic account of the nature of enquiry. But they very quickly part company.

The pragmatist often operates with the concept of an ideal, or unimprovable, justification and may define truth in such terms.[13] Pragmatism thus postulates a purposive end point to ethical enquiry and encourages a view of the history of enquiry as a narrative of converging, vindicatory, research programmes.[14] The contextualist sees enquiry as devolved into multiple, problem oriented contexts in which context sensitive epistemic norms are applied in a particularist way, falling under the generalizations of 'reasonable sufficiency' and 'definite lack'. We have only the resources of a belief being 'better than' and 'worse than' another belief in a context of comparative judgement. This cannot be iterated to generate the idea of a set of beliefs, which constitute a standpoint, than which no other is better. Contextualism does not represent the history of ethical enquiry as a set of converging research programmes. At that level of reflective generality, there is no unitary form of enquiry that can be assessed in terms of a 'point' to such enquiry as a whole. But the whole aim of contextualism is to insist that we take a more local view of the nature of enquiry and it does not follow that we do not, in specific contexts of appraisal, have good grounds to view one ethical belief as more likely to be true than another.

One way in which I would like to distance the kind of contextualism defended here from Putnam's view, then, is by resisting the claim that it is a form of pragmatism. But other aspects of his view also seem to me to be helpfully clarified or revised in the context of a more consistent contextualism. The contextual model of justification that Putnam actually defends combines a reflective equilibrium methodology with a view of morality as a code that promotes norms of flourishing, which also aim to reduce social conflict by subjecting it to rational regulation. This reasoning extends to ends as well as means; we rationally debate the nature of the good life for people as well as how best to attain it, individually and collectively. The reasoning involved can reasonably be regarded as objective:

The 'objectivity of ethical principles, or, more broadly, of moralities', is connected with such things as width of appeal, ability to withstand certain kinds of rational criticism . . . feasibility, ideality, and, of course, with how it actually feels to live by them or attempt to live by them.[15]

As Putnam developed his pragmatic realism, his later work found a role for an idea very similar to that of a background framework of belief:

---

[13] The idea that pragmatism is committed to explicating truth in terms of an unimprovable epistemic situation (while avoiding any reductive definition of truth) is central to the insightful arguments of Cheryl Misak in *Truth, Politics, Morality*, esp. 49 ff.

[14] Chris Hookway argues in 'Fallibilism and Objectivity, Science and Ethics', in Altham and Harrison (eds.), *World, Mind and Ethics*, 46–67 that a cognitivism influenced by a pragmatic model of human enquiry would end up presenting such a picture of ethical thought as constituted by such a set of converging research programmes. For that reason he is rightly sceptical of such a picture. But this book tries to develop a different account of the prospects for cognitivism, one more similar to the optimistic prospects for ethical objectivity at pp. 64–7 of Hookway's paper.

[15] Hilary Putnam, *Meaning and the Moral Sciences* (London: Routledge and Kegan Paul, 1978), 93.

A moral image . . . is not a declaration that this or that is a virtue, or this or that is what one ought to do; it is rather a picture of how our virtues and ideals hang together with one another and of what they have to do with the position we are in.[16]

This model of a background structure that organizes our 'virtues', 'ideals', or 'position' should, by my lights, be viewed as a background context of beliefs. That eliminates some of the vagueness in Putnam's account while also accepting that the expression of this class of beliefs can be difficult to separate from articulation.[17]

It should be clear, from the foregoing, which elements I object to in this pragmatic realist model. Putnam's use of the reflective equilibrium model seems resolutely centralist: it is fundamentally about principles, construed as using thin ethical concepts. Particular judgements are systematized into principles and it is the final defensibility of those principles that yields moral knowledge by those particular judgements being entailed by such thin, non-world guided general principles. It is this aspect of Putnam's view that leads Timmons, an insightful interpreter of Putnam's views, to describe them as a form of moral constructivism (and not as a form of realism). But this understanding of reflective equilibrium as a construction procedure is an optional one, as Chapter 8 demonstrated. It is, rather, better viewed as the taking up of *both* concrete (and more general) judgements, picked out solely by one's degree of confidence in them, and the supplementation of the direct justification they possess (if any), or the vitiations of this justification, by incorporation into a contextual model of justification.

It is the constructivist cast of Putnam's views that engenders the kinds of problems that lead Timmons ultimately to distance himself from Putnam's pragmatic realism. What troubles Timmons is the pluralism inherent in Putnam's view. Putnam argues that a natural consequence of his view is the reasonable pluralism internal to morality: that even in a cognitively unimprovable situation our ideal of human flourishing will be internally complex.[18] Timmons's concern is that there are no resources within Putnam's view for separating this claim, that a justified ethical outlook is internally complex, from a claim that a kind of constitutive *relativism* is true. On this latter view, there are competing and incommensurable ideals of human flourishing. This form of relativism (which Putnam clearly wants to reject) can be blocked off as an option, Timmons implies, only by bringing in 'externally realist' considerations to back up Putnam's avowed statement that not 'anything goes' in a moral justification that terminates on an ideal of human flourishing.

---

[16] Hilary Putnam, *The Many Faces of Realism* (La Salle, Ill.: Open Court Press), 51.

[17] Richard Moran, *Authority and Estrangement*, ch. 2, explains in some detail how the idea of articulation actually demands a background commitment to realism about the subject matter thus 'articulated', as discussed in Ch. 8, above. That is why I think we have to be appealing here to background *beliefs*, as I previously argued.

[18] I have switched over to Misak's idea of an unimprovable epistemic situation as an interpretation of Putnam's non-reductionist view of epistemic warrant. An oddity of Timmons's presentation of Putnam's views is that he gives a sympathetic and insightful treatment of Putnam's claims that we do not have a general theory of epistemic warrant and that all we can do is talk, in a context specific way, of being better or worse placed with regard to particular statements. But Timmons then goes on to assess Putnam's views in terms of the idea of an 'ideal limit', for example, at *Morality Without Foundations*, 103.

If we recast what Putnam says in more explicitly contextualist terms this genuine concern can be answered. Suppose, for the sake of argument (notwithstanding the fact that it is very probably true) that the background framework of belief we endorse after careful reflection is internally complex: it involves reasonable moral pluralism. Now a relativist competitor is proposed. Timmons puts forward the case of the 'rational Nazi', concerned that this is an alternative ideal of flourishing that is clearly morally outrageous, but which Putnam cannot rule out as wrong:

The case in question is one in which we have a group of fanatics who have worked out a coherent moral system. Granted, there may have been many actual Nazis who were such that, had they been made aware of and vividly reflected on the sorts of atrocities they were committing, they would have been led to give up their murderous ends . . . But there remain the true fanatics who, we are to suppose, have a 'coherently' worked out system.[19]

Note the importance here of coherence: this alternative ethical 'ideal' is coherent, so a viable candidate view. Timmons is worried that Putnam cannot say enough to rule out this view:

The situation looks difficult because (1) there doesn't seem to be a way of showing that 'rational' Nazis are really mistaken—we have a conception of rationality that reflects one conception of human flourishing; they have a different conception of rationality reflective of a different conception . . . Anything goes . . . one could insist that, in the ideal limit, Nazi outlooks would not survive, but getting to this result would seem to require going back on the claim that there are no norms of rationality that are the world's own norms (as Putnam submits), and would amount to embracing external realism.[20]

Recast in the contextualist terms defended in this book, there are several responses available here. First, abandon the centralism and commitment to abstract principles found in Putnam's version of reflective equilibrium and we have, in addition, the resources of experience and direct justification. We are not restricted to coherence alone, or minimal consistency of outlook. What the Nazi does to other people we can say, with a high degree of reflective confidence, is cruel, humiliating, and vicious. Secondly, without lapsing into external realism we can demand of a person espousing a Nazi outlook that he or she gives us the fully worked out details of this alternative way of arranging our collective lives together that can be represented as an ideal of human flourishing (and that does not depend on any false non-moral beliefs). The challenge a contextually justified background framework puts to any proposed sceptical alternative is for this alternative to be fully specified. This specification must be detailed, and based on a level playing field such that the alternative is fully internally consistent. I am quite confident that in the recurrent example of the 'rational Nazi' found in works of moral philosophy, this challenge to our outlook cannot be met.[21] We will retain the confidence we have earned that our outlook is true and that

---

[19] Ibid.

[20] Ibid. 104.

[21] Part of the problem here is that with false beliefs removed, there is not much left to Nazi ideology. Take the specific case of the 'principled' Nazis of Hitler's Germany. Remove false historical beliefs about the injustices imposed on Germany and its destiny as a nation. Remove false theories

the apparent competitor is not a genuine candidate. We did not do this by stand-ing outside our outlook in the way that Timmons suggests Putnam has to (thereby reintroducing external realism).[22]

Timmons's 'all things considered' response is that we can learn from Putnam not-withstanding the difficulties of his view. In particular, Putnam emphasizes that moral criticism is from an engaged perspective, we are allowed to reuse some of our moral beliefs in assessing some others, and we can expect to reuse our critical moral vocab-ulary in assessing proposed piecemeal changes to our moral beliefs:

> Notice that when we view things from a morally detached perspective, it certainly looks as if there are going to be multiple and incompatible sets of moral norms and values that are generally acceptable, relative to various incompatible set of idealized norms.[23]

I think that, once again, Timmons's commitment to generalism about moral prin-ciples leads him to overlook his own contextualist commitments in this passage. I took care to note, when discussing Michael Williams's views, that adjustment had to be made to apply his general thesis about the illusory object of disengaged epistemo-logical reflection to the specific case of ethics. Bernard Williams's hypertraditionalists were being foundationalist and reflecting in a detached way about ethical beliefs in particular, although in a thoroughgoing way that encompassed the whole of their ethical form of life. But once again I would argue that there is no blanket contrast between assessing competitor beliefs from a standpoint of ethical engagement and a detached perspective from which we are given the insight that there are 'multiple and incompatible sets of moral norms and values'. That insight is properly generated by prior presumptions of epistemological realism and rationalism, which together sup-port a commitment to a foundational perspective on moral beliefs. In the passage cited, these commitments seem to bias Timmons's reading of Putnam's views such that Putnam is appealing both to unsupported coherence amongst thin abstract prin-ciples, and doing so from a parochial perspective. If Putnam were to detach from his outlook, it seems that he would be delivered into the hands of the kind of 'anything goes' relativism dramatized by the threatened possibility of the rational Nazi. But I do not think that we have to see Putnam as in this position, and correcting some of his views about abstraction, the nature of reflective equilibrium and the availability of

---

in eugenics and false beliefs about Jews, Gypsies, gay people, and people with disabilities. What is left, as Putnam himself points out, is a caricature of a 'rational' person. We have a rational person in the sense that we have a minimally consistent person with some repellent, antisocial arbitrary preferences that lack any rational justification. I am happy to accept that many 'real world' Nazis in our own society meet this description rather well, while not really being in the business of rational argument. That is a separate point: what matters for the current argument is that such people represent no reasonable, fully worked out, ethical ideal that is an alternative to our own ideals.

[22] What Timmons says, precisely, is that 'one could insist that, in the ideal limit, Nazi outlooks would not survive, but getting to this result would seem to require going back on the claim that there are no norms of rationality that are the world's own norms (as Putnam submits) and would amount to embracing external realism'. Ibid. 104. The response I have suggested does claim that the Nazi outlook would not survive contextual justification, but I have not reintroduced the notion of an ideal limit, nor do I see anything in the proposal that I have put forward that suggests that rationality is in any way a reflection of the 'world's own norms'.

[23] Ibid. 105.

direct justifications makes this clearer. Timmons immediately goes on to qualify his slightly uncharitable reading of Putnam:

Evaluative statements . . . generally are immanent, in that they involve judgements made from a normatively engaged stance . . . On the other hand, truth is not just to be identified with our current outlook, or with any outlook. Our notions of truth and rationality have a kind of transcendence that blocks any attempt at some sort of naturalistic reduction of them. The immanence/transcendence dual aspect of such notions as truth and rationality is what needs preserving (so I think) in any plausible philosophical story about these notions.[24]

In my view, with these caveats entered, and with the revisions to existing versions of contextualism that I have proposed in this book, we have a fully defensible version of contextual justification that retains what is valuable in Putnam's and Timmons's discussions while avoiding those parts of their views which seem to me problematic. The key issues are supplementing indirect with direct justification (modulo the negative dependence of experience on theory) and undermining the deeply entrenched theses of epistemological realism from which the motivation for epistemological foundationalism flows. That preliminary task allows one to defend the view that moral justification proceeds from an engaged commitment to our own values without being either parochial or begging the questions against challenges to our outlook. I will go on, in the next chapter, to discuss how one might rationally determine which challenges to our moral outlook *are* genuine challenges and which are not. But it is important to emphasize that if an outlook can be given a further and detailed specification, it may turn out to result in a piecemeal revision of our outlook as a whole and indeed, such motivated scepticism is a vehicle of moral progress and development.

Does this overall model of moral knowledge meet the description of Jardine's precedent based account of ethical reasoning? It seems to me that the kind of contextual model I have outlined does meet Jardine's general proposal to develop a defence of ethical objectivity of this kind. However, there are immediate and obvious challenges that a view like this has to meet. The first challenge to the proposed model is that it does not allow for an entire series of precedents to be unfounded. This can be rebutted by arguing that there is no standpoint external to the ongoing tradition of enquiry from which such a charge could be levelled. There is no external point to the enquiry against which to calibrate its achievements. (I acknowledge that this may be another point of disanalogy with the scientific.)[25] Ethical enquiry is, in this sense, a process that sets its own ends in the course of its development: it is, in an interesting way, 'autotelic'.

I take it this is one way of interpreting Alasdair MacIntyre's much criticized account of the final end of a whole ethical life in *After Virtue*: MacIntyre implied that the ethical point or purpose of a whole life was to find out such a point or purpose,

---

[24] Ibid. 106.

[25] It does seem plausible to argue that problem solving has some independent weight as a metric of scientific progress. However, it seems to me unlikely to be the only such metric and furthermore to be itself an internally complex idea even for scientific reasoning. See Laurens Laudan, *Progress and Its Problems* (London: Routledge and Kegan Paul, 1977).

a view criticized on the grounds that it seemed to imply that those seeking the Holy Grail were after the search and not the Grail.[26] But the generally autotelic character of ethical objectivity casts light on MacIntyre's point here: that it is simply true that there is no substance to the idea of the ethical point of whole life independently of the reflective living of that life, a perspective from which its 'ends' are set, appraised, and (if possible) harmonized. Returning from the individual case to the collective one, the contextualist model of tradition based objectivity sees it as the fallible deployment of reliable rational methods. This deployment proceeds in the light of successful precedent and in that sense finding the whole tradition to be unfounded is not an alternative possibility that is up for appraisal. But that does not seem to me to be a damaging concession.

A second objection to my account of the legitimation of background frameworks is that the results it offers are too indeterminate. Our background frameworks of moral belief are internally reasonably pluralist and the evaluation of options proceeds by appealing to the idea of a more insightful development of our current outlook, without the further guarantee that this process can be iterated.[27] Is it not possible to be more precise? I fear not; after all, whatever ethical answers we come up with have to be delivered by the process of reflective living. What I can offer as a set of criteria is very limited, but adequate to reasonable expectations. The resources deployed in moral argument to advance the claims of a background framework are those of imagination as well as argument, and cannot be circumscribed in advance.[28]

A realistic view of contextualism does not view the incapacity of a model of moral knowledge fully to specify a set of criteria for belief revision as a problem for any sensible outlook. But then it would be unrealistic to expect that of any epistemological model for moral beliefs, contextualism included. I conclude, therefore, in the light of all the previous arguments of this book, that moral knowledge is possible at the reflective level. The challenge of non-objectivism can be met. But the extent of this knowledge is open to determination, and the enterprise of establishing this will not (I will argue in the next section) take the form of a global meta-narrative of the kind anticipated in the work of Alasdair MacIntyre and Charles Taylor. If Williams's non-objectivist scepticism about the ethical is reinterpreted as focusing on *how much* ethical knowledge we have, as well as on how it is possible at all, that question lies open. However, it seems beyond the powers of philosophy to determine how much moral knowledge is available in the distinctive conditions of modernity. To address that question requires the resources of historical and sociological understanding. On this point Williams and I were very much in agreement.

[26] MacIntyre, *After Virtue*, ch. 15, esp. 218–19.

[27] Detached from any implicit appeal to 'real interests', Charles Taylor's analogy between practical reasoning about values and 'gains in insight' in psychoanalytic therapy offers a helpful model of such a process. See Taylor, 'Explanation and Practical Reason', in Amartya Sen and Martha Nussbaum (eds.), *The Quality of Life* (Oxford: Oxford University Press, 1993), 208–41.

[28] This represents at the social level of our collective resource of moral knowledge an analogy for Kolnai's claims about the ineliminable role of imagination in practical reasoning discussed in Ch. 4 above. Bonevac's argument that reflective equilibrium has to be extended to the expansion of a person's moral experience in Chapter 8, above, also appeals to the moral use of the imagination, 'Reflection Without Equilibrium', 371.

3. COMPETING MODELS OF TRADITION BASED MORAL KNOWLEDGE: MACINTYRE AND TAYLOR

I have argued that the best response to scepticism as to whether or not we can reason objectively about ethical background frameworks of belief is to work out a contingent history of our actual moral ideas where some of those developments are represented as an epistemic gain over others. But whereas some contextualists have contented themselves with indicating the general form of a contextualist model of moral justification, others have gone further and have done the historical work needed to make such a contingent narrative of our actual moral identity plausible. In this section I want to consider the work of Alasdair MacIntyre and Charles Taylor in order to argue that in so far as their tradition based models of moral reasoning are plausible, they instantiate contextualism. Some of the implausibilities of their positions, particularly MacIntyre's, are conversely traceable to a model for moral knowledge that is tradition based but not contextualist, or alternatively, just based on false historical assumptions.

I believe that it would be fair to say that the starting point of both MacIntyre and Taylor's historicist analyses of the ethical was MacIntyre's interpretation of Kuhn's work on cognitive rationality.[29] MacIntyre interpreted Kuhn's *The Structure of Scientific Revolutions* in a non-relativistic way. He saw it as reinterpreting, rather than abandoning, the positivist distinction between 'the context of discovery' and 'the context of justification' of scientific theories. The emphasis that Kuhn's account gave to short run discontinuities in 'revolutionary' scientific history obscured a complementary emphasis on long run continuity.[30] In MacIntyre's interpretation such long run continuities are framed by a narrative justification of the relation between theories. Such narrative justifications are answerable to the constraint that a successor theory must be more inclusive than its predecessor. It must explain not only its predecessor's successes, but also its failures. MacIntyre took the further step of suggesting that such an account could, with qualifications, be extended to ethics and practical enquiry.[31]

MacIntyre argued that such a form of narrative justification, either within theoretical or practical reasoning, must take the form of a narrative which was, in a sense, cumulative: each successor theory must be more comprehensive than its

---

[29] This MacIntyrean meta-theory is presented in an important series of papers ancillary to his monographs: 'Epistemological Crises, Dramatic Narratives and the Philosophy of Science', *Monist*, 60 (1977), 453–72; 'Relativism, Power and Philosophy', in Kenneth Baynes, James Bohman, and Thomas McCarthy (eds.), *After Philosophy: End Or Transformation* (Cambridge, Mass.: MIT Press, 1987), 385–411.

[30] This emphasis on the difference between the long run and the short run claims about discontinuity in Kuhn has also been discussed by Gerald Doppelt, with conclusions similar to MacIntyre's, in 'Kuhn's Epistemological Relativism: An Interpretation and Defence', in Michael Krausz and Jack Meiland, *Relativism: Cognitive and Moral* (Notre Dame, Ind.: University of Notre Dame Press, 1982), 113–46. The requirement that successor theories should be more explanatorily inclusive than their predecessors was a view defended by Wilfred Sellars. See his 'Conceptual Change', in *Essays on Philosophy and Its History* (Dordrecht: Reidel, 1975), 172–88.

[31] Thus *After Virtue* marks precisely such an extension; the qualifications lie in the characterization of the 'internal discipline' of ethical discourse.

predecessor. Applied to ethics, MacIntyre argued that such historicist justification was the proper method of legitimating frameworks of moral belief. Taylor further develops this approach in the opening sections of *Sources of the Self*. He compares the kind of reasoning involved concerning background frameworks to psychoanalytic or practical reasoning:

Practical reasoning is reasoning in transitions. It aims to establish, not that some position is correct absolutely but rather that some position is superior to some other . . . We show one of these comparative claims to be well founded when we show that the move from A to B constitutes a gain epistemically . . . The nerve of rational proof consists in showing that this move is an error reducing one.[32]

This is a weakening of MacIntyre's comprehensiveness requirement; we no longer need to explain away *all* the failures of a predecessor theory, simply to 'reduce error'.

Taylor's version of that which can reasonably be expected when we move from one background framework of belief to another is, in my view, by far more defensible and is closer to the view defended here. MacIntyre's highly idealized account places great demands on theoretical progress and cannot cover cases where the move from one paradigm to another reopens old problems as the cost of theoretical innovation that is expected to be more fruitful in the future. MacIntyre's comprehensive requirement seems motivated less by a realistic picture of enquiry than by a residual 'eschatology of reason' in his account of rational progress. But there is no independent reason to believe that the progress of reason is a triumphal forward march, as opposed to a piecemeal story of gains and losses.

More congenial to contextualism, then, is Taylor's version of the argument, most fully developed in *Sources of the Self*. He argues that the move from one background framework of ethical belief to another may represent an epistemic gain. Such a gain is analogous to the kind of insight presented to a psychological subject by psychoanalytic therapy. A series of such epistemic gains is not envisioned as taking us to a standpoint from which, as it were, no further gains are to be made. That seems to be Taylor's putative stance, which is that *Sources of the Self* focuses on the historical origins of modern ethical pluralism, not on how such pluralism is to be overcome. However, those minded to detect the influence of Hegel on *Sources of the Self* could point to the very idea of a master narrative of the modern moral identity as suggesting that a final reconciliation of the plural cross-currents of modern moral thought can be envisaged. This is particularly so, given that Taylor indicates that he finds seriously problematic the epistemological basis of several frameworks of belief to which we contemporaries owe allegiance.

Disappointingly from the contextualist perspective, there is some looseness of fit between Taylor's plausible claim that in the move from one background framework to another we seek to 'reduce error' and the analogy he uses to explain this idea. To understand a psychological transition as a gain in insight without circularity, without simply assuming that a gain in insight can be indefeasibly judged to be so from the agent's later standpoint, it must be possible to characterize standing interests of

---

[32] Taylor, 'Explanation and Practical Reason'. See also *Sources of the Self*, 72–3.

importance in an individual's life. To gain leverage on a person's motivations, for example, to encourage me to undergo a painful and lengthy course of medical treatment that will ultimately save my life, we need to appeal to interests as authoritative over desire (while, I would add, respecting the criterion defended in Part II that we are still giving reasons *for* that particular agent). Taylor can draw on background assumptions here special to his own view. His residual Platonism sees the vindication of such narrative justifications in a vision of the good.[33] He can, therefore, define right reason as reasoning aligned with such a conception of the good. Taylor is sufficiently modern to be ambivalent about the kind of grand narrative he enacts in *Sources of the Self*, but nevertheless the entire text is expressive of his faith that a single background framework of belief can be vindicated as most consonant with our moral and political aspirations. Thus, the lacuna in Taylor's argument can be filled by his Platonic presupposition that we collectively have a real interest in being aligned with comprehensive conceptions of the good.

From a contextualist perspective I do not agree with these assumptions: they collectively represent, once again, precisely the chain fallacy about the justification of background frameworks of moral belief that the contextualist wants to avoid. Pluralism is unavoidable within a contextualist account of background frameworks and there is no reasonable prospect of its being overcome by the development of reason. The constraints that I place on rational transitions between background frameworks are weaker than those envisaged by MacIntyre and Taylor. It seems reasonable to impose the requirement that a background framework should be judged to represent a progressive development over its predecessor. However, this need not be an iterable operation that would generate a final ideally justified framework, nor need the requirement of explanatory exclusiveness be imposed. I believe that these are all residually Platonic or Hegelian commitments, which are not necessarily involved in the enterprise of evaluating background frameworks.

The contextualist has to make do with immanent moral sources, but any account that was restricted in this way would find considerable backing in the way that the argument of *Sources of the Self* actually proceeds. A feature that has misled several critics of *Sources of the Self* is Taylor's method of deploying ideal types, a methodological device with interesting parallels in Wittgenstein's later method.[34] Taylor structures his narrative along four thematic lines. These are described both synchronically and diachronically and are not intended to be literally true descriptions of actual historical processes, but idealized depictions of clusters of values and identities. The four lines are the development of a sense of inwardness, the affirmation of ordinary life, the rise of the idea of nature as an inner moral source in Romantic expressivism, and the

---

[33] See the discussion in Taylor, *Sources of the Self*, ch. 4, 'Moral Sources'. A representative quotation is as follows: 'The constitutive good does more than just define the content of the moral theory. Love of it is what empowers us to be good. And hence loving it is part of what it is to be a good human being. This is now part of the moral theory as well, which includes not only injunctions to act in certain ways and to exhibit certain moral qualities but also to love what is good', 93. For the substantive disagreement between this form of Platonism and my own view see the discussion in the conclusion to this chapter.

[34] Taylor's immediate influence is Weber's method of 'ideal types'.

complex cross-currents informing modernism in the twentieth century. In the concluding section of *Sources of the Self,* Taylor discusses the way the interwoven strands
of this account set the contemporary agenda, before suggesting his tentative proposal
for reconciling the conflicts of modernity.

Taylor sees us all as irrevocably committed to a range of fundamental moral
principles in the modern West, but commitment to these principles of right is
combined with protracted controversy over the goods which support them. The
distinctive feature of our contemporary predicament is that the three schematic views
which are in conflict, theism, naturalism, and the Romantic/Modernist axis, have
generated new problems. *Sources of the Self* maps out both the shared commitments
of principle distinctive of the moral outlook of the modern West, and the array
of evaluative sources that underpin those principles in many different ways. Since
the discussion is pitched at the level of ideal types to render the complexities of
the narrative manageable, the actual history of the modern moral identity is a far
more complex picture, with combinations of different evaluative frameworks yielding
further options, such as the combination of expressivism and naturalism that led
to modern Marxism. Add to this the fact that the ideal types are de-temporalized,
and that the modern world contains different temporal strata of moral outlook, and
the complexities of our current ethical situation become all too clear. Nevertheless,
Taylor maintains that we face rational decisions. He eschews the tempting alternative
diagnoses that we are confronted with various incoherent fragments of different
ethical outlooks, as claimed by Anscombe and MacIntyre. Neither are we faced with
the task of 'bricolage', piecing together these fragments as we choose. This complex
pluralism is a challenge to practical rationality but not a defeat for it and on that point
I very much agree with him.

An understandable reaction to the complexity of the modern moral identity would
be to conclude that in the face of such a kaleidoscope of ethical options, rationality can have little purchase. However, underneath the complexity lie the background
frameworks that Taylor identifies, and he argues that by working at the level of ideal
types, rationality can be extended to reasoning across such frames. The result is not
an answer that decisively vindicates one moral outlook, but that expectation is itself
too demanding. MacIntyre has given the correct response: the answer sought lies with
reflective living.[35] The contextualist shares this optimism on Taylor's part, which puts
some distance between his views and those of MacIntyre. MacIntyre's methodological work may have suggested a contextualist epistemology for ethics, but the way in
which he has actually pursued his project ought not to be welcome to the contextualist. The reasonable pluralism that the contextualist finds in contemporary ethics is,
for MacIntyre, the pitiful shuffling about of ultimately incoherent cultural fragments
one would expect in a post-apocalyptic ethical scenario.

---

[35] A conclusion which is echoed, ironically, by Williams's *Ethics and the Limits of Philosophy,*
which was sceptical about both philosophy and ethics, but not *as* sceptical about ethics. The
concluding call for that which Williams called social confidence placed him, with Taylor, on the
optimistic wing of Hegelianism and far from MacIntyre's Apocalyptic vision. But I have questioned
the extent to which Williams's optimistic vision of a confident society can withstand the corrosive
scepticism he takes to be distinctive of modernity in my discussion in Ch. 6.

MacIntyre makes two claims that are in fundamental tension with each other. MacIntyre's narrative claims both that the modern world is a scene of moral chaos and disorder, and that one tradition is uniquely placed to reconcile the conflicts of modernity, namely neo-Augustinian Thomism. If MacIntyre's narrative is correct, my entire project is misconceived as the attempt to restore rationality to practice is doomed to failure without a prior commitment to a comprehensive theory of the good in a Thomistic setting. Fortunately, however, I believe MacIntyre's claims can be resisted. The first point to be made is that MacIntyre is not, in fact, concerned with modernity in the usual sense. He understands the term as referring to any general cultural crisis involving the widespread breakdown in background frameworks of belief.[36] Thus, MacIntyre locates the modernity crisis that is his central concern in the ancient world, and the declining intellectual authority of the moral and political theory of Aristotle. The moral crisis, which MacIntyre maintains is our contemporary condition, has deep historical roots.

According to MacIntyre's narrative, moral life was once rational and unified, in the ancient Greek polis, as described in the ethical and political works of Aristotle. This was guaranteed by the relation Aristotle envisaged between his account of human beings as they are, the set of prescriptions directing them as to how to realize their essential nature, and the ideal of human excellence that would be the result. The discrediting of Aristotle's teleological metaphysics led to the loss of a sense that a human life had a unified purpose which could ground the value of that life. Thus all subsequent moral philosophy in the West is, in MacIntyre's view, a fruitless search for a means to connect the original elements of Aristotle's tripartite schema, given that the idea of the purpose of an individual life has been lost. This analysis culminates in MacIntyre's account of the contemporary moral situation which he views as being in complete intellectual disorder.

The reasons for this disorder are threefold. First, some traditions of thought are just incoherent: they fail to achieve the internal integrity required in MacIntyre's account of enquiry. Without a background context providing sense for their central concepts, such traditions of thought are intellectually fragmented. Secondly, even if traditions of enquiry are coherent, conflicts amongst them are pointless since without a matrix of commensurability, disagreement across traditions is, in principle, irresoluble. Thirdly, the contemporary world fails to recognize the intellectual authority of the neo-Augustinian Catholicism MacIntyre views as uniquely privileged in its relation to other traditions. It is from this neo-Augustinian basis that MacIntyre proposes that we resurrect Aristotelian ethics in the modern world. The key element of his proposed revival of Thomistic Aristotelianism is a new account of the overall purpose of a human life which permits the restoration of an ethic of virtue and the cultivation of appropriate forms of community. While MacIntyre's general position has remained constant, there have been shifts in his position as his trilogy of works has evolved, reflecting his increasing commitment to Catholicism. The main direction of this shift has been away from *After Virtue*'s modern emphasis on value pluralism,

---

[36] This was also Foucault's understanding of a 'modernity crisis' as set out in his insightful essay, 'What is Enlightenment?', in *The Foucault Reader* (London: Penguin Books, 1986), 32–50.

which influenced the book's account of the good life. The later works are less tolerant of pluralism, reflecting an increasing emphasis on the neo-Augustinian tradition that is, in MacIntyre's view, uniquely placed to present an ideal synthesis of past and present traditions.

MacIntyre's narrative is impressive in its scope and forcefulness, but his more pessimistic claims and the threat they pose to the idea of rationality extended across background frameworks are, I believe, quite unfounded. A central paradox vitiates the whole enterprise: when MacIntyre denounces the poverty of the moral knowledge available in modern conditions, he uses a foundationalist standard for knowledge.[37] However, when he explains the uniquely privileged standpoint of neo-Augustinianism, that tradition is the beneficiary of a move to contextualism. He keeps a double set of standards and shifts from one to the other. The problem is that MacIntyre wants to maintain both that the modern world is characterized by interminable moral disagreement of a distinctively severe and chronic sort, and that an intellectual tradition, when it is properly functioning, is characterized by lively internal debate and reflective reinterpretation. Thus, there are two kinds of disagreement: a pernicious kind involving incommensurability in concepts and epistemic norms and a valuable kind that is the basis of MacIntyre's admiration of the neo-Augustinian tradition. I would argue that the difference between these two kinds of disagreement is indeterminate, whereas for MacIntyre to indict the morals of modernity he must take the difference to be determinate. Furthermore, even if this is a difference of degree and not kind, I am not convinced that we have, in fact, any reason to conclude that contemporary ethical thinking is beset by the kind of corrosive incommensurability that MacIntyre alleges. I gave my reasons for this when trying to respond to Williams's similar non-objectivist claims: any such diagnosis seems tacitly to rest on foundationalist and epistemologically realist premises.

MacIntyre's approach to this issue is a subtle one, but it does not sustain the account he gives of the disagreements that he takes to be characteristic of the modern world. Taking the Wittgensteinian connection between agreement in judgements and canonical conditions of sense as his starting point, MacIntyre presses the question as to how much agreement must be in force for a tradition of thought to retain its integrity and for expressions to retain their sense. The Wittgensteinian answer should be, I take it, that this question is itself indeterminate. MacIntyre oscillates between correctly arguing that it is indeterminate, and incorrectly arguing that the question can be determinately settled to the disfavour of all contemporary moral traditions other than neo-Augustinianism. My concern is that this argument clearly threatens the rationality of interframework reasoning. MacIntyre offers the unattractive dichotomy of either finding determinate grounding in a theory of the good or abandoning the rationality of interframework reasoning.

---

[37] This was first pointed out by Charles Larmore, *Patterns of Moral Complexity*, ch. 2, sect. 3, 'A Modernist Malgré Lui', although Larmore was prepared to leave his criticism at that and not go on to accuse MacIntyre of using double epistemic standards. For Larmore he is merely a foundationalist, whereas I think it is more accurate to see him as a foundationalist about other views, but a contextualist very like Larmore when it comes to MacIntyre's own 'Neo-Neo-Augustinianism'.

MacIntyre's argument is further undermined by his inconsistent views on the relation of theory to practice. He claims that the modern world enacts, in its social fabric, its liberal politics, and its individualistic ethic the theoretical errors he has diagnosed. Thus, there is interaction between the sociology of modernity and our intellectual errors. However, if this is so, the obvious reply is that the ethics and the politics of the modern world are those most adjusted to modern conditions. Individualism and a retreat to a merely procedural view of reason have this to be said for them: they are adjusted to the society in which we find ourselves, and which we cannot escape. It would only be sensible for those of us trapped in Weber's 'iron cage' to make the necessary adjustments in our intellectual outlook.[38]

If MacIntyre's work can be reinterpreted in such a way that the charitable interpretation of the status of neo-Augustinianism can be extended to other traditions of ethical enquiry, there are many insights in his account that a contextualist theory would want to preserve. The most important of these have already been detailed: how criticism is from a standpoint of engagement, how creative reinterpretation of two competing traditions may produce synthesis of the insights of both from an initial standpoint of commitment to one of them. I have already argued that the adoption of contextualism allows one sympathetically to interpret one of MacIntyre's most criticized views, concerning the end point of a whole life. *After Virtue*'s picturesque metaphor of life as a quest was unobjectionable, but seemed hardly insightful. But, in fact, I think MacIntyre is giving, in this account, a similar view of the relationship between a life virtuously lived to the account I have defended in this book. The virtuous life does not stand to the good of that life as a means to an end. It is, rather, that the virtuous person, in the course of reflective living, sets him or herself various ends and yet, in the course of realizing them, finds other ends arising. To the extent that such ends can be brought together in the idea of a rational plan of life, to that extent it is possible to speak of a supervenient end of each individual good in the proper harmony and proportion. But, clearly, an end understood in such a sense cannot be an object of appraisal independently of the life virtuously lived.

How is the issue to be decided between Taylor's optimistic narrative, so congenial to the contextualist in its vindication of rationality in the face of conflict between background frameworks, and MacIntyre's deeply pessimistic alternative? I believe that this can be decided in two ways. First, MacIntyre's false theoretical assumptions have to be exposed. It is flatly inconsistent to argue that one ethical tradition should receive a contextual justification while others are subject to a foundationalist test that they cannot possibly meet. Secondly, the adoption of a consistent contextualism prevents a by now familiar question arising: the question of whether our best background framework is vindicated by moral sources that transcend it. MacIntyre seems to imply that if the answer to that question is 'no', then the rationality of interframework reasoning

---

[38] MacIntyre has a response in the political case, namely a political utopianism that opts out of the politics of the modern nation state entirely, but it is difficult to envisage what the moral counterpart of this move could be. (That is why MacIntyre is an unlikely 'communitarian': see his 'A Partial Response to My Critics', in Susan Horton and John Mendus (eds.), *After MacIntyre* (Notre Dame, Ind.: University of Notre Dame Press, 1994), 283–304.)

is threatened. But the foregoing discussions have revealed that this is a false dichotomy. It exactly parallels Timmons's worries about Putnam's view: that the view must collapse into relativism or external realism. But a carefully stated contextualism can avoid that dichotomy.

A fully satisfactory answer to MacIntyre would go on to contend with his arguments at the level of the historical details, but I cannot possibly undertake that task here. MacIntyre's own work has acted as catalyst for a narrative that reconceptualizes the connections between disagreement, conflict, and the distinctive conditions of modernity found in his work. In the complementary accounts given by J. B. Schneewind and Charles Larmore, the details of MacIntyre's narrative is challenged at many points.[39] Schneewind argues that MacIntyre's history of early modern moral philosophy simply ignores the extent to which it operated within a shared framework of Christian and Aristotelian assumptions in which teleology was subservient to a divine corporation conception of the moral world. Schneewind admits that this conception is now obsolete, and was problematized in the early modern period. However, his main point is that it sustained a legacy of shared understandings sufficient to block MacIntyre's incommensurability claim. Yet this resource of a common life available to the immediate inheritors of the divine corporation theory had to coexist, in Schneewind's narrative, with a new emphasis on the importance of resolving social conflicts. The key transitional figure is Kant, synthesizing his own emphasis on constructivism and autonomy with the remnants of the divine corporation model and an emphasis on social conflict based on 'unsociable sociability' taken from the natural law tradition of Grotius and Pufendorf.[40] Larmore's conclusions converge on those of Schneewind, and he too chooses to focus his argument on Kant. In particular, Larmore argues that Kant realized that he needed a further defence of his prioritization of principles of right over the theory of the good. Larmore argues that the basis for this position lies in Kant's 'modern' realization that given the plurality of conceptions of good, only principles of right could function as the basis of a common morality.[41]

Thus, two themes emerge from this work by Schneewind and Larmore which act as a counterweight to MacIntyre's narrative and its stress on incommensurable disagreement: namely, that as late as the eighteenth century an admittedly

---

[39] J. B. Schneewind, 'Moral Crisis and the History of Ethics', in Peter French, Theodore Uehling, and Howard Wettstein (eds.), *Midwest Studies in Philosophy*, 8 (1983), 525–42; 'Virtue, Narrative and Community', *Journal of Philosophy*, 79/11 (Nov. 1982), 653–63; 'The Divine Corporation and the History of Ethics', in Richard Rorty, Quentin Skinner, and J. B. Schneewind (eds.), *Philosophy in History* (Cambridge: Cambridge University Press, 1984), 173–92; 'The Misfortunes of Virtue', *Ethics*, 101/1 (Oct. 1990), 42–63; 'Kant and Natural Law Ethics', *Ethics*, 104/1 (Oct. 1993), 53–74; 'Natural Law, Skepticism and Methods of Ethics', *Journal of the History of Ideas*, 52/2 (Apr–June 1991), 289–308; Charles Larmore, 'The Right and the Good', *Philosophia* (Israel) 20/1–2 (July 1990), 15–32, and *Modernité et morale* (Paris: Presses universitaires de France, 1993).

[40] The classic account of the anthropological basis of Kant's ethics is that of Allen Wood, 'Unsociable Sociability: The Anthropological Basis of Kant's Ethics', *Philosophical Topics*, 19/1 (Spring 1991), 325–51.

[41] Larmore also emphasizes Kant's additional argument that obligations are directly known to us through conscience which marks another point at which Larmore's views converge with those of Bishop Butler.

problematized divine corporation view made available a set of shared understandings for ethical reflection, alongside increasing emphasis on value pluralism and social conflict. In this more nuanced historical narrative, modern ethical thought contains a fundamental 'contradiction' between an emphasis on shared understandings and a counter-emphasis on the inevitability of social conflict. The extent to which this shapes a distinctive account of the problems of modern politics will come into explicit focus in Part IV of this book, with particular focus on Larmore's views and parallel developments in the late work of John Rawls. However, the limited amount I want to take from these arguments in the ethical case is that at the level of historical fact, independently of any contestable theoretical errors MacIntyre may or may not make, it is possible to present a narrative of the emergence of the modern moral identity that does not sustain his account cast in terms of disintegration and loss. The contextualist belief that conflict can be resolved into reasonable disagreement can be sustained and does not rest on blind optimism about our collective prospects.

CONCLUSION

I have already argued that a very difficult challenge for the kind of contextualist view that I want to defend here is to maintain that there is scope for practical rationality across traditions of moral enquiry. But this claim can be substantiated. Substantiating it requires the construction of a contingent narrative of gains and losses of the kind developed by *Sources of the Self*, even if one takes issue with particular claims in that work. The aim of this book is not to present such a narrative, but to defend the possibility and the point of a narrative of this kind.

However, it would be complacent not to say more in defence of this general project. The non-objectivist stands prepared to remind us that he predicted that any objectivist construal of moral knowledge could not explain a certain kind of radical diversity of ethical outlook. For all my protestations that the position defended here is not a form of neo-Kantianism, Williams stands ready to accuse my view of smuggling back in to my account the transcendental 'we' standing for all makers of *ethical* judgements. This concept will indeed have been smuggled back in if all I can say is that we are committed to our tradition and that all other ethical outlooks of which we are reflectively aware are simply mistaken. That concept will have been implicitly in the background on the narrative of *Sources of the Self* if its overt narrative of pluralism points in the direction of a final reconciliation of this plurality. So, in the next chapter, I will address the issue of pluralism in more depth and, in particular, address the issues of developing a plausible theory of moral error and finding some truth in the thesis of the relativism of distance.

10

Moral Belief and the Possibility of Error

§1: When are two moral judgements in conflict? §2: The idea of a theory of error for moral beliefs. §3: Cognitivism explains error far better than non-cognitivism. §4: A model is outlined for the criticism of ideologically determined beliefs.

I have, throughout this book, insisted that the challenge of non-objectivism needs to be taken very seriously by anyone who wants to defend the idea of moral knowledge. It is a compelling form of a distinctively modern set of doubts about the ethical: that there is a radical plurality of ethical outlooks that goes beyond the reasonable pluralism within morality and destabilizes the claim of any one such outlook to represent the truth. An important aspect of this non-objectivist critique is the possibility it raises that our moral beliefs may, in fact, be nothing more than ideologically determined. This chapter addresses the problem of error in our moral beliefs in two ways. There is a generic problem: explaining how, within a cognitivist position, one can offer any explanation of the kinds of mistake that people make when they do not have true moral knowledge. This leads on directly to a more specific problem: how, among the false moral beliefs that people undoubtedly have, can we further pick out those that are merely ideologically determined? I will deal with these problems in turn, but there is an even more fundamental issue that needs to be addressed: how do we know when we have two options to compare? When is this a cognitive matter?

1. PLURALISM, INDETERMINACY, AND THE PRESUPPOSITIONS OF COMPARISON

A crucial step in the argument of this book was undermining the presuppositions of Williams's non-objectivist understanding of the ethical. That involved diagnosing a false assumption in the disaster scenario that befell the hypertraditionalists when we understood their ethical claims in an objectivist way. David Wiggins, too, has challenged Williams's understanding of how this thought experiment proceeds. His argument is that the thought experiment simply does not deliver the clear result that Williams assumed that it does. It was one possible instance of the effect of the reflective awareness of conflict among moral beliefs and Wiggins added that other results of such reflective awareness are possible. He describes three: a diagnosis that we have a case of incommensurability, a case of potential convergence, or a case of underdetermination.[1] Wiggins's interesting remarks on these alternative diagnoses are worthy of further consideration. He has focused on the key issue of whether or not, when we have two apparently competing sets of moral beliefs that are in conflict, this is, in fact, how we should acquiesce in describing the case—as one of conflict.

The first case that he describes is a kind of relativism that he regards as untroubling to cognitivism on the grounds that the latter claims cognitive status only for issues on which people share an understanding. (I will say more about relativistic confrontations below.) This first case is easily confused with the second kind of case, where initial disagreement suggests that the two parties should persevere in attempts to transcend their different starting points and arrive at a common standard. It has been independently pointed out that the idea of understanding another group itself masks two different senses: a sense in which understanding entails a capacity to understand and a sense in which it entails the ability to understand (those who are able to understand have the capacity to do so, but not vice versa).[2] You cannot determine at the outset whether two groups can understand each other (or, transposing the point, share a common standard or set of values) before attempts have been made to close the gap between them. Nothing of any interest follows from the fact that two groups cannot, at the moment, understand each other. Lacking the ability is not the point; lacking the capacity is. (For example, nothing significant follows from the fact that I cannot, now, speak Mandarin as I have not taken the time and trouble to learn it. It is more interesting if I do not have the capacity to do so and more interesting still if I could not have the capacity.) Whether two groups lack the capacity to understand each other is only determined after one has followed Wiggins's 'counsel of perseverance'.

In the third case, we have irresoluble disagreement, but again its impact on cognitivism is not clear:

> Relativization to circumstances does not help. Relativization to ethos represents distortion. And there is no manifest possibility of any winning set of considerations ever being mustered . . . If so, and if, where practical reason idles, it is pointless to look to it for a practical verdict, then—in so far as we persist in attributing to the disputants a common understanding of what is meant by the question of what one ought to do about this or that—well, indeterminacy or underdetermination is revealed in the reference and extension of certain moral words (understood in this way) or in certain combinations of them (so understood).[3]

The question of whether two candidate proposals are put forward by people who share the same understandings need not be a wholly determinate matter. Wiggins's underlying point, I believe, is that this kind of indeterminacy or underdetermination is not a special problem *about ethics*. Wiggins also reinforces a point that I made earlier

[1] This is the central focus of Wiggins, 'Moral Cognitivism, Moral Relativism and Motivating Moral Beliefs', 61–85.

[2] Susan Hurley discusses these points very insightfully in 'Intelligibility, Imperialism and Conceptual Scheme', in Peter French, Theodore Uehling, and Howard Wettstein (eds.), *Midwest Studies in Philosophy*, 17. *The Wittgenstein Legacy* (1992), 89–108 where she discusses the claim that there is an element of transcendental idealism in the later philosophy of Wittgenstein and connects this issue to Davidson's views about interpretation.

[3] Wiggins, 'Moral Cognitivism, Moral Relativism and Motivating Moral Beliefs', 77.

(a point also made by Timmons): it is one thing merely to point to an alternative ethical outlook that may have been held in some time or place, or could conceivably be held now, but that is not enough to view it as a genuine competitor to the outlook we now hold:

> Against the claim that, whatever conviction may be achieved, there will always be a tenable point of view that finds something consistent with our own best considered finding, its [cognitivism's] main defence will have to be to attack the insidious presumption of symmetry between points of view. Unless the non-cognitivist or the error theorist can show that there is an incoherence in the very idea of enlightenment and of refinement of moral conceptions, it is simply question begging to make this presumption.[4]

This point is, as I have argued, central to contextualism: what moves us to criticize and reconstruct a given context of enquiry is a challenge to it that is a real challenge, not merely another possible view. The moral sceptic can act as a catalyst for moral progress if he or she can put a specific, worked out competitor ethical conception forward for consideration; otherwise, sceptical doubt idles.

One of the most interesting questions is raised by Wiggins's first claim: that there is a certain kind of truth in moral relativism. I would interpret this claim, from the perspective of contextualism, as the claim that some apparently relevant alternative ethical outlooks are not, in fact, relevant as they fall under what both Wiggins and Williams call 'the relativism of distance'. Williams introduced this concept in the course of an attempt to set out the conditions for a consistent form of relativism which avoids Protagorean self-refutation.[5] First, one must have two theories which are more or less self-contained. Secondly, they must be incompatible, if only in a minimal sense. Thirdly, they must also be comparable, if only minimally. There must be some question, which they can both formulate, to which they give different answers. Finally, they must stand in a relation of real confrontation: there must be a group of people for whom the adoption of either theory is a genuine possibility. The truth that Williams thinks was badly expressed by relativism is that there is only point to appraising both theories if they are in a real confrontation.

Williams's claim has met with much critical discussion. My interpretation of it is that the reflective point of such evaluations varies according to the relative 'location' of the ethical option the culture supplies as an alternative to our own ethical point of view. A preliminary point is that in measuring this relativism of distance (where the ideas of distance and measurement are only metaphorical), the first task is to establish one's own location. That is the difficult achievement of individual and collective self-knowledge: an undeceived and honest view of what our ethical point of view actually is. Williams then argued that the ethical option presented by the other culture can either be a real or a notional option for us, its interpreters. This depends on whether or not the option of living that life is practically available to us without self-deception. Williams has been misunderstood on this point, but it was part of his view that the

---

[4] Wiggins, 'Moral Cognitivism, Moral Relativism and Motivating Moral Beliefs', 77.
[5] Bernard Williams, 'The Truth in Relativism', in *Moral Luck*, 132–43; Williams, *Ethics and the Limits of Philosophy*, ch. 9.

criticism of other cultures will continue, even if they do represent only a notional option for us. However, reflection on the *point* of that criticism will reveal it to have a different grounding from criticism directed at real options. Williams did not claim that universalist criticism of alternative ethical ways of life was impossible. His claim was not directed against aspiration to continue to condemn alternative practices even if that whole form of life is not a real option for us. Williams aimed, rather, to change our reflective understanding of its point. (Once again, this involves a denial of the claim that utterances that lack a pragmatic point are not truth-apt, a point that came up in my discussion of Cavell's response to the sceptic.) To borrow one of Williams's formulations from 'Wittgenstein and Idealism', in a notional confrontation groups are alternatives *for* us, not alternatives *to* us. Nevertheless, we will continue to criticize their practices, by our own lights, because it matters to how we understand our own critical appraisals that we continue to do so.

My interest in this argument is that it allows me to characterize the relevant range of ethical outlooks to our default 'home' outlook using some principled restrictions. Other cultures which we notionally confront are understandable and explicable, but not accessible to us in the sense that they can be seen as living by a genuinely competitor set of values. The accessibility relation I am appealing to here is not fixed in advance of attempts to determine its scope. A group can be more or less self-deceived in how it perceives its relations to other groups, and can take an option to be real when attempts to realize those values manifest the fact that the confrontation was, in fact, optional. In other words, the truth or falsity of whether we stand in a real or notional confrontation to another group is a cognitive matter: we can get it wrong. But the truth of the thesis as a whole indicates that there are some apparent sceptical alternatives to our current working ethical conceptions that do not, in fact, stand in the right kind of relation to our current conceptions to be an alternative to them.

2. THE AMBIVALENT IDEA OF A THEORY OF ERROR FOR MORAL BELIEF

So much, then, for the issue of whether or not we have two cognitive claims that are in competition with each other, such that we have to compare them. If we have two such claims, we have to declare what relation they stand in, and this could involve the diagnosis that one of them is a moral error. A plausible account of what *this* could mean is very important to contextualism. I have, throughout this book, argued that it is a mistake to try to claim too much on behalf of cognitivism. Traditions of moral enquiry ought not to be modelled as research programmes each independently searching for the moral truth such that we can expect them all eventually to converge on a single answer. That seems to misrepresent their character. But this is an anticipated consequence of the view defended in this book. I have argued that enquiry as a whole does not stand to judgement in the way that a means stands to an end. The most plausible form of cognitivist theory takes it that there is a reasonable objective pluralism within morality and this is not a single end to which enquiry leads. It is, indeed, not true that the history of ethical enquiry looks like a convergence of a set of research traditions on a single truth about the ethical, but it seems to me that this fact says as much about the nature of ethical truth as about the nature of enquiry. That is not a distinctive problem for cognitivism. The truth of objective pluralism is still a truth, and claims about values are still cognitive, claims that are also individually true.

Another reason for resisting the image that cognitivism may suggest of competing research traditions in ethical enquiry is, it seems to me, that we are already in possession of considerable amounts of moral knowledge. As I pointed out in response to Williams's 'no moral experts' argument, perhaps it just is not very difficult to get things right, morally speaking. We should not expect that we need to set up research teams to find out moral truth. Ethical traditions are not really in that business either; they are more in the business of articulating competing visions of the good. But that articulation, dependent as it is on expressive power, is impossible to separate from the expression of belief as I argued above in connection with Taylor's work. Changes in belief, in turn, offer possibilities for ethical critique and for the piecemeal replacement of beliefs that we already hold. That procedure can be developed until a fully developed competitor replaces a significant part of that which we believe. That process continues through time until we are, perhaps, some way from our starting point in the way that Nozick described in his image of a chain of intellectual transitions.[6] But these differences between the way that moral knowledge develops and the way that research in, say, biochemistry develops can be acknowledged without the claim that this is not a form of knowledge acquisition and use *at all*. I agree that a sudden revolutionary breakthrough in biochemistry could transform the field tomorrow, marking a radical change from existing theory. That is not a realistic prospect in the ethical case. But that marks off a difference between one kind of knowledge and another, not a difference between knowledge and non-knowledge.

The challenge that has recurred throughout this book is the challenge of developing a plausible theory of moral error within cognitivism. But I regard this challenge as ambivalent. Because while the cognitivist certainly has to say something about those who hold divergent beliefs, he or she should also point out that the existence of moral error may offer an argument *in support* of cognitivism. Mark Timmons has recently focused on this point and I believe that he is correct to do so.[7] That which Timmons and I have in mind is the possibility that our ordinary moral practices acknowledge within themselves the phenomenon of 'deep error'. This is error in moral beliefs that cannot be explained, in non-cognitivist terms, by invoking some extension of our critical practices as the non-cognitivist understands them. I will develop this point in the next section. However, as a necessary preliminary, it is worth pointing out the scope of the problem facing the contextualist. Not every disagreement calls for the application of a theory of moral error.

---

6 Nozick, *Invariances*, 2–3.

7 Timmons, *Morality Without Foundations*, ch. 3. Timmons devotes a chapter to the problem and argues that it forces non-cognitivism (he prefers the term 'irrealism') to take a non-reductive form. That non-reductive form is the attempt to defend an assertoric non-descriptivism, criticized in Ch. 5, above. While I do not accept Timmons's solution to the problem he poses, at least he poses it and recognizes it as the significant problem for non-cognitivism (irrealism) that it is.

The contextualist should chip away at what seems to be a very large and intractable problem, to show that, in fact, it is not as difficult a task as it seems to explain moral error on a cognitivist basis. There is a series of possible counter-considerations, none of which is decisive in itself, but which taken together have cumulative force and suggest that the development of a theory of error for ethical beliefs is not the problem it appears to be for cognitivism.

First, the error involved in a moral disagreement need not actually turn out to be moral. The moral beliefs that people hold can depend to a significant degree on other beliefs that they hold. Contextualism goes to some lengths to emphasize this.[8] But this has the consequence that if people hold false scientific, metaphysical, or religious beliefs they may also hold false moral beliefs as a consequence. Thus, divergence in moral belief may not result from diligent moral enquiry on the part of the two parties, but from a presupposition on the part of one party that the issue is already settled given other non-moral assumptions that they hold. Alternatively, those false assumptions may bias the direction of enquiry so that he or she has blamelessly conducted his or her moral enquiries, but in such a way as to derive a morally perverse result from prior false non-moral assumptions. A supplement to this point is that people may hold false moral beliefs because they make errors in processes of reasoning, such everyday fallacies as denying the antecedent of a conditional (in the case of deductive reasoning), or committing the gamblers' fallacy (in reasoning probabilistically).

The second response is that even within our quotidian theory of error, the kind that we use when we preliminarily screen our degree of confidence in our beliefs before they enter the process of narrow reflective equilibrium, we are sensitive to how difficult it is to get ethical beliefs right. Sometimes, to get things ethically right, you need to be emotionally engaged, perhaps even angry. In other cases you need to be calm and detached, devoid of emotion. Sometimes you need to be spontaneous; at other times, reflective. Common sense recognizes that getting things right, ethically, can be demanding in these ways and cognitivism is at least happy to acknowledge that it has common sense on its side on this point. (I believe that this is compatible with denying that there can be moral experts; I have not conceded that moral knowledge requires special expertise.)

The third response is that cognitivism only claims belief and truth for an important and central part of morality, not the whole of morality. I have already accepted that when it comes to the articulation of moral outlooks, there is an unclear line between belief and articulation or expression. My main emphasis has been on a consequence that I do *not* want drawn from this fact: I have argued that articulating and expressing are compatible with the expression of belief and, furthermore, are best explained as the expression of beliefs. But if there is a genuine continuity here and not a clear demarcation between expressions of belief and articulation, I can exploit that point too. Because there certainly seem to be areas of morality, like the discussion of personal ideals, where the emphasis falls more on the articulation of a vision than the expression of truth. Cognitivism claims plain truth for specific evaluations of persons,

---

[8] A point stressed, for example, in the contextualism of Larmore, *Patterns of Moral Complexity*, 29.

properties, and states of affairs, and this is the cognitive core of morality. Beyond this core there is a significant periphery where divergence between reasonable people is only to be expected. This is cognitively blameless divergence in expressions or articulations that are not yet, clearly, candidates for truth. But this divergence could be mistaken for a conflict that cognitivism is asked to explain away as an instance of a conflict between true belief and error. It is cases such as these that seem best to fit Wiggins's cases of 'cognitive underdetermination'. This term of art marks out the fact that whereas specific evaluations have all the marks of plain truth, the space of reasons does not, because it exhibits that which Wiggins once called 'cognitive underdetermination' in the sense of combining 'objectivity, discovery and invention'. Cognitivism not only tolerates this periphery, it explains it: as we move from the cognitive core of morality towards this periphery concerning, for example, personal ideals, so we find more and more cases of cognitive underdetermination.

A fourth response to explaining away divergent beliefs flows from this. Given competing ethical ideals, it is reasonable to expect that moral pluralism is as deep an ethical phenomenon as moral unity, as opposed to a conception of ethics as fundamentally unitary and only diverging into pluralism under the impact of cultural circumstance. Pretty much all sides to the argument agree on this; Williams, for example, is an ethical pluralist. The question is when the evidence can be read as sustaining more than this: the radical pluralism that Williams views as the typical ethical condition of modern societies. It is this *further* claim that I have tried to rebut in this book. But the underlying claim that ethical outlooks are reasonably internally plural, repeatedly defended by Stuart Hampshire, ought to be accepted by all sides to the debate. Hampshire was concerned with undoing the ancient, Sophistic, contrast between the unitary domain of nature, *physis*, and the plurality of the domain of cultural conventions, *nomos*, where morality is assumed to fall under the later classification.[9]

My fifth response is that one can reasonably expect central ethical concepts to be vague in their application.[10] Vagueness is a pervasive cognitive phenomenon and is no less of a problem in ethical enquiry than elsewhere. It may be vague whether a belief or its constituent concepts are indeed divergent, particularly without a commitment to a firm analytic/synthetic distinction.

I do not introduce these alternative diagnoses of divergence in order to evade a genuine issue, which is that some divergences in ethical reasoning are products of genuine error. But some divergences can be explained in the ways that I have described, with the consequence that not every divergence from a core tradition of ethical reasoning is automatically in error. The uphill task facing a theory of ethical error may be just that: an uphill task, not an impossible task. I have not sought in this book to overstate the case for the cognitive credentials of ethics, and one point of

---

[9] Stuart Hampshire, 'Morality and Conflict', in *Morality and Conflict* (Cambridge, Mass.: Harvard University Press, 1983), 140–70.

[10] There is surprisingly little discussion of this concept in connection with ethics, but see Russ Shafer-Landau, 'Vagueness, Borderline Cases and Moral Realism', *American Philosophical Quarterly*, 32 (1995), 83–96.

difference between the scientific and the ethical must be acknowledged. Christopher Hookway has argued that focusing on the various ways in which Williams deploys the concept of convergence fails to sharpen the necessary distinction between 'the scientific' and 'the ethical', but that reflection on the differing roles of the concept of fallibility in the two domains offers a defence of Williams's position in different terms.[11] Hookway argues that our attitude to the long-term project of scientific enquiry is that it is self-correcting. One feature of the world that scientific enquiry will cast light on is itself and its own failings. Acknowledging these failings will allow us to devise further methods to overcome them. However, the essential contestability and cognitive underdetermination that Hookway attributes to ethical enquiry prevents there being any close analogy for this point in ethics. He nonetheless argues for a form of weak objectivity in the ethical, which views it as beginning with the idea of forms of life that can be reasonably valued, as opposed to research traditions trying to track the objective truth. The features of pluralism and cognitive underdetermination will allow a range of possible developments of the ethical which are not rivals with each other as they would be within an objectivist model.

That point seems plausible to me, but from my perspective Hookway is overly pessimistic as to how much objectivity this strategy can secure. If one adopts a contextualist epistemology for ethical thought, then the kind of objectivity Hookway envisions looks considerably more robust. If the idea of justification by precedent has any hold within traditions of ethical reasoning, cannot they similarly be seen as self-correcting in an analogous way to scientific enquiry? Again, I am not trying to extend a model of objectivity across the board to all areas of enquiry, nor am I trying to deny obvious disanalogies between the scientific and the ethical. But if I can establish that there is not a principled gulf between the rational methods used in both scientific and ethical enquiry, how those methods are vindicated and their results justified, then a contextualist model of ethical objectivity can be sustained intact. Whereas Hookway takes cognitive underdetermination to be at the core of ethical cognitivism, I have argued that adopting contextualism allows one to explain this phenomenon as part of a periphery of ethical judgements best explained by treating the core of cognitive claims as robustly cognitive.

Part of this response to Hookway depends on defending the role of precedent within ethical enquiry. It seems to me that we very often reason morally by appealing to precedent. Wiggins's example of 'slavery being unjust and insupportable' is a very good example, as previous societies in different historical periods rationalized their practice of slavery as in some way right. It might be conceived of as 'natural', or as akin to a natural misfortune, or as in fact a benevolent form of paternalism. But all of these alleged justifications have been so utterly discredited that there is no prospect of their revival.[12] Changing attitudes to slavery are an example of collective social change that can only be described as an improvement and a precedent such as this offers critical

---

[11] Hookway, 'Fallibilism and Objectivity, Science and Ethics'.
[12] There may, nevertheless, be some point to rehearsing those arguments, in spite of their vindicatory character, to highlight the unreasonableness of those who fail to find them compelling. There is such a rehearsal in the case of slavery in Joshua Cohen, 'The Arc of the Moral Universe',

leverage on other forms of immoral practice within a society. At least since the time of the ancient Stoics, a moral case against slavery has been unanswerable and this looks like a plausible case of a self-correcting aspect in a moral outlook. Considerations of that kind are, indeed, part of the positive argument that a cognitivist can develop: that divergent ethical views are better explained by cognitivism than by non-cognitivism.

3. COGNITIVISM AND MORAL ERROR: THE POSITIVE CONNECTION

I noted in the previous section that while the existence of moral error is frequently presented as an embarrassment for cognitivism, the cognitivist has a powerful counter-argument. That argument is that *only* cognitivism can explain moral error whereas non-cognitivism cannot. Moral error is here understood as error in belief that does not depend on errors in non-moral beliefs or errors of reasoning. Very few non-cognitivists have taken this argument seriously, the exception being Mark Timmons. Focusing on our 'moral deliberations, debate and argument', which he summarizes under the umbrella term 'critical practices', Timmons points out that it seems to be a presupposition of our critical practices that a person can be in error, morally speaking.[13] Alternatively, we can speak of a moral outlook as improved or less erroneous. Closely related is the fact that we can speak of genuine disagreement between people over moral issues. Why do these facts lend support to cognitivism?

Because, once again, cognitivism offers a simple and compelling argument to the conclusion that the best explanation of *this* aspect of our critical practices is that they are concerned with truth and knowledge. The best way to extend this argument is to develop a case-by-case refutation of proposed rival views. To take a selective (but representative) range of examples: views which construct value, by a rational process, face the challenge of explaining the principled distinction between moral error and a rational proposal to revise the construction process. An intersubjective theory of value, I have argued, misplaces our relation to value and makes all values extrinsic. But a key idea in any such view is that we are being offered a transcendental insight into the possibility of the very category of the valuable.[14] The whole category depends on processes of rational construction. But in order for us to be externally constrained by value and to view our judgements about value to be capable of genuine error, we have voluntarily to will a forgetting of this insight. For only if we can feign amnesia in this way can we take moral errors to be errors and not, for example, revisionary proposals: that is because any construction out of the materials of our own sensibilities,

---

in Tommy Lott (ed.), *Subjugation and Bondage: Critical Essays on Slavery and Social Philosophy* (Totowa, NJ: Rowman and Littlefield Publishers, 1998), 281–328.

[13] Timmons, *Morality Without Foundations*, 82–85.

[14] The most subtle treatment of this point, that of Philip Stratton-Lake in *Kant, Duty and Moral Worth*, takes the moral law as constitutive of a certain space of reasons, that of deontic modality, and hence not as directly about value. But for that reason he takes his view to be incompatible with treating Kant as a justificatory constructivist and 'I have to concede that as I understand his account of moral worth the constructivist aspect of his [Kant's] view loses its centrality', 116. (Kant remains a 'criterial constructivist' in the sense explained by Stratton-Lake, ibid. 114–17.)

however idealized, lacks sufficient critical distance between our sensibilities and the facts of the matter to sustain the idea of genuine error. To use an analogy, if a player in a soccer match picks up the ball and runs with it in his hands, is that breaking the rules of soccer or inventing a new game altogether via a revisionary proposal, namely, the introduction of a new constitutive rule? There is a clear distinction between constitutive and regulatory rules, but is it clear, from within constructivism, how one is to classify a particular proposal as one or the other?[15]

Social code theories face a similar problem.[16] A view of this general kind identifies moral truths as licensed by a socially adopted set of norms. But how is one to understand a shift between sets of norms at the level of a whole society? Suppose one did want to argue that attitudes to slavery changed in the nineteenth century in several Western societies and changed in the sense of 'radically improved' from a moral perspective. If justification is internal to a code, what explains shifts at the level of the whole code? An appeal to presupposed values, such as human flourishing, lets in cognitivism by the back door as those values act as external constraints on codes which do not, in turn, explain them.[17] (Frequently the game is given away even earlier when social codes are described as instruments for the minimizing of conflict within or between individuals. This proposal wears on its sleeve a negative evaluation of conflict and a positive evaluation of its absence: values too obvious to state, perhaps, but values none the less.) The varieties of non-cognitivism surveyed in Chapter 5 attempt, similarly, to generate normativity out of subjective materials, most clearly in Blackburn's logic of the attitudes. Here, once again, the suspicion is that a collection of subjective attitudes can evolve in an unconstrained way and be described only as an improvement or a deterioration in an ethical sensibility relative to some prior interest that does not receive a subjectivist interpretation. This is inconsistent with the view being put forward.

Timmons usefully generalizes over these cases.[18] He argues that the problem for all varieties of non-cognitivism (irrealism) is not error, but that which he calls 'deep error'. The constructivist, social code theorist and non-cognitivist can, within their own views, develop 'ersatz' notions of correctness and error by appealing to hypothetical developments of their respective construction procedures, codes, and sensibilities under various idealized conditions. But that which escapes these manoeuvres is precisely the idea of a deep error that transcends any such conditions. Such deep error, however, is well described by contextualism, and on this point Timmons and I are in complete agreement. Contextualism keeps a balance between two points. First, it emphasizes how any background framework of belief can be transcended by a worked

---

[15] Brink, *Moral Realism and the Foundations of Ethics*, ch. 2, uses the argument from moral error against the restricted target of constructivism.

[16] The most sophisticated social code view I am aware of is David Copp's in *Morality, Normativity and Society*.

[17] I think this general line of objection could be applied, for example, to views which talk of social choice as meeting the rational satisfaction of needs, as in David Copp's 'Moral Knowledge in Society Centred Moral Theory', in Sinnott-Armstrong and Timmons (eds.), *Moral Knowledge?*, 243–66.

[18] Timmons, *Morality Without Foundations*, 76–93.

out competitor. It thus fully acknowledges the context breaking role of immanent reason. Secondly, it describes this role while denying the claim that critical pressure on any given outlook depends on there being an end point to enquiry as a whole. Our critical practices do not point to the idea of that context from which any other can be criticized, and it is a misrepresentation of them to infer that they do so.

Nicholas Sturgeon has developed a variation of this argument from the best explanation of error at the service of cognitivism.[19] He argues that non-cognitivist views, even if they do succeed in explaining error on their own terms, dangerously blur the lines between theoretical truth and falsity and the practical advantages and disadvantages of a view being true. Normally we recognize these as separate dimensions of assessment. To borrow a nice example from Peter Railton, everyone holds the view that they are a better than average driver of a car, although not much reflection shows that we cannot all be right about that.[20] But an accurate diagnosis of how bad a driver a person is may have deleterious practical consequences for them: for example, it may sap their confidence, which is an important part of driving. Perhaps it is for the best if this practice of driving cars proceeds on the basis of just enough overconfidence on the part of its participants to sustain it, while not being so overweening that its practitioners are so overconfident that they become as much of a danger as the underconfident. Even so, there is a fact of the matter as to how good a driver a person is independently of the benefits or costs of holding that belief. We normally separate this dimension of the theoretical truth of a belief from the question of its practical utility. Sturgeon argues, particularly in the case of social code theories, that their attempt to explain moral error fatally runs together these dimensions of assessment. My criticism was that to explain how an entire code is erroneous, the social code theorist must appeal to values such as well-being and flourishing about which we need not another set of norms, but some evaluative truths. Sturgeon can be seen as blocking a rejoinder to this argument that states that codes are justified solely as instrumental devices for the promotion of such values. That response simply vaults over the distinction between truth and acceptance value. It leaves a common sense distinction between the truth of a moral belief, and the value of believing in it, entirely unsupported in any principled way.

The positive connection between cognitivism and moral error could be put this way. In a manner paralleling the arguments of Chapter 5, the claim is not that it is impossible to come up with an explanation of an aspect of our critical moral practices that cognitivism also explains. It is, rather, that an argument to the best explanation shows that cognitivism is the simplest and most compelling explanation. In this context, too, function is most elegantly explained in terms of truth. Functional approaches to ethics emphasize its role in regulating conflict within the individual, or regulating conflict between individuals, or promoting other values such as well-being. The cognitivist does not deny this, on the contrary, he or she claims that these

[19] Nicholas Sturgeon, 'What Difference Does It Make Whether Moral Realism Is True?', *Southern Journal of Philosophy*, 24, suppl. (1986), 115–42.
[20] Peter Railton, 'Morality, Ideology and Reflection; Or The Duck Sits Yet', in *Facts, Values and Norms* (Cambridge: Cambridge University Press, 2003), 118.

functions are best explained as dependent on a prior notion of moral beliefs as *true*. This is shown by the fact that we understand that these two dimensions of assessment, truth and correct function, can come apart. Might a transition to a set of true beliefs on the part of an individual or a society lead to increased conflict with others or between that social group and another group? The answer is clearly 'yes', independently of whether or not one goes on to an all things considered judgement as to whether one would prefer to be in a society with more or less true belief and/or more or less conflict. Sturgeon's point is that we aware that we have two issues here, not one. That lends support to the view that cognitivism is best placed to explain not only how moral beliefs are true, but also how they function both within an individual and a social group or a whole society.

I conclude that the claim that moral cognitivism needs a theory of error is an ambivalent problem from the point of view of the cognitivist. It presents itself as an obstacle for cognitivism, but in its recognition of the phenomenon of deep error, cognitivism is better placed to explain how moral error is possible than its non-cognitivist rivals. I turn, now, to a related challenge. This is the challenge of recognizing moral error caused by the ideological determination of belief.

4. BELIEF AND IDEOLOGY: A GENERAL MODEL

A crucial aspect of Williams's critique of cognitivism was that he implied that the position was, to some extent, a little too complacent about moral knowledge. The view began from the internal perspective of participants in a given form of life and gave an excellent account of the commitments implicit in that internal perspective. However, it did not, Williams alleged, give a comparable account of the critical resources we need to ask certain questions about outlooks taken as a whole. The aim of this section is to address his concerns by explaining how, within cognitivism, it is possible to give an account of ideologically determined beliefs.

The issue is broader than this particular concern on Williams's part. Jürgen Habermas has similarly argued that contextualism is inherently local in a damagingly parochial way that makes it a hostage to ideologically determined sets of belief.[21] So the problem has a broader scope and is, indeed, central to the very idea of how we bring criticism to bear on sets of beliefs at the level of whole groups or societies. But it is not my aim, in this section, to offer any definitive account of the nature of 'ideology critique', a subject on which there is, unsurprisingly, a very substantial literature. My more limited aim is to point out that contextualism does not suffer from the damaging defect that Williams and Habermas suggest that it does. I will try to develop a simple model of how we deal with ideologically determined beliefs and then to work this model up into something adequate enough to address the non-objectivist's concerns. I am going to approach the issue of the ideological determination of belief from a 'bottom up' and 'top down' perspective, beginning with the 'bottom up' account of

---

[21] This criticism dates as far back as *On the Logic of the Social Sciences*, trans. Sherry Weber Nicholson and Jerry A. Stark (Cambridge, Mass.: MIT Press, 1988), but also presented in *Between Facts and Norms*, trans. William Rehg (Cambridge: Polity Press, 1996).

what it is, at the level of an individual, that constitutes the ideological determination of his or her beliefs.

Cases of ideological beliefs are a subclass of the general range of irrationally motivated phenomena, including self-deception, weakness of will, and so on. So some of the features of ideologically determined beliefs do not distinctively mark them off as a class, although their function or purpose might. Davidson explains the general class of irrational beliefs in this way:

> In standard reason explanations . . . not only do the propositional contents of various beliefs and desires bear appropriate logical relations to one another and to the contents of the belief, attitude or intention that they help explain; the actual states of belief and desire cause the explained state or event. In the case of irrationality, the causal relation remains, while the logical relation is missing or distorted. In the case of irrationality that we have been discussing, there is a mental cause which is not a reason for what it causes . . . A person is irrational if he is not open to reason—if, on accepting a belief or attitude on the basis of which he ought to make accommodating changes in his other beliefs, desires or intentions, he fails to make those changes. He has a reason which does not cause what it is a sufficient reason for.[22]

As an instance of this general class, an ideologically determined belief has the wrong kind of cause. That picks out two kinds of case: a case where the belief has another mental cause, but the belief and the cause do not stand in a rational relation, or a case where the belief has a non-mental cause which cannot stand in the right relation to belief.

Can the belief still be true? Yes, but it is a Gettier style case where the tracking condition for knowledge is not met: the belief and its truth are merely accidental. A criterion for this is that the belief does not respond to evidence in the right way. Held in place by non-rational causes, it will not respond to patterns of countervailing evidence in the right way. Beliefs entrenched in a way insensitive to patterns of rational belief revision form a general class, of which ideological beliefs are a subclass. Self-deceptive beliefs, for example, may fall under this general description. If there is to be anything distinctive about the class of ideological beliefs, then they are going to have to be picked out in terms of content. A natural suggestion is that they function as beliefs that sustain the power relations that cause them. Relations of power determine ideological beliefs, whose content supports that power in a vicious circle. That natural suggestion about the content and role of ideological beliefs serves to distinguish them from the broader class of irrational beliefs. Nevertheless, they do share with that larger class their non-responsiveness to evidence, itself reflecting their non-standard causal history.

What of the legitimate exercise of power? Suppose I believe that the liberal state in which I currently live exercises its power legitimately and that I acquired that belief (very indirectly) as a result of a causal chain terminating distantly in that

---

[22] Donald Davidson, 'Paradoxes of Irrationality', in Jim Hopkins and Anthony Savile (eds.), *Philosophical Essays on Freud* (Cambridge: Cambridge University Press, 1984), 289–305, quotation from 298–9.

power itself?[23] This is an instance of the point that the difference between legitimate and ideologically determined beliefs really only shows up counterfactually in terms of processes of belief revision. The belief in the legitimacy of the legislation of my liberal state is related to its cause as a good reason is related to a good reason. These normative relations, however, only show up criterially when I respond differentially to the impact of new information into my belief system in the 'right' way. But, one might add, the relation of good reason to good reason is one that holds in any case, even if the criteria for its presence are demonstrated, counterfactually, in how I would respond to certain kinds of new evidence. (This is particularly true if, as I believe, one ought not to adopt a causal theory of knowledge for all knowledge.)

The next problem for this basic account is that it demarcates a class of beliefs not all of which are ideological: for example, we are not disposed lightly to give up very central beliefs of logic or mathematics, those furthest away from the peripheral core of experience. It seems that they, too, will be held no matter what. That is just what their centrality comes to. They are the last beliefs an agent will rationally revise. But I think this is, as it were, an in-principle problem: such beliefs are revisable in the light of empirical confirmation or disconfirmation, whereas ideologically determined beliefs are not revisable as their place in the belief system of an agent is underwritten not by reasons but by the irrelevant intrusion into processes of rational belief revision by 'alien causes'.

A natural way to put some more flesh on the bare bones of this proposal is to say that the determination of a set of beliefs as ideological turns on how the acquisition and use of those beliefs is best explained. The correct explanation of an ideological belief or set of beliefs claims that they serve the interests of a powerful group or individual who is responsible for the inculcation of those beliefs in another or in others in a way that is insensitive to their truth. Typically, in the most directly political cases, the content of these beliefs concerns issues of legitimation. They legitimate, as necessary, a set of arrangements that are not only contingent but false or wrong. Alternatives may be represented, on the other hand, as impossible or impracticable. However, there are interesting cases that are, as it were, more diffuse. The core cases directly tie ideology to power, and power to a central authority or function that exerts that power. Moving out towards a periphery are effects of power that are less directly tied to a central executive authority. For example, the idea of a 'normal' or 'typical' individual features in beliefs that do not seem directly tied to the exercise of power or to any interest in particular. Yet this idea, which has attracted the critical attention of both Foucault and Habermas (particularly when connected to a class of experts in the social sciences qualified to classify people in this way), seems to be an instance of the internalization of power in an account of identity. It does not directly serve an interest, but it makes itself available to serve any of a number of interests.

The key idea in these explanations of ideological belief is that of an interest. The general structure of how we criticize such beliefs reflects epistemological truisms: that

---

[23] There is a very insightful discussion of this general problem in Bernard Williams, *Truth and Truthfulness*, ch. 9, sect. 5.

it is in the nature of belief to be a response to that which is the case, so deviant casual relations between that which is represented and the representation, for example, can undermine that belief as a candidate for knowledge. The distinctively ideological component is the function of such beliefs, the furthering of those interests that in turn hold them in place. **Interest** here is not a particularly individualistic concept: individuals can have interests, but so can social groups.

How, in the light of all the foregoing, does one explain a belief, or set of beliefs, in a context as ideologically determined? To take a specific thesis, Foucault claimed that the contemporary discourse of sexual liberation was in fact its opposite.[24] In claiming to liberate a person's desires, the impulse to a liberated sexuality is the latest in a succession of contingent social practices that place a person under the authority of an expert figure whose role it is to interpret your desire on your own behalf. (Foucault was most familiar with the practice of Roman Catholic confessional.) This was, for Foucault, the latest mask worn by power, specifically the power of others to interpret one's 'deep' or 'real' self which is represented as an object of articulation, but an articulation that is not transparently available to the passive subject. So liberation is in fact its opposite: our therapeutic culture is another expression of the drive to normalize the individual on the part of social institutions and those who play roles in them. In this case the role is that of therapeutic expert who interprets others and in doing so conceptualizes his or her own experience in terms of the normal and abnormal. This is not truth telling but its opposite; nevertheless it presents itself as a liberation.

It is an ironic thesis (it is the final irony if power masquerades as a form of personal liberation) and not an implausible one in a therapeutic and narcissistic culture.[25] But how might one assess beliefs in these terms? Suppose a person holds the belief that their sexuality is liberated and that this is a deep and important truth about who they really are (part of their politics of identity). However, having studied Foucault's arguments, from a third personal perspective a different person, a social critic, comes to the view that this person holds ideologically determined and false views about his or her own self-interpretation. This is not liberation but ideological determination of belief in an administered society. How might a person's beliefs be characterized in order to make this competing description of his or her beliefs manifest when those beliefs are the subject of debunking social criticism?

A first point is that the person's beliefs lack direct justification. In the account I have defended, theoretically laden experience gives a suitably equipped moral judge the capacity to make judgements about the values available to him or her in experience. When screened by a preliminary theory of moral error (what one might call a 'folk theory of error') we have considered judgements. These considered judgements have a prima facie direct justification that they do not lose unless overturned by theory. Ideological beliefs do not have this direct justification. They may seem to, but they do not. They will not survive integration into theory, but even worse, they do not have direct justification in the first place. (Any more than, to use Denise Meyerson's

---

[24] In Michel Foucault, *The History of Sexuality* (New York: Vintage Books, 1990).
[25] See also Phillip Reiff, *The Triumph of the Therapeutic* (Chicago: Chicago University Press 1987); Christopher Lasch, *The Culture of Narcissism* (New York: W. W. Norton, 1991).

example, the way to explain how it truly appears to you in a case of déjà vu that you have been in a place before is to argue that your really have. You can truthfully explain an appearance without explaining it as true.[26]) Secondly, in the individual case, the beliefs of a person are being determined by structures that run through the individual. The general category of individualistic explanations are being subverted by structural or historicist explanations.[27] Understanding how this is possible is a clue to how one might explain beliefs as ideologically determined.

The argument thus far has suggested that any account of how the beliefs of an individual may be ideologically determined has to extend to the embedding of that individual in social structures. General accounts of the relationship between the beliefs of an individual and social structures are standardly organized around three contrasts: between cultural and acultural theories, between structural/historical explanation and individualistic explanation, and between globally and locally debunking explanations. These three distinctions, much discussed in the literature, are standardly explained in the following ways. A cultural theory does not attempt to dispense with the self-understandings of social actors in explaining agency, whereas acultural theory regards such understandings as causally epiphenomenal. When individuals act in the light of their beliefs, a cultural theory of the explanation of social action takes it that the content of those beliefs, as avowed by the individual, has at least a prima facie claim to be the starting point of social explanation. An acultural theory hopes, by contrast, to explain that action in terms that the agent does not, or cannot, avow as the ostensible cause of his or her actions as expressed by his or her beliefs.[28]

A closely related distinction is between structural/historicist explanations and individualist explanations. The former class of explanations regard action by an individual as dominantly explained by the action exemplifying either a social structure viewed synchronically or viewed diachronically. In the former case we have a structuralist social explanation; in the latter case, a historicist explanation. In either case, the structuralist or the historicist views the explanation that he or she offers as dominant over an explanation pitched at the level of the individual's own intentional belief/desire psychology. This dominance, as Pettit explains, can consist in such explanations either 'overriding' or 'outflanking' ordinary intentional explanations.[29] According to the structuralist or the historicist, his or her explanation in terms of

---

[26] Denise Meyerson, *False Consciousness* (Oxford: Oxford University Press, 1996), 5.

[27] There is an excellent discussion of this general issue in Phillip Pettit, *The Common Mind: An Essay on Psychology, Society and Politics* (Oxford: Oxford University Press, 1992), ch. 3, to which I am indebted.

[28] Pettit discusses the structuralist/historicist and atomist/holist contrast, ibid., chs. 3 and 4 respectively; the contrast between cultural and acultural theories is emphasized by Charles Taylor, 'Two Theories of Modernity', *Hastings Center Report*, 25 (1995), 24–33.

[29] Pettit, *The Common Mind*, ch. 3. The overridingness thesis is the more familiar; by 'outflanking' Pettit intends to refer to views in which, for example, 'If socio-structural regularities outflanked intentional in this selectional way, then there would be a sense in which people lacked the autarchy assigned by intentional psychology . . . There would be predestinating factors in operation that would give lie to the autarchy that we naturally ascribe to them', 156. I will focus here on the overridingness argument. The less plausible outflanking argument is straightforwardly rebutted by Pettit in *The Common Mind*, 156–63.

social structure trumps the individualist explanation. Individualists argue for the opposite thesis: in his or her view, an individualist explanation takes the motivating states of the individual agent to be prior in the order of explanation to the relation of such states to a structural or historical cause.

The first two distinctions are closely related, and matters are further complicated by the relevance of yet a third distinction: the scope of such explanations can be explained as applying globally to all social actions or locally to social actions of some predetermined class.[30] So extant models of how individual explanations in terms of beliefs and desires relate to social explanations fall into six distinct classes corresponding to each of these three pairs of distinctions.

My suggestion is that a suitably methodologically modest account of social criticism need only align these three contrasts correctly. (For example, we do not need to go on to explain how an emancipatory social science differs from a social science per se).[31] On the first contrast, between cultural and acultural theory, it seems difficult to believe that cultural factors are epiphenomenal in the explanation of social action. It would be folly, on the other hand, and the lapse into what was traditionally called 'idealism', to see social explanations as cast in terms of cultural causes alone. An obvious compromise that seems, in addition, very plausible, is to argue that there is an asymmetry in the two cases. That asymmetry is to be explained by availing ourselves of the third distinction, that between local and global claims. Acultural theory makes the bold global claim that we need never appeal to the content of a social actor's beliefs and desires; cultural theory makes the equally bold claim that we must always do so. But to finesse the question, the obvious step is to argue that we need to abandon the global aspect of both claims. But at this point a key difference between the two views emerges.

The interesting asymmetry, in my view, is that acultural theories make only potentially global claims, whereas cultural theories can make either local or global claims. It is most implausible to argue that one class of cause globally dominates another, rendering the other epiphenomenal. But the asymmetry is that cultural theories can accommodate local cases whereas acultural causes operate via causes that appear to be cultural but are, in fact, epiphenomenal in that context. These would be local instances of false consciousness. We know that there are lots of good social explanations where the avowed causes of action at the level for an agent's beliefs and desires turn out to be a rationalization for actions caused in the wrong way by ideological beliefs. But from the fact that this is sometimes the case, one can hardly infer that it is always the case. From the perspective of cultural theory, you can make the concession that sometimes we do need to go outside the avowed content of an agent's beliefs or desires to explain her actions. But acultural theories cannot make the parallel concession. On that ground, cultural theories are more explanatory and, in my view, are generally to be preferred to their acultural competitors.

---

[30] This contrast is implicit in Pettit's analysis; for reasons that will become clear I think it needs to be highlighted.

[31] By way of contrast this is the primary concern of Raymond Geuss in his sceptical assessment of the prospects for a distinctively emancipatory social science in *The Idea of a Critical Theory: Habermas and the Frankfurt School* (Cambridge: Cambridge University Press, 1981).

So the third distinction helps to make sense of the first. There seems good reason to argue for the priority of cultural over acultural theory generally. With that matter settled, one can frame the key issue: can social or historical explanations globally debunk individualistic explanations? There seem to be good reasons to answer negatively. As Phillip Pettit has argued, it is difficult to see the individualist explanations of folk psychology being globally consigned to the explanatory scrap heap. Can social or historical explanations debunk individualistic explanations locally? The answer seems obviously 'yes', and in explaining how such explanations do locally debunk, one has, it seems to me, gone a long way towards explaining what is distinctive about social criticism. It is local, focused, improves as it becomes more detailed, and discriminates between appropriate and inappropriate causes for the formation of belief. That is not just the key to how we should give an account of ideology critique; it is also the key to explaining why contextualism dovetails neatly with any such account.

Discussion of the nature of social criticism has been dominated by the rejection of a conception of explanatory social theory as global, acultural, and structural/historicist in such a way as to undermine the status of individualistic explanation. Theories of this kind are arguably to be found in the work of Althusser and Foucault, although I would certainly like to relativize the claim in the case of Foucault to a limited number of works, notably the early and notably Manichaean *Discipline and Punish*.[32] In these works we seem to have the paradox of 'purposefulness without a purpose'; of the working out of a teleological scheme not realized in the avowed intentions of the agents who bring that end about. In the course of a response to Foucault's work Taylor sets up a criterion of acceptability for a formulation of the relationship between structural and individual explanations so insightful that it is worth setting out in full:

[P]urposefulness without purpose requires a certain kind of explanation to be intelligible. The undesigned systematicity has to be related to the purposeful action of agents in a way that we can understand . . . [T]he text of history, which we are trying to explain, is made up of purposeful human action. Where there are patterns in this action which are not on purpose, we have to explain why an action done under one description on purpose also bears this other, undesigned description. We have to show how the two descriptions relate. A strategic pattern cannot just be left hanging, unrelated to our conscious ends and projects. It is a mistake to think that the only intelligible relation between a pattern and our conscious purposes is a direct one where the pattern is consciously willed . . . But this must not be confused with the explanatory requirement outlined above. It is certainly not the case that all patterns issue from conscious action, but all patterns have to be made intelligible in relation to conscious action.[33]

This elegant constraint is a constraint of counterfactual intelligibility. It partially functions to moderate the ambitions of globally debunking historicist or structural explanations. They cannot, as they seem to, give us purposefulness wholly without purpose in the explanation of social action. They seek to dominate individual explanations, rendering them epiphenomenal, and Taylor's constraint explains why such global ambitions will not be realized. Pettit gives further insight into why

---

[32] Michel Foucault, *Discipline and Punish* (New York: Vintage Books, 1995).
[33] Charles Taylor, 'Foucault on Freedom and Truth', in *Philosophical Papers, ii. Philosophy and the Human Sciences* (Cambridge: Cambridge University Press, 1985), 152–84.

Taylor's constraint holds: in the relevant sense of 'individualism', individualism is vindicated by the observation that fully thought through alternatives to it must be taken to involve the global replacement of folk psychology, hardly a likely prospect.[34]

But Taylor and Pettit are equally clear that this vindication of individualism does not mean that there are not structural regularities, alongside intentionalist (individualist) ones. It does mean, however, that we do not, in this case, have two competing sets of laws, as Pettit clearly explains.[35] Both classes of generalization are supervenient on the causal properties of the natural and biological properties from which such regularities arise: we cannot end up with two laws jostling in the same explanatory space to explain what the other would explain, but in an exclusive way. The way that these two sets of regularities are brought together is in certain kinds of explanations, namely, explanations that vindicate or vitiate beliefs by examining the causal origins of their acquisition.

Here there is scope for a local versus global contrast. Whereas a global sceptical thesis tries to debunk all beliefs of a certain class by citing the undermining of such beliefs by, for example, socio-structural regularities, a local thesis would simply cite the dominant explanatory role of a socio-structural regularity in a particular case. There is no threat here of the generalization of such a strategy into either a global scepticism or a global anti-individualism. For this reason I believe that the path through the labyrinth is simply to get the three distinctions with which I began correctly aligned with each other.

I believe that there is an interesting analogy with Stanley Cavell's pragmatic refutation of scepticism, which I mentioned, but did not find finally convincing, in Chapter 8. Cavell claimed that the philosophical sceptic concentrated on certain kinds of case, chosen to be representative, namely, 'generic objects'.[36] If I cannot recognize that this generic object in front of me is a tomato, then I cannot recognize any external object at all. A failure to know such generic objects has a catastrophic effect on my claim to have knowledge of the external world. However, if I cannot recognize some obscure form of tomato in a horticultural competition even though I am the judge of the tomato class in that competition, that is a specific failure of knowledge that does not generalize to other cases. I am, in general, a good judge of the class, but in this case I am tripped up by a particularly exotic instance that outstrips my expertise. (Perhaps I fail to distinguish a Potentate from a Russian Red.) By contrast to the generic case, such failures to know 'Austinian objects', in Cavell's terminology, do *not* generalize. That leads to Cavell's diagnosis of the failure of scepticism, namely, that there is no pragmatic point to the sceptic's claim that one does not know a generic object. There is no issue that he or she can sensibly be raising in that kind of case. So, on Cavell's assumption of the priority of pragmatics to semantics, that sceptical doubt is not true because there is no point to raising that doubt (at this stage I part

[34] Pettit, *The Common Mind*, 144–6.
[35] Ibid. 146–52.
[36] See the critical discussion on precisely this aspect of Cavell's argument in McGinn, *Sense and Certainty*, ch. 5; Barry Stroud, 'Reasonable Claims: Cavell and the Tradition', in *Understanding Human Knowledge* (Oxford: Oxford University Press, 2000).

company from this critique of the sceptic as this claim of the priority of pragmatics to truth-aptness seems to me too strong). There *is* a pragmatic point to doubts about Austinian objects, but failures to know in that case do not generalize. So the sceptic cannot find a representative case where there is any point to his or her doubts, at which point Cavell concluded that the sceptic stood refuted. But even if this is not a promising line of argument against scepticism, I believe that it is a good analogy for a parallel issue in social explanation and I will explain why.

One might say that where a debunking approach undermines the claim of individualistic explanation by providing a conclusive and detailed case that an action is caused by a socio-structural regularity, the detail of the explanation is such that the case cannot generalize. There is no path from particular and local claims to a global claim that individualistic explanations *as a class* are headed for the dustbin of history.

This model of social criticism, then, takes the form of a cultural theory that takes the individualistic, intentional descriptions of agents seriously. But it can also accept that there are socio-structural regularities, provided such regularities meet Taylor's counterfactual intelligibility constraint. The patterns it postulates have to be intelligible as patterns of human agency that *could have* been consciously, deliberatively chosen, even if they actually were not so chosen in this particular case. Further, these regularities can be deployed sceptically to undermine, in a local way, particular formations of belief on the part of an intentional subject. These are local disruptions of the space of reasons by the order of causes that trade, precisely, on reasons being token identical with causes.[37] The interest and plausibility of such proposals will lie in the detail of the particular case which makes the claim that socio-structural regularity is a better explanation than an individual explanation in this particular case. But while prioritizing individual explanations, such a view finds an ethical point to citing certain socio-structural regularities, operating under an individualist constraint.

I have outlined, in necessarily summary form, a model for the critique of ideologically determined beliefs and its application to moral beliefs; a full development and defence of such a model is beyond the scope of this book. The question remains of what this model has to do, in particular, with contextualism. Are the two views not independent of each other? Independent, but in my view they are also mutually supportive. That is because of a distinctive feature of contextualist models of justification: the emphasis on localness. Contextualism domesticates scepticism. Global scepticism tries to derail an entire tradition of enquiry in an untenable way. Contextualism demonstrates the unacceptability of such global scepticism, but also invites the formulation of local sceptical hypotheses as an instrument of enquiry: pointful and specific doubts are precisely that which causes a taken for granted background belief itself to come into question. The onus that the contextualist places on the sceptic is to make an alternative hypothesis specific and detailed, so that it can develop into a genuine competitor of an existing outlook as opposed to a barely sketched-in possibility. But this is precisely the same responsibility placed upon the critic of ideologically determined belief. The argument of this chapter has shown that such critiques are most effective when they are local, detailed, and specific.

[37] Donald Davidson, 'Actions, Reasons and Causes', in *Essays on Actions and Events*, 261–75.

Another aspect of contextualism is a degree of local holism in beliefs, organized as they are into functional classes of background frameworks. The combination of localness, and a degree of moderate holism, supports a particular kind of critique of our ethical ideas. That is criticism based on other of our ethical ideas. If we move away from the abstract characterization of the non-objectivist in general to the particular case of Bernard Williams, one of his recurrent concerns was that excessive attention to whether or not ethics as a whole is globally 'objective' has obscured from view a far more interesting issue.[38] That more interesting issue offers a local critique in which some of our inherited moral ideas come under sceptical pressure from others to which we are more firmly committed. His critique of the 'morality system' (paralleled in the work of Charles Taylor) raised precisely this kind of concern.[39] The way in which it did so also exhibited some of the key features of the critique of ideological beliefs developed in this chapter. Williams argued that processes of modernization and increasing reflectiveness hold in place a set of ideas that depend on certain fictions. These fictions are not stable under reflection and so conflict with the aspiration to truthfulness.[40] The morality system has evolved in such a way as to protect itself from explanatory debunking by setting itself up as representing a higher set of values that cannot be explained in terms of the lower. This protective mechanism means that any attempt to explain this set of tightly interconnected ideas is itself represented as some kind of impugning of their authority; the morality system represents itself as beyond explanation, *tout court*, so clearly beyond debunking explanations in particular.

No view would be finally acceptable that prevented such interesting forms of local critiques about our ethical ideas from arising, but contextualism is in fact a hospitable setting for local, critical projects such as these which use some of our ethical ideas as the basis for a critique of a narrower set, such as those implicated in the morality system. The way in which contextualism handles the local versus global contrast is itself a guarantee that a cognitivist theory that embeds a contextualist model of justification will not be a hostage to ideological fortune in the way that troubled Williams. I believe that this legitimate concern of the non-objectivist has, in this chapter, been addressed.

CONCLUSION

A contextualist defence of cognitivism is open to the charge that it cannot supply a convincing theory of error for when moral judgements diverge. In this chapter I

---

[38] See esp. 'The Need to Be Sceptical', *Times Literary Supplement* (16–22 Feb. 1990), 163–4.

[39] Williams, *Ethics and the Limits of Philosophy*, ch. 10, 'Morality: The Peculiar Institution'. (I am grateful to Tim Chappell for pointing out to me that 'the peculiar institution' was the standard Confederacy euphemism for the institution of slavery in the ante-bellum South.) The best commentary on Williams's critique of the morality system is Taylor's 'A Most Peculiar Institution', in Altham and Harrison (eds.), *World, Mind and Ethics*, 132–55; for an effective response to Williams see Robert C. Louden, 'Williams' Critique of the Morality System', in Alan Thomas (ed.), *Bernard Williams* (forthcoming).

[40] Williams, *Truth and Truthfulness*, ch. 4.

have rebutted this concern: conditions have been set out for when apparent conflict between moral views really is such, or, alternatively, whether we should accept different diagnoses in any particular case. If a conflict between moral beliefs is genuinely a case of conflict, then various explanations have been supplied for why this might be so that do not, as yet, directly draw on the idea of moral error. This is to make the task facing a theory of moral error more manageable. In developing such a theory, it was argued that it is not a defect of cognitivism but a strength that it can explain moral error. This is because only cognitivism can give an account of deep moral error. Finally, the issue of social criticism was considered and a model described for the criticism of ideological beliefs that was, to a certain extent, independent of the truth of cognitivism. But it was further argued that this model of ideological critique and the epistemological model of cognitivism complemented each other in important ways and that the two views are mutually complementary.

PART IV

CONTEXTUALISM IN POLITICAL PHILOSOPHY

11

Political Liberalism and Contextualism

§1: Contextual justification and the problem of legitimacy in modern polit-ical theory. §2: Rawls's contextual justification of the politicization of justice and 'external' and 'internal' critics of Rawls's contexualism. §3: A revision is proposed of Rawls's conception of the political.

The final part of this book is a coda to my main argument, in which I shall examine the extent to which the arguments developed so far can be put to use in political philo-sophy. In these final chapters I will focus mainly on the work of John Rawls. There was some surprise when Rawls announced, in his work *Political Liberalism*, that he took the central theses of that work to be *contextually* justified.[1] My aim is to cast some light on that remark and to argue that contextualism may be of great value in resolv-ing some of the controversies surrounding Rawls's later work, which, as will become clear, I regard as the best political theory for a liberal society currently available. (At various points in my argument I will refer to Charles Larmore's parallel development of a contextually justified political liberalism and also consider his views.) I will, in the later parts of my argument, suggest the need for a development of Rawls's position. Taking Rawls's political liberalism as a starting point, I will defend a version of a view known as liberal republicanism. But I take the version of the position that I defend to be a natural development out of Rawls's views, not a repudiation of them. The start-ing point of my argument is Rawls's embedding of his account of justice within a far broader model of how one justifies a political outlook, such as liberalism, as politically legitimate.

The plan of part IV is as follows. In this chapter I will put contextualism to work in analysing Rawlsian liberalism. *Political Liberalism* marked a shift in focus in Rawls's project as a whole from the presentation of a conception of justice and its stability to the wider question of what constituted a *legitimate* conception of justice for a modern society marked by a certain kind of moral pluralism.[2] This transition has

---

[1] John Rawls, *Political Liberalism*, p. xxi–xxviii, 14, 43. See also Richard Dees, 'Living with Contextualism', *Canadian Journal of Philosophy*, 24/2 (June 1994), 243–60. Contextualism is not as out of favour in political philosophy as it is in moral philosophy, where it has struggled to dislodge coherentist interpretations of reflective equilibrium. In addition to Dees's work, see Don Herzog's *Without Foundations: Justification in Political Theory* (Ithaca, NY: Cornell University Press, 1989) and Arthur Ripstein, 'Foundationalism in Political Theory', *Philosophy and Public Affairs*, 16/2 (Spring 1987), 115–37. (Larmore's arguments in *Patterns of Moral Complexity* spanned both moral and political philosophy.)

[2] The kind of moral pluralism identified e.g. in *Political Liberalism*, 36–7.

been controversial. Some commentators have erroneously taken this shift to represent a revision in Rawls's initial presentation of his conception of justice.[3] Others have accepted that this part of the view remains unchanged while nevertheless expressing reservations as to whether the issue of legitimacy needed to be raised in the way in which Rawls raised it.[4] I will suggest that a focus on the contextualist model of justification underpinning Rawls's view can alleviate both sources of concern.

This discussion will, however, leave one important item of unfinished business that will be the subject of the next chapter. An important concept within a contextual model of justification is that of presupposition, a concept that I have used repeatedly in explaining some of the distinctive aspects of contextualism. In the present case of political liberalism one can once again ask the question of what such a theory presupposes about the kind of society to which it is intended to apply. The answer is that the theory presupposes a moral background culture, internally plural, of the kind associated with a typically modern society. 'Modern' here refers to a normative political ideal, not simply a sociological category.[5] Focusing on this presupposition, however, merely gives rise to further questions. What should our response be if, through time, the operation of political liberalism came to have marked effects on the nature of that moral background culture? Would that threaten political liberalism with a charge of damaging circularity, of merely unpacking its own presupposed truth from within a moral background culture that it has fashioned in its own image?[6]

This charge does *not* trouble a certain kind of liberal when it is levelled against his or her own brand of liberalism. So-called 'ethical liberals', such as William Galston and Stephen Macedo, openly acknowledge that liberal politics and liberal ethics are deeply interconnected.[7] A liberal society demands a certain kind of ethical outlook on the part of its citizens continuous with an ethical account of the good life for persons. The interconnectedness of an account of the good life and a view of that which

---

[3] While papers have been published rebutting this view their authors concede that this objection to Rawls's later views is more prominent in discussion than in print. One can point to Thomas Pogge's description of Rawls's later 'abstraction, vagueness and conservatism', *Realizing Rawls* (Ithaca, NY: Cornell University Press, 1989), 4.

[4] I will discuss these two 'internal' critics of the change in Rawls's thought below. The papers that I will discuss are Samuel Scheffler's 'The Appeal of Political Liberalism', in *Boundaries and Allegiances: Problems of Justice and Responsibility in Liberal Thought* (Oxford: Oxford University Press, 2002), 131–48, and Leif Wenar, 'Political Liberalism: An Internal Critique', *Ethics*, 106/1 (Oct. 1995), 32–62. Their criticism is 'internal' in that it challenges Rawls's own understanding of why he needed to shift his attention from justice and its stability to the wider topic of liberal legitimacy in his later work. These internal critics find this change in Rawls's own system poorly motivated; given their sympathy with the basic approach of his early work they are not external critics of the whole Rawlsian project as is, say, Alasdair MacIntyre.

[5] See e.g. Bernard Yack's distinction between philosophic, sociological, political, and aesthetic modernities, *The Fetishism of Modernities*, 32 ff.

[6] A line of concern expressed by both 'ethical liberals' and those more sympathetic to Rawls's own project. Representative of the first group are William Galston, *Liberal Purposes: Goods, Virtues, and Diversity in the Liberal State* (Cambridge: Cambridge University Press, 1991) and Stephen Macedo, *Liberal Virtues: Citizenship, Virtue, and Community in Liberal Constitutionalism* (Oxford: Oxford University Press, 1990). Representative of the latter point of view is John Tomasi, *Liberalism Beyond Justice* (Princeton: Princeton University Press, 2000).

[7] Galston, *Liberal Purposes*, ch. 10; Macedo, *Liberal Virtues*, chs. 6 and 7.

constitutes a liberal society seems to them unavoidable. A liberal politics demands a liberal virtue ethics at the level of individual ethics. But Rawls seemed to hold a different view from such 'ethical liberalisms'. His motive for politicizing justice in his later work was to *avoid* the claim that his principles of justice rested on a single comprehensive conception of the good. This was so even if (or particularly if) that comprehensive conception was the kind of liberal individualism found in Kant or Mill. Furthermore, this kind of liberal individualist conception is very similar to the autonomy based ethical liberalism defended by many contemporary ethical liberals.[8] I will consider those issues and a possible response to them in Chapter 12 of this book. They seem to me to constitute the most serious challenge to the Rawlsian project, but a criticism that requires a development of Rawls's views, not a rejection of them.

My view is that, properly understood, Rawls's theory of justice *does* place demands on the moral background culture of that society which it 'theorizes'. However, those demands can be interpreted in a certain way. They can be understood in terms compatible with Rawls's later explicit theory of legitimacy only if one adopts one form of liberal republicanism. The liberal republican argues that even a politicized conception of justice presupposes the liberal outlook that makes itself possible in the limited sense that it can, and ought, to give an account of citizenship and free associations. Civil society, that which Michael Walzer has called the 'setting of settings', is where the virtues associated with the centrally important social role of citizenship are learned and exercised.[9] Without such a normative ideal of citizenship and a context in which it can be learned and exercised, the very demanding conception of citizenship at the centre of Rawlsian liberalism would not be possible.[10] The key point, however, is that in describing these presuppositions of a liberal outlook one is not advancing a single and possibly exclusionary reasonable comprehensive conception of the good, but rather sustaining an option value.[11] Liberal republicanism is not indifferent to

[8] This motivation is, if anything, even more clear in the parallel work of Charles Larmore, 'The Right and the Good', *Philosophia*, 20/1-2 (July 1990), 15–32; 'Political Liberalism', *Political Theory*, 18/3 (Aug. 1990), 339–60, repr. in *The Morals of Modernity* (Cambridge: Cambridge University Press, 1996); 'The Moral Basis of Political Liberalism', *Journal of Philosophy*, 96/12 (Dec. 1999), 599–625.

[9] Michael Walzer, 'The Civil Society Argument', in Chantal Mouffe (ed.), *Dimensions of Radical Democracy: Pluralism, Citizenship, Community* (London: Verso, 1992), 89–107. There is now further discussion of civil society throughout Walzer's *Politics and Passion:Towards a More Egalitarian Liberalism* (New Haven and London: Yale University Press, 2004), but esp. ch. 4.

[10] For a very helpful treatment of the revival of interest in the theme of citizenship in political philosophy see Will Kymlicka and Wayne Norman, 'The Return of the Citizen: A Survey of Recent Work on Citizenship Theory', *Ethics*, 104/2 (1994), 352–81. There is (as usual) an excellent paper on this subject by Michael Walzer, to which I am indebted, 'Citizenship', in T. Ball, J. Farr, and R. Hanson (eds.), *Political Innovation and Conceptual Change* (Cambridge: Cambridge University Press, 1989), 211–19. See also Adrian Oldfield, *Citizenship and Community: Civic Republicanism and the Modern World* (London: Routledge, 1990).

[11] There are two points here: that the relevant value is an option value and that our attitude towards it should be one of honouring rather promoting, an argument that I first set out in 'Liberal Republicanism and the Role of Civil Society', *Democratisation*, 4/3 (Aug. 1997), 26–44. For the latter distinction see Elizabeth Anderson, *Value in Ethics and in Economics* (Cambridge, Mass.: Harvard University Press, 1993) and Christine Swanton 'Profiles of the Virtues', *Pacific Philosophical Quarterly*, 76 (1995), 47–72.

the very great social goods of free associations and active citizenship, but there is an important constraint on how it may promote them: they can only be promoted as an option value, not as part of the good life for persons.[12] To use a distinction more familiar from moral philosophy and discussions of our different relations to value, liberal republicanism honours, but does not promote, these values. Ethical liberalism correctly identifies a question: what does a constitutional liberal regime presuppose in a moral background culture such that it makes itself possible? The answer it gives to that question is too ambitious to the point of giving an answer that is too close to the question. Ethical liberalisms of different kinds give answers like autonomy, or the need for a perfectionist state to provide a choice worthy environment for the exercise of autonomy.[13] The liberal republican restricts him- or herself solely to those preconditions that make the widest possible set of liberal outlooks possible, namely, active citizenship in free associations, and honours those social goods as important option values. Within these general arguments about liberalism and legitimacy, there is then a separate case to be made for justice as fairness as our best conception of justice.

This looks like a communitarian corrective to Rawls's approach to justice, but that appearance is, I think, deceptive. He denied that the transition from *A Theory of Justice* to *Political Liberalism* marked any kind of acknowledgement of the correctness of the communitarian critique of his early work.[14] But it seems to me that a theme much discussed by communitarians can receive a parallel treatment from republican liberals in such a way as to take the sting from the communitarian charge that Rawls's two principles of justice presuppose strong ties of solidarity that were significantly underdetermined by his account of political identity.[15] If, in this most impure of areas in philosophy, appeal to context involves an appeal to our political traditions in the modern West, then that is still a contextualist form of justification. It remains within the general ambit of contextualism to extend an argument about political justification to these wider issues. In particular, contextual justification can extend to the relationship between a liberal theory and the moral background culture of a society.

1. CONTEXTUAL JUSTIFICATION AND THE PROBLEMS OF MODERN POLITICAL THEORY

Contextualism in general begins from the specification of a problem situation, the more narrowly defined, the better. What problems does a political theory

[12] My concept of an 'option value' does not place me in direct disagreement with the similar arguments of Richard Dagger, in ch. 3 of *Civic Virtues: Rights, Citizenship and Republican Liberalism*, (Oxford: Oxford University Press, 1997) where Dagger develops his moderately perfectionist version of Rousseauian liberalism. But my claim that our attitude to this value should be honouring does; Dagger argues that his republican liberalism seeks to *promote* (but not *maximize*) a republican virtue ethic.

[13] For the latter answer, see Joseph Raz, *The Morality of Freedom* (Oxford: Oxford University Press 1988), chs. 14, 15.

[14] Rawls, *Political Liberalism*, 27.

[15] This was the original charge levelled by Michael Sandel in *Liberalism and the Limits of Justice* (Cambridge: Cambridge University Press, 1998) against Rawls's arguments in *A Theory of Justice*.

face in a particular kind of context, namely, the special context of a modern society? That is the key question that the final phase of Rawls's work, and the parallel work of Charles Larmore, has put at the centre of contemporary debate in political philosophy. The argument of this book has, throughout, brought out the dependence of various assumptions about moral knowledge on a background conception of a modern society. It was demonstrated in Chapter 6 that Williams's non-objectivist critique of the ethical rested on a background theory of the nature of a distinctively modern society. The relevance of such a background model is also clearly a part of justification in that part of political philosophy that is explicitly focused on the legitimacy of forms of government. Here, too, analysing these assumptions about society can both cast light on contested issues in recent political philosophy and help to resolve them.

The view of a distinctively modern society found in Rawls's last works was that such a society is deeply pluralist. Rawls concluded that this fact about the kind of society for which he was advancing a conception of justice had implications for the feasibility of different kinds of liberal political theory. I should say immediately that one does *not* find in Rawls's work a commitment to recognizing the existence of a radical pluralism, correlative with the moral or political equivalent of a foundational 'view from nowhere in particular', that was criticized throughout Part III of this book. That is because Rawls's arguments *began* from the contextual point that social worlds cannot represent within themselves every possible objectively valuable form of life. Acknowledging the arguments of Isaiah Berlin, Rawls agreed that liberalism does not set itself this self-defeating aim.[16] Liberalism is not an attempt to take up an Archimedean point outside all valuable forms of life and to develop a mode of living together that is comprehensive enough to include them all. But when this illusion has been abandoned an objective value pluralism central to our conception of the ethical remains. It is this form of pluralism, a pluralism of objective reasonable comprehensive conceptions of the good, that Rawls emphasized was central to the problem of a liberal theory of legitimacy.

For this reason there is an important change of scope and emphasis when one comes to apply contextualism neither to knowledge as a whole, nor to moral knowledge in particular, but to the narrower domain of political justification. How can such justifications be legitimate given the fact of objective moral pluralism that is distinctive of modern societies? The first contextualist aspect to Rawls's views is that he begins by specifying the 'problem situation' characterized by this question: the task of a liberal theory of legitimacy is specified in terms of the problems arising from the kind of society whose political arrangements it seeks to theorize and justify. The contextual justification of a reflective account of the political begins by specifying a problem that candidate conceptions have to solve.

In common with others Rawls assumes that any political theory that aims at legitimacy has to provide a *reason* for the political arrangements that it proposes in the name of justice and that, furthermore, this reason is one that can be given *as* a reason

---

[16] Rawls, *Political Liberalism*, 57; lecture V, § 6. 2.

for each citizen.[17] Furthermore, each of these people has to receive the *same* reason: we cannot give different reasons to different people or different classes of people.[18] It is also worth noting that such justifications have to be truthful and not rest on deception or coercion.[19] This point is rarely stated because it seems to us so obvious, but our commitment to such truthfulness is also, it seems to me, a distinctively modern commitment.[20] The upshot of these considerations is that any account of political legitimacy operates under certain constraints. Its formulation has to be guided by an acknowledgement of the nature of the society for which it develops a theory. It also has to be guided by our modern commitments to both truthfulness in justification and the individual nature of each justification given to each citizen in terms that are the same for every member of a society. The arguments of this part will show that these constraints have some real cutting edge when it comes to deciding on which political theory we ought to endorse.

This issue of legitimacy was a central focus of Rawls's later work.[21] Modern societies, if they embed within themselves a constitutional and legislative securing of Rawls's two principles of justice, will through time develop a plurality of competing, reasonable, comprehensive conceptions of the good. Rawls came to view this development as threatening to the legitimacy of his original theory of justice in that it seemed to him (controversially) to be expressive of just *one* of these conceptions. It cannot, therefore, supply a justification of its own principles to adherents of other conceptions. It thereby fails the test of legitimacy as Rawls came to conceive of such a test. I will examine this argument, and the internal adjustments that Rawls made to his own theory, below. This set of adjustments marked the transition from his earlier work, *A Theory of Justice*, to his later work represented by *Political Liberalism* and *The Law of Peoples*.[22]

Rawls's motivation, whether correct or incorrect, was an attempt to respect constraints on the theory of legitimacy derived from his background account of the nature of a modern society. The way in which he did so contrasts instructively with the way in which Charles Larmore has, in parallel to Rawls, developed a version of political liberalism of his own.[23] Larmore has, even more explicitly, gone into the details of

[17] A point explicitly discussed by both Jeremy Waldron, 'Theoretical Foundations of Liberalism', *Philosophical Quarterly*, 37/147 (Apr. 1987), 127–50, and Nagel, *Equality and Partiality*, ch. 4.

[18] Nagel, *Equality and Partiality*, ch. 4.

[19] Williams, *Truth and Truthfulness*, ch. 9, sect. 5.

[20] Bernard Williams, 'From Freedom to Liberty: The Construction of a Political Value', *Philosophy and Public Affairs*, 30/1 (2001), 3–26, at 20. It does not follow, as Williams was keen to emphasize, that we can thereby help ourselves to a 'Whiggish' history in which the rise of liberal political arguments is best explained in terms of a history of winning decisive arguments that brought down its historical rivals. If liberalism is going to be based on truthfulness, Williams argues, it had better be able to be truthful about itself: 'Philosophy as a Humanistic Discipline'.

[21] As David Estlund puts it: 'It is no exaggeration to say that the two books [*A Theory of Justice* and *Political Liberalism*] are not about the same subject. The first is primarily about justice; the second is primarily about political legitimacy, a topic essentially ignored in *TJ*.' 'The Survival of Egalitarian Justice in John Rawls' *Political Liberalism*', *Journal of Political Philosophy* (Mar. 1996), 68–78 at 68.

[22] John Rawls, *Political Liberalism; The Law of Peoples* (Cambridge, Mass.: Harvard University Press, 1999).

[23] Larmore, 'Political Liberalism'; 'The Moral Basis of Political Liberalism'.

precisely what it is about modern societies that makes the problem of legitimacy so pressing. They are, he argues, functionally differentiated (in Niklas Luhmann's sense) and certain kinds of traditional legitimating narrative no longer command assent in a 'postmetaphysical' society.[24] The traditional value spheres of science, aesthetics, and morality/law have become increasingly autonomous, detaching from each other and developing their own specialized inner logics. This fact, plus the discrediting of traditional narratives of legitimation, makes the legitimation problem even more radical than Rawls envisaged in Larmore's version of political liberalism. Larmore, too, is a contextualist about justification.[25] His argument for political liberalism also begins from the specification of a problem situation. But the kind of pluralism that concerns Larmore is more radical than that described by Rawls and receives a much deeper philosophical articulation. However, for that reason, I think we should be cautious in taking Larmore's starting point as the basis for a contextual justification of political liberalism.

Rawls's later views about political justification seemed designed to maximize agreement by minimizing controversy. While there is a degree of truth in seeing the tasks of a theory of legitimacy in such terms, that does not mean that the view as a whole cannot be motivated by, and proceed in terms of, claims that are themselves controversial.[26] (This is equally important in the case of the subsidiary arguments that seek to determine which conception of justice any legitimate liberal view will implement, perhaps even more so.[27]) It is a recurrent mistake to view Rawls's later view as having abandoned normativity and controversy and to be a search, instead, for a deadening status quo based on a mutually accommodating bargain between the interest groups in a given society.[28] Not the least of the implausibilities of this view is that the very essence of Rawls's contractualism is abandoned: there is no longer a contrast between his contractualism and contractarian bargaining solutions based on pre-given interests fixed prior to, and independently of, rational dialogue. (Adopting this conception of pre-given interests would go a long way to undermining the distinction between contractualism and contractarianism.) But while this is the case, and Rawls was free to begin his argument from controversial assumptions, in fact I believe that Rawls's recognition of an objective value pluralism in modern societies is a more plausible assumption from which to start than the deeper form of pluralism found in Habermas and Luhmann. Their interest is in challenging the radical value pluralism that this entire book has sought to undermine. I have no objection to the basis for a theory of legitimacy being a controversial thesis about the nature of modern societies. It still remains the

---

[24] Niklas Luhmann, *The Differentiation of Society*, trans. Stephen Holmes and Charles Larmore (New York: Columbia University Press, 1990); Jürgen Habermas, *Postmetaphysical Thinking: Philosophical Essays*, trans. William Mark Hohengarten (Cambridge, Mass.: MIT Press, 1994).
[25] This is clearest in Larmore's earlier *Patterns of Moral Complexity*.
[26] A point made by Estlund, 'The Survival of Egalitarian Justice in John Rawls' Political Liberalism', 74–5 and which I will discuss further below.
[27] Ibid. 75.
[28] Rawls, *Political Liberalism*, 234. Rawls himself was sensitive to the charge that he had made political liberalism 'political in the wrong way' and denied that he had done so. He devoted sect. 56 of *Justice as Fairness: A Restatement*, ed. Erin Kelly (Cambridge Mass.: Harvard University Press, 2001) to the subject, entitling that section (unsurprisingly) 'Is Political Liberalism Political in the Wrong Way?'.

case that the less controversial the better, given that a plausible initial assumption is needed to sustain the radical changes in how one ought to conceive of the constraints on a theory of legitimacy. If, as I believe, such a background thesis about modern societies does some real work in constraining candidate reflective accounts of the political, then it ought it itself to be plausible and widely accepted.

Nevertheless, even beginning from Rawls's weaker assumptions, it does seem to me that Rawls highlighted a significant problem for any liberal political theory that aims to meet the constraints imposed by an independently plausible account of legitimacy. The justification of a set of political arrangements will have to give the same justification to each member of the society governed by such arrangements. This constraint must be met in spite of the truth of a pluralism about reasonable comprehensive conceptions of the good. Rawls's response to this problem was what he called the *politicization* of his concept of justice. In my view, the best way to approach the need to develop his views is to set out the narrative of why Rawls revised his own earlier position. It will turn out that this process of revision has further corollaries, some of which, I will argue, lead to a significant development of the scope of Rawlsian political liberalism.

2. RAWLS'S CONTEXTUAL JUSTIFICATION OF POLITICAL LIBERALISM

There are two strands to Rawls's later work that are analysable separately. The first strand concerns the epistemological model underpinning Rawls's views. The second concerns the politicization of justice in the face of what he viewed as the challenge facing the theory of legitimacy in the context of a modern society. As the discussions of Part III demonstrated, Rawls's epistemological commitments have been much discussed. He seems, from his earliest publications, to have been a moral cognitivist, certainly in the sense that he did not believe that criteria derived from reflection on other kinds of knowledge, such as knowledge in the natural sciences, posed any kind of threat to a *sui generis* model of that in which our knowledge of morality consists.[29] But when it came to the theory of justice, the method of reflective equilibrium was applied to develop a critique of a pluralism about principles of justice that lacked any internal order or priority relations. By contrast, Rawls's lexically ordered two principles were selected on the basis of what Rawls chose to call a construction procedure (where by 'lexical order' it is meant that the requirements of the first principle must be fully satisfied before proceeding to satisfy the requirements of the second). But, equally, he emphasized that construction requires materials that are not, themselves, constructed.

In his later work on political justification, Rawls emphasized both the contextual justification of his principles of justice and the peculiar role he envisaged for the complementary ideas of reasonableness and truth.[30] Rawls's contextualism came to

---

[29] This remains clear in *Political Liberalism*, see e.g. lecture III, §6.
[30] Rawls's later politicized conception of justice 'does without the concept of truth', ibid., p. 94 and the standard of correctness for his political liberalism is reasonableness, ibid., p. 127.

the forefront of his account of justification in several ways. His theory of justice was always internal to our traditions of enquiry, in the sense that he always sought to justify *a* theory of justice, relative to a set of admittedly contestable criteria, from our philosophical tradition of reflection on justice. His proposed principles were compared, primarily, to the treatment of justice in the consequentialist tradition. This relative internality became even more marked when justice was politicized in the way I will describe more precisely in the next section so as to meet the wider demands of a theory of legitimacy. The entire model is now relativized to certain political ideas that are already prevalent in the Western liberal constitutional tradition during the modern period.[31] Those ideas are shaped by the contingent history of their development in our societies. We start, as this book has emphasized we must start, with those of our ideas that withstand the test of reflective endorsement within our own ongoing tradition of enquiry where 'we' is not a foundational 'we' standing outside all possible forms of life. Rawls emphasized that any given social world contains an overlapping range of realizations of competing sets of values, such that not every conceivable set can share any one social world or (I would add) stand as a real option for any given social world. A claim of even broader scope is that this account of 'our' political traditions takes place against the backdrop of a wider theory of the nature of a distinctively modern society. Finally, the whole orientation of Rawls's approach is that politics is a cognitive matter. We are properly dealing here with truth, knowledge, and reasonableness, not merely preference satisfaction, or the satisfaction of pre-given interests that can be understood prior to the process of political deliberation.[32]

While Rawls's view is cognitivist, he does treat knowledge and truth, in the particular context of the theory of legitimacy, in an unusual way.[33] For reasons internal to the politicization of justice, he believed that in the context of the justification of the constitutional and legislative fundamentals represented by the two principles of justice, as applied to the special subject of the basic structure of society, we should restrain ourselves when we offer a justification for these principles. This self-restraint consists in an appeal not to truth, but rather to reasonableness. The basic idea is that if we are to justify these constitutional fundamentals in terms that everyone can accept (the constraint on the theory of legitimacy) then we cannot advance these fundamentals on the basis of reasons specific to any reasonable comprehensive conception of the good. (Including, allegedly, that conception that was expressed by the arguments of *A Theory of Justice*.) Each of us affirms these fundamentals from within whichever reasonable comprehensive conception of the good each of us endorses. However, these

---

[31] Ibid., pp. xxiv, 13 ff, 175, 223. There is a very insightful discussion of this aspect of Rawls's views in Richard Rorty, *Contingency, Irony and Solidarity*, 57–8 and 'The Priority of Democracy to Philosophy', in *Objectivity, Relativism and Truth: Philosophical Papers*, i (Cambridge: Cambridge University Press, 1991).

[32] For a defence of such a 'cognitivist' account of the materials of political theorizing, see Susan Hurley, 'Cognitivism in Political Philosophy', in Roger Crisp and Brad Hooker (eds.), *Morality and Well Being: Essays in Honour of James Griffin* (Oxford: Oxford University Press, 2000), 177–208.

[33] Rawls, *Political Liberalism*, 94.

reasonable comprehensive conceptions overlap, to form what Rawls calls an overlapping consensus.[34] This has the consequence that while we affirm each conception as
true, and can from within that conception affirm the constitutional fundamentals as
true, when we go on to affirm them to our fellow citizens we do not affirm them
as *true*. At that point we exercise epistemological self-restraint and we now, for the
special purposes of the political, affirm them as merely *reasonable*. Rawls has a range
of arguments for this self-restraint of differing degrees of plausibility.

His most implausible argument associates the speech act of asserting a claim as true
with 'zeal and intolerance'.[35] The problem with that argument is, as I noted in my
opening chapter, the unclear and indirect connection between objectivity and intolerance. After all, someone who intolerantly wants to force his or her views upon you
may do so because they regard you not as a false believer, but as an unreasonable one.
So restricting oneself to reasonableness, as opposed to truth, appears not to help in
undercutting the motivations of the intolerant. Conversely, Rawls's point cannot be
made independently of the content of the comprehensive reasonable conception that
a person asserts: for example, many ethical liberals, whose views will be described
below, affirm a conception which has, as an internal condition, that all good lives
realize within themselves the value of autonomy.[36] Imposing this view on others in
an intolerant and paternalistic way is not simply intolerant, but internally incoherent. Forcing people to be free, in the light of this conception, is simply a practical
inconsistency. The ethical liberalisms central to the political philosophy of the modern West, from Kant and Mill to Joseph Raz, emphasize that liberalism demands that
all good lives be autonomously chosen from within a choice worthy environment,
where the putting in place of such social conditions for autonomy is properly a matter for the liberal state.[37] For that reason such a form of liberalism is going to hold a
view of its own exceptional status. It is the *only* form of political theory that is internally protected from being illegitimate, in the sense of coercive, as political autonomy
cannot of its very nature be coercively imposed. For that reason it can be put forward
as true secure from the further claim that to do so is to put it forward in a spirit of
'zeal and intolerance'. That makes no sense: what, exactly, is a liberal zealot?

More plausibly, Rawls (and Larmore) argue that since, as it were, you have exhausted the resources of truth by affirming the constitutional essentials as true from

---

[34] Rawls, 'The Idea of an Overlapping Consensus', in *Collected Papers*, ed. Samuel Freeman
(Cambridge, Mass.: Harvard University Press, 1999), 421–48 and *Political Liberalism*, lecture IV.

[35] See e.g. *Political Liberalism*, 42–3 and 'The Idea of Public Reason Revisited', *University of
Chicago Law Review*, 64/3 (1997), 766. I have benefited a great deal from the discussion of Rawls's
attitude towards truth in Cheryl Misak, *Truth, Politics, Morality* (London: Routledge, 2000), 20–9.

[36] See, as a representative example, Joseph Raz, *The Morality of Freedom*, 369–78, 395.

[37] Ibid. 308 (on 'social forms'), 368–70 (on liberal involvement in such social forms). The social
forms thesis is amplified in a later publication, 'National Self-Determination', in *Ethics in the Public
Domain* (Oxford: Oxford University Press, 1996) where Raz wrote: 'Being social animals means not
merely that the means for the satisfaction of people's goals are more readily available within society.
More crucially, it means that the goals themselves are . . . the creatures of society, the products of
culture', 133.

within your particular comprehensive conception, there is no basis left on which to assert those fundamentals to others 'as true'.[38] All that can mean, Rawls seems to imply, is that it is 'true to you'. And you cannot expect that fact, in itself, to sway the conviction of others and if offered as a justification *for* others it is a violation of the requirement that you treat them with respect. Equal respect means that you must be sensitive to the kind of contractualist formulation discussed in Part II: that considerations must be put to your fellow citizens that they could not reasonably reject. Putting forward a justification of constitutional fundamentals grounded solely on its being asserted as true from within your distinctive comprehensive conception can only anticipate reasonable rejection. Hence you do not treat your fellow citizens with respect if you advance justifications of this sort and you ought rather to exercise, in the light of your duty of civility to others, a form of epistemological self-restraint.

The exact form of this restraint, and how it is best understood, will be discussed below. At this point I will simply note that the argument given thus far looks hopelessly question begging, or as simply making a mistake about the nature of assertion.[39] I make my assertions, but I do not make them simply as mine: to assert, after all, is to assert as true. You can infer from my assertion of a claim that I believe it, but even if the assertion is expressive of a form of self-knowledge, my asserting it is not merely noting a fact about my autobiography: it is, precisely, even in that limiting case, the expression of such a fact. That which I assert, I assert as true, and therefore communicate to you that I have endorsed the asserted content. That is what it *is* for you to treat me as an independent centre of conscious, rational agency and not simply a passive repository-cum-conveyor of truth-bearing representations.[40] Even if I am implicitly relying on you to take the content of the assertion on trust, that had better be on the basis of some objective epistemological authority to which I am entitled. Even in that case, my claim to authority had better rest on *something*. So to assert as true is not simply to announce that I believe a proposition, contrary to that which Rawls seems to suggest. Furthermore, if the basis of the entire exercise is a commitment to equal respect, something had better be said to justify *that* commitment. If, relative to the entire process of justification, that commitment is treated as foundational, then there are many figures central to the Western tradition of political philosophy (from Nietzsche to Carl Schmitt) who are not going to share that commitment. But the prospects for deriving a norm such as equal respect from the contractualist formulation *itself* do

---

[38] This is brought out most clearly in the interpretations/developments of Rawls's views by Thomas Nagel, 'Moral Conflict and Political Legitimacy', *Philosophy and Public Affairs*, 16/3 (Summer 1987), 215–40 and Joshua Cohen, 'Moral Pluralism and Political Consensus', in David Copp (ed.), *The Idea of Democracy* (Cambridge: Cambridge University Press, 1993), 281–4.

[39] Michael Dummett, *Frege* (London: Duckworth, 1973), ch. 10; Timothy Williamson, *Knowledge and Its Limits* (Oxford: Oxford University Press, 2000), ch. 11.

[40] A point emphasized by Richard Moran, in a paper 'Getting Told and Being Believed', presented to the philosophy department at the University of Kent, 22 June 2004, which forms part of a wider project on the subject of testimony. This paper is forthcoming in Jennifer Lackey and Ernest Sosa (eds.), *The Epistemology of Testimony* (Oxford: Oxford University Press, 2006).

not look hopeful. On the contrary, such a commitment looks prior to, and the basis for, what is attractive in the contractualist formulation.[41]

Furthermore, appealing to the oldest philosophical trick in the book, the Democritean 'reversal', David Estlund has pointed out that if Rawls wants to apply the political philosophy of toleration to political justification itself, so as to restrict that to which one may appeal to the reasonable, and not the true, the principle of restriction must itself be true and not merely reasonable.[42] Any attempt to claim that this principle is itself merely reasonable would be hopelessly question begging unless it is true and, I would argue, conceding this much is to concede that we need to break with Rawls's assumptions. We need to look for independent truths in a *sui generis* political morality to make the best overall sense of his position. I will develop this argument below.

It should be clear from this necessarily brief exposition that this is a subtle and controversial set of claims about why theory of legitimacy is, in Rawls's view, cut off from appraising views in terms of truth and is restricted to reasonableness.[43] But, in order to understand them more fully, I will now set out the complementary strand of Rawls's thought. I will explain what the politicization of justice involves and how it is supposed to work. Only with this parallel line of argument in place, together with the puzzles and controversy that it has caused, will I be able to demonstrate how contextualism makes the best sense of Rawls's views when contextualism is applied in a fully consistent way to the defence of politically liberal principles.

I will assume, for the purposes of this book, a general familiarity with the contents of Rawls's original presentation of a theory of justice. The indefinite article in Rawls's title marked out the fact that it was presented as one candidate conception, 'justice as fairness', to be selected from a range of other candidates internal to our own intellectual traditions. Some of the general methodological presuppositions of Rawls's initial presentation were described in Part III of this book: the method of reflective equilibrium and Rawls's claim that in the specific case of justice, a pair of lexically ordered principles could be devised to model the intuition of justice as fairness that went beyond a pluralist view lacking any internal priority relations. The basic form of this argument for the original conception was a 'bootstrapping' one, to borrow Joshua Cohen's helpful phrase.[44] In a manner that already anticipated the explicit adoption of contextualism, Rawls's methodology was to appeal to our inchoate intuitions about freedom, equality, and justice and to regiment them by supplying a model that captured most of our reflectively stable intuitions. That model was always intended to

---

[41] I would interpret Larmore's political liberalism as a view that is explicit on this point. Larmore is very clear that the moral basis of his version of political liberalism is a moral principle of *equal respect*. I will argue below that it is better viewed as a principle of political morality.

[42] David Estlund, 'The Insularity of the Reasonable: Why Political Liberalism Must Admit the Truth', *Ethics*, 108/2 (Jan. 1998), 252–75 at 253.

[43] A full consideration of the argument would have to take into account the alternative defences of a broadly Rawlsian approach by Nagel, 'Moral Conflict and Political Legitimacy' and Cohen, 'Moral Pluralism and Political Consensus'. There is a well-known scepticism about this family of arguments, different from my own, in Joseph Raz, 'Facing Diversity: The Case of Epistemic Abstinence', *Philosophy and Public Affairs*, 19/1 (Winter 1990), 3–46.

[44] Cohen, 'Moral Pluralism and Political Consensus', 277–81.

be an explication of that which, in a sense, we already believed. It gives insight by modelling our intuitions in order clearly to articulate both the intuitions and their (sometimes no longer intuitively obvious) consequences that emerge from the modelling process.

The basic idea is this: we all agree on some widely held, because in a sense merely 'formal' accounts of the equal political liberties, equality of opportunity, and the shared goods of social life.[45] We are asked to conduct a thought experiment in which we seek to justify these commitments politically and to see, in doing so, that which we are assuming about the relevant properties of people. These turn out to be certain abstract potentialities and in explaining how we best protect their actual realization we are driven, by our own assumptions, to recognize a wider class of conditions that make this realization possible. So the actual egalitarian content of Rawls's conception of justice, namely, 'the fair value of political liberty, fair equality of opportunity, and the maximin criterion of distributive equity' emerge as implicit in our initial assumptions and are brought out by conducting a reflective enquiry into our initial assumptions.

But the idea that we begin from shared common ground is no threat to the content of Rawls's egalitarianism. The method thus described, and the abstract account of people's relevant features that it uncovers, is in no way exclusionary or distinctively 'Kantian'. And that account of people is embedded in shared common ground that is, as Cohen describes it, much more like a contextualist problem situation rather than a set of agreed-upon theoretical principles:[46]

What lies in the intersection of different moral conceptions is not simply a set of policies or a system of norms . . . Nor is it simply a determinate set of moral principles . . . The consensus extends to a view of persons, of the importance of fairness, and other political values, of what counts as an advantage, and of which practices are paradigmatically evil . . . In short, what lies at the intersection of different views is a (restricted) terrain on which moral and political argument can be conducted, and not simply a fixed and determinate set of substantive points of political agreement.[47]

This supplies the background to the application of the 'pluralistic consensus test' to a conception of justice. It is this test that has most concerned Rawls's critics and seemed to shackle Rawls's egalitarianism by being political, as Rawls put it, 'in the wrong way'.[48] But as Cohen points out, 'the bootstrap argument for the egalitarian view is itself meant to proceed on common ground shared by different moral conceptions in a well-ordered society governed by it'.[49] Thus it is no part of Rawls's view to assume that an overlapping consensus involves something like majoritarian agreement. There is disagreement about the substantive content of egalitarianism and that disagreement

---

[45] I here follow the excellent exposition of Rawls's procedure and substantive arguments, ibid. 277–8.

[46] This seems to me very similar to the role assigned to background beliefs in moral justification in part III, above.

[47] Cohen, 'Moral Pluralism and Political Consensus', 278.

[48] Rawls, *Political Liberalism*, 234.

[49] Cohen, 'Moral Pluralism and Political Consensus', 279.

will persist even in conditions that are more favourable to its resolution. In contextualist terms, an overlapping consensus describes a problem situation, not a particular solution to any such problem. Any particular proposed solution, and Rawls clearly takes his overall package of views to remain the most reasonable overall liberal political theory for a society to adopt, can contain elements that are controversial and will undoubtedly do so given the contested nature of the issues involved.[50]

Estlund has added a further exegetical support for this line of defence of Rawls pointing out that one aspect of Rawls's presentation which had misled his critics was the relative priority of constitutionally secured principles and those advanced at the level of a legislative stage.[51] Rawls clearly connected this distinction with that between principles which are more, or less, subject to reasonable disagreement. Just because a principle, such as Rawls's second principle, can reasonably be expected to remain a focus of political controversy does not mean that it cannot retain its role in his overall view, even though that is the ground given for seeing that principle secured not in the constitution, but at the legislative stage, a claim (as Estlund demonstrates) that neither weakens the content of the second principle nor represents any departure from the claims of *A Theory of Justice*, where it has exactly the same role.[52]

In summary, then, critical misunderstanding of Rawls's later views ignores the contextual element that was always present in Rawls's model of justification. 'Overlapping consensus', for example, is more like a contextualist problem situation than a list of shared beliefs or principles. It is shaped by agreement on such matters as relevant values, fixed points in our deliberations (such as the absolute unacceptability of slavery or racism), and background commitments. That is what we share, in spite of our commitment to different comprehensive conceptions of the good, and it constitutes a great deal. It is a very detailed and substantial political ideal.[53] The way that we reason from it is also contextualist. We are interested in those conditions that allow the 'moral powers' of subjects to flourish and that is the key, as Cohen puts it, to the 'bootstrapping' as 'we are naturally led from the more formal to the more substantively egalitarian requirements since the latter more fully elaborate the range of favourable conditions'.[54]

Contextualism can also, I believe, address some, if not all, of the concerns of Rawls's 'internal' critics, Samuel Scheffler and Leif Wenar.[55] By an internal critic I mean a person sympathetic to the original project expressed by *A Theory of Justice* who denies that the arguments of that work need to be revised or supplemented. These internal critics do not object to the politicization of justice because it represents a loss of the normative and critical content of Rawls's views. It is, rather, that they view the transition in Rawls's thinking as both unmotivated and not feasible in its own terms. Once again, a

[50] Estlund, 'The Survival of Egalitarian Justice in John Rawls's *Political Liberalism*', 76.
[51] Ibid. 73.
[52] Ibid. 75.
[53] Rawls, 'The Idea of an Overlapping Consensus'; Cohen, 'Moral Pluralism and Political Consensus', 279.
[54] Cohen, 'Moral Pluralism and Political Consensus', 278.
[55] Scheffler, 'The Appeal of Political Liberalism'; Wenar, 'Political Liberalism: An Internal Critique'.

full assessment of their arguments goes beyond the scope of the current discussion, but their basic argument is that Rawls was wrong to say that the convergence of reasonable people on the two principles of justice in *A Theory of Justice*, supplemented by a demonstration that that conception was stable, rested on a single reasonable comprehensive conception of the good.

The point that came to trouble Rawls was this: that a society that had successfully adopted his two principles of justice would, through time, come to have a certain character. It would exhibit, under conditions of freedom, a plurality of reasonable comprehensive conceptions of the good. That pluralism is not, itself, unwelcome as each of these comprehensive views is reasonable. But it suggested to Rawls a scepticism as to whether a society so characterized could be expected to endorse as legitimate the stable conception of justice specified in *A Theory of Justice*. If *that* theory rested on merely one such reasonable comprehensive conception how could it expect to be accepted by those committed to the other conceptions? So Rawls proposed to politicize justice: to present his account of justice as a 'free-standing' or 'modular' political conception that is disjoined from any reasonable comprehensive moral conception.[56] Modularity identifies how Rawls's later conception of politicized justice was supposed to function. A module in this sense is a detachable functional component. The analogy in the case of politicized justice is that each reasonable comprehensive moral conception is envisaged as affirming modular justice from within itself, but it is not the proprietary expression of any. It is supported, as I have just described, by the overlapping consensus of all reasonable comprehensive views.[57] The same module 'slots in', as it were, to different reasonable comprehensive moral views. Its function is always the same, but it is grounded in an overlapping consensus made up of different views.

Rawls's internal critics are not convinced: they argue that he was wrong to argue that the conception of justice stated in *A Theory of Justice* rested on such a single reasonable comprehensive conception in such a way that it made the theory as a whole lacking in legitimacy. That stable conception of justice suffices to ground its *own* legitimacy, Scheffler and Wenar argue, and a further demonstration of that legitimacy is redundant. That is fortunate, the internal critics argue, as Rawls builds into his own account of how one develops such an account of legitimacy false assumptions that show that the overlapping consensus which is central to his politicization of justice could reasonably be expected to be weaker than any consensus on the two principles of justice (and their stability) taken in isolation. Far from showing how his two principles and their stability could also be demonstrated to be legitimate Rawls inadvertently undermines the degree of legitimacy that the principles already enjoy.[58]

This internal critique is clearly the more threatening to the politicization of justice than external criticism as it casts doubt on the fundamental motivation of the transition in Rawls's thinking. Scheffler argues that considering the cases that Rawls first cites as exemplary of three views that may, for reasons that differ between themselves,

---

[56] For representative passages explaining the sense in which Rawls views his conception of justice as functioning in a modular way within political liberalism see *Political Liberalism*, 143, 147.

[57] Rawls, *Political Liberalism*, lecture IV.

[58] Scheffler, 'The Appeal of Political Liberalism', 139.

nonetheless affirm the same modular political conception of justice, we have been given no reason to assume that, in fact, the right kind of overlapping consensus actually exists. The passage Scheffler cites is this Rawlsian description of a model case of an overlapping consensus:

> It contains three views; one affirms the political conception because its religious doctrine and account of free faith lead to a principle of toleration and underwrite the fundamental liberties of a constitutional regime; while the second view affirms the political conception on the basis of a comprehensive liberal moral doctrine such as those of Kant or Mill. The third . . . is not systematically unified: besides the political values formulated by a freestanding political conception of justice, it includes a large family of non-political values.[59]

Scheffler objects that this list of reasonable comprehensive views is too narrow. It is unsurprising that these views should lead to the endorsement of the political conception of justice, but they are too close to it in content. It is an open question what *other* views could also form part of such a consensus.

I think this is representative of a criticism that does not take into account Rawls's commitment to contextualism. As I argued in the case of Timmons's criticisms of Putnam it is a reasonable contextualist requirement that any proposed candidate conception must be a fully worked out competitor to those reasonable comprehensive conceptions that Rawls *does* describe. I have noted Rawls's endorsement of Berlin's argument that no form of living together can accommodate all valuable forms of life and its importance in his overall argument. As Rawlsian liberalism entrenches itself through time, so certain admirable or valuable forms of life may find it increasingly difficult to sustain themselves. (I shall discuss this point in more detail in the next chapter.) Some blatantly unreasonable or objectionable forms of life will be permanently 'put out of business'. In the latter case it is not regrettable, in the former case of valuable or admirable forms of life it is, but contextualism requires Scheffler's sceptical worry to have more determinate content than the thought that there may be *a* candidate conception that could not be accommodated in a Rawlsian overlapping consensus. Is the proposed candidate a form of life that is tacitly racist or intolerant, whose passing is not to be regretted? Is it a form of life that is traditional or hierarchical, with an emphasis on fixed relations of authority which is going to find it difficult to reproduce itself in a liberal environment and whose loss might be regretted, even by liberals? Without the specification of further detail, it is not clear to what kind of candidate conception Scheffler can appeal and how it will fare through time in a politically liberal society.

Scheffler's other important argument is a redundancy argument. The politicization of justice is not necessary as the endorsement of the two principles of justice suffices to demonstrate the legitimacy of that conception. Furthermore, by asking citizens to affirm the two principles not simply in the light of their reasonable comprehensive moral conceptions but also in the light of a free-standing conception of justice, Rawls weakens the plausibility that such a consensus could even come into being. I concede that Rawls seems mistakenly to imply that the parties in the original position *itself* are sensitive to issues about legitimacy and select principles of justice taking

---

[59] Rawls, *Political Liberalism*, 145.

such factors into account.[60] Scheffler is surely correct that this is a mistake: legitimacy is not an issue for the parties in the original position.[61] It is an issue for those
who use the model as a device of justification, not for those who are represented as
within the model (the choosers in the original position). But if that is true, and the
structure of Rawlsian justification is first to select the two principles then address the
stability of the conception of justice that they represent and then their legitimacy,
what is the difference between Rawls's politicized conception of justice and Scheffler's
best case scenario in which that final move is redundant? I think Scheffler is drawing
attention to the very fact that I noted about ethical liberalism, namely, that for certain kinds of liberal outlook their very structure makes it impractical to see them as
coercively imposed on others. Agreement on the two principles carries within itself a
guarantee of legitimacy, in the sense that if we have that much agreement, then we
can dispense with the question of whether it is based on a particular reasonable comprehensive conception *as a concern about legitimacy.* Suppose that those who do *not*
subscribe to a morally individualist and reasonably comprehensive conception of the
good come to see the principles of justice as based on such a conception. Ought they
to be concerned that, for that reason, the principles are not legitimate? Scheffler cannot see why: agreement on the principles *is* legitimacy, and no one holding such a
view is going to be discriminated against in the sense that moral individualism could
not be used as a ground for coercing him or her or restricting his or her rights.

I think the correct response on Rawls's part is to deny that this is a scenario where
the issue of legitimacy does not arise. This issue is, of its very nature, of broader scope
than the acceptability or otherwise of a particular conception of justice. If we have
agreement on the latter, that can only be on the basis that, implicitly, we have already
agreed on the former issue. Scheffler's thought experiment cannot lead, as he suggests,
to an alternative in which one can simply dispense with the whole idea of politicizing justice. Scheffler argues that agreement on the two principles themselves, as an
exercise of political solidarity, achieves everything that an explicit and supplementary
theory of the legitimacy of justice and the permissible grounds of political argument
was supposed to provide:

Citizens are aware of the existence both of widespread agreement on the principles of justice
and of widespread disagreement in people's comprehensive moral doctrines. This awareness,
when coupled with the commitment to mutual respect that is implied by citizens' common
affirmation of the two principles, gives rise to an ethos of restraint, a reluctance on the part
of many citizens to appeal in the public arena to their own comprehensive moral doctrines.
After all, the fact that they are in agreement about the principles . . . is what matters for fundamental political purposes . . . they have no need and little desire to alienate those they respect
by insisting on divisive moral or religious claims.[62]

Charges that one or other side of an argument is begging the question tend not to be
very interesting; in this case it seems to me more helpful to argue that the difficulty

---

[60] The offending passage is Rawls, *Political Liberalism*, 223–5, on which see Scheffler, 'The
Appeal of Political Liberalism', 141.
[61] Scheffler, 'The Appeal of Political Liberalism', 141–2.
[62] Ibid. 143–4.

with Scheffler's alternative scenario is that it is extensionally equivalent to the conception of justice *as* modular and politicized. The two principles of justice are affirmed by Catholic citizens, Jewish citizens, secular citizens, and Muslim citizens but the reasons that are the basis of this affirmation differ for each representative citizen. In that way the issue of legitimacy can only be understood, in this thought experiment, as already settled. Modularity is, after all, a functional category: it is about the *role* that principles play, not their content. Scheffler's ideal scenario is not an alternative to Rawls's conception as this is a description of *how* the two principles play precisely the role of a modular conception of justice. If Scheffler is to draw a distinction between his appeal to how the two principles of justice are used to regulate political deliberation and action and Rawls's account of modular politicized justice, that can only be on the assumption that politicizing justice *changes the contents of the two principles, not their role*. But I have already given reasons why that ought not to be so: why we should not see the issue of legitimacy as irrelevantly intruding into the original position itself. (As Scheffler says, quite rightly, that it ought not to so intrude, to avoid damaging circularity.) All that Scheffler adds that appears to be distinctive in his alternative account is an 'ethos of restraint'. But what is the politicization of justice if not the affirmation of such an ethos? This ethos seems to introduce precisely the kind of reflectively aware restraint that Scheffler objects to in Rawls's proposal. Citizens in Scheffler's ideal scenario, as in Rawls's account, self-consciously restrain *themselves* and are aware of themselves as doing so. It is their 'ethos' that makes them do so.

Appeal to an 'ethos' suggests an appeal to the background moral culture of a society to which a particular conception of justice applies. It seems to me that Scheffler is raising two questions here: from an explanatory point of view, what resources are there within a background moral culture for such a duty of restraint? That is a very good question, it does identify a lacuna in Rawls's arguments and the next chapter attempts to remedy that lack, offering an account of how a political liberal can advance the option value of active citizenship in such a way as to make it intelligible how citizens might come to adopt such an ethos of restraint. Second, from a normative point of view, can Rawls give an account of the content of such a duty of restraint? It seems to me that this is precisely that which the politicization of justice aims to provide.

If Scheffler and Rawls are not simply to be interpreted as at cross-purposes, then the difference between them will have to be that Scheffler views his set of arrangements as capable of receiving an 'external' understanding, such that political agents may be interpreted as exercising an ethos of restraint where this is not part of their explicit self-understanding of their political agency. That argument seems to me to have very limited force: if an ethos of restraint self-consciously guides the duty of civility exercised by citizens, why cannot a similar awareness of such a restraint as guided by a fundamentally political civic duty be advanced in a similarly reflective way? But Scheffler's point undoubtedly has *some* force: it leads to his second and very important set of arguments (arguments interestingly complemented by the similar arguments of Leif Wenar).[63] If the politicized conception of justice is a moral conception with

---

[63] Wenar, 'Political Liberalism: An Internal Critique'.

particular restricted scope, and it is supported by reasonable comprehensive moral conceptions, is that very description of it not a proof of its own redundancy? It is trying to fill a gap in Rawls's arguments that does not exist. Scheffler's further argument is that he cannot see what role separable recognition by a political actor that his or her affirmation of the conception of justice from within their particular reasonable moral conception is *politicized* is supposed to achieve.

This is, I think, a more serious problem for Rawls. Rawls's view is only going to be defensible from this kind of internal critique if a sharper distinction is made between morality and politics. Scheffler's objection is, after all, conditional: *if* the politicized conception of justice consists solely in a moral conception with a certain kind of restricted scope, it seems redundant. Citizens *already*, in their grasp of the two principles and their role, exhibit a grasp of the different scope of comprehensive moral conceptions and the two principles. What is gained by redescribing the situation where this is a combination of two kinds of moral view of differing scope, such that the moral view with the more restricted scope is relabelled as 'politicized'? Before suggesting what I think will turn out to be the best way of answering this criticism, it is necessary clearly to distinguish it from a similar internal criticism of the transition within Rawls's views. Wenar insightfully points out that the one place where a contrast between internal and external understanding *does* seem to apply to Rawls's arguments, in a damaging way, is when Rawls builds into his model of a reasonable person not only that person's intrinsic features but an acknowledgement of those features which, Rawls believes, *explains* their capacity to participate in an overlapping consensus. That does appear to be simply a mistake. Rawls claimed, for example, that a ground for the restraint involved in liberal citizenship is a belief that there are ineliminable burdens of judgement. But acknowledging *that* is not itself part of that in which being a reasonable person consists. A conception of justice as modular can be advanced to a reasonable person, and accepted by such a person, without him or her accepting the grounds Rawls's adduces for him or her to do so.[64]

That holds open two appealing prospects from a Rawlsian perspective: that the view of the role of liberal citizenship and its self-restraint that Rawls advances could survive the falsity of his explanations for why it comes into being and the equally happy prospect that there may be further grounds for it, open to discovery independent of those grounds that Rawls advanced. We are sticking, strictly, to the functional role of modular justice without explaining how it plays that role in such a way that citizens themselves have, first personally, to acknowledge the truth of that explanation. I think, then, in order to develop a finally defensible view, further attention is needed to the way in which Rawls understands the concept of the political, to see if that understanding could be revised in a constructive way.

3. RAWLS AND THE CONCEPT OF THE POLITICAL

There is, then, one aspect of the internal critique of political liberalism that does seem to have force. In order to address it, one would need to develop a rationale for the

[64] Ibid. 43 ff.

duty of mutual restraint other than that developed by Rawls. Furthermore, whichever account one develops, it will have to dispense with his assumption that this rationale need necessarily figure in the first personal deliberations of citizens. It seems to me that in order to develop such a rationale it is also necessary to take a sceptical look at how Rawls uses the concept of the political. Ostensibly, political liberalism works precisely by marking out a distinction between morality and politics. But that appearance is misleading. It has often been argued, particularly by political philosophers influenced by Isaiah Berlin, such as John Gray and Bernard Williams, that Rawls's view is fatally flawed because of its inadequate conception of the political, viewed as simply a set of moral ideas with a restricted scope of application. This has been claimed to misrepresent the essentially agonistic nature of the political process, or to misrepresent the extent to which political principles involve evaluative trade-offs and losses.[65]

In the present context, it does look as if Rawls's politicization of justice is not political *enough*. One response as to why reasonable comprehensive conceptions are not in the business of what one might call comprehensive coverage, ranging from moral issues about interpersonal relations and private ideals to justice and the constitution, is that the latter are properly political matters and form part of a disjoint political morality.[66] Legislating for constitutional fundamentals from within one's reasonable comprehensive moral conception is to extend those views beyond their proper sphere. But, on closer examination, Rawls takes the domain of the political to be a set of moral ideas, with a particularly narrow scope of application. This does seem to me to make the modularization of justice an insufficient detachment of Rawls's political use of his theory from its motivational moorings in citizens' reasonable comprehensive conceptions of the good. Rawls takes the domain of the political to be a set of moral ideas, with a particularly narrow scope of application, in such a way as to invite Scheffler's objection that such a scope is *not* a sufficiently robust distinction to support the politicization of justice.[67] My view is that a sharper distinction between morality and the political will help to defend Rawls's substantive claims.

The argument of *Political Liberalism* as a whole, as Wenar points out, seems to imply that the concept of the political itself dictates that politics is more important than morality.[68] But because of Rawls's explanation of the concept of the political, what that amounts to, Wenar argues, is a particular Kantian interpretation of autonomy which operates in 'stealth mode'. Presented as a free-standing and independent political conception, Rawls in fact presents a doctrine that values autonomy and the free exercise of reason above all other values and his account of the political appears,

---

[65] Bernard Williams, 'From Freedom to Liberty: The Construction of a Political Value', a paper to which I am indebted. The charge against Rawls has also been levelled by John Gray, at the service of Gray's (then) 'agonistic' version of liberalism: see e.g. 'Agonistic Liberalism', in *Enlightenment's Wake* (London: Routledge, 1995), 64–86.

[66] A phrase taken from Mill, if not precisely the concept that I have in mind. The concept of a distinct political morality is central to the arguments of Richard Vernon, *Political Morality: A Theory of Liberal Democracy* (London and New York: Continuum Press: 2001).

[67] Scheffler, 'The Appeal of Political Liberalism', 143–5.

[68] Wenar, 'Political Liberalism: An Internal Critique', 58.

on those grounds, disingenuous. (Particularly, one might add, when compared to the explicit grounding of their views on an ideal of autonomy offered by those ethical liberals from whom Rawls seemed at particular pains to distance himself.) However, if one were not to follow him in that, but instead to argue both for the existence of a distinct concept of the political and for the existence of a *sui generis* political morality, then it becomes easier to describe the kind of interface between morality and politics envisaged by a modular conception of justice.

Bernard Williams argued that 'political philosophy is not just applied moral philosophy, which is what in our culture it is often taken to be'.[69] He further argued that political philosophy has a distinctive set of concepts, focused on the ideas of power and legitimation; that it has a distinctive notion of what constitutes a political disagreement; that it involves interpretation, but not in the limiting sense of determining what counts as particular instances of a political value; finally, that to make sense of politics you basically need to make sense of the idea of political *opposition*. Williams self-consciously echoed Carl Schmitt here, in particular his controversial definition of the concept of the political. Schmitt notoriously understood the concept of the political as 'reducible' to the criterial distinction between 'friend and enemy'.[70] On the least alarming interpretation, this view understands the political not in terms of actual conflict, but in terms of the permanent possibility of conflict centred on conflicting 'ways of life'.[71] Understanding how a certain kind of conflict is possible is integral to the concept of the political as a concept allegedly (in Schmitt's argument) distinct from the ethical.[72]

The basic point I want to take from Williams's insightful discussion is that making sense of the political involves, precisely, making sense of conflict explained via the idea of political opposition.[73] Conflicting political values are experienced as involving trade-offs and hence costs. Williams argued that if those costs are not to be resented by those who must bear them when they do not accept the justifications for them, a way must be found to accommodate this fundamental idea of political opposition. Legitimacy, here, is the acknowledgement of an authority that decides what will happen, but not, as Williams puts it, an authority that decides *what will happen rightly*, such that the opponents of the decision are revealed as merely intellectually confused

69 Williams, 'From Freedom to Liberty', 5.
70 Schmitt, *The Concept of the Political*, 26–9.
71 Nevertheless, Schmitt is concerned with actual conflict as opposed, he sardonically comments, to a 'moral and ethical' understanding of conflict in which there are only other 'debating adversaries', ibid. 28. He contrasts with this ethical sense a more fundamental sense in which 'the enemy concept belongs to the ever present possibility of combat', ibid. 32.
72 Leo Strauss pointed out the obvious conflict in Strauss between his emphasis on the distinctiveness of the concept of the political and yet its basis, in Schmitt, in an authentic, existential, and hence clearly ethical experience of 'the other' as enemy. Strauss's notes are printed as an 'Appendix' to the University of Chicago translation of *Concept of the Political*; see esp. para. 27.
73 As Williams puts it, 'The idea of the political is to an important degree focused in the idea of political disagreement: and political disagreement is significantly different from moral disagreement. Moral disagreement is characterized by a class of considerations, but the kinds of reasons that are brought to bear on a decision. Political disagreement is identified by a field of application—eventually, about what ought to be done under political authority, in particular through the deployment of state power', 'From Freedom to Liberty', 6.

all along.[74] Williams's explicit target is an over-moralized, or one might say, de-politicized notion of legitimacy.[75] If it is correct to connect the concept of the political to a certain kind of understanding of disagreement, then there is a basis for developing the claim that certain key uses of concepts can constitute part of political morality viewed as disjoint from an individual's reasonable comprehensive conceptions of the good.

The idea would be this: it is true that a citizen's allegiance to the modular conception of justice is motivated by his or her reasonable comprehensive conception of the good. But that motivation is balanced by the reflective recognition that the ideal of political legitimacy introduces a new and separate constraint on that motivation. There is the separate motivation to hold a legitimate conception where that prioritizes one's role as a citizen over one's private allegiances to a reasonable comprehensive conception, which is simply not appropriate as a basis for legitimate legislation. Each citizen understands that legitimacy is about managing and negotiating conflict and the restriction in the application of reasonable comprehensive moral views is not just a curtailment of their scope, but their subordination to the demands of political morality.

This recognition of the need for a clear distinction between politics and morality is the necessary first step towards what I believe is the most plausible ground for the politicization of justice put forward, namely, Charles Larmore's view that the rationale is *equal respect*.[76] But, once again, this is not the moral ideal of equal respect, but a political ideal. Modular justice and the duty of civility are precisely what eventuate when the reasonable comprehensive conception to which a citizen is attached is combined with equal respect for the point of view of each other citizen. My own view, which is undoubtedly controversial, is that this duty is grounded on the moral truth that we can reasonably attribute to comprehensive moral conceptions and the truth of the principle of equal respect as a principle of political morality.[77] (Thus I do not agree with Rawls that we need, in this case, to retreat from any truth claims to claims which are merely reasonable.) Taking the point of view of others seriously is to respect them equally and hence to make them all beneficiaries of our mutual restraint. Recall that the liberal views the two central problems of modern political theory as the determination of legitimate grounds of state authority and the formulation of political principles in a modern society. Such a society is characterized by a plurality of comprehensive conceptions of the good and a degree of overlapping consensus. This consensus is a framework for normal moral decision-making that does not draw on the elements of a comprehensive conception of the good. Political liberalism attempts a solution to these two problems, but can only proceed by adopting a principled distinction between morality and politics.

74 Williams, 'From Freedom to Liberty', 7, 14, esp. 15–16.

75 Ibid. 13–14.

76 Larmore, 'Political Liberalism', ch. 6 of *The Morals of Modernity*, pp. 127, 132.

77 Thus one keeps the modular conception of political liberalism, avoids Rawls's agnosticism about truth claims, but embeds his entire argument strategy within a recognition that, as Williams puts it, we are dealing with political values, 'In the sense that concerns these discussions, freedom is a political value . . . we must take seriously the point that because it is a political value, the most important disagreements that surround it are political disagreements', 'From Freedom to Liberty', 5.

A contrast with Larmore's views will make the same point more clearly: his avowed aim is to describe how the policy of political liberalism is to implement a policy of 'procedural neutrality' based on that minimal moral conception expressed in an overlapping consensus.[78] Larmore's distinctive contribution to the development of political liberalism is his argument that this minimal moral conception is adopted solely as a result of what he calls an 'underdetermination problem' within morality.[79] Our best conception of the good life is likely to yield an underdetermined outcome in view of the plurality of background frameworks available to reflection and the necessity for ongoing critical engagement in the formulation of moral frameworks. These facts of plurality and underdetermination are the basis for liberal abstention from contested conceptions of the good. It is not an account of the good on a par with rivals, such as moral pluralism, nor is it a form of scepticism. It is rather a recognition of the underdetermination problem:

Political neutrality is a moral principle, stipulating the conditions on which political principles can be justified . . . the reasons for the ideal of neutrality are not primarily epistemological . . . they are instead basically moral.[80]

The moral basis of neutrality cannot, on this view, be as controversial as those contested conceptions of the good from which the political justification of legislation abstains. Thus, perfectionist justifications of neutrality must be avoided.[81] I agree on that last point, but Larmore's strategy seems to follow Rawls's lead in treating political principles as the application of moral principles while restricting their scope. So my objection to Rawls's account extends to Larmore's account of the status of this principle. He has identified precisely the correct principle, but I view it as a principle of political morality, not a moral principle with a certain restricted scope.

There is at least one respect, then, in which a substantive revision needs to be made to Rawls's views in addition to emphasizing the crucial role played by contextualism in defence of the politicization of justice. But that substantive revision involves no more than taking a Rawlsian assumption and developing it: he claimed to have politicized the concept of justice, whereas in fact his understanding of the political is simply that it takes a moral idea and applies it with restricted scope. A more radically politicized account of the civic duty of self-restraint gives it, I would argue, a more defensible rationale. That leaves open, however, a question of how citizens can be appropriately motivated to observe such a duty. Scheffler raised that issue acutely when he identified this motivation as dependent on an ethos located in the moral background culture of a society. That is the subject of the next chapter.

[78] Larmore, 'Political Liberalism', 134–41.
[79] Larmore develops his earlier account of this phenomenon in 'Pluralism and Reasonable Disagreement', ch. 7 of *The Morals of Modernity*, esp. at 169–74
[80] Larmore, 'Political Liberalism', 342 of the original publication in *Political Theory* (Aug. 1990), 342–7.
[81] Larmore, 'Political Liberalism', in *The Morals of Modernity*, 128–32.

CONCLUSION

In this chapter I have broadly defended the strategy of the politicization of justice expressed in Rawlsian political liberalism. I have argued that the transition can be properly motivated and defended from both its internal, and some of its external, critics. However, there is one line of relatively internal critique that I do think needs further evaluation. That is the claim that the politicization of justice is self-defeating. It is not self-defeating in that it offers a conception of justice more controversial than the reasonable comprehensive moral conception that supplies its grounds, even when it is supposed to function in such a way as to defuse such controversy. It is self-defeating in that the point of a theory of legitimacy was to explain how the scope of liberalism goes beyond the theory of justice. Liberalism depends on a moral background culture in a society, which it presupposes and about which it deliberately does not theorize. In contextual terms, it is a presupposition of the availability of a distinctively liberal form of justification. Political liberalism makes that point particularly clearly: the fact of reasonable pluralism is its starting point. But when the politicization of justice is established, will it mould this moral background culture in an objectionably, or acceptably, circular way? Will something analogous to the communitarian critique of liberalism emerge after justice has been politicized? Those questions seem to me sufficiently important to warrant further consideration as they suggest a further revision to the defence of political liberalism. In answering these I will also address Scheffler's question regarding the basis of the demanding duty of self-restraint required of citizens in a politically liberal society. That is the subject of the final chapter of this book.

12

Political Liberalism and Civic Republicanism

§1: Motivating political liberalism as a contextual solution to the problems of modern political theory. §2: Picking out one, empirical, strand in the communitarian critique of liberalism. §3: Distinguishing Rousseau's and Machiavelli's different versions of liberal republicanism. §4: How the liberal republican appeals to civil society as the basis of a theory of citizenship. §5: The entrenchment of political liberalism through time in a moral background culture does not violate neutrality of effect in a damaging way.

In this final chapter I will address the unresolved problem for Rawls that I described at the end of the previous chapter. That problem is that, given the demanding nature of the duty of mutual restraint invoked when citizens deliberate about constitutional and legislative fundamentals some account is necessary of how people are actually motivated to act in accordance with such a demanding ideal of citizenship. It seems that a person's deepest convictions (which may be integral to his or her moral identity) have to be overridden by that person's duty, as a citizen, not to put forward reasons for legislation to his or her fellow citizens that they can reasonably reject. That is not an anaemic defence of the status quo, but a challenging account of the demands of liberal citizenship. How can ordinary people be motivated to act in this way? In this chapter I will consider this issue which I will refer to as the motivation problem.

I will argue that the problem can be solved by extending political liberalism to cover a specific set of claims drawn from the republican tradition. Given that the incorporation of these claims is subject to the constraints on a legitimate political theory that political liberalism makes explicit, these republican themes are a complement to, not a corrective for, the basic motivations for the politicization of justice. Republicanism, like Rawlsian political liberalism, emphasizes the preconditions of the kind of demanding liberal political culture that Rawls's views envisage in the background moral ethos of a society. I will argue, in a manner parallel to William Galston, Stephen Macedo, and John Tomasi, that even Rawls's later 'politicized' version of liberalism is committed to certain corollaries about how it views the wider culture of the society for which it is a theory: a politically liberal culture.[1] But they are interested in developing this argument in order to prove that the distinction Rawls perceived between his own view and explicitly ethical or perfectionist liberalisms *cannot* be defended. That, as will become clear, is certainly not my aim. I intend to vindicate Rawls's basic

---

[1] Galston, *Liberal Purposes*; Macedo, *Liberal Virtues*; Tomasi, *Liberalism Beyond Justice*.

approach while extending it to address this concern by invoking some of the central
themes usually associated with the republican tradition.

These various challenges arise because the way in which political liberalism presupposes a certain kind of moral background culture is both distinctive and open to challenge. It is open to direct challenge from those ethical liberals who argue that the kind
of culture that political liberalism presupposes must itself be a liberal background culture which inculcates a liberal virtue ethic in its citizens.[2] There is an inevitable and
non-objectionable circularity, they argue, in the fact that liberal political philosophy
rests on a moral background culture which places distinctively liberal ethical demands
on the citizens of that polity. The *political* liberal objects that such a view is tacitly
illegitimate. It is a canonical case of basing a political view, liberalism, on an exclusionary comprehensive conception of the good in a way that violates constraints on
legitimacy.

But this objection does raise the question of whether or not the political liberal
can simply presuppose the general character of the background moral culture upon
which it draws. This question has been raised and answered in a way threatening
to the ambitions of political liberalism by two kinds of critic. The first kind is the
communitarian critic of liberalism as a whole who argues that, empirically, citizens of
liberal democracies suffer from a radical motivational deficit.[3] Compared to 'visions
of the good' liberal polities offer anaemic grounds for political allegiance and for commitment to liberalism. Looking at the contemporary political reality in which we live
our lives it seems that very few people live solely by the ideals of cosmopolitan world
citizenship. Many people are, however, moved by more local and particular sources
of allegiance: nationalist identifications, ethnic identifications, or identity in the sense
of gender or sexual orientation. How does the liberal compete with these sources of
motivation, or co-opt them? Prima facie, liberalism seems an inherently cosmopolitan political view. How does liberalism avoid losing out in the competition for the
engagement of citizens' motivations? This is simply one strand in the complex set of
arguments that make up the communitarian critique of liberalism, but it has always
seemed to me the most plausible and the most challenging.

The second kind of critic, such as Scheffler, argues that the demanding ideal of
citizenship that political liberalism presupposes can only be located in a background
social ethos that, ironically, falls outside the scope of the type of justifications to which
political liberalism limits itself, as discussed in the previous chapter. The third kind of
critic, ethical liberals well represented in this debate by John Tomasi, argue that even
after the politicization of justice has taken place, the sort of criticism raised by both
the ethical liberal and the communitarian comes back to haunt political liberalism in
a new guise. This argument has been developed at length by Tomasi in an important monograph.[4] The operation of political liberalism through time will, once again,
entrench a damagingly circular presupposition of its own correctness in the moral

[2] Galston, *Liberal Purposes*, ch. 10; Macedo, *Liberal Virtues*, chs. 6 and 7.
[3] Charles Taylor, 'The Politics of Recognition', in *Philosophical Arguments* (Cambridge, Mass.:
Harvard University Press 1995), 225–56.
[4] Tomasi, *Liberalism Beyond Justice*, esp. ch. 3.

background culture upon which it draws. The political liberal aims solely at neutrality of aim, not neutrality of effect, dismissing the latter as not feasible.[5] But even the unintended spillover effects of political liberalism, this critic argues, lead to a circularity in its own justification as the politically liberal state shapes its background culture in its own image.

In this chapter I will argue for a single general response to these arguments. They are correct in their focus on the responsibilities, as well as the duties, of liberal citizenship. But I give that familiar communitarian refrain a precise and limited sense: the general structure of political liberalism needs to embed within itself a republican emphasis on active citizenship as an option value, not as an intrinsic part of a good life. This is a limited acknowledgement that political liberalism cannot simply presuppose an account of its moral background culture, but must address itself to how the demanding role of citizenship that it places at the centre of its account of legitimacy is to be sustained. (Thus addressing Scheffler's concerns.) It is sustained by active citizenship, as an option value, as expressed by those forms of associational life expressed by civil society.[6] Political liberalism cannot remain indifferent to whether the moral background culture it presupposes is a hospitable environment for such associational life. But I will go on to argue that at that point its responsibility stops, as it were. The reformulated 'neo-communitarian' objection (from Tomasi) that political liberalism will inevitably shape which forms of life can participate in that culture will merely have to be lived with. Tomasi's error, I will argue, is to take Rawls's views about responsibility in a political context, as applied to the basic structure of society, and apply those views with a much wider scope to all the effects that political liberalism fails to prevent in society as a whole.[7] Ironically, a very demanding thesis that Rawls develops specifically about the subject matter of his conception of justice will turn out to be appropriate only there; it is not appropriate to apply this stringent view to the very idea of a legitimate liberal theory.

I agree with these critics of Rawls that in spite of his avowedly restricted focus Rawls's views on legitimately and constitutionally securing the principles of justice must have implications for the wider moral background culture of any society that adopts these principles. Unlike these critics, however, I take Rawls's principles of justice to constrain how we are to construe this wider spillover from the theory

---

[5] Rawls, *Political Liberalism*, 192–3.

[6] See Walzer, 'The Civil Society Argument', esp. the discussion at 104.

[7] Tomasi's arguments here parallel a different discussion which attacks the normative content of Rawls's egalitarianism as insufficiently demanding, on the grounds that it applies to the basic structure of society as opposed directly to the conduct of individuals via their first personal deliberations about, for example, their economic decisions about marketing his or her labour. The most succinct statement of this critique is G. A. Cohen, 'Where the Action Is: On the Site of Distributive Justice', *Philosophy and Public Affairs*, 26/1 (Winter 1997), 3–30 and in the closing chapters of G. A. Cohen, *If You're An Egalitarian, How Come You're So Rich?* (Cambridge, Mass.: Harvard University Press, 2000). I have addressed some of the issues involved in 'Cohen's Critique of Rawls: A "Double Counting" Objection', unpublished MS (2005) and in the on-line publication 'The Permissibility of Prerogative Grounded Incentives in Liberal Egalitarianism', 'Straight to the Point', *Ethics and Economics* (2005): <http://mapage.noos.fr/Ethique-economique/html_version/> It should be clear from the subsequent discussion that these two apparently independent lines of critique actually have a great deal in common. See also nn. 70 and 77, below.

of justice to a view of liberalism more widely construed. Thus, where they see a problem for Rawls, I perceive merely a lacuna in his arguments that needs to be supplemented. That involves the incorporation within a generally politicized theory of justice of a complementary account of its social presuppositions: namely, a liberal republican account of the concepts of citizenship and civil society. Care will be taken to distinguish the way in which the liberal republican develops those concepts, a way that respects the constraints of political liberalism, as opposed to their development by ethical liberals or communitarians. I will also, in this chapter, explain why it is important to detach the kind of republicanism I want to endorse from its close relative, found in Rousseau, that has brought the entire tradition of civic republicanism into a certain amount of disrepute.[8]

1. POLITICAL LIBERALISM AND ITS RIVALS

The previous chapter focused on the internal structure of political liberalism and for a particular interpretation of which parts of the view are fundamental and which, I argued, needed to be revised. This chapter takes up a wider focus on this set of ideas, so it is prudent to begin with a restatement of precisely why I take political liberalism to be the political theory that is the most stable under reflection before I contrast the view with its rivals. I argued that political liberalism is the most successful form of liberal theory because it clearly identifies the problems inherent in a political theory for a distinctively modern society. It offers solutions that incorporate many of the strengths, and avoid many of the weaknesses, of other liberal theories. Historically, political liberalism is the successor to the Lockean 'modus vivendi' tradition which begins from, rather than tacitly presupposes, a historical and social thesis about the nature of modern societies. On such a Lockean view it is explicit that modern societies are primarily scenes of pluralism and potential conflict and the contribution of liberalism is a development of the impetus to toleration in the interest of a common life. However, it is clear from Chapter II that political liberalism goes beyond a merely modus vivendi conception, resting as it does on a conception of a shared moral framework for political legislation which rests on more than 'devices to get us to live together as alternatives to dying together'.[9] It expresses its own distinctive normative ideals.

---

[8] Unfortunately, even very distinguished commentators associate republicanism very strongly with Roussseau. Thus Adam Seligman, one of the leading contemporary theorists of civil society, discusses the relationship between civil society and the republican tradition solely in terms of its relation to Rousseau. Unsurprisingly, Seligman is pessimistic as to the extent to which republicanism in the Rousseauian tradition can accommodate genuine civic diversity. See Seligman, 'Animadversions upon Civil Society and Civic Virtue in the Last Decade of the Twentieth Century', in John Hall (ed.), *Civil Society: Theory, History, Comparison* (Cambridge: Polity Press), 200–23. More generally, Richard Dagger's arguments for civic republicanism try to defend the theory in its 'Rousseauian' version in that it contains as a central component a model of distinctive human excellence, see Dagger, *Civic Virtues: Rights, Citizenship and Republican Liberalism* (Oxford: Oxford University Press, 1997), esp. 194–201 for a summative discussion of the relationship between Dagger's view and perfectionism.

[9] Bernard Williams, 'A Fair State: Review of John Rawls, *Political Liberalism*', *London Review of Books*, 15/9 (13 May 1993), 7–8.

Chapter II also brought into focus the fact that the tradition of liberalism with which political liberalism is most clearly to be contrasted is ethical liberalism.[10] Ethical liberalism claims that a liberal political theory is a natural extension of a correct view of the nature of persons and that which constitutes a good life for such persons. Ethical liberalism is typically combined with *political expressivism*, a complementary view which forms the bridge to the idea that politics ought to express our best ethical theories.[11] Expressivist themes are found in the political philosophy of Kant and those political traditions he influenced, and also in the older tradition of neo-Aristotelianism. Expressivism is powered by some of the neo-Aristotelian assumptions that motivate certain of liberalism's external critics, such as Marxism. Expressivists seek an expressive harmony between individual and social conceptions of the good and prioritize conceptions of good over principles of right. They emphasize autonomy and moral perfectionism and argue that the ultimate grounding of their theory is in a distinctive account of human nature. Thus ethical liberalism and political expressivism are natural complements to each other. The ethical liberal and political expressivist both argue that the politicization of justice is fundamentally misconceived. Political truth consists in a recognition of the ethical truth about good lives. A liberal form of political life is one that expresses the truth about good lives, but a truth pitched at such abstraction that it does not lead to state support of private ideals. In that sense it remains a neutralist view. However, it does lead to the liberal state promoting the enabling conditions of good lives and dissuading citizens from bad or damaging lives, perhaps by providing its autonomous citizens with a choice worthy environment, or by forcing them to face up to the responsibilities of citizenship (or, conversely, the full social costs of irresponsibility).[12] There is, on this view, a distinctively liberal vision of the good, and an associated set of liberal virtues that the state has every reason to inculcate into its citizens.

However, the key point of controversy, in my view, is not this internecine dispute between ethical liberals and political liberals. That is because it seems to me that a certain kind of liberal can both acknowledge the demands on a legitimate theory of justice posed by political liberalism and also emphasize some of the issues of concern to ethical liberals. A *liberal republican* can draw on the historical inheritance of civic republicanism in a way that does not violate Rawls's argument for the politicization of modular justice.[13] Ethical liberals, or some communitarians, take the central themes

---

[10] Galston, *Liberal Purposes;* Macedo, *Liberal Virtues;* Raz, *The Morality of Freedom.*

[11] Larmore, *Patterns of Moral Complexity*, 73–7.

[12] There is an emphasis on the provision of a choice worthy environment to sustain the value of autonomy in Raz's *The Morality of Freedom*, chs. 4, 14, 15. There is an influential version of liberal egalitarianism that focuses on the issue of responsibility, the full assessment of which falls outside the scope of this book, namely, Ronald Dworkin's *Sovereign Virtue: The Theory and Practice of Equality* (Cambridge, Mass.: Harvard University Press, 2000).

[13] There are two strands to the contemporary revival of interest in republicanism: the historical work of Berlin, Skinner, and Pocock and the philosophical application of those ideas by Taylor, Pettit, and Skinner. For the former, see Berlin's seminal study, 'The Originality of Machiavelli', in Myron P. Gilmore (ed.), *Studies on Machiavelli* (Florence: Sansoni, 1972), 147–206; Quentin Skinner, 'The Republican Ideal of Political Liberty' and 'Pre-humanist Origins of Republican Ideas', both in Gisela Bock, Quentin Skinner, and Maurizio Viroli (eds.), *Machiavelli and Republicanism*

of the civic republican tradition to be uniquely accommodated within a distinct ethical liberal/expressivist tradition within liberalism.[14] They believe that to incorporate themes from republicanism one has to be a fully fledged ethical liberal. By contrast, I will argue that the central themes of republicanism, including the values of active citizenship and the importance of a flourishing civil society, are better accommodated within a view that is a natural extension of political liberalism. I will set out this latter line of argument and explain why a republican liberal will proceed to attach considerable strategic importance to the idea of civil society, one of the most intensely debated themes in contemporary political philosophy.[15]

My view is that Rawlsian political liberalism not only can, but must, accept a republican emphasis on the value of active citizenship. Such citizenship requires a functioning and flourishing civil society to provide appropriate spheres of voluntary association. Furthermore, given that liberalism must appeal to specific cultural circumstances to explain the basis of our allegiance to liberal principles, the invocation of civil society can also assist the liberal in solving a further problem, that of political motivation. Taking both points together, I will argue that the central strength of the idea of civil society lies in its combination of a common form and a variable, culturally specific, content. But that is the barest outline of a proposal whose more detailed elaboration is the subject of this chapter.

2. PARALLEL TRACKS: ONE STRAND IN THE COMMUNITARIAN CRITIQUE OF LIBERALISM

Thus far in my discussion of political liberalism I have not mentioned, at any great length, the communitarian critique of liberalism, save for my acceptance of how Charles Taylor understands the problem of political motivation. That omission has been deliberate: I have taken at face value Rawls's assertion that his own change of emphasis when he turned from the stability to the legitimacy of his own conception of justice was in no way a response to the communitarian critique of his earlier work.[16]

(Cambridge: Cambridge University Press, 1990) at 293–309 and 121–42 respectively; 'The Idea of Negative Liberty', in Richard Rorty, Jerome Schneewind, and Quentin Skinner (eds.), *Philosophy in History* (Cambridge: Cambridge University Press, 1984), 193–221.

[14] See e.g. Charles Taylor's seminal papers: 'What's Wrong with Negative Liberty?', in *Philosophical Papers, ii. Philosophy and the Human Sciences* (Cambridge: Cambridge University Press 1985), 211–29; *Sources of the Self*, 196–7; *Philosophical Arguments*, 141, 192; 'Democratic Exclusion (and Its Remedies?)', in Rajeev Bhargava, Amiya Kumar Bagchi, and R. Sudarshan (eds.), *Multiculturalism, Liberalism and Democracy* (New Delhi: Oxford University Press), 138–63.

[15] There is a very substantial literature on the theme of civil society. The discussions that have influenced this book the most are the monographs of John Keane, *Civil Society: Old Images, New Visions* (London: Polity Press, 1998); Adam B. Seligman, *The Idea of Civil Society* (Princeton: Princeton University Press, 1995); Andrew Arato and Jean Cohen, *Civil Society and Political Theory* (Cambridge, Mass.: MIT Press 1992); Robert D. Putnam, *Bowling Alone: The Collapse and Revival of American Community* (New York: Simon & Schuster, 2000). Two outstanding papers on the subject, to which I am greatly indebted, are Walzer's 'The Civil Society Argument' (see also his most recent discussion of civil society in *Politics and Passion*, ch. 4) and Charles Taylor's 'Invoking Civil Society', *Philosophical Arguments*, 204–24.

[16] Rawls, *Political Liberalism*, 27.

His rather pointed comment that his politicized conception of justice rests on no controversial metaphysical theses, in particular metaphysical theses about the nature of persons, might be taken as further evidence that the changes in Rawls's own views were not caused by any conviction that the communitarian critique of *A Theory of Justice* had any force.[17] That critique of Rawls's early formulations suffered from the central problem of bringing prior assumptions about the structure of the debate to the interpretation of Rawls's work. He was placed in the role of the neo-Kantian empty formalist, whose work stood in need of correction by an account of substantive ethical life, particularly our 'thickly constituted' ethical identities, that would update Hegel's critique of Kant.[18] But that did scant justice to Rawls's own communitarian vision of the 'social union of social unions', inspired by Wilhelm von Humboldt, in part 3 of *A Theory of Justice* and treated Rawls as both an atomist about persons and a foundationalist about justification, neither charge proving particularly plausible.[19] The charge of atomism confused the moral individualism expressed by Rawls's choice of a contractualist method with a particular subcomponent of the model used to develop that individualism. Only on that basis could one take a part of Rawls's model of the original position, understood as a 'device of representation', and understand it as his theory of what people essentially are. Properly understood, all that Rawls's model asks one to do is to think about oneself in a certain kind of abstract way, where abstraction is not, in this case, the route to the discovery of one's essence as a person.[20] And the charge of foundationalism levelled against Rawls was even weaker given Rawls's commitment to the methodology of reflective equilibrium.

However, I have also noted that if the critique of Rawls was not on target, there was a legitimate strand of argument (almost wholly empirical) within communitarianism that should be of concern to liberals of all persuasions. This concern should trouble political liberals and ethical liberals alike. That is Charles Taylor's argument that liberalism has, empirically, failed adequately to motivate its citizens' commitment to liberal principles and that it has, empirically, taken for granted a motivational basis in the institutions and structures of liberal political culture without thematizing or recognizing this fact sufficiently.[21] This is the motivation problem. (Taylor takes himself to be reformulating in contemporary terms a central argument of

[17] See also Rawls, 'Justice as Fairness: Political not Metaphysical', in Rawls, *Collected Papers*, 388–414 at 402.

[18] For a very clear statement of this interpretation see Albrecht Wellmer's paper, 'Conditions of a Democratic Culture: Remarks on the Liberal-Communitarian Debate', repr. in *Endgames: The Irreconcilable Nature of Modernity*, trans. David Midgley (Cambridge, Mass. and London: MIT Press, 1998), 39–61.

[19] Nagel, in his very perceptive early review of *A Theory of Justice*, noted the moral individualism implicit in Rawls's thought experiment but did not (correctly in my view) connect this claim to any atomistic theory of persons: 'Rawls On Justice', in Norman Daniels (ed.), *Reading Rawls* (New York: Basic Books 1975), 1–16. I argued in Ch. 11, above, that there was nothing distinctively 'Kantian' about this individualism, a claim made even more plausible by the very abstract account of the two moral powers in *Political Liberalism*. (However, see Wenar's discussion of Rawls's Kantianism that I drew upon in Ch. 11: 'Political Liberalism: An Internal Critique'.)

[20] I drew upon this understanding of abstraction as opposed to idealization in Ch. 4, above.

[21] See Charles Taylor, 'What's Wrong with Negative Liberty?'; 'Legitimation Crisis', both in *Philosophical Papers*, ii at 175–93 and 248–88 respectively.

de Tocqueville's.) Any survey of contemporary liberal societies, he argues, will find a severe motivational deficit, as the citizens of such societies fail to find liberal principles a focus of political attachment. Other particularist forms of attachment, which Taylor summarizes under the general heading of the 'politics of recognition', seem to have more motivational grip than the appeal of liberalism itself.[22] Taylor thinks that this problem, amongst others that he views as endemic to contemporary liberalism, can be solved only by making political participation itself a part of the good life. This is the central commitment of *his* version of civic republicanism.[23]

Since Taylor's views are clearly not illiberal this position can, with some justice, be called *a* form of liberal republicanism. It is a version of liberalism that maintains that liberals need to be articulate about the theory of good that underlies their view and, equally importantly, its social preconditions. They cannot, Taylor argues, rely simply on the intuitive appeal of certain rational principles generated by privileged rational procedures: the theory of right is not epistemically self-sufficient. As part of this recognition of the good, Taylor's version of liberalism will make a central good of a person's life his or her participation in the life of their political community, with whose central values he or she will be identified. An essential part of this view is that liberalism needs to be more articulate as to the nature of its social preconditions. There is an even stronger argument in Taylor's work that I will not engage with here as it would take the argument too far afield. Taylor has some deeply insightful arguments to the effect that liberalism ought to be more articulate about its moral sources, but it *cannot* be.[24] Modern liberals are, on this stronger view, doomed to a fatal inarticulacy about the most fundamental goods underpinning their outlook.

I accept Taylor's diagnosis of the limited problem of political motivation if not his particular solution to it (and I will not address his deeper concern about liberal inarticulacy about the 'moral sources' of contemporary liberalism as that would take the argument too far afield). I will suggest, instead, that it is possible to develop a contextual defence of a liberal republicanism that is not a rival to political liberalism as is Taylor's version. It is not a rival because it is a perfectly natural development of key themes that political liberalism itself emphasizes. This alternative version of liberal republicanism accepts that liberalism has, in the past, been insufficiently attentive to its own social preconditions. Liberals have been insufficiently explicit about the nature of a liberal political culture. Taylor was correct to pinpoint this weakness in liberalism. But his challenge can be met in a way that does not lead to the rejection of political liberalism. That view, political liberalism, sets some general constraints on an acceptable political theory. I will argue that Taylor's version of republican liberalism violates those

---

[22] Taylor, 'The Politics of Recognition'.

[23] Taylor, 'Cross-Purposes: the Liberal-Communitarian Debate', in *Philosophical Arguments*, 181–203; 'Between Democracy and Despotism: The Dangers of Soft Despotism', *Current*, 359 (Jan. 1994), 36–9.

[24] This aspect of Taylor's views is most prominent in the discussion in *Sources of the Self*, 88–90. Characteristically, however, this is balanced by the observation, 'But it is quite possible to be strongly in favour of a morality based on the notion of a good but lean to some procedural formula when it comes to the principles of politics . . . If in the end I cannot quite agree with some such procedural view . . . this is not because I don't see its force', 532 n. 60.

constraints and that my version does not. By taking the argument in this direction I will also suggest that there are aspects of ways that Rawls presents his views, indeed, perhaps, aspects of the views themselves, that I can present in a different light.

The form of liberalism that I defend, a liberal republicanism indebted to Machiavelli and not to Rousseau, is supplemented by the resources of history and sociology in its account of its own historical and social preconditions. This ensures that the theory is deficient in neither its historical nor social self-understanding. One point that is clear from recent discussion is how fragile and contingent are the conditions of a liberal polity. Part of the enhanced self-understanding of contemporary liberalism is its awareness of itself as a historical 'latecomer', as Larmore puts it, amongst the forms of political organization.[25] Just as the philosophy of science faces a start-up problem in explaining why the scientific enterprise has become so much more successful since the seventeenth century, so liberalism must explain its historical emergence. But, in the general historical narrative of the de-legitimizing of past regimes and the emergence of liberalism, it is also possible to trace an intertwined history of republicanism that can complement a significant lacuna in the argument for political liberalism. That lacuna is that political liberalism places very strong demands on the moral background culture of the society for which it is a theory, but then fails to acknowledge or explain how such demands are to be realized in practice.

3. THE TWO TRADITIONS OF LIBERAL REPUBLICANISM

Liberal republicanism is a form of liberal political theory that places citizen participation, and its social preconditions, at the centre of its account of political freedom. It is a marriage of two sets of ideas: a liberal set of ideas that emphasizes the liberties of citizens and a republican set that emphasizes their responsibilities. The way in which these two sets of ideas are complementary is that the liberal republican takes liberty as prior to responsibility and political participation, but also sees such participation as a necessary precondition of liberty. They thus form a package of ideas that are developed together.

The major challenge for the particular form of liberal republicanism that I want to defend in this book is to overcome the problem that the revival of interest in the tradition of republicanism has been presented by Taylor as a distinctively communitarian theme.[26] If Taylor is right, the civic republican tradition is intrinsically connected to ethical liberalism/political expressivism and my argument in this chapter is not going to succeed. If Taylor is correct about this then I believe that political liberalism would be at a severe disadvantage. If it cannot avail itself of these civic republican themes, centrally the concept of liberty and of active citizen virtue, then it is impoverished as a political tradition. It certainly will not be in a position to help us solve the motivation problem. However, I do not regard civic republicanism as inherently opposed to political liberalism and I shall explain why.

---

[25] Charles Larmore, 'The Foundations of Modern Democracy', *European Journal of Philosophy*, 3/1 (April 1995), 55–68.

[26] Taylor, 'Cross-Purposes: The Liberal-Communitarian Debate'.

There is a natural compatibility between that which liberals advocate in order to make their own view so much as possible and that which is advocated by the strand of civic republicanism that is *equally* opposed to the alliance between ethical liberalism and political expressivism. Political liberals and civic republicans can adopt the same policies for the promotion, or honouring, of the value of active citizenship. However, the important difference is that political liberalism must abstain from advocating the distinctive conception of the good life for persons at the centre of ethically liberal or expressivist political programmes.

It is important at this point to restate why the political liberal is opposed to the ethically liberal or expressivist view that a liberal polity depends on the political expression of a liberal account of moral life, viewed as a distinctively liberal set of ideals and virtues. As I have indicated, Taylor's kind of political republican holds a similar view to that of the ethical liberal. He sees political participation as itself part of the good life.[27] For political liberalism, however, this builds too much, namely a substantive ethical ideal, into the role of the citizen. On the alternative conception of citizenship that I will defend here, political activity need not be an essential component of any good life, even if the *possibility* of taking up the role of a citizen and giving that role authority over one's private use of reason is essential to a liberal conception of a good life. This is *not* a theory of persons or personal identity: it is an interest relativity thesis, in which a person is asked to take up a role relative to certain interests he or she possesses.[28] The distinction between the moral and the political invites citizens of a modern polity to be capable of adopting one social role which differs in importance from other roles they occupy. They must be capable of seeing themselves as citizens. As I argued in the previous chapter, that capacity is connected to the priority of politics recognized by the existence of a *sui generis* political morality.

Civic republicanism is not, in my view, essentially communitarian and it offers a model of citizenship that a political liberal can happily accept as an integral part of the self-understanding of liberalism. There are two quite distinct forms of civic republicanism on the contemporary political agenda, one allied to perfectionism and thus not compatible with political liberalism and a different version which is so compatible. That which is common to both traditions within this wider tradition, making it easy to overlook their differences, is an emphasis on active participation in political life by citizens, motivated by the honour of the political state, pride in one's political community, and a robust sense that the interests at stake in politics are too important to be left to other people. If you do not look to your own interests others will look after them for you in a way that contains a standing invitation to corruption and other political evils.

Other theorists draw attention to the distinctiveness of the republican tradition of liberty and take that to constitute the signal difference between any such view and

---

[27] Rawls commented that 'Participation is not encouraged as necessary for the protection of the basic liberties of democratic citizenship, and as in itself one form of good among others, however important for many persons. Rather, taking part in democratic politics is seen as the privileged locus of the good life. It is a return to giving a central place to what Constant called 'the liberty of the ancients' and has all the defects of that.' *Political Liberalism*, 206.

[28] This once again deflects the charge that political liberalism even tacitly appeals to a thesis about the nature of persons.

liberalism.[29] There is a line of argument, found more prominently in some contemporary theorists of republicanism than others, that claims that the distinctive part of republicanism is that it offers a 'third' concept of liberty. If you are sympathetic to this way of setting up the debate, then the civic republican identifies liberty not with the absence of constraint, but with a secure immunity from constraint. Phillip Pettit has argued that this is civic republicanism's distinctive commitment and a novel contribution to contemporary debates over freedom. I have some doubts about the wisdom of pinning too much on this idea on the grounds that the sceptically minded might conclude that as this is simply negative liberty with an added counterfactual, then there is not much distinctive about republicanism. I think that would allow disappointment with one aspect of republicanism to overshadow its other valuable features.

Within these broad areas of commonality across all forms of republicanism there is one absolutely fundamental difference. There are two very different versions of civic republicanism on the contemporary agenda.[30] Taylor's version makes political participation itself part of the good life for citizens, a formulation that reflects the ambiguous role in this debate of the historical influence of the republicanism of Rousseau. Rousseau is better characterized as an external critic of liberalism, one of those political thinkers who asks the seminal question for modern forms of 'total revolution', namely, what quality of person does our current set of political arrangements produce? This fateful and very dangerous question was answered by Rousseau in a way that, quite rightly, disconcerts contemporary liberals.[31] His concept of the general will takes political theory in an illiberal, holistic, and collectivist direction.[32] But that is not the only form of republicanism and it is certainly not the form that can be incorporated into liberal republicanism. The other tradition of republicanism is that of Machiavelli. As recovered for contemporary political theory by Quentin Skinner, Phillip Pettit, and Frank Michelman, this tradition emphasizes participation in political life, construed very broadly, as a necessary prudent protection of your own interests.[33] Failure to participate, even in this very broad sense, will place your interests at the mercy of others who do not necessarily have your best interests at heart. The difference between the form of civic republicanism advocated by Skinner and that preferred by Taylor is explained by the latter as follows:

[29] This line of argument is prominent in Quentin Skinner's work and particularly that of Philip Pettit. See esp., Pettit, *Republicanism: A Theory of Freedom and Government* (Oxford: Clarendon Press, 1997).

[30] As Taylor points out very clearly in 'Cross Purposes: The Liberal/Communitarian Dispute'.

[31] For an insightful account of the dangers attaching to this question and its role in the history of Western political theory see Bernard Yack, *The Longing for Total Revolution: Philosophic Sources of Social Discontent from Rousseau to Marx and Nietzsche* (Princeton: Princeton University Press, 1986).

[32] Thus I don't object to Adam Seligman's critical comments on the failings of this form of republican appropriation of civil society, but I do object to the implicit view that this is the *only* form of civic republicanism that represents an available option. Seligman, 'Animadversions upon Civil Society and Civic Virtue in the Last Decade of the Twentieth Century'.

[33] In addition to the previously cited papers on the Machiavellian tradition, see Dagger, *Civic Virtues: Rights, Citizenship and Republican Liberalism*; Pettit, *Republicanism: A Theory of Freedom and Government*; Frank Michelman, 'Law's Republic', *Yale Law Journal*, 97/8 (1988), 1493–1537.

According to this [view, i.e. Skinner's], the appeal of the theory [of freedom] is purely instrumental. The only way to defend any of my freedoms is to sustain a regime of active participation, because otherwise I am at the mercy of others who are far from having my interests at heart. On this version, we do without common goods altogether, and freedom is redefined as a convergent value. Skinner may be right about Machiavelli, but this interpretation could not capture, for example, Montesquieu, Rousseau, Tocqueville, Mill (in *On Representative Government*) or Arendt.[34]

Taylor has wider commitments, whose full examination cannot be undertaken here, which lead him to regard the value of liberty in his version of the republican tradition as superior to the alternative Machiavellian or Roman tradition. The crux of the dispute is liberty: for Taylor it is an intrinsic and convergent good, a good strongly 'held in common'.[35] In the alternative tradition of theorizing about liberty from a republican perspective, it is not strongly analogous to anything like positive liberty. I have noted that Pettit, in particular, has argued that republican liberty is not just freedom from interference (as in negative liberty) but also security from interference, a distinction epitomized by the Roman distinction between the liberty of a citizen and the liberty of a slave who quite accidentally happens to have no master. This is opposed to a communitarian notion of freedom, derived from the Rousseauian tradition of republicanism, as participation in collective self-determination:

Republicans are sometimes accused of requiring people to be spontaneously good: requiring them to be lovers of the common weal. But it is worth emphasising that all that freedom as citizenship requires is reliably beneficent behaviour, whether the reliability be a result of character or circumstance.[36]

I have already argued that, independently of the correct analysis of the concept of freedom, Taylor's version of republicanism is unacceptably demanding in the way in which it builds a controversial ethical ideal of political participation into the idea of citizenship itself. An alternative approach to citizenship from a republican perspective does not align that idea with a theory of irreducibly social, strongly convergent goods. Our best political theory must be adjusted to the prevailing conditions of the kind of society it is a theory for, in this case a sociologically complex modern society whose increasing differentiation makes the availability of shared conceptions of the good problematic, even in the particular form of an ideal of good citizenship.

This relationship between political theory and sociological description suggests a proper role for the communitarian emphasis on the priority of the conceptions of the good to principles of right. The strongest case for communitarianism is in special sociological circumstances, such as the place of aboriginal cultures in a modern society, or such political singularities as the place of Quebec, which views itself as a microcosmic nation state within a wider immigrant society.[37] These sociologically special

---

[34] Taylor, 'Cross Purposes: The Liberal/Communitarian Dispute', *Philosophical Arguments*, quotation from n. 15.

[35] Taylor 'Irreducibly Social Goods', repr. in *Philosophical Arguments*, 127–45.

[36] Pettit, *The Common Mind*, 313

[37] I here report the self-understanding of many Quebecois, without necessarily endorsing the truth of the sociological claim that I am in no position to assess.

conditions may require a particular conception of the good to be given political priority to avoid the application of principles of right failing to ensure the survival of the very identity of particular cultural forms of life. These cases seem plausible, and to require mixed constitutional solutions, but their very exceptionalism suggests that they represent supplements to political liberalism, not global replacements for such a liberalism.

This is why I view liberal republicanism as the most viable form of political organization and the importance of its central normative ideal of active citizenship as one that both political liberals and civic republicans should endorse. Both liberals and republicans will foster those spontaneous, freely associating groups that make up civil society. The key difference is that liberal republicans see themselves as defending an 'option value' whereas the Taylorian civic republicans take themselves to be defending stronger, 'goods based' conditions of any good life. I have suggested that this latter alternative is not feasible absent some very special sociological conditions. However, the essence of my argument in this chapter is that one cannot merely pay lip service to an option value. Sustaining an option requires commitment, in this case, the honouring of the normative ideal of citizenship in the context of civil society.

Thus far in this book, it seems that all that political liberalism demands from the ideal of citizenship is negative: a duty of restraint. But it does seem to me that in order to make plausible the claim that liberal citizens are capable of meeting the requirements of this demanding duty, one does have to say more about the ideal of citizenship itself. It is demanding in the sense that all citizens are required to place this duty of mutual restraint above the demands placed on them by their private convictions. This is so, no matter how important those convictions, unless that duty of restraint can *itself* be motivated from within those convictions. In explaining how this demanding duty is possible, liberal republicans point to a general social good of active citizenship as the basis for an account of how citizens can be motivated to act in solidarity with other citizens of their shared political community. Active citizenship is itself a demonstrable social good, a form of 'social capital', and societies are demonstrably better off when they exhibit a high degree of such capital and demonstrably worse off when it is impoverished.[38] Responsible citizenship helps to solve the paradox of governability: that a liberal society gives citizens a substantial scope for private discretion in a sphere of action outside the control of the state, but can nevertheless be ungovernable if citizens fail to act responsibly within this sphere. The virtues of citizenship, of cooperative activity towards a common goal in free associations outside the sphere of governmental control, are learnt in the context of associational life, located between the intimate sphere of the family and those areas of social life under direct state control.

The politically liberal state seeks to promote a sense of effective political agency amongst its citizens and to extend the possibilities of political participation. It does so while avoiding the imposition of comprehensive conceptions of the good life on its citizens. Thus the concept of citizenship becomes of central theoretical importance:

---

[38] This is one of the central claims of Robert D. Putnam's *Bowling Alone*.

the ongoing debate concerns how the ideal of citizenship is to be best interpreted. This concept can hardly be approached in a vacuum and must be set in the context of a consideration of associational life in civil society. In the next section I will say more about how a political liberal will deploy both of these concepts in his or her overall theory.

4. LIBERAL REPUBLICANISM, CIVIL SOCIETY, AND CITIZENSHIP

I have argued that political liberalism must address the problem of political motivation. If the sole basis for political motivation was the partial and incomplete account of citizenship offered by political liberalism, then an important dimension of citizens' motivation would have been ignored and the picture of liberal citizenship offered would be one-dimensional. Liberalism as a whole already faces a challenge in explaining its grip on the motivations of citizens given the alternative sources of motivation offered by the politics of identity and recognition in all its forms. That situation is exacerbated if all that political liberalism adds is that liberals are people who do not endorse constitutional and legislative fundamentals in such a way as to violate their duty of self-restraint towards those with whom they share a political community. Taken as it stands, that sounds too much like the old joke that liberals are people who cannot take their own side in an argument. There is a lacuna in the argument for political liberalism that has to be addressed. It is addressed by thematizing the traditional liberal emphasis on free associations and active citizenship that explains how any liberal view, but particularly the demanding view represented by political liberalism, makes itself possible.

This point about motivation is taken by Taylor and Walzer as fatal to political liberalism which requires, in their view, replacement by an expressivist emphasis on how political motivation can only rest on a shared conception of the goods of a life. Walzer argues further that the requisite concept of citizenship can only be learned within the context of a functioning civil society: 'the civility that makes democratic politics possible can only be learned in the associational networks [of civil society]'.[39] I agree with the latter claim, which may be a little exaggerated but contains a fundamental truth. However, the former view seems to me quite mistaken, and I shall explain why.

To explain political motivation one does not need to add a shared conception of the good to liberal principles of right. Rather, one can add the colouring that liberal principles take for a given society from the specific historical narrative of their adoption. One can also add the fact that the transition to liberalism involves the avoidance

---

[39] Walzer, 'The Civil Society Argument', 104. I am trying to attach some socially and politically realistic substance to Rawls's very schematic proposal that 'To realize the full publicity condition is to realize a social world within which the ideal of citizenship can be learned and may elicit an effective desire to be that kind of person. This political conception as educator characterizes the wide role'. *Political Liberalism*, 71; see also 84 on the 'ideal of citizenship' and the discussion at lecture VI § 2. Larmore has also argued that 'the virtue of active citizenship . . . plays therefore a necessary role in liberal thought, too', 'Political Liberalism', ch. 6 of *The Morals of Modernity*, 124.

of shared common evils. The former argument has been presented by Larmore and the latter by both Shklar and Hurley.[40] Liberalism has a role for active citizenship and a shared common life, although it abstains from contested conceptions of the good. The elements that are shared are a sense of common evils in our collective life together, such as intolerance, faction, and fanaticism, and sense of freedom under the rule of law as requiring active citizenship in civil society.

The political liberal certainly ought to endorse Walzer's point that the virtues of active citizenship have to be learnt and learnt in appropriate spheres.[41] However, for the republican liberal this takes us no further than an option value rather than an integral part of the good life. I concur with Walzer that these appropriate spheres for active citizenship outside the mechanism of the state and beyond the realm of the private are located within civil society, as that idea has been conceived since the early modern period. In a Western European context two models dominate: a conception of civil society which interpenetrates political society yielding the various forms of political corporatism and those political models motivated either by left wing or right wing hostility to corporatism which clearly separate a 'self-limiting' conception of civil society from any connection with the state.[42] Both models involve the crucial element of publicity that is central to the concept of civil society and links its rise in its distinctively modern form to that of the public sphere, another distinctive product of modernity.

Which concept of civil society is required by the argument I have traced so far? I take it that a tradition which emphasizes the virtues of active citizenship will look for a self-limiting conception of civil society to prevent its co-option into the apparatus of the state. The way in which the concept of **self-limitation** is so important to the new ways of theorizing civil society after the Velvet Revolution in Eastern Europe has been described by Cohen and Arato. It is the self-understanding of participants in democratic reform that civil society best serves its democratic function if it is counterposed to, rather than absorbed into, economic and political society.[43] Civil society does not seek to supply a model of how society as a whole is to be governed: it is, rather, a check on state power, a medium for linkages between a mass population and the political elite, a channel for citizen activism and the 'schoolhouse' of citizen virtue. The liberal requirement of active citizenship could be satisfied either by a corporatist

[40] See the discussion of this point in Ch. 11, above, and Larmore, 'The Foundations of Modern Democracy'; Shklar, 'The Liberalism of Fear'.

[41] This is the central claim of Walzer, 'The Civil Society Argument'. Kymlicka and Norman, 'The Return of the Citizen' expresses scepticism on this point. But I don't think anyone need deny that there are uncivil societies and that people can learn 'not in my back yard' attitudes and illiberal forms of parochialism in their associational lives. (By direct analogy no one need deny that community is a value but that there are illiberal communities.) The issue is justificatory interdependence: justifications of liberalism appeal to civil society, but clearly explaining the word 'civil' draws on the appeal of liberalism. But that circularity is not damaging, even if in the real world it poses the practical problem that we cannot appeal to uncivil societies as schoolhouses of civic virtues, but rather their opposites. A solution to this problem could appeal to the operations of state funded schooling systems—literal schoolhouses—but addressing that issue goes beyond the scope of this book. It is taken up and developed by Amy Guttmann in *Democratic Education* (rev. edn.: Princeton: Princeton University Press, 1999).

[42] See the analysis in Arato and Cohen, *Civil Society and Political Theory*, ch. 9.

[43] Ibid., pp. 57–8, 63.

model in which free public associations are co-opted into political society to reach common economic or political ends, or by a model in which spontaneously associating groups constitute a self-regulating sphere outside political society. The point is that both of these models contrast with a libertarian vision of civil society as simply a de-politicized zone within the social where the atoms of social and political life temporarily and transiently congeal into molecules of socially coordinated activity.[44]

Thus, my account of the liberal appropriation of the concept of civil society parallels the account of liberal citizenship in that the concept proves not to be the exclusive preserve of the communitarian. To complete the envisioned rapprochement between political liberalism and one tradition of civic republicanism requires a model of liberal citizenship, which in turn requires a model of the role of the citizen in modern society. It is at this point, I would argue, that the liberal should introduce the concept of civil society.

I have introduced the concept at this stage of my argument for two reasons. First, I have attempted to clarify which aspect of the problem of political motivation the concept of civil society is introduced to solve. Secondly, with this problem understood, I can explain why an apparent weakness of the idea of civil society is in fact its central strength. That apparent weakness is the vagueness and context sensitivity of the concept and its relation to particular cultural circumstances. These features of the concept have led to the concern that a common core cannot be extracted from it that does not lose its cultural specificity.[45] There certainly is such a common core, and it was paradigmatically described by Hegel in the *Philosophy of Right*.[46] Civil society is there defined as a differentiation of concrete ethical life that reinterprets two dualities, that of oikos/polis and state/society as a threefold classification of family, civil society, and the state. Civil society is also essentially public, although this represents one of the many ambiguities in Hegel's theory. A more complex model, such as that of Cohen and Arato, complements this core concept but does not significantly alter it. Cohen and Arato introduce the additional components of 'economic' and 'political' societies to their theoretical model.[47]

---

[44] It is this account of civil society as an 'apolitical' zone of primordial liberty that has attracted critiques from the Left, such as that of Nicholas Rose, *Powers of Freedom: Reframing Political Thought* (Cambridge: Cambridge University Press, 1999) which is highly critical of contemporary appeals to community or civil society as involving a 'natural, extra-political zone of human relations', 167. Unfortunately the influence of Foucault on Rose's project takes the form of sweeping, unsupported generalizations and the total pessimism of Foucault's early work, expressed by comments such as 'The communitarian thought of Putnam, and indeed of Etzioni, does indeed appear to wish to re-invent community in a disciplinary and normalizing form', 194. Suffice to say that I am not convinced by this interpretation of Putnam, Etzioni, or, more generally, those who explain civic diversity in terms of civil society.

[45] For extensive discussion of the prospects for extending an explanatory and normative category originally at home in the early modern period in Western Europe to other geographical regions, see the essays in Sudipta Kaviraj and Sunil Khilnani (eds.), *Civil Society: History and Possibilities* (Cambridge University Press, 2001).

[46] Georg Wilhelm Friedrich Hegel, *Elements of the Philosophy of Right*, ed. Allen Wood, Quentin Skinner, and Raymond Geuss, trans. H. B. Nisbet (Cambridge: Cambridge University Press, 1991), esp. 'Third Part: Ethical Life' sect. ii 'Civil Society'.

[47] Cohen and Arato, *Civil Society and Political Theory*, 74–81.

I take it that it is no accident that Rawlsian political liberalism should, at this stage of its development, end up appealing to a concept developed by Hegel. For, as Joshua Cohen insightfully points out, Rawls's emphasis on normative consensus recapitulates this concern expressed at an earlier stage of Western political theory:

Hegel [concluded] . . . that it was necessary to reformulate the classical ideal of a political community organized around a moral consensus in light of the modern distinction between the unity of political agency and the diversity of civil society.[48]

As Cohen points out, Hegel's particular solution to this problem divided two aspects of social life, placing civic diversity and political unity side by side. But he also accepted that the civic diversity that he envisaged would be 'substantially inegalitarian', as Cohen puts it. This seems to follow from the division of social life into these two aspects. Indeed, concern about this inegalitarianism and its socially disintegrative force was counterbalanced by a politically authoritarian and conservative account of monarchical power. The Rawlsian project has come to face a similar theoretical problem and is now, Cohen argues, confronted with a parallel objection to that which Marx developed against Hegel.[49] I have already, in the previous chapter, discussed the concern that Rawls's goal of normative consensus leads to a compromise with his egalitarianism and have sided with those, such as Estlund, who take this claim to be mistaken. This chapter focuses on the account of civic diversity implicit in Rawls's view that must be made explicit if one is to defend Rawls's demanding politically liberal conception of citizenship.

Another prominent line of criticism of any appeal to the idea of civil society is that the core sense of the concept fails to do justice to the historical specificity of its development. A recurrent concern of historicist critics is that the concept as it figures in contemporary discussion is too closely tied to the historical specificities of early modern Europe for it to be of general theoretical usefulness.[50] There is a parallel argument which one might describe as 'regionalist' rather than historicist, which ties the role of the concept to the way it structures the historical traditions of particular regions.[51] By contrast, the argument I have pursued suggests that this is, in fact, the central strength of civil society within liberal theory. Its role is to delimit that part of society, beyond the state, in which citizen virtue is developed and which is shaped by a common culture in such a way that it informs the basis of political motivation for those living in that very culture. My argument is that for the purposes of a theory of liberal

---

48 Cohen, 'Moral Pluralism and Political Consensus', 276–7.

49 Ibid.

50 The leading such sceptic is Adam Seligman. For a convincing reply see John Keane, who accuses Seligman—justly in my view—of an inappropriate kind of foundationalism concerning the justification of an appeal to civil society as an explanatory or normative category. Seligman's scepticism is the central theme of *The Idea of Civil Society* where he argues that civil society was so closely tied to the conditions of its historical emergence that it is a mistake to identity the same phenomenon in contemporary conditions; for Keane's reply see *Civil Society: Old Images, New Visions*, 56 ff.

51 For historicist and regionalist analyses, see Jenö Szücs, 'Three Historical Regions of Europe', *Acta Historica Scientiarum Hungaricae*, 29 (1983), 131–84 and Mihaly Vajda, 'East-Central European Perspectives', in John Keane (ed.), *Civil Society and the State* (London: Verso Press, 1988), 333–360.

democracy, this dual role of the concept is its central strength. It is an appropriate setting for the liberal normative ideal of active citizenship, while also being shaped by local and particular circumstances in the way that I have suggested individual liberal settlements for particular societies are shaped by their actual history. There is also a connection between invoking civil society and a liberalism based on a shared recognition of common political and social evils. One pathway through the plethora of competing definitions of civil society is to note its recurrent use as a contrastive term. Throughout modern Western political theory, civil society is usually contrasted with despotism, fanaticism, and factionalism.[52]

The model I have sketched shows how the liberal can appropriate the concept of civil society and the advantages of doing so. However, this will avail my overall argument little if the concept reproduces the same internal tension that generated the liberal/communitarian dispute in the first place. Taylor seems to present this argument in his important paper 'Invoking Civil Society'.[53] He traces the historical evolution of the concept and argues that the Hegelian analysis runs together two quite different conceptions stemming from Locke and Montesquieu. The Lockean conception of civil society is of a social reality that is not coterminous with sovereign power, as in Hobbes, but rather which is constituted by the following: a realm of subjective rights enjoined by natural law, an autonomous economy, and the public sphere, site of a novel modern concept of 'public opinion'. This permits the idea that secular social purposes can be carried on outside the sphere of the political, and it is a prescient concept that awaits reinforcement by another modern phenomenon, nationalism.

The Tocquevillean criticism of this form of civil society is reiterated by Taylor: that it leads to a conception of public, extra-political interests outside the state that can develop into either radical self-determination and the absorption of the state into the general will of society, or the marginalization of the political. In the latter case the concept of the political becomes so marginalized that citizens of a modern polity suffer from

[A] kind of mild despotism in which citizens fall prey to a tutelary power that dwarfs them; and this is both cause and effect of a turn away from the public to the private which, although tempting, represents a diminution of their human stature.[54]

Taylor invokes instead a communitarian concept of civil society indebted to Montesquieu and de Tocqueville. That tradition emphasizes the role of egalitarian free institutions as the bulwark against despotism. However, Taylor does not, in fact, find the concept of civil society to be internally incoherent. He does concede that the Lockean conception is so deeply entrenched in our understanding of civil society that the Tocquevillean tradition is at best a complement to it.

The real contrast is not between a communitarian and a liberal concept of civil society. It is, rather, between both those traditions and a libertarian conception of

---

[52] For one exploration of this approach to the concept see Dominique Colas, *Civil Society and Fanaticism: Conjoined Histories* (Stanford, Calif.: Stanford University Press, 1997).

[53] Taylor, 'Invoking Civil Society', *Philosophical Arguments*, 204–24.

[54] Ibid., 221.

a wholly privatized and de-politicized public sphere. Here again the liberal and the communitarian seem to have a great deal in common when opposed to a common enemy, in this case a libertarian refusal to develop a concept of civil society that interpenetrates political and economic society, replacing it with a purely privatized extra-political reality conjoined with an autonomous market mechanism. Once again, though, the distance Taylor puts between his position and that of the political liberal seems to me to be artificial. If the point is that the institutions of civil society must be egalitarian, that is secured by the liberal's insistence on the value of equal respect, which would be violated if there were inegalitarian institutions of civil society.[55]

An important functional role of civil society is to make public deliberation about politics possible: it is the place where the capacities of active citizenship are made available to those who wish to participate, understanding that idea as broadly as possible.[56] The role of public deliberation is to provide a channel for organizations in civil society to provide the kind of check on the exercise of political power that is a distinctive advantage of traditional republicanism. Citizens in a mass society require a means of communicating with a political elite; organizations in civil society which impinge on the political process either through the representation of interests or explicit lobbying offer such a channel. This is particularly true in the case of mass membership organizations, often called 'new social movements', such as feminism or environmentalism.[57]

But in each case civil society is self-limiting in that it forms part of a systematic arrangement of our collective political life, broadly conceived, that does not see its culmination in the form of a radically participatory democratic process. It rather supplies a constant flow of information, and hence political pressure, on a society's political and administrative elites. Alongside the other distinctively modern development, the public sphere, civil society offers a channel of communication between political elites and mass pressure. This leads both to the reshaping of political agendas and a check on the use of state power.[58] But it does not seek to replace that power and to become, itself, the basis of political authority. Alongside these generally valuable features of civil society I have argued, in particular, that civil society is the 'schoolhouse'

---

[55] A reminder that, not for the first time in this book, there is a virtuous circularity between civil society's role in explaining how political liberalism is possible, and the application of a conception of justice embedded within political liberalism to the question of what makes a society civil as opposed to uncivil.

[56] If participation is made as broad as active and ongoing political involvement then we are back with Taylor's perfectionist version of republicanism. The aim is to honour an option value and to give people the virtues and skills to participate if they choose to do so, and a sense, as MacIntyre might put it, of the goods internal to the social practice of involvement and participation.

[57] Such new social movements are central to the arguments of Cohen and Arato in *Civil Society and Political Theory*, ch. 10, who look to them to supply the emancipatory potential missing from neo-Marxist theory given the historically somewhat disappointing performance of the traditional proletariat. For a caustic evaluation of their appeal to this replacement for the proletariat see Hudson Meadwell, 'Post-Marxism: No Friend of Civil Society', in Hall (ed.), *Civil Society: Theory, History, Comparison*, 183–99.

[58] Interestingly discussed in an earlier textbook by Robert D. Putnam, esp. the chapter on 'elite-mass linkages' in his *The Comparative Study of Political Elites* (Englewood Cliffs, NJ and London: Prentice-Hall, 1976).

of political virtue in such a way that political liberalism can begin to develop a plausible case that its demanding account of citizenship and motivation can actually be realized. That is the central reason why a political liberal needs to extend his or her view to give an account of civil society and of citizenship. But he or she should be happy to accept the other beneficial aspects of a high level of development of associational life as a whole: increased impersonal trust, increased social capital, and a higher level of democratic accountability.[59]

5. LIBERALISM, NEUTRALITY, AND ENTRENCHMENT

The arguments set out so far here and in the previous chapter have sought to defend the claim that our best political theory, that which is most stable under reflection, is political liberalism. That theory is strengthened by its contextual justification. The politicization of justice and its modular function can be defended from internal critiques, modulo some of the necessary revisions to Rawls's views described in this part of my book.

This chapter has sought to remedy a damaging incompleteness in the theory. Part of this defence has been to acknowledge the fact that it is, in a sense, *reasonably* demanding and not a retreat from the commitments of *A Theory of Justice*. As John Tomasi has pointed out, any reflection on that which Rawls's later theory demands of a politically liberal citizen makes it an unlikely flaccid defender of the political status quo, devoid of any critical edge.[60] It is certainly a *demanding* view. The politically liberal state places strong demands on its citizens and in this way is implicitly committed to ensuring that the moral background culture of the society for which it is a theory must offer a hospitable basis for such citizenship. Working within, and not against, the central claims of political liberalism, I have attempted in this chapter to explain how the political liberal encourages associational life as an option value, not as the strongly convergent good of realizing an important aspect of one's identity in political participation. (Once again, as in the previous chapter, a clear distinction *between* morality and politics is important to this argument.)

However, Tomasi is also the author of an important critical argument that challenges any complacency as to whether the political liberal, having co-opted these key republican themes, has a fully defensible view.[61] What is deeply interesting about his arguments is that they seem closely analogous to the communitarian critique of liberalism, but come into play *after* justice has been politicized. I did not concede that the politicization of justice was itself a response to communitarianism, but I did argue

---

[59] For a characterization of these multiple benefits of a high level of social capital, see not only Putnam's *Bowling Alone* but also Arend Lijphart's *Patterns of Democracy: Government Forms and Performance in Thirty-Six Countries* (New Haven and London: Yale University Press, 1999) which argues that the more consensual, participative, and democratic a society, the more successful it is across a wide range of socio-economic indicators, conclusions summarized in ch. 16, 'The Quality of Democracy and a "Kinder, Gentler" Democracy: Consensus Democracy Makes A Difference'.

[60] Tomasi, *Liberalism Beyond Justice*, pp. xvii, 9.

[61] Ibid., ch. 3.

that there is one important line of communitarian argument, focused on the motivation problem, that should concern all liberals. In addition, there is clearly a close connection between the motivation problem and the issues of legitimacy that were a central motivation of the politicization of justice: which motivations is it unreasonably demanding to put before a politically liberal citizen?

Tomasi offers an insightful account of the politicization of justice and the way in which it is contextually justified.[62] But his concern is that, practically, there is little difference between the way in which political liberalism entrenches itself in the ethical background culture of a society and the way in which a more explicitly ethical liberalism does so. Ethical liberals are quite open about the way in which their view has an impact on how people lead their lives in a liberal state. Stephen Macedo once provocatively claimed that 'liberalism holds out the promise, or maybe the threat, of making all the world like California'.[63] The political liberal, however, claims to be in a different position. He or she claims that the motivation for politicizing justice was to broaden the appeal of liberal justification.[64] Political liberalism is explicit in promoting neutrality of aim, but not neutrality of effect. It openly acknowledges that the acceptance of a politically liberal system of justice in a society will have an impact on the ethical background culture of a particular society, but that seems to Rawls inevitable:

It is surely impossible for the basic structure of a just constitutional regime not to have important effects and influences as to which comprehensive doctrines endure and gain adherents over time, and it is futile to try to counteract these effects and influences, or even to ascertain for political purposes how deep and pervasive they are. We must accept the facts of commonsense political sociology . . . Neutrality of effect or influence political liberalism abandons as impracticable.[65]

It also seems that whatever impact political liberalism has on the ethical background culture of a society, it will have *less* impact than ethical liberalism. The ethical liberal is explicitly in the business of promoting a liberal form of life and its social preconditions and in dissuading other forms of life. But Tomasi argues that this contrast is misleading: political liberalism, in spite of its avowed breadth of appeal, will have 'spillover effects' on the ethical background culture of the society it governs that will undercut its broad appeal, make its own justification circular, and put certain forms of social life that are independently valuable in danger of social extinction. Tomasi argues that in fact political liberalism does clearly have a 'liberal virtue ethic' of its own; that which the justificatory structure of political liberalism achieves is simply to locate this part of the theory in a different place.[66]

The overall effect, then, of Tomasi's arguments is a position similar to my own. Tomasi adds to an account of political liberalism a view of citizenship, but one explicitly intended to be developed within the constraints of political liberalism. Furthermore, both he and I are concerned with the relationship between political liberalism and the background ethical culture of the society it governs, particularly

---

[62] Ibid., chs. 2 and 3.   [63] Macedo, *Liberal Virtues*, 278.
[64] See e.g. Rawls, *Political Liberalism*, p. xx.   [65] Ibid. 193.
[66] Tomasi, *Liberalism Beyond Justice*, 39.

as addressed to the question as to how the formation of politically liberal citizens is so much as possible. But at that point the similarity ends. I am not convinced by Tomasi's argument that, in practice, ethical liberalism and political liberalism come to the same thing and I will explain why.

I agree that there is more to liberalism than merely justice: if anything, the closer tie is between liberalism and dominant views of legitimacy current in our culture. Tomasi complains that some contemporary liberal theorizing has become fixated on justice or on egalitarianism to the exclusion of other liberal ideals and there is clearly some justice to that charge.[67] But as Estlund pointed out, the whole point of the shift in Rawls's thinking was to preserve a conception of justice and to embed it in a wider account of liberal legitimacy. However, in that widening of focus, there is no need, I would argue, to take Rawls's view about the stringency of the demands of political responsibility reflected in his conception of the subject matter of justice also to be extensible to that wider issue of legitimacy.

One major division between contemporary liberals concerns the relative funda-mentality of responsibility in his or her overall theory.[68] Rawls took the view that the theory of justice applied to what he called the basic structure of society; this was one of his radical innovations.[69] Familiarity with Rawls's work as a whole has led to this innovative proposal being taken for granted, although neo-Marxist criticism of the egalitarianism of Rawls's second principle, the difference principle, has led to explicit focus on whether this restriction on the scope of justice is defensible.[70] Rawls has various different arguments justifying how he conceives of the subject matter of justice, but it is clear that given how he does see that subject matter, issues of respons-ibility at the individual level arise after we have implemented a given conception of justice within a particular society and its institutional structures.[71] Once these struc-tures are in place, we can begin to talk about individual responsibility and legitimate expectation.[72] But at the level of society as a whole, the Rawlsian state functions as

---

[67] Tomasi, *Liberalism Beyond Justice*, 'High Liberalism', ch. 6.

[68] As insightfully discussed by Samuel Scheffler, in 'Responsibility, Reactive Attitudes and Liberalism in Philosophy and Politics', *Boundaries and Allegiances*, 12–31.

[69] See Rawls, 'The Basic Structure As Subject', in *Political Liberalism*, ch. 7.

[70] The neo-Marxist critique is that of G. A. Cohen. It is, in some respects, like Scheffler's critique of political liberalism in that it appeals to the need for a background social ethos to correct for perceived defects in Rawls's egalitarianism. However, Cohen's wider ranging critique appeals to an egalitarian ethos to remedy what he takes to be the inegalitarian implications of Rawls's conception of justice, particularly the difference principle (a conception unchanged between *A Theory of Justice* and *Political Liberalism*). I discuss Cohen's critique in 'Cohen's Critique of Rawls: A "Double Counting" Objection'.

[71] See Scheffler, 'Responsibility, Reactive Attitudes and Liberalism in Philosophy and Politics', 17–18, for an analysis of Rawls's 'institutional theory of desert'.

[72] Philippe van Parijs has also pointed out that the usual contrast between Rawls's responsibility insensitive form of liberal egalitarianism and other forms, such as Dworkin's 'responsibility sensitive' egalitarianism, is an overdrawn comparison. That is because, as van Parijs points out, 'correctly understood, the difference principle is therefore far more responsibility-friendly (or ambition sensitive) and hence less egalitarian in outcome terms than it is often taken to be', van Parijs, 'Difference Principles', in Samuel Freeman (ed.), *The Cambridge Companion to Rawls* (Cambridge: Cambridge University Press, 2003), 200–40 quotation from 216, summarizing the argument of 213–16.

our collective agent. The state is, at that level, as responsible for that which it fails to prevent as that which it brings about.[73] Rawls took this particular view of the relationship between political action and responsibility because he was solely concerned with justice and conceived of the basic structure as its subject matter.

Tomasi seeks, in his account of political liberalism, to exploit that aspect of Rawls's views and to turn it against the project of legitimizing political liberalism as a whole. He takes this approach to responsibility that seems integral to Rawls's conception of justice and applies it to the wider issue of legitimacy. The result is a parallel argument to Rawls's treatment of individual responsibility in which the state, as our collective agent, is as responsible for that which it fails to prevent as that which it brings about. This point is applied by Tomasi to the issue that ought to separate political liberalism from ethical liberalism, namely, the fate under political liberalism of those that Rawls called 'citizens of faith' and Larmore calls 'reasonable Romantics'.[74]

[They] may affirm some general ethical doctrine that is based on religious authority—for example, the Church or the Bible. [They] may affirm traditionalist doctrines that impose social roles on persons or generate moral conclusions regarding them, which turn on people's gender, religious heritage, or sexual orientation. . . . [They] do not demand that those elements of their worldview be enforced coercively against citizens who do not accept the 'truth' as they see it. Nor do they seek selectively to deny the primacy of political values whenever those values do not mirror the nonpublic view they affirm. For example, if [they] affirm a normative system of social roles based on gender, they do so only concerning the nonpublic aspects of their lives, the internal life of their families as well as more voluntary organizations such as clubs and churches.[75]

Tomasi argues that under the conditions of political liberalism, such forms of life, which are independently valuable, will fare badly. Furthermore, this undermines political liberalism because it has to be held accountable for spillover effects in the ethical background culture with which it is associated.[76] It cannot get itself off the hook by appealing to the distinction between neutrality of aim and neutrality of effect, arguing that the latter is simply impracticable and then appealing to Berlin's point that the aim was never to accommodate every valuable form of living together that people can devise. That distinction simply *is* the distinction between doing and allowing applied to the actions of the state.

This is a challenging argument, and political liberals have to take it seriously. It parallels wider concerns about Rawls's egalitarianism and raises many of the same issues as neo-Marxist critiques of the content of Rawls's view.[77] But it does seem to

[73] This is very helpfully discussed by Thomas Nagel, in *Equality and Partiality*, 99–100.

[74] Rawls, 'Introduction' to the paperback edn. of *Political Liberalism*, (1996) p. xlv.

[75] Tomasi, *Liberalism Beyond Justice*, 18.

[76] Ibid., 33–9.

[77] The central point of convergence is taking Rawls's coordinated accounts of responsibility and the subject matter of justice and denying that they are related as he supposed. This denial aims radically to expand the scope of responsibility, either at the level of our collective responsibility for the 'free erosion' of valuable forms of life, or at the level of individual economic decisions. But Jerry Cohen's arguments have met with some powerful objections based precisely on how Rawls conceives of the subject matter of justice, namely, as a society's basic structure. The most well-known 'basic

me equally ill-founded: the irony is that Rawls's demanding account of responsibility was restricted precisely to issues about justice and not extensible to the wider question of liberal legitimacy. After all, Rawls had very precise reasons for his innovation in the treatment of the subject matter of justice: the basic structure, as he conceives of it, has such a deep and long-lasting effect on people's life chances that he had basically a moral rationale for making it the exclusive subject matter of justice.[78] However, Rawls made very special assumptions about the society to which he applied his conception: one of the very misleading aspects of his self-presentation as a contract theorist is that a Rawlsian society is nothing like a voluntary association.[79] Political communities, as we know them, have boundaries, a value to membership, and processes of emigration and immigration: a Rawlsian society is an idealization that people enter with birth and leave with death. They do not, in that sense, 'contract in' to such a society.[80] These two points come together in the reflection that a basic structure is *not* a voluntary association, made up of individuals 'contracting in' to it, and that is precisely why such a demanding concept of responsibility is appropriate to it. It has a deep and lasting influence on people's life prospects and we would like a basic structure with such profound impact on people's lives to be voluntarily underwritten, but it cannot be so underwritten.[81] But within its scope, we are free to impose a demanding sense of political responsibility to reflect its unique nature and importance.

These very special assumptions of Rawls's conception seem to me damaging to any attempt to say that liberals as a whole, or political liberals in particular, have to obliterate the distinction between that which the liberal state brings about and that which

structure' response is that of Andrew Williams in 'Incentives, Inequality and Publicity', *Philosophy and Public Affairs*, 27/3 (Summer 1998), 225–47. I discuss this line of response in 'Cohen's Critique of Rawls: A Double Counting Objection'.

[78] Rawls gave his rationale as follows: '[the] basic structure is the primary subject of justice because its effects are so profound and present from the start', *A Theory of Justice*, 7.

[79] For another excellent reason why it is misleading to treat Rawls as a contract theorist see Jean Hampton, 'Contracts and Choices: Does Rawls Have a Social Contract Theory?', *Journal of Philosophy* 77/6 (June 1980), 315–38.

[80] For Rawls's most developed remarks on why he does not view society as a voluntary association in the usual sense, see *Political Liberalism*, ch. 1, § 7. In an influential series of papers on the liberal/communitarian dispute, Walzer criticizes traditional liberalism for overemphasizing a model of society as a contractual arrangement, leading to a misrepresentation of our contingent and involuntary associative obligations. See Liberalism and the Art of Separation', *Political Theory*, 12 (Aug. 1984), 315–30; 'Philosophy and Democracy', *Political Theory*, 9 (Aug. 1981), 379–99; 'The Communitarian Critique of Liberalism', *Political Theory*, 18/1 (Feb. 1990), 6–23; and *Politics and Passion*. What liberals ought more clearly to value, Walzer argues, is the right to break any such tie—a 'transgressive' model of the self. But these remarks cannot apply to Rawls, not simply because he makes no claims about the self, but because the subject matter of justice is not, for him, a voluntary association or significantly analogous to one. In his most recent *Politics and Passion* Walzer identifies the target of his critique as 'standard liberalism'. In fact the actual argument of his book, such as its insightful account of powerless, stigmatized, and hence unequal involuntary groups in ch. 2, seems to be a *supplement* to liberal optimism. It is a supplement that works by extending liberal accounts of emancipation (for example, through associational life) to involuntary groups unified solely by being stigmatized and oppressed as a group via an 'empowerment model'.

[81] There is once again a very insightful discussion of this point in Nagel's *Equality and Partiality*, e.g. 'The search for legitimacy can be thought of as an attempt to realise some of the values of voluntary participation, in a system of institutions that is unavoidably compulsory', 36.

it fails to permit in the restricted context of a theory of liberal legitimacy. On this wider issue Rawls's views are *less* demanding, but then the wider issue is precisely one on which every liberal has to have a view, not simply the Rawlsian. How a conception of liberal equality handles the issue of responsibility may well divide different kinds of liberal egalitarianism from each other, but that is no reason to take Rawls's distinctive treatment of the issue at the level of his particular conception of justice and to take him to apply those views to the theory of legitimacy itself. I conclude that Rawls is not guilty of any inconsistency when he claims that he *can* draw a distinction between neutrality of aim and neutrality of effect.

I have argued that political liberalism has to be extended to give an account of its own preconditions within the moral background culture, but I was careful to restrict that which the political liberal promotes, namely, associational life and the basis of active citizenship, viewed as an option value. But I do not see that process as extending to a refashioning of background culture in political liberalism's own image, as Tomasi seems to envisage. There is, on the view that I have defended, still a clear difference between the degree of impact that political liberalism will have on background culture and the degree of impact that ethical liberalism will have. There is nothing objectionable about political liberalism shaping background culture such as to make *itself* possible. It begins from a set of contextually basic ideas about political society, gives a bootstrapping justification from those ideas to a politicized conception of justice, and then goes on to supplement the overall view with an account of its own presuppositions. That is not damagingly circular: the only part of the ethical background culture that political liberalism directly affects is the very narrow set of ideas that makes itself possible. That is not to remould society as a whole in its own image. It supports only those 'weak and widely shared' political ideas from which it begins.

Tomasi concedes that his argument takes place on the uncertain 'sandy ground' of political sociology and I agree that there has to be some indeterminacy in claiming that one view or the other of the sociological effects of adopting political liberalism is correct or incorrect.[82] But I have reiterated two of Rawls's most important points about the relationship between a political theory and a moral background culture: that no political theory takes up a view from nowhere in which every valuable form of political life can be accommodated in a single political space and that it is unrealistic not to expect there to be sociological effects from the adoption of political liberalism. There is, then, an indeterminate range between the unrealizable ambition of incorporating every valuable form of life into a political society and the undesirable ideal of adopting an ethically liberal view that remakes its own social preconditions in its own image, such that it violates constraints on legitimacy. But I see no reason to concede that the political liberal does not get this right: that he or she puts forward a view which is, in a sense, self-sustaining in that it intervenes in an ethical background culture solely to make itself possible. But the associational life and active citizenship that it promotes makes other things possible too, and political liberalism

---

[82] Tomasi, *Liberalism Beyond Justice*, 18.

is importantly self-limiting or self-correcting.[83] As Tomasi argues, if its derived conception of citizenship is subject to its own strictures, then it cannot become in effect as self-entrenching through time as a reasonable comprehensive moral view.

The deep disagreement, then, between Tomasi and myself is over the role of citizenship which he sees as potentially undermining of political liberalism in the long run and which I have argued is a deliberately restricted option value for the political liberal. I take it Tomasi and I are in agreement that simply because Rawls treats of a restrictive subject matter, the basic structure of society, his position may need to draw on a far wider range of assumptions to make itself a plausible explanation of that precisely delimited subject matter. But Tomasi takes Rawls's claim that it is difficult, in the case of state action directed towards the basic structure, to separate acts from omissions, as a Trojan horse for reformulated communitarian critique. This is the much wider claim that Rawlsian liberalism cannot make this distinction between acts and omissions even when it deals more widely with its own preconditions. That is, I think, an unfounded extension of Rawls's claim and that is why, in this book, while I have extended Rawlsian liberalism towards an account of citizenship and civil society I have taken this account to be subject to the constraints on legitimacy central to the politicization of justice. It is only the liberal republicanism indebted more to Machiavelli than to Rousseau which treats political participation as an option value that liberal republicanism has to sustain that can both extend Rawls's views, as they need to be extended, but also respect the constraints on a legitimate political theory. I would argue that while Tomasi's identification of the problems that may arise after the politicization of justice is insightful, it is the view defended in this book that is the more defensible solution of those problems.

CONCLUSION

I have in this chapter sought to extend political liberalism in order to show how it can give an account of its own preconditions. The motivation problem can be solved by appropriating one tradition of civic republicanism, but doing so while observing the constraints on an acceptable theory developed in the contextual defence of political liberalism in the previous chapter. The motivation problem can be solved within the ambit of political liberalism by determining its own conceptions of citizenship and civil society. The upshot is a liberal republicanism that is, in a sense, self-embedding through time. But this kind of circularity, which is inherent in the project of contextual justification via traditions of enquiry, is not, I have argued, an objectionable circularity.

---

[83] It is 'self-limiting' in that it honours, and does not promote, those values of active citizenship and participation that make it possible, even if an attitude of promotion—perhaps via legal coercion—might be more practically effective measured in purely consequentialist terms.

Conclusion

In this book I have tried to put an epistemological outlook to work in resolving some of the most difficult issues surrounding the idea of moral objectivity and the justification of political principles. The aim was not to offer a complete defence of epistemological contextualism in its own right, but to show how existing arguments for contextual models of justification can be consolidated when that approach yields rich dividends in moral and political philosophy.

I have not, at any stage of this book, attempted a comprehensive account of 'the scientific' alongside my account of the 'ethical' and related issues in political philosophy. I have suggested, however, that properly to understand the deepest challenge to moral cognitivism, the non-objectivist critique developed by Bernard Williams, his views need to be detached from any argument that he is tacitly committed to an externally realist view which, of its nature, sets the demands for moral cognitivism too high. The non-objectivist critique of moral cognitivism has been the central thread of this book. Rebutting it has been a lengthy task, but valuable not least because any plausible defence of moral cognitivism has to incorporate the insights of Williams's critique. In particular, it has particularly to address the demands of giving an account of ethical justification in the distinctive context of a modern society. That issue proved equally central to the arguments in Part IV that were broadly supportive of a Rawlsian approach to liberalism, supplemented by aspects of the civic republican tradition. Overall, the argument of this book has attempted to vindicate cognitivism in moral and political philosophy by arguing that modernity is not a distinctively hostile place for such claims. That offers a limited degree of reassurance for a task beyond the scope of this book; the task, as Alasdair MacIntyre described it, of reflective living. Only in that task will the claim that we possess significant amounts of moral and political knowledge achieve a final vindication. That task, however, is beyond the scope of this book. It lies beyond the limits of philosophical reflection.

List of Works Cited

Altham, J. E. J., 'Reflection and Confidence', in Altham and Harrison (eds.), *World, Mind and Ethics*, 156–69.

_____ and Harrison, T. R. (eds.), *World, Mind and Ethics: Essays on the Ethical Philosophy of Bernard Williams* (Cambridge: Cambridge University Press, 1995).

Anderson, E., *Value in Ethics and in Economics* (Cambridge, Mass.: Harvard University Press, 1993).

Annis, D. B., 'A Contextualist Theory of Epistemic Justification', *American Philosophical Quarterly*, 15/3 (July 1978), 213–19.

Anscombe, G. E. M., *Intention* (Ithaca, NY: Cornell University Press, 1957).

_____ *An Introduction to Wittgenstein's Tractatus* (London: Hutchinson, 1967).

Arato, A., and Cohen, J., *Civil Society and Political Theory* (Cambridge, Mass.: MIT Press, 1992).

Aristotle, *Nicomachean Ethics*, trans. J. A. K. Thompson (London: Penguin Classics, 2004).

Audi, R., 'Intuitionism, Pluralism and the Foundations of Ethics', in Sinnott-Armstrong and Timmons (eds.), *Moral Knowledge?*, 101–36.

_____ 'A Kantian Intuitionism', *Mind*, 110/439 (July 2001), 601–35.

_____ *The Good in the Right: A Theory of Intuition and Intrinsic Value* (Princeton and Oxford: Princeton University Press, 2004).

Austin, J. L., *Philosophical Papers* (Oxford: Oxford University Press, 1961).

Baker, G., and Hacker, P., *Language, Sense and Nonsense* (Oxford: Basil Blackwell, 1984).

Ball, T., Farr, J., and Hanson, R. (eds.), *Political Innovation and Conceptual Change* (Cambridge: Cambridge University Press, 1989).

Bambrough, R., *Moral Scepticism and Moral Knowledge* (London: Routledge, 1979).

Batens, D., 'Do We Need a Hierarchical Model of Science?', in Earman (ed.), *Inference, Explanation and Other Frustrations*, 199–215.

Baynes, K., Bohman, J., and McCarthy, T. (eds.), *After Philosophy: End Or Transformation* (Cambridge, Mass.: MIT Press, 1987).

Beehler, R., *Moral Life* (Oxford: Basil Blackwell, 1978).

Berlin, I., *Four Essays on Liberty* (Oxford: Oxford University Press, 1969).

_____ 'The Originality of Machiavelli', in Gilmore (ed.), *Studies On Machiavelli*, 147–206.

Bhargava, R., Bagchi, A. K., and Sudarshan, R. (eds.), *Multiculturalism, Liberalism and Democracy* (New Delhi: Oxford University Press: 2000).

Black, M. (ed.), *The Importance of Language* (Englewood Cliffs, NJ: Prentice-Hall, 1960).

Blackburn, S., 'Rule Following and Moral Realism', in Holtzmann and Leich (eds.), *Wittgenstein: To Follow a Rule*, 163–87.

_____ *Spreading the Word* (Oxford: Oxford University Press, 1984).

_____ 'Making Ends Meet', *Philosophical Books*, 27/4 (Oct. 1986), 193–203.

_____ *Essays in Quasi-Realism* (Oxford: Oxford University Press, 1993).

_____ 'The Land of Lost Content', in Frey and Morris (eds.), *Value, Welfare and Morality*, 13–25.

_____ *Ruling Passions* (Oxford: Oxford University Press, 1999).

_____ 'Options for the World', unpublished MS (n.d.).

Bock, G., Skinner, Q., and Viroli, M. (eds.), *Machiavelli and Republicanism* (Cambridge: Cambridge University Press, 1990).

Boghossian, P., and Velleman, D., 'Colour as a Secondary Quality', *Mind*, 98/389 (Jan. 1989), 81–103.

——and Peacocke, C. (eds.), *New Essays on the A Priori* (Oxford: Oxford University Press, 2000).

Bonevac, D., 'Reflection Without Equilibrium', *Journal of Philosophy*, 101/7 (July 2004), 363–88.

Bonjour, L., *The Structure of Empirical Knowledge* (Cambridge, Mass.: Harvard University Press, 1985).

Boyd, R., 'Realism, Underdetermination, and a Causal Theory of Evidence', *Noûs*, 7 (Mar. 1973), 1–12.

——'How to Be a Moral Realist', in Sayre-McCord (ed.), *Essays on Moral Realism*, 131–98.

Brink, D., *Moral Realism and the Foundations of Ethics* (Cambridge: Cambridge University Press, 1989).

Broackes, J., 'The Autonomy of Colour', in Lennon and Charles (eds.), *Reduction, Explanation and Realism*, 421–67.

Brower, B., 'Virtue Concepts and Ethical Realism', *Journal of Philosophy*, 85/12 (Dec. 1988), 675–93.

——'Dispositional Ethical Realism', *Ethics*, 103/2 (Jan. 1993), 221–49.

Brown, S. C. (ed.), *Objectivity and Cultural Divergence* (Cambridge: Cambridge University Press, 1984).

Campbell, J., 'A Simple View of Colour', in Haldane and Wright (eds.), *Reality, Representation and Projection*, 257–68.

Carnap, R., *Meaning and Necessity: A Study in Semantics and Modal Logic*, 2nd edn. (Chicago: University of Chicago Press, 1988).

——*The Logical Syntax of Language*, trans. A. Smeaton (London: Routledge, 2000).

Cassam, Q., 'Transcendental Arguments, Transcendental Synthesis and Transcendental Idealism', *Philosophical Quarterly*, 37/149 (Oct. 1982), 355–78.

Cavell, S., *This New Yet Unapproachable America* (Albuquerque, N. Mex.: Living Batch Press, 1989).

——*Conditions Handsome and Unhandsome* (Chicago: University of Chicago Press, 1990).

——*The Claim of Reason: Wittgenstein, Scepticism, Morality and Tragedy* (Oxford: Oxford University Press, 1999).

——*Must We Mean What We Say?*, updated edn. (Cambridge: Cambridge University Press, 2002).

Child, W., *Causality, Interpretation and the Mind* (Oxford: Oxford University Press, 1995).

Coetzee, J. M., *The Lives of Animals* (Princeton and Oxford: Princeton University Press, 2001).

Cohen, G. A., 'Where the Action Is: On the Site of Distributive Justice', *Philosophy and Public Affairs*, 26/1 (Winter 1997), 3–30.

——*'If You're An Egalitarian, How Come You're So Rich?'*, (Cambridge, Mass.: Harvard University Press, 2000).

Cohen, J., 'The Arc of the Moral Universe', in Lott (ed.), *Subjugation and Bondage*, 281–328.

——'Moral Pluralism and Political Consensus', in Copp (ed.), *The Idea of Democracy*, 281–4.

Cohon, R., 'Are External Reasons Impossible?', *Ethics*, 96/3 (Apr. 1986), 545–56.

Colas, D., *Civil Society and Fanaticism: Conjoined Histories* (Stanford, Calif.: Stanford University Press, 1997).

Copp, D. (ed.), *The Idea of Democracy* (Cambridge: Cambridge University Press, 1993).

_____ 'Moral Knowledge in Society Centred Moral Theory', in Sinnott-Armstrong and Timmons (eds.), *Moral Knowledge?*, 243–66.

_____ *Morality, Normativity and Society* (Oxford: Oxford University Press, 1995).

_____ and Zimmerman, D. (eds.), *Morality, Reason and Truth* (Totowa, NJ: Rowman and Allenfeld, 1985).

Craig, E., *Knowledge and the State of Nature* (Oxford: Oxford University Press, 1990).

Crisp, R., 'Naturalism and Non-Naturalism in Ethics', in Lovibond and Williams (eds.), *Essays for David Wiggins*, 113–29.

_____ and Hooker, B. (eds.), *Morality and Well Being: Essays in Honour of James Griffin* (Oxford: Oxford University Press, 2000).

Cullity, G., and Gaut, B. (eds.), *Ethics and Practical Reason* (Oxford: Oxford University Press, 1997).

Dagger, R., *Civic Virtues: Rights, Citizenship and Republican Liberalism* (Oxford: Oxford University Press, 1997).

Dancy, J., *Moral Reasons* (Oxford: Blackwell Publishers 1993).

_____ *Practical Reality* (Oxford: Oxford University Press, 2000).

_____ *Ethics Without Principles* (Oxford: Oxford University Press, 2004).

Daniels, N. (ed.), *Reading Rawls* (New York: Basic Books, 1975).

_____ *Justice and Justification: Reflective Equilibrium in Theory and Practice* (Cambridge: Cambridge University Press, 1996).

Darwall, S., *The British Moralists and the Internal 'Ought', 1640–1740* (Cambridge: Cambridge University Press, 1995).

_____ Gibbard, A., and Railton, P., 'Toward *Fin de Siècle* Ethics: Some Trends', *Philosophical Review*, 101/1 (Jan. 1992), 115–89.

Davidson, D., *Essays on Actions and Events* (Oxford: Oxford University Press, 1980).

_____ *Inquiries into Truth and Interpretation* (Oxford: Oxford University Press, 1984).

_____ 'Paradoxes of Irrationality', in Hopkins and Savile (eds.), *Philosophical Essays on Freud*, 289–305.

Davies, M., and Humberstone, I., 'Two Concepts of Necessity', *Philosophical Studies*, 38 (July 1980), 1–30.

Dees, R., 'Living with Contextualism', *Canadian Journal of Philosophy*, 24/2 (June 1994), 243–60.

Dent, N., *The Moral Psychology of the Virtues* (Cambridge: Cambridge University Press, 1975).

DePaul, M., *Balance and Refinement: Beyond Coherence Methods of Moral Inquiry* (London, Routledge: 1986).

_____ 'Reflective Equilibrium and Foundationalism', *American Philosophical Quarterly*, 23 (Jan. 1986).

_____ 'Two Conceptions of Coherence Methods in Ethics', *Mind*, 96/384 (Oct. 1987), 463–81.

Diamond, C., 'Losing Your Concepts', *Ethics*, 98/2 (Jan. 1988), 255–77.

Divers, J., and Miller, A., 'Platitudes and Attitudes: A Minimalist Conception of Belief', *Analysis*, 55/1 (Jan. 1995), 37–44.

Doppelt, G., 'Kuhn's Epistemological Relativism: An Interpretation and Defence', in Krausz and Meiland (eds.), *Relativism*, 113–46.

Dummett, M., *Frege* (London: Duckworth, 1973).

_____ 'What Is a Theory of Meaning II?', in Evans and McDowell (eds.), *Truth and Meaning*, 67–137.

Dummett, M., *Truth and Other Enigmas* (Cambridge, Mass.: Harvard University Press, 1978).

Dupré, J., *Disorder of Things: Metaphysical Foundations of the Disunity of Science* (Cambridge, Mass.: Harvard University Press, 1993).

Dworkin, R., 'The Original Position', in Daniels (ed.), *Reading Rawls*, 16–52.

——*Sovereign Virtue: The Theory and Practice of Equality* (Cambridge, Mass.: Harvard University Press, 2000).

Earman, J., *Bayes or Bust* (Cambridge, Mass.: MIT Press, 1992).

——(ed.), *Inference, Explanation and Other Frustrations: Essays in the Philosophy of Science* (Berkeley and Los Angeles: University of California Press, 1992).

Ebbs, G., *Rule-Following and Realism* (Cambridge, Mass.: Harvard University Press, 1997).

Ebertz, R., 'Is Reflective Equilibrium a Coherentist Model?', *Canadian Journal of Philosophy*, 23/2 (June 1993), 193–214.

Estlund, D., 'The Survival of Egalitarian Justice in John Rawls' *Political Liberalism*', *Journal of Political Philosophy*, 4/1 (Mar. 1996), 68–78.

——'The Insularity of the Reasonable: Why Political Liberalism Must Admit the Truth', *Ethics*, 108/2 (Jan. 1998), 252–75.

Evans, G., and McDowell, J. (eds.), *Truth and Meaning: Essays in Semantics* (Oxford: Oxford University Press, 1976).

Everson, S., 'Aristotle and the Explanation of Evaluation', in Heinamann (ed.), *Aristotle and Moral Realism*, 173–99.

Fehige, C., and Wessels, U. (eds.), *Preferences* (Berlin: Walter de Gruyter, 1998).

Fitzpatrick, W. J., 'Reasons, Value, and Particular Agents: Normative Relevance Without Motivational Internalism', *Mind*, 113/450 (Apr. 2004), 285–318.

Foot, P., *Virtues and Vices* (Oxford: Basil Blackwell, 1978).

Foucault, M., *The Foucault Reader* (London: Penguin Books, 1986).

——*The History of Sexuality* (New York: Vintage Books, 1990).

——*Discipline and Punish* (New York: Vintage Books, 1995).

Freeman, S., 'Contractualism, Moral Motivation and Practical Reason', *Journal of Philosophy*, 88/6 (June 1991), 281–303.

——(ed.), *The Cambridge Companion to Rawls* (Cambridge: Cambridge University Press, 2003).

French, P., Uehling, T., and Wettstein, H. (eds.), *Midwest Studies in Philosophy*, 8. *Contemporary Perspectives on the History of Philosophy* (1992).

——(eds.), *Midwest Studies in Philosophy*, 17. *The Wittgenstein Legacy* (1992).

Frey, R., and Morris, K. (eds.), *Value, Welfare and Morality* (Cambridge: Cambridge University Press, 1993).

Fricker, M., 'Confidence and Irony', in Harcourt (ed.), *Morality, Reflection and Ideology*, 87–112.

Friedman, M., 'Carnap's *Aufbau* Reconsidered', *Noûs*, 21 (Dec. 1987), 521–45.

——'Philosophy and the Exact Sciences: Logical Positivism as a Case Study', in Earman (ed.), *Inference, Explanation and Other Frustrations*, 84–98.

——'Transcendental Philosophy and A Priori Knowledge: A Neo-Kantian Perspective', in Boghossian and Peacocke (eds.), *New Essays on the A Priori*, 367–83.

——*The Dynamics of Reason* (Stanford, Calif.: Center for the Study of Language and Information, 2001).

Gallie, W. B., 'Essentially Contested Concepts', in Black (ed.), *The Importance of Language*, 121–46.

Galston, W., *Liberal Purposes: Goods, Virtues, and Diversity in the Liberal State* (Cambridge: Cambridge University Press, 1991).

Gaut, B., 'Moral Pluralism', *Philosophical Papers*, 22/1 (Apr. 1993), 17–40.

_____ 'Rag Bags, Disputes and Moral Pluralism', *Utilitas*, 11/1 (Mar. 1999), 37–8.

_____ 'Justifying Moral Pluralism', in Stratton-Lake (ed.), *Ethical Intuitionism*, 137–60.

Geach, P., 'Ascriptivism', *Philosophical Review*, 69/2 (1960), 221–5.

_____ 'Assertion', *Philosophical Review*, 74/4 (1965), 449–65.

Geertz, C., *The Interpretation of Cultures* (New York: Basic Books, 1973).

Geuss, R., *The Idea of a Critical Theory: Habermas and the Frankfurt School* (Cambridge: Cambridge University Press, 1981).

Gibbard, A., *Wise Choices, Apt Feelings* (Oxford: Oxford University Press, 1990).

_____ 'Thick Concepts and Warrant for Feelings', *Proceedings of the Aristotelian Society*, suppl. vol. 66 (1992), 267–83.

_____ 'Reasons Thin and Thick: A Possibility Proof', *Journal of Philosophy*, 100/6 (2003), 288–304.

Gillespie, M. A., *Hegel, Heidegger and the Ground of History* (Chicago: University of Chicago Press, 1984).

Gillespie, N. (ed.), *Moral Realism: Proceedings of the 1985 Spindel Conference, Southern Journal of Philosophy*, suppl. 24 (1986).

Gilmore, M. G. (ed.), *Studies on Machiavelli* (Florence: Sansoni, 1972).

Goldfarb, W., 'I Want You to Bring Me a Slab', *Synthese*, 56 (Sept. 1983), 265–82.

_____ 'Wittgenstein On Understanding', in French, Uehling, and Wettstein (eds.), *Midwest Studies in Philosophy*, 17. *The Wittgenstein Legacy*, 109–22.

Gray, J., *Enlightenment's Wake* (London: Routledge, 1995).

Grice, P., *The Conception of Value* (Oxford: Oxford University Press, 1991).

Guttmann, A., *Democratic Education*, rev. edn. (Princeton and Oxford: Princeton University Press, 1999).

Habermas, J., *On the Logic of the Social Sciences*, trans. S. W. Nicholson and J. A. Stark (Cambridge, Mass.: MIT Press, 1988).

_____ *Justification and Application: Remarks on Discourse Ethics*, trans. C. P. Cronin (Cambridge, Mass.: MIT Press, 1993).

_____ *Postmetaphysical Thinking: Philosophical Essays*, trans. W. M. Hohengarten (Cambridge, Mass.: MIT Press, 1994).

_____ *Between Facts and Norms*, trans. W. Rehg (Cambridge: Polity Press, 1996).

_____ 'A Genealogical Analysis of the Cognitive Content of Morality', *Proceedings of the Aristotelian Society*, 96 (1996), 335–58.

_____ *Truth and Justification*, trans. B. Fultman (Cambridge, Mass.: MIT Press, 2003).

Haldane, J., and Wright, C. (eds.), *Reality, Representation and Projection* (Oxford: Oxford University Press, 1993).

Hale, R., 'Can there be a Logic of Attitudes?', in Haldane and Wright (eds.), *Reality, Representation and Projection*, 337–64.

_____ 'Can Arboreal Knotwork Help Blackburn Out of Frege's Abyss?', *Philosophy and Phenomenological Research*, 65/1 (July 2002), 144–9.

Hall, J. (ed.), *Civil Society: Theory, History, Comparison* (Cambridge: Polity Press, 1995).

Hampshire, S., 'Spinoza on the Idea of Freedom', *Proceedings of the British Academy*, 46 (1960), 195–215.

_____ 'Morality and Convention', in Sen and Williams (eds.), *Utilitarianism and Beyond*, 145–57.

_____ *Morality and Conflict* (Cambridge, Mass.: Harvard University Press, 1983).

Hampshire, S., *Innocence and Experience* (Cambridge Mass.: Harvard University Press, 1989).

Hampton, J., 'Contracts and Choices: Does Rawls Have a Social Contract Theory?', *Journal of Philosophy*, 77/6 (June 1980), 315–38.

Harcourt, E. (ed.), *Morality, Reflection and Ideology* (Oxford: Oxford University Press, 2001).

Hare, R. M., *The Language of Morals* (Oxford: Oxford University Press, 1952).

—— 'Rawls's Theory of Justice', in Daniels (ed.), *Reading Rawls*, 81–107.

Harman, G., *The Nature of Morality* (Oxford: Oxford University Press, 1977).

—— *Change in View* (Cambridge, Mass.: MIT Press, 1988).

Harrison, T. R., 'Transcendental Arguments and Idealism', in Vesey (ed.), *Idealisms*, 211–24.

Heal, J., 'Ethics and the Absolute Conception', *Philosophy*, 64 (1985), 49–65.

—— 'The Disinterested Search for Truth', *Proceedings of the Aristotelian Society*, 88 (1987–8), 97–108.

—— *Fact and Meaning* (Oxford: Blackwell, 1989).

Heil, J. (ed.), *Cause, Mind and Reality* (Dordrecht: Kluwer, 1989).

Heinamann, R. (ed.), *Aristotle and Moral Realism* (London: University College, London Press, 1995).

Hegel, G. W. F., *Elements of the Philosophy of Right*, ed. A. Wood, Q. Skinner, and R. Geuss, trans. H. B. Nisbet, (Cambridge: Cambridge University Press, 1991).

Henderson, D., 'Epistemic Competence and Contextualist Epistemology: Why Contextualism Is Not Just the Poor Person's Coherentism', *Journal of Philosophy*, 91/12 (Dec. 1994), 627–49.

Herman, B., *The Practice of Moral Judgement* (Cambridge, Mass.: Harvard University Press, 1993).

Herzog, D., *Without Foundations: Justification in Political Theory* (Ithaca, NY: Cornell University Press, 1989).

Holmgren, M., 'Wide Reflective Equilibrium and Objective Moral Truth', *Metaphilosophy*, 18/2 (Apr. 1987), 108–24.

—— 'The Wide and Narrow of Reflective Equilibrium', *Canadian Journal of Philosophy*, 19/1 (Mar. 1989), 43–60.

Holtzmann, S., and Leich, C. (eds.), *Wittgenstein: To Follow a Rule* (London: Routledge, 1981).

Honderich, T. (ed.), *Morality and Objectivity* (London: Routledge, 1985).

Hooker, B., 'Williams's Argument Against External Reasons', *Analysis*, 47/1 (Jan. 1987), 42–4.

—— (ed.), *Truth in Ethics* (Oxford: Blackwell Publishers, 1996).

—— 'Ross-Style Pluralism versus Rule-Consequentialism', *Mind*, 106/420 (Oct. 1996), 531–52.

Hookway, C., 'Fallibilism and Objectivity, Science and Ethics', in Altham and Harrison (eds.), *World, Mind and Ethics*, 46–67.

Hopkins, J., and Savile, A. (eds.), *Philosophical Essays on Freud* (Cambridge: Cambridge University Press, 1984).

Horton, S., and Mendus, J. (eds.), *After MacIntyre* (Notre Dame, Ind.: University of Notre Dame Press, 1994).

Horwich, P., 'Gibbard's Theory of Norms', *Philosophy and Public Affairs*, 22/1 (1993), 67–78.

Humberstone, I. L., 'Direction of Fit', *Mind*, 101/401 (Jan. 1992), 59–83.

Hurley, S., 'Objectivity and Disagreement', in Honderich (ed.), *Morality and Objectivity*, 54–97.

—— *Natural Reasons: Personality and Polity* (Oxford: Oxford University Press, 1992).

_____ 'Intelligibility, Imperialism and Conceptual Scheme', in French, Uehling, and Wettstein (eds.), *Midwest Studies in Philosophy*, 17. *The Wittgenstein Legacy*, 89–108.

_____ 'Cognitivism in Political Philosophy', in Crisp and Hooker (eds.), *Morality and Well Being*, 177–208.

Jackson, F., 'Realism, Truth and Truth Aptness', *Philosophical Books*, 35 (1994), 162–169.

_____ Oppy, G., and Smith, M., 'Minimalism and Truth Aptness', *Mind*, 103/411 (July 1994), 287–302.

Jacobson, S., 'Contextualism and Global Doubts about the World', *Synthese*, 129/3 (Dec. 2001), 381 404.

Jakobsen, R., 'Wittgenstein on Self-Knowledge and Self-Expression', *Philosophical Quarterly*, 46/182 (Jan. 1996), 12–30.

_____ 'Self-Quotation and Self-Knowledge', *Synthese*, 110/3 (Mar. 1997), 419–445.

_____ 'Semantic Character and Expressive Content', *Philosophical Papers*, 26/2 (Aug. 1997), 129–46.

Jardine, N., 'Science, Ethics and Objectivity', in Altham and Harrison (eds.), *World, Mind and Ethics*, 32–45.

Kaviraj, S., and Khilnani, S. (eds.), *Civil Society: History and Possibilities* (Cambridge: Cambridge University Press, 2001).

Keane, J. (ed.), *Civil Society and the State: New European Perspectives* (London: Verso Press, 1988).

_____ *Civil Society: Old Images, New Visions* (London: Polity Press, 1998).

Kirchin, S. T., 'Reasons and Reduction', conference paper, *The Space of Reasons* (Cape Town, July 2004).

Kitcher, P., 'A Priori Knowledge Revisited', in Boghossian and Peacocke (eds.), *New Essays on the A Priori*, 65–91.

Klagge, J., 'An Alleged Difficulty Concerning Moral Properties', *Mind*, 93/371 (July 1984), 370–380.

Kolb, D., *The Critique of Pure Modernity: Hegel, Heidegger and After* (Chicago: University of Chicago Press, 1986).

Kolnai, A., *Ethics, Value and Reality* (London and Indianapolis: Athlone Press, 1973).

Korsgaard, C., 'Skepticism about Practical Reason', *Journal of Philosophy*, 83/1 (Jan. 1986), 5–25.

_____ *Creating the Kingdom of Ends* (Cambridge: Cambridge University Press, 1996).

_____ *The Sources of Normativity* (Cambridge: Cambridge University Press, 1996).

_____ 'The Normativity of Instrumental Reason', in Cullity and Gaut (eds.), *Ethics and Practical Reason*, 215–55.

Krausz, M., and Meiland, J. (eds.), *Relativism: Cognitive and Moral* (Notre Dame, Ind.: University of Notre Dame Press, 1982).

Kymlicka, W., and Norman, W., 'The Return of the Citizen: A Survey of Recent Work on Citizenship Theory', *Ethics*, 104/2 (1994), 352–81.

Lackey, J., and Sosa, E. (eds.), *The Epistemology of Testimony* (Oxford: Oxford University Press, 2006).

Larmore, C., *Patterns of Moral Complexity* (Cambridge: Cambridge University Press, 1989).

_____ 'The Right and the Good', *Philosophia*, 20/1–2 (July 1990), 15–32.

_____ 'Political Liberalism', *Political Theory*, 18/3 (Aug. 1990), 339–60.

_____ *Modernité et morale* (Paris: Presses universitaires de France, 1993).

_____ 'The Foundations of Modern Democracy', *European Journal of Philosophy*, 3/1 (Apr. 1995), 55–68.

_____ *The Morals of Modernity* (Cambridge, Cambridge University Press, 1996).

Larmore, C., 'The Moral Basis of Political Liberalism', *Journal of Philosophy*, 96/12 (Dec. 1999), 599–625.

Lasch, C., *The Culture of Narcissism* (New York: W. W. Norton, 1991).

Laudan, L., *Progress and Its Problems* (London: Routledge and Kegan Paul, 1977).

Lear, J., 'Leaving the World Alone', *Journal of Philosophy*, 79/7 (July 1982), 382–403.

—— 'Ethics, Mathematics and Relativism', *Mind*, 83/92 (Jan. 1983), 38–60.

—— 'Moral Objectivity', in Brown (ed.), *Objectivity and Cultural Divergence*, 135–70.

—— 'On Reflection: The Legacy of Wittgenstein's Later Philosophy', *Ratio*, 2/1 (1989), 19–45.

—— *Open Minded: Working Out the Logic of the Soul* (Cambridge, Mass.: Harvard University Press, 1998).

Lennon, K., and Charles, D. (eds.), *Reduction, Explanation and Realism* (Oxford: Oxford University Press, 1992).

Levi, I., 'Conflict and Social Agency', *Journal of Philosophy*, 79/5 (May 1982) 231–47.

—— *The Fixation of Belief and Its Undoing: Changing Beliefs through Enquiry* (Cambridge: Cambridge University Press, 1991).

Lewis, D., 'Putnam's Paradox', *Australasian Journal of Philosophy*, 62/3 (Sept. 1984), 221–36.

Lijphart, A., *Patterns of Democracy: Government Forms and Performance in Thirty-Six Countries* (New Haven and London: Yale University Press, 1999).

Lott, T. (ed.), *Subjugation and Bondage: Critical Essays on Slavery and Social Philosophy* (Totowa, NJ: Rowman and Littlefield Publishers, 1998).

Louden, R. C., 'Williams' Critique of the Morality System', in Thomas (ed.), *Bernard Williams*.

Lovibond, S., *Realism and Imagination in Ethics* (Oxford: Basil Blackwell, 1983).

—— and Williams, S. (eds.), *Essays for David Wiggins: Identity, Truth and Value* (Oxford: Blackwells, 1996).

Luhmann, N., *The Differentiation of Society*, trans. S. Holmes and C. Larmore (New York: Columbia University Press, 1990).

Lyotard, J.-F., *The Postmodern Condition: A Report on Knowledge*, trans. B. Massumi, (Manchester: Manchester University Press, 1984).

MacDonald, G., and Wright, C. (eds.), *Fact, Science and Morality* (Oxford: Blackwell, 1986).

McDowell, J., 'Review of Bernard Williams, *Ethics and the Limits of Philosophy*', *Mind*, 95/379 (1986), 377–88.

—— 'Might There Be External Reasons?', in Altham and Harrison (eds.), *World, Mind and Ethics*, 68–85.

—— *Mind and World* (Cambridge, Mass.: Harvard University Press, 1994).

—— 'Responses', in Willaschek (ed.), *John McDowell*, 91–114.

—— *Meaning, Knowledge and Reality* (Cambridge Mass.: Harvard University Press, 2001).

—— *Mind, Value and Reality* (Cambridge, Mass.: Harvard University Press, 2001).

Macedo, S., *Liberal Virtues: Citizenship, Virtue, and Community in Liberal Constitutionalism* (Oxford: Oxford University Press, 1990).

McGinn, C., *The Subjective View* (Oxford: Oxford University Press, 1983).

McGinn, M., *Sense and Certainty: The Dissolution of Scepticism* (Oxford: Blackwell Publishers, 1989).

MacIntyre, A., 'Epistemological Crises, Dramatic Narratives and the Philosophy of Science', *Monist*, 60 (1977), 453–72.

—— 'Relativism, Power and Philosophy', in Baynes, Bohman, and McCarthy, (eds.), *After Philosophy*, 385–411.

—— *After Virtue* (London: Duckworth 1981).

_____ *Whose Justice? Which Rationality?* (London: Duckworth, 1988).

_____ *Three Rival Versions of Moral Enquiry: Encyclopaedia, Genealogy and Tradition* (London: Duckworth, 1990).

_____ 'A Partial Response to My Critics', in Horton and Mendus (eds.), *After MacIntyre*, 283–304.

_____ *A Short History of Ethics* (London: Routledge Classic, 2002).

Mackie, J. L., *Ethics: Inventing Right and Wrong* (London: Harmondsworth, 1977).

Malachowski, A. (ed.), *Reading Rorty* (Oxford: Basil Blackwell, 1990).

McMurrin, S. M. (ed.), *The Tanner Lectures on Human Values, i* (Cambridge: Cambridge University Press, 1980).

Mandelbaum, M., *The Phenomenology of Moral Experience* (Glencoe, Ill.: The Free Press, 1955).

Meadwell, H., 'Post-Marxism: No Friend of Civil Society', in Hall (ed.), *Civil Society*, 183–99.

Merrill, G. H., 'The Model-Theoretic Argument Against Realism', *Philosophy of Science*, 47 (Mar. 1980), 69–81.

Meyerson, D., *False Consciousness* (Oxford: Oxford University Press, 1996).

Michelman, F., 'Law's Republic', *Yale Law Journal*, 97/8 (1988), 1493–1537.

Milgram, E., 'Was Hume a Humean?', *Hume Studies*, 21/1 (Apr. 1995), 75–93.

_____ 'Williams' Argument Against External Reasons' *Noûs*, 30/2 (June 1996), 197–220.

_____ (ed.), *Varieties of Practical Reasoning* (Cambridge, Mass.: MIT Press, 2001).

Miller, R., *Fact and Method: Explanation, Confirmation and Reality in the Natural and the Social Sciences* (Princeton: Princeton University Press, 1987).

Misak, C., *Truth, Politics, Morality: Pragmatism and Deliberation* (London: Routledge, 2000).

_____ (ed.), *The Cambridge Companion to Peirce* (Cambridge: Cambridge University Press, 2004).

Moore, A. W., 'Transcendental Idealism in Wittgenstein, and Theories of Meaning', *Philosophical Quarterly*, 35/139 (Apr. 1985), 134–55.

Moore, A. W., 'Points of View', *Philosophical Quarterly*, 37/146 (Jan. 1987), 1–20.

_____ 'On Saying and Showing', *Philosophy*, 62 (Oct. 1987), 473–97.

_____ *Points of View* (Oxford: Oxford University Press, 1997).

_____ *Noble in Reason, Infinite in Faculty* (London: Routledge, 2003).

_____ 'Williams on Ethics, Knowledge and Reflection', *Philosophy*, 78/305 (July 2003), 337–54.

_____ 'Conative Transcendental Arguments and the Question Whether There Can Be External Reasons', in Stern (ed.), *Transcendental Arguments*, 271–92.

_____ 'Realism and the Absolute Conception', in Thomas (ed.), *Bernard Williams* (forthcoming).

_____ 'Maxims and Thick Ethical Concepts', *Proceedings and Addresses of the Central Division of the American Philosophical Association*, 78/4 (Feb. 2005), also forthcoming in *Ratio*.

Moran, R., *Authority and Estrangement* (Princeton and Oxford: Princeton University Press, 2001).

_____ 'Getting Told and Being Believed', in Lackey and Sosa (eds.), *The Epistemology of Testimony*.

Morawetz, T., *Wittgenstein and Knowledge: The Importance of On Certainty* (Brighton: Harvester Press, 1980).

Mouffe, C. (ed.), *Dimensions of Radical Democracy: Pluralism, Citizenship, Community* (London: Verso, 1992).

Moyal-Sharrock, D., *Understanding Wittgenstein's On Certainty* (London: Macmillan, 2004).

_____ and Brenner, W. H. (eds.), *Readings of Wittgenstein's On Certainty* (London: Macmillan, 2005).

Murdoch, I., *The Sovereignty of Good* (London: Routledge and Kegan Paul, 1970).

Nagel, T., *The Possibility of Altruism* (Oxford: Oxford University Press, 1970).

_____ 'Rawls on Justice', in Daniels (ed), *Reading Rawls*, 1–16.

_____ 'The Limits of Objectivity', in McMurrin (ed.), *The Tanner Lectures on Human Values*, i. 75–139.

_____ *The View from Nowhere* (Oxford: Oxford University Press, 1986).

_____ 'Moral Conflict and Political Legitimacy', *Philosophy & Public Affairs*, 16/3 (Summer 1987), 215–40.

_____ *Equality and Partiality* (Oxford: Oxford University Press: 1991).

Nielsen, K., 'Reflective Equilibrium and the Transformation of Philosophy', *Metaphilosophy*, 20/3–4 (1989), 235–46.

Nietzsche, F., *The Gay Science,* ed. Williams, trans. J. Nauckhoff and A. Del Caro (Cambridge: Cambridge University Press, 2002).

Norman, R., 'Making Sense of Moral Realism', *Philosophical Investigations*, 20/2 (Apr. 1997), 117–35.

_____ 'Particularism and Reasons', *Journal of Moral Philosophy* (forthcoming).

Nowell-Smith, P., *Ethics* (Oxford: Blackwell, 1957).

Nozick, R., *The Examined Life* (New York: Simon and Schuster, 1989).

_____ *Invariances* (Cambridge, Mass.: Harvard University Press, 2001).

Nussbaum, M., 'Aristotle on Human Nature and the Foundations of Ethics', in Altham and Harrison (eds.), *World, Mind and Ethics*, 86–131.

Oldfield, A., *Citizenship and Community: Civic Republicanism and the Modern World* (London: Routledge, 1990).

O'Neill, O., *Constructions of Reason* (Cambridge, Cambridge University Press, 1989).

Parfit, D., 'Reasons and Motivation', *Proceedings of the Aristotelian Society*, suppl. vol. 71 (1997), 98–146.

van Parijs, P., 'Difference Principles', in Freeman (ed.), *The Cambridge Companion to Rawls*, 200–40.

Peacocke, C. A. B., *A Study of Concepts* (Cambridge, Mass.: Bradford Books 1992).

Peterson, G. B. (ed.), *The Tanner Lectures on Human Values* (Salt Lake City: University of Utah Press, 1988).

Pettit, P., 'Humeans, Anti-Humeans, and Motivation', *Mind*, 96/384 (Oct. 1987), 530–3.

_____ *The Common Mind: An Essay on Psychology, Society and Politics* (Oxford: Oxford University Press, 1992).

_____ *Republicanism: A Theory of Freedom and Government* (Oxford: Clarendon Press, 1997).

_____ and McDowell, J. (eds.), *Subject, Thought and Context* (Oxford: Clarendon Press, 1986).

Phillips, D. Z., and Mounce, H., *Moral Practices* (London: Routledge, 1970).

Pippin, R. B., *Modernism as a Philosophical Problem*, 2nd edn. (Oxford: Blackwell Publishers, 1999).

Platts, M., *Ways of Meaning* (London: Routledge, 1979).

Pogge, T., *Realizing Rawls* (Ithaca, NY: Cornell University Press, 1989).

Preyer, G., and Peter, G. (eds.), *Contextualism in Philosophy: Knowledge, Meaning and Truth* (Oxford: Oxford University Press, 2005).

Price, A.W., 'Reasons and Desires', unpublished MS (1995).

Prichard, D., 'Two Forms of Epistemological Contextualism', *Grazer Philosophische Studien*, 64 (2002), 19–55.

_____ 'Wittgenstein's *On Certainty* and Contemporary Anti-Scepticism', in Moyal-Sharrock and Brenner (eds.) *Readings of Wittgenstein's On Certainty*, 189–224.

Putnam, H., *Meaning and the Moral Sciences* (London: Routledge and Kegan Paul, 1978).

_____ *Philosophical Papers, ii. Mind, Language and Reality* (Cambridge: Cambridge University Press, 1979).

_____ *Reason, Truth and History* (Cambridge: Cambridge University Press 1981).

_____ *The Many Faces of Realism* (La Salle, Ill.: Open Court Publishing, 1987).

_____ *Realism with a Human Face* (Cambridge, Mass.: Harvard University Press, 1992).

_____ *Renewing Philosophy* (Cambridge, Mass.: Harvard University Press, 1995).

_____ *The Collapse of the Fact/Value Dichotomy and Other Essays* (Cambridge, Mass.: Harvard University Press, 2002).

_____ *Ethics Without Ontology* (Cambridge, Mass.: Harvard University Press, 2004).

Putnam, R. D., *The Comparative Study of Political Elites* (Englewood Cliffs, NJ and London: Prentice-Hall, 1976).

_____ *Bowling Alone: The Collapse and Revival of American Community* (New York: Simon & Schuster, 2000).

Quine, W. V. O., *Ontological Relativity and Other Essays* (New York: Columbia University Press, 1969).

_____ *From a Logical Point of View*, 2nd edn. (Cambridge, Mass.: Harvard University Press, 1980).

Quinn, W., *Morality and Action* (Cambridge: Cambridge University Press, 1994).

Quinton, A., 'The Varieties of Value', in Peterson (ed.), *The Tanner Lectures on Human Values*, 185–210.

Railton, P., *Facts, Values and Norms* (Cambridge: Cambridge University Press, 2003).

Rawls, J., 'Outline for a Decision Procedure for Ethics', *Philosophical Review*, 40/2 (Apr. 1951), 177–197.

_____ *A Theory of Justice* (Cambridge Mass.: Harvard University Press, 1971).

_____ *Political Liberalism* (New York: Columbia University Press, 1993).

_____ 'The Idea of Public Reason Revisited', *University of Chicago Law Review*, 64/3 (1997), 765–807.

_____ *Collected Papers*, ed. S. Freeman (Cambridge, Mass.: Harvard University Press, 1999).

_____ *The Law of Peoples* (Cambridge, Mass.: Harvard University Press, 1999).

_____ *Justice as Fairness: A Restatement*, ed. E. Kelly (Cambridge Mass.: Harvard University Press, 2001).

Raz, J., *The Morality of Freedom* (Oxford: Oxford University Press, 1988).

_____ 'Facing Diversity: The Case of Epistemic Abstinence', *Philosophy and Public Affairs*, 19/1 (Winter 1990), 3–46.

_____ *Ethics in the Public Domain* (Oxford: Oxford University Press, 1996).

Reichenbach, H., *Experience and Prediction: An Analysis of the Foundations and Structure of Knowledge* (Chicago: Chicago University Press, 1961).

_____ *The Theory of Relativity and A Priori Knowledge* (Berkeley and Los Angeles: University of California Press, 1965).

Reiff, P., *The Triumph of the Therapeutic* (Chicago: Chicago University Press, 1987).

Richardson, H., *Practical Reasoning about Final Ends* (Cambridge: Cambridge University Press, 1997).

Ripstein, A., 'Foundationalism in Political Theory', *Philosophy and Public Affairs*, 16/2 (Spring 1987), 115–37.

van Roojen, M., 'Humean Motivation and Humean Rationality', *Philosophical Studies*, 79/1 (July 1995), 37–57.

—— 'Expressivism and Irrationality', *Philosophical Review*, 105/3 (July 1996), 311–36.

Rorty, R., *Philosophy and the Mirror of Nature* (Oxford: Basil Blackwell, 1979).

—— *The Consequences of Pragmatism* (Brighton: Harvester Press, 1982).

—— *Contingency, Irony and Solidarity* (Cambridge: Cambridge University Press, 1989).

—— *Objectivity, Relativism and Truth* (Cambridge: Cambridge University Press, 1991).

—— Skinner, Q., and Schneewind, J. B. (eds.), *Philosophy in History* (Cambridge: Cambridge University Press, 1984).

Rose, N., *Powers of Freedom: Reframing Political Thought* (Cambridge: Cambridge University Press, 1999).

Rosenblum, N. L. (ed.), *Liberalism and Moral Life* (Chicago and London: Chicago University Press, 1989).

Sacks, M., *The World We Found* (La Salle, Ill.: Open Court Publishing, 1989).

Sandel, M., *Liberalism and the Limits of Justice* (Cambridge: Cambridge University Press, 1998).

Sayre-McCord, G. (ed.), *Essays On Moral Realism* (Ithaca, NY: Cornell University Press, 1988).

—— 'Coherentist Epistemology and Moral Theory', in Sinnott-Armstrong and Timmons (eds.), *Moral Knowledge?*, 137–89.

Scanlon, T., 'Contractualism and Utilitarianism', in Sen and Williams (eds.), *Utilitarianism and Beyond*, 103–28.

—— 'The Aims and Authority of Moral Theory', *Oxford Journal of Legal Studies*, 12/1 (Spring 1992), 1–23.

—— *What We Owe to Each Other* (Cambridge, Mass.: Belknap Press, 1998).

Scheffler, S., *Human Morality* (Oxford: Oxford University Press, 1992).

—— *Boundaries and Allegiances: Problems of Justice and Responsibility in Liberal Thought* (Oxford: Oxford University Press, 2002).

Schmitt, C., *The Concept of the Political*, trans. G. Schwab (Chicago: University of Chicago Press, 1996).

Schneewind, J. B., 'Virtue, Narrative and Community', *Journal of Philosophy*, 79/11 (Nov. 1982), 653–663.

—— 'Moral Crisis and the History of Ethics', in French, Uehling, and Wettstein (eds.), *Midwest Studies in Philosophy*, 8. *Contemporary Perspectives on the History of Philosophy*, 525–42.

—— 'The Divine Corporation and the History of Ethics', in Rorty, Skinner, and Schneewind (eds.), *Philosophy in History*, 173–92.

—— 'The Misfortunes of Virtue', *Ethics*, 101/1 (Oct. 1990), 42–63.

—— 'Natural Law, Skepticism and Methods of Ethics', *Journal of the History of Ideas*, 52/2 (Apr.–June 1991), 289–308.

—— 'Kant and Natural Law Ethics', *Ethics*, 104/1 (Oct. 1993), 53–74.

Schueler, G. F., 'Modus Ponens and Moral Realism', *Ethics*, 98/3 (Apr. 1988), 492–500.

Searle, J., 'Meaning and Speech Acts', *Philosophical Review*, 71/4 (Oct. 1962), 423–432.

Seligman, A. B., *The Idea of Civil Society* (Princeton: Princeton University Press, 1995).

—— 'Animadversions upon Civil Society and Civic Virtue in the Last Decade of the Twentieth Century', in Hall (ed.), *Civil Society*, 200–23.

Sellars, W., *Science and Metaphysics: Variations on Kantian Themes* (London: Routledge and Kegan Paul, 1968).

—— *Essays on Philosophy and Its History* (Dordrecht: Reidel, 1975).

____*Empiricism and the Philosophy of Mind* (Cambridge, Mass.: Harvard University Press, 1997).

Sen, A., and Williams, B. (eds.), *Utilitarianism and Beyond* (Cambridge: Cambridge University Press, 1982).

____and Nussbaum, M. (eds.), *The Quality of Life* (Oxford: Oxford University Press, 1993).

Sencerz, S., 'Moral Intuitions and Justification in Ethics', *Philosophical Studies*, 50/1 (July 1986), 77–95.

Shafer-Landau, R., 'Vagueness, Borderline Cases and Moral Realism', *American Philosophical Quarterly*, 32/1 (1995), 83–96.

Shklar, J., 'The Liberalism of Fear', in Rosenblum (ed.), *Liberalism and Moral Life*, 21–38.

Shoemaker, S., *Identity, Cause and Mind* (Oxford: Oxford University Press, 2003).

Siewert, C., *The Significance of Consciousness* (Princeton: Princeton University Press, 1998).

Singer, P., 'Sidgwick and Reflective Equilibrium', *Monist*, 58 (July 1974), 490–517.

Sinnott-Armstrong, W., and Timmons, M. (eds.), *Moral Knowledge?: New Readings in Moral Epistemology* (Oxford: Oxford University Press, 1996).

Skinner, Q., 'The Idea of Negative Liberty', in Rorty, Schneewind, and Skinner (eds.), *Philosophy in History*, 193–221.

____'Pre-Humanist Origins of Republican Ideas', in Bock, Skinner, and Viroli (eds.), *Machiavelli and Republicanism*, 121–42.

____'The Republican Ideal of Political Liberty', in Bock, Skinner, and Viroli (eds.), *Machiavelli and Republicanism*, 293–309.

Skorupski, J., 'Internal Reasons and the Scope of Blame', in Thomas (ed.), *Bernard Williams* (forthcoming).

Smith, M., 'The Humean Theory of Motivation', *Mind*, 96/381 (Jan. 1987), 36–61.

____*The Moral Problem* (Oxford: Basil Blackwell, 1994).

____'Why Expressivists about Value Should Love Minimalism about Truth', *Analysis*, 54/1 (Jan. 1994), 1–12.

____'Minimalism, Truth-Aptitude and Belief', *Analysis*, 54/1 (Jan. 1994), 21–26.

Snowdon, P., 'On Formulating Materialism and Dualism', in Heil (ed.), *Cause, Mind and Reality*, 137–58.

Stern, R. (ed.), *Transcendental Arguments: Problems and Prospects* (Oxford: Oxford University Press, 2003).

van Straaten, Z. (ed.), *Philosophical Subjects* (Oxford: Clarendon Press, 1980).

Stratton-Lake, P., 'Can Hooker's Rule-Consequentialist Principle Justify Ross's Prima Facie Duties?', *Mind*, 106/424 (Oct. 1997), 751–8.

____*Kant, Duty and Moral Worth* (London: Routledge, 2000).

____(ed.), *Ethical Intuitionism: Re-Evaluations* (Oxford: Oxford University Press, 2002).

Strauss, L.,'Notes on Carl Schmitt: *The Concept of the Political*', in Schmitt, *The Concept of the Political*, 83–107.

Strawson, P. F., 'Scruton and Wright on Anti-Realism', *Proceedings of the Aristotelian Society*, 77 (1976–7), 15–21.

Stroud, B., 'Transcendental Arguments', *Journal of Philosophy*, 65/9 (May 1968), 241–56.

____*The Significance of Philosophical Scepticism* (Oxford: Oxford University Press, 1989).

____*Understanding Human Knowledge* (Oxford: Oxford University Press, 2000).

Sturgeon, N., 'Moral Explanations', in Copp and Zimmerman (eds.), *Morality, Reason and Truth*, 49–78.

____'Harman on Moral Explanations of Natural Facts', in Gillespie (ed.), *Moral Realism*, 69–78.

Sturgeon, N., 'What Difference Does It Make Whether Moral Realism Is True?', *Southern Journal of Philosophy*, 24, suppl. (1986), 115–42.

Sullivan, P., 'Problems for a Construction of Meaning and Intention', *Mind*, 103/410 (Apr. 1994), 147–68.

Svavarsdottir, S., 'Moral Cognitivism and Motivation', *Philosophical Review*, 108/9 (Apr. 1999), 161–219.

Swanton, C., 'The Rationality of Ethical Intuitionism', *Australasian Journal of Philosophy*, 65/2 (June 1987), 172–81.

——'Profiles of the Virtues', *Pacific Philosophical Quarterly*, 76 (1995), 47–72.

Szücs, J., 'Three Historical Regions of Europe', *Acta Historica Scientiarum Hungaricae*, 29 (1983), 131–84.

Taylor, C., *Philosophical Papers, i. Human Agency and Language* (Cambridge: Cambridge University Press, 1985).

——*Philosophical Papers, ii. Philosophy and the Human Sciences* (Cambridge: Cambridge University Press, 1985).

——*Sources of the Self* (Cambridge: Cambridge University Press, 1989).

——'Explanation and Practical Reason', in Sen and Nussbaum (eds.), *The Quality of Life*, 208–41.

——'Between Democracy and Despotism: The Dangers of Soft Despotism', *Current*, 359 (Jan. 1994), 36–9.

——*Philosophical Arguments* (Cambridge, Mass.: Harvard University Press, 1995).

——'A Most Peculiar Institution', in Altham and Harrison (eds.), *World, Mind and Ethics*, 132–55.

——'Two Theories of Modernity,' *Hastings Center Report*, 25 (1995), 24–33.

——'Democratic Exclusion (and Its Remedies?)', in Bhargava, Bagchi, and Sudarshan (eds.), *Multiculturalism, Liberalism and Democracy*, 138–63.

Taylor, Craig D., 'Williams on Moral Incapacity', *Philosophy*, 70/272 (Apr. 1995), 273–285.

Tenenbaum, S., 'Realists without a Cause: Deflationary Theories of Truth and Ethical Realism', *Canadian Journal of Philosophy*, 26/4 (Dec. 1996), 561–90.

Thomas, A., 'Review of Robert Brandom's *Making It Explicit*', *European Journal of Philosophy*, 4/3 (Dec. 1996), 394–6.

——'Liberal Republicanism and the Role of Civil Society', *Democratisation*, 4/3 (Aug. 1997), 26–44.

——'Minimalism and Quasi-Realism', *Philosophical Papers*, 26/3 (Nov. 1997), 233–9.

——'Kant, McDowell and the Theory of Consciousness', *European Journal of Philosophy*, 5/3 (Dec. 1997), 283–305.

——'Consequentialism and the Subversion of Pluralism', in B. Hooker, E. Mason, and D. Miller (eds.), *Morality, Rules and Consequences* (Edinburgh: Edinburgh University Press, 2000), 179–202.

——'An Adverbial Theory of Consciousness', *Phenomenology and the Cognitive Sciences*, 2/3 (2003), 161–85.

——'Nagel's Paradox of Equality and Partiality', *Res Publica*, 9/3 (2003), 257–84.

——'Kant's Practical Philosophy Considered', conference paper, *Kant's Practical Philosophy Reconsidered*, University of Kent (Mar. 2004).

——'Maxims and Thick Concepts: Reply to Moore', presented to the Central Division of the American Philosophical Association (2005) and available for download at <http://www.logical-operator.com/ReplytoMoore.pdf>

_____ 'Reasonable Partiality and the Agent's Personal Point of View', *Ethical Theory and Moral Practice*, 8/1–2 (Apr. 2005), 25–43.

_____ 'The Permissibility of Prerogative Grounded Incentives in Liberal Egalitarianism', 'Straight to the Point', *Ethics and Economics* (2005): <http://mapage.noos.fr/Ethique-economique/html_version>

_____ 'Cohen's Critique of Rawls: A "Double Counting" Objection', unpublished MS (2005).

_____ 'The Scope of the Agent-Relative', unpublished MS (2005).

_____ (ed.) *Bernard Williams* (Cambridge: Cambridge University Press, forthcoming).

_____ 'Practical Reasoning and Normative Relevance', *Journal of Moral Philosophy* (forthcoming).

Timmons, M., *Morality Without Foundations* (Oxford: Oxford University Press, 1999).

Tolhurst, W., 'On the Epistemic Value of Moral Experience', *Southern Journal of Philosophy*, 29, suppl. (1990), 67–87.

Tomasi, J., *Liberalism Beyond Justice* (Princeton: Princeton University Press, 2000).

Unwin, N., 'Quasi-Realism, Negation and the Frege-Geach Problem', *Philosophical Quarterly*, 49/196 (July 1999), 337–52.

Urmson, J. O., 'A Defence of Intuitionism', *Proceedings of the Aristotelian Society* (1975), 111–19.

Vajda, M., 'East-Central European Perspectives', in Keane (ed.), *Civil Society and the State*, 333–60.

Vernon, R., *Political Morality: A Theory of Liberal Democracy* (London and New York, Continuum Press: 2001).

Vesey, G. (ed.), *Idealisms: Past and Present* (Cambridge: Cambridge University Press, 1982).

Villanueva, E. (ed.), *Philosophical Issues*, 6 (Atascadero, Calif.: Ridgeview, 1995).

Waldron, J., 'Theoretical Foundations of Liberalism', *Philosophical Quarterly*, 37/147 (Apr. 1987), 127–50.

Walker, R. C. S., *The Coherence Theory of Truth: Realism, Anti-Realism, Idealism* (London and New York: Routledge, 1989).

Wallace, R. J., 'How to Argue about Practical Reason', *Mind*, 99/395 (July 1990), 355–385.

_____ 'Virtue, Reason, and Principle', *Canadian Journal of Philosophy*, 21/4 (Dec. 1991), 469–95.

Walzer, M., 'Philosophy and Democracy', *Political Theory*, 9/3 (Aug. 1981), 379–99.

_____ 'Liberalism and the Art of Separation', *Political Theory*, 12/3 (Aug. 1984), 315–30.

_____ 'Citizenship', in Ball, Farr, and Hanson (eds.), *Political Innovation and Conceptual Change*, 211–19.

_____ 'The Communitarian Critique of Liberalism', *Political Theory*, 18/1 (Feb. 1990), 6–23.

_____ 'The Civil Society Argument', in Mouffe (ed.), *Dimensions of Radical Democracy*, 89–107.

_____ *Politics and Passion: Towards a More Egalitarian Liberalism* (New Haven and London: Yale University Press, 2004).

Wellmer, A., *Endgames: The Irreconcilable Nature of Modernity*, trans. David Midgley (Cambridge, Mass. and London: MIT Press, 1998).

Wenar, L., 'Political Liberalism: An Internal Critique', *Ethics*, 106/1 (Oct. 1995), 32–62.

Wiggins, D., 'What Would Be a Substantial Theory of Truth?', in van Straaten (ed.), *Philosophical Subjects*, 189–221.

_____ 'On Singling Out an Object Determinately', in Pettit and McDowell, (eds.), *Subject, Thought and Context*, 169–80.

_____ 'Moral Cognitivism, Moral Relativism and Motivating Moral Beliefs', *Proceedings of the Aristotelian Society* (1991), 61–85.

____ 'Categorical Requirements: Kant and Hume on the Idea of Duty', *Monist*, 74/1 (1991), 83–106.

____ 'Cognitivism, Naturalism, and Normativity', in Haldane and Wright (eds.), *Reality, Representation and Projection*, 301–14.

____ 'A Neglected Position?', in Haldane and Wright (eds.), *Reality, Representation and Projection*, 329–38.

____ 'Objective and Subjective in Ethics, with Two Postscripts on Truth', in Hooker (ed.), *Truth in Ethics*, 35–50.

____ 'In a Subjectivist Framework, Categorical Requirements and Real Practical Reasons', in Fehige and Wessels (eds.) *Preferences*, 212–32.

____ *Needs, Values, Truth*, 3rd edn. (Oxford: Blackwells, 2000).

____ 'Reflections on Inquiry and Truth Arising from Peirce's Method for the Fixation of Belief', in Misak (ed.), *The Cambridge Companion to Peirce*, 87–126.

Willaschek, M. (ed.), *John McDowell: Reason and Nature (Lecture and Colloquium in Münster 1999)* (New Brunswick and London: Transaction Publishers, 2000).

Williams, A., 'Incentives, Inequality and Publicity', *Philosophy and Public Affairs*, 27/3 (Summer 1998), 225–47.

Williams, B., *Problems of the Self* (Cambridge: Cambridge University Press, 1973).

____ *Descartes: The Project of Pure Enquiry* (London: Penguin Books, 1978).

____ *Moral Luck* (Cambridge: Cambridge University Press, 1981).

____ *Ethics and the Limits of Philosophy* (London: Fontana, 1985).

____ 'Reply to Blackburn', *Philosophical Books*, 27/4 (Oct. 1986), 203–8.

____ 'Auto da fé', in Malachowski (ed.), *Reading Rorty*, 26–37.

____ 'The Need to Be Sceptical', *Times Literary Supplement* (16–22 Feb. 1990), 163–4.

____ 'Terrestrial Thoughts, Extraterrestrial Science: Review of Hilary Putnam, *Realism with a Human Face*', *London Review of Books* (7 Feb. 1991), 12–13.

____ 'A Fair State: Review of John Rawls, *Political Liberalism*', *London Review of Books*, 15/9 (13 May 1993), 7–8.

____ *Shame and Necessity* (Berkeley and Los Angeles: University of California Press, 1993).

____ *Making Sense of Humanity* (Cambridge: Cambridge University Press, 1995).

____ 'Replies', in Altham and Harrison (eds.), *World, Mind and Ethics*, 185–224.

____ 'Truth in Ethics', in Hooker (ed.), *Truth in Ethics*, 19–35.

____ *Der Wert der Warheit* (Vienna: Passagen Verlag, 1998).

____ 'Philosophy as a Humanistic Discipline', *Philosophy*, 75/294 (Oct. 2000), 477–96.

____ 'Postscript: Some Further Notes on Internal and External Reasons', in Milgram (ed.), *Varieties of Practical Reasoning*, 90–7.

____ 'From Freedom to Liberty: The Construction of a Political Value', *Philosophy and Public Affairs*, 30/1 (2001), 3–26.

____ *Truth and Truthfulness: An Essay in Genealogy* (Princeton: Princeton University Press, 2002).

____ *In the Beginning Was the Deed: Realism and Moralism in Political Argument*, ed. Hawthorn G. (Princeton: Princeton University Press, 2005).

Williams, Meredith, 'Wittgenstein, Kant and the Metaphysics of Experience', *Kant-Studien*, 81/1 (1990), 69–88.

____ 'Do We (Epistemologists) Need a Theory of Truth?', *Philosophical Topics*, 14/1 (Spring 1986), 223–42.

____ *Unnatural Doubts: Epistemological Realism and the Basis of Scepticism* (Oxford: Blackwell Publishers, 1991).

_____ 'Still Unnatural: A Reply to Vogel and Rorty', *Journal of Philosophical Research*, 22 (Apr. 1997), 29–39.

Williamson, T., *Knowledge and Its Limits* (Oxford: Oxford University Press, 2000).

Winch, P., 'Im Anfang war die Tat', in Block (ed.), *Perspectives on the Philosophy of Wittgenstein*, 159–78.

Wittgenstein, L., *Philosophical Investigations* (Oxford: Basil Blackwell, 1958).

_____ *Tractatus Logico-Philosophicus*, trans. D. Pears and B. McGuiness (London: Routledge and Kegan Paul, 1961).

_____ *On Certainty* (Oxford: Blackwell Publishers, 1975).

Wolf, S., *Freedom Within Reason* (Oxford: Oxford University Press, 1990).

Wood, A., 'Unsociable Sociability: The Anthropological Basis of Kant's Ethics', *Philosophical Topics*, 19/1 (Spring 1991), 325–51.

Woodfield, A., *Teleology* (Cambridge: Cambridge University Press, 1986).

Woods, M., 'Reasons for Action and Desires', *Proceedings of the Aristotelian Society*, suppl. vol. 46 (1972), 189–201.

Wright, C., *Realism, Meaning and Truth* (Oxford: Blackwell, 1986).

_____ 'Scientific Realism, Observation and the Verification Principle', in MacDonald and Wright (eds.), *Fact, Science and Morality*, 247–74.

_____ 'Moral Values, Projection and Secondary Qualities', *Proceedings of the Aristotelian Society*, suppl. vol., 62 (1988), 1–26.

_____ *Truth and Objectivity* (Cambridge, Mass.: Harvard University Press, 1992).

_____ 'Response to Jackson', *Philosophical Books*, 35 (1994), 169–75.

_____ 'Can there be a Rationally Compelling Argument for Anti-realism about Ordinary ("Folk") Psychology?', in Villanueva (ed.), *Philosophical Issues*, 6, 197–221.

_____ 'Truth in Ethics', *Ratio*, 8/3 (Dec. 1995), 209–26.

Yack, B., *The Longing for Total Revolution: Philosophic Sources of Social Discontent from Rousseau to Marx and Nietzsche* (Princeton: Princeton University Press, 1986).

_____ *The Fetishism of Modernities: Epochal Self-Consciousness in Contemporary Social and Political Thought* (Notre Dame, Ind.: University of Notre Dame Press, 1997).

Index